Ytr col
4/85

UC/EIS

# UNCOLLECTED PROSE
BY
## W. B. YEATS

*Also collected and edited by John P. Frayne*

UNCOLLECTED PROSE by W. B. YEATS 1
First Reviews and Articles 1886–1896

# UNCOLLECTED PROSE

## BY

# W. B. YEATS

*Collected and edited by*
## JOHN P. FRAYNE
*and*
## COLTON JOHNSON

## 2

REVIEWS, ARTICLES AND
OTHER MISCELLANEOUS PROSE
1897–1939

*First published 1975 by*
THE MACMILLAN PRESS LTD
*London and Basingstoke*
*Associated companies in New York*
*Dublin Melbourne Johannesburg and Madras*

SBN 0333 11280 6

*Printed in Great Britain by*
RICHARD CLAY (THE CHAUCER PRESS), LTD.,
Bungay, Suffolk

# Contents

CONTENTS9

# List of Illustrations

# Acknowledgement

THE quotations from the works of W. B. Yeats are reprinted by kind permission of Senator Michael B. Yeats and Miss Anne Yeats.

# Preface

IN the two volumes of this edition we have attempted to collect every piece of prose published in Yeats's lifetime which he acknowledged or which can reasonably be attributed to him and which is not currently in print—either in his own collections, in Allan Wade's edition of the letters[1] or in Mrs. Yeats's posthumous edition.[2] In the course of our work we have come to doubt that gathering together all such items is possible and we are sure that some interview or a brief letter to one of the dozens of newspapers whose columns were open to Yeats has escaped our notice. We have inspected Yeats's papers and Lady Gregory's, the files of contemporary periodicals and the bibliographical material in subsequent scholarship. We have failed to locate the writings in *The Gael* (Dublin) which also eluded Wade when he compiled his bibliography,[3] but the "unsigned report" of Wilfrid Blunt's "seventieth" birthday attributed to Yeats by Joseph Hone[4] is included here, thanks to the discovery that Blunt was in fact seventy-four.

Although we include in this volume several interviews, articles and letters which are not in Wade's bibliography, that work has again been an invaluable source for a great number of these fugitive pieces. These writings appear generally under the titles they bore in their original publication, and we have printed them as nearly as possible in the order in which they came before the public, since we felt that any grouping— by theme or by type, for example—might seem increasingly arbitrary and distracting as time went by and as the focus of interest in Yeats's work shifted.

We have excluded from this edition such writings as Yeats's prefaces to books by others because we felt that, in general, these texts would be available in many public and private libraries where most of the more obscure periodicals we have consulted would not be. A few other writings, such as the letter to *The Times* on "Maeterlinck and the Censor"[5] signed by Yeats and twelve others, and a few interviews

---

[1] *The Letters of W. B. Yeats*, edited by Allan Wade, London, 1954.

[2] W. B. Yeats, *Explorations*, selected by Mrs. W. B. Yeats, London, 1962.

[3] Allan Wade, *A Bibliography of the Writings of W. B. Yeats*, third edition, revised and edited by Russell K. Alspach, London, 1968, p. 11.

[4] Joseph Hone, *W. B. Yeats, 1865–1939*, New York, 1943, p. 291.

[5] Wade, *Bibliography*, p. 363.

where none of Yeats's words were quoted, are not included here because they lacked sufficient evidence of his authorship.

As we come into the years in which Yeats experimented more and more with expressing himself through interviews, the determination of the published text's authority becomes more important. The clipping books which Yeats and Lady Gregory kept in the years around the turn of the century and which are preserved in the National Library of Ireland—as well as Yeats's frequent "corrections" of published accounts of his words—are helpful here as they confirm Yeats's knowledge of the texts and sometimes supply his reactions to them. Our practice has been to include any texts where any substantial expression of Yeats's views appears in his own words. In a few instances, we reprint also Yeats's subsequent quarrels with editors and interviewers about just what his words had been.

The problems of textual inaccuracy discussed in the preface to the first volume of this edition continue to arise in Yeats's later writings. The suspicion stated there of his "innate indifference to accuracy of transcription" is strengthened as we compare his quotations in these writings with the original texts, which we have again supplied whereever possible. As the range of periodicals from which we have taken these writings is wider than in the first volume, we have been faced with an even greater range of possible textual inaccuracies. From the almost comical mangling of the identities of Yeats's allies in *L'Irlande Libre* to the impeccable texts of the *Fortnightly Review* we have attempted to give the closest possible rendering of Yeats's printed text. Where we have corrected what seem to be typographical errors, we have noted them, and in some cases where the magazine text is particularly difficult, we have let the original stand and suggested amendments in notes. In the few cases where a "typo" seemed clearly mechanical, we have silently emended the text.

While the preparation of the texts, the introductory and editorial material, and thus the responsibility for whatever value or mischief this volume contains result from thorough collaboration, Mr. Frayne has been primarily responsible for the material published between 1897 and 1900. Mr. Johnson has been most concerned with collecting and editing the writings published between 1900 and 1939. In a considerably different form, much of this material was included in his doctoral dissertation at Northwestern University, and for direction and encouragement in that work, as well as for friendly advice on the present volume, he is most grateful to Professor Richard Ellmann. He wishes also to acknowledge the many kindnesses of Senator and Mrs. Michael B. Yeats. Professors William Murphy and Michael O'Neill have kindly shared their knowledge of Yeats's times and his associations with Mr. Johnson, and he is grateful also to Dr. Lola Szladits, Curator of the Berg Collection of the New York Public Library, for permitting him to inspect Lady Gregory's books and papers. The Director and staff of the National Library of Ireland have answered many requests, both in person and by urgent air mail, for information and for copies of difficult-to-locate texts with kindness and efficiency.

Much of the material in the present volume was supplied from the collection of the Vassar College Library or through the efforts of its staff. Mr. Johnson is particularly thankful for the unfailingly cheerful aid of Miss Joan Murphy, Mrs. Marguerite Hubbard and Miss Rosalie Tucker. Among the students and friends at Vassar who have helped in important ways, Mr. Johnson wishes particularly to thank Sharon Pattyson Robinson, Mary E. McNichols, Sheila Broughel and Alison Cole. Professors Howard L. Green and Stanley J. H. Crowe have shared their knowledge and research with him, and he is grateful also for Lawrence Friedman's labors in aid of the index. He thanks Margaret Ryan, Deborah Thomson and Kathryn Sampson for help in the preparation of the text and he is also indebted to Geoff Smyth, who has several times run long-distance errands for him in Dublin.

For his part, Mr. Frayne wishes to thank first of all his graduate assistants: John Franson, to whom he is indebted for the tracing of many of Yeats's quotations from the works of Blake; and Michael Sawdey, who proof-read many of the original typescripts. Financial aid from the Graduate College of the University of Illinois made possible a trip to Ireland in the summer of 1967 and a sabbatical leave in 1971–2 which was used to complete this edition. For the articles in French which Yeats contributed to *L'Irlande Libre* he would like to thank Professor Victor Reed who helped to obtain copies of these pieces in the Bibliothèque Nationale in Paris, and Mrs. Catherine Majdiak for her assistance in estimating the idiomatic peculiarities of the French used in them.

His thanks are especially due to the National Library of Ireland and the exemplary courtesy of its staff. Much of the research materials for this second volume were obtained through the University of Illinois Library, and special thanks are due to Miss Eva Faye Benton for her solicitude and courtesy. The first pieces in this volume were part of a dissertation written at Columbia University and reflect the editorial advice of his sponsors Professors William York Tindall, James Lowry Clifford and John Unterrecker. He would like to thank his friends Gary Adelman, Daniel Majdiak and Ronald Rower for their advice and encouragement, and his wife, Eva, for debts too manifold to enumerate.

# UNCOLLECTED PROSE BY
# W. B. YEATS

# Introduction

THIS volume of Yeats's prose differs from the first collection in two important ways. Most of those writings were unified in purpose—the foundation of an Irish national literary movement—and they were all written during a scant ten years. The essays, articles, speeches and letters in this collection, however, trace several concerns over a much longer period of Yeats's life. One reason for this disparity—one decade against just over four—is that as Yeats grew older, more famous and surer of the uses of his prose, there was less and less which he did not intend from the outset for book publication or, if it appeared initially in the periodicals, which he did not reprint himself. The fact that the selections from the first three years of this volume's span outnumber those from the last twenty years of his life demonstrates this development.

These three years—1897 to 1900—also bring to a close the dozen or so years which Yeats spent as an active journalist, a career which produced a large body of prose of which he reprinted relatively little. In 1893 he collected some of his folklore articles and ghost-stories in *The Celtic Twilight*, which was revised and expanded in 1902. Some of his critical essays—largely from 1895–1900—he gathered into *Ideas of Good and Evil* (1903), and a selection of his fictional pieces makes up *The Secret Rose* (1897). But there is hardly a trace of his many book reviews of these years or of his propaganda for the Irish Literary Revival in his prose collections during this period. He ignored these writings when he assembled the 1908 collected edition and, from the evidence of his reticent introductory note to the collection of his American newspaper pieces of this period, *Letters to the New Island* (1934), we may conclude that Yeats wanted to forget the years of struggle and disappointment in the mid-nineties.

The development of Yeats's notions about his prose shows him to be, more clearly than his work in any other form, very much the "one that ruffled in a manly pose/For all his timid heart . . .", as he in retrospect saw himself in the years with which this volume begins. In the relative obscurity of his early years, Yeats had found considerable range for self-exploration and self-expression in his essays. His articles and reviews in the eighties and early nineties advanced, under the guise of reviews or researches into folklore and earlier Anglo-Irish writers, several critical positions about national literature, popular art and symbolic literature.

He spoke out on the question of nationalism and he carried on his personal quarrel with Trinity College, Dublin, in the articles on "Professor Dowden and Irish Literature" (1895). As his career gains momentum, however, his private remarks about his prose show him to be of several minds about it. In 1897, the veteran reviewer explained to Robert Bridges that "One has to give something of one's self to the devil, in order that one may live. I have given my criticisms."[1] While Yeats's articles *were* his bread and butter in these years, his airiness to Bridges about the ideas embodied there is part of a pose. He had much earlier dismissed his prose with a similar self-conscious insouciance in a letter to Katharine Tynan which Allan Wade dates December 21, 1888. There Yeats declares that he wishes to write prose, but only the sort required by the *Dictionary of National Biography*, so as to avoid "a compromise with my artistic conscience. When I cannot write my own thoughts . . . I want to get mechanical work to do."[2] The same letter, however, betrays a private worry—or perhaps a foreboding of troubles to come—about his prose writings: "All will go well if I can keep my own unpopular thoughts out of them. To be mechanical and workmanlike is at present my deepest ambition. I must be careful in no way to suggest that fairies, or something like them do veritably exist. . . ."[3] On this subject, then, there were two Yeatses—the poet of "unpopular thoughts" who protested to fellow poets his separate identity from the poor worker in prose who gave the devil and the public thoughts not his own.

However loudly he proclaimed his artistic aloofness from the mechanical work of the journalist in the nineties, Yeats had other worries about expressing himself in prose. He knew that his mysticism and his enthusiasm for magic, among his ideas on many subjects, were unpopular and he felt their unfriendly reception on all sides. The frequently noted vagueness and obscurity in his poems, which were regularly reviewed from the middle nineties onward, was often excused as appropriate for a dreamy Celt, wandering in the twilight. Thus, the *Fortnightly Review* declared in 1902 that his poetry was "Gaelic in its inward life, partaking of the Gaelic colour and shaped in the Gaelic mold; but he has the esoteric manner of those ancient ancestors of his who were renowned for their obscurity."[4] Despite its Paterian languor, however, Yeats's expository prose claimed no exotic lineage and thus it would find no such haven. His concern in 1890 over being

[1] *The Letters of W. B. Yeats*, edited by Allan Wade, New York, 1955, p. 286. This volume is henceforth referred to as *Letters*.

[2] *Letters*, p. 96.

[3] *Letters*, p. 97. Yeats referred to his articles on the distinction between Scots and Irish fairies for W. E. Henley's *Scots Observer*.

[4] *Fortnightly Review*, vol. LXXIII, N.S., p. 341.

"called all sorts of names—imposter, liar and the rest—"[5] if he published any notes on his "anti-materialist" experiments and his work with Blake was to some extent realized when he found himself defending these interests, once they were set forth in prose, to his father and such intimates as John O'Leary and Lionel Johnson. Similarly, *The Secret Rose*, the "book of phantastic stories",[6] some of which were "half prophecy of a very veiled sort",[7] provoked considerable "hostility" in Dublin, which was reported to Yeats, ominously, by his publisher. Further, he learned from his uncle that he was not to go near the Constitutional Club in Sligo. "Between my politics and my mysticism," he wrote to Lady Gregory shortly afterward, "I shall hardly have my head turned with popularity."[8]

One of the major influences on Yeats's mysticism was his work on the Blake edition with Edwin J. Ellis. This was a "prose" task, to be sure, but Yeats found that this kind of organized expository expression helped him in several distinct ways. Prose was becoming a part of his poetic process, and he was interested in the relation between the two activities. The work on Blake, he wrote to Katharine Tynan in 1890, had done his "mind a great deal of good in liberating me from formulas and theories of several kinds", a service probably as great as that for which he commended the work to her. "You will find it a difficult book," he wrote, "but one that will open up for you, as it did for me, new kinds of poetic feeling and thought. . . ."[9] Just two years earlier, he was content to speak of his essays and articles—when they were not "mechanical work"—as a supply of "plots and atmosphere", where one could "find plenty of workable subjects".[10] Within a year, however, he noted to John O'Leary that, in writing *The Countess Cathleen*, he had "made two complete prose versions before writing a line of verse".[11] By the turn of the century, Yeats was committed to the development of systems and formulations in prose to serve his poetic needs. This function of such "private" works as *Per Amica Silentia Lunae* (1918) and *A Vision* (1925, 1937) is well documented, but even in these public, occasional writings can be found the formulation of specific conflicts and often the very language from which the dramatic or poetic passage emerges.

Aside from deliberate system-building at the turn of the century, Yeats also at that period consciously looked to his prose for "veiled prophecy", a quality he attributed to "The Adoration of the Magi", which had been omitted from *The Secret Rose* at his publisher's urging. The story's undoing may have been its prediction of the passing of Christianity and its anticipation of the reign of the "Immortals", in a

[5] *Letters*, p. 150.       [6] *Letters*, p. 266.       [7] *Letters*, p. 279.
[8] *Letters*, p. 350.       [9] *Letters*, p. 153.
[10] *Letters*, p. 85.       [11] *Letters*, p. 125.

tone of urgency or advocacy, if not outright prophecy, which runs
through many of Yeats's earlier articles and reviews. The second part
of his essay on "The Poetry of Sir Samuel Ferguson", (1886), for
example, had turned from the appreciative mode of the first section to
assert that study of the Irish legends was "the duty of every Irish
reader",[12] The object of this declaration, however, was not prophecy
but the description of a personal redemption "from that leprosy of the
modern—tepid emotions and many aims".[13] Yeats found many allies
in these views in the years between 1886 and 1896, a decade in which he
joined and helped to found several small groups dedicated to his
various enthusiasms. No doubt, the "world of selfless passion in which
heroic deeds are possible and heroic poetry credible",[14] attained by only
a few according to the essay on Ferguson, seemed more likely in such
company, and hence the need for prophets more urgent.

The desire to utter prophecies, veiled or not, may be traced in Yeats's
letters and essays to Shelley. There is also something of Arnold's influence here as well, as there certainly is the effect of Yeats's sojourn in
the London household of that tireless prophet and pamphleteer,
William Morris. But a more compelling model was closer to hand in
the person of G. W. Russell (A.E.). Yeats's relationship with A.E. was
often troubled for, as he told Lady Gregory a few years later, his lifelong friend had "demoralized me as long as I can remember".[15] But
his admiration for "this most amazing person" in 1898 is clear in a letter
to his sister Lily: "He is . . . making up his case for an attack on
T[rinity] C[ollege] D[ublin] and is working with Osbourne and Miss
Purser and a lot of others to get up a loan exhibition of pictures which
he suggested. He also sees the gods as of old and preaches of them to a
group of young persons. He has begun to write very fine prose."[16]
Such prophecies as Russell's "The Awakening of the Fires" and "Priest
or Hero?" appeared in the Irish Theosophist in 1896 and 1897, calling
for a return "to the ideal Paganism of the past", and to "the reverence
for truth among the Fianna".[17] Betraying none of Yeats's concern about
his "unpopular thoughts", Russell allied Ossian, whose return was
"premature", with Standish O'Grady, predicting that the ancient hero,
unlike the lonely old man in Yeats's "Wanderings of Oisin", might now
"find comrades come back from Tir-ne-noge for the uplifting of their
race".[18] Simultaneously, Russell was urging Yeats to join him in doing
"what Emerson did for the New Englanders", a project which he had

[12] J. P. Frayne, ed., Uncollected Prose by W. B. Yeats, New York and London, 1970, p. 104.
Henceforth this book will be referred to as Uncollected Prose, I.
[13] Uncollected Prose, I, p. 104.          [14] Uncollected Prose, I, p. 104.
[15] Letters, p. 344.                       [16] Letters, pp. 306–7.
[17] "The Awakening of the Fires", The Irish Theosophist, vol. V, p. 850.
[18] "Priest or Hero?", The Irish Theosophist, vol. V, p. 150.

been "brooding the past year over". "Now what I propose to do is
this, that you, Lionel Johnson, Standish O'Grady, Douglas Hyde,
John Eglinton and myself do write a book containing a declaration of
our principles."[19] Partial realization of this project came with the publication in 1899 of essays by Yeats, Russell, "Eglinton", and William
Larminie as *Literary Ideals in Ireland*. And in the same year, when Yeats
contributed "The Literary Movement in Ireland" to the *North American
Review*, he put aside his poses and advanced with great urgency precisely
the same "unpopular thought" he had avoided earlier: ". . . if Ireland
can make us believe that the beautiful things that move us to awe . . .
are in truth, and not phantasy alone, the symbols, or the dwellings of
immortal presences, she will have begun a change that, whether it is
begun in our time or not for centuries, will some day make all lands
holy lands again" (see p. 195 below).

A.E.'s example was probably essential to Yeats's emerging prophecies, but Yeats had been pondering the uses of literary criticism well
before he came under the influence of his friend, for whom, in any case,
literature was always subservient to the forces of the spirit world. In
1889 Yeats had told Katharine Tynan of the "great want for a just
verdict on [Irish writers since Moore] and their use for Ireland",[20]
adding a few months later that "Much may depend in the future in
Ireland now developing writers who know how to formulate in clear
expression the vague feelings now abroad . . .".[21] Such concerns as this
show Yeats, despite his banishment of his "criticism" in the letter to
Bridges, troubling over the paradox of "disinterested" cultural advocacy which had engaged Arnold earlier in the century. In a letter to
*United Ireland* in 1894 he echoed Arnold's insistence upon a cosmopolitan view. Replying to the rising Nationalist sentiment which would
have Irish artists attend only to Irish criticism, he concluded that the
"true ambition is to make criticism as international and literature as
National, as possible".[22] In 1895 he had thought of a guide for readers
of Irish literature, made up of his articles in the *Bookman* on the subject[23]
but nothing came of the project. In the long run, however, Russell's
encouragement and the achievement, though it seemed to Yeats flawed,
of his friend Arthur Symons in *The Symbolist Movement in Literature*
(1899) helped confirm his growing evaluation of his critical purpose.

Yeats was sure from the outset that his prophetic criticisms would
always appeal to "the few", as he told John O'Leary in 1897,[24] and that

[19] W. B. Yeats, ed., *Some Passages from the Letters of AE to W. B. Yeats*, The Cuala Press,
1936, p. 1.
[20] *Letters*, p. 133.  [21] *Letters*, p. 139.  [22] *Letters*, p. 238.
[23] See *Uncollected Prose*, I, articles beginning on pp. 359, 366, 375, 382.
[24] *Letters*, p. 258.

they would seem to fail as prophecies. Thus, he concludes his procla-
mation of the power of mysticism to "make all lands holy again" with
a distinction between "mistaken" and "unfulfilled" prophecy: "[Ire-
land's destiny] can but express the accidents and energies of her past,
and criticism does its natural work in trying to prophesy this expression;
and, even if it is mistaken, a prophesy is not always made all untrue by
being unfulfilled."[25] His later realization that to "Be secret and exult"
was "of all things known . . . most difficult", is implicit in this position.
The Yeats of the turn of the century, determined to give public expression to his wishes for the future, would soon profess his belief in
magic and would much later make such unpopular annunciations as his
endorsement of an era of "authority" in 1924.

By his own reckoning, 1897 was a turning point in Yeats's life. ". . . in
1897 a new scene was set, new actors appeared",[26] he noted in 1934 as
he worked on the section of his autobiography which describes his
first important meeting with Lady Gregory and his encounter with
Edward Martyn and George Moore. His friendship with Lady Gregory,
however, had begun the year before and the writing in this volume
directly reflects the results of that friendship. In 1897, she offered
Yeats a subsidy, approximate to what he would otherwise have earned
in occasional journalism, which was to be paid back some day. Lady
Gregory, with other of his Irish friends, was intent on rescuing Yeats
not only from "money cares and fears", but also from the snares of his
English, symbolist friends. Her hope may well have been to wean him
entirely from critical writing, since she felt—as she wrote him a few
years later, regarding an attack on one of his essays by D. P. Moran—
that such censure was "little more than what A.E. is always calling out,
and indeed I myself, that we long to see you at your own genuine work
. . . your lyrics, and that essays on Shelley and Blake are after all only
your second best".[27] But such writing had become essential to Yeats, as
we have seen, and thus the subsidy resulted largely in the supplanting
of his journalism and his popular writing by more idiosyncratic essays,
occasional writings which served to identify his own feelings, and by
essays describing a theatre which would embody the sort of literary
nationalism adumbrated in his essays of the previous decade.
    But if 1897 marks a turning forward, generally, the prose writings
which begin this volume are a momentary turning back, a payment of
old debts or a settling of old scores. The collection begins with a review
of a book by Sir Charles Gavan Duffy—Yeats's major opponent (and

[25] *Ideals in Ireland*, p. 102.        [26] *Letters*, p. 820.
[27] From an unpublished letter in the Berg Collection of the New York Public Library.
The letter was probably written around the end of 1900.

the winner) in a struggle over control of an Irish publishing scheme in the nineties. The subject of Duffy's book was the 1848 movement, "Young Ireland", against the renewal of which much of Yeats's propaganda in the first volume of this collection is directed. The second selection here, a review of John O'Leary's memoirs, is also a sort of valediction. Although it attempts to honor the man who had most shaped Yeats's early nationalist ideals, this review's tone marks the waning of O'Leary's influence, and its replacement by, among others, Lady Gregory.

In all, this volume contains fourteen book reviews, and only two, Yeats's review of Lady Gregory's *Poets and Dreamers*, and that of Maurice O'Sullivan's *Twenty Years A-Growing*, which Yeats declared to be his last attempt at reviewing, were written after 1900.[28] The other reviews of 1897-9 reflect Yeats's varied literary enthusiasms prior to his establishment of the Literary Theatre. The reviews and articles on his friends, A.E., Johnson and Nora Hopper, seek to consolidate an Irish school of poetry which would combine Irish subject matter with a distinctive spiritual idealism. Other reviews attempt to show that a multinational Celtic revival is taking place. Yeats's appreciations of Arthur Symons and Althea Gyles, on the other hand, set forth the ideals of the symbolist movement which Yeats's tries, in the articles on Maurice Maeterlinck, to connect with the Celtic awakening.

The six long folklore articles in this volume are part of Yeats's own contribution to this awakening. At the same time they represent part of Lady Gregory's subsidy, since they are renderings into essay form of materials from her folklore collections. As with several other of the longer pieces in this volume, these articles are first studies for a more extensive project, a "big book about the commonwealth of faery" which Yeats promised in the preface to *The Celtic Twilight* but which never appeared. The notes upon which these essays are based are Lady Gregory's, and what finally emerged in book form from them were the two volumes of her *Visions and Beliefs in the West of Ireland* (1920), to which Yeats contributed notes and two long essays. The present reprinting of the folklore articles will serve several purposes. They contain some beautiful Yeatsian passages and they demonstrate how much Yeats learned under Lady Gregory's tutelage about peasant praeternatural beliefs. They also throw additional light on those works for which they served as basis—the second *Celtic Twilight* collection and the plays and poems about the Irish countryside and the old, pagan Irish supernatural—the imaginative counterparts to the emerging "declaration of our principles", for which Russell had called.

[28] One other later review, "My Friend's Book" (1932) is an appreciation of A.E.'s *Song and its Fountains*. See *Essays and Introductions*, New York, 1968, pp. 412–18.

"I suppose Willie Yeats is still in the West," Russell wrote in early October, 1897, to Lady Gregory. "I hope so, and may the Gods guard him there from the snares of Bridges who teaches him the false things in art, also from the symbolists who do not understand their own symbols; for which things I pray to Angus Oge to watch over him."[29] Under such inspiration Yeats and his allies produced the material for such "sacred books" as *Ideals in Ireland* and *Ideas of Good and Evil,* the most comprehensive alliance of Symons's symbolists with Angus Oge. The flesh was to be made word, the world was to experience a great spiritual revelation, new gods were to appear—probably Celtic ones—and the Irish were to lead in a revival of the arts parallel to ancient Greek culture at its height. Stated thus, without Yeats's visionary diction, his *fin-de-siècle* criticism seems, as he expected it might, exaggerated and faulty as prophecy. Visions of a holy Ireland giving birth to a new Aeschylus or Aristophanes were to give way, in real life, to riots over the word "shift" and the display of the Republican flag, the Plough and the Stars, in a public house. The splendid expressions of "unpopular thoughts" at the end of the century were to be followed by a decade-long dull awakening, during which Yeats's prose traces the course of several real triumphs and many sharp conflicts—calling the police into his theatre, alienation of old friends, placating Miss Horniman.

More of the articles in this collection are concerned with the Irish National Theatre than with any other topic. Yeats himself collected a good number of such writings in the section called "The Irish Dramatic Movement" of vol. IV of the collected edition of 1908, currently reprinted in *Explorations.* A note to the 1931 edition of this collection declares that the writings in such magazines as *Beltaine, Samhain,* and *The Arrow* "rang down the curtain so far as I was concerned on what was called 'The Celtic Movement'—An 'Irish Movement' took its place."[30] What Yeats may have meant by this opposition was the change from the twilight prophecy to speaking in the clear cold light of the real world—the battles of J. M. Synge instead of the ephemeral dramatic projects of "Fiona Macleod". It is also likely, however, that Yeats would have had to include among the plays superseded by the "Irish Movement" much of his own dramatic writing, those plays which he seeks in several of the essays in this collection to integrate with the successful and generally realistic works of which he had become more often the defender than the shaper.

When one considers what Yeats did not collect of the writings for his theatre, however, more than one principle of selection emerges. He

[29] In Lady Gregory, Ts. of Memoirs, ch. 19, Berg Collection, New York Public Library.
[30] W. B. Yeats, *Explorations*, New York, 1962, p. 72.

began the selection of them in the 1908 edition with the *Samhain* issue of 1901 and, thus, did not include the occasional pieces dealing with the start of the dramatic movement itself. In the opening controversies with John Eglinton over the suitability of Irish mythological materials, one sees some perennial problems, the same problems, in fact, which are implicit in the reaction of Yeats's audience at his earliest public formulations of his ideas, the lectures to the Irish Literary Society. Also, the first announcements of the project are modest, the beginning theoretical essays are exploratory, and in these previously uncollected pieces one can trace the shifting aims and goals that characterize any beginning project. It is perhaps this exploratory quality that prevented Yeats from including them in the 1908 collection.

In comparing these uncollected pieces with the ones which were included in "The Irish Dramatic Movement" one also notes that these deal with more topical problems, are concerned with details of production and management, or repeat what Yeats wrote in more finished form in his longer dramatic essays. In the writings collected here, one can trace minutely the growth, for example, of Yeats's admiration for the stage designs of Gordon Craig. And from the lowness of the attacks against which he defended, for example, Synge's *In the Shadow of the Glen*, one appreciates the nobleness of his defenses and the exasperation and bitterness which afflicted Yeats's middle years. One skirmish with Arthur Griffith, "the slanderer of Lane and Synge",[31] affords volumes of commentary on "the daily spite of this unmannerly town".

In fact, as his personal fame grew, Yeats found his personal role as the English-speaking spokesman for the Irish movement—usually resident in London—under increasing attack. His own theatre, the highly independent Gaelic League, and such national journals as Griffith's *United Irishman* and Moran's *Leader* inspired after the turn of the century a critical voice with a Gaelic authority he could not easily ignore. Meanwhile, the general critical reception in England of Celtic "glamour" began to refine its terms, and Yeats found himself experimenting in a form of personal public expression quite new to him, the interview. Several accounts, in the nineteenth-century fashion, of his lectures to the various literary societies appeared around the turn of the century, such as his address, reprinted here, on "The Irish Literary Theatre". But as his literary and dramatic projects gained attention, he actively sought interviews in the press.[32] At the same time, his fascination with the creation of an "artistic personality in the modern sense", as he later expressed it in a letter to John Quinn[33] was obviously served by these direct reflections of "Mr. W. B. Yeats". The degree to which

31 W. B. Yeats, *The Autobiography of William Butler Yeats*, New York, 1965, p. 278.
32 See *Letters*, p. 318.        33 *Letters*, p. 447.

Yeats seems to have shaped the text and that to which it purports to quote his actual words determine, in large part, which of the interviews are included in this volume. Also included, however, are some examples of "corrected" interviews where the personality evoked evidently varied too widely from Yeats's intention. The case of his interview with the *Free Lance*, for example, indicates the delicacy of Yeats's experiments in this genre. The "long, white, cadaverous clean shaven face, topped by a drooping lock of blue black hair", in which "you see a beautiful soul hungering after a perfect happiness that the world in which its lot is cast can never give", is a recognizable version of the Celt steeped in continental mysticism who lived in London at the turn of the century. Contemporary reviews frequently evoke this figure who "lures us away from the impetus towards action, and the desire of life, to watch with him the wraiths rising slowly from the abyss, carrying the immortal legacies of dead songs and hidden symbols".[34] But after 1899, Yeats increasingly sought the allegiance of Irish nationalists full, as they thought, of impetus towards action and motivated by not at all hidden symbols. Thus, their quick ridicule of this exotic creature provoked Yeats's immediate response. As time passed Yeats became more and more adept in this form so that his experiments with radio broadcasting, of which the final essay in this volume is an example, are a natural development.

The establishment, maintenance and defense of the Irish Literary (later the National) Theatre is Yeats's major theme during the first two decades of the century. Such a shift in purpose has distinct results in his major critical preoccupations. Curiously, he becomes less interested in poetry other than dramatic poetry and even less interested in prose fiction than ever. There are, both in these essays and letters and in those which are reprinted in book form, few words about poetry and fewer still about the subject of so many essays and collections of the eighties and nineties, the forms of prose writing. Yeats's attitude toward Ireland and Irish literature also changes, as he becomes less concerned with the merits or defects of the literature of the past. His efforts to define the goals of a national culture become concentrated upon the particular questions of embodying that ideal in a theatre, and upon the practical problems of keeping such a theatre open—rioting audiences, the theological scruples of colleagues, resigning players and managers, an enraged patroness, and half-empty houses.

The prose of Yeats's writings on the theatre, most of it written between 1899 and 1917, is simpler and more direct than most of his earlier writing. Perhaps this is the result of Lady Gregory's influence, for Yeats liked to characterize her manner by paraphrasing Aristotle, saying

[34] *Academy*, June 13, 1903, p. 589.

that she could think like a wise man but express herself like one of the common people. Certainly, she felt such an influence grow as their friendship developed. "I dreamed," she noted on the back of her journal for 1900, "that I had been writing some article and that W. B. Y. said 'It's not your business to write. Your business is to make an atmosphere.' "[35] But of course the instigation for these writings was different, as were the times and his audience. Shortly after the turn of the century, Yeats became committed to participate in the nationalist propagandizing of Maud Gonne, Arthur Griffith and Standish O'Grady, all of whom founded newspapers in 1900–1901. Thus, intermixed with Yeats's more theoretical statements, we find him writing in these years against the proposed visit of Queen Victoria in 1901, a piece which parallels Maud Gonne's suppressed essay on "The Famine Queen" and which Lady Gregory, returning from a continental holiday, dismissed as "a little article on Loyalty and Disloyalty".[36]

Many of the theatre writings themselves thus draw some of their directness from Yeats's other preoccupations, as well as from the considerable increase in political activity among the public into which he sent his plays. According to such eye-witnesses of his public, political controversies as Joseph Halloway, Yeats's published defenses are somewhat more tempered than his curtain lectures. In these writings we none the less see both the origins of the direct diction of such later poems as "Paudeen" or "To a Friend Whose Work Has Come to Nothing" and Yeats's first reactions to some of the personal frustrations which are the acknowledged subjects of these poems. When it appears in the poems written at the same time as these prose writings, this harder tone is usually subordinated to the twilit images and atmosphere of the earlier lyrics. But such examples as ". . . Tara uprooted/And new commonness upon the throne . . .", although they be vanquished by the peace "In the Seven Woods", gain value in the context of his public despair with Edward VII and his concern over the digging up of the old Royal site, both subjects of articles in this collection.

Significantly, the instigation of an outpouring of Yeats's prose nearly equivalent, in the later period, to his labors on behalf of his theatre is the collection of French paintings left to Ireland in an illegal bequest by Lady Gregory's nephew Hugh Lane. The cause is a complicated, personal one and the principles not ones served by propaganda but ones which, like the poems to come, accrete to themselves both Yeats's philosophical interests and quite specific public and private events. Of the nine separate articles or letters on this subject reprinted here, several

---

[35] Unpublished letters, Berg Collection, New York Public Library, #65B1808.
[36] Ibid.

are strategic moves in the struggle against both the representative of the English art establishment and the small-minded Dublin public. In his edition of Yeats's letters Allan Wade reprinted a single long letter as representative of the entire controversy, but from the supplementary writings we see the great expenditure of energy, the mass of detailed argument, and indeed the sometimes tedious reiteration of major points that make up this controversy—a controversy, incidentally, which still smoldered in the editorial columns of *The Irish Times* in January, 1973. For Yeats, these pictures were not only symbols of Ireland robbed of her treasure but also an exemplar of one of his major obsessions—the relationship of men of daring and of genius to the society that supports them and then degrades them.

These writings have their parallels in Yeats's several poems on this subject and we may see between the dull, effective letters and such magnificently defiant poems as "To a Wealthy Man" and "To a Friend" such a relationship as Yeats recognized in "A General Introduction for My Work:" "A poet writes always of his personal life . . .; he never speaks directly as to someone at the breakfast table, there is always a phantasmagoria . . . he is never the bundle of accident and incoherence that sits down to breakfast; he has been reborn as an idea, something intended, complete."[37] By the time of these writings, Yeats's prose had come to serve him as a necessary first expression both in his poetry and in his public life of "accident and incoherence"—the "accidents and energies" we have seen him seeking expression for nearly forty years earlier in his essay in *Ideals in Ireland.*

These poems share with many of the great last poems that remarkable rhetorical particularity in which Archibald MacLeish, to Yeats's delight, identified "the strong presentness, the urgent voice" of "a poet of public speech and the world".[38] Yeats called this tribute "the only article on [my work] which has not bored me for years".[39] A concurrent feature of several of Yeats's prose contributions to periodicals after, roughly, 1915 is a similar bold amalgamation of public events, facts of his personal life and his current readings with the durable, lifelong concerns of his writing. Increasingly, in Yeats's mature years, he assumed all these things within his personality as great poet, theatre director, thinker, Senator of the Free State and, after 1923, Nobel laureate. A very early example of this amalgamation is his performance—it is hardly less—before the British Association for the Advancement of Science in 1908. Under the guise of introducing a special performance of the

[37] *Essays and Introductions*, p. 509.

[38] Archibald MacLeish, "Public Speech and Private Speech in Poetry", *Yale Review*, Spring, 1938, p. 544.

[39] Dorothy Wellesley, ed., *Letters on Poetry from W. B. Yeats to Dorothy Wellesley*, London, 1940, p. 179.

Abbey company, Yeats, both in person and in an essay, spoke his mind on Science and Art, on his oft-stated thesis that "all life is battle", combining references to a ride on a train from Galway with comparisons of himself and the assembled and probably bemused scientists to Adam.

Several of the later writings in this volume, then, are interesting as they provide not so much a gloss on the poetry as coincidental responses to what Yeats called the need for audacity of thought. In the nineties he spoke rather abstractly of this need, opposing "national feeling" to lack of "impulse and momentum" in his assessment of the failure of William Allingham: "Allingham had the making of a great writer in him, but lacked impulse and momentum, the very things national feeling could have supplied . . . There is no great literature without nationality, no great nationality without literature."[40] In his last years, the abstraction has broken away and this need, allied to the irresponsible and self-illuminating gesture of genius he calls "gaiety" in several late poems, is expressed constantly and with great particularity. It is behind his reasoned attacks on the Irish Censorship Bill of 1928 and his defense of the "blasphemous" "Cherry Tree Carol" as well as his perfectly ambivalent dialogue on compulsory Gaelic and his anonymous editorial in *To-Morrow*—anonymous not because he wished to disown his "unpopular thoughts" but because he didn't want his fame to shield the young editors from the inevitable "enemies everywhere and . . . suppression, I hope a number of times . . .".[41]

Yeats's urgency in the *To-Morrow* essay to proclaim "the human soul restored to all its courage, to all its audacity", to "declare that it can do whatever it please . . .", may be traced to his faith in prophecy which is true though unfulfilled; and his assertion that "new form" and "new subject matter" flow only from such souls lies necessarily behind his affirmation that "All things fall and are built again,/And those that build them again are gay." Similarly, we read in "The Censorship and St. Thomas Aquinas" of the effect of "Platonizing theology", a separation of body and mind, upon the mosaics in "that little Byzantium chapel at Palermo". This explanation of the "saints with thought-tortured faces and bodies . . . but a framework to sustain the patterns and colours of their clothes" and of "a Christ with face of pitiless intellect, or a pinched, flat-breasted virgin holding a child like a wooden doll" is necessary formulation, between the accident and incoherence of personal life and the inhuman artifices in "Sailing to Byzantium" and the assertion in "Byzantium" that "A starlit or a moonlit dome disdains/All that man is,/All mere complexities,/The fury and the mire of human veins."

This formulative relationship between Yeats's later prose and poetry

[40] *Letters to the New Island*, edited by Horace Reynolds, Cambridge, Mass., 1934, pp. 103–4.
[41] *Letters*, p. 706.

is perhaps more immediately sensed in some of the writings in this
volume than in those brief essays and introductions or the broadcast
essay he included in the last two sections of *Essays and Introductions*. And
while it certainly is implicit in the texture of *A Vision*, the present writings, because they still bear more clearly the marks of the occasions
from which they arise, will help to define this relationship more closely.
The challenge lies in avoiding both the temptation to regard the prose
as the raw material, the "plots and atmosphere", of the poetry and that
of the settling upon an evaluation of which form better communicates
Yeats's experience. In the famous letter to Lady Elizabeth Pelham, near
the end of his life, Yeats seemed to rule out the possibility of any com-
municable wisdom or self-knowledge. Claiming he had "found" what
he "wanted", he concluded that "When I try to put all into a phrase I
say, 'Man can embody truth but he cannot know it'."[42] Clearly, writings
such as those in this collection, in which Yeats attempts to discover his
responses by public analysis of public events, are part of the embodiment of a kind of truth, significant in itself and as it throws light on
Yeats's other writings.

[42] *Letters*, p. 922.

# Young Ireland

In 1892, despite Yeats's strenuous objections, Sir Charles Gavan Duffy had gained the editorship of the "New Irish Library" book series, a post which Yeats very likely wanted for himself (see p. 238 below). Yeats's revenge was long and leisurely. He reviewed some of the "New Irish Library" books favourably, but those volumes produced by Duffy and his coterie received slighting reviews, such as that of Duffy's *Young Ireland* in *The Bookman* for January, 1897. With Duffy's appropriation of the library scheme in mind, Yeats criticized Thomas Davis for dragooning his friends into writing plays for the "Young Ireland" movement. Within a year after this review Yeats, who was a better hunter than either Davis or Duffy, was beating the bushes for any talents to contribute to the Irish Literary Theatre.

THE period of Irish history most studied in Ireland is the period between the foundation of the *Nation* newspaper in 1842 and the Rebellion of 1848. During this period the national feeling was expressed for the first time in a definite political philosophy, and the writers and speakers through whose minds it was expressed are sacred names in Ireland. "Young Ireland," of which Sir Charles Gavan Duffy has just issued a final edition,[1] illustrated with many portraits, is the standard history of their writings and speeches, their plans and their hopes, and without it there is no understanding of modern Ireland.

I can only concern myself here with the literary influence of "Young Ireland," which has been almost as great as its political, and is, though much weakened of late among educated nationalists, still the one powerful literary influence in Ireland. The "Young Irelanders" very consciously and deliberately endeavoured to create a literature which was to be "racy of the soil," and they persuaded every man and woman they could lay hands on to join in their big endeavour. "Have you ever tried dramatic writing?" Thomas Davis, their inspiring spirit, wrote to the biographer Maddyn,[2] who was certainly the least dramatic and perhaps the dullest writer of any note Ireland has produced. "Do you know

---

[1] *Young Ireland* appeared in two volumes (1880–3). An "Irish People's Edition" appeared in 1884–7.

[2] Daniel Owen Madden (1815–59)—Duffy spelled it "Maddyn" in *Young Ireland*—was the author of *The Age of Pitt and Fox* and *Ireland and Her Rulers*.

Taylor's 'Philip Van Artevelde'[3] and Griffin's 'Gissipus?' [*sic*][4] I think them the two best serious dramas written in English since Shakespeare's time. A drama equal to either of them with an Irish subject would be useful and popular to an extent you can hardly suppose." It seemed to them possible for any clever man to write a good song, a good history, a good drama, if he only would; for literature meant to them an exposition of certain opinions about which they were agreed and hoped to make others agreed, and of certain types of character which all men might be expected to admire, and not a capricious inspiration coming with an unforeseen message out of the dim places of the mind. They published in *The Library of Ireland*[5] hastily written books of Irish history and Irish biography and Irish ballad poetry, and in the *Nation* articles on the poets and politicians and revolutionists of many lands; and this writing, which is inspired by a didactic purpose, and is but excellent journalism for the most part, seems to thousands of young men in Ireland a great ideal literature. It is only a minority of Irishmen who understand that nearly all of it that is not politics is now in one of those infirmaries of the human mind where, M. Maeterlinck says, all truths which are not mystic truths, which are not truths come out of a solitary and mysterious ideal, go at last and to die.

The "Young Irelanders" were of necessity buried in those heterogeneous occupations which Arthur Hallam[6] believed more dangerous to a writer than the most immoral of lives; and they were too preoccupied with public conduct to attend to the persuasions of their own temperaments, and all good literature is made out of temperaments. To be preoccupied with public conduct is to be preoccupied with the ideas and emotions which the average man understands or can be made to understand, and out of the ideas and emotions of the average man you can make no better thing than good rhetoric. A characteristic fruit of their moral and practical lives was the blazing rhetoric of "The Spirit of the Nation,"[7] just as a characteristic fruit of the immoral and unpractical but solitary and individual life of Clarance [*sic*] Mangan was the impassioned poetry of "The Dark Rosaleen" and of "O'Hussy's

[3] Sir Henry Taylor (1800–86) published *Philip van Artevelde, a Dramatic Romance, in Two Parts*, in 1834.

[4] *Gisippus* by Gerald Griffin (1803–40) was produced at Drury Lane in 1842.

[5] "The Library of Ireland" was a series of books written mainly by the "Young Irelanders" published by James Duffy (1809–71) in the later 1840s.

[6] In 1893, Yeats had reviewed *The Poems of Arthur Henry Hallam*. (See J. P. Frayne, ed., *Uncollected Prose by W. B. Yeats*, vol. I, New York and London, 1970, pp. 276–8.) Hallam's essay on the early poems of Tennyson became for Yeats a major critical text and he often quoted Hallam throughout the nineties.

[7] "The Spirit of the Nation" was the collection of patriotic poetry edited by Thomas Davis (1814–45) and first published in 1843.

Ode for the Macguire".[8] Clarance Mangan might doubtless have been a less unequal poet, and a poet of a more ample and serene inspiration, had he drunk less whisky and smoked less opium, but had he been buried in heterogeneous occupations or preoccupied with public conduct, he would have been no more than a good rhetorician. It is probable, however, that even if public needs had left the "Young Irelander" free to make a national literature, the season to make it had not come, for a national literature can only be painted, as it were, against a background of patient and minute scholarship, and patient and minute scholarship in Irish things had only just begun in their day. They did the one excellent thing, the one seasonable thing, that cried out to be done—they taught fervour, and labour, and religious toleration, and left their memory for an inspiration to the young men of Ireland.

W. B. Yeats

# Mr. John O'Leary

In his *Autobiography* (New York, 1965, pp. 63ff.) as well as in the last essay in this volume, Yeats ascribed to the influence of John O'Leary (1830–1907) the native force of his entire career. The *Autobiography* also records Yeats's severe disappointment when O'Leary's *Recollections of Fenians and Fenianism*, which he had been writing when the two men lived together briefly, was published in 1896. "In the evening, over his coffee, he would write passages for his memoirs . . . taking immense trouble with every word and comma, for the great work must be a masterpiece of style. When it was finished, it was unreadable, being dry, abstract, and confused; no picture had ever passed before his mind's eye." (p. 142.) Thus when Yeats, responding to the urging of his father, undertook his review of *Recollections* for the February 1897 issue of *The Bookman* his approach was to praise the author and ignore the work.

[8] Yeats had written an appreciation of James Clarence Mangan (1803–49) in 1887 (*Uncollected Prose*, I, pp. 114–19) and although he often, as here, chose the introverted Mangan over his more rhetorical contemporaries, he mistrusted the effect on Mangan of his poverty and of the tragic love affair which Yeats had documented in 1891 in his essay on "Clarence Mangan's Love Affair" (*Uncollected Prose*, I, pp. 194–8). Writing to John Quinn in 1905, Yeats assessed Mangan as a national poet: "Irish national literature . . . has never produced an artistic personality in the modern sense of the word. Tom Moore was merely an incarnate social ambition. And Clarence Mangan differed merely from the impersonal ballad writers about him in being miserable. He was not a personality as Edgar Poe was. He had not thought out or felt out a way of looking at the world peculiar to himself." (Allan Wade, ed., *The Letters of W. B. Yeats*, London, 1954, p. 447.)

A very close paraphrase of this article appeared in *L'Irlande Libre*, the Parisian political journal sponsored by Maud Gonne (1866–1953) on June 1, 1898. (See pp. 113–15 below.)

IN Ireland we sometimes celebrate the memories of our national heroes by little suppers, at which we sit round a long table and drink coffee and listen to speeches and patriotic songs. I remember talking a couples of years ago to the man who sat next me at a supper in honour, I think, of Thomas Davis, and his saying, "Our public men, with the exception of Mr. John O'Leary, have been afraid to differ from the people in anything, and now we haven't got a pinsworth of respect for anybody but for Mr. John O'Leary." This man was, if I remember rightly, a clerk in a big shop, and typical of many of the younger generation in Dublin. He had probably given his adhesion in practical things to some leader who had more eloquence, or a firmer hold on the questions of the hour, or who had shown him some immediate thing to be done, but he had only given his adhesion in practical things. As long as he could remember, Mr. John O'Leary had been denouncing this or that political expedient, this or that popular leader, and affirming, because manhood is greater than nations, that there are things which a man should not do, perhaps even to save a nation.[1] Had anyone who had not suffered, like Mr. John O'Leary, years of imprisonment and of exile, said these things, my neighbour would not have listened; but as things were, Mr. John O'Leary represented to his imagination the national conscience. There were plenty of others, he would perhaps have said, who could give you better advice as to whether a thing was expedient or inexpedient, but there was only Mr. John O'Leary to tell you whether it was right or wrong, and to tell it not only in the quiet light of your fire, but, if it were necessary, before a raging mob out in the street. To me it has always seemed that the passion for abstract right, which has made the letters to press, the occasional speeches, and above all the conversation of Mr. John O'Leary so influential with the younger generation, is the Celtic passion for ideas, intensified by that mistrust of the expedient which comes to men who have seen the failure of many hopes; and that as Irish men and women become educated they will inherit a like passion, if not in a like degree. Certainly the young men I meet in "Young Ireland" societies, in Irish literary societies, and in the Irish art schools are more like him than like the loose-

---

[1] Yeats quotes this saying of O'Leary's in his *Autobiography* as an example of O'Leary's gift for saying "things that would have sounded well in some heroic Elizabethan play". "'There are things that a man must not do to save a nation.' He would speak a sentence like that in ignorance of its passionate value, and would forget it the moment after." (p. 64.)

lipped, emotional, sympathetic, impressionable Irishman, who is the only Irishman of whom many Englishmen have ever heard. The very inhumanity of Irish journalism and of Irish politics comes from a tendency to judge men not by one another, not by experience of the degree of excellence one may hope to meet in life and in politics, but by some abstract standard.

Mr. John O'Leary's detachment from his own enthusiasms has not come to him with old age, but has given his whole life a curious and solitary distinction. His patriotism was first, he tells us, awakened by the verse of Davis, like the patriotism of so many Irishmen, but he has never so far confused literary with moral qualities as to call Davis a great or even a considerable poet. When very young he organised a band of peasants to attempt the rescue of Magher [*sic*],[2] but was able to criticise Magher's speech from the dock as calmly as though indifferent to his fate. He entered the Fenian organisation, and worked for it with energy and devotion, with no great hope for any better success that a renovation of the national spirit, and when his time came suffered imprisonment and exile without complaining. He is of that supreme type, almost unknown in our heady generation, the type that lives like the enthusiasts, and yet has no other light but a little cold intellect. And his book has a strange impartiality, which must make it, ill-arranged, rambling even, as it is, of the utmost importance both to Irish and to English historians. It has called up for me, who am more interested in the history of the soul than in the history of things, the picture of an impressive personality, and is a new example of that sense of abstract ideas, of abstract law, which I believe the Celtic peoples have preserved, together with a capacity for abstract emotion, longer than more successful and practical races.

W. B. Yeats

# The '98 Centenary

Yeats's letter on "The '98 Centenary" in *United Ireland* for March 20, 1897, is a fragmentary memento of his efforts to organize a centennial celebration of the uprising of 1798 which would unite all the warring Irish factions. On March 4, 1897, he attended a plenary meeting at Dublin City Hall as one of

[2] Thomas Francis Meagher (1823–67) was a "Young Irelander" tried for revolutionary activities in 1848, sentenced to death, reprieved, transported to Van Diemen's Land, escaped to America where he became a brigadier-general in the Civil War. He was drowned in the Missouri River while going to become temporary governor in the territory of Montana.

two representatives of the English centenary committee. As might be expected, Yeats's motives were suspect to some of the parties. Here, he is stressing his independence from the Fuath-na-Gall, a revolutionary party whose "Irish Executive in Great Britain" had published a fiery report of the meeting, denouncing the organizers for their failure to launch the project along geographically representative lines and for their failure to include in their plans "the ancient chief of the Fenian movement", James Stephens (1824–1901). In August 1898, the "Wolf Tone Memorial Association", of which Yeats was president, succeeded in laying a foundation stone at a mass demonstration in memory of the hero of the " '98".

The other representative mentioned here, Frank Hugh O'Donnell (1848– 1916), was to become a persistent antagonist of Yeats and Maud Gonne. Joseph Hone, Yeats's biographer, describes him as "a very clever man but half mad with vanity, long political contention and the strain of impecuniosity". (Hone, *W. B. Yeats, 1895–1939*, 2nd edition, New York, 1962, p. 161.) Yeats was amused by O'Donnell at first but broke with him when he attacked the reputation of Michael Davitt (1846–1906), the founder of the Land League. O'Donnell responded by writing a pamphlet, *Souls for Gold*, in which the words of the demons in *The Countess Cathleen* who bought Irish souls were quoted as being Yeats's own opinions. All this precipitated the theologico-political battle over the play. (See p. 337 below.)

TO THE EDITOR OF *UNITED IRELAND*

DEAR SIR—The otherwise admirable article, signed "By Order, Fuath-na-Gall," in UNITED IRELAND of the 13th of March, may lead a headlong reader to imagine that Mr. Frank Hugh O'Donnell and myself were sent to the meeting in the City Hall by the political body your correspondent calls "The Irish Executive of Great Britain." We were sent by "The Central Centenary Committee of Great Britain" alone, and had no purpose but to secure a representative celebration, believing that the memory of the men of '98 is a National and not a party memory.—Yours very sincerely,

W. B. Yeats

# Mr. Arthur Symons' New Book

The second review by Yeats of Arthur Symons's work, a review of *Amoris Victima* (1897) in *The Bookman* for April, 1897, contains his most impassioned defense of the decadents, a group with which Yeats, by his insistence on a literature expressing a philosophy of life and race, had as many differences as opinions in common. Symons's identification with the movement dated from his essay, "The Decadent Movement in Literature", which he had published in 1893, in reply to Richard Le Gallienne, who had declared that "decadence is merely limited thinking, often insane thinking". (*Retrospective Reviews*, London, 1896, vol. 1, p. 25.)

The catalog here of Yeats's contemporaries is his most explicit attempt to create an anti-Victorian school and demonstrates Yeats's power of organizing disparate talents under one banner. In the summer of 1896, Yeats had toured the west of Ireland with Arthur Symons (1865–1945). The introduction to the second edition of Symons's *London Nights* was dated "Rosses Point, Sligo: September 2, 1896" and there is in Symons's later volume of verses *Images of Good and Evil* a five-poem cycle, "In Ireland".


MR. ARTHUR SYMONS attempts in his latest book, "Amoris Victima," "to deal imaginatively with what seems" to him "a typical phase of modern love, as it might affect the emotions and sensations of a typical modern man, to whom emotions and sensations represent the whole of life."[1] The book is divided into four sections—"Amoris Victima," a group of fourteen sonnets; "Amoris Exsul," a group of fourteen lyrics; "Amor Triumphans," a group of sixteen lyrics; "Mundi Victima," a poem in heroic couplets divided into eleven sections of irregular length; and all these poems, though he hopes "able to stand alone," are related to "the general psychology of the imaginary hero." It is difficult and dangerous to define the movements and epochs of anything so much a part of oneself as contemporary literature, but when popular criticism, which does not consider anything difficult and dangerous, has given certain names to certain kinds of work, and hated the work for the name's sake, one is compelled to define. Popular criticism having agreed that poetry like that of Mr. Arthur Symons is "decadent," and therefore "immoral," "insincere," and "shallow," it is necessary to try and find out what distinguishes poetry like that of Mr. Arthur Symons from the poetry popular criticism has learned to honour. It seems to me that the poetry which found its greatest expression in Tennyson and Browning pushed its limits as far as possible, tried to absorb into itself the science and philosophy and morality of its time, and to speak through the mouths of as many as might be of the great persons of history; and that there has been a revolt—a gradual,[2] half-perceptible revolt, as is the fashion of English as contrasted with French revolts—and that poetry has been for two generations slowly

---

[1] This quotation is from Symons's foreword to this book (p. vii) and echoes the subtitle of Pater's *Marius the Epicurean, His Sensations and Ideas* (1885).

[2] gradual: *The Bookman* prints "gradaul".

contracting its limits and becoming more and more purely personal and lyrical in its spirit. Mr. Lang, and Mr. Dobson, and Mr. Gosse began the change by their delight in the most condensed of lyric forms; while Mr. Bridges, with his reiteration of the most ancient and eternal notes of poetry and of them alone; Mr. Francis Thompson, with his distinguishing catholic ecstasy and his preoccupation with personal circumstance; Mr. Henley, with his noisy, heroic cry; Mr. Lionel Johnson, with his ecstatic stoicism; Mr. Davidson, with his passionate insistence on a few simple ideas, whose main value is in his passionate insistence; Mr. Le Gallienne, with his fanciful attitude towards life and art; Mr. Watson, with his continual pronouncements on public affairs; and Mr. Symons, with his pleasure in "the typical modern man, to whom emotions and sensations represent the whole of life," and in "the typical modern man" alone, are but, according to their very various powers, carrying this change to its momentous fulfilment: the calling of what is personal and solitary to the supreme seat of song. Some of these poets embody this change more than others, and popular criticism seems to me to dislike a poet just in so far as he embodies this change, for popular criticism has learned the importance of the science and philosophy and morality of its time, and of the great persons of history; but a poetry which is personal and solitary, and must therefore be judged by the poetical instinct alone, leaves it puzzled and angry. Mr. Symons, who is not only, in his verse, less of a savant, or a philosopher, or a moralist, or an historian than any poet of his time, but has certain very personal preoccupations which popular criticism has never learned to associate with poetry, has endured the whole burden of its indignation.

Though this book may not decrease the indignation of popular criticism, it will set Mr. Symons' name much higher with the dozen or so of men and women to whom poetry is the first interest in life, for it has far less of that occasional aridity which was the shadow of his particular excellence. Mr. Symons in "Silhouettes" and "London Nights" was often too anxious to make his readers feel as his "typical modern man" felt at some particular moment, let us say, under the leaves in the Luxembourg gardens; and the inspiration that comes, when one is holding the pen, is despotic, and will not share its dominions with any memory of sensation and circumstance. In this book, however, he writes under a far more fiery influence than memory, than even the most moving, exquisite memory, and the lines at their best leap and live with a strange glowing and glimmering life. The blank verse lyric which his "typical modern man" addresses to "the wanderers" is as perfect as his "La Mélanite: Moulin Rouge,"[3] one of the most perfect lyrics of our time, and has greater intensity.

[3] In Symons, the title is "La Mélinite: Moulin-Rouge".

> *Theirs is the world and all the glory of it,*
> *Theirs because they forego it, passing on*
> *Into the freedom of the elements;*
> *Wandering, ever wandering,*
> *Because life holds not anything so good*
> *As to be free of yesterday, and bound*
> *Towards a new to-morrow; and they wend*
> *Into a world of unknown faces, where*
> *It may be there are faces waiting them,*
> *Faces of friendly strangers, not the long*
> *Intolerable monotony of friends.*

"La Melanite" [*sic*] was an exquisite impression, and "The Javanese Dancers," in an earlier book, was an exquisite impression, but here is the supreme emotion expressed supremely. The whole book is indeed preoccupied with the great issues and the great emotions of life, with the overmastering things, while "Silhouettes" and even "London Nights" were preoccupied with those little issues and little emotions which one can master and forget. This change of substance is most marked in "Mundi Victima," which, being the last section, and a logical climax for the other sections, is probably the latest written. "Mundi Victima" is a long ecstasy of sorrow, a long revery of that bitter wisdom which comes only to those who have a certain emotional distinction, and which is much older than philosophies and sciences, and moralities and histories, which can be taught and understood and perhaps believed by the most undistinguished people.

> *Even in our love our love could not suffice*
> *(Not the rapt silence whose warm wings abound*
> *With all the holy plenitude of sound,*
> *At love's most shadowy and hushed hour of day)*
> *To keep the voices of the world away.*
> *O subtle voices, luring from the dream*
> *The dreamer, till love's very vision seem*
> *The unruffled air that phantom feet have crossed*
> *In the mute march of that processional host*
> *Whose passing is the passing of the wind;*
> *Avenging voices, hurrying behind*
> *The souls that have escaped and yet look back*
> *Reluctantly along the flaming track;*
> *O mighty voices of the world, I have heard*
> *Between our heart-beats your reiterate word,*
> *And I have felt our heart-beats slackening.*

One may say of Mr. Symons that he is in no accurate sense of the word a "decadent," but a writer who has carried further than most of his contemporaries that revolt against the manifold, the impersonal, the luxuriant, and the external, which is perhaps the great movement of our time, and of more even than literary importance. Popular criticism, which prolongs the ideals and standards of a school of literature, which has finished its great work for this epoch of the world, is, on the other hand, in the most accurate sense of the word, "decadent."

W. B. Yeats

# Miss Fiona Macleod

Yeats's review of "Fiona Macleod's" *Spiritual Tales* (1897) in *The Sketch* for April 28, 1897, attests to the durability of the feminine guise of his friend, William Sharp (1855–1905), who was a critic and biographer under his own name (see *Uncollected Prose*, 1, p. 421). By 1897, Yeats's hopes for a Celtic revival had become a fervent conviction and, although he was later to mistrust a multinational "Pan-Celticism" (see p. 241 below), in this essay his two major examples of the new Celtic, spiritual art were the Scots "Fiona Macleod" and the Belgian Maurice Maeterlinck (1862–1949). Yeats was beginning to see all signs pointing in the direction of his desires, and even R. L. Stevenson (1850–94) and Kipling (1865–1936), seldom praised by Yeats, fit into his vision.

CRITICISM is essentially a civilised thing, and the last age of the world, being very civilised, defined literature as a criticism of life, and expressed itself in certain great writers whose work was full of criticism. Its typical writers—perhaps because the criticism of science was all about in them—had no constant and tranquil belief in the divinity of imagination, no matter how great their imaginations, but were vehement with gospels of all kinds. An English literary revolution, unlike a French one, is so gradual that we have hardly yet begun to understand how completely their heavens have been rolled up and how new an earth has come in the place of their earth. Romance-writers like Mr. Stevenson, with his delight in adventurous circumstance for its own sake, and Mr. Kipling, with his delight in the colour and spectacle of barbarous life, and those countless collections of fairy-tales which are so marked a feature of our times, are but among the most obvious of the signs of change. We no longer complicate imagination with criticism, and we have begun to recover the ancient trust in passion and in

beauty, and will soon have forgotten that we ever doubted. I am convinced that this change is bringing new kinds of temperaments into our
literature—temperaments that have been too wild and hasty for deliberate criticism of life, and that it is this change which is making
countries like Ireland and like the Highlands, which critical civilisation
has forgotten, begin to be full of voices. And of all these voices none
is more typical than the curious, mysterious, childlike voice that is in
these stories of Miss Fiona Macleod. Mr. Stevenson and Mr. Kipling
have written many simple, passionate tales, but they have written them
as men write, who are too conscious of having been born to write of
simple, passionate things to be themselves simple and passionate.
They have never forgotten, and in this lies the very value of their art,
that they have observed picturesque and barbarous things with the
keen eyes of the people of a civilised and critical land; but Miss Macleod sees everything with the eyes of the personages of her tales, and
they have not any dream too extravagant, any passion too wild, any
hope too impossible, for her heart to be in it as though there had never
been any other dream, any other passion, any other hope in the world.
Her very faults—even the faults which made, as I think, "Pharais" and
"The Mountain Lover,"[1] her earlier books, no better than books of
great promise—come from this absolute absorption in the dreams and
passions and hopes of her personages. She forgets, in following some
spectacle of love and battle, that she is using words and phrases, paragraphs and chapters, rhythms and cadences; and so "thou" and "you"
get mixed together, and words altogether out of the true key mix
themselves into her rushing sentences. She is, however, gradually
learning that writing is not all a spiritual enthusiasm, and these three
books, in which she has collected the best tales out of her "Sin-Eater"[2]
and "Washer of the Ford," with certain new tales, are constantly almost
perfect of their kind. I have put them to a hard test, for I read the tales in
"The Washer of the Ford," which are reprinted here, on the deck of an
Arran[3] fishing-boat and among the grey stones of Arran Island; among
the very people of whom she writes, for the Irish and Highland Gael
are one race; and when I laid down the book I talked with an Arran
fisherman of the very beliefs and legends that were its warp and woof. I
read of St. Colum and the seal in the hot sun on the deck—

The holy man had wandered on to where the rocks are, opposite to Soa.
He was praying and praying, and it is said that whenever he prayed aloud the
barren egg in the nest would quicken, and the blighted bud unfold, and the
butterfly cleave its shroud.

[1] Sharp's book was called *The Mountain Lovers*.    [2] Sharp's title had no hyphen.
[3] Arran: usually spelled "Aran". Yeats had visited the Aran Islands the previous year in
search of material for his unfinished novel, "The Speckled Bird".

Of a sudden he came upon a great black seal lying silent on the rocks with wicked eyes.

"My blessing upon you, O Ròn!" he said, with the good, kind courteousness that was his.

"*Droch spadadh ort*," answered the seal. "A bad end to you, Colum of the Gown!"

"Sure, now" said Colum angrily, "I am knowing by that curse that you are no friend of Christ, but of the evil pagan faith out of the North. For here I am known even[4] as Colum the White, or as Colum the Saint, and it is only the Picts and wanton[5] Normen who deride me because of the holy white robe I wear."

"Well, well," replied the seal, speaking the good Gaelic as though it were the tongue of the deep sea, as, God knows, it may be for all you and I[6] or the blind wind can say; "well, well, let that thing be; it's a wave-way hear or a wave-way there. But now, if it is a Druid you are, whether of Fire or of Christ, be telling me where my woman is, and where my little daughter."

At this Colum looked at him for a long while; then he knew.

"It is a man you were once, O Ròn?"

"Maybe ay and maybe no."

"And with that thick Gaelic that you have it will be out of the North isles you come?"

"That is a true thing."

"Now, I am for knowing at last who and what you are. You are one of the race of Odrum the Pagan."

And so on, until it is told that the seal is Judas, looking for his wife Lilleth through all the wastes of the sea. When I had done, I talked to an old man of the mystery of the seals, or of the Ròns, for he did not know them by their English name, and of their human-like eyes and human-like voices, and it was plain to me that he was not altogether at all times certain that they were mere beasts of the sea. And then I read "The Dan-nan-Ròn," which tells of a man that was descended from the seals, and how he rushed into the sea that he might be a seal again; and when I had done, I talked with another old man, who told me that his own family were come of the seals, but it might "be all talk." It seemed to me that Miss Macleod had not, like the rest of us, taken a peasant legend and made it the symbol of some personal phantasy, but that she felt about the world, and the creatures of its winds and waters, emotions that were of one kind with the emotions of these grave peasants, the most purely Celtic peasants in Ireland, and that she had become their voice, not from any mere observation of their ways, but out of an absolute identity of nature. The truth is that she, like all who have

---

[4] even: Sharp reads "ever".
[5] wanton: Sharp reads "the wanton".
[6] you and I: Sharp reads "you, I, or".

Celtic minds and have learnt to trust them, has in her hands the keys of those gates of the primeval world, which shut behind more successful races, when they plunged into material progress.

Criticism, and the art which is of criticism, deal with visible and palpable things; but her art belongs in kind, whatever be its excellence in its kind, to a greater art, which is of revelation, and deals with invisible and impalpable things. Its mission is to bring us near to those powers and principalities, which we divine in mortal hopes and passions, although we cannot see them or feel them, and which M. Maeterlinck has told us in his beautiful "Treasure of the Lowly"[7] are pressing in upon us to-day with a patient persistence, perhaps unknown since the founding of Christendom.

W. B. Yeats

# The Treasure of the Humble

One of Yeats's golden books, for a time, was Maurice Maeterlinck's volume of essays, *The Treasure of the Humble* (*Le Trésor des humbles*, 1896), the English translation of which he reviewed in *The Bookman* for July, 1897. Maeterlinck's prophesies of the millennium agreed with Yeats's own announcements of the coming age of anti-realistic, symbolic art. Yeats shared with Maeterlinck an admiration for Plotinus, and the Belgian dramatist probably introduced him to the work of the medieval Flemish mystic Jan van Ruysbroeck (1293–1381).

What Yeats found lacking in Maeterlinck—"the definiteness of the great mystics"—he found in Blake, and he tried to emulate this definiteness later in his own philosophy, *A Vision*. His attack on A. B. Walkley's introduction to Maeterlinck's volume not only reflects his irritation with profane triflers with mysticism but also his experience of almost a decade as an introducer of books.

A slightly changed version of this review appeared in the American edition of *The Bookman* (August, 1897, pp. 518–19).

W E are in the midst of a great revolution of thought, which is touching literature and speculation alike; an insurrection against everything which assumes that the external and material are the only fixed things, the only standards of reality. There have indeed been always plenty of men to write and to say that "thought is the only reality," but since the rise of the scientific philosophers they have said it with a merely aca-

---

[7] Actually *The Treasure of the Humble*, which Yeats reviewed in *The Bookman* issue of July, 1897 (see pp. 45–7, below).

demic conviction, and all their criticisms of life and of literature have
assumed that the world and nature were alone realities. But this insurrection has come with a generation young enough to have escaped from
servitude to the scientific philosophers, and M. Maeterlinck, who took
the red bonnet from the hands of Villiers de Lisle Adam [*sic*], is among
the most inspired of its leaders. The soul is to-day, he says, "clearly
making a mighty effort. Its manifestations are everywhere, and they are
strangely urgent. . . . I will say nothing of the occult powers, of which
signs are everywhere. . . . These things are known of all men, and can
easily be verified,[1] and truly they may well be the merest bagatelle by
the side of the vast upheaval that is actually in progress, for the soul is
like a dreamer, enthralled by sleep, who struggles with all his might to
move an arm or raise an eyelid. . . . In the work-a-day lives of the
humblest[2] of men spiritual phenomena manifest themselves—mysterious direct workings that bring soul nearer to soul; and of all this we
can find no record in former times." His book is an exposition of the
"mysterious direct workings" of which "we can find no record in former times"; and the wonder of the book is that M. Maeterlinck has
dwelled so long with these dim powers, these mysterious principalities,
which are the deep below all deeps, that he writes of them, not with the
arid vehemence of a combatant or an innovator, but with a beautiful
pathos and tenderness. "What[3] avail to cultivate an *ego* on which we
have little influence? It is our star which it behoves us to watch. It is
good or bad, pallid or puissant, and not by all the might of the sea can
it be changed. Some there are who may confidently play with their
star as one might play with a glass ball. They may throw it and hazard
it where they list; faithfully will it ever return to their hands. They know
full well it cannot be broken. But there are many others who dare not
even raise their eyes towards their star, without it detach itself from the
firmament and fall in dust at their feet." The book lacks the definiteness
of the great mystics, but it has countless passages of this curious pathetic
beauty, and shows us common arts and things, with the light of the
great mystics, and a new light that was not theirs, beating upon them.
It is very tolerably translated by Mr. Alfred Sutro, and had not Mr.
A. B. Walkley[4] written an absurd introduction would have been worthy

[1] Maeterlinck reads "verified. And truly . . .". Quotation is from "The Awakening of
the Soul".
[2] Maeterlinck reads "very humblest".
[3] Maeterlinck reads "Of what avail". Quotation is from "The Star".
[4] Despite his scolding here of Arthur Bingham Walkley (1855–1926), the influential
drama critic for *The Star* and *The Times*, Yeats came eventually to value him among his
converts to his ideas about drama. In 1902, Walkley again aroused Yeats when, in a review
of Gordon Bottomley's *The Crier by Night*, he attributed the production's "completely
stupid insolence towards the playhouse and its audience" to the influence of Yeats "and his

to be a book of those that have few books and turn to them year after year. Mr. A. B. Walkley has done great service to dramatic literature by his analysis of modern drama, but he has no mystical knowledge and no mystical sympathy. He has introduced a book, which would charm that it may persuade, with a story from Dickens about Mr. Squeers and how his pupils spelled w-i-n-d-e-r before they cleaned the windows. Apart from his special subjects Mr. Walkley is but a popular journalist, and would probably think a quotation from Dickens and a quotation from Dr. Johnson, unfailing symptoms of popular journalism, the only necessary prelude to "The Imitation of Christ." If publishers would frankly recognise that popular journalism has but a trade value, and perforate the inner margins of the pages of its introductions, no man would have a reason to complain. To merely slip the introductions in like circulars would be to go too far, for numbers will always prefer them to the books themselves.

W. B. Yeats

# Mr. Standish O'Grady's *Flight of the Eagle*

Yeats has given to Standish O'Grady's *History of Ireland* (1878–80) the credit for starting the Irish Literary Revival. He had cited the *Bog of Stars* (1893) as one of the "two or three good books" published by the ill-fated New Irish Library and six books by O'Grady (1846–1928) appeared on Yeats's list of thirty essential Irish books in 1895. Although he was a Unionist and the principal leader writer for the *Daily Express*, "the most conservative paper in Ireland", Yeats admired O'Grady's gentle, implacable reiteration of his Protestant heritage. "All round us people talked or wrote for victory's sake, and were hated for their victories," Yeats recalled in his *Autobiography* (p. 148), "but here was a man whose rage was a swan-song over all that he had held most dear, and to whom for that very reason every Irish imaginative writer owed a portion of his soul." In two of his last essays, the "General Introduction for my Work" and "I Became an Author", as well as in the late poem called "Beautiful Lofty Things", Yeats coupled O'Grady with John O'Leary as the two powerful influences upon him at the time when his commitment to poetry was being formed.

---

foolish friends". "The insolence . . . is our wicked defiance," Yeats wrote to Lady Gregory, "I sent him a copy of *Samhain.*" (*Letters*, p. 388.)

Walkley's enthusiastic and sympathetic article about the Irish National Theatre Society's performance in May, 1903 (reprinted in *Drama and Life*, New York, 1908) pleased Yeats greatly. In *Samhain* for September, 1903, he cited Walkley's "subtle and eloquent words", and he alluded to them in speaking before his American audiences in 1904 and in his letter on the Irish National Theatre to *The Times* of June 16, 1910 (see p. 381, below).

Yeats's awe of O'Grady as an historian seems, however, to have lessened with the years, and by the time he reviewed *The Flight of the Eagle* in *The Bookman* for August, 1897, he had his own ideas about the Irish past. His basic disagreement with O'Grady was that Yeats could not accept an account of Irish noblemen cooperating with their Elizabethan conquerors—whether O'Grady had evidence to support this feeling or not. Although the historical figures from the period covered by O'Grady's book seemed to appeal strongly to Yeats's sensibilities, that age of Irish history figures very little in his writings. Yeats's taste was less secure in prose than in poetry, and his admiring final quotation from O'Grady shows his occasional admiration for fustian prose when the manner was Miltonic and the matter was Celtic.

MR. STANDISH O'GRADY is the first historian who has written Irish history in a philosophic spirit and as an imaginative art. Many have made long lists of kings and battles, and one or two, like Mr. Lecky,[1] have weighed and measured political and economical movements; but Mr. O'Grady alone has looked for the great tides of passion and thought that are the substance of life. One goes to other historians to support a political argument, and, indeed, for all those things which, to use a phrase of William Blake's, are "something other than human life;" but one goes to him to enlarge one's imagination, and to have the more of that philosophy that comes of imagination, and these things are human life itself. One need not always agree with him, and I certainly do not yet agree with more than half of the theory, that is, in the foundations of much of his writings on the Elizabethan age in Ireland. Roused into hostility by the extreme view of the popular Irish historians, who talk of an Elizabethan Ireland, united, but for a few knaves and dastards, in a last struggle against English rule, Mr. O'Grady sees a feudal Ireland, with feudal ideas of freedom, struggling against a modern Ireland, with modern ideas of freedom, and all, ancient and modern Ireland alike, loyal to the crown. When the great chiefs went into rebellion, they went, he holds, mourning that they had been loyal in vain; and when they were pulled down they were pulled down by modern Ireland with England helping. I do not find it difficult to follow Mr. O'Grady, when he explains that the crown had so long been the most powerful of the clans, that its rule, and all the more because it was hitherto little but a nominal rule, was accepted, or half accepted, by the great chiefs, in place of that strong native rule which, but for it, would have come to silence their disorders; but I find it difficult to follow him when he says, or seems to say, that this loyalty was more than the cold

[1] William Edward Lecky (1838–1903), British historian, born and educated in Ireland. His most famous work dealt only indirectly with Ireland—*History of England in the Eighteenth Century* (8 volumes, 1878–90). He also wrote *The Leaders of Public Opinion in Ireland* (1861).

and fitful loyalty born of expediency and necessity, and that Ireland, speaking a different language and having different traditions from England, had, I will not say no national antagonism, for nationality is a modern idea, but no racial antagonism to England. Mr. O'Grady may be right, for I am no historian, and human nature is a nearly incalculable thing, but I will find it difficult to follow him, until the Gaelic tongue has given up its dead and I know what was sung and repeated at the hearths of the people, and how the traditions of hunters and shepherds magnified or diminished policies and battles. Some of the evidence on which he relies does not seem to me as strong as it does to him, though it is all interesting enough to have made its discovery a great service to history. He tells in this book how Perrot,[2] the Viceroy, boasted that there was no man in Ireland that would not come to Dublin if he but bade him; and calls the speech "not less true than proud;" and yet there was one, Feagh MacHugh, also told of in this book, and more vividly than ever before in any Irish history, who lived but a few miles from Dublin, and would not have budged an inch for all the Perrots in the world, and Feagh MacHugh had a son that would not have budged either, although Perrot had long wanted him, and had "passionately sought him." Then, too, in *Pacata Hibernica*,[3] of which Mr. O'Grady has given us the best edition, and on which he relies for much of his evidence, there is a saying of a certain "loyal" man, that if the Spaniards came there would be no more loyal men. I make these criticisms, not because I am weary of praising Mr. O'Grady, but because I do not wish to be misunderstood by my Irish readers, who see nothing in Mr. O'Grady's, or in anybody else's, histories, but help or hindrance to some political argument; and return to my praising.

There is in no Irish book, except in Mr. O'Grady's own "Bog of Stars,"[4] which should be read with this book, so long a procession of great historical persons: Perrot, with his proud and boastful ways, and his fierce hardihood; the noseless married priest who digs Perrot's grave; the Lady O'Donnell, the "dark daughter," keeping the lands of her imprisoned son at the sword's point; Feagh MacHugh, the masterful feudal dynast among his hills; Sir Felim O'Toole, politic or half-craven; Art O'Toole, living a disorderly drunken life in Dublin taverns, and denouncing and mocking his brother Felim; Viceroy

[2] Sir John Perrot (1527?–92) was president of Munster from 1570 to 1573, and Lord Deputy of Ireland from 1584 to 1588. He was found guilty of high treason and died in the Tower of London in 1592.

[3] *Pacata Hibernica* by Sir Thomas Stafford (*fl.* 1633) was, according to the sub-title, "a history of the wars in Ireland during the reign of Queen Elizabeth". O'Grady's edition appeared in 1896.

[4] *The Bog of Stars*, a book of stories and sketches of Elizabethan Ireland, appeared in the New Irish Library series in 1893.

FitzWilliam[5] with his ailments and his many venoms; and among these, and with all these to hurt or to hinder him, Red Hugh O'Donnell,[6] twice a captive in Dublin Castle and twice a fugitive. The book is of somewhat new a kind in modern days and hard to class. It is not an historical romance, for all of it that is imagination was made for the sake of history; and it is not a history in our modern sense, for much of it is but inference, and Mr. O'Grady does not always check his story to say when it is but inference. It would have met with no complaints in the day of Herodotus, but our timid day will in all likelihood abuse it roundly. It is written with vigour and music, but with less of sustained style than Mr. O'Grady's legendary books, perhaps because he has not the example of the great epics to guide him. Here and there the commentary is a little obvious, but here and there commentary and style alike are lifted up into an almost lyric simplicity and intensity, and never so truly as when he has to tell of that sea of ancient Celtic legend whose flood-gates he was the first to lift. Red Hugh O'Donnell rides into the North to begin his war upon the Government, "the last great secular champion of the Gaelic tradition—the foiled champion too—such is the power of the weaving stars;" and as he rides comes upon Sleive Fuad,[7] most legendary of hills, and Sleive Fuad becomes a person of the history, a symbol of "the Gaelic tradition." "Here Ossian's sire slew the enchanter Alwain,[8] son of Midna, who once a year,[9] to the sound of unearthly music, consumed Taru[10] with magic flames. On this mountain Cuculain seized the wild faery steed, the Leath[11] Macha, new risen from the Grey Lake, ere steed and hero in their giant wrestlings and reelings encompassed Bunba,[12] and in the quaking night the nations trembled. Here, steeped in Lough Lieth's[13] waters, Finn's golden tresses took on the hue and glitter of radiant snow. From the spilled goblet of the god sprang the hazels whose magic clusters might assuage that hunger of the spirit which knows no other assuagement. The Fead[14] Fia was shed around them. Here shined and trembled the wisps[15] of druid-grasses,

[5] Sir William Fitzwilliam (1526–99) was Lord Deputy of Ireland from 1572 to 1575 and from 1588 to 1599.

[6] Red Hugh O'Donnell (1571?–1602), lord of Tyrconnel, fought sometimes victoriously against the English in the 1590s, and died of poison in Spain.

[7] According to P. W. Joyce in *Old Celtic Romances*, "Sleive Fuad was the ancient name of the highest of the Fews mountains, near Newtown Hamilton, in Armagh; but the name is now lost."

[8] Alwain: O'Grady reads "Almain".

[9] once a year: O'Grady reads "once every year".

[10] Taru: O'Grady reads "Tara".

[11] Leath: O'Grady reads "Liath".

[12] Bunba: O'Grady reads "Banba".

[13] Lieth's O'Grady reads "Liath's".

[14] Fead: O'Grady reads "Faed".

[15] wisps: O'Grady reads "wisp".

from whose whisperings with the dawn wind pure ears might learn
the secrets of life and death. Here beneath those hazels, their immortal
green and their scarlet clusters, sprang the well of the waters of all
wisdom. Three dreadful queens guarded it. Sometimes they smile
seeing afar some youth wandering unconsoled o'er-laden with the
burthen of his thoughts, rapt with visions, tormented by the gods, a
stranger in his own household, scorned by those he[16] cannot scorn, out-
cast from the wholesome cheerful life of men—they smile, and smiling
dart from rosy immortal fingers one radiant drop upon his pallid lips,
and lo the word out of his mouth becomes a sword wherewith he
cleaves[17] through mountains; with his right hand he upholds the weak,
and with the left prostrates powers, and tyrants tremble before the light
of his mild eyes." The enchanted catalogue is long, much longer than
my extract, but I at any rate would not tire were it far longer than it is.

W. B. Yeats

# Aglavaine and Selysette

Yeats had a higher regard for Maurice Maeterlinck as a philosopher and
prophet than as a dramatist. As with those of John Todhunter, however, he
praised the plays of Maeterlinck as symptoms of a change in public taste
toward a poetic and away from naturalistic drama. He had been acquainted
with Maeterlinck's plays since the early nineties and he had formed his
opinion of Maeterlinck much earlier than his review of "Aglavaine and Selysette", in *The Bookman* for September, 1897. In a letter to Olivia Shakespear of
April 7, 1895, he had stated his reservations:

> I feel about his things generally however that they differ from really
> great work in lacking that ceaseless revery about life which we call
> wisdom. . . . I said to Verlaine, when I saw him last year, "Does not
> Maeterlinck touch the nerves sometimes when he should touch the heart?"
> "Ah yes," said Verlaine, "he is a dear good fellow and my very good friend,
> but a little bit of a mountebank." This touching the nerves alone, seems to
> me to come from a lack of reverie. He is however of immense value as a
> force helping people to understand a more ideal drama. (*Letters*, p. 255.)

Yeats thought for a time that he had found "that ceaseless reverie about life"
in Maeterlinck's *Treasure of the Humble* (see p. 45 above).
The opening section of this review, contrasting Flaubert with Villiers de

---

[16] those he: O'Grady reads "those whom he".
[17] cleaves: O'Grady reads "shears".

l'Isle Adam and Maeterlinck, was revised for inclusion in the first part of Yeats's essay, "The Autumn of the Flesh", which appeared in 1898.

THE literary movement of our time has been a movement against the external and heterogeneous, and like all literary movements, its French expression is more intelligible and obvious than its English expression, because more extreme. When one compares "La Tentation de Saint Antoine" of Flaubert, the last great work of the old romantic movement, with the "Axël" of Villiers de L'Isle Adam, the first great work of the new romantic movement, one understands the completeness of the change. A movement which never mentions an external thing except to express a state of the soul, has taken the place of a movement which delighted in picturesque and bizarre things for their own sakes. M. Maeterlinck has called himself a disciple of Villiers de L'Isle Adam, who, in the words of a recent French critic, "opened the doors of the beyond with a crash that our generation might pass through them"[1]— I quote from memory—but he has carried his master's revolt farther than his master, and made his persons shadows and cries. We do not know in what country they were born, or in what period they were born, or how old they are, or what they look like, and we do not always know whether they are brother and sister, or lover and lover, or husband and wife. They go hither and thither by well-sides, and by crumbling towers, and among woods, that are repeated again and again, and are as unemphatic as a faded tapestry; and they speak with low, caressing voices which one has to hold one's breath to hear. The old movement was full of the pride of the world, and called to us through a brazen trumpet; and the persons of "Axël" were lifted above the pride of the world, by the pride of hidden and august destinies, the pride of the Magi following the star over many mountains; but these souls are naked, and can little but tremble and lament. They have not hitherto needed to do more, for they were made to prolong the sense of terror Shakespeare put into the line, "the bay trees in my country are all withered,"[2] the terror at we do not know what, mixed with a pity for we do not know what, that we come to in contemplation when all reasons, all hopes, all memories have passed, and the Divine ecstasy has not found us. M. Maeterlinck has, however, made the persons of

---

[1] The French critic was Remy de Gourmont (1858–1915). In *Le Livre des masques* (1895) de Gourmont said of Villiers de l'Isle Adam, ". . . c'est qu'il a rouvert les portes de l'an delà closes avec quel fracas, on s'en souvient, et par ces portes toute une génération s'est ruée vers l'infini". (*Pages Choisies*, Paris, 1922, p. 240.) Yeats quotes this passage more accurately in his essay on "John Eglinton and Spiritual Art". (See p. 129 below.)

[2] *Richard II*, Act 2, scene 4, l. 8.

"Aglavaine and Sélysette"[3] with a partly different purpose, for he has found a philosophy in his search for the quintessence, the philosophy of his beautiful "Trésor des Humbles," and he would have his persons speak out of its wisdom. It will make his plays more beautiful in time, for the serious fault of his best plays, even of "Les Aveugles" and "L'Intruse," is that they have not the crowning glory of great plays, that continual revery about destiny that is, as it were, the perfect raiment of beautiful emotions. Its immediate effect is mischievous, for Meleander and Aglavaine, his most prominent persons, continually say things, which they would say differently or not at all, if their maker were only thinking of them as persons in the play. The first act and part of the second act are a little absurd, because Meleander and Aglavaine explain when they should desire and regret; and because their overmastering sense of certain spiritual realities has blinded them to certain lesser realities, which natures of so high a wisdom could not have been blinded to; and because the art, which should be of a cold wisdom, has shared in their delusions and become a little sentimental. One is not indeed moved until the play begins to eddy about Meligrane, an old grandmother, Yssalene[5], a child, and Sélysette, a childlike woman, persons whose natures are so narrowed because of forgotten and unknown things, that M. Maeterlinck cannot speak through their lips, but must let them speak as their destinies would have them speak. They speak more movingly than the persons of "Les Aveugles" or "L'Intruse," for though still hardly more than shadows and cries, they have each, as the persons in Shakespeare have, their portion of wisdom, while all they say is beautiful with the pathos of their little interests and their extreme weakness. I do not think M. Maeterlinck has indeed written anything as beautiful as one thing that is said by old Meligrane to her granddaughter, Sélysette.

"So do I often think of those days, Sélysette. I was not ill, then, and I was able to carry you in my arms or run after you. . . . You wandered to and fro, and your laughter rang through the house, then suddenly you would fling open the door and shriek in terror, 'She is coming, she is coming, she is here!' And no one knew whom you meant, or what it was that frightened you; you did not know yourself; but I would pretend to be frightened too, and would go through the long corridors with you till we reached the garden. And it all went for so little, and served no purpose, my child; but we understood each other, you and I, and smiled at each other, night and morning. . . . And thus, thanks to you, have I been a mother a second time, long after my beauty had left

[3] In the English translation of this play, Alfred Sutro dropped the accent from Sélysette, but Yeats retains it throughout the review.
[4] Yssalene: spelled Yssaline in the play.

me; and some day you will know that women never weary of mother-
hood, that they would cherish death itself, did it fall asleep on their
knee."

W. B. Yeats

# The Tribes of Danu

Yeats's article entitled "The Tribes of Danu" in *The New Review* for November, 1897, is the first of six long essays on various aspects of Irish folklore and
supernatural experience. The other articles in the series are:

> The Prisoners of the Gods (*Nineteenth Century*, January, 1898)
> The Broken Gates of Death (*Fortnightly Review*, April, 1898)
> Ireland Bewitched (*Contemporary Review*, September, 1899)
> Irish Witch Doctors (*Fortnightly Review*, September, 1900)
> Away (*Fortnightly Review*, April, 1902).

As the first result of his friendship and collaboration with Lady Augusta
Gregory (1852–1932), this essay represents a milestone in Yeats's career. They
had met in the summer of 1896, and during the following year their friendship
ripened, as Lady Gregory started her endeavour to help the sick, discouraged
and unhappy Yeats. He spent part of the summer of 1897 at Coole where he
accompanied Lady Gregory on her rounds of the peasant cottages. She had
been collecting folktales for some time in the past, and Yeats, who had
published his collection of folktales from the Sligo region in 1894, happily
joined in the project.

Yeats regarded the folklore materials in these articles as much Lady
Gregory's as his own. In a letter of December 22, 1898, he described a direct
collaboration on a "big book of folklore"—a project not to be completed
until 1916 and not to be published until 1920:

> One hand should do the actual shaping and writing—apart from peasant
> talk—and I would wish to do this. In some cases my opinions may be too
> directly mystical for you to accept. In such cases I can either initial the
> chapters containing them or make a general statement about them in the
> preface. If you agree to this, all future essays can either appear over our two
> signatures or I can add a footnote saying that a friend, whose name I do
> not give, because it is easier to collect if one is not known to be writing, is
> helping me throughout. Please agree to this arrangement as I dislike taking
> credit for what is not mine and it will be a great pleasure to do this work
> with you. (*Letters*, p. 305.)

In the 1902 preface to *The Celtic Twilight* he told his readers that a more
ambitious folklore project was under way: "I shall publish in a little while a

big book about the commonwealth of faery, and shall try to make it system-
atical and learned enough to buy pardon for this handful of dreams." (*The
Celtic Twilight and a Selection of Early Poems*, intro. by Walter Starkie, New
York, p. 32, 1962.) But the only book to come from the collaboration was the
two volumes of *Visions and Beliefs in the West of Ireland, Collected and Arranged
by Lady Gregory; with Two Essays and Notes by W. B. Yeats* (1920). These two
essays, which might have been, as Yeats put it in the letter quoted above,
"too mystical for you" were "Witches and Wizards and Irish Folk-lore" and
"Swedenborg, Mediums and the Desolate Places", both dated 1914. Yeats's
involvement with Lady Gregory's two volumes can be traced in his letters.
On May 9, 1911, he wrote to his father that he was settling down to work on
the project—"Finding myself unfitted for verse, which is always a strain . . .".
(*Letters*, p. 558). On March 5, 1912, he told his father that he was writing a
lecture on the supernatural world which would serve as introduction to the
Lady Gregory work—probably one of the last two essays reprinted here (*ibid.*,
pp. 567–8). And, three years later, on June 24, 1915, he told John Quinn,
"I have also nearly finished my Notes for Lady Gregory's book, and that has
laid the ghost for me. I am free at last from the obsession of the supernatural,
having got my thoughts in order and ranged on paper" (*ibid.*, p. 595). With
all of *A Vision* before him, this must be surely the most inconclusive "at last"
in Yeats's lifetime.

The footnotes to these articles indicate some parallels in the Lady Gregory
volumes, but the similarities cited are by no means complete. Lady Gregory
arranged her material under rather simple headings such as "Biddy Early"
and her presentation of this material is direct and without much commentary.
Yeats's essays begin and end with his interpretations, but the central portions
of these articles are mainly direct reportage of folklore.

Such an allegation as this article makes—that the peasants of the west of
Ireland have a widespread and deep belief in the pagan Irish supernatural—
could not fail to arouse clerical reaction, and Yeats tells Lady Gregory in a
letter of November 17, 1897, that there was "rather a blow" about it (*Letters*,
p. 290). For whatever reason, all the other articles appeared in other journals.

The rhythm of the opening sentence of this article is as beautiful as any in
Yeats's prose. His assurance in his knowledge not only that Homer was
happy but why he was happy is that of a man who speaks not only as *a* poet
but as *the* poet.

## I.—THE LANDS OF THE TRIBES OF DANU

THE poet is happy, as Homer was happy, who can see from his door
mountains, where the heroes and beautiful women of old times were
happy or unhappy, and quiet places not yet forsaken by the gods. If a
poet cannot find immortal and mysterious things in his own country,
he must write of far-off countries oftener than of his own country, or
of a vague country that is not far off or near at hand, for even the most

fleeting and intelligible passions of poetry live among immortal and mysterious things; and when he does not write of his own country the waters and mountains about him, and the lives that are lived amongst them, are less beautiful than they might be. He will be more solitary too, for people will find little in their lives to remind them of him, and he will find little in his writings to remind him of them, and the world and poetry will forget one another. The more he has of spiritual passion the more solitary he will be, for who would not think *Prometheus Unbound* better to read and better to remember if its legends and its scenery were the legends and the scenery they had known from child-hood, or that Shelley had known from childhood and filled with the passion of many memories? Indeed, I am certain that the writers of a spiritual literature, if it is not a literature of simple prayers and cries, must make the land about them a Holy Land; and now that literature which is not spiritual literature is, perhaps, passing away, we must begin making our lands Holy Lands, as the Jews made Palestine, as the Indians made Northern India, as the Greeks made the lands about the Ionian Sea. I think that my own people, the people of a Celtic habit of thought, if genius which cannot be whistled for blow their way, can best begin, for they have a passion for their lands, and the waters and mountains of their lands remind them of old love tales, old battle tales, and the exultant hidden multitudes. There is no place in Ireland where they will not point to some mountain where Grania[1] slept beside her lover, or where the misshapen Fomor were routed, or to some waters where the Sacred Hazel once grew and fattened the Salmon of Wisdom with its crimson nuts; nor is there, I think, a place outside the big towns where they do not believe that the Fairies, the Tribes of the goddess Danu, are stealing their bodies and their souls, or putting unearthly strength into their bodies, and always hearing all that they say. Nothing shows more how blind educated Ireland—I am not certain that I should call so unimaginative a thing education—is about peasant Ireland, than that it does not understand how the old religion which made of the coming and going of the greenness of the woods and of the fruitfulness of the fields a part of its worship, lives side by side with the new religion which would trample nature as a serpent un-der its feet; nor is that old religion faded to a meaningless repetition of old customs, for the ecstatic who has seen the red light and white light of God smite themselves into the bread and wine at the Mass, has seen the exultant hidden multitudes among the winds of May, and if he were

---

[1] Yeats refers to the famous legend of Grania, who was pursued with her lover Diarmuid by her original betrothed, Finn MacCool. The "mishapen Fomor" were a race of monsters who battled with the Firbolg in Ireland before the coming of the Tuatha de Danaan. They are, according to a note which Yeats wrote for the 1895 edition of his poems, the ancestors of evil faeries, giants and leprechauns. (*Variorum Poems*, p. 795.)

philosophical would cry with the painter, Calvert:[2]—"I go inward to God, outward to the gods."

## II.—THE PERSONS OF THE TRIBES OF DANU

The old poets thought that the tribes of the goddess Danu were of a perfect beauty, and the creators of beautiful people and beautiful arts. The hero Fiachna[3] sang when he came from among them:—

> They march among blue lances,
> Those troops of white warriors with knotted hair,
> Their strength, great as it is, cannot be less.
> They are sons of queens and kings,
> On the heads of all a comely
> Harvest of hair yellow like gold.
> Their bodies are graceful and majestic,
> Their eyes have looks of power and blue pupils,
> Their teeth shine like glass,
> Their lips are red and thin.

And "every artist harmonious and musical" is described in an old book by one Duald mac Firbis,[4] of Laccan, as of the Tribes of the goddess Danu, that is to say, inspired by the Tribes of the goddess Danu. It took me a long time to find out that they still kept their beauty, for the peasant visionaries have never been from their own countrysides, and can only compare what they have seen to commonplace things and tell you that they have seen rooms "grander" than some commonplace room "up at the Lodge," or marching people, who looked (as a poteen-maker, who had praised their magnificence, said to me) "for all the world like policemen." But now I ask careful questions, and am told, as I was told the other day by a woman, who was telling of a sight one

[2] Edward Calvert (1799–1883), an artist who was a disciple of Blake, is mentioned in "Under Ben Bulben" in the company of "Wilson, Blake and Claude".

[3] This quotation is from Fiachna's song describing the "Plain of the Two Mists" (the land of the dead) which he sings to Loegaire Liban. The passage is from "The Legend of Loegaire Liban" and is translated in *The Irish Mythological Cycle and Celtic Mythology* by H. D'Arbois de Jubainville, translated by Richard Irvine Best (Dublin, 1903, pp. 201–5). Yeats omits a quatrain after the second line of his quotation. The original tale is in the Book of Leinster. Lady Gregory's version, "Laegaire in the Happy Plain" is in *Gods and Fighting Men* (London, 1910, pp. 136–9). Yeats's translator could not be discovered.

[4] Yeats refers not to the MacFirbis who compiled the Book of Lecan but to Duald Mac Firbis (1585–1670), compiler of *The Book of Genealogies*. Douglas Hyde quotes the passage Yeats refers to: "Everyone who is fair-haired, vengeful, large, and every plunderer, every musical person, the professors of musical and entertaining performances, who are adepts in all druidical and magical arts, they are the descendants of the Tuatha De Danann in Erin." (Douglas Hyde, *A Literary History of Ireland*, new edition with introduction by Brian Ó'Cuív, London, 1967, p. 563.) Hyde notes wryly that no Irish family can trace ancestry to those wonderful people.

Martin Roland saw in a bog, that "their women had their hair wound round their heads, and had a wild look, and there were wreaths of flowers upon their horses"; or, as I was told when I asked an old man who has seen them, and whose uncle used to be away among them, if their great people had crowns of one shape:—"O no, their crowns have all kinds of shapes, and they have dresses of all kinds of colours"; or, as I was told by the same old man, when the friend who was with me held up a sapphire ring and made it flash, and asked if their dresses were as beautiful:—"O, they are far grander than that"; or, as I was told by a blind piper, when I asked if he had any of their music:—"I have no music like theirs, for there is no music in the world like theirs."

Many have thought that the Tribes of the goddess Danu have become little, like the fairies in the *Midsummer Night's Dream*, and some have built a theory on their littleness; but they are indeed tall and noble, as many have told me. They have among them monsters and grotesque persons who are now big and now little; but these are their old enemies, the Fomor,[5] the Caetchen, the Laighin, the Gailioin, the Goborchin, the Fir Morca, the Luchorpain, the Firbolg, and the Tribes of Domnu, divinities of darkness and death and ugliness and winter cold and evil passion; and they[6] can take shapes and sizes that are not their true shapes and sizes, as they and the Druids do in the poems, and become "very small and go into one another, so that all you see might be a sort of a little bundle"; or become "like a clutch of hens," or become like "a flock of wool by the road," or become like a tar-barrel "flaming and rolling," "or look like a cow and then like a woman"; but all the while "they are death on handsome people because they are handsome themselves." The Country of the Young, as the poets call their country, is indeed the country of bodiless beauty that was among the Celtic races, and of which (if D'Arbois de Jubainville[7] has written correctly) the Greek mythology and all that came of it were but the beautiful embodiment; and it still lives, forgotten by proud and learned people, among simple and poor people. When the Irish peasant passes into a

---

[5] These pre-Danaan gods of Ireland are discussed in detail in Best's translation of de Jubainville's *Irish Mythological Cycle* (pp. 51–78). The Formorians were a race of giants and monsters, analogous in de Jubainville's estimation to the Titans who warred with Zeus in Greek mythology. The Fir-Domnann inhabited Munster and Connacht, the Gailioin and the Laighin lived in Leinster, and the Firbolg in Ulster. The "Goborchin" are Formorians with goats' heads (Jubainville–Best, p. 54). The Fir Morcha may be followers of Morc, a Formorian being (Jubainville–Best, p. 57). "Luchorpains" are dwarfs which Jubainville claimed were rare in Irish mythology (Jubainville–Best, p. 53).

[6] The sequence here is unclear, but "they" probably returns to the Tuatha de Danaan.

[7] De Jubainville drew extended parallels between Greek and Celtic mythology, but also noted important differences. Yeats's statement here is unclear. He may be suggesting a common source of inspiration for both Greek and Celtic mythology, or he may be claiming a primacy of Celtic mythology over the Greek. The latter possibility is not suggested by de Jubainville.

sudden trance and, sleeping, is yet awake and awake is yet sleeping, it is still that bough of golden apples, whose rustling cast Cormac, son of Art, into a Druid sleep, whose rustling has overcome him;[8] and its beauty is not the less beautiful because Christianity has forbidden its rustling, and made Eve's apple grow among its golden apples.

## III.—THE HOUSES OF THE TRIBES OF DANU

Although a man has told me that "the Others," as the Galway peasant, like the Greek peasant, has named the gods, can build up "in ten minutes and in the middle of a field a house ten times more beautiful than any house in the world," and although some have told me that they live everywhere, they are held by most to live in forts or "forths," the little fields surrounded by clay ditches that were the places of the houses of the ancient people. Every countryside is full of stories of the evils that have fallen upon the reckless or unbelieving people, who have broken down the ditches of the forts, or cut the bushes that are in them. A man, who has a mill and a farm near Gort, in Galway County, showed me where a fort on his farm had been cut through to make a road, and said:—"The engineer must have been a foreigner or an idolater, but he did not live long anyway"; and the people of a neighbouring townland tell how an old man, who is not long dead, cut a bush from one behind his house, and "next morning he had not a blade of hair on his head— not one blade, and he had to buy a wig and wear it all the rest of his life." A distant relation of my own bid his labourers cut down some bushes in a fort in Sligo, and the next morning they saw a black lamb among his sheep, and said it was a warning, and would not cut the bushes; and the lamb had gone the morning after that. A great number of the people of every countryside have seen some fort lighted up, with lights which they describe sometimes as like torches, and sometimes as like bonfires; but once, when I questioned a man who described them as like a bonfire, I found that he had seen a long thin flame, going up for

[8] Cormac, son of Art, trades his wife and children to Manannan MacLir (in disguise) in exchange for a magic branch with nine golden apples, "And whoever heard it forgot forthwith sorrow and care; and men, women, and children would be lulled to sleep by it." (Jubainville–Best, p. 185.)

Yeats refers to it in this poem "The Dedication to a Book of Stories Selected from the Irish Novelists"—the earlier version of this poem opens:

> There was a green branch hung with many
> a bell
> When her own people ruled in wave-worn Eire;
> And from its murmuring greeness, calm of faery,
> A Druid kindness, on all hearers fell.

(*Variorum Poems*, p. 129.)

thirty feet and whirling about at the top. A man, who lives near the fort
where the old man lost his hair, sees a woman lighting a fire under a
bush in the fort; but I do not know what the fire is like, as I have not
been able to question him; but a girl says the fires come with a sudden
blaze "like a man lighting his pipe." Somebody in almost every family
that lives near a fort has heard or seen lights or shadows, or figures that
wail or dance, or fight or play at hurling, which was a game among the
Tribes of Danu in old days, or ride upon horseback, or drive in strange
carriages that make a muffled sound. I know one fort where they hear
the galloping of horses, as if from underground, but "the Others" are
generally supposed to live in the forts, as the ancient people lived in
them and are indeed sometimes said to be the ancient people doomed to
await the end of the world for their redemption, because they had (as
a man said to me) "Freemasons and all sorts of magicians among them,"
or, as another said to me, "because they used to be able to put souls
into rocks and to make birds and fishes speak, and everybody who has
read about the old times knows that fishes and birds used to speak."

Certain queerly-shaped bushes, not near forts and often alone in the
middle of fields, and certain trees, are also frequented and protected.
The people say that you must not hurt these bushes and trees, because
"the Others" have houses near them; but sometimes it seems that, if
you hurt one of them, you hurt one of "the Others," for I have been
told of a man who went to cut a bush on the road to Kinvara, in Galway
County, "and at the first blow he heard something like a groan coming
from beneath it; but he would not leave off, and his mouth was drawn
to one side all of a sudden, and two days after he died."[9] A man[10] has
told me that he and another went in their boyhood to catch a horse in a
certain field full of boulders and bushes of hazel and rock roses and
creeping juniper that is by Coole Lake; and he said to the boy who was
with him:—"I bet a button that if I fling a pebble on to that bush, it will
stay on it," meaning that the bush was so matted that the pebble would
not be able to pass through it. So he "took up a pebble of cowdung, and
as soon as it hit the bush, there came out of it the most beautiful music
that ever was heard." They ran away and, when they had gone about
two hundred yards, they looked back, and saw a woman dressed in
white walking round and round the bush:—"First it had the form of a
woman and then of a man, and it going round the bush." He said that
some time afterwards "the master[11] sent men to cut down the bushes in
that part of the field, and a boy was cutting them near the matted bush,

[9] Lady Gregory tells the same story in *Visions and Beliefs*, vol. II, p. 233.
[10] In Lady Gregory, *Visions and Beliefs*, vol. II, p. 229, the man's name is "John Mangan",
and her version differs in some details.
[11] In Lady Gregory, "the master" is "Sir William".

and a thorn ran into his eye and blinded him." There is an old big elm[12] at the corner of a road a couple of miles from the field; and a boy, who who was passing before daylight with a load of hay, fell from his cart, and was killed just beside it, and people say that the horse was standing quite still by him when he was found, and that a shower of rain, which fell just after he was taken away, wet everything except the dust where he had lain. Many places have bad names, because people have fallen from their carts at them, and "the Others" are said to have these people among them. The old big elm has not altogether a bad name, because it is said that one day a man was passing by it, who had come from Galway with "a ton weight in his cart," and "the lynching of his wheel came out, and the cart fell down, and a little man about two and a half feet high came out of the wall, and lifted up the cart, and held it up until he had the lynching put up again, and never said a word, but went away as he came." This may be a story come out of old times; but it may not, for simple people live so close to trance that the lynching may never have come off, and the carter may have seen it all awake and yet asleep or asleep and yet awake; or the lynching may have come off, and the carter may have put it on with his own hands, and not have known that he put it on. There is a plantation of younger trees near the big old elm which they protected also; and when a man called Connellan went a while ago to cut trees there, "he was prevented, and never could get the hand-saw near a tree, nor the man that was with him" (but I have not been able to find out how he was prevented); and there is a whole wood bordering on the field where the matted bush used to be, which Biddy Early, a famous wise woman,[13] used to call a "very bad place"; and many see sights in it, and many go astray in it, and wander about for hours in a twilight of the senses. Souls are sometimes said to be put into the trees for a penance; for there was a woman who was "for seven years in a tree at Kinadyfe, and seven years after that in the little bridge beyond Kilcreest, below the arch with the water running under her; and while she was in the tree, whether there was frost or snow or storm, she hadn't so much as the size of a leaf to shelter her."

A woman has told me that people only see "the Others" in the forts and by the bushes and trees, because "they are thinking of them there," but that "they are everywhere like the blades of the grass"; and she showed me a corner of a road, where there was neither a fort nor a bush nor a tree, and said that they had put her brother "into a faint" there, and that the young men were afraid to come home at night from card playing till there were a number of them together. She herself has seen

---

[12] The elm was "outside Raheen" according to Lady Gregory, vol. II, p. 234.

[13] Biddy Early is mentioned in other articles in this folklore series, and much space is given to tales about her in the fourth article, "Ireland Bewitched".

something far from a fort or a bush or a tree:—"I was walking with another girl, and I looked up, and saw a tall woman dressed in black, with a mantle of some sort, a wide one, over her head, and the waves of the wind were blowing it off her, so that I could hear the noise of it. All her clothes were black and had the appearance of being new." She asked the other if she could see the woman, but she could not:—"For two that are together can never see such things, but only one of them." They ran away then, and the woman followed them until she came to a running stream. They thought the woman was one who had been "taken," for they were coming from "a house of the Kearneys, where the father and mother had died, but it was well known they often came back to look after the children." She is confident, however, that you must not question a dead person till you come to a bush, showing, as indeed everything shows, that half the dead are believed to have gone to the houses of "the Others," lured thither by sweet music or by the promise of unearthly love, or taken captive by their marching host.

They live also in certain hills like the hill behind Corcamroe Abbey,[14] in which they have "a town," and they are very plentiful under waters. A woman at Coole, in Galway, says:—"They are in the sea as well as on the land. That is well known by those that are out fishing by the coast. When the weather is calm, they can look down sometimes, and see cattle and pigs and all such things as we have ourselves. And at night their boats come out and they can be seen fishing; but they never last out after one o'clock."

## IV.—THE FRIENDS OF THE TRIBES OF DANU

Though hundreds in every countryside that I know in Ireland have seen them, and think of seeing them as but a common chance, the most are afraid to see them, because they may not wish to be seen. The people about Inchy, at Coole, point out an old blind man, and say that he was not blind when he was a boy; but one day he heard the coach of "the Others," the coach-a-bower, or deaf coach, as it is called, because it makes a deaf or muffled sound, and stood up to look at them instead of sitting still and looking another way. He had only time to see beautiful ladies, with flowers about them, sitting in the coach before he was smitten blind. Some of the old books call Midir the king of the fairies; and one of the old books says that three herons stand before his door, and when they see anybody coming, the first heron cries:—"Do not come, do not come"; and the second heron cries:—"Go away"; and the third heron cries:—"Go by the house, by the house." There are, however, people that the gods favour, and permit to look upon them

---

[14] Corcamroe Abbey, founded in 1194, is on the western coast of County Clare.

and go among them. A young man in the Burren Hills told me that he remembers an old poet, who made his poems in Irish, and who met, when he was young, one who called herself Maive, and said she was a queen among them, and asked him if he would have money or pleasure. He said he would have pleasure, and she gave him her love for a time, and then went from him, and ever after he was very sad. The young man had often heard him sing the poem of lamentation that he made, but could only remember that it was "very mournful," and that it called her "beauty of all beauties." "The Others" are often said to be very good to many people, and to make their crops abundant, and to do them many services. I have been told "there was a family at Tirneevan, and they were having a wedding there; and when it was going on the wine ran short, and the spirits; and they didn't know what to do to get more, Gort being two miles away; and two or three strange people came in, that they never had seen before, but they made them welcome; and when they heard what was wanting they said they would get it, and in a few minutes they were back with the spirits and the wine, and no place to get it nearer than Gort!" But the people they let look upon them often live in poor and tumble-down houses. I asked a man once if a neighbour of his, who could see things, had the cure that is made out of seven common things, and can end "all the evils that are in the world"; and he answered:—"She has the scenery for it, but I do not know that she has it"—meaning that his neighbour's house was a poor and tumble-down house.

[15]There was an old Martin Roland, who lived near a bog a little out of Gort, who saw them often from his young days, and always towards the end of his life. He told me a few months before his death that "they" would not let him sleep at night with crying things at him in Irish and with playing their pipes. He had asked a friend of his what he should do, and the friend had told him to buy a flute, and play on it when they began to shout or to play on their pipes, and maybe they would give up annoying him, and he did, and they always went out into the field when he began to play. He showed me the flute, and blew through it, and made a noise, but he did not know how to play; and then he showed me where he had pulled his chimney down, because one of them used to sit up on it and play on the pipes. A friend of his and mine went to see him a little time ago, for she heard that "three of them" had told him he was to die. He said they had gone away after warning him, and that the children (children they had "taken," I suppose) who used to come with them, and play about the house with them, had "gone to some other place," because "they found the house too cold for them, maybe"; and

[15] Here begins the section reprinted by Yeats as "The Friends of the People of Faery" in *The Celtic Twilight* (1902) and reprinted in *Mythologies* (1959, pp. 117-24).

he died a week after he said these things. His neighbours were not certain that he really saw anything in his old age, but they were all certain that he saw things when he was a young man. His brother said:—"Old he is, and it's all in his brain the things he sees. If he was a young man we might believe in him." But he was improvident and never got on with his brothers. A neighbour said:—"The poor man! they say they are mostly in his head now, but sure he was a fine fresh man twenty years ago, the night he saw them linked in two lots, like young slips of girls walking together. It was the night they took away Fallon's little girl"; and she told how Fallon's little girl had met a woman "with red hair that was as bright as silver" who took her away. Another neighbour, who was herself "clouted over the ear" by one of them for going into a fort where they were, said:—"I believe it's mostly in his head they are, and when he stood in the door last night I said:— 'The wind does be always in my ears and the sound of it never stops,' to make him think it was the same with him; but he says:—'I hear them singing and making music all the time, and one of them is after bringing out a little flute, and it's on it he's playing to them'. And this I know, that when he pulled down the chimney where he said the piper used to be sitting and playing, he lifted up stones, and he an old man, that I could not have lifted when I was young and strong." The people often tell one, as a proof that somebody is in communication with "the Others," that nobody can do so much work as he does, or that nobody can lift such weights as he does, or that nobody can play so well at the hurling as he does. The Country of the Gods is called "the Country of the Young," and the strength of their youth is believed to fall about those they love just as it fell about Cuchullin and the other heroes in the poems, and as the strength of Apollo was believed to fall about his priests at Hylae, so that they could leap down steep places and tear up trees by the roots, and carry them upon their backs over narrow and high places. When one has crossed the threshold of trance, it may be that one comes to the secret Waters of Life, where Maeldun[16] saw the dishevelled eagle bathing till it had grown young again, and that their drifting spray can put strength into our bodies.

Those who can see "the Others" as easily as Martin Roland saw them, look on them very much as we look on people from another townland; and indeed many among those who have seen them but seldom, think of their coming and going as of a simple and natural thing and not a thing to surprise anybody. I have often been told in Galway that the people in the North of Ireland see them easily; and a friend[17] has

[16] Maeldun is the hero of an ancient Irish saga which Tennyson used as subject for "The Voyage of Maeldune".

[17] Probably the friend was Lady Gregory.

written for me an account of a talk she had with an old woman in
Tyrone, who considers their coming and going a very small and natural
thing. It is quite accurate, for my friend, who had heard the old woman's
story some time before I heard of it, got her to tell it over again, and
wrote it out at once. She began by telling the old woman that she did
not like being in the house alone because of the ghosts and fairies; and
the old woman said:—"There's nothing to be frightened about in
fairies, Miss. Many's the time I talked to a woman myself that was a
fairy or something of the sort, and no less and more than mortal anyhow. She used to come about your grandfather's house, your mother's
grandfather that is, in my young days. But you'll have heard all about
her." My friend said that she had heard about her, but a long time
before, and she wanted to hear about her again; and the old woman
went on:—"Well, dear, the very first time ever I heard word of her
coming about was when your uncle, that is, your mother's uncle,
Joseph, was married, and building a house for his wife, for he brought
her first to his father's, up at the house by the Lough. The foundations
were marked out, and the building stones lying about, but the masons
had not come yet, and one day I was standing with my mother fornent
the house, when we sees a smart Wee Woman coming up the field over
the burn to us. I was a bit of a girl at the time, playing about and sport-
ing myself, but I mind her as well as if I saw her there now!" My
friend asked how the woman was dressed, and the old woman said:—
"It was a grey cloak she had on, with a green Cashmere skirt and a
black silk handkercher tied round her head, like the countrywomen
did use to wear in them times." My friend asked:—"How wee was
she?" And the old woman said:—"Well, now, she wasn't wee at all when
I think of it, for all we called her the Wee Woman she was bigger than
many a one, and yet not tall as you would say. She was like a woman
about thirty, brown-haired, and round in the face. She was like Miss
Betty, your grandmother's sister, and Betty was like none of the rest,
not like your grandmother nor any of them. She was round and fresh
in the face, and she never was married, and she never would take any
man, and we used to say that the Wee Woman, her being like Betty, was
maybe one of their own people that had been took off before she grew
to her full height, and for that she was always following us and warning
and foretelling. This time she walks straight over to where my mother
was standing:—'Go over to the Lough this minute'—ordering her like
that!—'go over to the Lough, and tell Joseph that he must change the
foundation of this house to where I'll show you forenenst the thorn
bush. That is where it is to be built, if he is to have luck and prosperity,
so do what I'm telling ye this minute.' My mother goes over to the
Lough, and brings Joseph down and shows him, and he changes the

foundations, the way he was bid, but didn't bring it exactly to where was pointed, and the end of that was, when he came to the house, his own wife lost her life with an accident that come to a horse that hadn't room to turn right with a harrow between the bush and the wall. The Wee Woman was queer and angry when next she come, and says to us : —'He didn't do as I bid him, but he'll see what he'll see.' " My friend asked where the woman came from this time, and if she was dressed as before, and the woman said:—"Always the same way, up the field beyant the burn. It was a thin sort of shawl she had about her in summer, and a cloak about her in winter, and many and many a time she came, and always it was good advice she was giving to my mother, and warning her what not to do if she would have good luck. There was none of the other children of us ever seen her unless me, but I used to be glad when I seen her coming up the burn, and would run out and catch her by the hand and the cloak, and call to my mother:—'Here's the Wee Woman!' No man body ever seen her. My father used to be wanting to, and was angry with my mother and me, thinking we were telling lies and talking foolish-like. And so one day when she had come, and was sitting by the fireside talking to my mother, I slips out to the field where he was digging, and 'Come up,' says I, 'if ye want to see her. She's sitting at the fireside now talking to mother.' So in he comes with me and looks round angry-like and sees nothing, and he up with a broom that was near hand and hits me a crig with it, and 'Take that now,' says he, 'for making a fool of me,' and away with him as fast as he could, and queer and angry with me. The Wee Woman says to me then:—'Ye got that now for bringing people to see me. No man body ever seen me and none ever will.' There was one day, though, she gave him a queer fright anyway, whether he seen her or not. He was in among the cattle when it happened, and he comes up to the house all trembling-like. 'Don't let me hear you say another word of your Wee Woman. I have got enough of her this time.' Another time all the same he was up Gortin to sell horses, and, before he went off, in steps the Wee Woman, and says she to my mother, holding out a sort of a weed: —'Your man is gone up by Gortin, and there's a bad fright waiting him coming home, but take this and sew it in his coat, and he'll get no harm by it.' My mother takes the herb but thinks to herself:—'Shure there's nothing in it,' and throws it on the floor, and lo and behold and sure enough! coming home from Gortin, my father got as bad a fright as ever he got in his life. What it was I don't right mind, but anyway he was badly damaged by it. My mother was in a queer way, frightened by the Wee Woman, after what she done, and sure enough the next time she was angry. 'Ye didn't believe me,' she said, 'and ye threw the herb I gave ye in the fire, and I went far enough for it. Ye'll believe me when I tell ye this now.' " She then told them of a time they were in Edinburgh and of a countrywoman that came up and talked to them. They did not remember at first, but when she told them what they had talked about, they remembered.

"There was another time she came and told how William Hearn was dead in America. 'Go over,' she says, 'to the Lough, and say that William is dead, and he died happy, and this was the last Bible chapter ever he read,' and with that she gave the verse and chapter. 'Go,' she says, 'and tell them to read them at the next class-meeting, and that I held his head while he died.' And sure enough word came after that how William had died on the day she named. And, doing as she bid about the chapter and hymn, they never had such a prayer meeting as that. One day she and me and my mother was standing talking, and she was warning her about something, when she says of a sudden:—'Here comes Miss Letty in all her finery, and it's time for me to be off.' And with that she gave a swirl round on her feet, and raises up in the air, and round and round she goes, and up and up, as if it was a winding stairs she went up, only far swifter.[18] She went up and up, till she was no bigger nor a bird up against the clouds, singing and singing the whole time the loveliest music I ever heard in my life from that day to this. It wasn't a hymn she was singing, but poetry, lovely poetry, and me and my mother stands gaping up, and all of a tremble. 'What is she at all, mother?' says I. 'Is it an angel she is or a fairy woman, or what?' With that up come Miss Letty, that was your grandmother, dear, but Miss Letty she was then, and no word of her being anything else, and she wondered to see us gaping up that way, till me and my mother told her of it. She went on gay dressed then, and was lovely looking. She was up the lane where none of us could see her coming forward when the Wee Woman rose up in that queer way, saying:—'Here comes Miss Letty in all her finery.' " Who knows to what far country she went or to see who dying?

"It was never after dark she came, but daylight always as far as I mind, but wanst, and that was on a Hallow Eve night. My mother was by the fire, making ready the supper, she had a duck down and some apples. In slips the Wee Woman. 'I'm come to pass my Hallow Eve with you,' says she. 'That's right,' says my mother, and thinks to herself:—'I can give her supper nicely.' Down she sits by the fire awhile. 'Now I'll tell you where you'll bring my supper,' says she. 'In the room beyond

[18] On this important matter of winding stairs, Yeats added the following note to the *Celtic Twilight* reprinting: "A countryman near Coole told me of a spirit so ascending. Swedenborg, in his *Spiritual Diary*, speaks of gyres of spirits, and Blake painted Jacob's Ladder as an ascending gyre." (*Mythologies*, p. 123, note dated 1924. It was added to the version printed in *Early Poems and Stories*, 1925.)

there beside the loom, set a chair in and a plate.' 'When ye're spending the night, mayn't ye as well sit by the table and ate with the rest of us?' 'Do what you're bid, and set whatever you give me in the room beyant. I'll eat there and nowhere else.' So my mother sets her a plate of duck and some apples, whatever was going, in where she bid, and we got to our supper and she to hers; and when we rose I went in, and there, lo and behold ye, was her supper plate a bit ate of each portion, and she gone!"[19]

The old woman went on to tell how her mother made the Wee Woman angry "off and on like she did about the herb, and asking questions that way. The Wee Woman said one day:—'You're in trouble now, but it is in thicker trouble you will be, and you'll mind this warning, and believe what I tell you.' And after this she quit coming." But the old woman saw her once more, and before the "thick trouble" came, as it did: "One night I was over on some errand to your uncle's people's place. Rightly I mind it was a basket of praties we were carrying, me and a girl called Rosanna M'Laren, and coming over the stile by the haggard, I leaped over first, the better to help with the basket, and what do I see across the burn, over by a haystack, but the Wee Woman with all her hair hanging about her, lovely long brown hair, and she combing away at it; and I gives a screech, startled like, and Rosanna drops the basket, and all the praties spilt, but when I turned my head back, she was clean gone, while you would take time to wink, and the two of us took to our heels as hard as we could, and round the end of the house. I don't know what came over me to be scared that way at seeing her, but maybe she was angered, for from that day to this I never seen or heard tell of her, but once that she came to my mother in Belfast. She was always friendly with me, and I was always glad to see her, and I would run out to meet her; but none of the children ever seen her except myself, only my mother and me, and no man body at all at all, as I have told ye."

"Uncle Joseph's" house had to be moved, one has no doubt, because it was "on the path"; for there are stories everywhere of houses that had to be pulled down, because they were "on the path" or "in the way," or were pulled down by the whirling winds that are "the Others" journeying in their ways. There is a house in Gort, for instance, on which, people say, it is impossible to keep a roof, although the roofs keep on the houses beside it. I have no doubt either that the old woman's mother threw the herb away, because she was afraid of it, for the gifts of "the Others" are often believed to bring ill-luck in the end. The people say:—"O, yes, it is best to be without them anyway." If the "Wee Woman" was, as I think she was, one of the dead, she came

[19] Section excerpted as "The Friends of the People of Faery" ends here.

on Hallow Eve because it was the beginning of the old Celtic winter,[20] and the time when many old nations held a festival of the dead amid the dropping leaves and gathering cold. In Brittany a table covered with food and a warm fire are left for them even now on "All Souls Night," which is but two days from Hallow Eve. "The Others," however, are said also to be busier, on Hallow Eve and on the first of November, than at any other time, except the first of May, the beginning of the old Celtic summer.[21] The Wee Woman ate by herself, because "the Others," and the dead, and even the living, that are among them, may not eat while mortal eyes are looking. The people put potatoes on the door-step for them, often night after night throughout the year, and these potatoes must not have been "put on the table," for they would not eat them if they had been "put before any common person"; and there is a young man near Gort who is believed to go out of our world at night, and it is said, though not correctly, that he will not let anybody see him eating. All ancient people set food for the dead, and believed that they could eat as we do, and about this and about the possibility of them and of "the Others" bringing and taking away solid things I have much to say, but at present I hold a clean mirror to tradition. They often go away as the Wee Woman did by going up and round and round in the air. A woman who lives by Kiltartan bog says:—" I often saw a light in the wood at Derreen. It would rise high over the trees going round and round. I'd see it maybe for fifteen minutes at a time, and then it would fall like a lamp"; and the whirling winds that are their winds, but were called the dance of the daughters of Herodias in the middle ages, show how much their way is a whirling way.

All of us are said to have a great many friends among them—relations and forbears snatched away, and they are said to come at times like the Wee Woman to warn us and protect us, and lament over us. I have been told that nobody can tell how many have been snatched away, for that two or three years ago "eighteen or nineteen young men and young girls" were taken out of one village. The Country of "the Others," "the Country of the Young," is in truth the heaven of the ancient peoples, and I can discover, and will show[22] in the stories told of it, the ancient thoughts, plausible and complex thoughts, about life and death. It has been the Celt's great charge to remember it with ancient things, among forgetful peoples; and it may be his charge to speak of it and of ancient sanctities to peoples who have only new things. It was perhaps for this that the Roman went by him afar off, and that the Englishman is beating in vain upon his doors and wondering how doors of dreams can be so greatly harder than doors of iron; and that his days pass among grey

---

[20] Samhain.          [21] Beltaine.
[22] Presumably in the following articles, although this article did not promise a sequel.

stones and grey clouds and grey seas, among things too faint and seemingly frail to awaken him from the sleep, in which the ancient peoples
dreamed the world and the glory of it, and were content to dream.

W. B. Yeats

# Three Irish Poets

Yeats's encomium for his friends A.E., Lionel Johnson and Nora Hopper
appeared as "Three Irish Poets" in "A Celtic Christmas" issue of *The Irish
Homestead* in December, 1897. This year was the peak of Yeats's Pan-Celtic
propaganda, and the opening paragraph, envisaging the birth of a Celtic,
symbolist, occult Messiah at the turn of the century, is one of his most fervent
annunciations.

Yeats wrote separate articles on all three of these poets during the following
year for the Dublin *Daily Express*. The present article was accompanied by a
sketch of Yeats, presumably by A.E., who had begun in November, 1897, his
association with Horace Plunkett's Irish Agricultural Organisation Society
and who was to edit *The Homestead*, the Society's journal, from 1905 onward.

I T is hardly an exaggeration to say that the spiritual history of the world
has been the history of conquered races. Those learned in the traditions
of many lands, understand that it is almost always some defeated or
perhaps dwindling tribe hidden among the hills or in the forests, that is
most famous for the understanding of charms and the reading of dreams,
and the seeing of visions. And has not our Christianity come to us from
defeated and captive Judea? The influence of the Celt, too, has been a
spiritual influence, and men are beginning to understand how great it
has been. The legends of King Arthur and the Holy Grail, which had so
great an influence on the whole of Europe in the twelfth century, and so
great a part in the foundation of chivalry, were Celtic legends, and some
say Irish legends transformed by Welsh and Breton story-tellers. The
legends that gave Dante the structure of his poems are believed to have
been Irish legends of the visions seen by devout persons in a little
island in Lough Dearg;[1] and but for the legends and history of the
Highlanders, who are in all things of one stock with ourselves, Sir
Walter Scott could hardly have begun that great modern mediaeval

---

[1] C. S. Boswell's *An Irish Precursor to Dante*, London, 1908, which discusses the vision of
the eighth century Irish Saint Adamnan, mentions visions seen at St. Patrick's Purgatory on
Lough Derg by the knight Owen in 1153 and written down by Henry of Saltrey (Boswell,
p. 234).

movement, which has influenced all the literature and art and much of the religion of the nineteenth century. Until our day the Celt has dreamed half the dreams of Europe, while others have written them but to-day he is beginning to write his own dreams, and such great Bretons as Lamennais,[2] Chateaubriand, Renan, and Count Villiers de Lisle Adam [sic], the founder of the present spiritual movement in French literature, and the great Welshman, William Morris, the founder of the decorative movement in English art, prove that he can write persuasively. The bulk of the poets of modern Ireland has been so exclusively political, or so exclusively national, in a political sense, that it has hardly busied itself like the poets of Wales and Brittany with the spiritual part of life, but now we have several poets who are speaking with what I think is the truest voice of the Celt. I call them spiritual, not because they are religious, in the dogmatic sense of the word, but because they touch our deepest and most delicate feelings, and believe that a beauty, not a wordly beauty, lives in worldly things. "A.E.," Miss Nora Hopper, and Mr. Lionel Johnson are good types of this new school. "A.E." takes our ancient legends just as the story-teller of the twelfth century took the legends of the Holy Grail and shows us their spiritual meaning. For instance, we read somewhere of a certain well called "Connla's well," and how a sacred hazel tree grew over it and dropped nuts, that were nuts of wisdom to all who eat of them; and in his dream the well seemed to fill the world, and the thoughts that came to him from the beauty of nature, seemed but its dropping berries; and he made this poem about it.

> *A cabin on the mountain side hid in a grassy nook,*
> *With door and windows open wide where friendly stars may look;*[3]
> *The rabbits*[4] *shy can patter in; the winds may enter free,*
> *Who throng around the mountain throne in living ecstasy.*
> *And when the sun sets dimmed in eve and purple fills the air,*
> *I think the sacred hazel tree*[5] *is dropping berries there,*
> *From starry fruitage waved aloft where Connla's well*[6] *o'erflows;*
> *For sure the enchanted water runs*[7] *through every wind that blows.*

---

[2] Félicité Robert de Lamennais (1782–1854), born at St. Malo, was a French priest, writer and philosopher. He was a strong supporter of the ultra-montanist or papal position against the Gallicanist or national French position in Roman Catholicism. His views were condemned by the Pope and he left the church.

[3] This version of "The Nuts of Knowledge" differs in a number of details from the version printed in "A.E.'s" *The Divine Vision and Other Poems*, London, 1904, pp. 28–9. This line reads in *The Divine Vision*: "Where door and windows open wide that friendly stars may look".

[4] rabbits: *The Divine Vision* reads: "rabbit".

[5] hazel tree: *The Divine Vision* reads "Hazel Tree".

[6] well: *The Divine Vision* reads "Well".

[7] water runs: *The Divine Vision* reads "waters run".

> *I think when night towers up aloft and shakes the trembling dew,*
> *How every high and lonely thought that thrills my being through,*
> *Is but a shining berry* [8] *dropped down through the purple air,*
> *And from the magic tree of life the fruit falls everywhere.*

To Irish people accustomed to the eloquent and argumentative poetry of *The Nation*[9] newspaper, this new poetry will sometimes seem strange and difficult, but it is really very like the Celtic legends that influenced the world long ago. Miss Hopper has written of many beautiful legends and read into them many tender and beautiful meanings, but her "Fairy Fiddler" must be my one example.

> *'Tis I go fiddling, fiddling,*
> *By weedy ways forlorn;*
> *I make the blackbird's music*
> *Ere in his breast 'tis born;*
> *The sleeping larks I waken*
> *Twixt the midnight and the morn,*
>
> *No man alive has seen me*
> *But women hear me play*
> *Sometimes at door or window*
> *Fiddling the souls away:*
> *The child's soul and the colleen's*
> *Out of the covering clay.*
>
> *None of my fairy kinsmen*
> *Make music with me now:*
> *Alone the raths I wander,*
> *Or ride the whitethorn bough,*
> *But the wild swans, they know me,*
> *And the horse that draws the plough.*

That is a little snatch of song that will not soon pass away. Mr. Lionel Johnson is before all else a Catholic poet, and many of his poems are hymns, many of them written in Latin, like the medieval hymns; but he is not the less for that, but rather so much the more for that—an Irish and a Celtic poet. His "Christmas and Ireland" begins with these passionate verses:—

> *The golden stars give warmthless fire,*
> *As weary Mary goes through night,*
> *Her feet are torn by stone and briar;*
> *She hath no rest, no strength, no light:*
> *O Mary, weary in the snow,*
> *Remember Ireland's woe!*

[8] shining: *The Divine Vision* reads "ruddy".

[9] *The Nation*, as edited by Thomas Davis, was the major organ of the "Young Ireland" movement of the 1840s.

*O Joseph, sad for Mary's sake!*
  *Look on our earthly mother[10] too :*
*Let not the heart of Ireland break,*
  *With agony its[11] ages through :*
*For Mary's love, love also thou*
  *Ireland, and save her now!*

*Harsh were the folk, and bitter stern,*
  *At Bethlehem, that night of nights.*
FOR YOU NO CHEERING HEARTH SHALL BURN:[12]
WE HAVE NO ROOM HERE, YOU NO RIGHTS.
*O Mary and Joseph! hath not she,*
  *Ireland, been even as ye!*

His political poetry cannot be quoted here, but it is not less exalted
and passionate, and would sound well in our ballad books.

This new school cannot fail to influence Irish thought very strongly,
for it is full of the dreams that we dream in our most exalted moments.
Few who have not read deeply in the history of literary movements,
know how strong is the influence of the highest kind of poetry, for it
does not directly influence many minds, but it influences the finest
minds and through them many minds. This new school, and the ever
increasing knowledge of the old poetry in Gaelic, must in time make
many strong and delicate minds spend themselves in the service of
Ireland that would else have spent themselves in alien causes, and
Ireland may become again a spiritual influence in the world.

W. B. Yeats

---

[10] In the version printed in Lionel Johnson's *Ireland with Other Poems*, London, 1897,
p. 53, the word "mother" is capitalized, thus making the allusion to "Mother Ireland"
clearer.

[11] its ages. *Ireland with Other Poems*, p. 53, reads "the ages".

[12] In *Ireland with Other Poems*, p. 53, this and the following line are italicized and not
capitalized.

# The Prisoners of the Gods

The second in the group of six articles which Yeats organized from the folk materials gathered by himself and Lady Gregory was "The Prisoners of the Gods" in *Nineteenth Century* for January, 1898.

NONE among people visiting Ireland, and few among the people living in Ireland, except peasants, understand that the peasants believe in their ancient gods, and that to them, as to their forbears, everything is inhabited and mysterious. The gods gather in the raths or forts, and about the twisted thorn trees, and appear in many shapes, now little and grotesque, now tall, fair-haired and noble, and seem busy and real in the world, like the people in the markets or at the crossroads. The peasants remember their old name, the *sheagh sidhe*, though they fear mostly to call them by any name lest they be angry, unless it be by some vague words, 'the gentry,' or 'the royal gentry,' or 'the army,' or 'the spirits,' or 'the others,' as the Greek peasant calls his Nereids; and they believe, after twelve Christian centuries, that the most and the best of their dead are among them.

A man close by the bog of Kiltartan said to the present writer: 'I don't think the old go among them, when they die, but, believe me, it's not many of the young they spare, but bring them away till such time as God sends for them;' and a woman at Spiddal, in northwestern Galway, where the most talk nothing but Gaelic, said: 'There are but few in these days that die right. The priests know all about them, more than we do, but they don't like to be talking of them, because they might be too big in our minds.' Halloran[1] of Inchy, who has told me and told a friend of mine many stories, says: 'All that die are brought away among them, except an odd old person.' And a man at Spiddal says: 'Is it only the young go there? Ah, how do we know what use they may have for the old as well as for the young?' A fisher woman among the Burren hills says: 'It's the good and the handsome they take, and those that are of use, or whose name is up for some good action. Idlers they don't like; but who would like idlers?' An old man near Gort has no fear of being taken, but says: 'What would they want with the like of me? It's the good and the pious they come for.' And an old

---

[1] These names are not, of course, the real names. It seems better to use a name of some kind for every one who has told more than one story, that the reader may recognize the great number of strange things many a countryman and woman sees and hears. I keep the real names carefully, but I cannot print them. [Yeats's notes.]

woman living on a bog near Tuam says: 'I would hardly believe they'd take the old, but we can't know what they might want of them. And it's well to have a friend among them, and it's always said you have a right not to fret if you lose your children, for it's well to have them there before you. They don't want cross people, and they won't bring you away if you say so much as one cross word. It's only the good and the pious they want; now, isn't that very good of them?'

There are countless stories told of people who meet 'the others' and meet friends and neighbours among them. This old woman tells of 'a man living over at Caramina, Rick Moran was his name, and one night he was walking over the little green hill that's near his house, and when he got to the top of it he found it like a fair green, just like the fair of Abbey with all the people that were in it, and a great many of them were neighbours he used to know when they were alive, and they were all buying and selling just like ourselves. And they did him no harm, but they put a basket of cakes into his hand and kept him selling them all through the night. And when he got home he told the story, and the neighbours, when they heard it, gave him the name of the cakes, and to the day of his death he was called nothing but Richard Crackers.'

A Spiddal man says: 'There was a man told me he was passing the road one night, near Cruach-na-Sheogue, where they are often seen dancing in the moonlight, and the walls on each side of the road were all crowded with people sitting on them, and he walked between, and they said nothing to him. And he knew many among them that were dead before that time.' And a weatherbound boatman from Roundstone had a friend who was 'out visiting one night, and coming home across the fields he came into a great crowd of them. They did him no harm, and among them he saw a great many that he knew that were dead, five or six out of our own village. And he was in his bed for two months after that. He said he couldn't understand their talk, it was like the hissing of geese, and there was one very big man that seemed the master of them, and his talk was like a barrel when it is being rolled.' Halloran of Inchy knew a man that was walking along the road near the corner where Mr. Burke and the soldier who was with him were shot in the time of the land troubles, and he saw 'in the big field that's near the corner a big fire and a lot of people round about it, and among them a girl he used to know that had died.'

The old inhabitants of the forts dug caves under the forts, in which they kept their precious things, one supposes, and these caves, though shallow enough, are often believed to go miles. They are thought pathways into the country of the dead, and I doubt not that many who have gone down into them shaking with fear, have fallen into a sudden trance, and have had visions, and have thought they had walked a great

way. The fisher woman among the Burren Hills tells this story, that has
doubtless come of such a trance, and would be like the visions of St.
Patrick's Purgatory[2] if it were at all Christian:

'There's a forth[3] away in the county Clare, and they say it's so long
that it has no end. And there was a pensioner, one Rippingham, came
back from the army, and a soldier has more courage than another, and
he said he'd go try what was in it, and he got another man to go with
him, and they went a long, long way and saw nothing, and then they
came to where there was the sound of a woman beetling.[4] And then they
began to meet people they knew before, that had died out of the village,
and they all told them to go back, but still they went on. And then they
met the parish priest of Ballyvaughan, Father Ruane, that was dead,
and he told them to go back, and so they turned and went. They were
just beginning to come to the grandeur when they were turned away.'

The dead do not merely live among their captors as we might among
a strange people, but have the customs and power which they have, and
change their shapes and become birds and beasts when they will. A
Mrs. Sheridan said to me, 'Never shoot a hare, for you wouldn't
know what might be in it. There were two women I knew, mother and
daughter, and they died, and one day I was out by the wood and I saw
two hares sitting by the wall, and the minute I saw them I knew well
who they were. And the mother made as though she'd kill me, but the
daughter stopped her. Bad they must have been to be put into that
shape, and indeed I knew that they were not too good. I saw the mother
another time come up near the door as if to see me, and when she got
near she turned herself into a big red hare.' The witches are believed to
take the shape of hares, and so the hare's is a bad shape. Another time
she saw 'the old Captain standing near the road, she knew well it was
him, and while she was looking at him he was changed into the shape
of an ass.'

Young children are believed to be in greater danger than anybody
else, and the number of those whose cries are heard in the wind shows
how much 'the others' have to do with the wind. A man called Martin,
who lives by Kiltartan bog, says: 'Flann told me he was by the hedge
up there by Mr. Gerald's farm one evening, and a blast came, and as it
passed he heard something crying, crying, and he knew by the sound it
was a child that they were carrying away.'

All the young are in danger, however, because of the long lives they

[2] St. Patrick's Purgatory is on Station Island in Lough Derg, Co. Donegal. There St.
Patrick is supposed to have seen a vision of Purgatory. It has been a famous place of pilgrimage since the Middle Ages.
[3] Yeats explains this term above, p. 59.
[4] "Beetling" may be a dialect word, or it may be the verb derived from "beetle"—"a
wooden pestle or bat for domestic purposes" (*Webster's Seventh New Collegiate Dictionary*).

have before them, and the desire of 'the others' to have their lives devoted to them and to their purposes. When I was staying with a friend in Galway a little time ago, an old woman came from the Burren Hills to ask for help to put a thatch on her cottage, and told us, crying and bemoaning herself, of the snatching away of her five children. One of us asked her about a certain place upon the road where a boy had fallen from his cart and been killed, and she said:

'It's a bad piece of the road. There's a forth near it, and it's in that forth my five children are that were swept from me. I went and I told Father Lally I knew they were there, and he said, "Say your prayers, my poor woman, that's all you can do." When they were young they were small and thin enough, and they grew up like a bunch of rushes, but then they got strong and stout and good-looking. Too good-looking they were, so that everybody would remark them and would say, "Oh! look at Ellen Joyce, look at Catherine, look at Martin! So good to work and so handsome and so loyal to their mother!" And they were all taken from me; all gone now but one. Consumption they were said to get, but it never was in my family or in the father's, and how would they get it without some privication? Four of them died with that, and Martin was drowned. One of the little girls was in America and the other at home, and they both got sick at the one time, and at the end of nine months the both of them died.

'Only twice they got a warning. Michael, that was the first to go, was out one morning very early to bring a letter to Mr. Blake. And he met on the road a small little woman, and she came across him again and again, and then again, as if to humbug him. And he got afraid, and he told me about her when he got home. And not long after that he died.

'And Ellen used to be going to milk the cow for the nuns morning and evening, and there was a place she had to pass, a sort of an enchanted place, I forget the name of it. And when she came home one evening she said she would go there no more, for when she was passing that place she saw a small little woman with a little cloak about her, and her face not the size of a doll's face. And with the one look of her she got, she got a fright and ran as fast as she could and sat down to milk the cow. And when she was milking she looked up and there was the small little woman coming along by the wall. And she said she'd never go there again. So to move the thought out of her mind I said, "Sure that's the little woman is stopping up at Shemus Mor's house." "Oh, it's not, mother," says she. "I know well by her look she was no right person." "Then, my poor girl, you're lost," says I, for I knew it was the same woman that Michael saw. And sure enough, it was but a few weeks after that she died.

'And Martin, the last that went, was stout and strong and nothing ailed him, but he was drowned. He'd go down sometimes to bathe in the sea, and one day he said he was going, and I said, "Do not, for you have no swim." But a boy of the neighbour's came after that and called to him, and I was making the little dinner for him, and I didn't see him pass the door. And I never knew he was gone till when I went out of the house the girl from next door looked at me some way strange, and then she told me two boys were drowned, and then she told me one of them was my own. Held down, they said he was, by something underneath. They had him followed there.

'It wasn't long after he died I woke one night, and I felt some one near, and I struck the light, and there I saw his shadow. He was wearing his little cap, but under it I knew his face and the colour of his hair. And he never spoke, and he was going out the door and I called to him and said, "O Martin, come back to me, and I'll always be watching for you!" And every night after that I'd hear things thrown about the house outside, and noises. So I got afraid to stop in it, and I went to live in another house, and I told the priest I knew Martin was not dead, but that he was still living.

'And about eight weeks after Catherine dying I had what I thought was a dream. I thought I dreamt that I saw her sweeping out the floor of the room. And I said, "Catherine, why are you sweeping? Sure you know I sweep the floor clean and the hearth every night." And I said, "Tell me where are you now?" and she said, "I'm in the forth beyond." And she said, "I have a great deal of things to tell you, but I must look out and see are they watching me." Now, wasn't that very sharp for a dream? And she went to look out the door, but she never came back again.

'And in the morning, when I told it to a few respectable people they said, "Take care but it might have been no dream but herself that came back and talked to you." And I think it was, and that she came back to see me and to keep the place well swept.

'Sure we know there were some in the forth in the old times, for my aunt's husband was brought away into it, and why wouldn't they be there now? He was sent back out of it again, a girl led him back and told him he was brought away because he answered to the first call, and that he had a right only to answer to the third. But he didn't want to come home. He said he saw more people in it than he ever saw at a hurling, and that he'd ask no better place than it in high heaven.'

Mystics believe that sicknesses and the elements do the will of spiritual powers, but Mrs. Joyce had not heard this, and so could only deny that her children had died of consumption or were drowned by the unaided waters. Her aunt's husband was doubtless called by a voice into the fort, and he went at the first call, instead of waiting, as the country people say all should, for the third call, which it seems cannot be called except by the living; and doubtless wandered about there in a dream and a sleep until it seemed in his dream that a girl of 'the others' led him out of the fort and he awoke.

Next to young children women after childbirth are held to be in most danger. I hear often of a year in which many were taken out of South Galway. A man about Tillyra said to me: 'It's about fourteen years since so many young women were brought away after their child being born. Peter Regan's wife of Peterswell, and James Jordan's wife of Derreen, and Loughlin's wife of Lissatunna—hundreds were carried off in that year. They didn't bring so many since then; I suppose they brought enough then to last them a good while.' And a man near Gort says: 'And it's not many years ago that such a lot of fine women were taken from Gort very sudden after childbirth—fine women. I knew them all myself.'

These women are taken, it is believed, to suckle children who have been made captive or have been born from the loves of spirits for mortals. Another man from near Gort says: 'Linsky the slater's mother was taken away, it's always said. The way it's known is, it was not long after her baby was born, but she was doing well. And one morning very early a man and his wife were going in a cart to Loughrea one Thursday for the market, and they met some of those people, and they asked the woman that had her child with her, would she give a drink to their child that was with them. And while she was doing it they said, "We won't be in want of a nurse to-night; we'll have Mrs. Linsky of Gort." And when they got back in the evening, Mrs. Linsky was dead before them.'

A fisherman from Aasleagh showed a correspondent, who was sailing along by the Killeries, a spot on the side of Muel Rae where there was a castle 'haunted by evil spirits' who were often heard 'making a noise like screeching and crying and howling and singing,' and 'Peter's brother's wife' was there; 'she was taken in her labour. It was an evil spirit that was in her, she couldn't bring it to the birth alive. In the morning when her crying was done they went to see her. There wasn't a bit of her there.' Evil spirits had 'fetched her away, and they took the sack of potatoes to put her in, and the potatoes were running all over the road even down to the water. She's there shut up to nurse the queen's child. A fine creature she was.' The tales of fishermen are full of the evil powers of the world.

The old woman who lives on the bog near Tuam says: 'There are many young women taken by them in childbirth. I lost a sister of my own in that way. There's a place in the river at Newton where there's stones in the middle you can get over by, and one day she was crossing, and there in the middle of the river, and she standing on a stone, she felt a blow on the face. And she looked round to see who gave it, and there was no one there, so then she knew what had happened, and she came to my mother's house, and she carrying at the time. I was but a little slip at that time, with my books in my hand coming from the school, and I ran in and said, "Here's Biddy coming," and my mother said, "What would bring her at this time of the day?" But she came in and sat down on a chair, and she opened the whole story. And my mother, seeing she got a fright, said to quiet her, "It was only a pain you got in the ear, and you thought it was a blow." "Ah," she said, "I never got a blow that hurted me like that did."

'And the next day and every day after that, the ear would swell a little in the afternoon, and then she began to eat nothing, and at the last her baby wasn't born five minutes when she died. And my mother used to watch for her for three or four years after, thinking she'd come back, but she never did.'

Many women are taken, it is believed, on their marriage day, and many before their babies are born, that they may be born among 'the others.' A woman from the shore about Duras says: 'At Aughanish there were two couples came to the shore to be married, and one of the new-married women was in the boat with the priest, and they going back to the island. And a sudden blast of wind came, and the priest said some blessed words that were able to save himself, but the girl was swept.'

This woman was drowned, doubtless. Every woman who dies about her marriage day is believed to die, I think, because a man of 'the others' wants her for himself. Next after a young child and a woman in childbirth, a young, handsome and strong man is thought in most danger. When he dies about his marriage day he is believed to die, I think, because a woman of 'the others' wants him for herself. A man living near Coole says: 'My father? Yes, indeed, he saw many things, and I'll tell you a thing he told me, and there's no doubt in the earthly world about it. It was when they lived in Inchy they came over here one time to settle a marriage for Peter Quin's aunt. And when they had the marriage settled they were going home at dead of night. And a wedding had taken place that day, of one Merrick from beyond Turloughmore, and the drag was after passing the road with him and his party going home. And in a minute the road was filled with men on horses riding along, so that my father had to take shelter in Carthy's big haggard. And the horsemen were calling on Merrick's name. And twenty-one days after he lay dead. There's no doubt at all about the truth of that, and they were no riders belonging to this world that were on those horses.'

The hurling was the game of the gods in old times, and 'the others' are held everywhere to-day to delight in good hurlers and to carry them away. A man by the sea-shore near the Connemara hills in western Galway says: 'There was a man lived about a mile beyond Spiddal, and he was one day at a play, and he was the best at the hurling and the throwing and at every game. And a woman in the crowd called out to him, "You're the strongest man that's in it." And twice after that a man that was beside him and that heard that said, saw him pass by, with his coat on, before sunrise. And on the fifth day after he was dead. He left four or five sons, and some of them went to America, and the eldest of them married and was living in the place with his wife. And he was going to Galway for a fair, and his wife was on a visit to her father and her mother on the road to Galway, and she bid him to come early, that she'd have commands for him. So it was before sunrise when he set out, and he was going up a little side road through the fields to make a short cut, and he came on the biggest fair he ever saw, and the most people in it, and they made a way for him to pass through. And a man with a big coat and a tall hat came out from them and said, "Do you know me?" And he said, "Are you my father?" And he said, "I am, and but for me you'd be sorry for coming here, but I saved you; but don't be coming out so early in the morning again." And he said, "It was a year ago that Jimmy went to America." And that was true enough. And then he said, "And it was you that drove your sister away, and gave her no peace or ease, because you wanted the place for yourself." And he said, "That is true." And he asked the father, "Were you all these years here?" And he said, "I was. But in the next week I'll be moved to the west part of Kerry, and four years after that my time will come to die." It was the son himself told me all this.'

This man was taken according to the traditional philosophy because someone praised him and did not say 'God bless him,' for the admiration of a sinner may, it says, become the admiration of 'the others,' who do many works through our emotions, and become as a rope to drag us out of the world.

They take the good dancers too, for they love the dance. Old Langan, a witch doctor on the borders of Clare, says: 'There was a boy was a splendid dancer. Well, one night he was going to a house where there was a dance. And when he was about half way to it, he came to another house where there was music and dancing going on. So he turned in, and there was a room all done up with curtains and with screens, and a room inside where the people were sitting, and it was only those that were dancing sets that came to the outside room. So he danced two or three sets and then he saw that it was a house they had built up where there was no house before for him to come into. So he went out, but there was a big flagstone at the door, and he stumbled on it and fell down. And in a fortnight after he was dead.'

I know a doctor who met one day among the Burren Hills the funeral of a young man he had been attending some time before. He stopped and asked the sister why he had not been sent for of late, and she said, 'Sure you could do nothing for him, doctor. It's well known what happened, him such a grand dancer, never home from a wedding or a wake till three o'clock in the morning, and living as he did beside a forth. It's *they* that have him swept.'

All the able-bodied, however, should fear the love of the gods. A man who lives by Derrykeel, on the Clare border, says of a friend and neighbour of fifty years ago: 'We were working together, myself and him, making that trench you see beyond to drain the wood. And it was contract work, and he was doing the work of two men, and was near ready to take another piece. And some of the boys began to say to him, "It's a shame for you to be working like that, and taking the bread out of the mouth of another," and I standing there. And he said he didn't care what they said, and he took the spade and sent the scraws out flying to the right and to the left. And he never put a spade into the ground again, for that night he was taken ill and died shortly after. Watched he was and taken by *them*.'

Even the old and feeble should not feel altogether safe. I have been told at Coole that 'there was a man on this estate, and he sixty years, and he took to his bed and the wife went to Biddy Early, a famous wise woman of whom I have many stories, and said, "It can't be by *them* he's taken. What use would he be to them, being so old?" And Biddy Early is the one that should know, and she said, "Wouldn't he be of use to them to drive their cattle?"'

But all are not sad to go. I have heard 'there were two men went with poteen to the island of Aran. And when they were on the shore they saw a ship coming as if to land, and they said, "We'll have the bottle ready for those that are coming." But when the ship came close to land it vanished. And presently they got their boat ready and put out to sea. And a sudden blast came and swept one of them off. And the other saw him come up again, and put out the oar across his breast for him to take hold of it. But he would not take it, but said, "I'm all right now," and sank down again, and was seen no more.'

There is indeed no great cause why any should fear anything except in the parting, for they expect to find there things like the things they have about them in the world, only better and more plentiful. A man at Derrykeel says: 'There was a woman walking in the road that had a young child at home, and she met a very old man having a baby in his arms. And he asked would she give it a drop of breast milk. So she did, and gave it a drink. And the old man said, "It's well for you you did that, for you saved your cow by it; but to-morrow look over the wall into the field of the rich man that lives beyond the boundary, and you'll see that one of his was taken in the place of yours." And so it happened.'

Mrs. Colahan of Kiltartan says: 'There was a woman living on the road that goes to Scahanagh, and one day a carriage stopped at her door and a grand lady came out of it, and asked would she come and give the breast to her child. And she said she wouldn't leave her own children, but the lady said no harm would happen them, and brought her away to a big house, but when she got there she wouldn't stop, but went home again. And in the morning the woman's cow was dead.'

And because it is thought 'the others' and the dead may need the milk for the children that are among them, it is thought wrong to 'begrudge' the cows. An old farmer at Coole says: 'The way the bad luck came to Tommy Glyn was when his cow fell sick and lay for dead. He had a right to leave it or to kill it himself. But his father-in-law was covetous, and he cut a bit of the lug off it, and it rose again, and he sold it for seven pound at the fair of Tubber. But he never had luck since then, and lost four or five bullocks, near all he owned.' To 'cut a bit of the lug off it' is, it seems, a recognised way of breaking the enchantment.

A man at Gortaveha says: 'There was a drunkard in Scariff, and one night he had drink taken he couldn't get home, and fell asleep by the roadside near the bridge. And in the night he woke and heard them at work, with cars and horses, and one said to another, "This work is too heavy; we'll take the white horse belonging to Whelan" (that was the name of a rich man in the town). So, as soon as it was light, he went to this rich man, and told him what he heard them say. But he would only laugh at him and said, "I'll pay no attention to what a drunkard dreams." But when he went out after to the stable, the white horse was dead.'

A woman near Spiddal says: 'We had a mare, the grandest from this to Galway, had a foal there on that floor, and before long both mare and foal died. And I often hear them galloping round the house, both mare and foal, and I not the only one, but many in the village can hear them too.'

Roots and plants are taken too. I have heard of their pulling the nuts in the woods about Coole, and a woman who lives on the side of the road between Gort and Ardrahan says: 'There was a girl used to come with me every year to pick water grass, and one year I couldn't go and she went by herself, And when she looked up from picking it she saw a strange woman standing by her with a red petticoat about her head and a very clean white apron. And she took some of the water in her hand

and threw it in the girl's face and gave her a blow and told her never to come there again. Vexed they were the water grass to be taken away; they wanted it left to themselves.'

A Galway lady tells of great noises that she and her household heard coming out of the apple room, and I asked a friend's gardener if he every heard noises of the kind, and he said, 'For all the twelve nights I slept in the apple house I never say anything, and I never went to bed or stripped off my clothes all the time, but I kept up a good turf fire all the night. But every night I could hear the sound of eating and of knives and forks, I don't know, was it the apples they were eating or some dinner they brought with them. And one night one of them jumped down from the granary over the bed, I could hear him scraping with his hands, and I went out and never came in again that night, and ever since that time I am a bit deaf.' Once he was in the grape house and there came a great wind and shook the house, and when it had gone by one of the bunches had been 'swept.' He has often heard that the pookas, a kind of mischievous spirits that come mostly in the shape of animals and are associated with November, take away the blackberries in the month of November, and he says: 'Anyway, we know that when the potatoes are taken it's by "the gentry," and surely this year they have put their fancy on them.'

Kirwan, the faery man of a place opposite Aran, under the Connemara hills, who learns many things from his sister who is away among them, says: 'Last year I was digging potatoes, and a boy came by, one of *them*, and one that I knew well before. And he said, "They're yours this year, and the next two years they will be ours." And you know the potatoes were good last year, and you see how bad they are this year, and how they have been made away with. And the sister told me that half the food in Ireland goes to them, but that if they like they can make out of cow dung all they want, and they can come into a house and use what they like, and it will never be missed in the morning.'

The woman on the bog near Tuam says: 'There's a very loughy woman living up that boreen beyond, is married to a man of the Gillanes, and last year she told me that a strange woman came into her house and sat down, and asked her had she good potatoes, and she said she had. And the woman said, "You have them this year, but we'll have them next year." And she said, "When you go out of the house it's your enemy you'll see standing outside." And when she went away the woman went to the door to see what way did she go, she could see her nowhere. And sure enough there was a man standing outside that was a near neighbour and was her most enemy.' A correspondent found a man on the Killeries cutting oats with a scissors, and was told that they had seen his scythe the year before, and to keep him from taking the oats they 'came in the middle of the night and trampled it all down, so he was cutting it quietly this year.'

It is, I think, a plausible inference that, just as people who are taken grow old among them, so unripe grain and fruits and plants that are taken grow ripe among them. Everything, according to this complex faith, seems to have a certain power of life it must wear out, a certain length of life it must live out, in either world, and the worlds war on one another for its possession.

A sound of fighting is often heard about dying persons, and this is thought to come of fighting between their dead friends who would prevent their being taken, and those who would take them. An old man died lately near Coole, and some of the neighbours heard fighting about his house, though one neighbour of his own age will not believe it was for him, because he was 'too cross and too old' to be taken; and last year I met a man on the big island of Aran who heard fighting when two of his children died. I did not write his story down at the time, and so cannot give his very words. One night he heard a sound of fighting in the room. He lit the light, but everything became silent at once and he could see nothing. He put out the light and the room was full of the sound of fighting as before. In the morning he saw blood in a box he had to keep fish in, and his child was very ill. I do not remember if his child died that day, but it died soon. He heard fighting another night, and he tried to throw the quilt on the people who were fighting, but he could not find anybody. In the morning he found blood scattered about and his second child dead. A man he knew was in love with a girl who lived near and used to sleep with her at night, and he was going home that morning and saw a troop of them, and the child in the middle of them. Once, while he was telling this story, he thought I was not believing him, and he got greatly excited and stood up and said he was an old man and might die before he got to his house and he would not tell me a lie, before God he would not tell me a lie.

A man near Cahir-glissane [5] says: 'As to fighting for those that are dying, I'd believe in that. There was a girl died not far from here, and the night of her death there was heard in the air the sound of an army marching and the drums beating, and it stopped over her house where she was lying sick. And they could see no one, but could hear the drums and the marching plain enough, and there was like little flames of lightning playing about it.'

A woman at Kiltartan [6] says: 'There does often be fighting heard when a person is dying. John King's wife that lived in this house before

---

[5] This story appears in Lady Gregory, *Visions and Beliefs*, vol. II, p. 83.

[6] In Lady Gregory, *Visions and Beliefs*, vol. II, p. 82, this story is attributed to "Tom Smith" and in her version "John King's wife" is "John Madden's wife".

I came to it, the night she died there was a noise heard, that all the village thought that every wall of every garden round about was falling down. But in the morning there was no sign of any of them being fallen.'

A woman at Spiddal [7] says: 'There are more of them in America than what there are here, and more of other sort of spirits. There was a man came from there told me that one night in America he had brought his wife's niece that was sick back from the hospital, and had put her in an upper room. And in the evening they heard a scream from her, and she called out, "The room is full of them, and my father is with them and my aunt." And he drove them away, and used the devil's name and cursed them. And she was left quiet that night, but the next day she said, "I'll be destroyed altogether to-night with them." And he said he'd keep them out, and he locked the door of the house. And towards midnight he heard them coming to the door and trying to get in, but he kept it locked and he called to them by way of the keyhole to keep away out of that. And there was talking among them, and the girl that was upstairs said she could hear the laugh of her father and of her aunt. And they heard the greatest fighting among them that ever was, and after that they went away, and the girl got well. That's what often happens, crying and fighting for one that's sick or going to die.'

A woman at Coole [8] says: 'There was an old woman the other day was telling me of a little girl was put to bake a cake, for her mother was sick in the room. And when she turned away her head for a minute the cake was gone. And that happened the second day and the third, and the mother was vexed when she heard it, thinking some of the neighbours had come in and taken it away. But the next day an old man appeared, and they knew he was the grandfather, and he said, "It's by me the cake was taken, for I was watching the house these three nights, where I knew there was one sick in it. And you never knew such a fight as there was for her last night, and they would have brought her away but for me that had my shoulder to the door." And the woman began to recover from that time.'

The woman on the bog near Tuam says: 'It's said to be a very good place, with coaches and all such things, but a person would sooner be in this world, for all that. And when a man or a woman is dying, the friends and the others among them will often gather about the house and will give a great challenge for him.'

And Langan, the faery man on the borders of Clare and Galway, says:

[7] This story is attributed to "An Islander" in Lady Gregory's *Visions and Beliefs*, vol. II, p. 81.

[8] In Lady Gregory, *Visions and Beliefs*, vol. II, p. 82, this story is attributed to Mrs. Meagher.

'Everyone has friends among them, and the friends would try to save when others would be trying to bring you away.'

Sometimes those they are trying to take seem to have a part in the fight, for they tell about Kiltartan of a woman who seemed dying, and suddenly she sat up and said, 'I have had a hard fight for it,' and got well after; and they understood her words to mean that she was fighting with the host of 'the others.'

Sometimes, too, the friends and neighbours and relations who are among them are thought to help, instead of hindering, the taking away. The fisherwoman from Burren says: 'There was my own uncle that lived on the road between Kinvara and Burren, where the shoemaker's shop is now, and two of his children were brought away from him. And the third he was determined he would keep, and he put it to sleep between himself and the wife in the bed. And one night a hand came in at the window and tried to take the child, and he knew who the hand belonged to, and he saw it was a woman of the village that was dead. So he drove her away and held the child, and he was never troubled again after that.'

And Kirwin the faery man says: 'One night I was in the bed with the wife beside me, and the child near me, next the fire. And I turned and saw a woman sitting by the fire, and she made a snap at the child, and I was too quick for her and got hold of it, and she was at the door and out of it before I could get hold of her.' The woman was his sister, who is among them and has taught him his unearthly knowledge.

In November 'the others' are said to fight for the harvest, and I may find, when I know more, that this fight is between the friends of the living among the dead, and those among the dead who would carry it away. The shadow of battle was over all Celtic mythology, for the gods established themselves and the fruitfulness of the world, in battle against the Fomor, or powers of darkness and barrenness; and the children of Mill,[9] or the living, and perhaps the friends of the living, established themselves in battle against the gods and made them hide in the green hills and in the barrows of the dead, and they still wage an endless battle against the gods and against the dead.

W. B. Yeats

9 Mill, usually spelled "Mile", was the legendary progenitor of the human inhabitants of Ireland called "Milesians".

# Mr. Lionel Johnson's Poems

Lionel Johnson (1867–1902) was one of Yeats's closest friends of the nineties. He taught Yeats some Latin and Greek, a little of the Church Fathers, and the deportment of a gentleman. Yeats gave in his autobiography some of Johnson's dicta: "One should be quite unnoticeable", and "Life is ritual". (*Autobiography*, pp. 113 and 201.) A master of some arts such as punctuation which Yeats had never mastered, he once told his friend, ". . . you need ten years in a library, but I have need of ten years in the wilderness". (*Ibid.*, pp. 204–5.)

Johnson was not Irish although he claimed that his family had once thought of themselves as Irish. He seems to have acquired at the time of his conversion to Catholicism a passionate devotion to Ireland—his only radicalism, as he called it. His learned orthodoxy enabled Yeats to demonstrate to the Irish clergy that the Irish literary revival was friendly to the Church. Yeats, however, never liked those poems inspired by Johnson's Irish patriotism. They reminded him too strongly of Thomas Davis and the *Nation* school.

Before Johnson's sudden, accidental death in 1902, he and Yeats had drifted apart. His excessive drinking whenever they met caused Yeats to feel himself morally implicated and thus Yeats avoided visiting him. Still, Johnson appears as an exemplar in the "tragic generation" in Yeats's autobiography and in the poem "In Memory of Major Robert Gregory".

While Yeats does not seem to have reviewed Johnson's 1895 volume of poems, he reviewed *Ireland, with Other Poems* (1897) in "Mr. Lionel Johnson's Poems" in *The Bookman* for February, 1898. A poem in the 1895 collection had been dedicated to Yeats and several of the poems in the present collection were dedicated to distinguished people, among them Thomas Hardy, Edmund Gosse, George Santayana, E. K. Chambers, Louise Imogen Guiney, Roger Fry, Dr. Birkbeck Hill and Will Rothenstein.

ARTHUR HALLAM distinguishes in the opening of his essay[1] on Tennyson between what he calls "the aesthetic school of poetry," founded by Keats and Shelley, and the various popular schools. "The aesthetic school" is, he says, the work of men whose "fine organs" have "trembled with emotion, at colours and sounds and movements unperceived by duller temperaments,"[2] "a poetry of sensation rather

---

[1] For Yeats's devotion to Arthur Henry Hallam's essay "On Some of the Characteristics of Modern Poetry, and on the Lyrical Poems of Alfred Tennyson" (1893), see p. 34 above.

[2] This passage reads in Hallam, ". . . their fine organs trembled into emotions at colours, and sounds, and movements, unperceived or unregarded by duller temperaments". *The Poems of Arthur Henry Hallam, Together with His Essay on the Lyrical Poems of Alfred Tennyson*, ed. by R. Le Gallienne, pp. 93–4.

than of reflection,"[3] "a sort of magic producing a number of impressions too multiplied, too minute, and too diversified to allow of our tracing them to their causes, because just such was the effect, even so boundless and so bewildering, produced on their imaginations by the real appearance of nature." Because this school demands the most close attention from readers whose organs are less fine, it will always, he says, be unpopular compared to the schools that "mix up" with poetry all manner of anecdotes and opinions and moral maxims. This little known and profound essay defines more perfectly than any other criticism in English the issues in that war of schools which is troubling all the arts, and gradually teaching us to rank such "reflections" of the mind as rhetorical and didactic verse, painted anecdotes, pictures "complicated with ideas" that are not pictorial ideas, below poetry and painting that mirror the "multiplied" and "minute" and "diversified" "sensation" of the body and the soul. Mr. Johnson, like Wordsworth and Coleridge, has sometimes written in the manner of the "popular schools," and "mixed up" with poetry religious and political opinions, and though such poetry has its uses everywhere, and in Ireland, for which Mr. Johnson has written many verses, and where opinion is still unformed, its great uses, one must leave it out when one measures the poetical importance of his poetry. I find poetry that is "a sort of magic," in "Poems," published in 1895, and in the present book, "Ireland" (Elkin Mathews), and the most unpopular "sort of magic," for it mirrors a temperament so cold, so austere, so indifferent to our pains and pleasures, so wrapped up in one lonely and monotonous mood that one comes from it wearied and exalted, as though one had posed for some noble action, in a strange *tableau vivant*, that casts its painful stillness upon the mind instead of upon the body. Had I not got Mr. Johnson's first book when I was far from books, I might have laid it down scarcely begun, I found the beginning so hard, and have lost much high pleasure, many fine exaltations; and though I have kept his new book as long as I could before reviewing it, I do not know if I admire the first book more merely because I have had longer to make its sensations my own sensations. In a poem that changes a didactic opinion to a sensation of the soul, Mr. Johnson sings the ideal of his imagination and his verse.

> *White clouds embrace the dewy fields*
> *Storms lingering mist and breath:*[4]
> *And hottest heavens to hot earth yield*
> *Drops from the fire of death.*

[3] Hallam said, "They [Keats and Shelley] are both poets of sensation rather than reflection." *ibid.*, p. 93.

[4] Storms: Johnson reads "Storm's", *Ireland, with Other Poems*, London, 1897, p. 81. The poem, entitled "An Ideal" was dated 1888 and dedicated to Standish O'Grady.

Come! *sigh the shrouding airs of earth:*
Be with the burning night;
Learn what her heart of flame is worth,
And eyes of glowing light.

*I come not. Off, odorous airs!*
*Rose-scented winds, away!*
*Let passion garnish her wild lairs,*
*Hold her fierce holiday.*

*I will not feel her dreamy toils*
*Glide over heart and eyes:*
*My thoughts shall never be her spoils,*
*Nor grow sad memories.*

*Mine be all proud and lonely scorn,*
*Keeping the crystal law*
*And pure air of the eternal morn:*
*And passion, but of awe.*

Poetry written out of this ideal can never be easy to read, and Mr. Johnson never forgets his ideal. He utters the sensations of souls too ascetic with a Christian asceticism to know strong passions, violent sensations, too stoical with a pagan stoicism to wholly lose themselves in any Christian ecstasy. He has made for himself a twilight world where all the colours are like the colours in the rainbow, that is cast by the moon, and all the people as far from modern tumults as the people upon fading and dropping tapestries. His delight is in "the courtesy of saints," "the courtesy of knights," "the courtesy of love," in "saints in golden vesture," in the "murmuring" of "holy Latin immemorial," in "black armour, falling lace, and altar lights at dawn," in "rosaries blanched[5] in Alban air," in all "memorial melancholy" things.[6] He is the poet of those peaceful, unhappy souls who, in the symbolism of a living Irish visionary, are compelled to inhabit when they die a shadowy island paradise in the West, where the moon always shines, and a mist is always on the face of the moon, and a music of many sighs always in the air, because they renounced the joy of the world without accepting the joy of God.

The poems, which are not pure poetry according to Arthur Hallam's definition, will, I think, have their uses in Catholic anthologies, and in those Irish papercovered books of more of less political poetry which

[5] Johnson reads "Ivories blaunched" instead of "rosaries blanched", *Poems*, London, 1895, p. 44.
[6] This pastiche of quotations is from "The Age of a Dream", p. 85, "The Church of a Dream", pp. 84–5, and "Glories", p. 44—all poems from Johnson's 1895 volume.

are the only imaginative reading of so many young men in Ireland. "Parnell," "Ways of War," "Ireland's Dead," "The Red Wind," "Ireland," "Christmas and Ireland," "Ninety-Eight," "To the Dead of '98," and "Right and Might," even when they are not, as they are sometimes, sensations of the body and the soul, will become part of the ritual of that revolt of Celtic Ireland which is, according to one's point of view, the Celt's futile revolt against the despotism of fact[7] or his necessary revolt against a political and moral materialism. The very ignorance of literature, among their Irish readers, will make the formal nobility of their style seem the more impressive, the more miraculous.

W. B. Yeats

# Mr. Rhys' Welsh Ballads

As "Fiona Macleod" proved valuable to Yeats by showing how the Celtic Movement had spread to Scotland, so Ernest Rhys supplied him with a Welsh ally for the movement. In "Four Years: 1887–1891", he remembers Rhys (1859–1946), whose *Welsh Ballads* (1898) he reviewed in *The Bookman* for April, 1898, as "a writer of Welsh translations and original poems, that have often moved me greatly, though I can think of no one else who has read them". "Between us we founded The Rhymers' Club . . ." (*Autobiography*, p. 111). Aside from his work as novelist, poet, autobiographer and translator, Rhys was most famous as the longtime editor of "Everyman's Library". During the nineties he was an editor of a series called "The Camelot Classics" and had helped to publish in that series some of Yeats's first anthologies of Irish fairy tales and fiction.

THE movement that found a typical expression in the consolations of "In Memoriam," in the speculations of "Locksley Hall," in the dialectics of "Bishop Blougram's Apology,"[1] in the invective of "Les Châtiments,"[2] and found its explanation when Matthew Arnold called art a criticism of life, has been followed by a movement that has found a typical expression in the contentment of "The Well at the World's End,"

[7] The famous phrase "to react against the despotism of fact" is from Matthew Arnold's *The Study of Celtic Literature* where Arnold attributed it to M. Henri Martin in his *Histoire de France*.

[1] Robert Browning's dramatic monologue "Bishop Blougram's Apology", was first published in *Men and Women*, 1855.

[2] Victor Hugo, while in exile on the island of Jersey, arranged to have published *Les Châtiments* in Brussels (1853). The book contains versified invectives against Napoleon III.

in the ecstasy of "Parsifal," in the humility of "Aglavaine and Selysette," in the pride of "Axel," [3] and might find its explanation in the saying of William Blake that art is a labour to bring again the golden age. The old movement was scientific and sought to interpret the world, and the new movement is religious, and seeks to bring into the world dreams and passions, which the poet can but believe to have been born before the world, and for a longer day than the world's day. This movement has made painters and poets and musicians go to old legends for their subjects, for legends are the magical beryls in which we see life, not as it is, but as the heroic part of us, the part which desires always dreams and emotions greater than any in the world, and loves beauty and does not hate sorrow, hopes in secret that it may become. Because a great portion of the legends of Europe, and almost all of the legends associated with the scenery of these islands, are Celtic, this movement has given the Celtic countries a sudden importance, and awakened some of them to a sudden activity.

Wales, which gives us so much excellent scholarship, seems alone untouched by a propagandist fire, for since Lady Guest's "Mabenogian," [*sic*] [4] she has given us little of her old literature, except prose translations from Taliesin and Davyth ap Gwilym and Lywarch Hen [5] and the like, by men so ignorant of any meaning in words finer than the dictionary meaning, that were it not for one or two delicate and musical translations in "The Study of Celtic Literature," [6] Welsh poetry would not even be a great name to most of us; while unlike Ireland and Celtic Scotland, she has never made a new literature in English. Mr. Ernest Rhys' poems, with the exception of a few poems by Mr. Lionel Johnson, [7] which follow far less closely in the manner of the old Welsh poetry, are, so far as I know, the first Welsh poetry in the English language which is moving and beautiful. Mr. Rhys' book contains ten free translations from the Welsh, some dozen poems inspired by Welsh legends, and some eighteen or nineteen poems more or less inspired by Welsh scenery, and one translation from the Irish. The translations are particularly excellent, and make one look eagerly for

[3] With the exception of Wagner's *Parsifal*, Yeats's examples are all works he reviewed in *The Bookman*: William Morris's romance *The Well at the World's End* (see *Uncollected Prose*, I, pp. 418–20), Villiers de l'Isle Adam's *Axel* (*ibid.*, 320–5) and Maeterlinck's play *Aglavaine and Selysette* (see pp. 51–4 above).

[4] Lady Charlotte Elizabeth Guest (1812–95) was the translator of a famous collection of Welsh romances called (and spelled) the *Mabinogion* (3 vols., 1838–49).

[5] Songs of Urien's victories, attributed to Taliesin, the Welsh bard of the sixth century, were collected in *The Book of Taliesin*. Dafydd ap Gwilym, a Welsh bard of the fourteenth century, is chiefly famous for his poem to the woman with whom he eloped, Morvydd of Anglesey. Llywarch Hên was also a sixth-century Welsh bard.

[6] Matthew Arnold's famous study, first published in 1867.

[7] In Johnson's volume, *Ireland with Other Poems*, London, 1897, were included such poems as "Cyhiraeth" and "To Morfydd Dead".

the life of Davyth ap Gwilym, the greatest of the mediaeval Welsh poets, illustrated with translations, which he announces as in preparation, in his notes on "The Poet of the Leaves." These stanzas from different parts of "The Song of the Graves," a condensation of a poem of seventy-three (Mr. Rhys says seventy-two) stanzas in "The Black Book of Carmarthen," are an example of his manner at its best.

> *In graves where drips the winter rain,*
> *Lie those that loved me most of men :*
> *Cerwyd, Cywrid, Caw, lie slain.*
>
> *In graves where the grass grows rank and tall,*
> *Lie, well avenged ere they did fall:*
> *Gwrien, Morien, Morial.*
>
> *In graves where drips the rain, the dead*
> *Lie, that not lightly bowed the head:*
> *Gwrien, Gwen, and Gwried.*
>
> *Seithenin's lost mind sleeps by the shore,*
> *'Twixt Cinran and the grey sea's roar;*
> *Where Caer Cenedir starts up before.*
>
> *In Abererch lies Rhyther' Hael,*
> *Beneath the earth of Llan Morvael;*
> *But Owain ab Urien in lonelier soil.*
>
> *Mid the dreary moor, by the one oak tree,*
> *The grave of stately Siawn may be;*
> *Stately, treacherous, and bitter was he!*
>
> *Mid the salt-sea-marsh where the tides have been,*
> *Lie the sweet maid, Sanaw; the warrior Rhyn;*
> *And Henin's daughter, the pale Earwyn.*
>
> *And this may the grave of Gwythur be;*
> *But who the world's great mystery,—*
> *The grave of Arthur shall ever see?* [8]

And so on, for the remembrance of Arthur is not the climax, but only a passing moment of a more unearthly sorrow in a dirge which must fade out with the same impassioned monotony in which it began. "The Calends of Winter," in which Mr. Rhys has certainly improved his original by giving appropriateness to the moral saying which seems to have been added to each stanza by some mediaeval copyist without

---

[8] Yeats omitted many intermediate stanzas from this quotation.

thought of the meaning of the stanza, is almost as fine; and "The Song of the Wind," and "The Lament of Lywarch Hen,"⁹ and "The Lament for Cyndylan," and, indeed, all the translations are beautiful in their different ways. "The House of Hendré," which is inspired by some legend of a poet who saw in a vision the seven heavens, and Merlin and Arthur there, and the heroes and the poets about them, and his own seat waiting, and so longed for death, the best of the original poems, has a melancholy, like that of curlews crying over some desolate marsh, which is partly in the words and partly in the very singular metre. The poems whose association with Wales is slighter, the mere link of the name of some Welsh village or mountain side at times, are much less successful. It is as though Mr. Rhys' imagination, which, like the imagination of a child, delights in a fanciful prettiness, needs the gravity of some old legend or old model before it can rise to a high argument. This fanciful prettiness, which, like all fanciful prettiness, is sometimes a little conventional, and an occasional indecision in the words and rhythm, is the defect of a temperament, which is shaping itself gradually, and with much labour, for beautiful expression.

W. B. Yeats

# The Broken Gates of Death

The third article of the folklore series based on materials collected by Lady Gregory was "The Broken Gates of Death", published in the *Fortnightly Review*, April, 1898. Most of this article appears to be Yeats's arrangement of Lady Gregory's materials, but the ending sounds distinctly like Yeats's own work. It seems curious that the first three articles of this more or less connected series appeared in three different periodicals. The fourth was to appear in still a fourth periodical—the *Contemporary Review*—but the fifth and sixth also appeared in the *Fortnightly Review*.

This third article aroused a touch of controversy. The magazine *Outlook* of April 16, 1898, contained a paragraph which accused Yeats of being unable to separate his "dreams and poetic fancies from the realities" he had witnessed (quoted in *Letters*, p. 297). The writer doubted Yeats's facts, and said that Yeats's article was "the dream of a poetical folk-lorist". Presuming his adversary was a Catholic, Yeats promised him that if he read the remaining articles, "he will find that the Irish peasant has invented, or that somebody has invented for him, a vague, though not altogether unphilosophical, reconciliation between his Paganism and his Christianity" (*Letters*, pp. 297–

⁹ The full title of this poem is "The Lament of Llywarch Hën in his Old Age".

8). The article "Irish Witch Doctors" (September, 1900) speaks briefly of such a reconciliation at the very beginning of the essay (see p. 219 below).


THE most of the Irish country people believe that only people who die of old age go straight to some distant Hell or Heaven or Purgatory. All who are young enough for any use, for begetting or mothering children, for dancing or hurling, or even for driving cattle, are taken, I have been told over and over again, by "the others," as the country people call the fairies; and live, until they die a second time, in the green "forts," the remnants of the houses of the old inhabitants of Ireland, or under the roots of hills, or in the woods, or in the deep of lakes. It is not wonderful, when one remembers this nearness of the dead to the living, that the country people should sometimes go on half-hoping for years, that their dead might walk in at the door, as ruddy and warm as ever, and live with them again. They keep their hopes half-living with many stories, but I think only half-living, for these stories begin mostly: "There was an old man on the road," or "There was one time a tailor," or in some like way; and not with the confident, "There was a sister of Mick Morans, that is your own neighbour," or "It happened to a young brother of my own," of the mere fairy tales. I once heard them called in the partly Elizabethan speech of Galway, "Maybe all vanities," and have heard many sayings like this of a woman at Inchy, "Did I know anyone that was taken by them? Well, I never knew one that was brought back again." Such stories have the pathos of many doubts. Numbers of those said to have been brought back, were children. A fisherwoman among the Burren Hills says: "There was an old man on the road one night near Burren, and he heard a cry in the air over his head, the cry of a child that was being carried away. And he called out some words, and the child was left down into his arms and he brought it home, and when he got there he was told that it was dead. So he brought in the live child, and you may be sure it was some sort of a thing that was good-for-nothing that was put in its place."

And another woman among the Burren Hills says: "There was one time a tailor, and was a wild card, always going to sprees. And one night he was passing by a house, and he heard a voice saying, 'Who'll take the child.' And he saw a little baby held out, and the hands that were holding it, but he could see no more than that. So he took it and he brought it to the next house, and asked the woman there to take it in for the night. Well, in the morning, the woman in the first house found a dead child in the bed beside her. And she was crying and wailing, and called all the people. And when the woman from the neighbouring house came, there in her arms was the child she thought was dead.

But if it wasn't for the tailor that chanced to be passing by, and to take it, we may know well what would have happened to it."

Sometimes a spell, like the spell of fire, even where used by accident, is thought to have brought the dead home, as in this tale, another Burren woman told a friend of mine:—

"There was a man lived beyond on the Kinvara road, and his child died and he buried it. But he was passing the place after, and he'd asked a light for his pipe in some house, and after lighting it, he threw the sod, and it glowing, over the wall where he had buried the child. And what do you think, but it came back to him again, and he brought it to its mother. For they can't bear fire."

Most of the stories are about women who are brought back by their husbands, but almost always against their will, because their will is under enchantment.

An old man at Lisadell, in county Sligo, who told me also a number of tradition[al] tales of the kind that are told generation after generation in the same words and in the same chanting voice, told me one tale, full of that courtesy between "the others" and the living which endures through all the bitterness of their continuous battles.

His father had told him "never to refuse a night's lodging to any poor travelling person," and one night "a travelling woman" or beggar woman, told him that in her place, a woman died, and was taken by "the gentry," and her husband often saw her after she was dead, and was afraid to speak to her. He told his brother, and his brother said he would come and speak to her, and he came, and at night lay on a settle at the foot of the bed. When she came in, he laid hold of her and would not let her go, although she begged him to let her go because "she was nursing the child of the King." Twelve messengers came in one after the other, and begged him to let her go, but he would not; and at last the King came himself, and said that she had been always well treated, and let come and nurse her own child, and that if she might stay until his child was weaned, he would send her home again, and leave, where they could find it, money to pay a debt of some forty pounds that "was over" her husband. The man said, "Do you promise this on your honour as a King?" and the King said, "I do," and so the man let her go, and all happened as the King had promised.

They are brought back more violently in most of the stories, as in this story told to a friend of mine by a man at Cool[e]: "And I'll tell you a thing I heard of in the country. There was a woman died and left her child. And every night at twelve o'clock she'd come back, and bring it out of the bed to the fire, and she'd comb it and wash it. And at last six men came and watched and stopped her at the door, and she went very near to tear them all asunder. But they got the priest, and he took it off her. Well, the husband had got another wife, and the priest came and asked him, 'Would he put her away and take the first wife again?' And so he did, and brought her to the chapel to be married to her again, and the whole congregation saw her there." When my friend asked if that was not rather hard on the second wife, he said: "Well, but wasn't it a great thing for the first poor creature to be brought back. Sure there's many of those poor souls wandering about."

Those who are brought back are sometimes thought to bring with them unholy knowledge. A woman at Kiltartan says: "There's a man in Kildare that lost his wife. And it was known that she would come back at twelve o'clock every night to look at her baby. And it was told the husband that if he had twelve men with him with forks when she came in, they would be able to keep her from going out again. So the next night he was there and all his friends with forks, and when she came in they shut the door, and when she saw she could not get out, she sat down and was quiet. And one night as she sat by the hearth with them all, she said to her husband: 'It's a strange thing that Leuchar would be sitting there so quiet with the bottom after bein' knocked out of his churn.' And her husband went to Leuchar's house, and he found it was true as she had said. But after that he left her, and would not go back to her any more."

Sometimes the women themselves tell how they are to be brought back, but they have sometimes to be seized and held before they will speak, as though a human touch broke the enchantment, as in this story told by a woman at Gort. "There was a woman beyond at Rua died, and she came back one night, and her husband saw her at the dresser looking for something to eat. And she slipped away from him that time, but the next time she came he got hold of her, and she bid him come for her to the fair at Eserkelly, and watch for her at the Custom Gap, and she'd be on the last horse that would pass through. And then she said: 'It's best for you not to come yourself, but send your brother.' So the brother came, and she dropped down to him, and he brought her to the house. But in a week after he was dead and buried. And she lived a long time; and she never would speak three words to anyone that would come into the house, but working, working all the day. I wouldn't have liked to live in the house with her after her being away like that."

I heard a story from a man at Doneraill, in county Cork, of a woman who bade a man go and look for her in a certain fort, and told him to hold her, even though she would struggle to escape, and scream out, either because the enchantment would have returned again, or because she would not have "the others" think her willing to leave them. I have only heard one story of a woman who came back of her own will, and without the help of anybody. A woman at Kiltartan says: "Mick Foley was here the other day telling us newses [?], and he told the strangest thing ever I heard that happened to his own first cousin. She died and was buried, and a year after, her husband was sitting by the fire, and she came back and walked in. He gave a start, for she said, 'have no fear of me, I was never in the coffin and never buried, but I was kept away for the year.' So he took her again, and they reared four children after that. She was Mick Foley's own first cousin, and he saw the four children himself."

The dead body was but an appearance made by the enchantment of "the others," according to the country faith.

If the country people sometimes doubt that those they have seen die can come and live with them as before, they never doubt that those they have seen die constantly visit them for a little while. A woman at Kiltartan says: "It's well known that a mother that's taken from her child will come back to it at night, and that's why a light is kept burning all night for a good while after a woman dying that has left young children in the house." And I have even been told that a mother always comes to her children; and because of the greater power of the dead, a dead mother is sometimes thought better than a living one.

Another woman at Kiltartan[1] says: "Did the mother come to care them? Sure an' certain she did, an' I'm the one that can tell that. For I slept in the room with my sister's child after she dyin'—and as sure as I stand here talkin' to you, she was back in the room that night. An' a friend o' mine told me the same thing. His wife was taken away in childbirth, an' the five children she left that did be always ailin' an' sickly, from that day there never was a ha'porth ailed them."

And another woman at Kiltartan[2] says: "My own sister was taken away, she an' her husband within twenty-four hours, an' not a thing upon them, an' she with a baby a week old. Well, the care of that child fell upon me, an' sick or sorry it never was, but thrivin' always."

Sometimes nothing but a chance is believed to prevent the dead being kept in the world for good. A woman at Sligo knew a Mayo man who was told to wait for his wife in a certain yard at night, and that she would come riding on a white horse, and would stay with him if he would snatch her from her horse, but the owner of the yard laughed at him and would not give him the key; while the terror of the husband did the mischief in a story told by an old man at Gortavena. "There was a man and he a cousin of my own, lost his wife. And one night he heard her come into the room where he was in the bed with the child beside

---

[1] Lady Gregory tells this story in *Visions and Beliefs in the West of Ireland*, vol. I, pp. 181–2.
[2] Lady Gregory, in the same passage cited in footnote 1, attributes this story of "Martin Rabbitt".

him. And he let on to be asleep, and she took the child and brought her out to the kitchen fire, and sat down beside it, and suckled it. And she put it back then into the bed again, and he lay still and said nothing. The second night she came again, and he had more courage and he said, 'Why are you without your boots?' for he saw that her feet were bare. And she said, 'Because there's nails in them.' So he said, 'Give them to me,' and he got up and drew all the nails out of them, and she brought them away. The third night she came again, and when she was suckling the child, he saw she was still barefoot, and he asked why didn't she wear the boots? 'Because,' said she, 'you left one sprig in them, between the upper and lower sole. But if you have courage,' says she, 'you can do more than that for me. Come to-morrow night to the gap up there beyond the hill, and you'll see the riders going through, and I'll be the one you'll see on the last horse. And bring with you some fowl droppings and urine, and throw them at me as I pass, and you'll get me again.' Well, he got so far as to go to the gap and to bring what she told him, but when they came riding through the gap he saw her on the last horse, but his courage failed him, and he let what he had in his hand drop, and he never got the chance to see her again. Why she wanted the nails out of the boots! Because it's well known they will have nothing to do with iron. And I remember when every child would have an old horse-nail hung round its neck with a bit of string, but I don't see it done now."

The mother comes sometimes out of hate of the second wife or the second wife's children. A man near Gort says: "There was a little girl I knew, not five years of age, and whenever the second wife would bid her rock the cradle or do anything for her children, she'd just get as far as the bed, and lie down asleep. It was the mother put that on her, she wouldn't have her attending to the children of the second wife."

A woman at Kiltartan says: "There was a man had buried his wife, and she left three children; and when he took a second wife she did away with the children, hurried them off to America and the like. But the first wife used to be seen up in the loft, and she making a plan of revenge against the other wife. The second one had one son and three daughters. And one day the son was out digging in the field, and presently he went into what is called a fairy hole. And there a woman came before him, and says she, 'What are you doing here, trespassing on my ground?' And with that she took a stone and hit him in the head, and he died with the blow of the stone she gave him. And all the people said, it was by the fairies he was taken."

And a woman at Inchy says: "There was a woman in Ballyderreen died after her baby being born. And the husband took another wife, and she very young, that everybody wondered she'd like to go into the house. And every night the first wife came in the loft, and looked down at her baby, and they couldn't see her, but they knew she was there by the child looking up and smiling at her. So at last someone said that if they'd go up in the loft after the cock crowing three times, they'd see her. And so they did, and there she was, with her own dress on, a plaid shawl she had brought from America, and a cotton skirt with some edging at the bottom. So they went to the priest, and he said mass in the house, and they didn't see so much of her after that. But after a year the new wife had a baby, and one day she bid the first child to rock the cradle. But when she sat down to do it, a sort of a sickness came over her, and she could do nothing, and the same thing always happened, for her mother didn't like to see her caring the second wife's baby. And one day the wife herself fell in the fire and got a great many burns, and they said that it was she did it. So they went to the blessed well of Tubber Macduagh; and they were told to go there every Friday for twelve weeks, and they said seven prayers and gathered seven stones every time. And since then she doesn't come to the house, but the little girl goes out and meets her mother at a fairy bush. And sometimes she speaks to her there, and sometimes in her dreams. But no one else but her own little girl has seen her of late."

People indeed come back for all kinds of purposes. I was told at Sligo about four years ago of a man who was being constantly beaten by a dead person. Sometimes it was said you could hear the blows as he came along the road, and sometimes he would be dragged out of bed at night and his wife would hear the blows, but you could never see anything. He had thought to escape the dead person by going to a distant place, Bundoran I think, but he had been followed there. Nobody seemed to give him any pity, for it was "an old uncle of his own that was beating him."

Sometimes people come back out of mere friendliness, though the sight of them is often an unwholesome sight to the living. A man on the coast opposite Arran, in Western Galway, told a friend and me this tale as we were coming from a witch-doctor's. "There was a boy going to America, and when he was going, he said to the girl next door, 'Wherever I am when you're married, I'll come back to the wedding.' And not long after he went to America he died. And when the girl was married and all the friends and neighbours in the house, he appeared in the room, but no one saw him but his comrade he used to have here; and the girl's brother saw him too, but no one else. And the comrade followed him and went close to him, and said, 'Is it you indeed?' And he said, 'It is, and from America I came to-night.' And he asked how long did that journey take, and he said 'three-quarters of an hour,' and then he went away. And the comrade was never the better of it; either he got the touch, or the other called him, being such friends as they were, and soon he died. But the girl is now middle-aged, and is living in that house we're just after passing, and is married to one Bruen."

Many and many are believed to come back to pay some debt, for, as a woman at Gort says: "When some one goes that owes money, the weight of the soul is more than the weight of the body, and it can't get away till someone has courage to question it."

A man who lives close to the witch-doctor says: "There was a man had come back from Boston, and one day he was out in the bay, going to Arran with £3 worth of cable he was after getting in M'Donough's store, in Galway. And he was steering the boat, and there were two turf boats along with him, and all in a minute the men in them saw he was gone, swept off the boat with a wave, and it a dead calm. And they saw him come up once, straight up as if he was pushed, and then he was brought down again and rose no more. And it was some time after that a friend of his in Boston, and that was coming home to this place, was in a crowd of people out there. And he saw him coming to him, and he said, 'I heard you were drowned.' And the man said, 'I am not dead, but I was brought here, and when you go home bring these three guineas to Michael M'Donough, in Galway, for its owed him for the cable I got from him. And he put the three guineas in his hand and vanished away."

Only those the living retake in their continuous battle against "the others," and those "the others" permit to return for an hour, are thought to come in their own shape; but all the captives of "the others," according to some tellers of tales, return in a strange shape at the end of their unearthly lives. I have been told about Gort that nobody is permitted to die among "the others," but everybody, when the moment of their death is coming, is changed into the shape of some young person, who is taken in their stead, and put into the world to die, and to receive the sacraments.

A woman at Kiltartan says: "When a person is taken, the body is taken as well as the spirit, and some good-for-nothing thing left in its place. What they take them for is to work for them and to do things they can't do themselves. You might notice it's always the good they take. That's why when we see a child that's good-for-nothing we say 'Ah, you little fairy.' "

A woman near Gort says: "There was a woman with her husband passing by Eserkelly, and she had left her child at home. And a man came and called her in, and promised to leave her on the road where she was before. So she went, and there was a baby in the place where she was brought to, and they asked her to suckle it. And when she was come out again, she said, 'One question I'll ask, what were those two old women sitting by the fire?' And the man said, 'We took the child to-day and we'll have the mother to-night, and one of those will be out in her place, and the other in the place of some other person, and then he left her where she was before. But there's no harm in them, no harm at all."

She said "there's no harm in them" because they might be listening to her.

Death among "the others" seems not less grievous than among us, for another woman near Gort says: "There was a woman going to Loughrea with a bundle of flannel on her head, was brought into the castle outside Roxborough gate to give the breast to a child, and she saw an old woman beside the fire, and an old man behind the door, who had eyes red with crying. They were going to be put in the place of people who were to be taken that night. 'The others' gave her a bottle, and when she'd put a drop of what was in it on her eyes, she'd see them hurling, or whatever they were doing. But they didn't like her to be seeing so much, and after a little time the sight of one of her eyes was taken away from her."

A man who lives near Gort was coming home from a fair, "And there were two men with him, and when three persons are together, there's no fear of anything, and they can say what they like." One of the men pointed out a place they were passing: "And it was a fairy place, and many strange things had happened there," and the other "told him how there was a woman lived close by had a baby. And before it was a week old her husband had to leave her because of his brother having died. And no sooner was she left alone than she was taken, and they sent for the priest to say Mass in the house, but she was calling out every sort of thing they couldn't understand, and within a few days she was dead. And after death the body began to change, and first it looked like an old woman and then like an old man, and they had to bury it the next day. And before a week was over, she began to appear. They always appear when they leave a child like that. And surely she was taken to nurse the fairy children, just like poor Mrs. Gleeson was last year."

And a woman from Kiltartan says: "My sister told me that near Cloughballymore, there was a man walking home one night late, and he had to pass by a smiths' forge, where one Kenealy used to work. And when he came near he heard the noise of the anvil and he wondered Kenealy would be working so late in the night. But when he went in he saw they were strange men that were in it. So he asked them the time and they told him, and he said, 'I won't be home this long time yet.' And one of the men said, 'You'll be home sooner than what you think,' and another said, 'There's a man on a grey horse gone the road, you'll get a lift from him.' And he wondered that they'd know the road he was going to his own house. But sure enough, as he was walking, he came up with a man on a grey horse and he gave him a lift. But when he got home his wife saw he looked strange-like, and she asked what ailed him, and he told her all that had happened. And when she looked at him, she saw that he was taken. So he went into the bed, and the next evening he was dead. And all the people that came in knew by the appearance of the body that it was an old man that had been put in his place, and that he was taken when he got on the grey horse. For there's something not right about a grey or a white horse, or about a red-haired woman. And as to forges, there's some can hear working and hammering in them all the night."

Forges and smiths have always been magical in Ireland. S. Patric prayed against the spells of women and smiths, and the old romances are loud with the doings of Goibnui,[3] the god of the smiths, who is remembered in folktale as the Mason Goban, for he works in stone as in metal.

Another woman from Kiltartan says: "Near Tyrone there was a girl went out one day to get nuts near the wood. And she heard music inside the wood, and when she went home she told her mother. But the next day she went again, and the next, and she stopped so long away that her mother sent the other little girl to look for her, but she could see no one. She came in after a while, and she went inside in to the room, but, when the girl came out, she said she heard nothing. But the next day after that she died. The neighbours all came in to the wake, and there was tobacco and snuff there, but not much, for it's the custom not to have so much when a young person dies. But when they looked at the bed, it was no young person in it, but an old woman with long teeth, that you'd be frightened, and the face wrinkled and the hands. So they didn't stop, but went away, and she was buried the next day. And in the night the mother could hear music all about the house, and lights of all colours flashing about the windows. She was never seen again, except by a boy that was working about the place; he met her one evening at the end of the house, dressed in her own clothes. But he couldn't question her where she was, for it's only when you meet them by a bush you can question them there. I'll gather more stories for you, and I'll tell them some time when the old woman isn't in the house, for she's that bigoted, she'd think she'd be carried off there and then."

Tyrone is a little headland in the south of Galway Bay.

Sometimes the "old person" lives a good time in the likeness of the person who has been taken, as in this tale, told by a woman at Ardrahan:[4] "My mother told me that when she was a young girl, and before

---

[3] The skill of the smith Goibnui (spelled "Goibniu" by Douglas Hyde) in making and repairing weapons quickly enabled the Tuatha de Danaan to defeat the Formorians at the second battle of Moytura.

[4] In Lady Gregory, *Visions and Beliefs*, vol. I, p. 176, the story is attributed to "Mrs. Donnely".

the time of side-cars, a man that lived in Duras married a girl from Ardrahan side. And it was the custom then, for a newly-married girl to ride home on a horse behind her next of kin. And she was on the pillion behind her uncle. And when they passed Ardrahan churchyard, he felt her to shiver and nearly to slip off the horse. And he put his hand behind for to support her, and all he could feel was like a piece of tow. And he asked her what ailed her, and she said she thought of her mother when she was passing the churchyard. And a year after her baby was born, and then she died. And everyone said, the night she was taken was her wedding night.'

An old woman in the Burren Hills says: "Surely there are many taken. My own sister that lived in the house beyond, and her husband and her three children, all in one year. Strong they were, and handsome and good and best, and that's the sort that are taken. They got in the priest when first it came on the husband, and soon after a fine cow died, and a calf. But he didn't begrudge that if he'd get his health, but it didn't save him after. Sure Father Leraghty said, not long ago in the chapel, that no one had gone to heaven for the last ten years.

"But whatever life God has granted them, when it's at an end, go they must, whether they're among them or not. And they'd sooner be among them than go to Purgatory.

"There was a little one of my own taken. Till he was a year old, he was the stoutest and the best, and the finest of all my children, and then he began to pine, till he wasn't thicker than a straw, but he lived for about four years. How did it come on him? I know that well. He was the grandest ever you saw, and I proud of him, and I brought him to a ball in this house, and he was able to drink punch. And soon after I stopped one day at a house beyond, and a neighbouring woman came in with her child, and she says: 'If he's not the stoutest, he's the longest.' And she took off her apron and the string of it to measure them both. I had no right to let her do that, but I thought no harm of it at the time. But it was that night he began to screech, and from that time he did no good. He'd get stronger through the winter, but about the Pentecost, in the month of May, he'd always fall back again, for at that time they're at the worst. I didn't have the priest in, it does them no good but harm, to have a priest take notice of them when they're like that. It was in the month of May, at the Pentecost, he went at last. He was always pining, but I didn't think he'd go so soon. At the end of the bed he was lying with the other children, and he called to me and put up his arms. But I didn't want to take too much notice of him, or to have him always after me, so I only put down my foot to where he was. And he began to pick straws out of the bed, and to throw them over the little sister that was beside him till he had thrown as much as would thatch a goose. And when I got up, there he was, dead, and the little sister asleep, and all covered with straws."

She believed him to fall under the power of "the others," because of the envy of the woman who measured him, for "the others" can only take their prey through "the eye of a sinner." She dwelt upon his getting worse, and at last dying, in May, because "the others" are believed to come and go a great deal in May.

Sometimes "the old person" is recognised by the living, as in this tale told by another woman in the Burren Hills: "There were three women living at Ballindeereen: Mary Flaherty, the mother, and Mary Grady, the daughter, and Ellen Grady, that was a by-child of hers. And they had a little dog, called Floss, that was like a child to them. And the grandmother went first, and then the little dog, and then Mary Grady, within a half-year. And there was a boy wanted to marry Ellen Grady that was left alone. But his father and mother wouldn't have her, because of her being a by-child. And the priest wouldn't marry them not to give the father and mother offence. So it wasn't long before she was taken too, and those that saw her after death knew it was the mother that was there in place of her. And when the priest was called the day before she died, he said, 'She's gone since twelve o'clock this morning, and she'll die between the two masses to-morrow.' For he was Father Hynes that had understanding of these things. And so she did."

Sometimes "the old person" is said to melt away before burial. A woman near Cork[5] says:—"There were two brothers, Mullallys, in Ballaneen. And when one got home one night and got into the bed, he found the brother cold and dead before him. And not a ha'porth on him when he went out. Taken by them he surely was. And when he was being buried in Kiltartan, the brother looked into the coffin, finding it so light, and there was nothing in it but the clothes that were around him. Sure if he'd been a year in the grave he couldn't have melted away like that."

A woman from Kiltartan says:—"There was a girl buried in Kiltartan, one of the Joyces, and when she was laid out on the bed, a woman that went in to look at her saw that she opened her eyes, and made a sort of face at her. But she said nothing but sat down by the hearth. But another woman came in after that and the same thing happened, and she told the mother, and she began to cry and roar that they'd say such a thing of her poor little girl. But it wasn't the little girl that was in it at all, but some old person. And the man that nailed down the coffin left the nails loose, and when they came to Kiltartan churchyard he looked in, and not one they saw inside it but the sheet and a bundle of shavings."

[5] Cork: probably a misprint for "Gort".

"The others" sometimes it seems take this shape; a woman in the Burren Hills tells of their passing her in the shape of shavings driven by the wind. She knew they were not really shavings, because there was no place for shavings to come from.

Even when cattle are taken, something or someone is put in their place. A man at Doneraill told me a story of a man who had a bullock that got sick, and that it might be of some use, he killed it and skinned it, and when it was in a trough being washed it got up and ran away. He ran after it and knocked it down and cut it up, and after he and his family had eaten it, a woman, that was passing by said: "You don't know what you have eaten. It is your own grandmother that you have eaten."

A man in the Burren Hills, says: "When anyone is taken something is put in his place, even when a cow or the like goes. There was one of the Nestors used to be going about the country skinning cattle, and killing them, even for the country people, if they were sick. One day he was skinning a cow that was after dying by the roadside, and another man with him. And Nestor said, 'It's a pity we couldn't sell the meat to some butcher, we might get something for it.' But the other man made a ring of his fingers, like this, and looked through it, and then bade Nestor to look, and what he saw was an old piper that had died some time before, and when he thought he was skinning the cow, what he was doing was cutting the leather breeches off the piper. So it's very dangerous to eat beef you buy from any of those sort of common butchers. You don't know what might have been put in its place."

And sometimes cattle are put in the place of men and women, and Mrs. Sheridan, a handsome old woman who believes herself to have been among "the others," and to have suckled their children, tells many stories of the kind; she says: "There was a woman, Mrs. Keevan, killed near the big tree at Raheen, and her husband was after that with Biddy Early, and she said it was not the woman that died at all, but a cow that died and was put in her place."

Biddy Early was a famous wise woman, and the big tree at Raheen is a great elm tree where many mischiefs and some good fortunes have happened to many people. Few know as much as Mrs. Sheridan about "the others," and if she were minded to tell her knowledge and use the cure they have given her for all the mischiefs they work, she would be a famous wise woman herself, and be sought out, perhaps, by pilgrims from neighbouring counties. She is, however, silent, and it was only when we had won her confidence, that she came of her self, with some fear of the anger of "the others," and told a friend and myself certain of the marvels she had seen. She had hitherto but told us tales that other people had told her, but now she began:

"One time when I was living at Cloughauish, there were two little boys drowned in the river there. One was eight years and the other eleven years. And I was out in the fields and the people looking in the river for their bodies, and I saw a man coming over the fields and the two little boys with him, he holding a hand of each and leading them away. And he saw me stop and look at them, and he said: 'Take care, would you bring them from me (for he knew I had power to do it), for you have only one in your house, and if you take these from me, she'll never go home to you again.' And one of the boys broke from his hand and came running to me, but the other cried out to him, 'O Pat, will you leave me!' So then he went back, and the man led them away. And then I saw another man, very tall he was, and crooked, and watching me like this, with head down; and he was leading two dogs, and I knew well where he was going and what he was going to do with the dogs. And when I heard the bodies were laid out, I went to the house to have a look at them, and those were never the two boys that were lying there, but the two dogs that were put in their place. I knew them by a sort of stripes on the bodies, such as you'd see on the covering of a mattress. And I knew the boys couldn't be in it, after me seeing them led. And it was at that time I lost my eye, something came on it, and I never got the sight of it again."

"The others" are often described as having striped clothes like the striped hair of the dogs.

The stories of the country people, about men and women taken by "the others," throw a clear light on many things in the old Celtic poems and romances, and when more stories have been collected and compared, we shall probably alter certain of our theories about the Celtic mythology. The old Celtic poets and romance writers had beautiful symbols and comparisons that have passed away, but they wrote of the same things that the country men and country women talk of about the fire,—the country man or country woman who falls into a swoon, and sees in a swoon a wiser and stronger people than the people of the world, but goes with less of beautiful circumstance upon the same journey Etain went when she passed with Midher into the enchanted hills;[6] and Oisin when he rode with Niam on her white horse over the sea;[7] and Conla when he sailed with a divine woman in a ship of glass to "the ever-living, living ones";[8] and Cuchallain when he sailed in a

[6] The god Midher carries off Etain, his wife in a previous incarnation, from the palace of Eochaid, her husband. Midher and Etain fly off as swans. (de Jubainville, *The Irish Mythological Cycle and Celtic Mythology*, trans. R. I. Best, pp. 176–82.)

[7] The subject of Yeats's "The Wanderings of Oisin".

[8] The beautiful young woman is the messenger of the god of death Tethra, and she comes to summon Conla, son of Conn, the High King, to the land of the dead (de Jubainville-Best, p. 108).

ship of bronze to a divine woman;[9] and Bran, the son of Feval, when a
spirit came through the closed door of his house holding an apple-
bough of silver, and called him to "the white-silver plain";[10] and
Cormac, the son of Art, when his house faded into mist, and a great
plain, and a great house, and a tall man, and a crowned woman, and
many marvels came in its stead.[11] And when the country men and
country women tell of people taken by "the others," who come into
the world again, they tell the same tales the old Celtic poets and romance
writers told when they made the companions of Fion compel, with
threats, the goddess Miluchra to deliver Fion out of the Grey Lake on
the Mountain of Fuad; and when they made Cormac, the son of Art, get
his wife and children again from Mananan, the son of Lir; and, perhaps,
when they made Oisin sit with Patric and his clergy and tell of his life
among the gods, and of the goddess he had loved.

W. B. Yeats

# *Le Mouvement Celtique*: Fiona Macleod

Yeats's articles on the Celtic Movement, a term he came to abhor, appeared in
April of 1898 in *L'Irlande Libre* which, as the *"Organe de la colonie irlandaise à
Paris"*, was the principal means of propaganda for Maud Gonne's *Association
Irlandaise*. Although Yeats joined the league shortly after its founding in
1896, two essays, *"Le Mouvement Celtique*: Fiona Macleod" (April 1) and
*"Le Mouvement Celtique* II: M. John O'Leary" (see p. 113 below), translated
into French by an unknown hand, were his only contributions to the paper.

JE base ma foi en l'influence prochaine des races celtiques dans la
littérature, principalement sur les innombrables légendes encore
enfouies dans de vieux manuscrits irlandais, comme aussi sur les
traductions peu connues et les traditions populaires.

La littérature se renouvelle sans cesse au moyen des légendes et par le

---

[9] The woman is Fand, wife of Manannan mac Lir. This spelling of the hero's name is
unusual. In these folklore articles Yeats usually spelled it "Cuchullain".

[10] Bran is summoned by a goddess with a silver branch to make a journey, during which
he encounters Manannan mac Lir. Bran arrives with his band of thirty comrades at an
island peopled only by women, whose queen is the goddess who had given him the silver
branch (de Jubainville–Best, p. 183).

[11] These wonders take place during the story of how Cormac traded his wife and children
to Manannan mac Lir for a magic branch with golden apples, and how Cormac eventually
regained them (de Jubainville–Best, pp. 185–8).

souvenir que celles-ci conservent de la manière dont ont pensé et imaginé des races plus passionnées que nos races modernes.

De ces antiques races, la mine féconde des légendes slaves et finlandaises est loin d'être aussi riche que le foyer celtique: Wagner, Morris et leur précurseur Ibsen ont fait main base sur les fables scandinaves, qu'ils se sont appropriées; de même, les fables grecques et latines ont été mises au pillage par des centaines de générations.

Les antiques légendes celtiques sont à la fois originales et d'une beauté extraordinaire. Il se peut qu'elles aient encore sur la littérature une influence aussi grande qu'ont eue celles du pays de Galles, aux douzième et treizième siècles.

Leur traduction et leur mise en lumière absorbent la pensée de beaucoup d'érudits, tels que: Herr Windron, en Allemagne; M. de Joubanville en France; les professeurs Nuts et Rhys, en Angleterre; le docteur Hyde et M. Kayse O'Grady, en Irlande; dans le même temps que, pour fonder la nouvelle littérature romantique, M. Standish O'Grady, Miss Hoper, MM. Hinkson,[1] et enfin Miss Fiona Macleod, ont commencé à utiliser les dites légendes. En d'autres pays encore d'autres écrivains vont, je crois, se mettre aussi à l'oeuvre' et alors, peut-être quelque littérateur étranger, quelque Wagner ou Morris, donnera-t-il à ce réveil enivrant sa forme parfaite et définitive.

Miss Fiona Macleod est le nom le plus intimement lié à ce mouvement, à cette renaissance celtique, comme disent les journaux. Ses contes, puisés tantôt dans les écrivains irlandais, tantôt parmi d'autres vieux auteurs qu'on appelle les Irlandais-Ecossais (population des îles à l'ouest de l'Ecosse, au milieu de laquelle elle est née), ses contes, dis-je, renferment l'âme même du peuple.

Je fus grandement désappointé par ses premières oeuvres: "Pharaïs" et le "Vaurien de la Montagne",[2] il me semblait qu'elle n'y tenait aucunes des promesses qu'on attendait de son jeune talent. On y trouvait une continuelle véhémence, une monotonie de passion, une prolixité de langage qui me déplurent. Il me semblait entendre un de nos incultes paysans politiques irlandais déversant en phrases confuses ses interminables lamentations, et je me dis: "Voici un esprit qui court

---

[1] Yeats's list here contains several figures, their identities somewhat obscured by translator or typesetter, whom Yeats cites frequently as his authorities on Celtic matters. Among these are W. O. Ernst Windisch ("Herr Windron") (1844–1918), the German philologist, Marie Henri d'Arbois de Jubainville (see p. 226 below), whose courses at the Sorbonne J. M. Synge was to attend in 1898 and 1902, Alfred T. Nutt ("Nuts") (see p. 118 below), the publisher and folklorist, John Rhys (see p. 227 below), principal of Jesus College, Oxford, and Standish Hayes O'Grady ("M. Kayse O'Grady") (1832–1915). "Miss Hoper" is, of course, Nora Hopper (see p. 124 below) and Mrs. Hinkson is Yeats's friend and confidante Katharine Tynan Hinkson (1861–1931).

[2] *Pharaïs* was published in 1894 and, while there was no *Vaurien of the Mountains* by "Fiona Macleod", her *The Mountain Lovers* appeared in 1895.

à sa perte, faute de mesure". Je ne fus vraiment conquis qu'après avoir lu quelques-unes de ces courtes nouvelles dénommées: "Contes Spirituels", "Contes Barbares" et "Romans Tragiques" que j'emportai avec moi dans l'ile méridionale d'Arran,[3] où vivent les plus primitifs et les plus simples des paysans irlandais.

Alors je jugeai Miss Macleod en pleine possession de son art,—un art où désormais régnait la mesure. Bien plus! je reconnus que les personnages de ses contes étaient ceux-là mêmes qui m'entouraient. Après avoir fermé le livre, il m'arrive de conserver les croyances et les légendes dont parlent ces histoires, la foi en des êtres qui furent des phoques avant de devenir des hommes, des esprits qui se meuvent autour de nous, des grands saints et des héros qui sont plus "vivants" dans l'esprit de ce peuple que ne le sont les hommes publics dont il est question dans les journaux. Il m'apparut que Miss Macleod avait sur le monde exactement les mêmes instincts que ces graves paysans avec lesquels je m'entretenais; qu'elle était devenue comme leur propre voix, non par une étude plus approfondie de leurs saveurs, mais par suite d'une identité de nature.

Dans ces courtes nouvelles, elle ne reproduit pas littéralement les vieilles légendes; elle compose, d'après les mêmes croyances populaires, des contes nouveaux qu'elle fait ressortir de ce fonds commun, comme d'une forêt fantastique, mystérieusement hantée. Mais son dernier ouvrage *The Laughter of Petekin*,[4] reproduit assez fidèlement les légendes les plus fameuses de la vieille Irlande, et cette reproduction est la meilleure de toutes celles que notre "mouvement" a produites.

Ce livre ne peut manquer d'aider à l'union de sentiments que nous souhaitons créer entre les Celtes irlandais et écossais, en leur rappelant tout à la fois leurs origines semblables et ces trésors d'héroïques légendes.

Une communauté de sentiments, non seulement entre ces deux peuples, mais encore avec les Celtes gallois, sera peut-être l'un des résultats décisifs du "Mouvement Celtique", et bien des événements sociaux, politiques, aussi bien que littéraires, en peuvent dériver.

W. B. Yeats

---

[3] The stories in "Fiona Macleod's" *The Sin-Eater* (1895) and *The Washer of the Ford* (1896) were reissued, slightly augmented, as a three-volume set called *Barbaric Tales, Dramatic Tales*, and *Spiritual Romances* in March, 1897. It is probable, however, that Yeats read the stories in their original format during his first trip to the Arans in August, 1896, as he suggests in his review of the tales and romances in *The Sketch* for April, 1897. (See pp. 42–45 above.)

[4] "Fiona Macleod's" story was entitled *The Laughter of Peterkin*.

# "A.E.'s" Poems

Yeats's review, in *The Sketch* of April 6, 1898, of the book *The Earth Breath and other poems* (1897), was accompanied by a small self-portrait sketch by A.E. Although Yeats's criticism that ". . . without a convention, there is, perhaps, no perfect spiritual art" was here applied only to A.E.'s paintings, we know from Yeats's autobiography that he had much the same criticism of A.E.'s poetry. Yeats wanted him to submit his visions to the questions of the intellect and he was impatient that A.E. seemed unable or unwilling to distinguish between his visions and reality. A.E., in his turn, thought that Yeats's theory of the masks was the attempt of a style to create a personality and hence a reversal of the natural order. In a letter to George Moore, A.E. said of what he considered Yeats's artistically created personality, "The error in his psychology is that life creates the form, but he seems to think that the form creates life." (*Letters from AE*, ed. Alan Denson, New York, 1961, p. 110.) Both men admired each other and quarreled with the special privilege of old friends. *The Earth Breath* was dedicated to Yeats.

UPON the walls of a certain lecture-room in Dublin,[1] where men who are themselves visionaries lectured until lately upon Indian and Neoplatonic and Christian visionaries, "A.E." has painted some very fantastic pictures: a young man looking at his own image in the scales of a serpent; a vast stone figure sitting on a mountain with a devotee prostrating his body in adoration before it, while his soul rises up threatening it with a spear; a man huddled up in darkness while his soul rushes out and grasps a star; a company of little figures moving among mushrooms and long grasses: picture everywhere melting into picture. They are the work of a hand too bewildered by the multitudinous shapes and colours of visions to narrow its method to a convention, and, without a convention, there is, perhaps, no perfect spiritual art. It has sought unavailingly, despite much talent, to make of unmoving and silent paint a mirror for the wandering, exultant processions that haunt those margins of spiritual ecstasy, where colours are sounds, and sounds are shapes, and shapes are fragrances. The poems of "A.E.," the little paper-covered book published by a friend who hired a garret for that purpose, and this larger book, "The Earth Breath," published by Mr. John Lane, are a more perfect mirror, because poetry changes with the changing of the dream. All things in these elaborate and subtle verses

---

[1] These paintings were on the walls of a room at the Dublin Lodge of the Theosophical Society at 3 Upper Ely Place (Ella Young, *Flowering Dusk, Things Remembered Accurately and Inaccurately*, New York, 1945, p. 30).

are perpetually changing, and all things are the symbols of things more unsubstantial than themselves. The poet looks at the heavens, and they become a great bird with a blue breast and wings of gold, and at the wood, and it becomes a great sheep shaking its shadowy fleece, and then bird and sheep become, through some vague wisdom floating in the rhythm and in the colour of the words, moments of the divine tenderness. A bird with diamond wings passes through his imagination, and he knows it a soul wandering from its body in a deep sleep; and when he thinks of the girdle of twilight eyes in the moon may see about the earth, where day and night mingle, he thinks of beauty hung between death and life, eternity and time, sleep and waking. He would bring before his eyes the eternal house of the soul, and calls up a burning diamond, and, while he watches it, it has changed, as in the changes of a hashish dream, to islands fringed with flames. All things that have shape and weight change perpetually, being, indeed, but symbols. "For every star and every deep" filled with stars "are stars and deeps within." [2] It is the doctrine of all mystics, the doctrine that awakened Plotinus to his lonely and abstract joy. "In the particular acts of human life," he wrote, "it is not the interior soul and the true man, but the exterior shadow of the man alone, which laments and weeps, performing his part on the earth as in a more ample and extended scene, in which many shadows of souls and phantom forms appear." [3] Even when we are in love, "A.E." would have us love the invisible beauty before the visible beauty and make our love a dream.

> *Let me dream only with my heart,*
> *Love first, and after see:*
> *Know thy diviner counterpart*
> *Before I kneel to thee.*

> *So in thy motions all expressed*
> *Thy angel I may view;*
> *I shall not on thy beauty rest,*
> *But beauty's ray in you,*

[2] This quotation is from A.E.'s "Star Teachers", p. 89 of *The Earth Breath*.

[3] Yeats had probably read some Plotinus at this time in the 1895 *Selected Works* edited by Thomas Taylor (1758–1835). The nearly lifelong discontent with the "lonely and abstract joy" of Plotinus of which this remark is the first evidence culminates in "The Tower" (1925) with Yeats's refusal to "Choose Plato and Plotinus for a friend / Until imagination, ear and eye, / Can be content with argument and deal / in abstract things . . ." (Peter Allt and Russell K. Alspach, eds., *The Variorum Edition of the Poems of W. B. Yeats*, New York, 1957, p. 409). The defiant decision in that poem to ". . . mock Plotinus' thought / And cry in Plato's teeth, / Death and life were not / Till man made up the whole . . ." (*ibid.*, p. 415) is softened by a note dated 1928 which reflects Yeats's enthusiastic study of the new translation of Plotinus by Stephen McKenna (1871–1934). "When I wrote the lines about Plato and Plotinus I forgot that it is something in our own eyes that makes us see them as all transcendence" (*ibid.*, p. 826).

he writes in verses that have a Jacobean music, and a nobility of thought that is not Jacobean. He would have our love, too, end as well as begin in the invisible beauty, and in another poem sings to the visible beauty of the woman—

> *O beauty, as thy heart o'erflows*
> *In tender yielding unto me,*
> *A vast desire awakes and grows*
> *Unto forgetfulness of thee.*

It is this invisible beauty that all life seeks under many names, and that makes the planets "break in woods and flowers and streams," and "shake" the winds from them "as the leaves from off the rose," and that "kindles" all souls and lures them "through the gates of birth and death," and in whose heart we will all rest when "the shepherd of the ages draws his misty hands[4] away through the glimmering deeps to silence" and "the awful fold." It kindles evil as well as good, for it awakens "the fount of shadowy beauty" that pours out those "things the heart would be" and "chases" "in the endless night."[5] All things are double, for we either choose "the shadowy beauty," and our soul weeps, or the invisible beauty that is our own "high ancestral self," and the body weeps. Many verses in this little book have so much high thought and they sing it so sweetly and tenderly that I cannot but think them immortal verses.

W. B. Yeats

# Le Mouvement Celtique: II. M. John O'Leary

The first section of "*Le Mouvement Celtique*" (see p. 108 above) was an original essay which borrowed little from an earlier review of "Fiona Macleod's" prose. The second part, however, "M. John O'Leary", which appeared in *L'Irlande Libre* on June 1, 1898, is, with the exception of the two introductory

[4] hands: A.E. reads "hordes" (from "A Vision of Beauty", in *The Earth Breath*, pp. 15–16). This same quotation appeared in Yeats's May, 1895 review. Yeats then inserted "herds" for "hordes". The line is quoted correctly in Yeats's later essay in the Dublin *Daily Express* on "The Poetry of A.E." (see p. 123 below).

[5] in the endless night: in A.E., this phrase reads "in endless flight". (*The Earth Breath* p. 39.) From "The Fountain of Shadowy Beauty", these phrases are from the lines:

> *The Fount of Shadowy Beauty throws*
> *Its magic round us all the night;*
> *What things the heart would be, it sees*
> *And chases them in endless flight. . . .*

paragraphs, a direct translation of most of the first paragraph of Yeats's review of *Fenians and Fenianism* which had appeared in *The Bookman* for February, 1897 (see p. 35 above).

M. JOHN O'LEARY est aujourd'hui président du Conseil central exécutif de l'organisation qui se prépare à célébrer la révolte de 1798, et, il y a dix ou douze ans, il eut une influence prédominante sur les débuts de ce mouvement littéraire irlandais qui, maintenant qu'il a rencontré comme alliés les mouvements écossais et gallois, est devenu le mouvement celtique. De jeunes nationalistes qu'éloignait le mouvement utilitaire de Parnell: M. Rolleston, l'editeur de la *Revue de l'Université*, qui fut de courte durée, et ou furent publiés tant d'écrits de notre nouvelle école; Miss Catherine Tynan, qui venait à peine de publier son premier volume de poésie lyrique; le docteur Douglas Hyde, lequel n'avait pas encore commencé a publier les ouvrages qui ont fait de lui le plus fameux de nos savants gaëliques, et d'autres, qui ont plus ou moins de notoriété, apprenaient chez lui à se comprendre et à connaître leurs communes aspirations.

Les qualités mêmes qui ont empêché M. O'Leary d'être un véritable homme d'action, l'ont rendu propre à exercer une influence sur ces mouvements de pensée et de sentiment qui sont les sources de l'action.

Je me souviens d'une conversation que j'eus, il y a une couple d'années, avec mon voisin de table, a un souper en l'honneur, je crois de Thomas Davis: "Nos hommes publics, me disait-il, à l'exception de John O'Leary, ont eu peur de différer du peuple en quoi que ce soit; aussi pas un, à part John O'Leary, ne nous inspire-t-il le moindre respect." Cet homme était, si nos souvenirs sont exacts, commis dans un grand magasin, et c'était le type de la jeune génération de Dublin. Il avait probablement donné son adhésion pour les choses pratiques à quelque leader qui avait plus d'éloquence ou qui s'attachait avec plus de force aux questions du moment, mais il ne lui avait donné son adhésion que pour les choses pratiques. D'aussi loin qu'il pouvait se souvenir, M. John O'Leary avait dénoncé tel ou tel expédient politique, tel ou tel leader populaire, et affirmé que, l'humanité étant supérieure aux nations, il y a des choses qu'un homme ne doit pas faire, peut-être même pour sauver une nation.

Si cela eût été dit par quelqu'un qui n'eût pas souffert comme M. John O'Leary des années d'emprisonnement et d'exil, mon voisin n'y eût pas prêté l'oreille; mais, les choses étant comme elles étaient, M. John O'Leary représentait à son imagination la conscience nationale. Il y en a quantité d'autres, aurait-il dit peut-être, qui pourraient nous donner un meilleur avis sur la question de savoir si une chose est utile ou ne l'est pas, mais il n'y a que M. John O'Leary pour dire si cela est juste ou injuste, et pour le dire, non seulement à la tranquille lumière de votre foyer, mais, s'il est nécessaire, dehors, sur la voie publique, devant une foule furieuse. Il m'avait toujours semblé que sa passion pour la justice abstraite est la passion celtique pour les idées, intensifiée par la défiance à l'égard des expédients qui vient aux hommes dont les espérances ont été maintes fois déçues, et que les Irlandais, hommes et femmes, à mesure qu'ils deviennent instruits, doivent hériter d'une pareille passion, sinon à un degré pareil. Certainement, les jeunes gens que j'ai rencontrés dans les sociétés de la "Jeune Irlande" dans les sociétés littéraires irlandaises et dans les écoles d'art irlandaises, lui ressemblent plus qu'ils ne ressemblent à cet Irlandais aux lèvres mobiles, prompt à l'émotion et à la sympathie, impressionnable, qu'est le seul Irlandais dont quelques Anglais aient jamais entendu parler.

La cruauté même du journalisme irlandais et de la politique irlandaise vient d'une tendance à juger les hommes, non les uns par les autres, non par l'expérience du degré de supériorité qu'on peut espérer rencontrer dans la vie et dans la politique, mais par quelque étalon abstrait.

W. B. Yeats

# Mr. Lionel Johnson and Certain Irish Poets

Yeats's article on "Mr. Lionel Johnson and Certain Irish Poets" in the Dublin *Daily Express* for August 27, 1898, was reprinted with changes and deletions as an introduction to a selection of Johnson's poems in *A Treasury of Irish Poetry* (1900 and later editions), edited by Stopford A. Brooke and T. W. Rolleston. Yeats included in vol. 8 of his *Collected Works* (1908) a version very much like that included in *A Treasury*, but the piece was dropped from later prose collections. In the *Collected Works* it was dated 1899.

Yeats had reviewed Johnson's *Ireland with Other Poems* for *The Bookman*, February, 1898 (see p. 88 above). This article represents a softening of Yeats's views of Johnson's esoteric Catholicism. In *The Bookman*, Yeats had said that Johnson's religion was too ascetic in a Christian sense for passion and too stoic in a pagan way for ecstasy. By the time he wrote the present article Yeats had learned that Johnson's "ecstasy was the ecstasy of combat" and hence the dilemma was solved.

IF I were asked to say what distinguishes the little school of contemporary Irish poets, I would say they believe, with a singular fervour of belief, in a spiritual life, and express this belief in their poetry.[1] Contemporary English poets are interested in the glory of the world like Mr. Rudyard Kipling, or in the order of the world like Mr. William Watson,[2] or in the passion of the world like Mr. John Davidson,[3] or in the pleasure of the world like Mr. Arthur Symons. Mr. Francis Thompson, who has fallen under the shadow of Mr. Coventry Patmore,[4] the poet of an older time and in protest against that time, is alone preoccupied with a spiritual life; and even he, except at rare moments, has less living fervour of belief than pleasure in the gleaming and scented and coloured symbols that are the footsteps where the belief of others has trodden. Ireland which has always believed, and has never even held her mind, as I think, more than a moment in a balance between two beliefs, and has spoken her beliefs in all kinds of headlong movements, is creating in English a poetry which, whatever be its merits, is as full of spiritual ardour as the poetry that praised in Gaelic, "the ever living living ones," and "the country of the two mists," and "the country of the young,"[5] and "the country of the living heart."

Mr. George Russell, "A.E.," as he still signs himself, has written an ecstatic pantheistic poetry which reveals in all things a kind of scented flame consuming them from within, a poetry that finds its fitting interpretation in the singular and involved, but as I think, profound prose of "John Eglinton."[6] Miss Hopper,[7] an unequal and immature poet, whose best verses are delicate and distinguished, has no clear vision of spiritual things, but makes material things as frail and fragile as if they were already ashes, and that we stirred them in some mid-world of dreams, as "the gossips" in her poem "stir their lives' red ashes." Mrs. Hinkson,[8] uninteresting at her worst, as only uncritical and unspecula-

---

[1] The version of this essay in *The Collected Works* begins, "Contemporary Irish poets believe in a spiritual life, invisible and troubling, and express this belief in their poetry" (vol. VIII, p. 185).

[2] William Watson (1858–1935) was a voluminous poet in the tradition of Wordsworth. After Tennyson's death in 1892, he had been considered for the laureateship, but it was given to Alfred Austin. Yeats's article on him, "A Scholar Poet", in the *Providence Sunday Journal*, June 15, 1890, was collected in *Letters to the New Island* (ed. Horace Reynolds, Cambridge, Mass., 1934, pp. 204–13).

[3] John Davidson (1857–1909), best known for his *Fleet Street Eclogues* (1893), was, with Yeats, a member of the Rhymers' Club.

[4] Both Coventry Patmore (1823–96) and Francis Thompson (1859–1907) were Catholic poets. Thompson reviewed some of Yeats's books in the early nineties.

[5] The Gaelic name for the country of the young in *Tir-nan-Og.*

[6] See pp. 128 and 255, below, for Yeats's controversy with "John Eglinton" over the use of mythology as subject matter for drama. Later versions of this article omit mention of Eglinton.

[7] Nora Hopper was to be the subject of a separate article in the *Daily Express*. (See p. 124 below.)

[8] Mrs. Hinkson (Katharine Tynan) had received much more charitable comment from Yeats when they were young and good friends. (See his review of *Shamrocks* in *Uncollected*

tive writers are uninteresting has sometimes expressed an impassioned and instinctive Catholicism in poems that are, as I believe, a permanent part of our literature. And Mr. Lionel Johnson, of whom I wish to speak at some length, has in his poetry completed the trinity of the spiritual virtues by adding stoicism to ecstasy and asceticism. He has renounced the world out of which Mr. Kipling and Mr. Davidson have made their verses. He has built up a twilight world where all the colours are like the colours in the rainbow that is cast of the moon, and all the people as far from modern tumults as the people upon fading and droping tapestries. He has so little interest in our pains and pleasures, and is so wrapped up in his own world, that one comes from his books wearied and exalted as though one had posed for some noble action in a strange *tableau vivant* that cast its painful stillness upon the mind instead of the body. He might have cried with Axel, "as for living, our servants will do that for us."[9] As Axel chose to die, he has chosen to live among his books and between two memories—the religious tradition of the Church of Rome and the political tradition of Ireland—and from these he gazes upon the future. Whether he writes of Sertorius, or of Lucretius, or of Parnell, or of "Ireland's dead," or of '98,[10] or of St. Columba, or of Leo XIII, it is always with the same cold or scornful ecstasy. He has made out of these things a kind of "Church of a Dream," that were it not half Pagan, would be like "The Church of a Dream"[11] in his own poem:

> *Sadly the dead leaves rustle in the whistling wind,*
> *Around the weather-worn, gray church, low down the vale:*
> *The Saints in glorious*[12] *vesture shake before the gale;*
> *The glorious windows shake, where still they dwell enshrined;*
> *Old Saints, by long dead, shrivelled hands, long since designed;*
> *There still, although the world autumnal be, and pale,*
> *Still in their golden vesture the old Saints prevail;*
> *Alone with Christ, desolate else, left by mankind.*[13]

---

*Prose*, vol. I, pp. 119–22.) The phrase at the end of this sentence, "a permanent part of our literature", becomes "as perfect as they are beautiful" in the version of this essay in *A Treasury of Irish Poetry*, London, 1923, p. 466.

[9] This quotation from Villiers de l'Isle Adam's *Axël* is a favourite of Yeats's.

[10] Yeats referred to a number of Johnson's poems: "Sertorius" is an apostrophe to Quintus Sertorius, a Roman general and ally of Sulla, assassinated in 70 B.C. "Lucretius" is a trilogy of short poems on the author of the *De Rerum Natura*. "Parnell" is an 1893 lament for "the Chief". "Ninety-Eight" is a poem on the uprising of 1798 which uses as a first line of each stanza the famous opening of "The Memory of the Dead" by John Kells Ingram (1823–1907): "Who fears to speak of '98?"

[11] "The Church of a Dream" appeared in Johnson's 1895 *Poems*, and was dedicated to Bernhard Berenson.

[12] glorious: Johnson's *Poems* reads "golden".

[13] In Johnson's *Poems* there is a stanza break between octave and sestet.

> *Only one ancient Priest offers the Sacrifice,*
> *Murmuring holy Latin immemorial:*
> *Swaying with tremulous hands the old censer full of spice,*
> *In grey, sweet incense clouds; blue, sweet clouds mystical;*
> *To him, in place of men, for he is old, suffice*
> *Melancholy remembrance*[14] *and vesperal.*[15]

His ecstasy is the ecstasy of combat, not of submission to the Divine will, and even when he remembers that "the old Saints prevail"; he sees the "one ancient Priest" who alone offers the Sacrifice, and remembers the loneliness of the Saints. Had he not this ecstasy of combat he would be[16] the poet of those peaceful and unhappy souls, who, in the symbolism of a living Irish visionary, are compelled to inhabit when they die a shadowy island paradise in the west, where the moon always shines, and a mist is always on the face of the moon, and a music of many sighs is always in the air because they renounced the joy of the world without accepting the joy of God.

W. B. Yeats

# Celtic Beliefs About the Soul

Yeats's article on "Celtic Beliefs About the Soul" in *The Bookman* for September, 1898, was a review of *The Voyage of Bran* (1895, 1897), edited by Kuno Meyer and Alfred Nutt. Meyer's translation of the early Irish saga furnished the title for both volumes of this work although it served only as an example for Nutt's long essay. More than half of the first volume was devoted to the first part of the essay, "The Happy Otherworld", and almost all of the second volume to the other part, "The Celtic Doctrine of Re-birth".

Alfred T. Nutt (1856–1910), editor of the *Folk-lore Journal* and manager of his father, David Nutt's, publishing firm, had been a useful irritant to Yeats on the subject of folklore. In 1888, Yeats did some copying work for the Nutt firm in the Bodleian library and in the British Museum. Although Nutt specialized in the publication of folklore, none of Yeats's work was published by his company. On the occasion of a bad review of Lady Wilde's *Ancient*

---

[14] remembrance: Johnson's *Poems* reads "remembrances".

[15] In the later versions of this essay, the poem is omitted and this passage reads: "He has made a world full of altar lights and golden vestures, and murmured Latin and incense clouds, and autumn winds and dead leaves, where one wanders remembering martyrdoms and courtesies that the world has forgotten." (*Treasury of Irish Poetry*, p. 467.)

[16] In Yeats's review of *Ireland* in *The Bookman* of February, 1898 (see p. 90 above), he is unequivocal about Johnson's escapism. There Yeats says, "He is the poet of those peaceful, unhappy souls. . . ."

*Cures, Charms and Usages of Ireland* in the *Academy* of 1890, Yeats wrote a letter to this journal defending the more imaginative retelling of folktales in contrast to the scientific approach, typified for Yeats by Nutt's *Folk-lore Journal* (see *Uncollected Prose*, vol. I, p. 173). In his reply, Nutt reminded Yeats that he had borrowed a tale from the *Folk-lore Journal* for his *Fairy and Folk Tales of the Irish Peasantry*.

Nutt had published Douglas Hyde's translation of Gaelic folktales *Beside the Fire* in 1890, and in Yeats's review of this book for the *National Observer*, February 28, 1891 (*ibid.*, p. 185), he complained that Hyde was too much a scholar and too little an artist to finish fragmentary folktales. Yeats asked, "Is it the evil communications of that very scientific person, Mr. Alfred Nutt (he contributes learned notes), which have robbed us of the latter page of *Guleesh na Guss Dhu?*" (p. 188.)

Nutt's assertion in his essay of the striking similarities in Greek and Irish primitive folklore and religion added to Yeats's conviction that Ireland was entering a literary golden age to match that of Greece. Once out of its epic stage, Ireland would soon enter the next stage according to the tripartite development set forth in 1893 in Yeats's lecture on "Nationality and Literature" (*ibid.*, p. 266) and this stage would be its dramatic age. That Yeats intended Ireland to rival the Attic stage is stated explicitly in two essays gathered in *Ideas of Good and Evil*: "Ireland and the Arts", and "The Galway Plains". As Greek drama originated in the cult of Dionysus, so Irish drama would be based upon legends of the *Tuatha de Danaan* still current among the peasants.

CELTIC legends are, according to certain scholars, our principal way to an understanding of the beliefs out of which the beliefs of the Greeks and other European races arose. Mr. Nutt has written a masterly book upon the most important of all old beliefs—the beliefs about the destiny of the soul and the light Celtic legends have thrown upon it. His book is indeed so masterly that I have no doubt that D'Arbois De Joubainville's "Mythologie Irlandais,"[1] Professor Rhys' "Celtic Heathendom,"[2] and it are the three books without which there is no understanding of Celtic legends. Mr. Nutt published the first volume in 1895 as a commentary on "The Voyage of Bran," an old Celtic poem translated and annotated by Kuno Meyer for the purpose; and described with much detail "the happy other world" in Celtic and Greek and Anglo-Saxon and Jewish and Scandinavian and Indian literature. He showed "that Greek and Irish alone have preserved the early stages

---

[1] The usual spelling of this name is Jubainville. The second volume of D'Arbois de Jubainville's series, *Cours de Littérature Celtique*, was *Le Cycle Mythologique Irlandais, et la Mythologie Irlandais* (1884).

[2] John Rhys's *Lectures on the Origin and Growth of Religion as Illustrated by Celtic Heathendom* (1886).

of the happy other world conception with any fulness,"[3] and that Ireland has preserved them "with greater fulness and precision" than the Greeks. He describes in "The Voyage of Bran," vol. 2, the Celtic and Greek doctrine of the rebirth of the soul, of its coming out of the happy other world of the dead, and living once more, and of its power of changing its shape as it desires. By comparing the Greek cult of Dionysius [*sic*] and the Irish cult of the fairies, he concludes that its rebirth and its many changes are because "the happy other world" is the country of the powers of life and increase, of the powers that can never lay aside the flame-like variability of life. He describes the old orgaic[4] dances, in which the worshippers of the powers of life and increase believed themselves to take the shapes of gods and divine beasts, and first, he thinks, imagined "the happy other world," in which their momentary and artificial ecstasy was a continual and natural ecstasy. If the fairy legends of the Irish peasants were better collected, he would have even more copious evidence to prove the association of continual change and of the continual making of new things with the inhabitants of the other world, with the dead as well as with the fairies. I have been often told that "the fairies" change their shapes and colours every moment, and that they can build their houses in a moment and that they can make the fields fruitful and make the milk abundant, and that they can make food or money out of cow dung, and change apples into eggs, or anything into any other thing; and all that is told of the fairies is told of the dead who are among them. The traditional explanation of the battle fought by the fairies in autumn for the harvest is probably less allegorical and less simple than Mr. Nutt's, who explains it as a battle between the powers of life and increase against the powers of death and decay. The peasants are very positive—I have given their words in the January *Nineteenth Century*[5]—that a bad harvest with us is a good harvest among the fairies, and the analogy of a battle fought about the dying makes one inclined to believe that the battle is between the guardians of the living who would leave the harvest for the living, and the fairies and the dead who would take the harvest for themselves. The main argument of Mr. Nutt's book is the argument of Mr. Frazer's "Golden Bough"[6] applied to Celtic legends and belief, and being itself a deduction from peasant custom and belief, and not, like the solar myth theory, from the mythology of cultivated races, it must look always

---

[3] On page 241 of volume 2, Nutt says, ". . . that Greeks and Irish alone have preserved the early stage of the Happy Otherworld conception in any fulness".

[4] *orgaic*: Yeats probably meant "orgiac".

[5] The January, 1898, issue of the *Nineteenth Century* contained "The Prisoners of the Gods", the second of Yeats's long quarterly articles on Irish fairy lore which he had collected with Lady Gregory (see p. 74 above).

[6] Frazer's *Golden Bough* had been published in a two-volume edition in 1890.

for the bulk of its proofs and illustrations to peasant custom and belief. Mr. Nutt seems to imply in a foot-note [7] that the solar myth mythology is a later development and is based upon the harvest mythology, and this shows an accommodating spirit not to be found in Mr. Lang and Mr. Frazer. Mr. Nutt is indeed so tolerant that I am filled with wonder when I find him writing, like other folklorists, as if you had necessarily discovered the cause of a thing when you had discovered its history. Man may have first perceived "the happy other world" in the orgaic dance or in some other ecstasy, but to show that he has done so, though important and interesting, is not to make a point in the great argument about the mystery of man's origin and destiny.

W. B. Yeats

# The Poetry of "A.E."

In his article on "The Poetry of 'A.E.'" in the Dublin *Daily Express* of September 3, 1898, Yeats brushed aside the several criticisms he had made of the "Dublin Mystics", his friends Russell and Magee, and of the "lonely and abstract joy" of Plotinus. A version of this appreciation which introduces the selection of A.E.'s verse in Brooke's and Rolleston's *A Treasury of Irish Poetry* (1900), is very similar except for the omission of the poem beginning "Image of beauty, when I gaze on thee, . . .".

A LITTLE body of young men hired a room in York street, some dozen years ago, and began to read papers to one another on the Vedas, and the Upanishads, and the Neoplatonists, and on modern mystics and spiritualists.[1] They had no scholarship, and they spoke and wrote badly, but they discussed great problems ardently and simply and unconventionally as men, perhaps, discussed great problems in the mediaeval Universities. When they were scattered by their different trades and professions, others took up the discussions where they dropped them, moving the meetings, for the most part, from back street to back street, and now two writers of genius—"A.E." (Mr. George Russell) and "John Eglinton"—seem to have found among them, without, perhaps,

[7] The editors have been unable to locate this footnote. Nutt states at some length the priority of the cult of Dionysus to that of Apollo.

[1] Yeats is referring to the Dublin Hermetical Society, founded in 1885, a group which subsequently grew into the Dublin Theosophical Society.

agreeing with them in everything, that simplicity of mind and that belief in high things, less common in Dublin than elsewhere in Ireland, for
whose lack imagination perishes. "John Eglinton" in "Two Essays on
the Remnant"² and in the essays he has published in the little monthly
magazine,³ they print and bind themselves, analyses the spiritual elements that are transforming and dissolving the modern world; while
"A.E.," in "Homeward Songs by the Way" and in "The Earth Breath,"
repeats over again the revelation of a spiritual world that has been the
revelation of mystics in all ages, but with a richness of colour and a
subtlety of rhythm that are of our age. Plotinus⁴ wrote—"In the particular acts of human life it is not the interior soul and the true man, but
the exterior shadow of the man alone, which laments and weeps,
performing his part on the earth, as in a more ample and extended
scene in which many shadows of souls and phantom forms appear;"
and so these poems cry out that "for every deep filled with stars" there
"are stars and deeps within,"⁵ and that "our thought" is but "the
echo of a deeper being," and that "we kiss because God once for beauty
sought amid a world of dreams,"⁶ and that we rise by "the symbol
charioted" "through loved things" to "love's own ways."⁷ They are
full of the sadness, that has fallen upon all mystics, when they have
first come to understand that there is an invisible beauty from which
they are divided by visible things. How can one be interested in the
rising and in the setting of the sun, and in the work men do under the
sun, when the mistress that one loves is hidden behind the gates of
death, and it may be behind a thousand gates beside—gate beyond
gate?

> *What of all the will to do?*
> *It has vanished long ago,*
> *For a dream-shaft pierced it through*
> *From the Unknown Archer's bow.*

---

² *Two Essays on the Remnant* (1895) had been reviewed by Yeats, along with editions of
poems by A.E., in *The Bookman*, May, 1895 (see *Uncollected Prose*, vol. I, p. 356).

³ Probably *The Irish Theosophist*; Eglinton's own magazine, *Dana*, appeared in 1904.

⁴ Yeats used this quotation from Plotinus (*c.* A.D. 203–62), the neo-Platonist and author
of the *Enneads*, in his review of A.E.'s *Poems* (*The Sketch*, April 6, 1898; see p. 112 above).
A.E.'s initials were taken from the neo-Platonic word AEON, meaning "emanation of the
Divine".

⁵ Paraphrase of a stanza of "Star Teachers", p. 89 of *The Earth Breath*, London, 1897:

> *For this, for this the lights innumerable*
> *As symbols shine that we the true light win:*
> *For every star and every deep they fill*
> *Are stars and deeps within.*

⁶ Paraphrase of "Echoes", p. 17 in *Homeward Songs by the Way* (1895, Dublin edition).

⁷ Paraphrase of "Symbolism", p. 48 in *Homeward Songs by the Way*.

*What of all the soul to think?*
  *Some one offered it a cup*
*Filled with a diviner drink,*
  *And the flame has burned it up.*

*What of all the hope to climb?*
  *Only in the self we grope*
*To the misty end of time:*
  *Truth has put an end to hope.*[8]

It is this invisible beauty that makes the planets "break in woods and flowers and streams" and "shake" the winds from them "as the leaves from off the rose," and that "kindles" all souls and lures them "through the gates of birth and death," and in whose heart we will all rest when "the shepherd of the ages draws his misty hordes away through the glimmering deeps to silence"[9] and to "the awful fold." But this invisible beauty kindles evil as well as good, for its shadow is "the fount of shadowy beauty" that pours out those things "the heart," the merely mortal part of us, "would be," and "chases" in "the endless night." All emotions are double, for either we choose "the shadowy beauty," and our soul weeps, or the invisible beauty that is "our high ancestral self,"[10] and the body weeps.

*Image of beauty, when I gaze on thee,*
*Trembling I waken to a mystery,*
*How through one door we go to life or death*
*By spirit kindled or the sensual breath.*

*Image of beauty, when my way I go;*
*No single joy or sorrow do I know:*
*Elate for freedom leaps the starry power,*
*The life which passes mourns its wasted hour.*

*And, ah, to think how thin the veil that lies*
*Between the pain of hell and paradise!*
*Where the cool grass my aching head embowers*
*God sings the lovely carol of the flowers.*[11]

These poems, perhaps the most beautiful and delicate that any Irishman of our time has written, seem to me all the more interesting

---

[8] These stanzas are the first three of a four-stanza poem, "Sung on a By-way", p. 23 in *Homeward Songs by the Way.*

[9] From "A Vision of Beauty", p. 15 of *The Earth Breath.*

[10] This passage is loosely paraphrased from "The Fountain of Shadowy Beauty", p. 39 of *The Earth Breath.*

[11] This poem is entitled "Janus", p. 48 of *The Earth Breath.*

because their writer has not come from any of our seats of literature and scholarship, but from among sectaries and visionaries whose ardour of belief and simplicity of mind has been his encouragement and his inspiration.

W. B. Yeats

# The Poems and Stories of Miss Nora Hopper

Yeats had recognized his first real disciple when he had read the *Ballads in Prose* (1894) of Nora Hopper (1871–1906), a young woman of Irish descent who had lived all her life in England. "I have read Miss Hopper and like her," he wrote to his sister in January, 1895, in response, evidently to a letter suggesting that Miss Hopper's "Celtic" poems borrowed too much from his own and others'. Yeats, however, found most of the borrowings to be "plagiarisms of inexperienced enthusiasm. . . . She had take[n] us as documents, just as if we had written hundreds of years ago." (*Letters*, pp. 244–5.) A more serious fault, however, her lack of "solidity and clearness" (*ibid.*), was a feature of his repeated, faint praise of her work in the nineties. Thus, in "The Poems and Stories of Miss Nora Hopper", which appeared in the Dublin *Daily Express* on September 24, 1898, he identified the "filmy vagueness" which had troubled him in 1895 (see *Uncollected Prose*, vol. I, p. 370) with her "uncertainty" "about the places of her legends". In a letter to Katharine Tynan at the time of Nora Hopper's death, Yeats spoke more directly of the failure of this transplantation of Irishness: "I have been reading your old letter and I agree with what you say about Nora [Hopper], and the way our Irish fairyland came to spoil her work . . ." (*Letters*, p. 483).

A shortened version of this essay introduced Nora Hopper's poems in Brooke's and Rolleston's *Treasury of Irish Poetry*, and parts of it appeared in *Literary Ideals in Ireland*, the volume which resulted from the controversy to which Yeats alludes in the postscript (see p. 128 below).

ALL great poets—Dante not less than Homer and Shakespeare—speak to us of the hopes and destinies of mankind in their fulness; because they have wrought their poetry out of the dreams that were dreamed before men became so crowded upon one another, and so buried in their individual destinies and trades, that every man grew limited and fragmentary. If you were to take out of the great poets the personages and stories and metaphors, that first, it may be, visited the shepherds and hunters, who lived before men tilled the ground, not merely the

substance but the language of their poetry would crumble to nearly
nothing. Modern poetry grows weary of using over and over again the
personages and stories and metaphors that have come to us through
Greece and Rome, or from Wales and Brittany through the middle
ages, and has found new life in the Norse and German legends. William
Morris's "Sigurd," if it is as fine as it seemed to me[1] some years ago,
may yet influence the imagination of Europe, and Henrik Ibsen's
"Peer Gynt" and "The Heroes of Heligoland"[2] are already great influences, while Richard Wagner's dramas of "The Ring," are, together
with his mainly Celtic "Parsival" and "Lohengrin," and "Tristan and
Iseult,"[3] the most passionate influence in the arts of Europe. The Irish
legends, in popular tradition and in old Gaelic literature, are more
numerous, and as beautiful as the Norse and German legends, and
alone among great European legends have the beauty and wonder of
altogether new things. May one not say, then, without saying anything
improbable, that they will have a predominant influence in the coming
century, and that their influence will pass through many countries?

The latest of a little group of contemporary writers, who have begun
to found their work upon them, as the Trouveres founded theirs upon
the legends of Arthur and his knights, is Miss Nora Hopper, whose two
books—"Ballads in Prose" and "Quicken Boughs"[4]—though they
have many of the faults of youth, have at their best an extraordinary
delicacy and charm. I got "Ballads in Prose" when it came out two or
three years ago, and it haunted me as few new books have ever haunted
me, for it spoke in strange wayward stories and birdlike little verses of
things and of persons I remembered or had dreamed of; it did not speak
with the too emphatic manner that sometimes mars the powerful stories
Miss Fiona Macleod has told of like things and persons, but softly—
more murmuring than speaking. Even now, when the first enchantment
is gone and I see faults I was blind to, I cannot go by certain brown bogs
covered with white tufts of bog cotton—places where the world seems
to become faint and fragile—without remembering the verses her
Daluan—a kind of Irish Pan—sings among the bogs, and when once
I remember them, they run in my head for hours—

> *All the way to Tir nan'Og are many roads that run,*
> *But the darkest road is trodden by the King of Ireland's son.*

[1] The *Daily Express* printed "Segurd" but it was corrected to "Sigurd" in *Literary Ideals*.
In a recording of a radio talk for the BBC (recording dated April 10, 1932), Yeats described
how he had heard William Morris read *Sigurd the Volsung* in Dublin in the mid-1880s.

[2] *Haermeendene pa Helgeland*, translated into English as *The Vikings at Helgeland*, was first
published and produced in 1858.

[3] The usual spelling of two of these operas by Wagner is "Parsifal" and "Tristan and
Isolde".

[4] Nora Hopper's second book was *Under Quicken Boughs*, London, 1896.

*The world wears on to sundown, and love is lost and won,*
*But he recks not of loss or gain, the King of Ireland's son.*
*He follows on for ever, when all your chase is done,*
*He follows after shadows—the King of Ireland's son.*[5]

One does not know why he sings it, or why he dies on November Eve, and why the men cry over him, "Daluan is dead—dead! Daluan is dead!" and the women, "Da Mort is king," for "Daluan" is but Monday, and "Da Mort" is but Tuesday;[6] nor does one well know why any of her best stories, "Bahalaun and I," "The gifts of Aodh and Una," "The Four Kings," or "Aonan-nan Righ"[7] shaped itself into the strange drifting dreamy thing it is, and one is content not to know. They delight us by their mystery, as ornament full of lines, too deeply interwoven to weary us with a discoverable secret, delights us with its mystery; and as ornament is full of strange beasts and trees and flowers, that were once the symbols of great religions, and are now mixing one with another, and changing into new shapes, this book is made out of old beliefs and stories, mixing and changing in an enchanted dream. Their very mystery, that has left them so little to please the mortal passionate part of us, which delights in the broad noon light,[8] men need if they would merely act and live, has given them that melancholy which is almost wisdom. Does not this melancholy, as of twilight, brood over the passage, where Aodh gives to the heroes, in the temple of the heroes, all that he has to give, to deliver his land from Famine?[9] "The door at which he was striving opened wide, and from the dark shrine swept out a cloud of fine grey dust. The door clanged to behind him, and he went up the aisle walking ankle deep in the fine dust, and straining his eyes to see through the darkness if indeed figures paced beside him, and ghostly groups gave way before him as he could not help but fancy. At last his out-stretched hands touched a twisted horn of some smooth, cold substance, and he knew that he had reached the end of his journey. With his left hand clinging to the horn, he turned towards the dark temple, saying aloud: 'Here I stand, Aodh, with gifts to give the Fianna and their gods. In the name of my mother's God,

[5] This song, Yeats's "one exception" to the destructive effects of "our Irish fairyland" (*Letters*, p. 483) on Nora Hopper's verses, is from the story "Daluan", and it should begin "All away", not "All the way". (*Ballads in Prose*, London, 1894, p. 97.)

[6] p. 101 in *Ballads in Prose*.

[7] Spelled "Aonan-na-Righ" in *Ballads in Prose*.

[8] The comma after "light" printed in the *Daily Express* confuses the passage and was corrected in *A Treasury of Irish Poetry*.

[9] The *Daily Express* had no quotation marks here to signify that a long quotation follows from "The Gifts of Aodh and Una", pp. 138–40 of *Ballads in Prose*. Yeats had quoted this same passage in "Irish National Literature, II, Contemporary Prose Writers", in *The Bookman*, August, 1895 (see *Uncollected Prose*, vol. I, pp. 370–1).

let them who desire my gifts come to me.' 'Aodh, son of Eochaidh,' a shivering voice cried out, 'Give me thy youth.' 'I give,' Aodh said quietly. 'Aodh,' said another voice, reedy and thin and[10] sweet, 'give me thy knowledge. I, Grania, loved much and knew little.' There was a grey figure at his side, and without a word Aodh turned and laid his forehead on the ghost's cold breast. As he rested thus, another voice said, 'I am Oisin; give me thy death, O Aodh.' Aodh drew a deep breath, then he lifted his head, and clasped a ghostly figure in his arms, and holding it there felt it stiffen and grow rigid, and colder yet. 'Give me thy[11] hope, Aodh!' 'Give me thy faith, Aodh!' [ . . . ] 'Give me thy dreams, Aodh!' So the voices called and cried, and to each Aodh answered and gave the desired gift. 'Give me thine heart, Aodh!' cried another. 'I am Maive, who knew much and loved little.' '" Miss Hopper merely describes the Temple of the Heroes as being on an island of the Shannon, and is sometimes even less certain about the places of her legends, though she has much feeling for landscapes; and this uncertainty is, I believe, a defect in her method. Our legends are always associated with places, and not merely every mountain and valley, but every strange stone and little coppice has its legend, preserved in written or unwritten tradition. Our Irish romantic movement has arisen out of this tradition, and should always, even when it makes new legends about traditional people and things, be haunted by places. It should make Ireland, as Ireland and all other lands were in ancient times, a holy land to her own people. Had Aodh brought his gifts to any of the traditional sacred places, and had the emotion of the place and its history been in the story, the dreamy beauty of his sacrifice would have grown more beautiful from mixing with ancient beauty and with the beauty of sun and moon burning over an island or hill or hollow, that is a part of the scenery of our lives.

W. B. Yeats

P.S.—I had some thought of replying to an article headed, "What should be the subject of a National Drama?"[12] in your issue of last Saturday, but found, when I considered the matter, that this article, which I had already finished, answered the most important of your contributor's arguments. He said that "these subjects (ancient legends) obstinately refuse to be taken out of their old environment and be transplanted into the world of modern sympathies. The proper mode of treating them is a secret lost with the subjects themselves." And I have given the example of Ibsen, whose "Peer Gynt" founded on "these subjects" is not only "national literature," the very thing your con-

---

[10] and: *Ballads* reads "but".                 [11] thy: *Ballads* reads "thine".
[12] By John Eglinton. See headnote.

tributor said it could not be, but the chief glory of "the national literature" of its country, and the example of Wagner, whose dramas, also founded upon "these subjects," are becoming to Germany what the Greek Tragedies were to Greece.

# John Eglinton and Spiritual Art

In late October, 1898, Yeats and his friends undertook a public controversy designed, as Yeats noted in a letter to Lady Gregory, to "keep people awake until we announce The Irish Literary Theatre in December . . ." (*Letters*, p. 304). The initial points at issue were John Eglinton's rejection of ancient Irish myth and saga as subjects for an Irish national school of drama and Yeats's affirmation of them. Yeats's hope of expanding the discussion "into a discussion of the spiritual origin of the arts" (*ibid.*) was realized in a second round of essays in which Eglinton supported a philosophical view of poetry, exemplified by Wordsworth—in opposition to such aesthetic models as Keats, the early Tennyson and the French symbolists—and Yeats's rejection of Arnold's view of poetry as a criticism of life.

The exchange began with John Eglinton's "What Should be the Subjects of a National Drama?" in the September 18, 1898, issue of the Dublin *Daily Express*, a paper which usually carried a number of literary articles each Saturday. Yeats partially answered Eglinton in "The Poems and Stories of Miss Nora Hopper" on September 24, 1898. Although only the postscript of this article dealt directly with Eglinton, Yeats probably meant his introductory remarks for him as well. Eglinton's reply in the *Daily Express* of October 8, 1898, "National Drama and Contemporary Life", provoked the present essay, Yeats's "Mr. John Eglinton and Spiritual Art", in the *Daily Express* for October 29, 1898. Eglinton's next salvo was "Mr. Yeats and Popular Poetry", on November 5, 1898. A.E. joined the controversy on November 12, 1898 with "Literary Ideals in Ireland". William Larminie entered the lists with "Legends as Materials for Literature" on November 19, 1898.

Yeats's final contribution was "The Autumn of the Flesh" on December 3, 1898, which he reprinted as "The Autumn of the Body" in *Ideas of Good and Evil* (1903). The controversy ended with A.E.'s "Nationality and Cosmopolitanism in Literature" on December 10, 1898, and on January 12, 1899, Yeats published his "Important Announcement—Irish Literary Theatre" in the *Daily Express* (see p. 137 below). *Literary Ideals in Ireland* was published in May, 1899. Yeats wrote in John Quinn's copy: "This was a stirring row while it lasted and we were all very angry. W. B. Yeats. New York, 1904." (Allan Wade, ed., *A Bibliography of the Writings of W. B. Yeats*, third edition, London, 1968, p. 286.)

Althea Gyles: The Knight Upon the Grave of his Lady. *See p.136 for Yeats's comments*

Althea Gyles: Noah's Raven. *See pp. 135-6 for Yeats's comments*

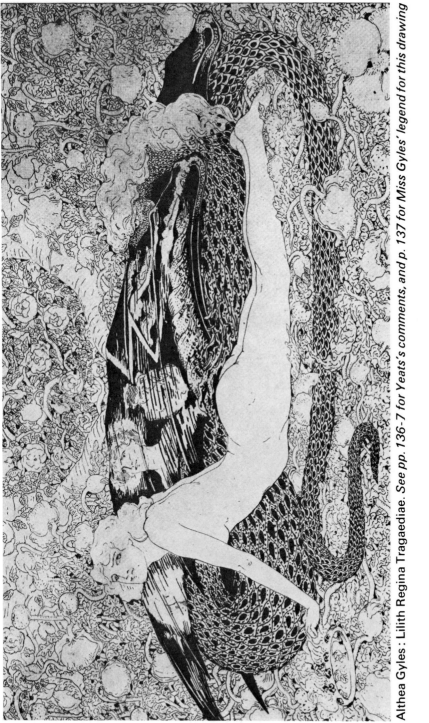

Althea Gyles: Lilith Regina Tragaediae. *See pp. 136–7 for Yeats's comments, and p. 137 for Miss Gyles' legend for this drawing*

Althea Gyles: Deirdré. The Gaelic phrase above the drawing means "The Tragedy of the Children of Uisneach". *See p.137 for Miss Gyles' legend for this drawing*

"JOHN EGLINTON" wrote recently that though "the ancient legends of Ireland undoubtedly contain situations and characters as well suited for drama as most of those used in Greek tragedies," yet "these subjects," meaning old legends in general, "refuse to be taken up out of their old environment, and be transplanted into the world of modern sympathies. The proper mode of treating them is a secret lost with the subjects themselves."[1] I might have replied by naming a good part of modern literature; but as he spoke particularly of drama I named Ibsen's "Peer Gynt," which is admittedly the chief among the national poems of modern Norway; and Wagner's musical dramas, which I compared to the Greek tragedies, not merely because of the mythological substance of "The Ring" and of "Parsifal," but because of the influence both words and music are beginning to have upon the intellect of Germany and of Europe, which begins to see in them the soul of Germany.

He replied by saying that he preferred Ibsen's dramas, which are "not ideal," which is nothing to the point, and that "the crowd of elect persons seated in curiously devised seats at Bayreuth does not seem very like the whole Athenian democracy thronging into their places for a couple of obols supplied by the State, and witnessing in good faith the deeds of their ancestors."[2] He is in error about the facts, for Wagner's musical dramas are not acted only or principally at Bayreuth, but before large crowds of not particularly elect persons at Vienna and at Munich and in many places in Germany and other countries. I do not think the point important, however, for when I spoke of their influence I thought less of the crowds at Vienna or at Munich than of the best intellects of our time, of men like Count Villiers de L'Isle Adam, the principal founder of the symbolist movement, of whom M. Remy de Gourmont has written,[3] "He opened the doors of the unknown with a crash, and a generation has gone through them to the infinite." The crowds may applaud good art for a time, but they will forget it when vulgarity invents some new thing, for the only permanent influence of any art is a gradual and imperceptible flowing down, as if through orders and hierarchies.

His second article abandons the opinion—an opinion that I thought from the beginning a petulance of rapid writing—that ancient legends "cannot be transplanted into the world of modern sympathies," and thinks that a poet "may be inspired by the legends of his country," but goes on to distinguish between "two conceptions of poetry mutually

[1] These statements are quoted from Eglinton's first essay in this controversy, "What Should be the Subjects of National Drama?"

[2] Quoted from Eglinton's second article, "National Drama and Contemporary Life".

[3] Yeats quoted this statement in his review of Maeterlinck's *Aglavaine and Selysette*, *Bookman*, September, 1897 (see p. 52 above).

antagonistic," two ways of treating legends and other things. I am glad to discuss these distinctions with him, for I think it a misfortune that "John Eglinton," whose influence on Irish opinion may yet be great, should believe, as I understand him to believe, in popular music, popular painting, and popular literature. He describes the "conception" of poetry, he believes me to prefer, as preferred "by those who are rather in sympathy with art than with philosophy," as regarding the poet as "an aristocratic craftsman," as looking for "the source of inspiration" to "the forms and images, in which old conceptions have been embodied—old faiths, myths, dreams," and as seeking "in poetry an escape from the facts of life;" and he describes the "conception" he himself prefers and calls Wordsworthian, as looking "to man himself as the source of inspiration," and as desiring a poetry that expresses "its age" and "the facts of life," and is yet, strange to say, "a spiritual force" and the work of "a seer."

I will restate these distinctions in the words of the younger Hallam, in his essay on Tennyson—one of the most profound criticisms in the English language.[4] Arthur Hallam described Tennyson, who had then written his earlier and greater, but less popular, poems, as belonging to "the aesthetic school," founded by Keats and Shelley—"A poetry of sensation rather than of reflection," "a sort of magic producing a number of impressions too multiplied, too minute, and too diversified to allow of our tracing them to their causes, because just such was the effect, even so boundless and so bewildering, produced" on the imagination of the poet "by the real appearance of nature." This poetry, the work of men whose "fine organs" "have trembled with emotion at colours and sounds and movements unperceived by duller temperaments," must always, he thinks, be unpopular, because dull temperaments shrink from, or are incapable of the patient sympathy and exaltation of feeling needful for its understanding. He contrasts it with the popular school, the school he thinks Wordsworth belonged to, in all but his highest moments, which "mixes up" anecdotes and opinions and moral maxims for their own sake—the things dull temperaments can understand, with what is sometimes the poetry of a fine temperament, but is more often an imitation.

This poetry of the popular school is the poetry of those "who are rather in sympathy" with philosophy than with art, and resembles those paintings one finds in every Royal Academy surrounded by crowds, which "are rather in sympathy" with anecdotes or pretty faces or babies than with good painting. It is the poetry of the utilitarian and the rhetorician and the sentimentalist and the popular journalist and the popu-

---

[4] See p. 34 above, for Yeats's lifelong enthusiasm for A. H. Hallam's essay on Tennyson's lyric poetry.

lar preacher, but it is not the poetry of "the seer," the most "aristocratic" of men, who tells what he alone has tasted and touched and seen amid the exaltation of his senses; and it is not a "spiritual force," though it may talk of nothing but spiritual forces, for a spiritual force is as immaterial and as imperceptible as the falling of dew or as the first greyness of dawn. Why, too, should "John Eglinton," who is a profound transcendentalist, prefer a poetry which is, like all the lusts of the market place, "an expression of its age" and of "the facts of life," the very phrases of the utilitarian criticism of the middle century—to a poetry which seeks to express great passions that are not in nature, though "the real appearance of nature" awakens them—"ideas" that "lie burningly on the divine hand," as Browning calls them, "the beauty that is beyond the grave," as Poe calls them?[5]

The Belgian poet, M. Verhaeren,[6] has also discussed these "two conceptions of poetry," and has described the one as founded on physical science and the other as founded upon transcendental science, and has shown that "the bias of belles lettres at present," of which John Eglinton complains, has accompanied a renewed interest in transcendental science, and it may well be that men are only able to fashion into beautiful speech the most delicate emotions of the soul, spending their days with a patience like the patience of the middle ages, in the perfect rounding of a verse, or in the perfect carving of a flower, when they are certain that the soul will not die with the body and that the gates of peace are wide and that the watchers are at their places upon the wall.

I believe that the renewal of belief—which is the great movement of our time—will more and more liberate the arts from "their age" and from life, and leave them more and more free to lose themselves in beauty, and to busy themselves, like all the great poetry of the past and like religion of all times, with "old faiths, myths, dreams"—the accumulated beauty of the ages. I believe that all men will more and more reject the opinion that poetry is "a criticism of life," and be more and more convinced that it is a revelation of a hidden life, and that they may even come to think "painting, poetry, and music" "the only means of conversing with eternity left to man on earth." I believe, too, that, though a Homer or a Dante or a Shakespeare may have used all knowledge—whether of life or of philosophy, or of mythology or of

[5] "Inspired by an ecstatic prescience of the glories beyond the grave, we struggle, by multiform combinations among the things and thoughts of Time, to attain a portion of that Loveliness whose very elements, perhaps, attain to eternity alone." ("The Poetic Principle", p. 98 in *The Poems of Edgar Allan Poe with a Selection of Essays*, Everyman's Library, 1927.)

[6] Emile Verhaeren (1855–1916), Belgian poet and dramatist, wrote almost no criticism. Verhaeren expressed ideas like these in a speech "French Poetry of Today" delivered at the Taylorian Institute, Oxford, March, 1901. It was reprinted, translated by C. H. Heywood, in the *Fortnightly Review*, vol. 69, April, 1901, pp. 723–38. Where Yeats had encountered these ideas by 1898 is unknown.

history—he did so, not for the sake of the knowledge, but to shape to a familiar and intelligible body something he had seen or experienced in the exaltation of his senses. I believe, too, that the difference between good and bad poetry is not in its preference for legendary, or for un-legendary subjects, or for a modern or for an archaic treatment, but in volume and intensity of its passion for beauty, and in the perfection of its workmanship; and that all criticism that forgets these things is mischievous, and doubly mischievous in a country of unsettled opinion.

W. B. Yeats

# A Symbolic Artist and the Coming of Symbolic Art

Yeats's article on "A Symbolic Artist and the Coming of Symbolic Art" first appeared in *The Dome* of December, 1898, where it was accompanied by three drawings. (See plates between pp. 128 and 129.) The ideas on symbolism expressed here are a further development of those in his essays "Symbolism in Painting" and "The Symbolism of Poetry" written about the same time and collected in *Ideas of Good and Evil* (1903).

The subject of this article, the artist and the poet Althea Gyles, was the eccentric bohemian offspring of an old and wealthy family in Kilmurry, Co. Waterford. She had studied art in Dublin around 1890, and in London during the years 1891 or 1892. Rather little was known about Miss Gyles's life until the publication in the first issue of *Yeats Studies* (Bealtaine, 1971) of Ian Fletcher's "Poet and Designer: W. B. Yeats and Althea Gyles" (pp. 42–79).

In the early nineties Miss Gyles lived for a time at the Dublin Theosophical Society's rooms at number 3 Upper Ely Place, and Yeats has given, without naming her, a memorable picture of the "strange, red-haired girl" at that time, starving and neurotically driven (*Autobiography*, p. 160). During the period of her closest association with Yeats, she designed covers for *The Secret Rose* (1897), the 1899 edition of *Poems*, and the book which bears her most famous design, *The Wind Among the Reeds* (1899). During 1899 her friendship with Yeats was strained because of her affair with Leonard Smithers (1861–1907), who was, among other things, a publisher of porno-graphic books. "A very unpleasant thing has happened," Yeats wrote to Lady Gregory. "Althea Gyles, after despising Symons and Moore for years because of their morals, has ostentatiously taken up with Smithers, a person of so immoral a life that people like Symons and Moore despise him" (*Letters*, p. 330). In the same year, she sided with Yeats in a schism in The Order of

the Golden Dawn against Aleister Crowley (1875–1947). Crowley published
in his magazine *Equinox* in 1909 a story, "At the Fork of the Roads", in
which Yeats is called "Will Bute", Althea Gyles bears the name "Hypatia
Gay" and Crowley is "Count Swanoff".

Yeats thought highly enough of Miss Gyles's poetry to write an introduction to the poem "Sympathy" for the 1900 edition of Rolleston and Brooke's
*A Treasury of Irish Poetry*. After the present article, *The Dome* magazine printed
in the December, 1898 issue of Yeats's "Aodh Pleads with the Elemental
Powers", Miss Gyles's "Sympathy" and a poem by Nora Hopper. After
1900, Miss Gyles published poems in various magazines. The latter years of
her life were marked by poverty and failure, mainly caused by her eccentric
personality. She died in a London nursing home in 1949.


THE only two powers that trouble the deeps are religion and love,
the others make a little trouble upon the surface. When I have written
of literature in Ireland, I have had to write again and again about a
company of Irish mystics[1] who have taught for some years a religious
philosophy which has changed many ordinary people into ecstatics and
visionaries. Young men, who were, I think, apprentices or clerks, have
told me how they lay awake at night hearing miraculous music, or
seeing forms that made the most beautiful painted or marble forms
seem dead and shadowy. This philosophy has changed its symbolism
from time to time, being now a little Christian, now very Indian, now
altogether Celtic and mythological; but it has never ceased to take a
great part of its colour and character from one lofty imagination. I do
not believe I could easily exaggerate the direct and indirect influences
which "A.E." (Mr. George Russell), the most subtle and spiritual
poet of his generation, and a visionary who may find room beside
Swedenborg and Blake, has had in shaping to a definite conviction the
vague spirituality of young Irish men and women of letters. I know that
Miss Althea Gyles, in whose work I find so visionary a beauty, does not
mind my saying that she lived long with this little company, who had
once a kind of conventual house; and that she will not think I am taking
from her originality when I say that the beautiful lithe figures of her
art, quivering with a life half mortal tragedy, half immortal ecstasy, owe
something of their inspiration to this little company. I indeed believe
that I see in them a beginning of what may become a new manner in
the arts of the modern world; for there are tides in the imagination of
the world, and a motion in one or two minds may show a change of
tide.

Pattern and rhythm are the road to open symbolism, and the arts

---

[1] The Dublin Theosophical Society.

have already become full of pattern and rhythm. Subject pictures no longer interest us, while pictures with patterns and rhythms of colour, like Mr. Whistler's, and drawings with patterns and rhythms of line, like Mr. Beardsley's in his middle period, interest us extremely. Mr. Whistler and Mr. Beardsley have sometimes thought so greatly of these patterns and rhythms, that the images of human life have faded almost perfectly; and yet we have not lost our interest. The arts have learned the denials, though they have not learned the fervours of the cloister. Men like Sir Edward Burne-Jones and Mr. Ricketts[2] have been too full of the emotion and the pathos of life to let its images fade out of their work, but they have so little interest in the common thoughts and emotions of life, that their images of life have delicate and languid limbs that could lift no burdens, and souls vaguer than a sigh; while men like Mr. Degas, who are still interested in life, and life at its most vivid and vigorous, picture it with a cynicism that reminds one of what ecclesiastics have written in old Latin about women and about the world.

Once or twice an artist has been touched by a visionary energy amid his weariness and bitterness, but it has passed away. Mr. Beardsley created a visionary beauty in *Salome with the Head of John the Baptist*,[3] but because, as he told me, "beauty is the most difficult of things," he chose in its stead the satirical grotesques of his later period. If one imagine a flame burning in the air, and try to make one's mind dwell on it, that it may continue to burn, one's mind strays immediately to other images; but perhaps, if one believed that it was a divine flame, one's mind would not stray. I think that I would find this visionary beauty also in the work of some of the younger French artists, for I have a dim memory of a little statue in ebony and ivory. Certain recent French writers, like Villiers De L'Isle Adam, have it, and I cannot separate art and literature in this, for they have gone through the same change, though in different forms. I have certainly found it in the poetry of a young Irish Catholic who was meant for the priesthood, but broke down under the strain of what was to him a visionary ecstasy; in some plays by a new Irish writer; in the poetry of "A.E."; in some stories of Miss Macleod's; and in the drawings of Miss Gyles; and in almost all these a passion for symbol has taken the place of the old interest in life.

---

[2] Yeats's interest in these artists was a durable one. (See p. 383 below for his appreciation of Charles Ricketts, the artist and stage designer.) Nearly forty years after this essay, describing his study at Riverdale, he noted that "in the window into the greenhouse hangs a lovely Burne-Jones window (Ricketts's gift). Through the glass door into the flower garden I see the bare boughs of apple trees and a few last flowers . . ." (*Letters*, p. 901).

[3] The publication of the drawing entitled "'J'ai baisé ta bouche, Iokanaan'", in *The Studio* for April, 1893, brought Beardsley the commission to illustrate Lord Alfred Douglas's translation of Wilde's *Salomé* (1894). This drawing, which was also known as "Salome with John the Baptist's Head", is a more ornate version of "The Climax" in the Wilde volume.

These persons are of very different degrees and qualities of power, but their work is always energetic, always the contrary of what is called "decadent." One feels that they have not only left the smoke of human hearths and come to The Dry Tree, but that they have drunk from The Well at the World's End.[4]

Miss Gyles' images are so full of abundant and passionate life that they remind one of William Blake's cry, "Exuberance is Beauty,"[5] and Samuel Palmer's command to the artist, "Always seek to make excess more abundantly excessive."[6] One finds in them what a friend, whose work has no other passion, calls "the passion for the impossible beauty"; for the beauty which cannot be seen with the bodily eyes, or pictured otherwise than by symbols. Her own favourite drawing, which unfortunately cannot be printed here, is *The Rose of God*, a personification of this beauty as a naked woman, whose hands are stretched against the clouds, as upon a cross, in the traditional attitude of the Bride, the symbol of the microcosm in the Kabala; while two winds, two destinies, the one full of white and the other full of red rose petals, personifying all purities and all passions, whirl about her and descend upon a fleet of ships and a walled city, personifying the wavering and the fixed powers, the masters of the world in the alchemical symbolism. Some imperfect but beautiful verses accompany the drawing, and describe her as for "living man's delight and his eternal revering when dead."[7]

I have described this drawing because one must understand Miss Gyles' central symbol, the Rose, before one can understand her dreamy and intricate *Noah's Raven*.[8] The ark floats upon a grey sea under a grey sky, and the raven flutters above the sea. A sea nymph, whose slender swaying body drifting among the grey waters is a perfect symbol of a soul untouched by God or by passion, coils the fingers of one

---

[4] "The Dry Tree" is a symbol of decadence in *The Well at the World's End*, a romance by William Morris (London, 1896) which Yeats had reviewed for *The Bookman* in November, 1896 (see *Uncollected Prose*, I, pp. 418–20).

[5] One of the proverbs of Hell in Blake's *The Marriage of Heaven and Hell*. (Geoffrey Keynes, ed., *The Writings of William Blake*, London, 1925, vol. 1, p. 186.)

[6] Palmer's (1805–81) "command" comes from one of his sketchbooks in which he explains Blake's figures: "There are many mediums in the *means*—none, O! not a jot, not a shadow of a jot, in the *end* of great art. . . . We must not begin with medium, but think always to excess, and only use medium to make excess more abundantly excessive . . ." (A. H. Palmer, *The Life and Letters of Samuel Palmer, Painter and Etcher*, London, 1892, p. 16).

[7] Fletcher reprints the verses in *Yeats Studies*, pp. 52–3. The phrase Yeats quotes is a distortion of the two lines:

> *Wrapt Thee round him for living men's delight*
> *And his eternal reverie when dead.*

[8] See accompanying illustration. Yeats's interpretations are based upon Miss Gyles's explanations, given in a letter to Yeats quoted by Fletcher, pp. 53–4.

hand about his feet and offers him a ring, while her other hand holds a shining rose under the sea. Grotesque shapes of little fishes flit about the rose, and grotesque shapes of larger fishes swim hither and thither. Sea nymphs swim through the windows of a sunken town and reach towards the rose hands covered with rings; and a vague twilight hangs over all. The story is woven out of as many old symbols as if it were a mystical story in "The Prophetic Books."⁹ The raven, who is, as I understand him, the desire and will of man, has come out of the ark, the personality of man, to find if the Rose is anywhere above the flood, which is here, as always, the flesh, "the flood of the five senses." He has found it and is returning with it to the ark, that the soul of man may sink into the ideal and pass away; but the sea nymphs, the spirits of the senses, have bribed him with a ring taken from the treasures of the kings of the world, a ring that gives the mastery of the world, and he has given them the Rose. Henceforth man will seek for the ideal in the flesh, and the flesh will be full of illusive beauty, and the spiritual beauty will be far away.

*The Knight upon the Grave of his Lady* tells much of its meaning to the first glance; but when one has studied for a time, one discovers that there is a heart in the bulb of every hyacinth, to personify the awakening of the soul and of love out of the grave. It is now winter, and beyond the knight, who lies in the abandonment of his sorrow, the trees spread their leafless boughs against a grey winter sky; but spring will come, and the boughs will be covered with leaves, and the hyacinths will cover the ground with their blossoms, for the moral is not the moral of the Persian poet: "Here is a secret, do not tell it to anybody. The hyacinth that blossomed yesterday is dead."¹⁰ The very richness of the pattern of the armour, and of the boughs, and of the woven roots, and of the dry bones, seems to announce that beauty gathers the sorrows of man into her breast and gives them eternal peace.

It is some time since I saw the original drawing of *Lilith*, and it has been decided to reproduce it in this number of *The Dome* too late for me to have a proof of the engraving; but I remember that Lilith, the ever-changing phantasy of passion, rooted neither in good nor evil, half crawls upon the ground, like a serpent before the great serpent of the world, her guardian and her shadow; and Miss Gyles reminds me that Adam, and things to come, are reflected on the wings of the serpent; and that beyond, a place shaped like a heart is full of thorns and roses. I remember thinking that the serpent was a little confused,

⁹ Yeats refers to Blake. "The Prophetic Books" was not Blake's title but was added later by his editors.
¹⁰ The Persian poet is Omar Khayyam. The translation is not Fitzgerald's, but corresponds to part of quatrain LXIII in Fitzgerald's version.

and that the composition was a little lacking in rhythm, and upon the whole caring less for this drawing than for others, but it has an energy and a beauty of its own. I believe that the best of these drawings will live, and that if Miss Gyles were to draw nothing better, she would still have won a place among the few artists in black and white whose work is of the highest intensity. I believe, too, that her inspiration is a wave of a hidden tide that is flowing through many minds in many places, creating a new religious art and poetry.

W. B. Yeats

NOTE.[11]—*The following are the legends for two of Miss Gyles' drawings, as chosen by herself:—*

DEIRDRE. *"There is but one thing now may comfort my heart, and that thing thy sword, O Naisi."*

LILITH REGINA TRAGAEDIAE. *"O Lilith, tristissima, cujus in corde terrae prima magna tragaedia acta est, propter te adhuc amoris manam tenet invidia."* *("O most sorrowful Lilith, in whose heart was played Earth's first great tragedy, still for thy sake does Hatred hold Love's hand.")*

# Important Announcement—Irish Literary Theatre

The first public notice of the national dramatic project which Yeats and Lady Gregory had undertaken in the autumn of 1897 was Yeats's letter, "Important Announcement—Irish Literary Theatre", in the Dublin *Daily Express* for January 12, 1899. In addition to the impressive roll of guarantors he, Lady Gregory, and Edward Martyn (see p. 197 below) had drawn into their plan, the notice marked two other achievements. In the summer of 1898 a way had been found by William E. H. Lecky, the historian and a member of the House of Commons, to alter, by an insertion in the Local Government (Ireland) Bill, a century-old prohibition of dramatic presentations anywhere in Dublin except in the prohibitively expensive licensed theatres. Finally, at a meeting of the National Literary Society in the Leinster Lecture Hall on January 9, Martyn agreed to accept whatever financial responsibility might arise beyond the amount already guaranteed.

[11] This note appeared at the end of the article in *The Dome* printing.

## TO THE EDITOR OF THE *DAILY EXPRESS*

SIR—Something over a year ago some friends of mine and myself endeavoured to found an "Irish Literary Theatre," to do for Irish dramatic literature, as was hoped, what the Theatre Libre and the Theatre l'Oeuvre have done for French dramatic literature.[1] We intended to take a theatre, or a hall, for a few days in the spring of every year, and to perform plays upon Irish subjects, which would at any rate aim at being literature. We found, however, that Dublin had no small and inexpensive theatres, like those in which such adventures are made elsewhere, and that the law prevented our performing plays in a hall. It was necessary to change the law, and by uniting our efforts to those of the Dublin amateurs, we have succeeded in changing it. The Lord Lieutenant has now the power, on an application through the new Council, to grant a temporary license to perform plays in a hall, whether the actors are professionals or amateurs, provided the profits go to some artistic or literary object. We are only waiting for the meeting of the Council to make our application, and we propose to give our first performance in May, a week before the Feis Concerts, when "The Heather Field," a play of modern Irish life by Mr. Edward Martyn, and "The Countess Kathleen," a play of medieval Irish life by myself, will, we hope, be produced under the management of Miss Florence Farr, late manageress of the Avenue Theatre, London.[2] Mr. Standish O'Grady, Mr. George Moore, and Miss Fiona Macleod have written or are writing plays for our use in subsequent years.[3] Among those who have already sent their names as guarantors to Lady Gregory, who has acted as provisional Hon. Sec., are the Right Hon. W. E. H. Lecky, M.P.; Dr. Douglas Hyde, Mr. J. Dillon, M.P.; Lord Plunket, Right Hon. Horace Plunkett, M.P.; Lord Castletown, Mr. John Redmond,

---

[1] Like Yeats and his collaborators, André Antoine (1858–1943) had little experience with the theatre and little capital when he founded the Théâtre Libre in Montmartre in 1877. Unlike Yeats's enterprise, Antoine's theatre was dedicated to the production of modern realistic plays, a distinction Yeats noted in a letter written a few years after this essay to Frank Fay. "Be just to Antoine's genius, but show the defects of his movement. Art is art because it is not nature, and he tried to make it nature." (*Letters*, p. 440.)

The Théâtre de l'Œuvre, established in 1893 in Paris by Aurelien-Marie Lugné Poë (1869–1940), was one of the first experiments in the art theatre movement. As the Abbey's was to be only after many years, its program was thoroughly cosmopolitan, featuring Ibsen and Tolstoy, as well as Chinese and Indian plays.

[2] For the first productions, in May, 1899, of the Irish Literary Theatre, see p. 153 below.

[3] Of these three exemplars of the Celtic awakening, only George Moore contributed to the National Theatre. "I think the word 'Celtic'," Lady Gregory wrote, "was put in [the 1899 proposal] for the sake of Fiona Macleod whose plays however we never acted, though we used to amuse ourselves by thinking of the call for 'author' that might follow one, and the possible appearance of William Sharp in place of the beautiful woman he had given her out to be, for even then we had little doubt they were one and the same person." (Lady Gregory, *Our Irish Theatre*, New York and London, 1913, p. 9.)

M.P.; the Hon. Emily Lawless, the Marquis of Dufferin and Ava, the Right Hon. C. T. Redington, the Lord Chief Justice of Ireland, Mr. William O'Brien, Miss Jane Barlow, Miss Maud Gonne, Sir Frederick Burton, the Duchess of St. Albans, Mr. John O'Leary, Miss Margaret Stokes, Lord and Lady Ardilaun, and many other representatives of all sections of opinion. As soon as some necessary arrangements can be made with the National Literary Society, which is assisting us in our project, and a permanent hon. sec. selected, the full list of guarantors will be published, and the support of your readers will be asked for.— Yours truly,

W. B. Yeats

# The Irish Literary Theatre

On January 14, 1899, Yeats followed the announcement of his theatre project with an essay on "The Irish Literary Theatre" in the Dublin *Daily Express*.

NORWAY has a great and successful school of contemporary drama, and Spain and Germany, though they have an admiration for bad work, which Norway has not, have good dramatists whom they admire. Elsewhere—and there is no difference of opinion on this matter among men of letters—vulgarity and triviality have an almost perfect possession of the theatre. Now and then a play is better than the others, and when it is nearly as good as a good, but still ephemeral novel, the critics, who are not men of letters, call it a great play, and common playgoers believe them, because "it does not accuse them of want of wit," being but the image of a passing fashion. One finds the literary drama alone, when some great work, old enough to be a national superstition, is revived with scenery and costume so elaborate that nobody need listen to the words unless he likes, or in little and unexpensive theatres which associations of men of letters hire from time to time that they may see upon the stage—the plays of Henrik Ibsen, Maurice Maeterlinck, Gerard Hauptmann, Jose Echegaray, or of some less famous dramatist who has written, in the only way literature can be written, to express a dream which has taken possession of his mind.[1] These associations, the Theatre

---

[1] To his dramatic models Ibsen and Maeterlinck, Yeats adds Gerhart Hauptmann (1862–1946), the German playwright and Nobel laureate (1912), and José Echegaray y Eizaguirre

Libre and the Independent Theatre especially,[2] have, in the face of violent opposition, trained actors who have become famous, and had a powerful influence even upon those plays, which are written to please as many people as possible that they may make as much money as possible. We are about to attempt in Dublin what has been done in London and Paris, and we will, if we have even the smallest success, produce every Spring a play or two founded upon some Irish subject. We believe that common playgoers will not dislike us very much, certainly nothing like as much as they dislike those who make similar attempts in other countries, and that they will come in time to like us; for even if they do not understand that we offer them plays written in a more sincere spirit than plays which are written to please as many people as possible, they will understand that we are writing about the country in which they live, and re-telling those ancient, heroic tales which are chief among its treasures. We believe, too, that the people who read books and have ceased to go to the theatre will find out about us gradually, as they have found out about similar attempts in other countries, and will come to see our plays, and will even stay a little longer in town for their sake. There is no feeling, except religious feeling, which moves masses of men so powerfully as national feeling, and upon this, more widely spread among all classes in Ireland to-day than at any time this century, we build our principal hopes. It will give us just that help which men of letters have lacked for similar attempts elsewhere, and keep us out of the shadow of dilletantism [*sic*]. About six weeks ago an anonymous play in four acts about an old Irish story and a musical play with words by a nun, and about an old Irish story, were acted in Letterkenny before enthusiastic audiences.[3] I have no way of knowing whether these plays had literary merit, but I am certain that their audiences did not find in them, or expect to find in them, that superficial appeal to the nerves and to vulgar appetites which has made sincere drama impossible in the ordinary modern theatre. They appealed

---

(1832–1916), the Spanish dramatist who dominated the Madrid stage during the period 1875–1900 and who shared the Nobel Prize for literature in 1904. Yeats met Hauptmann in Italy in 1929.

    [2] The Théâtre Libre (1877) of André Antoine was the model for the Independent Theatre, founded in London in 1891 by J. T. Grein (1862–1935). Grein's productions, staged at the Royalty Theatre, included Shaw's first successful play, *Widowers' Houses* (1892).

    [3] In connection with an autumn fair, Douglas Hyde, Alice Milligan, and Cardinal Logue, among others, had attended a performance of "Finola, or the Borrowed Bride", a Gaelic play with music written by a sister at the Loretto Convent National School in Letterkenny, County Donegal, on November 22, 1898. According to the *Donegal Independent* for Friday, November 25, the play centered around the rescue of the princess Finola from the fairies by O'Boyle, chieftain of the Rosses of Donegal. "The little play was plainly but effectively staged . . . [and] the school children who did the ballads and solo dances acquitted themselves very creditably indeed . . ." (p. 3).

to the national feeling, and because all feeling is more or less imaginative, were understood, as plays were understood before modern vulgarity began its inventions. Although we have for the moment decided
to produce no plays not upon Irish subjects, we know that when Irish
literature is more developed Irishmen will utter the personality of their
country, no matter what subjects they write about. When they have
learned their lesson, when they have come to understand the country
they live in, they will write admirably about other countries. All literature and all art is national.[4] The Eastern poets, Homer and the Greek
dramatists, the writers of the Icelandic Sagas, Dante, Shakespeare in
"King Lear" and in the historical plays, Goethe in "Faust," the only
one among his works which has moved the imagination of the world,
and Ibsen at almost all times, have written about the history and legends
of their own countries. Shakespeare, Calderon, Milton, in writing of the
history and legends of other countries, have written out of emotions
and thoughts that came to them because of their profound sympathy
with the life about them. Egyptian art differs from Greek, Dutch art
differs from Italian, French art differs from English, because they have
come out of different nationalities. The curious imaginative sterility
of what are called the Irish educated classes has its source in that spirit
of antagonism to the life about them, which until recently has cut them
off from the foundations of literature, and left their imaginations cold
and conventional. That small minority, which from time to time, has
divided itself from its class, has been so fruitful in imagination that one
understands how much evil has been worked by a bad theory and how
great the flood may be once the flood-gates have been lifted. Victor
Hugo has said that in the theatre the mob became a people,[5] and, though
this could be perfectly true only of ancient times when the theatre was a
part of the ceremonial of religion, I have some hope that, if we have
enough success to go on from year to year, we may help to bring a
little ideal thought into the common thought of our times. The writers,
on whom we principally depend, have laboured to be citizens, not
merely of that passing and modern Ireland of prosaic cynicism and
prosaic rivalries which it may be their duty to condemn, but of that
eternal and ancient Ireland which has lived from old times in tender and
heroic tales and in the unwearied love of many thousand men and
women who have been poor in all other things. And they have laboured
to write of Irish and all other things, as men should write who have

---

[4] Yeats echoes his pronouncement, in February, 1890, on the failure of William Allingham to achieve greatness: "Allingham had the making of a great writer in him, but lacked
impulse and momentum, the very things national feeling could have supplied. . . . There is
no great literature without nationality, no great nationality without literature." (*Letters to
the New Island*, pp. 103–4.)

[5] See p. 286 below for this favourite quotation from Hugo.

never doubted that all things are shadows of spiritual things, and that men may come to the gates of peace by beautiful and august thoughts.

W. B. Yeats

# High Crosses of Ireland

Yeats's abilities to draw together disparate ideas and enthusiasms are everywhere manifest in his work of the late nineties. Despite dissimilarities, the Irish Literary Theatre, as it took shape in his essays, would recreate the theatre of the ancient Greeks on a model given by the French realist Antoine. Similarly, his essay on "High Crosses of Ireland", a review of a lecture by Margaret MacNair Stokes (1832–1900) to the National Literary Society on January 14, 1899, welded the research of this archaeologist and artist to Yeats's masters in Celtic studies—Rhys, Nutt and Jubainville—as well as to his studies of Blake and mysticism. Yeats's review, signed "Rosicrux", appeared in the Dublin *Daily Express* on January 28, 1899.

MOST of us who are writing in Ireland now are dreaming of a literature at once romantic and religious, and as the country housewife rakes among the ashes at dawn for the still glowing embers of yesterday's fire—for the seed of the fire, as she calls it—we search for the religious life of other times among old Irish monuments and legends. The work of Mr. Nutt and Professor Rhys and M. De Joubainville has made known something of the religious life in the Pagan legends, and the greater part of contemporary Irish and Highland literature has come of the discovery. Until I heard Miss Stokes's lecture to the National Literary Society on "The High Crosses of Ireland," I did not know how much had been done to make intelligible much of what was most naive and charming in the religious life of the first Christian centures in Ireland. Though she has only published her drawings and photographs of two crosses, she has drawn and photographed a very great number, and hopes to do all the crosses of Ireland.[1] The four walls of the Leinster Lecture Hall were covered with photographs and drawings, reproducing, on a large scale, the ornaments and scenes sculptured in the panels

---

[1] Yeats here refers to Miss Stokes's *The High Crosses of Castledermot and Durrow*, Dublin, 1898. Prior to this folio volume, however, Miss Stokes had published drawings of two crosses in her *Early Christian Architecture in Ireland*, London, 1878.

of the crosses. She has found explanations of many of the panels in "The Byzantine Guide to Painters," and in other mediaeval works, in which artists found subjects and their traditional treatment.[2] She has found repeated over and over again on different crosses such things as Noah entering the Ark, Daniel in the Lion's Den, the Fall of Man, David playing upon his harp, Jacob wrestling with the Angel, and chariots and hunting scenes to describe Heaven to people who still remembered "the great plain," "the land of the ever living," "the land of the living heart," where the dead heroes lived in the delight of war and of the chase.

One does not find the more profound life of the middle age in these simple things, but I think one finds it in a curious diagram, which Miss Stokes has copied from Mr. Lawlor's edition of "The Book of Mulling," and, like him, believes to be the ground plan of an Irish Monastery of the 9th or 10th century, and of the high crosses set about it.[3] Two concentric circles, with their edges close together, mark the double foss of the monastery, and outside these circles are marked the places of six [*sic*] crosses—two to the south, two to the west, two to the north, two to the east; inside the circles are marked the places of three more; and the place of another is marked upon the double foss. There are half-obliterated words in Irish at the places of the crosses, to explain that the two southern crosses are dedicated to S. Mark and Jeremiah, and the two western to S. Matthew and Daniel, and the two northern to S. John and Ezekiel, and the two eastern to S. Luke and Isaiah, while the three crosses inside the circle are dedicated to Father, Son, and Holy Spirit. The words explaining the cross between the circles have been obliterated altogether. The whole figure is a mystical symbol. The Evangelists and their anti-types have their crosses in the four quarters of the heavens, because of the lion and man and eagle and ox, which they inherit from the Old Testament and from Paganism, and the attributions of these creatures to the strength of God, to His incarnation, to

[2] Miss Stokes had translated the latter half of the "Byzantine Guide to Painting", a manual for artists which dates to the Byzantine School of the twelfth century, from a French version and included it as an appendix to the second volume of Adolph Napoléon Didron's *Christian Iconography*, London, 1886, which she helped compile. That portion of the manual prescribes in elaborate detail how Biblical scenes such as Yeats names here were to be painted.

[3] *Chapters on the Book of* [*St.*] *Mulling* by Hugh J. Lawlor (1860–1938), Dean of St. Patrick's, was published in Edinburgh, 1897. St. Mulling (sometimes spelled Moling, Mullins, or Mullen) was an Irish saint of the seventh century (d. 697) who founded the monastery (now in ruins) of St. Mullins, Co. Carlow. A slip-sheet which prefaces Lawlor's eighth chapter, "The Last Page—II. The Circular Device", notes that "Miss Stokes . . . has discovered near the Cross of Christ and His Apostles what seems to be an indication of the entrance to the cashel, reminding us, as she remarks, of the words 'I am the door'" (p. 167). Miss Stokes's reproduction and explanation of "the circular device" taken from Lawlor is on pp. x–xiv of her *High Crosses*.

His revelation in the darkness of the world, and to His sacrifice when the incarnation ended at the crucifixion; and because of the resemblance of these things to the sun in his southern strength, to his setting in the west, to his journey under the earth, and to his rising in the east. I have no doubt that this, or something like it, is the meaning; but I am about to make, with much doubt, a suggestion about the cross between the circles. Miss Stokes suggests that all the crosses were once on the edges of circles, and by supposing that one circle went through all the places of the crosses of the Evangelists and another through all the places of the crosses of the prophets, and by counting the two circles of the double foss, she discovers seven circles, which she compares with the seven heavens and with the seven rings of petals in the mystical rose. In spite of a passion for the symbolism of the mystical rose, which has saddened my friends, I do not believe this, for I think if this were true the double foss would have two crosses. I suggest that the whole diagram represents a paradise, more remote than the seven heavens, containing the Trinity guarded by the Prophets and the Evangelists; and that the double foss and its single cross symbolise its walls.[4] Medieval mystics represented this ultimate paradise as a round mirror, and Jacob Boehmen, who gathered into himself the dying mysticism of the Middle Ages, made it almost a fourth person of the Trinity.[5] It was almost certainly a familiar symbol in ancient Ireland, for two years ago an old man on the north island of Arran told me of it. Nobody, he said, might look into it but God and this vexed Satan, who was then an angel, and Satan looked in "and Hell was made in a minute." Jacob Boehmen describes God the Father as seeing Himself in it as God the Son, and meditating about what He saw, and so making God the Holy Spirit. Blake called it "the looking-glass of Enitharmon," his name for the mother of all, and "the imagination of God," and many names besides.[6] It is notable, too, that the cross on the double foss is to the south-east, where S. Adamnan—or was it S. Furza?—one of the earliest of Chris-

---

[4] Yet Miss Stokes likewise proposes, as Yeats does here, that the diagram represents not only the plans for a monastery, but also the plans for a paradise as well, St. Mulling's ideal "City of Life" (*High Crosses*, p. xiv).

[5] Yeats's use of the writings of "the greatest of the Christian mystics" (*Letters*, p. 262), Jakob Böhme (1575–1624), dates back to the early nineties. While the name of the German theologian is sometimes spelled Behmen, Boehm, or Bohm, this spelling is peculiar to this essay and Yeats's commentary on Blake's symbolic system (see below).

[6] Yeats draws here on the discussion in his and Ellis's *The Works of William Blake* of the similar conception of paradise as mirror for Böhme and Blake (London, 1893, vol. I, pp. 246–7). Blake's "Looking Glass of Enitharmon" appears only in *Jerusalem* (63: 21, 38), and "the imagination of God" is not Blake's phrase but Yeats's own (see Yeats and Ellis, *Blake*, vol. I, p. 246). Yeats comments further on Böhme, Blake, and imagination in "William Blake and the Imagination" (*Essays and Introductions*, New York, 1961, p. 112). The description of Enitharmon as Blake's Great Mother symbol occurs on pp. 329–30, 339 of the first volume of the Yeats–Ellis *Blake*.

tian missionaries,[7] and William Blake, one of the latest, saw Paradise, perhaps because the sun in the south-east has put off the chill of night without putting on the fierceness of noon, and because of all that was symbolised by this mildness. I have given my explanation doubtfully, for the mystics I have read, wrote either much earlier or much later than the time to which Miss Stokes refers this diagram, and I have read their mysticism for its own sake, and not with any thought of its historical changes. I have met young Catholics of deep piety, and some that have heard voices and seen visions, and I am certain that some day one among them, having become scholour [sic] as well as visionary, and having mastered the mysticism of the Middle Ages, will tell us how much of it is reflected in the crosses and illuminated missals of this country.

Rosicrux

# Notes on Traditions and Superstitions

Yeats published the folklore materials he and Lady Gregory had collected (see p. 54 above) at regular intervals in the later nineties, and in 1899 he was asked for his comments on the "Traditions and Superstitions collected at Kilcurry, County Louth, Ireland", by Bryan J. Jones. Jones's material, his descriptions of his peasant "authorities", Yeats's notes and brief rejoinders by Jones appeared in the March, 1899, issue of *Folk-Lore*, the journal of The (London) Folk-Lore Society.

Yeats commented by number on ten of Jones's eleven items:

1. Sightings of the "Dead Coach", a silent black coach drawn by headless horses and driven by a headless driver over a certain route "whenever anyone in the parish is about to die" (*Folk-Lore*, vol. X, 1, p. 119).

2. The "Church of Fire" at Faughart which, while under construction on the site of an ancient fort, appeared to be consumed in flames one night, in manifestation of the fairies' displeasure.

3. The appearance, one moonlit night, of several hundred soldiers of the "gentry", the fairies, returning to the fort at Faughart after "some fight between themselves" (*ibid.*, 120).

4. The ghost of a hired man which returns to his former employer's yard as a big black dog.

7 St. Adamnan or Eunan (624–704), Abbot of Iona (an island off the west coast of Scotland, Co. Argyll), founded a number of churches in Ireland and Scotland; his most well-known work is *Vita Sancti Columbae*.

St. Fursa or Fursey (d. 648/50): early Irish missionary who founded monasteries in Europe which became scholastic centers affecting the development of the entire Continent.

6. The fairy transportation "toward daybreak" of a man, who flew from his doorstep to the top of Faughart Hill and was returned "when the half-past five horn blew" (*ibid.*, 120–1).

7. A boarded-up cottage, attached to a modern farmhouse, where the ghost of the farmer's father is said to have been trapped because it had "haunted the family so constantly" (*ibid.*, 121).

8. The story of a woman who was carried away for a time when she crossed a stream to help "what appeared to be a woman sitting on the opposite bank, wailing and 'batting the water with its hands'" (*ibid.*, 121).

9. The belief that upon death a spirit travels "over all the ground he travelled over while alive", during which time it is visible (*ibid.*, 121).

10. "If the first lamb you see in the season be white it is lucky, but if it be black you will die within the year" (*ibid.*, 121).

11. The "death warning" given a family when a pigeon flew into their house and out again "while at the same time there was a tap on the window" (*ibid.*, 122).

MR. CLODD[1] having shown the above notes to Mr. W. B. Yeats, the latter gentleman kindly forwarded the following memoranda upon them:—

I have stories about most of the things in the slip of folklore you send. I will be dealing with a good many of the subjects in a month or two.[2]

(1.) The coach is very common; Mr. Jones is perhaps wrong in calling it "the Dead Coach." The people of Co. Galway usually call it "the *Deaf* Coach," because it makes a "deaf" sound. They describe "deaf" as muffled or rumbling. I never heard before of its being soundless. Has he mistaken "deaf" for "dead"?

(2.) I am always hearing of forts and of certain rooms in houses being seen as if on fire. It is the commonest phenomenon in connection with forts, in all parts of Ireland I know.

(3.) I am collecting material about fairy battles, and am trying to find out when they coincide with May Day, or November Day, or thereabouts, or else with death.

(4.) A Newfoundland dog, according to my uncle's old servant, is "a very quiet form to do your penance in," She is a Mayo woman and very much of a saint.[3]

---

[1] Edward Clodd (1840–1930) was an amateur folklorist and at this time Vice-President of The Folk-Lore Society.

[2] Yeats published "Ireland Bewitched" in September, 1899 (see p. 167 below). However, the "deaf coach", as well as accounts of fairy troops and of people who are taken "away", appears in "Irish Witch Doctors" (p. 231 below) which was published a year later.

[3] In his *Autobiography* Yeats declares that "much" of *The Celtic Twilight* is "but [the] daily speech" (p. 46) of Mary Battle, George Pollexfen's second-sighted servant.

(6.) It is always dangerous to go out late at night. I have a number of Galway and Sligo stories of people being carried to a distance, including one in which I myself am supposed to have been carried four miles in County Sligo. Compare the spiritualistic medium, Mrs. Guppy, being carried across London with a saucepan in one hand and an egg in the other. She weighed about nineteen stone.[4] I have met about four peasants who believe in fairies but not in ghosts. I have never met the converse, though I have met a man in Co. Roscommon who denied both, but believed in water-horses.

(7.) A ghost has to go anywhere it is sent; but if you send it to an unpleasant place, you have to do your own penance there when you die. My uncle's old servant again.

(8.) Am greatly interested in the fairy "batting the water with her hands." A man at Ballesodare, Paddy Flynn, used the same phrase about the Banshee.[5]

(9.) I never heard this about the soul travelling where it had gone in life. It is very interesting.

(10.) I have heard of the fairies putting a black lamb into a flock as a warning to a Sligo relation of my own who had cut a fairy bush. In a couple of days the lamb had vanished. I suppose therefore that black lambs are uncanny.

(11.) I have a friend whose family (an old Kerry family, I think) has this death-warning.

W. B. Yeats

[4] Yeats refers to the famous "transit of Mrs. Guppy" on June 3, 1871, when the English medium appeared in the center of a spiritualist's table during a seance. Mrs. Samuel Guppy's career, which had begun in the late sixties with the materialization of flowers, fruit and live eels at her seances, culminated in "spirit photography", the practice of sitting for photographic portraits so that a spirit's image would also appear, which Yeats was much later to undertake. The "transit" was widely reported, but Yeats's egg and saucepan are confusing. Contemporary accounts of Mrs. Guppy's feat reported that, having been doing her accounts at the time, she appeared with pen and paper, on which she had just written the word "onions".

[5] Yeats includes this description of the Banshee in his sketch of Paddy Flynn, "A Teller of Tales", in *The Celtic Twilight* (p. 33).

# The Academic Class and the Agrarian Revolution

The hearings of the Intermediate Education Committee, which began on January 13, 1899, aroused great controversy over the teaching of Irish in the schools. An interview in the Dublin *Daily Express* on February 16, with J. P. Mahaffy (1839–1919), the Provost of Trinity College, Dublin, provoked letters in defence of instruction in Gaelic from Alice Milligan and others. Tensions rose when the testimony towards the end of the hearings, on February 22, of Robert Atkinson (1839–1908), professor of Romance languages, Sanskrit and comparative philology at Trinity was answered on February 25 by Douglas Hyde, who called Atkinson "a prig, and one of the first order". Atkinson had discouraged the teaching of Gaelic both because of the "unsettled" state of the language and because of "the smallness of the element of idealism" in the ancient stories. Atkinson's "ethical objection", the *Daily Express* reported on February 23, "referred only to ancient Irish literature. Dr. Hyde had published some stories, but they were so low— about a dirty wretch who never washed his feet and married the princess So and So (laughter)." Hyde's language "was not good enough for a patois", and "asked if it was improbable to find an ancient Irish text book which was not silly or indecent, witness said he would not put it that way, but what he desired to say was that it would be difficult to find a book in which there was not some part in it of that sort. The 'Book of Leinster' was not a book for children to read. All folklore was at bottom abominable."

Yeats enlisted in the "war between Dr. Atkinson and Dr. Hyde", as it became known in the *Daily Express*, on March 11, with his letter on "The Academic Class and the Agrarian Revolution". For Yeats, the combatants were familiar enough: the "agrarian revolution", by which he evidently meant the Gaelic League and the National Literary Society as much as Fenianism and the old Land League of Michael Davitt, were pitted against the moribund Anglo-Irish culture represented by Trinity College. In 1895, in the "Introduction" to *A Book of Irish Verse* Yeats had deprecated Trinity College, noting she had "been the mother of many verse-writers and of few poets . . . because she has set herself against the national genius, and taught her children to imitate alien styles and choose out alien themes" (p. xxv). By 1899, however, Yeats was describing a more desperate opponent—"that Death whose most manifest expression . . . is Trinity College," as he was to call it (see p. 243 below)—whose desperation he saw signalled by the virulence of its reaction against Irish language and literature. The subjects of this essay were to trouble Yeats for thirty years (see "Compulsory Gaelic: A Dialogue," p. 439 below, and part IV of "Ireland, 1921–1931", p. 489 below).

THERE are opinions and manners so memorable as indications of movements of thought that one longs to put them into some shape in which they may be read after the discussion that gave them birth is forgotten. I would gladly give such permanence to certain literary opinions of Dr. Atkinson and to a certain violence of manner in his expression of them. He has said "All folklore is essentially abominable," and of Dr. Hyde's imaginative and often beautiful stories "they are so very low," and of "the whole range of Irish literature" (including those tales of Cuchullin which "made an epoch" in the life of Burne-Jones, and many tales that are the foundation of much in contemporary Irish literature),[1] that it has "very little of the ideal, and very little imagination"; and, in what one must conclude to have been a paroxysm of political excitement, that there was a book of Irish tales "with translations" published the other day which "no human being could read without being absolutely degraded by contact with it, of the filth which I won't even demean myself to mention"—a book which every folklorist knows to have no existence outside the imagination of Dr. Atkinson.[2] "All folk-lore is essentially abominable." If a Professor at and English University were to say these things in any conspicuous place, above all before a Commission which he hoped would give his opinion an expression in action, he would not be reasoned with, but his opinion would be repeated with a not ill-humoured raillery and his name remembered at times with a little laughter. Dr. Hyde has understood, however, and perhaps rightly understood, that the conditions of Ireland are so peculiar that it is necessary to answer Dr. Atkinson, lest, as I should imagine, some imperfectly educated priest in some country parish might believe that Irish literature was "abominable," or "indecent"—to use another favourite word of Dr. Atkinson's—and raise a cry against the movement for the preservation of the Irish language. I prefer principally to inquire how a philologist and archaeologist of eminence comes to hold and to express violently such opinions upon matters that are neither philological nor archaeological, and which he would under ordinary circumstances have approached with some

---

[1] The English artist and engraver, Sir Edward Burne-Jones, Bart. (1833–98), who was best known for his romantic neo-medieval works, was in his youth so taken by Macpherson's *Ossian* that he later devoted a decade of his spare time to the study of Celtic romance, the mood of which pervades many works (see G. Burne-Jones, *Memorials of Edward Burne-Jones*, New York, London, 1904, vol. II, 42–3).
"Cuchullin" is Cuchulain or, in Macpherson, "Cuthullin".

[2] Atkinson's citation of "a book published not very long ago . . . that no human being could read . . . without feeling that he had been absolutely degraded . . ." provoked an accompanying letter to Yeats's in the *Daily Express* from Alfred Nutt, who attested that he had "purchased and read through every scrap of Irish text with English translation issued during the last 20 years, and that [he knew] of none to which Dr. Atkinson's words could by the utmost stretch of the most extravagant exaggeration apply for one moment".

modesty and timidity. I remember repeating to William Morris some twelve years ago an opinion of Dr. Atkinson's about Irish literature very like his present opinions, and William Morris answering: "People who talk that way"—or some such words—"know nothing of the root thoughts of literature." I do not think this is the explanation; for a certain lack of fine literary instinct, a certain lack of real understanding of the ideas and passions that give a literature importance, is common among men who spend their lives with words rather than ideas, with facts rather than emotions; and yet I do not think there is a Professor of any eminence at any English University who would not be as incapable of Dr. Atkinson's intemperate opinions as of his quaint manner of expressing them.

The true explanation is that Dr. Atkinson, like most people on both sides in politics of the generation which had to endure the bitterness of the agrarian revolution, is still in a fume of political excitement, and cannot consider any Irish matter without this excitement. If I remember my Bible correctly, the children of Israel had to wander forty years in the wilderness that all who had sinned a particular sin might die there; and Ireland will have no dispassionate opinion on any literary or political matter till that generation has died or has fallen into discredit. One watches with an irritation, that sometimes changes to pity, members of Parliament, Professors, eminent legal persons, officials of all kinds, men often of great natural power, who cannot talk, whether in public or private, of any Irish matter in which any living affection or enthusiasm has a part without becoming bitter with the passion of old controversies in which nobody is any longer interested. When the ideality of the National movement, as "Young Ireland" shaped it, faded before the inevitably imperfect ideals of the agrarian revolution, those streams of fruitful thought, which had begun to flow in Nationalist Ireland under "Young Ireland," became muddy; but the class, among whom Dr. Atkinson lives and from whom he takes his emotions, dried up the springs of all streams that had any sweet water for human thirst. The academic class in Ireland, because the visible enthusiasm of the time threatened its interests or the interests of the classes among whom it dined and married, set its face against all Irish enthusiasms in the first instance, and then, by perhaps slow degrees, against all the great intellectual passions. An academic class is always a little dead and deadening; and our political rancours may long have made our academic class even quicker in denial than its association with undeveloped minds, and its preoccupation with words rather than ideas, with facts rather than emotions, made unavoidable; but I am persuaded, from much that I have heard and read, that it only came to its full maturity of bitterness in the agrarian revolution.

One would be content to wait in silence the change that must already have begun within itself, had it not in part destroyed, and was it not still destroying, the imaginative life of the minds that have come under its influence. An American publisher of great experience said to me the other day: "I have noticed that quite a number of young men, who have come to the States from your Dublin University, try literature or art, but that they always take to commerce in the end. They are very clever— smart, we say—and they make a pot of money; but why do they do it?" I answered, so far as I remember, "Trinity College, Dublin, makes ex- cellent scholars, but it does not make men with any real love for ideal things or with any fine taste in the arts. One does not meet really cultivated Trinity College men as one meets really cultivated Oxford and Cambridge men. The atmosphere of what is called educated Dublin is an atmosphere of cynicism—a cynicism without ideas which expresses itself at the best in a wit without charm." I might have said that our academic class has had the educating of the great majority of Irishmen who are educated at all, and yet that almost all Irishmen who have any fine taste in the arts, any gift for imaginative writing, any mastery over style, have come from beyond its influence, or have a fierce or smoul- dering anger waiting to thrust it to its fall. It might have opposed the often narrow enthusiasm of nationalism with the great intellectual passions of the world, as I think Professor Dowden would have pre- ferred;[3] but it chose the easier way, that brings the death of imagination and at last the death of character.

"All folk-lore is essentially abominable": in that mood it has lived and worked, and of that mood its influence is dying. Fortunately for its country it has raised up powerful enemies, perhaps the most power- ful of all enemies. "Imagination," as an old theologian has written, "cannot be hindered because it creates and substantiates as it goes." Imagination and style are the only things that can, as it were, root and uproot the heart and give men what loves and hates they will; and our academic class understands in some dim way that its influence is passing into the hands of men who are seeking to create a criticism of life which will weigh all Irish interests, and bind rich and poor into one brother-

[3] Yeats often used the character of his father's friend and his own early idol, Edward Dowden (1845–1913), the Shakespearean critic and Professor of English at Trinity, to represent the stultifying influence of Trinity and of Anglo-Irish culture. In 1886, in Yeats's defense of "The Poetry of Sir Samuel Ferguson" (see *Uncollected Prose*, vol. I, p. 88 ff.), in the direct attacks in 1895 on "Professor Dowden and Irish Literature" (*ibid.*, pp. 346–9, 351–3), and in the *Autobiography* (pp. 56–64), where he is opposed to John O'Leary, Dowden per- sonifies the ironic, learned, balanced antithesis to Yeats's own point of view. In asides, however, such as this remark and in Yeats's exception of his mystical friends and "Prof. Dowden at an odd moment" from his denunciation in the "Introduction" to *A Book of Irish Verse* (p. xxv) of poets not self-consciously Irish, Yeats continually betrayed his recognition of Dowden's distinction from whatever class Yeats sometimes used him to represent.

hood; and a literature which will bring together, as Homer and Dante
and Shakespeare and all religions have brought together, the arranging
and comparing powers of the man of books, and the dreams and
idealisms of the man of legends. Our academic class has worked against
imagination and character, against the mover and sustainer of manhood;
and eternity is putting forth its flaming fingers to bring its work to
nothing. It understands that a movement which has published and sold
in seven years more books about Ireland and of all kinds than were
published and sold during the thirty years before it began, and that has
published and sold fifty thousand Gaelic text books in a single year,
must be taking away the attention and perhaps the respect of all
young minds that have a little literature and a little ideality.[4] Our academic class has hated enthusiasm, and Irish enthusiasm above all, and
it has scorned the Irish poor; and here is a movement which has made a
religion of the arts, which would make our hills and rivers beautiful
with memories, and which finds its foundations in the thoughts and
the traditions of the Irish poor. Hence that angry voice, sounding so
strange in the modern world, and crying that "all folk-lore is essentially
abominable," that a charming and admired book "is so very low," that
an old literature, which has inspired many poets, has very "little of the
ideal and very little imagination," and that a book of folk tales, which
no folklorist has ever heard of, is full of "filth," which he will not "even
demean himself to mention." Nor is this a solitary voice, for one finds
the same violence of petulance, or a brawling or chuckling cynicism,
which is perhaps worse, at many tables and in the mouths of Judges,
Professors, and politicians. Until the young have pushed these men from
their stools or have come to think of them as many, younger than I, do
already, and as I perhaps am too deep in the argument to do with the
good-humoured indifference with which one remembers Jacobins and
Jacobites, we shall not have a natural and simple intellectual life in
Ireland.

W. B. Yeats

4 The Gaelic League was founded in 1893.

# Irish Literary Theatre
# Lecture by Mr. W. B. Yeats

Part of Yeats's campaign to draw attention in London to the first productions of the Literary Theatre, his *The Countess Cathleen* and Edward Martyn's *The Heather Field*, was his address on the "Ideal Theatre" before the Irish Literary Society on April 23, 1899. The audience included Yeats's sister "Lily" (Susan Mary, 1866–1949), the poets Dora Sigerson Shorter (1866–1918), John Todhunter (1839–1916), Susan Mitchell (1868–1930) and A. P. Graves (1846–1931), W. P. Ryan (1867–1942), the author of *The Irish Literary Revival* (1894) and Yeats's sometime antagonist D. P. Moran (see pp. 236–7 below). The speech they heard, as reported in the Society's paper, *The Irish Literary Society Gazette*, in the issue of June, 1899 (vol. 1, no. 4), contained most of the elements of Yeats's current announcements and pronouncements about the Irish Literary Theatre. Significantly, the objections raised by some members at the end of Yeats's speech almost perfectly embody the several objections to his vision of an Irish poetic drama appealing at once to peasant and aristocrat which were to arise repeatedly during the following decades.

A MOST interesting lecture on the "Ideal Theatre," with special reference, to the Irish Literary Theatre, was delivered on the evening of Saturday, April 23rd, by Mr. W. B. YEATS, to the Irish Literary Society in the hall of the Society of Arts, Adelphi.

MR. EDMUND GOSSE presided and the members present were: —Miss Patricia Dillon, Mr. J. B. Yeats, Miss Lilly [*sic*] Yeats, Miss S. Mitchell, Miss Fannie J. Mason, Miss A. M. O'Dwyer, Miss T. Dempsey, Mr. Alfred P. Graves, Mrs. A. H. Wheeler, Miss E. D. Bertram, Miss MacMahon, Mr. Wm. Coates and Mrs. Coates, Mr. Frank MacDonagh, Miss A. Butler, Mrs. E. Aylmer Gowing, Miss F. Lynch, Miss A. Lynch, Mr. E. E. Brennan, Mrs. Dora Sigerson Shorter, Dr. J. Todhunter, Mr. F. Norreys Connell, Mrs. A. Rushton, Miss E. Drury, Miss J. Buchanan, Miss C. M. Reburn, Mr. A. Lucy, Mr. Rickard M. J. Burke, Miss Evelyn Gleeson, Mr. Nicholas P. H. Murphy, Mr. J. F. McNamara, Mr. Whittington Howley, Mr. W. P. Ryan, Miss Katie Hayes, Miss E. T. Phelan, Mr. D. P. Moran, Mr. Edward Mooney, Miss N. G. Feeney, Miss E. D'Esterre-Keeling, Mr. J. R. Cox and Mrs. Cox, Miss G. L. Griffin, Mr. J. W. Molloy, Mr. Hubert J. Sweeney, Mr. C. J. Kilgallin, Miss H. M. Madden, Mr. D. Lehane, Mr. J. MacMahon, Mr. W. Boyle, Miss E. Breen, Miss Ethel Wheeler, Miss M. Hayes, Miss M. Fitzpatrick, Mr. J. A. O'Sullivan, Mr. P. H. MacEnery, Miss B. M. O'Reilly.

MR. YEATS said most of them were aware that they were getting up in Dublin, next month, a series of performances. From the 8th of May they would have a week, during which would be performed two plays—one by Mr. Edward Martyn, and one of his own. He could not ask them to listen to what he had to say if their programme simply ended with those plays, for certainly he did not wish to push his own wares. He hoped if they had the slightest welcome at all, they would go on next year and the year after, until gradually the people who cared for the particular kind of thing offered would come to hear of them. They proposed to give next year a play upon an Irish subject by the great Spanish dramatist, Calderon, translated by Denis Florence Mac-Carthy.[1] They could also promise a romantic drama by Mr. Standish O'Grady, whom he had for years thought to have a great dramatic capacity, and a play by Miss Fiona MacLeod.[2] They had elected to give their plays in the Ancient Concert Rooms in Dublin rather than in any big theatre. A year ago when they began inquiries they found that the expenses of the ordinary theatre would be so considerable that they could not hope to succeed unless they got the ordinary crowd of people, and unless they were able to please very much the average man. By going to a small hall they had reduced their expenses enormously, and they would be able to succeed by joining to them the exceptional man—he did not mean the man of any class or the man who read books, though he meant principally the man who reads and who loves the old Irish legends. There were a certain number of those men in Ireland, as elsewhere, and he believed they would get them in sufficient numbers and finally make the experiment pay its expenses. The scenery and costumes would be simple and inexpensive, the actors would be professional, and good actors, and he thought it would be found that their performances would be vigorous and harmonious. Passing to the subject of the lecture proper, he said there was some hope that the ideal theatre might come about in time. First of all, they must remember that Ireland was not a country of great towns. Ireland, like ancient Greece, was a country of scattered population, and he thought that by working together with the musical festival in Dublin ("the Feis")[3] and with the Gaelic language movement there might grow up every spring about the time of the old festival of Baltaine [*sic*] a national, perhaps he should say a racial, festival, where they would have a sufficient number of people who were enthusiastic

---

[1] The translation by Denis Florence McCarthy (1817–82) of Calderon's "The Purgatory of Saint Patrick" was never produced by the Literary Theatre.

[2] These possibilities were discussed in more detail in *Beltaine* for May, 1899 (see p. 160 below). The plays were not produced.

[3] The modern *Feis Ceoil* (Music Festival) was inaugurated in 1897.

and sympathetic in those Celtic things to make it possible for the little
theatre with its limited resources to gradually grow up to a theatre of
sufficiently large resources for them all to be thinking seriously about
what was the ideal theatre. The theatre of Scandinavia was the nearest
approach to an ideal theatre in modern Europe. It was the only theatre
whose plays were at once literary and popular. Elsewhere one never
saw a literary play upon the stage unless it was old enough to be a
superstition or had been produced by some Association of men of
letters. It was only in the middle of this century that a rare and exceptional enthusiasm made it possible for the average Norwegian to understand great and sincere drama. Between 1840 and 1860 there arose a
national literary movement in Norway founded like ours upon the old
legends and the folk songs and the folk traditions of the country. Like
ours, too, it had to conquer the opposition of a cosmopolitan and
denationalised class. A semi-amateur theatre was founded in Bergen.
under the management of Ibsen, when 23, and later on a Norwegian
theatre as it was called, was founded in Christiania under the same
management. Ibsen and Bjornson, respectively vice-president and
president of the Scandinavian Society, a Society with the same objects
as the society he was now addressing, warred against the cosmopolitan
drama, and with so much success that a famous Danish actor left the
stage in disgust, and another was hissed off it.[4] He knew well that
neither Mr. Martyn nor himself nor any of the writers who have promised plays could claim to be Ibsens or Bjornsons, but they might
follow in the way those great men had gone, and in all humility. Heroic
ideas and interest in great passions spread abroad among the mass of the
people, and the only condition of the drama was at once literary and
popular. The ordinary man disliked to take trouble, disliked having to
think and to feel in new ways. He disliked the heroic and unadorned
sincerity of a play like "Ghosts" or the "Wild Duck," as much as he
disliked the unfamiliar magnificence of plays like "Peer Gynt" or the
"Heroes of Heligoland." [*sic*] But let a whole people be touched by an
intensity, and they would share in the creative impulse of the poets,
and every kind of great drama would spring up. Civilisation unchecked

---

[4] The Bergen Theatre had been started by Ole Bull (1810–80) in 1850, the year before the
23-year-old Ibsen—who never managed it—came to work there. Ibsen left in 1857 to
become manager of the Christiania (Oslo) Norwegian Theatre, which had been started five
years before his arrival.

He and Björnstjerne Bjørnson (1832–1910), the Norwegian poet, dramatist, reformer and
Nobel laureate (1903), founded in 1859 the Norwegian Society to promote nationalism in
literature and art. The Scandinavian Society, founded five years later, had as its purpose the
uniting of the Scandinavian states.

One of the actors Yeats speaks of was the Dane Vilhelm Wiehe whose resignation, provoked by the newspaper articles of Bjørnson, resulted in a battle in the press involving Ibsen
and Bjørnson.

by this rare and exceptional enthusiasm killed great drama by teaching people to live upon the surface, to seek easy pleasures, and to meditate little. The actor who spoke his lines like something out of the newspaper drove out that art of oratory which the stage inherited from the rhapsodists. If we were to restore drama to the stage—poetic drama, at any rate—our actors must become rhapsodists again, and keep the rhythm of the verse as the first of their endeavours. The music of a voice should seem more important than the expression of face or the movement of hands, for poetry spoken as prose, spoken without music, as the performance of Mr. Swinburne's "Loch Ryne" the other day, sounded like bad, florid prose.⁵ The conception of the drama had changed like the conception of acting. The modern drama was all action, the ancient drama was all words about action. Nothing at all happened in many of the greatest of Greek plays, and it was Hamlet's soliloquies and not his duel that were of the chief importance in the play. Even in life itself the dramatic moments were those that were inseparable from splendid and appropriate words. The object of the drama was to be a revelation of lofty and heroic life, whether in the mind of the writer alone, as with the great realists, or in the persons that move before one upon the stage, as with the Greek dramatists. It had, therefore, but a passing moment for all but a few imaginative natures. They would, therefore, do their part, according to their limited power, in building up in Ireland a dramatic tradition that would remember the purpose of drama in the world, and they threw themselves upon the national literary movement that they might have an audience. (Applause.)

DR. TODHUNTER, in proposing a vote of thanks to the lecturer, said that he sympathised with some of Mr. Yeats's heresies. (Laughter.) He had not read Mr. Martyn's work, but he had read "The Countess Kathleen," and he considered it would be extremely difficult to put it on the stage in any way. It was not that a poetical play of the kind might not be sympathetically given by sympathetic actors; but to produce it adequately the actors would require a special training for about a year. How Mr. Yeats was going to get the actors—who, he believed, were to be English and not Irish—to give perfect form to this play of "Countess Kathleen" he did not know. Mr. Yeats began at the beginning of drama—that was to say, a drama which was really chiefly lyrical. He thought that was the right way to begin such a movement; but he did not think that the purely lyrical drama was the greatest drama. With regard to the way of putting on the stage plays which were lyrical in character, he thought the great point was to give up all idea of realistic scenery. The experiment was tried at a theatre in London, when Maeter-

---

⁵ *Locrine: A Tragedy* was published in London in 1887.

linck's "Pelleas and Melisande," was performed with scenery of the simplest character. To him it was one of the most intensely interesting performances he had ever seen. It was done by a French company, who gave the speeches most beautifully. When he saw the same play produced at the Lyceum by Forbes Robertson with all the adjuncts of stage craft it had not for him anything like the charm of the other performance with the perfectly simple scenery.[6]

MR. NORREYS CONNELL[7] seconded the vote of thanks. He did not think that Mr .Yeats' idea of the theatre could ever successfully appeal to the people for support, and as a modern imitation of the old theatre it seemed impossible. (Applause.)

MR. CLEMENT SHORTER[8] said that everyone, whatever his nationality, must wish the utmost possible success to the scheme which Mr. Yeats had at hear[t]. (Hear, hear.) It was really a matter not so much of being zealous in Ireland to produce a play which should have certain touches of Irish romance in it, but of writing in English to capture the whole English-speaking world upon lines that were strictly Irish. (Hear, hear.) The more popular Mr. Yeats's plays were the greater would be the success of the Irish theatre movement, for the plays would be performed not only in Ireland, but in England, in America, and the Colonies. He did not think that mere attempts to appeal to a limited audience was the way in which Mr. Yeats could render the largest and most thorough service to the country which he loved so well. (Applause.)

Miss D'ESTERRE–KEELING, Mr. EDWARD MOONEY and Mr. H. SWEENEY also joined in the discussion, and dissented from the lecturer's views.

The CHAIRMAN[9] ventured to join issue with Mr. Yeats in the illustration that he gave with regard to the Norwegian theatre. In the first place, there was an element, if he might put it so, of the fairy tale in Mr. Yeats' picturesque and charming account of the birth of the Norwegian Theatre. (Laughter.) Mr. Yeats represented Ibsen as sweeping away cosmopolitan drama and starting with Saga drama. As a matter of fact Ibsen during the period mentioned produced an enormous quantity of cosmopolitan plays—Danish, Swedish, and German,

[6] Sir Johnston Forbes-Robertson (1853–1937), one of the most famous Hamlets of his period, was from 1895 the manager of the London Lyceum, where he produced "Pelleas and Melisande" in 1898.

[7] See pp. 361–63 below for the controversy nine years later over the Abbey Theatre's production of *The Piper* by Norreys Connell (Conal O'Riordan).

[8] See Yeats's quarrel, pp. 327–8 below, with his friend Clement Shorter, the husband of Dora Sigerson.

[9] The friendship, despite fundamental differences, which marks these observations by Edmund Gosse (1849–1928), persisted in his relationship with Yeats, whose Civil List pension in 1910 came about largely through Gosse's efforts.

and even French vaudevilles and farces. It was on the basis of the practical stage and its requirements that Ibsen built up the drama which
was such an extraordinary exemplification of his own individuality. If
Mr. Yeats represented his ideal theatre more or less on the lines of the
national Norwegian theatre he must not forget the commercial play,
because it was on the commercial play in the very fullest sense that the
present national theatre of Norway was based. But they all knew exactly
what Mr. Yeats meant, and they all sympathised with him. Mr. Yeats
meant to call them back from the base sense of animalism and commercialism to what was noble and dignified in the art of drama. He shared
with some of those who had spoken a certain scepticism as to whether
the scheme suggested by Mr. Yeats was really the practical mode of
carrying out the idea. As to the question of chanting dramatic verse,
he thought, with Dr. Todhunter, that that should be confined solely to
the primitive forms of lyrical drama. There was a country where it had
been used from immemorial times, Persia, where the purely lyrical
drama was habitually performed by actors who chanted slowly in
recitative to appropriate music, and that he believed was what Mr.
Yeats would be glad to see. He could not conceive of a drama in which
comedy did not exist. There were many things they had not got; they
had not got tragedy, except bastard melodrama; but comedy they had
as purely, as exquisitely, as it had ever been except in the palmiest days
of the seventeenth century. He could not but think that a people satur-
ated with humour like the Irish would feel it to be a very imperfect
thing if an ideal theatre were given them in which there was no room
found for comedy. (Hear, hear, and applause.)

Mr. YEATS, in returning thanks for the vote of thanks, said one of
the missions of the drama was to mould and perfect national feeling.
They would have no chance of success in Dublin but for national feeling. The people would be offered plays that would put before them the
life, the ideals, and the legends of Ireland, and the people would come to
see that which they would not find anywhere else.

A vote of thanks to the Chairman concluded the proceedings.

# Plans and Methods

Yeats set forth the guiding principles and immediate "Plans and Methods" of the Literary Theatre in the May, 1899, issue of *Beltaine*, a journal, named after the Celtic spring festival, which appeared only twice again—in February and April of 1900—before giving way to *Samhain* in 1901. The first two paragraphs of this piece appeared in altered form as "The Irish Literary Theatre" in the Dublin *Daily Express* on January 14, 1899 (see p. 139 above).

NORWAY has a great and successful school of contemporary drama, which grew out of a national literary movement very similar to that now going on in Ireland. Everywhere critics and writers, who wish for something better than the ordinary play of commerce, turn to Norway for an example and an inspiration. Spain and Germany, indeed, though they have a taste for bad dramatists, which Norway has not, have good dramatists, whom they admire. Elsewhere one finds the literary drama alone, when some great work, old enough to be a national superstition, is revived, with scenery and costumes so elaborate that nobody need listen to the words unless he likes; and in little and inexpensive theatres, which associations of men of letters hire from time to time that they may see upon the stage the plays of Henrik Ibsen, Maurice Maeterlinck, Gerard Hauptmann, Jose Echegaray, or some less famous dramatist who has written, in the only way literature can be written, to express a dream which has taken possession of his mind. These associations, the Theatre Libre and the Independent Theatre especially, in the face of violent opposition, have trained actors who have become famous, and have had a powerful influence even upon those plays which are written to please as many people as possible, that they may make as much money as possible.

The Irish Literary Theatre will attempt to do in Dublin something of what has been done in London and Paris; and, if it has even a small welcome, it will produce, somewhere about the old festival of Beltaine at the beginning of every spring, a play founded upon an Irish subject. The plays will differ from those produced by associations of men of letters in London and in Paris, because times have changed, and because the intellect of Ireland is romantic and spiritual rather than scientific and analytical, but they will have as little of a commercial ambition. Their writers will appeal to that limited public which gives understanding, and not to that unlimited public which gives wealth; and if they interest those among their audience who keep in their memories the songs of Callanan and Walsh,[1] or old Irish legends, or who love the good books of any country, they will not mind greatly if others are bored.

The Committee think of producing in 1900 Denis Florence Mac-Carthy's translation of Calderon's *St. Patrick's Purgatory*, a play about the conversion of Ireland. Miss Fiona Macleod has written, or is writing, three plays, *The Hour of Beauty, Fand and Cuchullain*, and *The Tanist*, an Irish historical play, and Mr. Standish O'Grady has promised an Irish historical play.[2] Others, too, have written or are writing plays, so that there will be no lack of work to select from. In all or almost all cases the plays must be published before they are acted, and no play will be produced which could not hope to succeed as a book.

In a play like Mr. Martyn's,[3] where everything is subordinate to the central idea, and the dialogues as much like the dialogues of daily life as possible, the slightest exaggeration of detail, or effort to make points where points were not intended, becomes an insincerity. An endeavour has therefore been made to have it acted as simply and quietly as possible. The chief endeavour with Mr. Yeats' play[4] has been to get it spoken with some sense of rhythm.

The two lyrics,[5] which we print on a later page, are not sung, but spoken, or rather chanted, to music, as the old poems were probably chanted by bards and rhapsodists. Even when the words of a song, sung in the ordinary way, are heard at all, their own proper rhythm and emphasis are lost, or partly lost, in the rhythm and emphasis of the music. A lyric which is spoken or chanted to music should, upon the other hand, reveal its meaning, and its rhythm so become indissoluble in the memory. The speaking of words, whether to music or not, is, however, so perfectly among the lost arts that it will take a long time before our actors, no matter how willing, will be able to forget the ordinary methods of the stage or to perfect a new method.

Mr. Johnson, in the interpretative argument which he has written for *The Countess Cathleen*, places the events it describes in the sixteenth

[1] James Joseph (sometimes given as Jeremiah) Callanan (1795–1829) was a collector and translator of Irish peasant songs. Edward Walsh (1805–50) published his collections in *Reliques of Irish Jacobite Poetry* (1844) and *Irish Popular Songs* (1847).
[2] "Fiona Macleod" completed two plays, *The Immortal Hour* and *The House of Usna*, and a third, *The Enchanted Valleys*, was not finished. None of these plays nor any by Standish O'Grady was performed by the Irish Literary Theatre.
[3] *The Heather Field.*
[4] *The Countess Cathleen.*
[5] Yeats printed in *Beltaine* "Impetuous heart, be still, be still" (Russell K. Alspach, ed. *The Variorum Edition of the Plays of W. B. Yeats*, London, 1966, p. 129) and "Who will go drive with Fergus now" (*ibid.*, pp. 52–6).

Yeats's American tour, 1903-4, in Boston

Yeats as seen by Kate Carew in the *New York World* (22 Nov 1903)

Honoring Wilfred Scawen Blunt on his seventy-fourth birthday, 18 January 1914. From left: Victor Plarr, Sturge Moore, Yeats, W. S. Blunt, Ezra Pound, Richard Aldington, F. S. Flint. *See p. 410. (By courtesy of the Humanities Research Center, University of Texas)*

Yeats at Casa Pastor, Palma-de-Mallorca, in 1936. "This villa is a charming but melodramatic house — tall marble pillars, white walls ornamented with stucco panels, a wide balcony going all the way round . . . I spend much of each day in an arm-chair on the balcony looking out over miles of coast and sea . . ." (*Letters,* p. 850)

century.[6] So Mr. Yeats originally wrote, but he has since written that he tried to suggest throughout the play that period, made out of many periods, in which the events in the folk-tales have happened. The play is not historic, but symbolic, and has as little to do with any definite place and time as an *auto* by Calderon. One should look for the Countess Cathleen and the peasants and the demons not in history, but, as Mr. Johnson has done, in one's own heart; and such costumes and scenery have been selected as will preserve the indefinite.

There are many allusions in *The Countess Cathleen* to old Celtic legends. Usheen, or Oisin, was a legendary poet who journeyed to the Land of Youth with Niam, an immortal woman. Adene, or Etain, was a legendary queen who left the world and found an immortal husband. Fergus was the poet of the Red Branch cycle of legends, as Oisin was of the Fenian cycle. He was the King of Uladh, but, as the legend was shaped by Ferguson, whom Mr. Yeats has followed in his lyric, he gave up his throne that he might live at peace, hunting in the woods.[7] 'The Shee,' 'The Sheogues,' 'The Danaan Nations,' 'The People of the Raths' are different names for the faëry people, the great gods of an earlier time. A Thivish is a ghost, a wandering and earthbound spirit. A Sowlth is a misshapen or shapeless spirit, sometimes identified with the Jack o' Lanthorn. 'Barach the traitor' was the man who made the feast for Fergus that the sons of Usna might lack his protection. The Clan Cailitin was a family of wizards among the troops of Maive, who at last brought about the death of Cuchullain, 'Sualtams' and old Dectera's child. 'The great king' who 'killed Naisi and broke Deirdre's heart,' was, of course, Concobar. Orchil was a Celtic goddess, who is always imagined as a kind of Lilith in Mr. Yeats' poetry. 'The bright spear' which Aleel sees in his frenzy driven through the eye of Balor, the old Celtic divinity of cold and darkness, is, of course, the spear flung by Lug, the god of warmth and light and order. The battle of Moytura was to the old Celts the battle in which the gods of light and life overcame the gods of cold and darkness and chaos. It is necessary to explain these things, as the old Irish mythology is still imperfectly known in modern Ireland.[8]

[6] Lionel Johnson's "interpretive argument", in which he noted that in Yeats's play "we never lose sight of the spiritual side of things: the dark, gross vapors of the rotting woods . . . are as the fumes and clouds of evil and sin . . ." was printed in this issue of *Beltaine* (pp. 10–11).

[7] Yeats's reference is to "The Abdication of Fergus MacRoy" in *Lays of the Western Gael* by Sir Samuel Ferguson (1810–86). For Yeats's earlier appreciation of Ferguson, see *Uncollected Prose*, vol. I, pp. 81–104.

[8] The explanations given here are similar to those in the glossary which Yeats furnished with the 1895 edition of *Poems*, which included *The Countess Cathleen* (see *Variorum Plays*, pp. 1284–7).

If any money is made by the performances it will be paid into the funds of the National Literary Society, to go towards the expenses of the Irish Literary Theatre in future years.

Editor of Beltaine

# The Irish Literary Theatre

Yeats continued his publicity for the "Irish Literary Theatre" with an article which appeared in *Literature* on May 6, 1899, two days before the initial performances. The article repeats many of Yeats's themes as he stated them in his lecture to the Irish Literary Society (p. 153 above) and in the first issue of *Beltaine* (see p. 159 above), but here these views are directed to a wider audience for whom Yeats's usual direct appeal to national pride must be altered to envisage an audience "touched . . . by a world-wide movement of thought and emotion".

THE last few months have been of an extreme importance to that Irish intellectual movement, which began with the break up of the political movement of Parnell, for they have done more than the preceding ten years to interest the Irish leisured classes in Irish thought and Irish literature. Certain political impulses have helped; but the *Irish Daily Express*, a paper whose policy is under the direction of Mr. Horace Plunkett, has been the chief mover in what had seemed an almost impossible change.[1] The intellectual movement has created a great number of books of all kinds, but most of us thought it would have to find its principal readers for years to come among the Irish in England, who read the English literary papers; for nothing but its Gaelic text books— and fifty thousand of these have been sold in a single year—had a considerable sale in Ireland. Now, however, the sons and daughters of the landlords and officials are beginning to read, and at the same time old rancours are dying down; and that sense of something going to happen, which alone gives creative spirits their opportunity, whether in action or thought, has begun to spread among all classes. A year or

---

[1] Yeats's reference should be to the Dublin *Daily Express*, owned during the nineties by Horace C. Plunkett (1854–1932), the Irish agricultural reformer and statesman, who bought the paper to publicize his farm policies. During the later nineties his paper gave much space to contemporary Irish literature, and A.E., John Eglinton, William Larminie, as well as Yeats, contributed articles.

two ago Mr. Martyn and myself would have found few helpers for our theatrical experiment; while to-day we have found so many helpers and so few hinderers, and hinderers are usually plentiful in Ireland, that, despite a despondent disposition, which astrologers trace to the moon having risen at my birth among a trouble of hostile stars, I have begun to hope for a measure of success.

And yet we are uncompromising enough. We have called our experiment "The Irish Literary Theatre," although we knew that "literary" sounded ill in playgoers' ears; and we have issued a circular describing the Norwegian theatre, which hatched "that northern phantom" Dr. Ibsen, as the only theatre at once literary and popular.[2] We have appealed to the imaginative minority and not to the majority which is content with the theatre of commerce; and, if we do not fail too badly, we will make a like appeal next spring, and so from spring to spring, for, though we have engaged good and experienced actors, we have economized sufficiently on our scenery, and on our stage, to be able to wait for a full success.

Our plays will all be about Irish subjects; and, if we can find enough writers, and I have little doubt we will find them, who will write with some depth and simplicity about legends associated with the rivers and mountains of Ireland, or about Irish historic personages and events, or about modern Irish life, an increasing number of persons will desire to hear a message that will so often illustrate the circumstance of their lives. On the 8th of May we give a play of mine, *The Countess Cathleen*, which is founded on old legends, and the next night a play of Mr. Martyn's, *The Heather Field*, a very profound and simple criticism of modern life; and next year, in all likelihood, Calderon's *St. Patrick's Purgatory*, which is about the conversion of Ireland; and a play by either Mr. Standish O'Grady or Miss Fiona Macleod.[3] I think that nearly all our little group of Irish or Celtic writers will try their hands at playwriting, and, as our political disorders and a double share of the medieval-man in our blood have given us a dramatic temper, our intellectual movement may begin to speak through the theatre. The first weeks of May, being also the date of our Musical Festival, and in most years (though not in this) of the festival of the Gaelic League, the most vigorous and powerful of our organizations, will perhaps become the season of a great racial gathering, drawing enthusiasts from far scattered towns and hill-sides as by a triple evocation. It may happen that the imaginative minority will spread their interests among the majority, for even the majority becomes imaginative when touched by enthusiasm.

[2] Yeats probably means the "Plans and Methods" section of *Beltaine* (see p. 159, above).
[3] For information about these projects and about the "Music Festival", see the notes to Yeats's lecture of April 23, 1899 (p. 153 above) and to his article in *Beltaine* (p. 159 above).

Men who are not more intelligent than London theatre-goers listen with sympathy and understanding to quiet and sincere miracle-plays in Brittany; and the crowds who went in procession when Cimabue had the cry, or who chanted the ballad of "Chevy Chase,"[4] or who filled the play-houses for Shakespeare, only differed from the crowds who think Rossetti's women "guys," and poetry of kinds "a bore," and Ibsen an "immoral" and inexpert writer, because they were touched by the fervour of religion, or by the delight of a familiar legend, or by a world-wide movement of thought and emotion.

W. B. Yeats

# The Dominion of Dreams

His third and last article on "Fiona Macleod", the review of *The Dominion of Dreams* (1899) in *The Bookman* for July, 1899, found Yeats still convinced that "hers" was a salutary and necessary kind of literature, although he was growing more restless over the deficiencies of "her" style. It seems likely that in 1899 Yeats was still unaware that "Fiona" was the feminine *alter ego* of William Sharp, for two years later he was still addressing letters to "her". However, Yeats may have suspected the truth but still used letters to "her" to reach that part of Sharp's personality.

ONE of Miss Macleod's new stories tells how a certain shepherd, wandering at night over a lonely marshland, sees a piper piping among a flock of sheep. He had a black feather in his bonnet and black streamers from his pipes, and his music was now full of mockery and now full of melancholy, and when the shepherd tried to go towards him he seemed always as far off as ever. The shepherd stood to listen, and suddenly he found that the piper was quite close, and that what he had thought sheep were but shadows of all shapes and sizes. They were, and he did not know how he knew this, the shadows of all the piper had seen that day—the shadows of trees and plants and cattle, and of a dead man in a corrie, and of the shepherd himself, as he had lost it an hour ago at the set of the sun. Being terrified, and angry because he was

---

[4] The Italian artist Giovanni Cimabue (1240–1301/2) was so popular that his Madonna was carried through the streets of Florence during religious processions. "The Ballad of Chevy Chase", one of the oldest English ballads, has been traced back as far as the fifteenth century.

terrified, he tried to seize the piper with his hands, and fell against a rock, striking his head, and as he fell he saw the shadows change to a flock of curlews and fly away. Presently he awoke out of a swoon and began wandering here and there, looking for the curlew that had been his shadow, until being at last worn out, he lay down and slept, and as he slept the piper came, but looking different, for now he had long black hair, and stood beside him and took up the shadow of a reed and played upon it. A curlew came nearer and nearer, and the piper played it back into a shadow and played the shadow into the mind of the shepherd. When day had come the shepherd awoke and gave "three cries of the curlew," and began to wander back aimlessly in the way he had come. People explained his madness by saying that the Dark Fool, the Amadan Dhu, had "touched" him.

I give this story, which loses much of its mystery in my bare chronicle, because it is easier to unwind it than to unwind her more complicated stories, and I am anxious to discover the thoughts about which her art is wound. Other writers are busy with the way men and women act in sorrow or in joy, but Miss Macleod has re-discovered the art of the myth-makers, and gives a visible shape to joys and sorrows, and makes them seem realities and men and women illusions. It was minds like hers that created Aphrodite out of love and the foam of the sea, and Prometheus out of human thought and its likeness to leaping fire. We understand in some dim way that her Amadan Dhu is some half-inspired madness such as marked men out in early times for a terrified worship, and that the shadows that gather about him like sheep are but our own memories, the things that make us ourselves and bind us to the world, in some peaceful mood, and that the shadows changed into curlews are our memories in some wilder mood; and because the links of resemblance are subtle and the full meaning beyond our reach, we understand with our emotions rather than with our reason, and the story is not allegory, but symbolism, and not prose, but poetry. Swedenborg and Jacob Boehme have begun to cast off the manners of the schools, and to talk the fairy tales of children, and from this union of the lofty with the simple religious myth has been re-born.

A change in thought in the world makes us understand that we are not walled up within our immediate senses, but bound one to another, and to some greater life, by a secret communion of thought and emotion that can in a moment fling up into the waking mind some dream or vision of a far-off friend, and of his circumstance, or of a hidden and consoling loveliness; and at once a kind of literature, which passed away with the ancient world and its witchcraft, begins to arise in every European country. This literature has a power over strange effects, for it can trust itself to dim emotions of beauty, as no literature can, which believes its revelation comes out of the waking mind. One of these stories tells of Eoan and Finola, whose house is "on a sun-swept mound in the wood." "Long ago he had eaten mistletoe berries in moonshine, and had not waked again. Finola, loving him more than life, had changed herself into the white stillness of sleep, and was a dream in his mind, and lay quiet and glad and at rest." And in another we are told of Aevgrain the daughter of Deirdre. "Then her white hands moved like swans through the shadowy flood that was her hair, and she put sleep from her."

Every kind of inspiration has its besetting faults, and perhaps because those who are at the beginning of movements have no models and no traditional restraints, Miss Macleod has faults enough to ruin an ordinary writer. Her search for dim resemblances sometimes brings her beyond the borders of coherence; and she has a way of using literary words, when the right words are the words of daily speech, that often makes some beautiful invention seem unreal. There is scarcely a story that would not be the better for the crossing out of many words. Before her shepherd sees the Dark Fool he hears the crying of sheep, and it is called a "lamentable melancholy sound, like children crying in some forlorn place."[1] How much better this would have been without "lamentable" and with "lonely" or the like instead of "forlorn"! At another place she spoils a beautiful old Gaelic saying, that calls the cry of the wind and the cry of the wave and the cry of the curlew, the three oldest cries in the world, by calling them "the three lamentable elder voices of the world." The bent of nature, that makes her turn from circumstance and personalities to symbols and personifications, may perhaps leave her liable to an obsession from certain emotional words, which have for her a kind of symbolic meaning, but her love of old tales should tell her that the great mysteries are best told in the simpler words.

W. B. Yeats

---

[1] In the uniform edition, arranged by Mrs. William Sharp, of *The Dominion of Dreams* and *Under the Dark Star*, New York, 1911, this passage in *Dalua*, p. 4, reads "that melancholy sound as of lost children crying in a forlorn place".

# Ireland Bewitched

The fourth of the six articles Yeats assembled from Lady Gregory's folk collections is "Ireland Bewitched", which appeared in *The Contemporary Review* for September, 1899. (See p. 54 above regarding this collaboration.)

Some of the parallels between stories given in this article and the versions in Lady Gregory's *Visions and Beliefs* (1920) are indicated in the footnotes. The names of the tale-tellers and of the characters in the stories are usually changed from Yeats's version in Lady Gregory's. While Yeats probably gave false names to his informants to protect them, there is no evidence that Lady Gregory's names are any more authentic.

WHEN one talks to the people of the West of Ireland, and wins their confidence, one soon finds that they live in a very ancient world, and are surrounded by dreams that make the little round fields that were the foundations of ancient houses (forts or forths as they call them), a great boulder up above on the hillside, the more twisted or matted thorn trees, all unusual things and places, and the common crafts of the country always mysterious and often beautiful. One finds the old witches and wisemen still busy, and even the crafts of the smith and of the miller touched with a shadow of old faiths, that gives them a brotherhood with magic. The principal crafts were once everywhere, it seems, associated with magic, and had their rites and their gods; and smith-craft, of which one hears much from Galway story-tellers, that was once the distinguishing craft of races that had broken many battles upon races whose weapons were of stone, was certainly associated with a very powerful magic. A man on the borders of Clare and Galway tells how his house was enchanted and filled with smoke that was like the smoke of a forge, and a man living by the sea in North Galway says: "This is a fairy stream we're passing; there were some used to see them by the side of it, and washing themselves in it. And there used to be heard a fairy forge here every night, and the hammering on the iron could be heard and the blast of the furnace." A man at Kiltartan says: "Black-smiths are safe from these things," meaning fairy mischiefs, "and if a blacksmith was to turn his anvil upside down and say malicious words he could do you great injury."[1] A man in the Burren Hills says: "Yes, they say blacksmiths have something about them. And if there's a seventh blacksmith in succession from seven generations, he can do

---

[1] The stories told about blacksmiths from this point on to p. 169 were given by Lady Gregory in *Visions and Beliefs*, vol. II, pp. 239–41 in chapter XI, "Blacksmiths".

many strange things, and if he gave you his curse you wouldn't be the better of it. There was one at Belharbour, Jamsie Finucane,[2] but he did no harm to any one, but was as quiet as another. He is dead now and his son's a blacksmith, too." A woman near Coole says: "A seventh son has the power to cure the ringworm, and if there is a seventh black-smith in a family he can do his choice thing." And an old man near Kiltartan says: "Blacksmiths have power, and if you could steal the water from the trough in the forge, it would cure all things." And a woman from Ardrahan says: "A blacksmith can do all things. When my little boy was sick I was told to go to a forge before sunrise and to collect some of the dust from the anvil. But I didn't after, he was too far gone." A drunken blacksmith at a village in the county of Clare, when asked by a friend who has collected many of these and other stories for me, if he had ever been to the famous wise woman, Biddy Early, answered: "I never went to Biddy Early for a cure myself, for you should know that no ill or harm ever comes to a blacksmith."

Iron is believed to be the great dissolver of all charms, and one hears stories of enchanted people and creatures that take their right shape when you point a gun at them and look along the iron of the barrel. It seems to be this property of iron that makes blacksmiths invulnerable. A woman from near Feakle says: "There was a man one time that was a blacksmith, and he used to go every night playing cards. And for all his wife could say he wouldn't leave off doing it. So one night she got a boy to go stand in the old churchyard he'd have to pass, and to frighten him.

"So the boy did so, and began to groan and to try to frighten him when he came near. But it's well-known that nothing of that kind can do any harm to a blacksmith. So he went in and got hold of the boy, and told him he had a mind to choke him, and went his way.

"But no sooner was the boy left alone than there came about him something in the shape of a dog, and then a great troop of cats. And they surrounded him, and he tried to get away home, but he had no power to go the way he wanted, but had to go with them. And at last they came to an old forth and a fairy bush, and he knelt down and made the sign of the cross and said a great many Our Fathers. And after a time they went into the fairy bush and left him.

"And he was going away and a woman came out of the bush, and called to him three times to make him look back. And he saw it was a woman he knew before, that was dead, and so he knew she was among the fairies. And she said to him, 'It's well for you I was here, and worked hard for you, or you would have been brought in among them, and be like me.' So he got home."

[2] In Lady Gregory, his name is given as "Pat Doherty".

"And the blacksmith got home, too, and his wife was surprised to see he was no way frightened. But he said, 'You might know that there's nothing of the sort that could harm me.'

"For a blacksmith is safe from all, and when he goes out in the night he keeps always in his pocket a small bit of iron, and they know him by that.

"So he went on card playing, and they grew very poor after."

Millers, too, have knowledge and power. An old man I knew, who believed himself to be haunted, went to the nearest miller for a cure; and a woman among the Slieve Echtge hills says that "a miller can bring any one he likes to misfortune by working his mill backwards," and adds, "just as the blacksmith can put his anvil upside down."

The people who have most knowledge, however, are not thought to have it from a craft, but because it has been told them, revealed to them, as it might be told or revealed to anybody. Once everybody almost had it, for as an old man in Kiltartan says: "Enchanters and magicians they were in the old times, and could make the birds sing and the stones and the fishes speak." But now only a few have it. One hears comparatively little of magic of the old wonder-working kind, but one does hear something of it. An old woman from the borders of Sligo and Mayo says that she remembers seeing, when she was a child, "a wild old man in flannel who came from Erris." He and the men used to sit up late at night sometimes, playing cards in a big barn. She was not allowed to go into the barn because children kneel down and look up under the cards, and a player has bad luck if anybody kneels when he is playing, but her father often told her that when they had been playing a long time "the wild old man" would take up the cards and move them about and a hare would leap out of the cards, and then a hound would leap out after the hare and chase it round and round the barn and away.

One hears sometimes of people who can see what is happening at a distance, or what is happening among "the others" (the fairies), or what is going to happen among us. A woman at Coole says: "There was a man at Ardrahan used to see many things. But he lost his eyesight after. That often happens, that those who see those things lose their earthly sight."

A man of the large island of Aran says: "There was a strange woman came to the island one day and told some of the women down below what would happen them. And they didn't believe, she being a stranger, but since that time it's all been coming true." And it is sometimes said that if you have the habit of walking straight on the road, and not of wavering a little from side to side, you are more likely to "see things" than another, which means, I suppose, that you should be in good health and strength if you are "to see things." The gift most valued seems to be the power of bringing back people who are in the power of "the others," or of curing the many illnesses that "the others" are believed to give us, that they may take us into their world. It is possible that all illness was once believed to come from them, but I am not sure, because a distinction is now made between the illnesses they make and ordinary illnesses. A man on one of the Aran Islands told my friend, with many other stories which I have, how he got a little of the knowledge and the use he made of it. He has not, however, the whole of the knowledge, for the people are at this moment looking out for a "knowledgeable" man or woman, to use their own words, as at present they have to go to Roundstone in Galway. The man says: "There are many can do cures because they have something walking with them, what we may call a ghost, from among the Sheogue (the fairies). A few cures I can do myself, and this is how I got them. I told you I was for five quarters in Manchester, and where I lodged were two old women in the house, from the farthest side of Mayo, for they were running from Mayo at that time because of the hunger. And I knew they were likely to have a cure, for St. Patrick blessed the places he was not in more than the places he was in, and with the cure he left, and the fallen angels, there are many in Mayo, can do them.

"Now it's the custom in England never to clear the table but once in the week, and that on a Saturday night. And in that night all is set out clean, and all the crusts of bread and bits of meat and the like are gathered together in a tin can and thrown out in the street. And women that have no other way of living come round with a bag that would hold two stone, and they pick up all that's thrown out, and live on it for a week. But often I didn't eat the half of what was before me, and I wouldn't throw it out, but I'd bring it to the two old women that were in the house, so they grew very fond of me.

"Well, when the time came that I thought I'd draw towards home, I brought them one day to a public-house, and made a drop of punch for them, and then I picked the cure out of them, for I was wise in those days. There was a neighbour's child was sick and I got word of it, and I went to the house, for the woman there had showed me kindness, and I went in to the cradle and I lifted the quilt off the child's face, and you could see by it, and I saw the signs, that there was some of their work there. And I said, 'You're not likely to have the child long with you, ma'am.' And she said, 'Indeed, I know I won't have him long.' So I said nothing, but I went out, and whatever I did and whatever I got there, I brought it in again and gave it to the child, and he began to get better. And the next day I brought the same thing again and gave it to the child, and I looked at him and I said to the mother, 'He'll live to comb his hair grey.' And from that time he got better, and now there's no stronger child in the island, and he the youngest in the house.

"After that the husband got sick, and the woman said to me one day: 'If there's anything you can do to cure him, have pity on me and my children, and I'll give you what you'll ask.' But I said, 'I'll do what I can for you, but I'll take nothing from you, except maybe a grain of tea or a glass of porter, for I wouldn't take money for this, and I refused £2 one time for a cure I did.' So I went and brought back the cure, and I mixed it with flour and made it into three little pills that it couldn't be lost, and gave them to him, and from that time he got well.

"There was a woman lived down the road there, and one day I went into the house when she was after coming from Galway town, and I asked charity of her. And it was in the month of August when the bream fishing was going on, and she said, 'There's no one need be in want now, with fresh fish in the sea and potatoes in the gardens,' and she gave me nothing. But when I was out the door, she said, 'Well, come back here.' And I said, 'If you were to offer me all you brought from Galway I wouldn't take it from you now.'

"And from that time she began to pine and to wear away and to lose her health. And at the end of three years she walked outside her house one day, and when she was two yards from her own threshold she fell on the ground, and the neighbours came and lifted her up on a door and brought her into the house, and she died.

"I think I could have saved her then—I *think* I could. But when I saw her lying there I remembered that day, and I didn't stretch out a hand and I spoke no word.

"I'm going to rise out of the cures and not to do much more of them, for *they* have given me a touch here in the right leg, so that it's the same as dead; and a woman in my village that does cures, she is after being struck with a pain in the hand. Down by the path at the top of the slip, from there to the hill, that is the way they go most nights, hundreds and thousands of them some nights; sleeping in that little cabin of mine I heard them ride past, and I could hear by the feet of the horses that there was a long line of them there."

Of all who have had this gift in recent years in the south-west of Ireland, the most famous was Biddy Early, who had most other fairy gifts likewise. She is dead some twenty years, but her cottage is pointed out at Feakle in Clare. It is a little rough-built cottage by the roadside, and is always full of turf-smoke, like many others of the cottages, but once it was sought out by the sick and the troubled of all the south-west of Ireland. My friend[3] went to Feakle for me a while back, and found it

[3] Yeats's "friend" is almost certainly Lady Gregory. The visit is described in the foreword to the "Seers and Healers" section of *Visions and Beliefs*, vol. I, pp. 35-7.

full of memories of Biddy Early's greatness. Nobody there denies her power, but some of the better off think her power unholy, and one woman says: "It is against our religion to go to fortune-tellers. She did not get her power from God, so it must have been from demons." The poor think better of her, and one man[4] says: "She was as good to the poor as to the rich. Any poor person she'd see passing the road she'd call in and give them a cup of tea or a glass of whisky and bread and all they wanted. She had a big chest within in that room, and it was full of pounds of tea and bottles of wine and of whisky and of claret and all things in the world." "I knew her well," says one, "a nice fresh-looking woman she was. It's to her the people used to be flocking, to the door and even to the window, and if they'd come late in the day they'd have no chance of getting to her, they'd have to take lodgings for the night in the town. She was a great woman. If any of the men that came into the house had a drop too much drink taken, and said an unruly word, she'd turn them out. And if any of them were disputing or fighting or going to law, she'd say, 'Be at one and you can rule the world.' The priests were against her, and used to be taking the cloaks and the baskets from the country people to keep them from going to her." An old pensioner[5] at Kiltartan says: "When I was in the army, whenever a Clare man joined, we were sure to hear of Biddy Early;" and another man[6] says that people came to her "from the whole country round, and from Limerick and Loughrea, and even from England and Wales. She had four or five husbands, and they all died of drink, one after another. They had the temptation, for maybe twenty or thirty people would be there in the day looking for cures, and every one of them would bring a bottle of whisky. Wild cards they were or they wouldn't have married her." Everybody tells of her many husbands, though not always of the same number. A man in Burren says: "She had three husbands; I saw one of them the day I was there, but I knew by the look of him he wouldn't live long." She is believed to have journeyed all over the country with the fairies, and she seems to have first seen and thrown her enchantment on one of the men she married, when on one of these journeys.

A woman near Roxborough says: "There was a Clare woman with me when I went there, and she told me there was a boy from a village near her brought tied in a cart to Biddy Early, and she said: 'If I cure you, will you be willing to marry me;' and he said he would. So she cured him and married him; I saw him there at her house. It might be

---

[4] In Lady Gregory's version this statement is attributed to "The Little Girl of Biddy Early's House", vol. I, pp. 46-7.

[5] In Lady Gregory, the pensioner is "A Blacksmith I met near Tulla", vol. I, pp. 47-8.

[6] The man's name in Lady Gregory's account is "Daniel Curtin", vol. I, p. 41.

that she had the illness put on him first." One man at Feakle seems to think that she had a lover or a husband among "the others" also, for he says: "Surely she was away herself, and as to her son, she brought him with her when she came back, and for eight or nine years he was lying on the bed. And he'd never stir as long as she was in it, but no sooner was she gone away anywhere than he'd be out down the village among the people, and then back again before she'd get to the house." Some, however, say that this boy was not her son but her brother. Most of the country people think she got her knowledge from this boy, though a witch doctor in Clare, whom I have described elsewhere, says that she told him her knowledge came to her from a child she met when she was at service. A woman at Burren says: "He was a little chap that was astray. And one day when he was lying sick in the bed, he said: 'There's a woman in such a house has a hen down in the pot, and if I had the soup of the hen I think it would cure me.' So Biddy Early went to the house, and when she got there, sure enough there was a hen in the pot on the fire. But she was ashamed to tell what she came for, and she let on to have only come for a visit, and so she sat down. But presently in the heat of talking she told what the little chap had said. 'Well,' says the woman, 'take the soup and welcome, and the hen too, if it'll do him any good.' So she brought them with her, and when the boy saw the soup, 'It can't save me,' says he, 'for no earthly thing can do that. But since I see how kind and how willing you are, and did your best for me all these years, I'll leave you a way of living.' And so he did, and taught her the cure. That's what's said at any rate."

But others say that after his death she was always crying and lamenting for the loss of him, and that she had no way of earning her bread, till at last he appeared to her and gave her the gift. One man who was cured by her thinks that she got her knowledge through having been among the fairies herself, and says: "She was away for seven years; she didn't tell it to me, but she told it to others;" and adds, "any how it is certain that when the case was a bad one, she would go into a stable, and there she would meet her people and consult with them." An old man near Coole says: "Biddy Early surely did thousands of cures; out in the stable she used to go, there her friends met her, and they told her all things." Another says: "She used to go out into a field and talk with her friends through the holes in the walls." Many tell, too, of a bottle in which she looked and found out whatever she wanted to know. A young man at Feakle, too young to remember her, says: "The people do be full of stories of all the cures she did. It was by the bottle she did all. She would shake it, and she'd see everything when she looked at it." She would say at once whether the sickness she was asked to cure was a common sickness or one of those mysterious sicknesses the people lay at the door of the fairies. A woman at Kiltartan says: "It's I was with this woman here to Biddy Early. And when she saw me she knew it was for my husband I came, and she looked in her bottle, and said: 'It's nothing put upon him by my people that's wrong with him.' And she bid me give him cold vinegar and some other things—herbs. He got better after. And sometimes she would see in the bottle that the case was beyond her power, and then she would do nothing." An old woman near Feakle says: "I went there but once myself, when my little girl that was married was bad after her second baby being born. I went to the house and told her about it. And she took the bottle and shook it and looked in it, and then she turned and said something to himself (her husband) that I didn't hear, and she just waved her hand to me like that, and bid me go home, and she would take nothing from me. But himself came out and told me that what she was after seeing in the bottle was the face of my little girl and her coffin standing beside her. So I went home, and sure enough on the tenth day after she was dead." Another woman tells a like story, but does not mention the bottle: "Often I heard of Biddy Early, and I know of a little girl was sick, and the brother went to Biddy Early to ask would she get well. And she said: 'They have a place ready for her, it's room for her they have.' So he knew she would die, and so she did."

A woman at Feakle [7] says: "I knew a man went to Biddy Early about his wife, and as soon as she saw him she said, 'On the fourth day a discarded priest will call in and cure your wife.' And so he did, one Father Ford." A woman at Burren [8] says: "I went up to Biddy Early one time with another woman. A fine stout woman she was, sitting straight up in her chair. She looked at me, and she told me my son was worse than what I was, and for myself she bid me to take what I was taking before, and that's dandelions. Five leaves she bid me lay out on the table, with three pinches of salt on the three middle ones. As for my son, she gave me a bottle for him, but he wouldn't take it; and he got better without." One does not know whether this was a common illness, but in most of the stories the illness is from the fairies. Somebody has been "overlooked"—that is, looked at with envy or with unbridled admiration by some one who would not say, or forgot to say, "God bless him," or its like; and because this emotion has given the persons looked at into the power of the fairies, who can only take people "away" "through the eye of a sinner," he has been given "the touch" or "the stroke" that is the definite beginning of their power. I have been told that only those who have been or are themselves "away"—that is, in the world of fairy, a changeling taking their place upon the earth—can

---

[7] In Lady Gregory the woman's name is "Mrs. McDonagh", vol. I, p. 53.
[8] This story is attributed to "An Old Woman" in Lady Gregory, vol. I, p. 55.

cure those who are "away," though many can cure "the touch" or
"the stroke." There are, however, stories of cures that contradict this.
A woman near Gort says: "There was a boy of the Brennans in Gort
was out at Kiltartan thatching Heniff's house. And a woman passed
by, and she looked up at him, but she never said, 'God bless the work.'
And Brennan's mother was on the road to Gort, and the woman met
her, and said, 'Where did your son learn thatching?' And that day he
had a great fall, and was brought home hurt. And the mother went to
Biddy Early, and she said, 'Didn't a red-haired woman meet you one
day going into Gort, and ask where did your son learn thatching; and
didn't she look up at him as she passed? It was then it was done.' And
she gave a bottle, and he got well after a time." "The touch" or "the
stroke" often show themselves by a fall. A red-haired woman is always
unlucky, and a woman near Gort who had told a friend and neighbour
about an old man who lost his hair all at once in a fairy fort after he had
cut down some bushes, says: "The old man here that lost his hair went
to Biddy Early, but he didn't want to go, and we forced him and
persuaded him. And when he got to the house she said, 'It wasn't of
your own free will you came here,' and at the first she wouldn't do
anything for him. And then she said, 'Why did you go to cut down the
phillibine (magpie) bush—that bush you see out of the window?' And
she told him an old woman in the village had overlooked him—Daly's
sister—and she gave him a bottle to sprinkle about her house. I suppose
it was the bush being interfered with she didn't like." Another woman
near Gort says: "There was a man I knew sick, and he sent to Biddy
Early, and she said, 'Was Andy in the house?' And they said he was,
'Well,' says she, 'the next time he comes in ask him his name and his
Christian name three times.' And so they did, and the third time he
turned and went out. And the man got better, but Andy's stock all
went from him, and he never throve from that time."

The asking the name is, no doubt, connected with the belief that if
you know a person's name you have power over him. I have a story of
a Tipperary woman who was tormented by fairies, who were always
trying to get her name from her that they might have power over her.

A woman near Coole[9] says: "It was my son was thatching Heniff's
house when he got the touch, and he came back with a pain in his back
and his shoulders, and took to the bed. And a few nights after that, I
was asleep, and the little girl came and woke me, and said, 'There's
none of us can sleep with all the cars and carriages rattling round the
house.' But, though I woke and heard that said, I fell into a sound sleep
again, and never woke till morning. And one night there came two
taps to the window, one after another, and we all heard it, and no one

[9] In Lady Gregory, the woman's name is "Mrs. Locke", vol. I, pp. 60-1.

there. And at last I sent the other boy to Biddy Early, and he found her in the house; she was then married to her fourth man. And she said he came a day too soon, and would do nothing for him; and he had to walk away in the rain. And the next day he went back, and she said, 'Three days later and you'd have been too late.' And she gave him two bottles; the one he was to bring to boundary water and to fill it up, and that was to be rubbed to the back, and the other was to drink. And the minute he got them he began to get well; and he left the bed, and could walk, but he was always delicate. When he rubbed the back we saw a black mark, like the bite of a dog, and as to his face, it was as white as a sheet. I have the bottle here yet, though it's thirty year ago I got it. She bid the boy to bring whatever was left of it to a river, and to pour it away with the running water. But when he got well I did nothing with it and said nothing about it, and here it is now for you to see, and you the first I ever showed it to. I never let on to Father Curran[10] that I went to her, but one time the bishop came. I knew he was a rough man, and I went to him and made a confession, and I said, 'Do what you like with me, but I'd walk the world for my son when he was sick.' And all he said was, 'I wouldn't have wondered if your messenger had had the two feet cut off from him.' And he said no more."

An old man near Coole says: "I got cured by her myself one time. Look at this thumb. I got it hurted, and I went out into the field after, and was ploughing all the day, I was that greedy for work. And when I went in, I had to lie on the bed with the pain of it, and it swelled, and the arm with it, to the size of a horse's thigh. I stopped two or three days in the bed, and then my wife went to see Biddy Early; and she came home; and the next day it burst, and you never saw anything like all the stuff that came away from it. A good bit after I went to her myself, where it wasn't quite healed, and she said, 'You'd have lost it altogether if your wife hadn't been so quick to come.' She brought me into a small room, and said good words and sprinkled water from a bottle, and told me to believe. The priests were against her, but they were wrong. How could that be evil doing that was all charity and kindness and healing? She was a decent-looking woman, no different from any other woman of the country. The boy she was married to at the time was lying on the bed drunk. There were side cars and common cars and gentry and country people at the door, just like Gort market, and dinner for all that came. And every one would bring her something, but she didn't care what it was. Rich farmers would bring her the whole side of a pig. Myself I brought a bottle of whisky and a shilling's worth of bread, and a quarter of sugar, and a quarter pound of tea. She was very rich, for there wasn't a farmer but would give her the grass of a

[10] In Lady Gregory the priest's name is "Folan".

couple of bullocks or a filly—she had the full of a field of fillies if they'd all been gathered together.

"She died a good many years ago. I didn't go to the wake myself, but I heard that her death was natural."

A well-to-do man near Kilchriest[11] says: "It was all you could do to get to Biddy Early with your skin whole, the priests were so set against her. I went to her one time myself, and it was hard when you got near to know the way, for all the people were afraid to tell it.

"It was about a little chap of my own I went, that some strange thing had been put upon. When I got to her house there were about fifty to be attended to before me, and when my turn came, she looked in her bottle, a sort of a common greenish one that seemed to have nothing in it, and she told me where I came from, and the shape of the house and the appearance of it, and of the little lake you see there, and everything round about. And she told me of a limekiln that was near, and then she said the harm that came to him came from the forth beyond that. And I never knew of there being a forth there; but after I came home I went to look, and there, sure enough, it was.

"And she told me how it had come on him, and bid me remember a day that a certain gentleman stopped and spoke to me when I was out working in the hayfield, and the child with me playing about. And I remembered it well; it was old John Lydon, of Carrig,[12] that was riding past, and stopped and talked, and was praising the child. And it was close by that forth beyond that John Lydon was born.

"I remembered it was soon after that day that the mother and I went to Loughrea, and when we came back the child had slipped on the threshold of the house and got a fall, and he was screeching and calling out that his knee was hurt, and from that time he did no good, and pined away and had the pain in his knee always.

"And Biddy Early said: 'While you're talking to me now the child lies dying.' And that was at twelve o'clock in the day. And she made up a bottle for me, herbs, I believe, it was made of, and she said, 'Take care of it going home, and whatever may happen, don't drop it,' and she wrapped it in all the folds of my handkerchief. So when I was coming home and got near Tillyra, I heard voices, and the man that was with me said, 'Did you see all the people beyond the wall?' And I saw nothing, but I kept a tight hold on the bottle. And when we got to the Roxborough gate, there were many people talking and coming to where we were. I could hear them and see them, and so could the man that was with me; but when I heard them I remembered what she had said, and

[11] In Lady Gregory, the following two stories, on pp. 177–78, are attributed to Daniel Shea, vol. I, pp. 55–8.

[12] In Lady Gregory, he is "old James Hill of Creen".

I took the bottle in my two hands and held it, and so I brought it home safely. And when I got home they told me the child was worse, and that at twelve o'clock the day before he lay, as they thought, dying. And when I brought in the bottle to him he pulled the bed-clothes up over his head, and we had the work of the world to make him swallow it. But from the time he took it the pain in his knee left him and he began to get better. And Biddy Early had told me not to let May Day pass without coming to her again when she gave me the bottle. But seeing him so well, I thought it no use to go again, and he got bad again, and it was not on May Day, but was in the month of May he died. He took to the bed before that, and he'd be always calling to me to come inside the bed where he was, and if I went in he'd hardly let me go. But I got afraid, and I didn't like to be too much with him.

"He was not eight years old when he died, but Mark Spelman,[13] that used to live beyond there at that time, told me privately that when I'd be out of the house and he'd come in, the little chap would ask for the pipe and smoke it, but he'd never let me see him doing it. And queer chat he had, and he was old-fashioned in all his ways." The child was evidently "away," and a changeling believed to have taken his place. May Day, Midsummer Day, and November Eve, which are old Celtic festivals, are thought times of great activity among the fairies, and that is why he was to bring the child to Biddy Early before May Day. One story tells how she offered to show a mother the child the fairies had taken from her and whom she thought dead. A woman from Kiltartan[14] says: "My mother got crippled in her bed one night, God save the hearers! And it was a long time before she could walk again with the pain in her back, and my father was always telling her to go to Biddy Early, and so at last she went. But she would do nothing for her, for, she said, 'What ails you is nothing to do with my business.' And she said, 'You have lost three, and one was a grand little fair-haired one, and if you'd like to see her again I'll show her to you.' And when she said that, my mother had no courage to look and to see the child she lost, but fainted then and there. And then she said, 'There's a field with corn beyond your house, and a field with hay, and it's not long since the little fellow that wears a Lanberis cap fell asleep there on a cock of hay. And before the stooks of corn are in stacks he'll be taken from you, but I'll save him if I can. And it was true enough what she said; my little brother that was wearing a Lanberis cap had gone to the field and fallen asleep on the hay a few days before. But no harm happened him, and he's all the brother I have living now. And it was Bruen from Gort went with my mother where his sister was sick. And she turned to

---

[13] In Lady Gregory, Mark Spelman is "Ned Cahel".
[14] The following story is attributed to "Mrs. Dillon" in Lady Gregory, vol. I, pp. 59-60.

him and she said, 'When you get home, the coffin will be level with the door before you.' And sure enough when he got home the sister had died, and the coffin had been brought and left at the door.''

The people always believed, I think, that whenever she saved anyone the fairies were trying to take, somebody or something was taken instead. She would sometimes ask people who came to her if they were ready to pay the penalty, and there is a story of one man who refused to lose a cow to save the wife he had come about, and when he got home she was dead before him. A well-to-do farmer near Gort, says, however: —"It was Donovan gave his life for my sister that was his wife. When she fell sick he said he'd go to an old woman, one Biddy Early, that lived in the mountains beyond, and that did a great deal of cures, but the priests didn't like any one to be going to her. So he brought her there and she cured her the first time, but she says, 'If you bring her again you'll pay the penalty.'

"But when she fell sick again, he brought her the second time, but he stopped a mile from the house himself. But she knew it well and told the wife where he was, but she cured her, and that time the horse died. And the third time she fell sick he went again, knowing full well he'd pay the penalty. And so he did and died. But she married again, one O'Mara, and lives over there towards Kinvara.''

A cow or a horse or a fowl was generally sufficient. A man at Corcomroe says: "Did I ever hear of Biddy Early? There's not a man in this country side over forty years of age that hasn't been with her some time or other.

"There's a man living in that house over there was sick one time, and he went to her and she cured him, but, says she, 'You'll have to lose something, and whatever it is, don't fret after it.' So he had a grey mare and she was going to foal, and one morning when he went out he saw that the foal was born and was lying by the side of the wall. So he remembered what she had said to him, and he didn't fret." Sometimes, however, the people believed that many lives were given instead of one. A man at Burren whom she cured says: "I didn't lose anything at the time, but sometimes I thought afterwards it came on my family, when I lost so many of my children. A grand stout girl went from me, stout and broad, what else would ail her to go?"

One often hears of the difficulty of bringing the bottle Biddy Early gave safe home, because of the endeavours of the fairies to break it. A man near Gort says: "Sometimes she'd give a bottle of some cure to people that came, but if she'd say to them, you'll never bring it home, break it they must on the way back with all the care they'd take of it."

A man near Gort says: "There was a boy I knew went to Biddy Early and she gave him a bottle, and she told him it would cure him if he did not lose it in the crossing of some road. And when he came to that place, for all he could do, the bottle was broke."

A woman in Burren says: "Himself went one time to Biddy Early, for his uncle Donoghue that was sick, and he found her, and her fingers all covered with gold rings, and she gave him a bottle, and she said, 'Go into no house on the way home, or stop nowhere, or you'll lose it.'

"But going home he had a thirst on him, and he came to a public-house, and he wouldn't go in, but he stopped and bid the boy bring him a drink. But a little farther on the road the horse got a fall and the bottle was broke."

And one story implies that the bottle was likely to be broken if you went "too late." A man from between Gort and Kiltartan says: "Biddy Early didn't like you to go too late. Brien's sister was sick a long time, and when the brother went to her at the last she gave him a bottle with a cure. But on the way home the bottle broke, and the car and the horse got a fright and ran away. And when Dr. Nolan was sent for to see her, he was led astray, and it's beyond Ballylee he found himself. And surely she was *taken* if ever any one was."

Her "second sight" seems to have been even more remarkable than her cures, and every one who ever went to her speaks of it with wonder. A very old woman in Kiltartan[15] says: "I went to Biddy Early one time myself, about my little boy that's now in America, that was lying sick in the house. But on the way to her I met a sergeant of police, and he asked where I was going, and when I told him, to joke like he said, 'Biddy Early's after dying.' 'Then the devil die with her,' said I. Well, when I got to the house, what do you think, if she didn't know that, and what I said. And she was vexed, and at the first she would do nothing for me. I had a pound for her here in my bosom, but when I held it out she wouldn't take it, but she turned the rings on her fingers, for she had a ring for every one, and she said, 'A shilling for one, sixpence for another.' But all she told me was that the boy was nervous, and so he was, she was right in that, and that he'd get well, and so he did.

"There was a man beyond, one Coen, was walking near the gate the same day, and he turned his foot and hurt it, and she knew that. She told me she slept in Ballylee Mill last night, and that there was a cure for all things in the world between the two wheels there."

The witch doctor Kerwin says that "the cure for all ills" was the moss on the stones, but that it cured evils done by the fairies and not common evils. When Biddy Early spoke of sleeping in Ballylee Mill, which is a great many miles from Feakle, she meant that she had been "away" the night before and journeyed about where she would. A

---

[15] In Lady Gregory, the following story is attributed to "The Spinning Woman", vol. I, pp. 51–2.

woman near Derrykeil in the Slieve Echtge hills, says: "I went to her myself one time to get a cure for myself where I was hurt with a fall I got coming down that hill over there. And she gave me what cured me, and she told me all about the whole place, and that there was a bowl broken in the house, and so there was." A fall is often believed to be the work of the fairies. A woman at Tillyra says: "There was a boy of the Saggartons in the house beyond went to Biddy Early, and she told him the name of the girl he would marry, and he did marry her after. And she cured him of a weakness he had and cured many, but it was seldom the bottle she'd give could be brought home without being spilled. I wonder did she go to *them* when she died? She got the cure among them any-way."

A woman in Gort says: "There was a man went to Biddy Early, and she told him that the woman he'd marry would have her husband killed by her brother. And it happened, for the woman he married was sitting by the fire with her husband and the brother came in having a drop of drink taken, and threw a pint pot at him that hit him in the head and killed him. It was the man that married her that told me this. One time she called in a man that was passing, and gave him a glass of whisky, and then she said to him, 'The road you were going home by, don't go by it.' So he asked why not, and she took the bottle, a long shaped bottle it was, and looked at it, holding it up, and then she bid him look through it and he'd see what would happen. But her husband said: 'Don't show it to him, it might give him a fright he wouldn't get over.' So she only said: 'Well, go home by another way,' and so he did and got home safe, for in the bottle she had seen a party of men that wouldn't have let him pass alive.

"She got the rites of the Church when she died, but first she was made to break the bottle."

A man at Corcomroe says: "There was a man, one Flaherty, came to his brother-in-law's house one day to borrow a horse. And the next day the horse was sent back, but he didn't come himself. And after a few days more they went to ask for him, but he had never come back at all. So the brother-in-law came to Biddy Early's. And she and some others were drinking whisky, and they were sorry that they were at the bottom of the bottle. And she said, 'That's no matter; there's a man on his way now, there soon will be more.' And sure enough there was; for he brought a bottle with him. So when he came in he told her about Flaherty having disappeared. And she described to him a corner of a garden at the back of a house, and she said, 'Go look for him there and you'll find him.' And so they did, dead and buried."

"Another time a man's cattle was dying, and he went to her and she said: 'Is there such a place as Benburb?' naming a forth up on the hill

beyond there, 'for it's there they're gone.' And sure enough it was toward that forth they were straying before they died." The cattle were
in Benburb "forth" or rath, for cattle are taken by the fairies as often as
are women.

She was consulted about all kinds of things, for she knew all fairy
things. A man at Doneraile, co. Cork, tells how a man asked her to
help him to find a buried treasure, but the story is vague, and he did
not know the name of the man. He indeed knows much about her, but
it is all vague, and he thinks that she is still living. He says: "A man
dreamed there was treasure in a certain 'forth,' and he went to her and
asked what he should do. She said it must not be more than four that
would dig for it. He and she and two others went, and they dug until
they came to the lid of a big earthen pot, and she killed a black cock. A
thing like a big ox came at them, and she said it was no use and that
they must go home, because five and not four had come. They found a
man watching behind the ditch, and they beat him before they went
home. The next day the hole they had dug was filled up."

The priests tried vainly to keep the people from going to her.

An old man on the beach at Duras says: "The priests were greatly
against Biddy Early, and there's no doubt at all it was from the fairies
she got her knowledge. But who wouldn't go to hell for a cure when
one of his own is sick?"

An old woman at Feakle[16] says: "There was a man I knew, living
near the sea, and he set out to go to her at one time. And on the way
he went into his brother-in-law's house, and a priest came in there and
bid him not to go. 'Well, Father,' says he, 'cure me yourself if you won't
let me go to her to be cured.' And when the priest wouldn't do that, he
said: 'Go on I will,' and he went to her. And the minute he came in:
'Well,' says she, 'you made a great fight for me on the way.' For though
it's against our creed to believe it, she could hear every earthly thing
that was said in every part, miles off. But she had two red eyes, and some
used to say, 'If she can cure so much, why can't she cure her own
eyes?' "

When she spoke of the red eyes, an old man who was listening said:
"She had no red eyes, but was a nice clean-looking woman. Any one
might have red eyes at a time they'd have a cold, or the like"; this man
had been to see her. A woman at Burren says: "There was one Casey,
in Kinvara, and he went to her one time for a cure. And Father Xavier
came to the house and was mad with him for going, and, says he, 'You
take the cure out of the hand of God.' And Mrs. Casey said, 'Your
reverence, none of us can do that.' 'Well,' says Father Xavier, 'then I'll

---

[16] This story is attributed to "Bartley Coen" in Lady Gregory, vol. I, p. 44. Coen is
mentioned on p. 180 of this article.

see what the devil can do, and I'll send my horse to-morrow that has a sore on his leg this long time, and try will she be able to cure him.'

"So next day he sent a man with his horse, and when he got to Biddy Early's house she came out, and she told him every word Father Xavier had said, and she cured the sore. So after that he left the people alone. But before it he'd be dressed in a frieze coat, and a whip in his hand, driving away the people from going to her."

A woman near Coole[17] says: "The priests took the bottle from Biddy Early before she died, and they found some sort of black things in it." The bottle was of course merely a bottle of some kind of liquid in which she looked as "crystal gazers" look into their crystals. She was surrounded all her life by a great deal of terror and reverence, but perhaps the terror was the greatest. She seems to have known how greatly she was feared, for a man who lived by the roadside near Tillyra says: "I was with her myself one time and got a cure from her for my little girl that was sick. A bottle of whisky I brought her, and the first thing she did was to give me a glass out of it, 'For,' says she, 'you'll maybe want it, my poor man.' But I had plenty of courage in those days."

A little while ago I met in Dublin a young man not at all of the people, and he told me that an uncle of his had once been her landlord, but had evicted her because of the scandal of seeing such great crowds drawn to her by what he held superstition, or diabolical power, I am not sure which. She cursed him, and in a very little time a house he was visiting at was burned to the ground and he was burned to death.

The "knowledgeable" men and women may leave their knowledge to some one before they die, but few believe that Biddy Early left her knowledge to any one. One woman said to my friend, "It's said that at a hurling the other day, there was a small little man seen, and that he was a friend of hers, and that she had left him the gift;" but the woman's husband said "No; the bottle was broken, and, anyhow, she had no power to pass it on; it was given to her for the term of her life."

W. B. Yeats

[17] In Lady Gregory, the woman is "Mrs. McDonagh", vol. I, p. 53.

# The Literary Movement in Ireland

On April 27, 1899, Yeats wrote to Lady Gregory that he had accepted a commission of £30 "to do an article . . . on The Intellectual Movement in Ireland for the *North American Review*" (*Letters*, p. 318). The result, "The Literary Movement in Ireland", in the issue for December, 1899, is an extended statement of the major sources of inspiration of the movement. A revised version was included by Lady Gregory—along with essays by A.E., D. P. Moran, George Moore, Douglas Hyde, and Standish O'Grady—in her *Ideals in Ireland* (1901). The present text is the revised version, with the major variations of the earlier version given in notes. Most of Yeats's changes have the effect of qualifying his earlier assertions or placing his ideas in a less immediate and narrow chronology. Also, the second version quotes less from Douglas Hyde and more from Lady Gregory, in anticipation, perhaps, of the appearance of her collection of translations, *Poets and Dreamers*.

For Yeats's other contribution to *Ideals in Ireland*, a "Postscript", see p. 244 below.

I HAVE just come to a quiet Connaught house from seeing a little movement, in a great movement[1] of thought which is fashioning[2] the dreams of the next generation in Ireland, grow to a sudden maturity. Certain plays, which are an expression of the most characteristic ideals of what is sometimes called the "Celtic movement," have been acted in Dublin before audiences drawn from all classes and all political sections, and described at great length in every Nationalist newspaper.[3] Whatever be the merit of these plays, and that must be left to the judgment of time, their success means, as I think, that the "Celtic movement," which has hitherto interested but a few cultivated people, is about to become a part of the thought of Ireland.

Before 1891, Unionists and Nationalists were too busy keeping one or two simple beliefs at their fullest intensity for any complexity of thought or emotion; and the national imagination uttered itself, with a somewhat broken[4] energy, in a few stories and in many ballads about the need of unity against England, about the martyrs who had died at the hand of England, or about the greatness of Ireland before the coming of England. They built up Ireland's dream of Ireland, of an ideal

---

[1] *N.A.R.* reads "a movement" instead of "a little movement, in a great movement . . . .

[2] For "is fashioning" *N.A.R.* reads "may do much to fashion".

[3] *N.A.R.* continued this sentence with the clause, "that the people in the cottages here in this quiet place are talking about them over the fire".

[4] broken: *N.A.R.* reads "uncertain".

country weighed down by immemorial sorrows and served by heroes and saints, and they taught generations of young men to love their country with a love that was the deepest emotion they were ever to know; but they built with the virtues and beauties and sorrows and hopes that would move to tears the greatest number of those eyes before whom the modern world is but beginning to unroll itself; and, except when some rare, personal impulse shaped the song according to its will, they built to the formal and conventional rhythm which would give the most immediate pleasure to ears that had forgotten Gaelic poetry and not learned[5] the subtleties of English poetry. The writers who made this literature or who shaped its ideals, in the years before the great famine, lived at the moment when the middle class had brought to perfection its ideal of the good citizen, and of a politics and a philosophy and a literature which would help him upon his way; and they made a literature full of the civic virtues and, in all but its unbounded patriotism, without inconvenient ardours. They took their style from Scott and Campbell and Macaulay, and that "universally popular" poetry which is really the poetry of the middle class, and from Beranger[6] and that "peasant poetry" which looks for its models to the Burns of "Highland Mary" and "The Cottar's [sic] Saturday Night." Here and there a poet or a story-writer found an older dream among the common people or in his own mind, and made a personality for himself,[7] and was forgotten; for it was the desire of everybody to be moved by the same emotions as everybody else, and certainly one cannot blame a desire which has thrown so great a shadow of self-sacrifice.

The fall of Parnell and the wreck of his party and of the organisations that supported it were the symbols, if not the causes, of a sudden change. They were followed by movements and organisations that brought the ideas and the ideals which are the expression of personalities[8] alike into politics, economics, and literature. Those who looked for the old energies, which were the utterance of the common will and hope, were unable to see that a new kind of Ireland, as full of energy as a boiling pot, was rising up amid the wreck of the old kind, and that

[5] N.A.R. reads "to ears that have forgotten Gaelic poetry, and have not yet learned . . .".

[6] Pierre-Jean Béranger (1780–1857) was regarded during his lifetime to be the national poet of France.

[7] In N.A.R. this passage reads to the end of the paragraph as follows: ". . . and got shoved away and forgotten; for everybody wanted to be moved by the same emotions as everybody else; and nobody who understands how much self-sacrifice is the shadow of their desire will blame it".

[8] N.A.R. version reads to the end of the sentence: "into Irish political, economic and literary interests".

the national life was finding a new utterance. This utterance was so necessary that it seems as if[9] the hand that broke the ball of glass, that now lies in fragments full of a new iridescent life, obeyed some impulse from beyond its wild and capricious will. More books about Irish subjects have been published in these last eight years than in the thirty years that went before them, and these books have the care for scholarship and the precision of speech which had been notoriously lacking in books on Irish subjects. An appeal to the will, a habit of thought which measures all beliefs by their intensity, is content with a strenuous rhetoric; but an appeal to the intellect needs an always more perfect knowledge, an always more malleable speech. The new writers and the new organisations they work through—for organisations of various kinds take the place held by the critical press in other countries—have awakened Irish affections among many from whom the old rhetoric could never have got a hearing, but they have been decried for weakening the national faith by lovers of the old rhetoric. I have seen an obscure Irish member of Parliament rise at one of those monthly meetings of the Irish Literary Society, when the members of the society read sometimes[10] their poems to one another, and ask their leave to read a poem. He did not belong to the society, but leave was given him, and he read a poem in the old manner, blaming the new critics and praising the old poems which had made him patriotic and filled his imagination with the images of the martyrs, and, as he numbered over their names, Wolfe Tone, Emmet, Owen Roe, Sarsfield,[11] his voice shook, and many were angry with the new critics.

The organisations that are making this change are the Irish Literary Society in London, the National Literary Society in Dublin, which has founded,[12] or rather sheltered with its influence, the Irish Literary Theatre, and the Feis Ceoil Committee in Dublin, at whose annual series of concerts of Irish music, singers and pipers from all parts of Ireland compete; and more important than all,[13] the Gaelic League, which has worked for the revival of the Gaelic language with such success that it has sold fifty thousand of its Gaelic text-books in a year. All these organisations have been founded since the fall of Parnell; and all are busy in preserving, or in moulding anew and without any thought of the politics of the hour, some utterance of the national life,

[9] In the *N.A.R.* version this sentence begins at this point with the phrase, "May be, the hand . . .".

[10] The *N.A.R.* version had no "sometimes".

[11] Owen Roe O'Neill (*c.* 1590–1649) commanded the Ulster forces which fought Cromwell. Patrick Sarsfield (?–1693), an Irish Jacobite nobleman and soldier, died in the service of the King of France.

[12] The *N.A.R.* version read "which has just founded", and lacked the following "or rather sheltered with its influence . . .".

[13] The phrase "more important than all" was not in the earlier *N.A.R.* version.

and in opposing the vulgar books and[14] vulgarer songs that come to us from England. We are preparing, as we hope,[15] for a day when Ireland will speak in Gaelic, as much as Wales speaks in Welsh, within her borders, but speak, it may be, in English to other nations of those truths which were committed to her when "He set the borders of the nations according to His angels";[16] as Dionysius the Areopagite[17] has written. Already, as I think,[18] a new kind of romance, a new element in thought, is being moulded out of Irish life and traditions, and this element may have an importance for criticism, even should criticism forget the writers who are trying to embody it in their work, while looking each one through his own colour in the dome of many-coloured glass.

Contemporary English literature takes delight in praising England and her Empire, the master-work and dream of the middle class; and, though it may escape from this delight, it must long continue to utter the ideals of the strong and wealthy. Irish intellect has always been preoccupied with the weak and with the poor, and now it has begun to collect and describe their music and stories, and to utter anew the beliefs and hopes which they alone remember. It may never make a literature preoccupied with the circumstance of their lives, like the "peasant poetry," whose half deliberate triviality, passionless virtue, and passionless vice has helped so many orderly lives; for a writer who wishes to write with his whole mind must knead the beliefs and hopes, which he has made his own, with the circumstance of his own life. Burns had this preoccupation, and nobody will deny that he was a great poet; but even he had the poverty of emotions and ideas of a peasantry that had lost, like the middle class into which it would have its children absorbed, the imagination that is in tradition without finding the imagination that is in books. Irish literature may prolong its

---

[14] In the *N.A.R.* version this sentence ends, "and the music-hall songs, that keep pouring in from England".

[15] In the *N.A.R.* version this sentence begins: "All but the Gaelic league, which considers language and nationality inseparable, use the English language, preparing, as some think, . . .".

[16] In the *N.A.R.* version, no source is given for the quotation and the sentence ends, ". . . and, as it seems, believing that the use of English, now it has become the language of so different countries, need no more make Irishmen think like Englishmen than did the use of Latin make the lettered classes of the Middle Ages think like Romans".

[17] A passage in the *Celestial Hierarchy*, one of four treatises attributed to the unknown mystical theologian who claimed to be St. Paul's Athenian convert, Dionysius (*fl.* 500), explains the establishment of a guardian angel over each nation. For Yeats's other uses of this quotation, see *Uncollected Prose*, vol. I, pp. 297, 367, and p. 199 below.

*The Hierarchies of Dionysius Areopagite*, usually now called the "Pseudo-Areopagite", were translated into English by J. Parker in 1894.

[18] In the *N.A.R.* version, this sentence begins, "But this is a dispute which concerns us principally; for what concerns others is that a new kind of romance . . .".

first inspiration without renouncing the complexity of ideas and emotions which is the inheritance of cultivated men, for it will have learned from the discoveries of modern learning that the common people, wherever civilization has not driven its plough too deep, keep a watch over the roots of all religion and all romance. Their poetry trembles upon the verge of incoherence with a passion all but unknown among modern poets, and their sense of beauty exhausts itself in countless legends and in metaphors that seem to mirror the energies of nature.

Dr. Hyde has collected many old Irish peasant love-songs, and, like all primitive poetry, they foreshadow a poetry[19] whose intensity of emotion, or strangeness of language, has made it the poetry of little coteries. His peasant lover cries—[20]

*It is happy for you, O blind man, who do not see much of women.*
*O! if you were to see what I see, you would be sick even as I am.*
*It is a pity, O God, that it was not blind I was before I saw her twisted hair.*
*I always thought the blind were pitiable, until my calamity grew beyond the grief of all,*
*Then though it is a pity I turned my pity into envy.*
*In a loop of the loops in a loop am I.*
*It is sorrow for whoever has seen her, and it is sorrow for him who does not see her every day.*
*It is sorrow for him who is tied in the knot of her love, and it is sorrow for him who is loosed out of it.*
*It is sorrow for him who is near her, and it is sorrow for him who is not near her.*

Or he cries—

*O Maurya! you are my love, and the love of my heart is your love—*
*Love that is without littleness, without weakness,*
*Love from age till death,*
*Love growing out of folly,*
*Love that will send me close beneath the clay,*
*Love without a hope of the world,*
*Love without envy of fortune,*
*Love that has left me withered in captivity,*
*Love of my heart beyond women;*
*And a love such as that, it is seldom to be got from any man.*

[19] The *N.A.R.* version of this sentence reads up to this point, "Dr. Hyde has collected much old Irish peasant love-poetry, and, like all primitive poetry, it foreshadows the unmeasured emotion, the ideal passion, of poetry . . .".

[20] This poem, "Happy It Is", was translated in Hyde's *Love Songs of Connacht* in a version in the original meter. The text quoted by Yeats is an adaptation of the literal translation given in Hyde's footnote to his verse version (pp. 131–2 of 1893 edition of *Love Songs*).

The next poem, "O Maurya", is also an adaptation of the version given by Hyde in a footnote to his verse version (p. 83 of *Love Songs*). Yeats reviewed *Love Songs of Connacht* in *The Bookman*, October, 1893 (see *Uncollected Prose*, vol. I, pp. 292–5).

[21]And Lady Gregory has translated a lament, that Raftery[22] the wandering fiddler made for a fiddler some sixty years ago, into the simple English of the country people of to-day—

*The swans on the water are nine times blacker than a blackberry, since the man died from us that had pleasantness on the top of his fingers;*
*His two grey eyes were like the dew of the morning that lies on the grass;*
*And since he was laid in the grave, the cold is getting the upper hand.*
*There are young women, and not without reason, sorry and heartbroken and withered, since he was left at the church;*
*Their hair, thrown down and hanging, turned grey on their head.*
*No flower in any garden, and the leaves of the trees have leave to cry, and they falling on the ground;*
*There are no green flowers on the tops of the tufts since there did a boarded coffin go on Daly.*

All are not like this, but the most inspired and, as I think, the most characteristic are like this. There is a square stone tower called Ballylee Castle, a couple of miles from where I am writing. A farmer called Hynes, who had a beautiful daughter, Mary Hynes, lived near it some sixty years ago; and all over the countryside[23] old men and old women still talk of her beauty,[24] and the young and old praise her with a song made by Raftery—

*O star of light, and O sun in harvest,*
*O amber hair, O my share of the world;*
*There is no good to deny it or to try and hide it,*
*She is the sun in the heavens who wounded my heart.*

*There was no part of Ireland I did not travel,*
*From the rivers to the tops of the mountains,*
*To the edge of Lough Greine, whose mouth is hidden,*
*And I saw no beauty but was behind hers.*

*It is Mary Hynes, the calm and easy woman,*
*Has beauty in her mind and in her face;*
*If a hundred clerks were gathered together*
*They could not write down a half of her ways.*[25]

[21] At this point in the *N.A.R.* version Yeats quoted Hyde's translation of "My love, O, she is my love" and did not quote the poem translated by Lady Gregory ("The swans on the water, *etc.*") which appears in the *Ideals in Ireland* version.
[22] For Yeats's interest in Anthony Raftery, the blind poet, see p. 239 below. The translation by Lady Gregory which follows is given in another version in her *Poets and Dreamers* (pp. 32–3). Yeats quotes it in part in his review of that volume (see p. 302 below).
[23] In the *N.A.R.* version, at this point a phrase was interpolated, ". . ., songs are still sung in her honor, and old men . . .".
[24] In the *N.A.R.* version, the sentence ends here and Lady Gregory's translation is not quoted.
[25] A different version of this poem appears in *Poets and Dreamers* (p. 25).

This song, though[26] Gaelic poetry has fallen from its old greatness, has come out of the same dreams as the songs and legends, as vague, it may be, as the clouds of evening and of dawn, that became in Homer's mind the memory and the prophecy of all the sorrows that have beset and shall beset the journey of beauty in the world. A very old woman who remembers Mary Hynes said to me, and to a friend who was with me: "I never saw one so handsome as she was, and I never will until I die. There were people coming from all parts to look at her, and maybe some of them forgot to say, 'God bless her.'* Any way she was young when she died, and my mother was at her funeral, and as to whether she was taken, well, there's others have been taken that were not handsome at all, and so it's likely enough she might have been, for there is no one to be seen at all that is handsome like she was." The spirit of Helen moves indeed among the legends that are told about turf-fires, and among the legends of the poor and simple everywhere. A friend of mine was told a while ago, in a remote part of Donegal, of a young man who saw a light before him on the road, and found when he came near that it was from a lock of hair in an open box. The hair was so bright that, when he went into the stable where he slept, he put the box into a hole in the wall and had no need of a candle. After many wanderings he found her from whose head it had been taken, and after many adventures married her and reigned over a kingdom.

The peasant remembers such songs and legends, all the more, it may be, because he has thought of little but cows and sheep and the like in his own marriage, for his dream has never been entangled by reality. The beauty of women is mirrored in his mind, as the excitement of the world is mirrored in the minds of children, and like them he thinks nothing but the best worth remembering. The child William Blake said to somebody who had told him of a fine city, that he thought no city fine that had not walls of gold and silver.[28] It may be that poetry is the utterance of desires that we can only satisfy in dreams, and that if all our dreams were satisfied there would be no more poetry. Dreams pass from us with childhood, because we are so often told they can never come true, and because we are taught with so much labour to admire the paler beauty of the world. The children of the poor and simple learn

---

* They should have said, "God bless her," so that their admiration might not give the fairies power over her.[27]

[26] In the *N.A.R.* version, this sentence begins, "The songs are not very good for Gaelic poetry has fallen from its old greatness, but they come . . .".

[27] [Yeats's note.]

[28] "One day, a traveller was telling bright wonders of some foreign city. 'Do you call *that* splendid?' broke in young Blake; 'I should call a city splendid in which the houses were of gold, the pavement of silver, the gates ornamented with precious stones!'" (Alexander Gilchrist, *Life of William Blake*, London, 1893, vol. I, p. 7.)

from their unbroken religious faith, and from their traditional beliefs, and from the hardness of their lives, that this world is nothing, and that a spiritual world, where all dreams come true, is everything; and therefore the poor and simple are that imperfection whose perfection is genius.

The most of us think that all things, when imagined in their perfection, that all images which emotion desires in its intensity, are among the things nobody has ever seen or shall ever see; and so we are always reminding one another not to go too far from the moderation of reality. But the Irish peasant believes that the utmost he can dream was once or still is a reality by his own door. He will point to some mountain and tell you that some famous hero or beauty lived and sorrowed there, or he will tell you that Tir-nan-og, the country of the young, the old Celtic paradise,—the Land of the Living Heart, as it used to be called,—is all about him. An old woman close by Ballylee Castle said to a friend of mine the other day, when someone had finished a story of the poet Usheen's return from Tir-nan-og, where he had lived with his fairy mistress: "Tir-nan-og? That place is not far from us. One time I was in the chapel of Labane, and there was a tall thin man sitting next to me, and he dressed in grey; and after the mass I asked him where he came from. 'From Tir-nan-og.' he said. 'And where is that?' I asked him. 'It's not far from you,' he said. 'It's near the place where you live.' I remember well the look of him, and he telling me that. The priest was looking at us while we were talking together."

There are many grotesque things near at hand, the dead doing their penance in strange shapes, and evil spirits with terrible and ugly shapes, but people of a perfect beauty are never far off; and this beauty is often, I know not how often, that heroic beauty "which changes least from youth to age," and which has faded from modern painting and poetry before a fleeting voluptuous beauty. One old Mayo woman, who can neither read nor write, described it to me, though with grotesque comparisons. She has been long in service, and her language has not the simplicity of those who live among fields. She was standing in the window of her master's house looking out toward a mountain where Queen Maeve, the Queen of the Western Spirits, is said to have been buried, when she saw "the finest woman she ever saw" travelling right across from the mountain and straight to her. The woman had a sword by her side and a dagger lifted up in her hand, and was dressed in white, with bare arms and feet. She looked "very strong and warry and fierce, but not wicked"; that is, not cruel, at all. The old woman had seen the Irish giant, and "though he was a fine man, he was nothing to this woman, for he was round, and could not have stepped out so soldierly." She told me that she was like a certain[29] stately lady of the neighbour-

[29] The *N.A.R.* version reads up to this point, "She was like Mrs. ——, naming a . . .".

hood, "but she had no stomach on her, and was slight and broad in the shoulders, and was handsomer than anyone you ever saw now; she looked about thirty." The old woman covered her eyes with her hands, and when she uncovered them the apparition had vanished. The neighbours were "wild" with her for not waiting to see if there was a message, for they are sure it was Queen Maeve, who often shows herself to the pilots. I asked the old woman if she had seen others like Queen Maeve, and she said: "Some of them have their hair down, but they look quite different, like the sleepy-looking ladies you see in the papers. Those with their hair up are like this one. The others have long white dresses, but those with their hair up have short dresses, so that you can see their legs right up to the calf." After some careful questioning I found that they wore what appeared to be buskins. She went on: "They are fine and dashing-looking, like the men one sees riding their horses in twos and threes on the slopes of the mountains, with their swords swinging." She repeated over and over: "There is no such race living now, none so fine proportioned," or the like, and then said: "The present queen is a nice, pleasant-looking woman, but she is not like her. What makes me think so little of the ladies is that I see none as they be," meaning the spirits; "when I think of her and of the ladies now, they are like little children running about, without being able to put their clothes on right. Is it the ladies? Why, I would not call them women at all!"

There are many old heroical tales about Queen Maeve, and before she was a queen she was a goddess and had her temples, and she is still the most beautiful of the beautiful. A young man among the Burren Hills of Clare told me, a couple of years ago, that he remembered an old poet who had made his poems in Irish, and had met in his youth one who had called herself Queen Maeve, and asked him if he would have money or pleasure. He said he would have pleasure, and she gave him her love for a time, and then went from him and ever after he was very sad. The young man had often heard him sing a lamentation he had made, but could only remember that it was "very mournful," and called her "Beauty of all Beauty."[30] The song may have been but a resinging of a traditional theme, but the young man believed it.

Many, perhaps most, of those that I have talked with of these things have all their earthly senses, but those who have most knowledge of these things, so much indeed that they are permitted, it is thought, to speak but broken words, are those from whom the earthly senses have fallen away. "In every household" of the spirits even, there is "a queen and a fool, and, maybe, the fool is the wisest of all." This fool, who is held to wander in lonely places and to bewitch men out of the world,—for the touch of the queen and of the fool give death,—is the type of

[30] In *N.A.R.* version, paragraph ends here.

that old wisdom from which the good citizen and the new wisdom have led the world away, forgetting that "the ruins of time build mansions in eternity."[31] The poetry that comes out of the old wisdom must turn always to religion and to the law of the hidden world, while the poetry of the new wisdom must not forget politics and the law of the visible world; and between these poetries there cannot be any lasting peace. Those that follow the old wisdom must not shrink too greatly from the journey described in some verses Miss Hopper, a poet of our school,[32] has put into the mouth of Dalua [*sic*], the fairy fool—

> *The world wears on to sundown, and love is lost or won,*[33]
> *But he recks not of loss or gain, the King of Ireland's son.*
> *He follows on for ever when all your chase is done,*
> *He follows after shadows, the King of Ireland's son.*

Alone among nations, Ireland has in her written Gaelic literature, in her old love tales and battle tales, the forms in which the imagination of Europe uttered itself before Greece shaped a tumult of legend into her music of the arts; and she can discover, from the beliefs and emotions of her common people, the habit of mind that created the religion of the muses. The legends of other European countries are less numerous, and not so full of the energies from which the arts and our understanding of their sanctity arose, and the best of them have already been shaped into plays and poems. "The Celt," as it seems, created romance, when his stories of Arthur and of the Grail became for a time almost the only inspiration of European literature, and it would not be wonderful if he should remould romance[34] after its oldest image, now that he is recovering his possessions.

The movement of thought which has made the good citizen, or has been made by him, has surrounded us with comfort and safety, and with vulgarity and insincerity. One finds alike its energy and its weariness in[35] churches which have substituted a system of morals for spiritual

---

[31] Blake wrote in a letter to William Hayley, May 6, 1800, "The ruins of Time builds [*sic*] Mansions in Eternity" (Keynes, p. 797).

[32] The preceding phrases in the *N.A.R.* version read ". . . which Miss Hopper, the latest poet of our school . . .". And at this point the editor of the *N.A.R.*, George B. M. Harvey (1864–1928), contributed the following note: "The reader will find, in the collection of recent poems by Miss Hopper which immediately follows this article, a most attractive illustration of the theme discussed by Mr. Yeats in such an interesting manner."

[33] This poem is from the story "Daluan" in Nora (Hopper) Chesson's *Ballads in Prose*, London, 1894, and Yeats changed the phrase "lost and won" to "lost or won" (p. 97 of *Ballads in Prose*).

[34] The *N.A.R.* version reads from this point on ". . . after its most ancient image, now that he is recovering his ancient possessions".

[35] The sentence begins at this point in the *N.A.R.* version, and "in churches", "in pictures" and "in poets" reads in *N.A.R.* "Churches", "pictures", and "poets".

ardour; in pictures which have substituted conventionally pretty faces for the disquieting revelations of sincerity; in poets who have set the praises of those things good citizens think praiseworthy above a dangerous delight in beauty for the sake of beauty.[36] The Romantic movement, from the times of Blake and Shelley and Keats, when it took a new form, has been battling with the thoughts of the good citizen, as moss and ivy and grass battle with some old building, crumbling its dead stone and mortar into the living greenery of earth. The disorders of a Shelley or[37] of a Heine in their art, and in their lives that mirror their art, are but a too impetuous ardour of battle, a too swift leaping of ivy or of grass to window ledge or gable end; and the intensity and strangeness of a picture by Rossetti or of an early picture[38] by Watts are but a sudden falling of stones. Moss and ivy and grass gather against stone and mortar in unceasing enmity, for while the old is crumbling the new is building; and the Romantic movement will never have perfect victory unless, as mystics have thought, the golden age is to come again, and men's hearts and the weather to grow gentle as time fades into eternity. Blake said that all art was a labour to bring that golden age,[39] and we call romantic art romantic because it has made that age's light dwell in the imaginations of a little company of studious persons.

Because the greater number of persons are too busy with the work of the world to forget the light of the sun, romantic art is, as I think, about to change its manner and become more like the art of the old poets, who saw the golden age and their own age side by side like substance and shadow. Ever since Christianity turned men's minds to Judea, and learning turned them to Greece and Rome, the sanctity has dwindled from their own hills and valleys, which the legends and beliefs of fifty centuries had filled so full of it that a man could hardly plough his fields or follow his sheep upon the hillside without remembering some august story, or walking softly lest he had divine companions. When the valleys and the hills had almost become clay and stone, the good citizens plucked up their heart and took possession of the world and filled it with their little compact thoughts; and romance fled to more and more remote fairylands, and forgot that it was ever more than an old tale which nobody believes. But now we are growing interested in

---

[36] In the *N.A.R.* this sentence ends, "are a part of its energy and its weariness".

[37] The *N.A.R.* version reads, instead of the phrase "or of a Heine in their art", the phrase ", of a French romanticist of our own time, in art, . . .".

[38] The phrase "of an early picture" is not in the *N.A.R.* version. George Frederick Watts, whose early work Yeats admired because he was then "least a moralist" (*Autobiography*, p. 371), is the subject of a lecture by Yeats in 1906 (see p. 342 below).

[39] In his notebook to "A Vision of the Last Judgment" Blake said "The Nature of My Work is Visionary or Imaginative; it is an Endeavour to Restore what the Ancients call'd the Golden Age." (Keynes edition, p. 605.)

our own countries, and discovering that the common people in all countries that have not given themselves up to the improvements and devices of good citizens, which we call civilization, still half understand the sanctity of their hills and valleys; and at the same time a change of thought is making us half ready to believe with Ecclesiasticus, that "all things are made double one above another,"[40] and that the forms of nature may be temporal shadows of realities.

In a little time places may begin to seem the only hieroglyphs that cannot be forgotten, and poets to remember that they will come the nearer the old poets, who had a seat at every hearth, if they mingle their own dream with a story told for centuries of some mountain that casts its shadows upon many doors, and if they understand that the beauty they celebrate is a part of the paradise men's eyes shall look upon when they close upon the world. The paradise of the Christian, as those who think more of the order of communities than of the nature of things have shaped it, is but the fulfilment of one dream; but the paradise that the common people tell of about the fire, and still half understand, is the fulfilment of all dreams, and opens its gates as gladly to the perfect lover as to the perfect saint, and only he who understands it can lift romance into prophecy and make beauty holy. Their paradise, Tirnan-og, the Land of the Living Heart, the Grass Green Island of Apples, call it what you will, created that religion of the muses which gave the arts to the world; and those countries whose traditions are fullest of it, and of the sanctity of places, may yet remould romance till it has become a covenant between intellectual beauty and the beauty of the world. We cannot know how many these countries are until the new science of folklore and the almost new science of mythology have done their work; but Ireland, if she can awake again the but half-forgotten legends of Slieve Gullion, or of Cruachmagh, or of the hill where Maeve is buried, and make them an utterance of that desire to be at rest amid ideal perfection which is becoming conscious in the minds of poets as the good citizen wins the priests over to his side; of if she can make us believe that the beautiful things that move us to awe, white lilies among dim shadows, windy twilights over grey sands, dewy and silent places among hazel trees by still waters, are in truth, and not in phantasy alone, the symbols, or the dwellings, of immortal presences, she will have begun a change that, whether it is begun in our time or not for centuries, will some day make all lands holy lands again.

Ireland has no great wealth, no preoccupation with successful persons to turn her writers' eyes to any lesser destiny. Even the poetry which

---

[40] Eccl. 42: 24. The 1888 edition of *The Apocrypha* edited by Henry Wace, London, 1888, reads: "All things are double one against another" (vol. 2, p. 205).

had its form and much of its matter from alien thought dwelt, as the Gaelic ballads had done before it, on ideas living in the perfection of hope, on visions of unfulfilled desire, and not on the sordid compromise of success. The popular poetry of England celebrates her victories, but the popular poetry of Ireland remembers only defeats and defeated persons. A ballad that is in every little threepenny and sixpenny ballad book asks if Ireland has no pride in her Lawrences[41] and Wellingtons, and answers that these belong to the Empire and not to Ireland, whose "heart beats high" for men who died in exile or in prison; and this ballad is a type of all. The popular poetry, too, has made love of the earth of Ireland so much a part of her literature that it should not be a hard thing to fill it with the holiness of places. Politics are, indeed, the forge in which nations are made, and the smith has been so long busy making Ireland according to His will that she may well have some important destiny. But whether this is so or not, whether this destiny is to make her in the arts, as she is in politics, a voice of the idealism of the common people, who still remember the dawn of the world, or to give her an unforeseen history, it can but express the accidents and energies of her past, and criticism does its natural work in trying to prophesy this expression; and, even if it is mistaken, a prophecy is not always made all untrue by being unfulfilled. A few years will decide if the writers of Ireland are to shape themselves in our time for the fulfilment of this prophecy, for need and much discussion will bring a new national agreement, and the political tumult awake again.

# The Irish Literary Theatre

Yeats announced the second season of the Irish Literary Theatre in a letter to the editor, Michael MacDonagh (1860–1946), in the issue of the *Irish Literary Society Gazette* for January, 1900.

## TO THE EDITOR OF THE *I. L. GAZETTE*

DEAR SIR,

I write to ask members of the Irish literary Society to support in every way they can the Irish Literary Theatre, which begins its per-

---

[41] Alexander Lawrence (1764–1835) led the attack on Seringapatam, India, in 1799.

formances this year on the 19th of February. The performances will be
given, as before, under the auspices of the National Literary Society,[1]
and in the Gaiety Theatre instead of in a hall as last year. We will produce three plays, "Maive," by Mr. Edward Martyn[2]—a play in which,
I think, I am right in seeing a symbolic expression of clashing Irish
and English ideals; "The Last Feast of the Fianna," by Miss Milligan,[3]
a one-act play about Usheen and Niam; and "The Bending of the
Bough," by Mr. George Moore,[4] a comedy in five acts, which expounds
through its movements and persons a national ideal, with which no
member of our Societies will quarrel, and satirises certain follies that
have begun to weigh upon the national conscience. These plays are
written to expound Irish characters and Irish ideas, and with no thought
of any but an Irish public; and whatever be their merit they are written
with sincerity, as one writes literature, and not as one writes for the
Theatre of Commerce. If they succeed nobody will be a penny the
richer, but Ireland will have found a new vehicle of expression.

Yours sincerely,<br>W. B. Yeats

[1] The National Literary Society was the Dublin organization founded by Yeats and John
O'Leary in 1892. It was allied with the Irish Literary Society which Yeats and T. W. Rolleston had founded in London in the same year. The aim of both organizations was to re-
awaken Ireland and the English-speaking world to Irish literature, language and folklore.

[2] Edward Martyn (1859-1923), was a wealthy Galway neighbour of Lady Gregory and a
distant cousin of George Moore. After his first play, *The Heather Field*, was successfully
produced during the first season of the Literary Theatre in 1899, he wrote *Maeve* for the
second season, of which he was also the benefactor. The action of this poetic drama centers
around a modern Irishwoman, the title-character, who hesitates in accepting the proposal of
a man of Norman descent, Fitzwalter, because their natures are not akin. Eventually Queen
Maeve appears and carries her namesake off to Tir-nan-og—the Land of the Ever-Young.

[3] Alice Milligan (1880-1953) wrote poems, plays and historical studies about Ireland. Her
play about the dissolution of the band of warriors loyal to Finn MacCool was not well
received. Yeats called it "a narrative, undramatic play" (*Autobiography*, p. 288), and plans by
W. G. Fay and Edward Martyn to revive it for the second part of the 1902 season of the
Irish National Dramatic Company in October of that year were abandoned.

[4] The return of George Moore (1852-1933) to Ireland was vigorous, and his active participation in the literary revival was brief. This play, like his contribution of the following
year, was a collaboration. It was based on a "comedy of affairs in five acts" by Edward
Martyn entitled *The Tale of a Town*, which in turn was somewhat indebted to Ibsen's *An
Enemy of the People*. When the other Directors of the Literary Theatre had found Martyn's
play unsuitable, Moore and Yeats rewrote it. No one was pleased with the final production
but Yeats noted that it "was the first dramatization of an Irish problem" and in her diary
Lady Gregory set down that "The Gaelic League, in great force, sang "*Fainne geal an lae*"
between the acts, and 'The Wearing of the Green' in Irish". (*Autobiography*, p. 288.)

# The Irish Literary Theatre, 1900

At the same time as his brief announcement of the Literary Theatre's new season in the Irish Literary Society Gazette (p. 196 above) Yeats offered a more elaborate description of his plans in "The Irish Literary Theatre, 1900", which appeared in *The Dome* for January, 1900. His point of departure is George Moore's ubiquitous declaration at this time of his quest, in his return to Ireland, after some elusive center of creative energy. Moore himself recreates, in *Ave*, one such pronouncement made at a dinner given for the Theatre by T. P. Gill (1858–1931), the energetic editor of the *Daily Express*:

> After some words hastily improvised . . . I explained the reason for my return to Ireland: how in my youth I had gone to France because art was there, and how, when art died in France, I had returned to England; and now that art was dead in England I was looking out . . . to find which way art was winging. Westward, probably, for all the countries of Europe had been visited by art, and art never visits a country twice. . . . so my native country had again attracted me. (*Hail and Farewell*, 3 vols.: *Ave, Salve, Vale*, vols. 8, 9, 10 of the "Uniform Edition", London, 1947, vol. I, p. 115.)

While Yeats agrees here with Moore about the demise of art in England, his vision of a vast Celtic awakening hardly allowed for such rootless ego-centricity. Thus, he is at pains to find in each of the Theatre's three, quite dissimilar plays—including Moore's own—the realization of a racial prophecy which "has come upon us not because we have sought it out but because we share . . . the intellectual traditions of the race . . .".

MR. MOORE has given reasons elsewhere why the founders of the Irish Literary Theatre believe good plays more possible in Ireland than in London; but I think he makes too much of these reasons when he makes them our chief impulse. I know that he and Mr. Martyn and myself, and those who are working with us, believe that we have things to say to our countrymen which it is our pleasure and our duty to say. If we write plays that are literature, and find people to like them, it will be because that strong imaginative energy, which is needed to fill with life the elaborate circumstance of a play, has not often come except as from a Sinai to some nation wandering as in the wilderness; but that strong imaginative energy comes among men, as I think, not because they have followed it from country to country, but because a genius greater than their own, and, it maybe, without their knowledge or their consent, has thrown its shadow upon them. Dionysius, the Areopagite, wrote that "He has set the borders of the nations according to His angels."[1] It is these angels, each one the genius of some race about to be unfolded, that are the founders of intellectual traditions; and as lovers understand in their first glance all that is to befall them, and as poets and musicians see the whole work in its first impulse, so races prophesy at their awakening whatever the generations that are to prolong their traditions shall accomplish in detail. It is only at the awakening—as in ancient Greece, or in Elizabethan England, or in contemporary Scandinavia—that great numbers of men understand that a right understanding of life and of destiny is more important than amusement. In London, where all the intellectual traditions gather to die, men hate a play if they are told it is literature, for they will not endure a spiritual superiority; but in Athens, where so many intellectual traditions were born, Euripides once made hostility enthusiasm by asking his playgoers whether it was his business to teach them or their business to teach him. New races understand instinctively, because the future cries in their ears, that the old revelations are insufficient, and that all life is revelation beginning in miracle and enthusiasm and dying out as it unfolds in what we have mistaken for progress. It is one of our illusions, as I think, that education, the softening of manners, the perfecting of law—countless images of a fading light—can create nobleness and beauty, and that life moves slowly and evenly towards some perfection. Progress is miracle, and it is sudden, because miracles are the work of an all-powerful energy; and nature in herself has no power except to die and to forget. If one studies one's own mind, one comes to think with Blake, that "every time less than a pulsation of the artery is equal to six thousand years, for in this period the poet's work is done; and all the great events of time start forth and are conceived in such a period, within a pulsation of the artery."[2]

Scandinavia is, as it seems, passing from her moments of miracle; and some of us think that Ireland is passing to hers. She may not produce any important literature, but because her moral nature has been aroused by political sacrifices, and her imagination by a political preoccupation with her own destiny, she is ready to be moved by profound thoughts that are a part of the unfolding of herself. Mr. Martyn lit upon one of them in his "Heather Field," which shares it with old Celtic legends. He described a man who attained the divine vision as his brain perished, and our Irish playgoers had so much sympathy with this man that they hissed the doctors who found that he was mad. The London playgoers, whose life, as must be wherever success is too highly valued, is established in a contrary thought, sympathised with the doctors and held the

---

[1] See p. 187 above for Yeats's use of this quotation from Dionysius the Pseudo-Areopagite.
[2] *Milton*, bk. I, pl. 28 ll. 62–63 and pl. 29 ll. 1–3.

divine vision a dream.[3] This year Mr. Martyn will return to the same thought with his "Maive," which tells of an old woman, who begs her way from door to door in life and is a great and beautiful queen in faery, and who persuades a young girl to renounce life and seek perfection in death. Miss Milligan, not influenced by Mr. Martyn, or by anything but old legends, has the same thought in her "The Last Feast of the Fianna," which, as I think, would make us feel the mortality and indignity of all that lives. Her bard Usheen goes to faery, and is made immortal like his songs; while the heroes and Grania, the most famous of the beautiful, sink into querulous old age. Mr. Moore, in his "The Bending of the Bough," the longest and most elaborate of our three plays, has written of the rejection of a spiritual beauty, which his play expounds as the ideal hope not of individual life, but of the race, its vision of itself made perfect; and the acceptance of mere individual life. His story, which pretends to describe the relations between two towns, one in the Celtic north and one in the Saxon south of a Scotland as vague as the sea-coast of Bohemia, describes the war of this vision with surrounding circumstance, and its betrayal by the light-souled and the self-seeking. It shows many real types of men and women in the fire of an impassioned satire, and will awaken some sleeping dogs. This thought of the war of immortal upon mortal life has been the moving thought of much Irish poetry, and may yet, so moving and necessary a thought it is, inspire many plays which, whether important or unimportant, shall have the sincerity of youth. It has come upon us not because we have sought it out, but because we share, as I think, a moiety of the blood and of the intellectual traditions of the race that give romance and the kingdom of faery to European literature; and which has always waited with amorous eyes for some impossible beauty. Our daily life has fallen among prosaic things and ignoble things, but our dreams remember the enchanted valleys.

W. B. Yeats

[3] As Martyn's play had not been produced outside Dublin at this time, Yeats must refer to "London playgoers" visiting Dublin.

# Plans and Methods

Revealing the Irish Literary Theatre's "Plans and Methods" for the 1900 season—in *Beltaine* for February 1900—Yeats again divined in the Theatre's offerings a "unity" which not only transcended the many differences he had with George Moore and Edward Martyn, but also gathered together Irish nationalists of all stripes. Remembering, no doubt, his unfulfilled promise in the previous year of plays by O'Grady Calderon and "Fiona Macleod" (see p. 160 above), he forecast the Theatre's programs more cautiously.

OUR plays this year have a half deliberate unity. Mr. Martyn's *Maive*,[1] which I understand to symbolise Ireland's choice between English materialism and her own natural idealism, as well as the choice of every individual soul, will be followed, as Greek tragedies were followed by satires and Elizabethan masques by antimasques, by Mr. George Moore's *The Bending of the Bough*,[2] which tells of a like choice and of a contrary decision. Mr. Moore's play, which is, in its external form, the history of two Scottish cities, the one Celtic in the main and the other Saxon in the main, is a microcosm of the last ten years of public life in Ireland. I know, however, that he wishes it to be understood that he has in no instance consciously satirised individual men, for he wars, as Blake claimed to do, with states of mind and not with individual men. If any person upon the stage resembles any living person it will be because he is himself a representative of the type. Mr. Moore uses for a symbol of any cause, that seeks the welfare of the nation as a whole, that movement for financial equity which has won the support of all our parties. If the play touches the imagination at all, it should make every man see beyond the symbol the cause nearest his heart, and its struggle against the common failings of humanity and those peculiar to Ireland. I do not think the followers of any Nationalist leader, on the one hand, or of Mr. Lecky or Mr. Plunkett,[3] on the other, can object to its teaching, for it is aimed against none but those persons and parties who would

---

[1] *Maive* was Edward Martyn's play for the 1900 season of the Irish Literary Theatre (see p. 197 above). Yeats consistently spells the title "Maive".

[2] This is the collaboration of Moore with Yeats mentioned on p. 197 above.

[3] Yeats combines the acceptable extremes of Irish national feeling in this reference. Although both W. E. H. Lecky, the historian, and Horace Plunkett, the agricultural reformer, were Unionists, Yeats's accommodation with them at this time resulted in their early support of the Irish Literary Theatre. He had suggested that Lecky read Lionel Johnson's prologue at the opening performance of "The Countess Cathleen"—which had not come about—and he had been influential in A.E.'s accepting a position as organizer for Plunkett's agricultural programme. Although Lecky withdrew much of his support after Yeats's protest over the visit of Queen Victoria (see pp. 208, 211 below), Plunkett and Yeats remained cordial.

put private or English interests before Irish interests. As Allingham[4] wrote long since,—

*We are one at heart if you be Ireland's friend,*
*Though leagues asunder our opinions tend:*
*There are but two great parties in the end!*

The Last Feast of the Fianna[5] has an antiquarian as well as an artistic interest. Dr. Hyde is of the opinion that the Usheen and Patric dialogues were spoken in character by two reciters, and that had Irish literature followed a natural development a regular drama would have followed from this beginning. Miss Milligan has added other characters while preserving the emotions and expressions of the dialogues; and if her play were acted without scenery it would resemble a possible form of old Irish drama. But for the extreme difficulty of the metre of the dialogues we would have acted this play in Irish, but the translator gave up after a few verses. We are anxious to get plays in Irish, and can we do so will very possibly push our work into the western counties, where it would be an important help to that movement for the revival of the Irish language on which the life of the nation may depend.

Mr. Moore and Mr. Martyn have put into their plays several eloquent things about the Celtic race, and certainly, if one were to claim that there is something in sacred races, and that the Celt is of them, and to found one's claim on Mr. Nutt's[6] pamphlets alone, one would not lack arguments. I am myself, however, more inclined to agree with Renan[7] and to set store by a certain native tradition of thought that is passed on in the conversations of father and son, and in the institutions of life, and in literature, and in the examples of history. It is these that make nations and that mould the foreign settler after the national type in a few years; and it is these, whether they were made by men of foreign or of Celtic blood, that our theatre would express. If I call them Celtic—

[4] For Yeats's early appreciation of William Allingham (1824–89), see his review of the "poet of Ballyshannon", "A Poet We Have Neglected" (*Uncollected Prose*, vol. I, pp. 208–12). His citation of Allingham's nationalist sentiments here is somewhat ironic in view of the reservation he expressed in some paragraphs in the *Boston Pilot* in 1890. "Allingham had the making of a great writer in him, but lacked impulse and momentum, the very things national feeling could have supplied. . . . There is no great literature without nationality, no great nationality without literature." (*Letters to the New Island*, pp. 103–4.) In fact, as early as 1888, Yeats seems to have made this determination. On September 18 of that year he wrote in his diary: "Miss Tynan sends me criticisms from *Providence Journal*—'The Poet of Ballyshannon'. (non-national, how sad!)" (quoted in John Hewitt, ed., *Poems of William Allingham*, Dublin, 1967, p. 19).

[5] This play, by Alice Milligan, is described on p. 197 above.

[6] Yeats's reference is to Alfred T. Nutt, the publisher, folklorist and Celtic scholar. Yeats had reviewed the edition of *The Voyage of Bran* by Nutt and Kuno Meyer in *The Bookman* in 1898 (see p. 118 above).

[7] Ernest Renan (1823–92), the French philosopher and historian.

and I think Mr. Moore and Mr. Martyn would say the same—it is because of common usage, because the men who made them have less foreign than Celtic blood, and because it is the only word that describes us and those people of Western Scotland who share our language and all but what is most modern in our national traditions.

Prophecies are generally unfortunate, and I made some last year that have not come true; but I think I may say that we will have no difficulty in getting good plays for next year. Mr. Martyn has finished a new play, Mr. Bernard Shaw promises us a play which he describes as an Irish Rogue's Comedy,[8] and Mr. George Moore and myself are half through a three-act play in prose on the legend of Dermot and Grania.[9] I have also finished a play in verse,[10] but I rather shrink from producing another verse play unless I get some opportunity for private experiment with my actors in the speaking of verse. The acting of the poetical drama should be as much oratory as acting, and oratory is a lost art upon the stage. Time too will, doubtless, bring us other plays to choose among, and we have decided to have a play in Irish if we can get it.

Mr. Moore and Mr. Martyn have sent me articles that see the decline of England in the decline of her drama. Shelley had a like thought when he said, 'In periods of the decay of social life the drama sympathises with that decay . . . it is indisputable that the highest perfection of human society has ever corresponded with the highest dramatic excellence; and that the corruption or the extinction of the drama in a nation, where it has once flourished, is a mark of the corruption of manners and an extinction of the energies which sustain the soul of social life.'[11] I myself throw the blame for that decline of the spiritual and intellectual energies of which Mr. Martyn and Mr. Moore are convinced, as were Ruskin and Morris and Arnold and Carlyle, upon that

[8] Bernard Shaw had proposed "a play on the contrast between Irish and English character" to Yeats on March 12, 1900 (Yeats, Letters, p. 335). The play, which became John Bull's Other Island, was finished and offered to the Abbey Theatre in 1904 but was refused on the ostensible grounds that there was no actor in the company talented enough to play Broadbent. When it was eventually produced by Granville Barker in London, in November, 1904, Yeats found that it was "immensely long . . . fundamentally ugly and shapeless, but certainly keeps everybody amused" (Letters, p. 442).

[9] Diarmuid and Grania was produced in October, 1901, by the Irish Literary Theatre.

[10] The play to which Yeats refers, The Shadowy Waters, had been under way since he was a boy. A version seems to have been ready for publication as early as 1896 (Letters, p. 237 n.). It first appeared, however, in May, 1900, in the North American Review. The first production of the play was by the Irish National Theatre Society in 1904. A revised version was published in October, 1906, and produced by the Abbey Theatre in December of that year.

[11] Shelley makes this observation in A Defence of Poetry, where he calls the drama "that form under which a greater number of modes of expression of poetry are susceptible of being combined than any other . . ." (Shelley, Complete Works, London, 1930, vol. VII, p. 122).

commercialism and materialism on which these men warred; and not upon race as do certain of my countrymen. It should be our business to bring Ireland from under the ruins, appealing to her, as Grattan[12] appealed to her in his speech on the tythes, by her own example and her own hopes.

If any money should be made by our plays, which is extremely unlikely, it will be paid into a fund for the production of plays in future years.

The Irish Literary Theatre works under the auspices of the National Literary Society.

Editor of *Beltaine*

# 'Maive' and Certain Irish Beliefs

*BELTAINE*, FEBRUARY, 1900

I THINK I remember Mr. Martyn telling me that he knew nothing, or next to nothing, about the belief in such women as Peg Inerny[1] among the Irish peasants. Unless the imagination has a means of knowledge peculiar to itself, he must have heard of this belief as a child and remembered it in that unconscious and instinctive memory on which imagination builds. Biddy Early,* who journeyed with the people of faery when night fell, and who cured multitudes of all kinds of sickness, if the tales that one hears from her patients are not all fancy, is, I think, the origin of his Peg Inerny; but there were, and are, many like her. Sometimes, as it seems, they wander from place to place begging their bread, but living all the while a noble second life in faery. They are sometimes called 'women from the North,' because witchcraft, and

* See my article in the *Contemporary Review* for September, 1899.[2]

[12] At the conclusion of his speech urging the commutation of tithes before the Irish parliament on February 14, 1788, Henry Grattan (1746–1820) had appealed to an indigenous Irish wisdom. "I speak this to you, from a long knowledge of your character, and the various resources of your soil; and I confide my motion to those principles not only of justice, but of fire, which I have observed to exist in your composition, and occasionally to break out in a flame of public zeal . . . those warm susceptible properties which abound in your mind, and qualify you for legislation." (Madden, ed., *Select Speeches of Grattan*, Dublin, 1845, p. 141.)

[1] In Edward Martyn's *Maeve*, which the Irish Literary Theatre produced in 1900, the character called Peg Inerny, a cunning vagrant, is an incarnation of Queen Maeve.

[2] Yeats's note. He referred to "Ireland Bewitched", p. 167 above.

spirits, and faeries come from the North. A Kitarton [*sic*] woman said to
a friend who has got me many tales: 'One time a woman from the North
came to our house, and she said a great deal of people are kept below
there in the lisses. She had been there herself, and in the night-time, in
one moment, they'd be all away at Cruachma, wherever that may be—
down in the North, I believe. And she knew everything that was in the
house, and told us about my sister being sick, and that there was a
hurling match going on that day, and that it was at the Isabella Wood.
I'd have picked a lot of stories out of her, but my mother got nervous
when she heard the truth coming out, and told me to be quiet. She had
a red petticoat on her, the same as any country woman, and she offered
to cure me, for it was that time I was delicate, and her ladyship sent
me to the salt water. But she asked a shilling, and my mother said she
hadn't got it. "You have," said she, "and heavier metal than that you
have in the house." So then my mother gave her the shilling, and she
put it in the fire and melted it, and, says she, "after two days you'll see
your shilling again;" but we never did. And the cure she left, I never
took it; it's not safe, and the priests forbid us to take their cures. No
doubt at all she was one of the ingentry (I have never heard this word
for the faeries from anybody else) that can take the form of a woman by
day and another form by night.' Another woman in the same neighbourhood said: 'I saw myself, when I was but a child, a woman come to the
door that had been seven years with the good people, and I remember
her telling us that in that seven years she'd often been glad to come
outside the houses and pick the bits that were thrown into the trough
for the pigs; and she told us always to leave a bit about the house for
those that could not come and ask for it: and though my father was a
cross man, and didn't believe in such things, to the day of his death we
never went up to bed without leaving a bit of food outside the door!'
Sometimes, however, one hears of their being fed with supernatural
food, so that they need little or none of our food.

I have two or three stories of women who were queens when in
faery; I have many stories of men and women, and have even talked
with some four or five among them, who believed that they had had
supernatural lovers. I met a young man once in the Burren Hills who
remembered an old Gaelic poet, who had loved Maive, and was always
very sorrowful because she had deserted him. He had made lamentation for her, but the young man could only remember that it was sorrowful, and that it called her 'beauty of all beauty;' a phrase that makes one
think that she had become a symbol of ideal beauty, as the supernatural lover is in Mr. Martyn's play. One of the most lovely of old
Gaelic poems is the appeal of such a lover to his beloved. Medhir, who
is called King of the Sidhe (the faeries), sang to the beautiful Etain,

wife of the King who was called Eochaid the ploughman. 'O beautiful woman, come with me to the marvellous land where one listens to a sweet music, where one has spring flowers in one's hair, where the body is like snow from head to foot, where no one is sad or silent, where teeth are white and eyebrows are black . . . . cheeks red, like foxglove in flower. . . . . Ireland is beautiful, but not so beautiful as the Great Plain I call you to. The beer of Ireland is heady, but the beer of the Great Plain is much more heady. How marvellous is the country I am speaking of: Youth does not grow old there; streams of warm blood flow there, sometimes meed, sometimes wine. Men are charming, and without a blot there. O woman, when you come into my powerful country, you will wear a crown of gold upon your head. I will give you the flesh of swine, and you will have beer and milk to drink, O beautiful woman. O beautiful woman, come with me!'

Maive (Medb is the Irish spelling) is continually described as the queen of all western faeries, and it was probably some memory of her lingering in western England, or brought home by adventurers from Ireland, that gave Shakespeare his Queen Mab. But neither Maive, nor any of our Irish faeries are like the fairies of Shakespeare; for our fairies are never very little, and are sometimes taller and more beautiful than mortals. The greatest among them were the gods and goddesses of ancient Ireland, and men have not yet forgotten their glory.

I recently described in the *North American Review* a vision of Queen Maive that came to an old Mayo woman. 'She was standing in the window of her master's house, looking towards a mountain, when she saw "the finest woman you ever saw" travelling right across from the mountain and straight to her.[3] The woman had a sword by her side and a dagger lifted up in her hand, and was dressed in white with bare arms and feet. She looked "very strong, and fierce, but not wicked"—that is, not cruel. (She was one of "the fair, fierce women" of the Irish poem quoted in Mr. Martyn's play.) The old woman had seen the Irish giant, and "though he was a fine man" he was nothing to this woman, "for he was round and could not have stepped out so soldierly." "She was like Mrs. ———," naming a stately lady of the neighbourhood; "but she had no stomach on her, and was slight, and broad in the shoulders, and was handsomer than any one you ever saw; she looked about thirty." The old woman covered her eyes with her hands, and when she uncovered them the apparition had vanished. The neighbours were wild with her for not waiting to see if there was a message, for they were

---

[3] Yeats recounted this story in the essay entitled "The Literary Movement in Ireland", which appeared in *North American Review* for December, 1899. The last paragraph of this essay is, with slight insertions and omissions, taken from the concluding part of section III of that essay (see pp. 191–92 above). Yeats also describes this vision by Mary Battle, his uncle's servant, in his *Autobiography* (p. 178).

sure it was Queen Maive, who often shows herself to the pilots. I asked the old woman if she had seen others like Queen Maive, and she said, "some of them have their hair down, but they look quite different, like the sleepy-looking ladies one sees in the papers. Those with their hair up are like this one. The others have long white dresses; but those with their hair up have short dresses, so that you can see their legs right up to the calf." After some careful questioning I found that they wore what appear to be buskins. She went on, "They are fine and dashing-looking, like the men one sees riding their horses in twos and threes on the slopes of the mountains with their swords swinging." She repeated, over and over, "There is no such race living now, none so finely proportioned," or the like, and then said, "The present queen is a nice, pleasant-looking woman, but she is not like her. What makes me think so little of the ladies is that I see none as they be," meaning the spirits. "When I think of her and of the ladies now, they are like little children running about without knowing how to put their clothes on right. Is it the ladies? Why, I would not call them women at all!" '
This old woman, who can neither read nor write, has come face to face with heroic beauty, that 'highest beauty,' which Blake says, 'changes least from youth to age,' a beauty that has been fading out of the arts, since that decadence, we call progress, set voluptuous beauty in its place.

W. B. Yeats

# A Correction

Yeats and his friends had contributed regularly to the Dublin *Daily Express* in the late nineties, when the paper was under the control of Horace Plunkett. ". . . AE, Yeats, John Eglinton, all contributed articles; economics and folklore, Celtic and Indian Gods, all went into the same pot—an extraordinary broth . . .", as George Moore recalled (*Hail and Farewell, Salve*, p. 90). By 1900, however, with control passing to Lord Ardilaun, head of the Guinness family, the paper was Unionist and conservative, and Yeats found himself quibbling with the *Daily Express*, as he did in "A Correction" which appeared in the issue for March 30, 1900.
In a letter in the *Freeman's Journal* on March 20, Yeats noted the political motivation for the approaching Irish visit by Queen Victoria, asserting that "the advisors of the Queen have not sent into Ireland this woman of eighty-one, to whom all labours must be weariness, without good reason, and the reason is national hatred—hatred of our individual national life . . .". He

proposed a public meeting with John O'Leary as chairman on April 2nd to protest the Queen's departure for Ireland on that day and the introduction into Parliament, a hundred years earlier on that day, of the Articles of Union (*Letters*, pp. 335–7).

Some paragraphs of his letter appeared in the *Daily Express* on March 21, suggesting that Yeats was "somewhat sensitive to insult" in his reference to a cartoon on the subject of the Queen's visit entitled "Outflanked By Jabers" in the issue of *Punch* for March 14. The sketch alludes to Irish support of the Boers and shows the Irish leaders standing dismayed before the announcement of the Queen's visit while a poster bearing an ape-like caricature of Paul Kruger, the Boer President, inscribed "Kruger for Iver—Down with the British", lies unnoticed at their feet.

## TO THE EDITOR OF THE *DAILY EXPRESS*

SIR,

A Press cutting agency has just sent me your paragraphs on my letter to the Nationalist papers about the Royal visit. Your quotations from my letter contain the following remarkable sentence—"If the people are left to organise their own protest, as they did on Jubilee night, there will be no broken glass and batoned crowds. The people will ask themselves, as they did on Jubilee night, 'Is it worth troubling about leaders who are afraid to lead?'" The word "no" was inserted by your printer; for I look for both "broken glass and batoned crowds" if the leaders do not arrange some orderly and disciplined protest.[1] And may I point out that your attempt to describe my opinions has not been more successful than your attempt to quote my words? I did not draw attention to the "Punch" picture, because it was insulting to the Nationalist party; but because it pictured this Royal visit with a really admirable candour as working for the English party in Ireland, and as a movement in a party game. Thanking you in advance for the insertion of this correction of mistakes that have doubtless arisen from the hurry of journalism, I remain, yours truly,

W. B. Yeats

[1] In a note to this letter, "Ed. D. E." admits to a "typographical error", the insertion of "no", and defends his paper's interpretation of Yeats's citation of the *Punch* cartoon: "Our inference that Mr. Yeats felt offended by the *Punch* cartoon appears to have been natural in view of his statement that the Nationalist Members introduced into it 'are made as hideous as President Kruger is made and the whole is inspired by National hatred.'" This defence is weakened by another typographical inaccuracy: "National" is not capitalized in Yeats's original letter.

# 'The Last Feast of the Fianna',
# 'Maive', and 'The Bending of the Bough',
# in Dublin

*BELTAINE*, APRIL, 1900

I REMEMBER somebody, who had nothing to do with any propaganda, saying once that everything becomes a reality when it comes to Ireland. We have brought the 'literary drama' to Ireland, and it has become a reality. If you produce the literary drama in London, you can get an audience for a night or two, but this audience will be made up of the professed students of the drama, of people who are, like yourself, in protest against their time, and who have no personal relations with that which moves upon the stage. In Ireland, we had among our audience almost everybody who is making opinion in Ireland, who is a part of his time, and numbers went out of the playhouse thinking a little differently of that Ireland which their work is shaping: some went away angry, some delighted, but all had seen that upon the stage at which they could not look altogether unmoved. Miss Milligan's little play, whose persons are the persons of numberless Irish folk tales; Mr. Martyn's *Maive*, whose heroine typifies Ireland herself wavering between idealism and commercialism; and Mr. Moore's *Bending of the Bough*, which leaves no class, no movement, that has had any part in these last ten years of disillusionment, out of the wide folds of its satire, touched the heart as greater drama on some foreign theme could not, because they had found, as I think the drama must do in every country, those interests common to the man of letters and the man in the crowd, which are more numerous in a country that has not passed from its time of storm, than in a long-settled country like England. As I came out of the theatre, after the first night of *The Bending of the Bough*, I heard these three sentences, in which there was perhaps a little of the extravagance of the Celt, spoken by three men, one of whom is among the most influential in Ireland. 'I wonder will people dare to come and see so terrible a satire.' 'I feel, as I have never felt before in my life, that there is a new soul come into Ireland.' 'No young man who came into this theatre to-night will go out of it the same man.' The cheaper parts of the house were the loudest in their applause, for our enthusiasts are poor; and their applause did not pick out mere obvious patriotic thoughts, but was discriminate and subtle. The gallery, which sang Gaelic songs between the acts, applauded thoughts like these: 'At all events we have no proof that spiritual truths are illusory, whereas we know that the world is.' 'Respectable causes, is a cause ever respectable'; and this thought very loudly: 'There is always a right and a wrong way, and the wrong way always seems the most reasonable.'[1] All the Irish papers, with the exception of the *Irish Times,* and our little Society papers, which are very proud to represent what they believe to be English interests, have written of all three plays with enthusiasm and at great length. The *Daily Independent* described Mr. Moore's play as 'the most remarkable drama which has been given to the nation for many years,' and said, when our week was over, 'a new intellectual life has arisen in Ireland'; and the other papers had as much, or nearly as much, to say. I do not speak of these opinions because I would agree with them, for I am too closely associated with this movement to measure the worth of the plays it has produced; but to show that we have made the literary drama a reality. The only correspondents of English papers who were present do not differ from the Dublin papers upon this point. The correspondent of the *Times* said of the reception of *The Last Feast of the Fianna* and of *Maive,* 'The plays were enthusiastically received;' and the correspondent of the *Observer* said of the reception of *The Bending of the Bough,* 'People really had to go to see it. Never, it was said, had such an Irish play been seen on the boards of an Irish theatre. If the business of a dramatist is to hold the mirror up to nature, here, said everybody, it was held up in our faces unflinchingly . . . When the curtain falls every one feels that there has been no such serious commentary on Irish life and Irish politics given to the world in our time; and on the whole no such just commentary either.' The English critics who have read the play and not seen it, and who do not know Ireland, have not understood it, for you must know Ireland and her special temptations to understand perfectly even such a sentence as, 'There is always a right and a wrong way, and the wrong way always seems the most reasonable.' On the whole, therefore, I have a good hope that our three years of experiment, which is all we proposed to ourselves at the outset, will make literary drama permanent in Ireland during our time, and give the Irish nation a new method of expression.

W. B. Yeats

[1] In his *Life of George Moore* (New York, 1936), Joseph Hone notes that, speaking of his conversion to the cause of the Boers, Moore paraphrased his play's hero, Jaspar Dean: "It is such joy to allow truth into one's mind. It was like a sudden change of light, all that had seemed right was suddenly changed to wrong, and what I had thought despicable became right and praiseworthy." (p. 223)

# Noble and Ignoble Loyalties

Yeats's early alliance with Arthur Griffith (1872–1922), the nationalist leader who founded *The United Irishman*, a weekly paper, in 1899, is reflected in his essay on "Noble and Ignoble Loyalties" in the issue for April 21, 1900. In an essay expressing ideas resembling those in his *Cathleen ni Houlihan* (1902), Yeats seeks to rationalize the generally enthusiastic reception of Queen Victoria during her Irish visit, despite the contrary efforts of Yeats, Griffith, Maud Gonne and others (see p. 207 above).

Yeats's friendship with Griffith deteriorated as Yeats's nationalism became more complicated and as nationalism in Ireland, which Griffith came to represent, became a less flexible concept. The paper's attack on Synge's *In the Shadow of the Glen*, for example, is behind Yeats's summary description of Griffith in *Dramatis Personae* as the "slanderer of Lane and Synge, founder of the Sinn Fein movement, first President of the Irish Free State . . ." (*Autobiography*, p. 278).

I HAVE written a couple of letters to the Irish papers on the visit of Queen Victoria to Ireland, but they have been very short, for I do not find that I have much to say upon such matters. Kings and queens come and go, and men wear emblems in their button-holes and cannons fire; and we all grow excited, and forget how little meaning there is in the cheers that such things buy. On the day after the taking of the Bastile, Louis XVI sent a message to the French Assembly, saying that he would address it in person. The members took council how the king should be received, and Mirabeau advised that a "mournful respect" best became that "hour of grief," for "the silence of the people is the lesson of kings." But because the desire to cheer a king lies deep in human nature, all cheered the king; and everybody knows what followed those cheers. Did the cheers that greeted Queen Victoria mean more than those that greeted Louis XVI? But for her fleet and her soldiers, and her great Empire, that watches over her, would she or any representative of English rule sleep easy under an Irish roof? She was here before, and was greeted with louder and more plentiful cheers, for I learn from certain English papers that this time the poor kept silent. She came in 1849, and though we had the great Famine to forget, and though Mitchel and Meagher and Smith O'Brien[1] had been transported a few months

[1] John Mitchell (1815–75) was one of the Young Irelanders, the group of young nationalists active at the time of the Great Famine (1845–9). He founded a journal, the *United Irishman*, in 1847, which urged radical agrarian reform through the agency of armed uprising. He was arrested, charged with sedition and transported in May, 1848. In August

before she came, she was met by cheering crowds. The streets were as full as they were a couple of weeks ago, and yet she had scarce gone when the Tenant League was founded and the Land War in its modern shape began. She came again in 1853 and opened an exhibition, amid cheering crowds, and five years later the Fenian Organisation was founded. In August, 1861, she paraded the streets again, amid cheering crowds, and two years, after she had gone, the *Irish People*[2] was founded, and after that came State Trials, and insurrection, and suspension of Constitutional Law. Her visits to Ireland have indeed been unfortunate for English power, for they have commonly foreshadowed a fierce and sudden shaking of English power in Ireland. I do not think this last visit will be more fortunate than the others, for I see all round me, among the young men who hold the coming years in their hands, a new awakened inspiration and resolve. It is for the best that they should have the two loyalties, loyalty to this English Queen, loyalty to her we call Kathleen Ny Hoolihan, called up before them, that they may choose with clear eyes the harder way, for man becomes wise alone by deliberate choice and deliberate sacrifice. There is a commandment in our hearts that we shall do reverence to overflowing goodness, wisdom, and genius, and to the nobler kinds of beauty, and to those immortal ideals that will accept none but arduous service, and to the Maker of these things; and that we shall do reverence to nothing else under Heaven. Was it for any of these that those thousands stood cheering by the roadway, and that those numberless children, in the stands, were brought together from all over Ireland, that they might some day tell their children what they had seen? It was to see a carriage with an aged woman, who is so surrounded by courtiers that we do not know with any certainty, whether she is wise or foolish, bitter or magnanimous, miserly or generous; and who, unlike the great kings and queens of a greater time, has certainly used her example and her influence to cherish mediocrity in music and in painting and in literature. In a few years crowds will gather, in as many thousands, to see a carriage with an elderly man, her son, who has used his example and his influence to make the love of man and woman seem a light and vulgar thing among great numbers in his islands.[3]

---

of that year, two other leaders of the Young Irelanders, William Smith O'Brien and Thomas Francis Meagher, were arrested and subsequently transported to Van Diemen's Land, an island near Australia.

[2] The *Irish People*, a Fenian paper, was founded in Dublin by James Stephens (1824–1901) in 1863. It lasted less than two years and one of the editors, John O'Leary, who was to become Yeats's teacher and friend, spent nine years in prison for subversion.

[3] In the title poem of *In the Seven Woods* (1904) Yeats reinforces this estimation of Edward VII, whose succession of Victoria in 1901 he terms "new commonness / Upon the throne and crying about the streets / And hanging its paper flowers from post to post, / Because it is alone of all things happy." (*Variorum Poems*, p. 198.)

Is it, then, that although this Royalty, that England sends as her messenger, is vulgar, the loyalty it would have from us is so ennobling, that we should close our eyes and do it reverence? No, for this royalty comes among us, with all the bribes of the world upon its knees, and a shopkeeper has but to cheer loudly enough and to fly flags enough, and he will fill his shop. And if a man has some half shame-faced hope to sit at rich men's tables, he has but to cheer loudly enough and to fly flags enough and he will find the way made easy before him. And even the blockhead who finds all other worships to be his enemies can go away more confident than heretofore, for has he not found a worship that does not try to change the heart or the mind? Is it because of these things that the cheers Royalty buys go down the wind so soon? They do not come out of any high resolve, but are the bought service of intellectual sloth and self-applauding egotism. Contrast this loyalty with the loyalty that has been the supreme emotion of so many thousands of poor Irish men and women. It gave them nothing, but the peace of heart that comes to those who serve high things, and for its sake they have gone to prison and exile and death, and endured the enmity and the scorn of the great and the wealthy. What can these Royal Processions mean to those who walk in the procession of heroic and enduring hearts that has followed Kathleen Ny Hoolihan through the ages? Have they not given her their wills and their hearts and their dreams? What have they left for any less noble Royalty?

W. B. Yeats

# The Freedom of the Press in Ireland

YEATS was a frequent contributor to *The Speaker*, the Liberal weekly edited, for a time, by Richard Barry O'Brien (1847–1918), a co-founder of the Irish Literary Society. In a letter on "The Freedom of the Press in Ireland" in the issue for July 7, 1900, Yeats presents his charges against George Henry, 5th Earl Cadogan (1840–1915), who, as Lord Lieutenant of Ireland, was both a constant supporter within the Government of Liberal policies and an implacable opponent of civil outbreaks and seditious journals.

Cadogan had seized the *United Irishman* for February 17, 1900, which contained quotations from a letter by the Reverend Patrick F. Kavanagh (1834–1916), under the title "Father Kavanagh on the War". In his letter, which had first appeared in the issue for December 23, 1899,

Kavanagh, the author of *A Popular History of the Insurrection of 1798* (2nd ed., 1874), set forth six points as "doctrine of the Catholic Church" to demonstrate that Irish men serving in the "unjust" war against the Boers must suffer the loss of their souls. In printing the excerpts "By Order, Irish Transvaal Committee", Griffith was adding to tensions which had begun with the letter of December 23 and had continued with declarations by Kavanagh in the *Irishman* throughout January. On February 3, the paper's "All Ireland" column had praised Kavanagh, announcing a lecture by him in Dublin "in aid of the Wicklow movement", and in the issue for February 24, Griffith denounced Cadogan by name, daring "that interesting nobleman" to "play the thief again".

Queen Victoria arrived in Dublin on April 5, 1900, and on April 7 Griffith published a translation from *La Patrie* of an article by Maud Gonne called "The Famine Queen", which portrayed the Queen "Taking the Shamrock in her withered hand [and daring] to ask Ireland for soldiers—for soldiers to protect the exterminators of their race". Cadogan moved against the paper again, and amid the violence of that week was Griffith's assault on Ramsey Colles (1862–1919), the editor of the Dublin *Figaro*, for slandering Maud Gonne. Griffith was found guilty, Colles later retracted, and the Lord Lieutenant continued to interrupt the paper's publication, confiscating the issue for May 26, which contained some correspondence about the earlier seizures. A week later, on June 2, Griffith reprinted the exchange, dared Cadogan to act again, and included the following in the short notes under his editorial: "At one o'clock on Friday last Earl Cadogan knighted Mr. Joseph Downes [1848–1925, High Sheriff of Dublin]; at 2:45 the noble Earl siezed the *United Irishman*. 'Sir Joseph' was within the precincts of the 'Lodge' when the joyful news arrived, and in a voice choked with emotion murmured, 'All hail, great Seizer!' "

## TO THE EDITOR OF *THE SPEAKER*

SIR,

It should be a principle of political life that all acts which involve public liberties should be done publicly; and the Irish Government has hitherto so far observed this principle as to prosecute papers when it suppresses them.

Lord Cadogan, who wishes to seem to be at peace with Ireland, has, however, adopted a different method with a newspaper, which certain friends of mine write and edit in the interests of a very uncompromising nationalism. The issues of this paper have been from time to time either partly or wholly seized in the post, and twice seized in the office of the paper; and always without any reason being given. The seizures in the post are unusually interesting to those who would study the methods of Irish government. As a rule a certain number of papers have been stopped each week, especially papers directed to America, with the desire, as many Dublin journalists believe, of making the subscribers think that the management is either incapable or anxious to keep their money without sending their papers. The seizure of a part of each issue attains this end at once quietly and sufficiently.

However, all copies posted of the issue of February 17th were seized, and, though no reason was given, it is tolerably certain that this unusual measure was adopted because of an article by Father Kavanagh explaining that according "to the doctrine of the Catholic Church" "No human authority can justify those who take part in an unjust war"—a doctrine which Count Tolstoy has preached continually. Mr. Henry Dixon wrote to the General Post-office [sic] asking why his copy had not reached him. The Secretary of the General Post Office replied:—

Sir—With reference to your application of the 22nd inst., I have to inform you that the copy of the *United Irishman* of the 17th, and addressed to you, has been detained by order of the Lord-Lieutenant.

Mr. Dixon then wrote to the Lord-Lieutenant sending a letter to each of his addresses, and registering the letters—such thoughts have we of our rulers—asking the reason of the seizure and pointing out that the papers at the newsagents had not been seized. He received an answer from the Lord-Lieutenant's secretary merely stating that the Lord-Lieutenant had ordered the Post Office not "to deliver the copy of the *United Irishman* newspaper to which you refer". It is obvious that the papers at the newsagents were not seized, because that would have made a noise and shown that Lord Cadogan was not at peace with Ireland. Mr. Dixon published this correspondence with a further letter of expostulation in the *United Irishman* of May 26th; upon which all copies of that day's issue were seized in the office of the paper. The paper reprinted the correspondence the week after, and called upon Lord Cadogan to prosecute; but this time it was not even seized, for it is most necessary that Lord Cadogan should seem to be at peace with Ireland.

One other issue was seized, the issue of April 7th, which contained a translation of an article on the Queen which Miss Gonne had written for a French paper, but this time Lord Cadogan, being supported by the presence of his Sovereign, ventured to ransack the newsagents and even the railway trains.

I ask your readers to watch Lord Cadogan and his Government, for history has told us that no Government can be entrusted with secret powers and when a Government is using them to persuade a somewhat

mocking world that it is at peace where it is indeed at war, secret powers
do not grow the less dangerous because they have grown absurd.

Yours sincerely,

W. B. Yeats

Dublin, June 27, 1900

# Irish Fairy Beliefs

Yeats's enthusiasm for the life led by such native Gaelic writers as Maurice
O'Sullivan, the subject of his last review (see p. 492 below), continued
throughout his life. But as early as "Irish Fairy Beliefs", his review of Daniel
Deeney's *Peasant Lore from Gaelic Ireland* (1900), in *The Speaker* for July 14,
1900, Yeats is troubled by the overriding problems of style and of finding, in
the native writer, necessary cultural sophistication. With his own work as a
folklorist largely behind him, Yeats uses this opportunity to frame the great
difficulties facing even someone like Deeney who, unlike Yeats himself,
knows Gaelic and dwells "at the gates of primitive and barbaric life".

SOME ten or eleven years ago, when I was compiling a little anthology
of Irish fairy and folk tales,[1] somebody asked an eminent authority to
advise me. He replied that there was little Irish folklore in print, that
could be trusted as one could trust the books of Scottish folklore, and
went on to moralise over the defects of Irish character. A couple of
years ago this eminent authority described the works of the Irish folklorists as more exhaustive and valuable than the works of the Scottish
folklorists. The truth is that moralising over defects and virtues of
national character is for the most part foolish, for the world is shaped
by habits of thought and habits of expression, and these, in young nations at any rate, can change with extreme swiftness. Ireland learned to
do in about five years the work she had neglected for a century, and the
intellectual awakening, which has given us so much, gave us Mr. Larminie, Mr. Curtin, Dr. Hyde,[2] the most admirable of all that have trans-

---

[1] Yeats published his *Fairy and Folk Tales of the Irish Peasantry* in 1888.

[2] William Larminie (1849–1900), an Irish poet, had published his *West Irish Folk Tales and
Romances* in 1893. His essay "Legends as Materials for Literature" had been published along
with pieces by Yeats, A.E. and John Eglinton as *Literary Ideals in Ireland* in 1899.
Jeremiah Curtin (1840–1906), a translator of works on folklore, was a collector of tales

lated out of the Gaelic of the country people, and some whose work is in magazines and newspapers. But because these writers, with the exception of Mr. Curtin in one little book,[3] have devoted themselves to the traditional tales and rather neglected the traditional beliefs one has a quite unworn welcome for Mr. Daniel Deeney, a National school teacher of Spiddal, in Western Galway, and a Gaelic speaker, who has got together a little bundle of tales of omens and charms and apparitions. He follows his masters wisely too, though here and there he shows a defect of the evil days of Croker and Lover,[4] and, while making some little incident vivid with characteristic dialogue, uses a word or phrase which has not come out of the life he is describing, but out of the life of some other place, or out of books. He should know the English dialect of Galway as few know it, and yet I am certain that "indade" is out of some novelist. The Irish countrypeople do not mispronounce, but rather over pronounce, the sound of the "ees" in "indeed," and surely "till" for "to" belongs to the north of Ireland, where Mr. Deeney was born, I believe, and not to Galway. He has heard many of his stories in Irish, I should imagine, for the countrypeople where he lives talk Irish principally, and, concluding very rightly that literary English is not a natural equivalent for the Irish of the countrypeople, has translated them into a dialect which even those who know it perfectly must continue to write imperfectly until it is classified and examined by learned men, as English and Scottish dialect has been. No merely instinctive knowledge can quite overcome a convention which

and legends. He collected Irish folk tales, some of which were published in book form and others of which appeared in the New York *Sun.*

Douglas Hyde (1860–1949), poet, folklorist and statesman, was the first president of Ireland (1938–45). He had been a founder of the Gaelic League in 1893 and its first president. His translations of Gaelic tales and poetry and his own poetry in Gaelic were primary instances of the revival of the Irish language and literature. Yeats cited Hyde's *Short History of Gaelic Literature* as one of the "two or three good books" published by the New Irish Library, the publishing venture of the Irish Literary Society.

[3] *Tales of the Fairies and of the Ghost World Collected from Oral Tradition in Southwest Munster*, London, 1895.

[4] Thomas Crofton Croker (1798–1854) was an early collector of Irish tales and legends. His several collections, which appeared in the 1820s and 1830s, were admired by Sir Walter Scott, among others. Samuel Lover (1797–1868), the Irish ballad-writer and novelist, published his collection of *Songs and Ballads* in 1839, and his comic novel about Irish character, *Handy Andy*, in 1842. "Croker and Lover," Yeats wrote in the "Introduction" to the *Fairy and Folk Tales of the Irish Peasantry*, "full of the ideas of harum-scarum Irish gentility, saw everything harmonised. The impulse of the Irish Literature of their time came from a class that did not—mainly for political reasons—take the populace seriously, and imagined the country as a humorist's Arcadia; its passion, its gloom, its tragedy, they knew nothing of." Yeats, however, appreciated each man's attempts to give "what was most noticed in his day"; he drew from Croker's *Fairy Legends and Traditions of the South of Ireland* (1825–8) and Lover's *Legends and Stories of Ireland* (1831) for the *Fairy and Folk Tales*. Lover's "Barney O'Reirdan" from *Legends and Stories of the Irish Peasantry* appeared in Yeats's list of thirty "Irish books" which was published in the *Daily Express* for February 27, 1895.

innumerable novelists and journalists have imposed upon the imagination. A safer equivalent would have been that English, as full of Gaelic constructions as the English of the countrypeople but without a special pronunciation, which Dr. Hyde has adopted in *Beside the Fire*,[5] the one quite perfect book of Irish folklore. Once, too, in telling a very wild and curious story of the Cladagh of Galway, he allows himself to look through the clouds of a literary convention. Lily-white fingers and flowing golden hair cannot be typical of the Cladagh, though they are typical of the heroines of forty years ago.

I point out these faults because Mr. Deeney, living in the middle of a primitive people and with a real knack in story and dialogue and a perfect knowledge of Gaelic, has only to work carefully at his craft to be of great importance to the intellectual awakening of Ireland. As it is he has made a book which makes one understand better than any book I know of the continual communion of the Irish countrypeople with supernatural beings of all kinds. A man who lives not far from Mr. Deeney once said to me, "There is no man mowing a meadow but sees them one time or another." These country people have seen what a king might give his crown and the world its wealth to have seen, and the doubts and speculations, that are in our eyes so great a part of the progress of the world, would be in their eyes, could they understand them, but dust in the hollow of a hand. Already some that have devoted themselves to the study of the visions and the beliefs of such people are asking whether it is we, still but very few, or primitive and barbaric people, still a countless multitude, who are the exceptions in the order of nature, and whether the seer of visions and hearer of voices is not the normal and healthy man. It may be that but a few years shall pass before many thousands have come to think that men like these mowers and fishers of Mr. Deeney's, who live a simple and natural life, possess more of the experience on which a true philosophy can be founded than we who live a hurried, troubled, unhealthy life. I am convinced, as I am convinced by no other thing, that this change will come; and it may be that this change will make us look to men like Mr. Deeney, who are at the gates of primitive and barbaric life, for a great deal of the foundations of our thought.

W. B. Yeats

[5] Douglas Hyde's *Beside the Fire* was published in London in 1890.

# Irish Witch Doctors

Yeats's article on "Irish Witch Doctors", in *The Fortnightly Review* for September, 1900, is the fifth in the series of folklore pieces which he prepared from materials collected, with his assistance, by Lady Gregory. (See pp. 54–55 above, about this series.)

THE Irish countryman certainly believes that a spiritual race lives all about him, having horses and cattle, and living much the same life that he does, and that this race snatches out of our life whatever horse or cow, or man or woman it sets its heart on; and this belief, harmonised with Christianity by certain ingenious doctrines, lives side by side with Christianity and has its own priesthood. This priesthood, sometimes called "faery doctors," sometimes "knowledgeable men," and sometimes "cow doctors," from its curing cows that have been "swept," as the word is, has secrets which no folklorist may ever perhaps wholly discover, for it lives in terror of the spiritual race who are, it believes, the makers and transmitters of its secrets. I have questioned these men, and some of them have talked to me pretty freely, so freely, indeed, that they were afraid for themselves afterwards, but I feel that there is more to be known about them, and that I know less about them than about anything else in Irish folklore. I met one man, whom I will call Kirwan, on the Galway coast last year. I cannot tell his whereabouts more freely, for he is afraid of the priests, and has made me promise to tell nobody where he lives. A friend of mine, who knew I was curious in these matters, had asked some of the coast people if there was anyone who did cures through the power of the faeries, as I wanted a cure for a weakness of the eyes that had been troubling me. A man I will call Daly said, "There's a man beyond is a great warrior in this business, and no man within miles of the place will build a house or a cabin or any other thing without going there to ask if it's a right place. He cured me of a pain in my arm I couldn't get rid of. He gave me something to drink, and he bid me to go to a quarry and to touch some of the stones that were lying outside it, and not to touch others of them. Anyway, I got well."

The country people are always afraid of building upon a path of "the Others," as they call the spirits, and one sometimes hears of houses being deserted because of their being "in the way," as the phrase is. The pain in the arm was doubtless believed to be what is called "the touch," an ailment that is thought to come from "the Others," and to be the beginning of being carried away. The man went on to give another example of Kirwan's power, a story of a horse that seemed possessed, as we would say, or "away" and something else put in its place, as he would say. "One time down by the pier we were gathering in the red seaweed; and there was a boy there was leading a young horse the same way he had been leading him a year or more. But this day, of a sudden, he made a snap to bite him; and, secondly, he reared and made as if to jump on top of him; and, thirdly, he turned round and made at him with the hoofs. And the boy threw himself on one side and escaped, but with the fright he got he went into the bed and stopped there. And the next day Kirwan came, and told him everything that had happened, and he said, 'I saw thousands on the strand near where it happened last night.' "

The next day my friend went to see the wife of "the great warrior in this business," to find out if he would cure my eyes. She found her in a very small cottage, built of very big stones, and of a three-cornered shape that it might fit into a crevice in the rocks. The old woman was very cautious at first, but presently drew her stool over to where my friend was sitting, and said, "Are you *right?* you are? then you are my friend. Come close and tell me is there anything Himself can do for you?" She was told about my eyes, and went on, "Himself has cured many, but sometimes *they* are vexed with him for some cure he has done, when he interferes with the herb with some person they are meaning to bring away, and many's the good beating they gave him out in the field for doing that. Myself they gave a touch to here in the thigh, so that I lost my walk; vexed they are with me for giving up the throwing of the cup." She had been accustomed to tell fortunes with tea-leaves. "I do the fortunes no more, since I got great abuse from the priest for it. Himself got great abuse from the priest, too, Father Peter, and he gave him plaster of Paris. I mean by that he spoke soft and humbugged him, but he does the cures all the same, and Father Maginn gave him leave when he was here." She asked for my Christian names, and when she heard them went on, "I'll keep that, for Himself will want it when he goes on his knees. And when he gathers the herb, if it's for a man, he must call on the name of some other man, and call him a King, *Righ*. And if it's for a woman, he must call on the name of some other woman, and call her a Queen. That is calling on the king or the queen of the plant." My friend asked where her husband had got the knowledge, and she answered, "It was from his sister he got the cure. Taken she was. We didn't tell John of it, where he was away caring horses. But he knew of it before he came home, for she followed him there one day he was out in the field, and when he didn't know her, she said, 'I'm your sister Kate.' And she said, 'I bring you a cure that you may cure both yourself and others.' And she told him of the herb, and the field he'd find it growing, and he must choose a plant with seven branches, the half of them above the clay and the half of them covered up. And she told him how to use it. Twenty years she's gone, but she's not dead yet, but the last time he saw her he said she was getting grey. Every May and November he sees her; he'll be seeing her soon now. When her time comes to die, she'll be put in the place of some other one that's taken, and so she'll get absolution. A nurse she has been all the time among them."

May and November, the beginning and end of the old Celtic year, are always times of supernatural activity in Ireland. She is to be put back as a changeling to get absolution when she is too old to be any more use among "the Others." All, one is almost always told, are put back in this way. I had been told near Gort that "the Others" had no children of their own, but only children they stole from our world. My friend, hearing her say that Kirwan's sister was a nurse, asked her about this. She said, "Don't believe those that say they have no children. A boy among them is as clever as any boy here, but he must be matched with a woman from earth; and the same way with their women, they must get a husband here. And they never can give the breast to a child, but must get a nurse from here." She was asked if she had herself seen "the Others," and if "Himself" saw them often. She said, "One time I saw them myself in a field, and they hurling. Bracket caps they wore, and bracket clothes of all colours. Some were the same size as ourselves, and some looked like gossoons that didn't grow well. But Himself has the second sight, and can see them in every place. There's as many of them in the sea as on the land, and sometimes they fly like birds across the bay. There is always a mistress among them. When one goes among them they would be all laughing and jesting, but when that tall mistress you heard of would tap her stick on the ground, they'd all draw to silence."

The clothes of "the Others" are always described as "bracket," which is the Irish for variegated, but is explained to mean striped by the country people when talking of "the Others." The old inhabitants of Ireland who have become "the Others," the people say, because they were magicians, and cannot die till the last day, wore striped clothes. The famous story of "The Quest of the Bull of Cualgne," preserved in in a manuscript of the eleventh century, makes its personages wear "striped" and "streaked" and "variegated" jackets of many colours.

It was arranged that I should go to Daly's house, and that Kirwan should go there to meet me after dark, that our meeting might not be noticed. We went to Daly's next evening, but found that Kirwan had been there earlier in the day to leave a bunch of herbs, which a botanist has since identified as the dog violet, for me to drink in boiled milk, which was to be brought to the boil three times; and to say that he could do nothing more for me, for what was wrong with my eyes "had nothing to do with that business," meaning that it was not the work of spirits. We left an urgent message asking Kirwan to come and talk to us, and next day Daly, who had been very doubtful if he would come, brought us word that he would come as soon as it was dark. We reached the cottage amid a storm of wind, and the door was cautiously opened, and we were let in. Kirwan was sitting on a low stool in a corner of a wide hearth, beside a bright turf fire. He was short and broad, with regular features, and had extraordinary dark and bright eyes, and though an old man, had, as is common among these sea people, thick dark hair. He wore a flannel-sleeved waistcoat, cloth trousers, patched on the knees with darker stuff, and held a soft felt hat in his hands, which he kept turning and squeezing constantly. Unlike his wife he spoke nothing but Irish. Daly sat down near us with a guttering candle in his hands, and interpreted. A reddish cat and a dog lay beside the fire, and sometimes the dog growled, and sometimes the woman of the house clutched her baby uneasily and looked frightened. Kirwan said, stopping every now and then for Daly to interpret, "It's not from *them* the harm came to your eyes. There's one of the eyes worse than the other" (which was true) "and it's not in the eyes that the trouble began" (which was true). I tried to persuade him that it might be "from them," to find out why he thought it was not, and I told him of a certain vision I had once, to make him feel that I was not a mere prying unbeliever. He said my eyes would get well, and gave me some more of the herb, but insisted that the harm was not "from *them*." He took the vision as a matter of course, and asked if I was ever accustomed to sleep out at night, but added that some might sleep out night after night and never fall into their power, or even see them. I asked if it was his friends among them who told what was wrong with anybody, and he said, "Yes, when it has to do with their business, but in this case they had nothing to do with it." My friend asked how he got his knowledge first, and he said, "It was when I was in the field one day a woman came beside me, and I went on to a gap in the wall, and she was in it before me. And then she stopped me, and she said, 'I'm your sister that was taken, and don't you remember how I got the fever first and you tended me, and then you got it yourself, and one had to be taken, and I was the one?' And she taught me the cure and the way to use it. And she told me she was in the best of places, and told me many things that she bound me not to tell. And I asked was it here she was kept ever since, and she said it was, but, she said, in six months I'll have to move to another place, and others will come where I am now, and it would be better for you if we stopped here, for the most of us here now are your neighbours and your friends. And it was she gave me the second sight."

I asked if he saw "them" often, and he said: "I see them in all places, and there's no man mowing a meadow that doesn't see them at some time or other. As to what they look like, they'll change colour and shape and clothes while you look round. Bracket caps they always wear. There is a king and a queen and a fool in each house of them, that is true enough, but they would do you no harm. The king and the queen are kind and gentle, and whatever you'll ask them for they will give it. They'll do no harm at all, if you don't injure them. You might speak to them if you'd meet them on the road, and they'd answer you, if you'd speak civil and quiet, and not be laughing or humbugging—they wouldn't like that."

He told a story about a woman we knew, who had been taken away among them to nurse their children, and how she had come back after— a story that I am constantly hearing—and then suddenly stopped talking and stooped to the hearth, and took up a handful of hot ashes in his hand, and put them into the pocket of his waistcoat, and said he'd be afraid going home, because he'd "have to tell what errand he had been on." I gave him some whisky out of my flask, and we left him.

The next day we saw Daly again, and he said, "I walked home with the old man last night, he was afraid to go by himself. He pointed out to me on the way home a graveyard where he got a great beating from them one night. He had a drop too much taken, after a funeral, and he went there to gather the plant, and gathered it wrong, and they came and punished him, that his head is not the better of it ever since. He told me the way he knows, in the gathering of the plant, what is wrong with the person that is looking for a cure. He has to go on his knees and to say a prayer to the king and the queen and to the gentle and the simple among them, and then he gathers it; and if there are black leaves about it, or white (withered) ones, but chiefly a black leaf folded down, he knows the illness is some of their doing. But for this young man the plant came fresh and clean and green. He has been among them himself, and has seen the king and the queen, and he says they are no bigger than the others, but the queen wears a wide cap, and the others have bracket caps. He never would allow me to build a shed beside the house here, though I never saw anything there myself."

We found an old man on the borders of Clare and Galway who knew English,[1] and was less afraid of talking to us, from whom we heard a

---

[1] In Lady Gregory's *Visions and Beliefs in the West of Ireland* (New York, 1920, vol. II, p. 92), this man's name is given as "Mr. Saggarton". Yeats also met on the borders of Clare and Galway a man—whom he called "Hearne"—who was the source for an article, "The Fool of Faery", which was reprinted in *The Celtic Twilight* (1902) as "The Queen and the Fool".

great deal. We went through a stony country, a good way from any town, and came at last to the group of poor cottages which had been described to us. We found his wife, a big, smiling woman, who told us that her husband was haymaking with their children. We went to the hay-field, and he came, very well pleased, for he knew my friend, to the stone wall beside the road. He was very square and gaunt, and one saw the great width of his chest through his open shirt, and recognised the great physical strength, supposed constantly to mark those who are in the service of "the Others." We talked of some relations of his, who were in good circumstances and tenants of my friend, and I think I told him some visionary experiences of my own. It was evident that he lived in great terror of "the Others," but gradually he began to talk. We asked him where he got his power to work cures, and he replied, "My uncle left me the power, and I was able to do them, and did many, but my stock was all dying, and what could I do? So I gave a part of the power to Mrs. Merrick, who lives in Gort, and she can do a great many things."

His stock died because of the anger of "the Others," or because some other life had to be given for every life saved. We asked about his uncle, and he said, "My uncle used to go away amongst them. When I was a young chap, I'd be out in the field working with him, and he'd bid me to go away on some message, and when I'd come back it might be in a faint I'd find him. It was he himself was taken, it was but his shadow or something in his likeness was left behind. He was a very strong man. You might remember Ger Kelly, what a strong man he was, and stout, and six feet two inches in height. Well, he and my uncle had a dispute one time, and he made as though to strike at him, and my uncle, without so much as taking off his coat, gave one blow that stretched him on the floor. And at the barn at Bunnahow he and my father could throw a hundredweight over the collar beam, what no other man could do. My father had no notion at all of managing things. He lived to be eighty years, and all his life he looked as innocent as that little chap turning the hay. My uncle had the same innocent look. I think they died quite happy."

He pointed out to us where there was a lake, and said, "My uncle one time told, by name, of a man that would be drowned there that day at 12 o'clock; and so it happened." We asked him if his uncle's knowledge was the same kind of knowledge as the knowledge of a famous wise woman called Biddy Early; and he said, "Surely I knew Biddy Early, and my uncle was a friend of hers. It was from the same they got the cures. Biddy Early told me herself that where she got it was, when she was a servant-girl in a house, there was a baby lying in the cradle, and he went on living for a few years. But he was friendly to her, and used to play tunes for her, and when he went away he gave her the bottle and the power. She had but to look in the bottle and she'd see all that had happened and all that was going to happen. But he made her give a promise that she'd never take more than a shilling for any cure she did, and she wouldn't have taken £50 if you had offered it to her, though she might take presents of bread and wine, and such things. The cure for all things in the world? Surely she had it, and knew where it was, and I knew it myself, too, but I could not tell you of it. Seven parts I used to make it with, and one of them's a thing that's in every house."

He had only told us of one spirit he had himself seen. He was walking with another man on the road to Galway, and he saw "a very small woman in a field beside the road, walking down towards us, and she smiling and carrying a can of water on her head, and she dressed in a blue spencer." and he asked the other man if he saw her, "but he did not, and when I came up to the wall she was gone." I have since heard, however, that he was "away" among them himself. He would only talk of what his uncle or somebody else had seen. I showed him some water-colour drawings of men and women of great beauty, and with very singular halos about their heads, which had been drawn and painted from visions by a certain Irish poet[2] who, if he lives, will have seen as many wonders as Swedenborg; and rather to my surprise, for I had thought the paintings too idealised for a peasant to understand, he became evidently excited. "They have crowns like that and of other shapes," he said, pointing to the halo. I asked if they ever made their crowns out of light, and he said, "They can do that." He said one of the paintings was of a queen, and that they had "different queens, not always the same, and clothes of all colours they wear." My friend held up a sapphire ring, and made it flash, and asked if their clothes were as beautiful. He said, "Oh, they are far grander than that, far grander than that. They have wine from foreign parts, and cargoes of gold coming in to them. The houses are ten times more beautiful and ten times grander than any house in this world, and they could build one of them up in that field in ten minutes. Coaches they make up when they want to go out driving, with wheels and all, but they want no horses. There might be twenty going out together sometimes, and all full of them. Youngsters they take mostly to do work for them, and they are death on handsome people, for they are handsome themselves. To all sorts of work they put them, digging potatoes, and the like. The people they bring

[2] The "certain Irish poet" is A.E. (George William Russell) (1867-1935), with whom Yeats had attended art school. In his *Autobiography*, Yeats gives a portrait of Russell at that time: "Men watched him with awe or with bewilderment; it was known that he saw visions continually, perhaps more continually than any modern man since Swedenborg . . ." (p. 163).

away must die some day, but as to themselves they were living from past ages, and can never die till the time when God has his mind made up to redeem them. And those they bring away are always glad to be brought back again. If you were to bring a heifer from those mountains beyond and to put it into a meadow, it would be glad to get back again to the mountain, because it's the place it knows."

And he showed us a sign with the thumb that we were never to tell to anybody, but that we were to make if we ever felt "a sort of shivering in the skin when we were walking out, for that shows that something is near." If we held our hand like that we might go "into a forth itself" and get no harm, but we were not to neglect that, "for if they are glad to get one of us they'd be seven times better pleased to get the like of you. And they are everywhere around us, and now they may be within a yard of us on this grass. But if I ask you, What day's to-morrow? and you said Thursday, they wouldn't be able to overhear us. They have the power to go in every place, even on the book the priest is reading!"

To say, "What day is to-morrow?" and be answered "Thursday," or to say, "What day is this?" and be answered "Thursday," or to say, "God bless them Thursday," is a common spell against being overheard, but in some places the country people think that it is enough to be told what day the next day, or that day, really is. There is no doubt some old pagan mystery in Thursday, and if we knew more about the old Celtic week of nine nights we might understand it.

We went to see old Langan, as I will call him, another day, and found him hay-making as before, but he went with us into his house, where he gave us tea and home-made bread, both very good. He would take no money either that time or the time before, and his manner was very courteous and dignified. He told much more about "the Others," this time. He said: "There are two classes, the Dundonians, that are like ourselves, and another race more wicked and more spiteful. Very small they are and wide, and their belly sticks out in front, so that what they carry, they don't carry it on the back, but in front, on the belly, in a bag."

The Dundonians are undoubtedly the Tuatha de Danaan, and Folk of the Goddess Danu, the old gods of Ireland, and the men with the bags on their stomachs undoubtedly the Firbolg, or Bag Men, as it is commonly translated, who are thought by M. de Jubainville an inferior Divine race, and by Prof. Rhys[3] an inferior human race conquered by

[3] Yeats refers to Marie Henri d'Arbois de Jubainville (1827–1910), the author of a twelve-volume *Cours de littérature celtique* (1883–1902), and specifically to the second volume, *Le cycle mythologique irlandais et la mythologie celtique* (1884), translated into English by Richard Irvine Best (1872–1959) and published in Dublin in 1903. Jubainville was a friend of Maud Gonne

the Celts. The old Irish epic tales associate the Megalithic ruins upon
Aran with the Firbolg, and a friend, Mr. Synge,[4] tells me that the people
of Aran call the builders of the ruins belly-men. Bolg in Irish means bag
or belly.

He went on: "There are fools among them, dressed in strange clothes
like mummers, but it may be the fools are the wisest after all. There is a
queen in every regiment or house of them. It is of those they steal away
they make queens for as long as they live, or that they are satisfied with
them. There were two women fighting at a spring of water, and one hit
the other on the head with a can and killed her. And after that her children began to die. And the husband went to Biddy Early, and as soon as
she saw him she said, 'There's nothing I can do for you. Your wife was
a wicked woman, and the one she hit was a queen among them, and she
is taking your children one by one, and you must suffer till twenty-one
years are up.' And so he did."

We asked him if he ever knew anybody "the Others" had given
money to, and he said, "As to their treasure, it's best be without it.
There was a man living by a forth, and where his house touched the
forth he built a little room and left it for them, clean and in good order,
the way they'd like it. And whenever he'd want money, for a fair or the
like, he'd find it laid on the table in the morning. But when he had it
again he'd leave it there, and it would be taken away in the night. But
after that going on for a time, he lost his son.

"There was a room at Cregg where things used to be thrown about,
and every one could hear the noises there. They had a right to clear it
out and settle it the way they'd like it." Then he turned to my friend
and said, "You should do that in your own big house. Set out a little
room for them with spring water in it always, and wine you might
leave—no, not flowers, they wouldn't want so much as that, but just
what will show your good will."

A man at Kiltartan had told us that Biddy Early had said to him,
"There is a cure for all the evil in the world between the two millwheels
at Ballylee," and I asked what cure that could be. He said, "Biddy Early's
cure that you heard of, between the two wheels of Ballylee, it was the

and an early influence upon J. M. Synge, who had attended his lectures at the Sorbonne in
February and March of 1898.

Professor John Rhys (1840–1915) was the author of *Lectures on the Origin and Growth of
Religion as Illustrated by Celtic Heathendom* (The Hibbert Lectures, 1886), published in
London in 1888, to which Yeats refers in a letter of that year (*Letters*, p. 92). In the second
lecture, "The Zeus of the Insular Celts", Rhys identifies the "Bag Men" as the race conquered by the Celts.

4 This is one of Yeats's earliest public citations of John Millington Synge (1871–1909).
Although he had met Synge in Paris in 1896, Yeats was writing to Lady Gregory about him
in February, 1899, as if the two men were only then becoming well acquainted (*Letters*,
p. 314).

moss on the water of the millstream. It can cure all things brought about by *them*, but not any common ailment. But there is no cure for the stroke given by a queen or a fool."

We told him of an old man who had died a little time before, and how fighting was heard by the neighbours before he died. He said, "They were fighting when Stephen Gorham died, that is what often happens. Everyone has friends among them, and the friends would try to save, when the others would be trying to bring you away. Youngsters they pick up here and there, to help them in their fighting or in their work. They have cattle and horses, but all of them have only three legs. The handsome they like, and the good dancers, and the straight and firm; they don't like those that go to right and left as they walk. And if they get a boy amongst them, the first to touch him, he belongs to her. They don't have children themselves, only the women that are brought away among them have children, but those don't live for ever like the Dundonians. They can only take a child, or a horse, or such a thing, through the eye of a sinner. If his eye falls on it, and he speaks and doesn't say 'God bless it,' they can bring it away then. But if you say it yourself in your heart, it will do as well. They take a child through the eye of its father, a wife through the eye of her husband." The meaning was that if you look at anybody or anything with envy or desire of admiration, it may be used by "the Others," as a link between them and the thing or person they are coveting. One finds this thought all over Ireland, and it is probably the origin of the belief in the evil eye. Blake thought that everything is "the work of spirits, no less than digestion and sleep;" [5] and this thought means, I think, that every emotion, which is not governed by our will, or suffused with some holy feeling, is the emotion of spirits who are always ready to bring us under their power. Langan had himself been accused once of giving a chicken into the power of "the Others." "One time myself, when I went to look for a wife, I went to the house, and there was a hen and a brood of small chickens before the door. Well, after I went home, one of the chickens died. And what do you think they said, but that it was I overlooked it."

This seems to have broken off the marriage for a time, but he married her in the end, and has had to suffer all kinds of misfortunes because of her. "The Others" tried to take her first, the day after her marriage using, as I understand, his feelings about her as their link between her and them. "My wife got a touch from them, and they have a watch on her ever since. It was the day after I married, and I went to the fair of

---

[5] Yeats paraphrases a passage from *Jerusalem*: "We who dwell on Earth can do nothing of ourselves; every thing is conducted by Spirits, no less than Digestion or Sleep" (in "To the Public", a prefatory letter to *Jerusalem*, vol. III, p. 167 of *The Writings of William Blake*, ed. Geoffrey Keynes, London, 1925).

Clarenbridge. And when I came back the house was full of smoke, but there was nothing on the hearth but cinders, and the smoke was more like the smoke of a forge. And she was within lying on the bed, and her brother was sitting outside the door crying. And I took down a fork from the rafters, and asked her was it a broom, and she said it was. So then I went to the mother and asked her to come in, and she was crying too, and she knew well what had happened, but she didn't tell me, but she sent for the priest. And when he came, he sent me for Geoghagan, and that was only an excuse to get me away, and what he and the mother tried was to get her to face death. But the wife was very stout, and she wouldn't give in to them. So the priest read mass, and he asked me, would I be willing to lose something. And I said, so far as a cow or a calf, I wouldn't mind losing that."

Smiths are often associated with "the Others," and with magic in Ireland, and so the room filled "with the smoke of a forge." S. Patrick prayed against the spells of smiths. The question about the fork was to find out if she was in what we would call an hypnotic state, receptive to every suggestion. "Well, she partly recovered, but from that day no year went by, but I lost ten lambs maybe, or other things. And twice they took my children out of the bed, two of them I have lost. And the others they gave the touch to. That girl there, see the way she is, and she is not able to walk. In one minute it came on her, out in the field, with the fall of a wall." He told the girl to come out from where she sat in the corner of the chimney, with the dazed vacant look that one saw on the faces of the other children. She staggered for a foot or two, and then sat down again. From our point of view, her body was paralysed and her mind gone. She was tall and gentle-looking, and should have been a strong, comely, country girl. The old man went on: "Another time the wife got a touch, and she got it again, and the third time she got up in the morning, and went out of the house and never said where she was going. But I had her watched, and I told the boy to follow her, and never lose sight of her. And I gave him the sign to make if he'd meet any bad thing. So he followed her, and she kept before him, and while he was going along the road, something was up on top of the wall with one leg. A red-haired man it was, with a thin face and no legs [sic]. But the boy got hold of him and made the sign, and carried him till he came to the bridge. At first he could not lift him, but after he had made the sign he was quite light. And the woman turned home again, and never had a touch after. It's a good job the boy had been taught the sign. It was one among them that wanted the wife. A woman and a boy we often saw coming to the door, and she was the matchmaker. And when we would go out, they would have vanished."

He told us some other little odds and ends about a warning his uncle had given against cutting down a certain bush before his house, and how, when it was cut down twenty years after his uncle's death, a bullock died; and that "Danes hate Irishmen to this day," and that "when there is a marriage in Denmark," he has been told, "the estates they owned in Ireland are handed down" (I have heard something like this in Sligo also); and then, evidently feeling that he was telling us a great mystery, he said, "The cure I made with seven parts, and I took three parts of each, and I said, Father, Son, and Holy Spirit be on it, and with that I could go into a forth or any place. But as to the ingredients, you could get them in any house."

We did not ask him for the ingredients, nor do I believe that any threat or any bribes would ever get them from him. When we were going, he said, and we were both struck by his dignity as he said it, "Now I've told you more than ever I told my wife. And I could tell you more, but I'd suffer in my skin for it. But if ever you, or one belonging to you, should be in trouble, come to me, and what I can to do relieve you, I'll do it."

Kirwan spoke of seeing his spirits, and Langan his, while in their ordinary state; but only those who are at times "away," that is, who are believed to go away among the spirits, while their bodies are in a trance, are thought to be able to bring back those who are "away." In ancient Ireland it was only a *File* who had the knowledge of a certain ritual called the *imbas forosna*, or great science which enlightens, whereby he could pass as many as nine days in trance, who had the full knowledge of his order. It was long before we could find anyone who was "away" and would tell us what it was like, for almost all who are "away" believe that they must be silent. At last an old woman, whom I will call Mrs. Sheridan, after telling many lesser things, told us what it was like. My friend had gone to see her one day, and been told a few curious things, but cautiously, for her daughter, who was afraid of such things, was there. She had said, "Come here close, and I'll tell you what I saw at the old castle there below.[6] I was passing there in the evening, and I saw a great house and a grand one, with screens at the end of it, and windows open. Coole House is nothing to what it was for size or grandeur. And there were people inside, and a lady leaning out of the window, and her hair turned back, and she made a sign to me, and ladies walking about, and a bridge over the river. For they can build up such things all in a minute. And two coaches came driving up and across the bridge to the house, and in one of them I saw two gentlemen, and I knew them both well, and both of them had died long before. One was Redmond Joyce, and the other was the master's own father. As to the coach

[6] Lady Gregory tells this story in the "Mrs. Sheridan" chapter of *Visions and Beliefs* (vol. I, pp. 74-5), where the "old castle there below" is "Ballinamantane".

and horses, I didn't take much notice of them for I was too much taken up with looking at the gentlemen. And a man came and called out to me and asked, would I come across the bridge, and I said I would not. And he said it would be better for you if you did; you'd go back heavier than you came. I suppose by that he meant they'd give me some good thing. And then two men took up the bridge and laid it against the wall. Twice I've seen that same thing, the house and the coaches, and the bridge, and I know well I'll see it a third time before I die."

This woman had never seen a drawbridge, and she had not read about one, for she cannot read. "It would have cost a penny a week to go to school," she explains, and it is most unlikely that she has ever seen a picture of one. The peasants continually see in their visions the things and costumes of past times, and this can hardly be tradition, for they have forgotten the names of their own great-grandfathers, and know so little about ancient customs that they will tell you about Finn MacCool flinging a man over a haystack on his way to the assizes in Cork.

They had met another day on the road, and as they came opposite to a very big twisted thorn-tree, the old woman had curtsied very low to the bush, and said, "And that's a grand bush we're passing by— whether it's a bush belonging to them I don't know, but wherever they get shelter, there they might be, but anyway it's a fine bush, God bless it." But she had not said anything about being "away." At last, one day she came and sat with us and talked and seemed very glad to talk. She is one of the handsomest old country-women I have ever seen, and though an old woman, is vigorous in mind and body. She does not seem to know the cures that Kirwan and Langan know, and has not, I think, any reputation for doing cures. She says, however[7]—"I know the cure for anything *they* can do to you, but it's few I'd tell it to. It was a strange woman came in and told it to me, and I never saw her again. She bid me to spit and to use the spittle, or to take a graineen of dust from the navel, and that's what you should do if anyone you care for gets a cold or a shivering, or they put anything upon him.

"All my life I've seen them, and enough of them. One day I was with John Cuniff by the big hole near his house, and we saw a man and a woman coming from it, and a great troop of children, little boys they seemed to be, and they went through the gate into Coole, and there we could see them running and running along by the wall. And I said to John Cuniff, 'It may be a call for one of us,' and he said, 'Maybe it's for some other one it is.' But on that day next week he was dead."

She has seen the coach-a-baur, or deaf coach, as it is called from the deaf or rumbling sound it makes, in which they drive about.

"I saw the coach one night near the chapel. Long it was, and black,

[7] Lady Gregory gives this statement in *Visions and Beliefs* (vol. I, p. 85).

and I saw no one in it. But I saw who was sitting up driving it, and I knew it to be one of the Fardys that was taken some time before. I never saw them on horses, but when I came to live at Martin Macallum's, he used to bring in those red flowers that grow by the road, when their stalks were withered, to make the fire. And one day I was out in the road, and two men came over to me, and one was wearing a long grey dress, and he said to me, 'We have no horses to ride on, and we have to go on foot, because you have too much fire.' So then I knew it was their horses we were burning."

She seems to confuse red and yellow, and to have meant the yellow *bucalauns* or ragweeds, believed to be the horses of "the Others." Ragweed is given as a medicine to horses, and it may have got its association with the horses of "the Others" through its use in witch medicine.

"One day I saw a field full of them, some were picking up stones to clear it, and some were ploughing it up. But the next day, when I went by, there was no sign of it being ploughed up at all. They can do nothing without some live person is looking at them, that's why they were always so much after me."

One is constantly hearing that "the Others" must have a mortal among them, for almost everything they do, and one reads as constantly in the old Irish epic tales of mortals summoned by the gods to help them in battles. The tradition seems to be that, though wisdom comes to us from among spirits, the spirits must get physical power from among us. One finds a modification of the same idea in the spiritualistic theory of mediumship. Mrs. Sheridan went on: "One time I went up to a forth to pick up a few sticks for the fire, and I was breaking one of the sticks on the ground, and a voice said from below, 'Is it to break down the house you want?' and a thing appeared that was like a cat, but bigger than any cat ever was. And one time I was led astray in Coole, where I went to gather sticks for the fire. I was making a bundle of them, and I saw a boy beside me and a little dogeen with me, a grey one. And at first I thought it was Andrew Healy, and then I saw it was not. And he walked along with me, and I asked him did he want any of the sticks, and he said he did not, and as we were walking he seemed to grow bigger. And when we came to where the caves go underground he stopped, and I asked him his name, and he said, 'You should know me, for you've seen me often enough.' And then he was gone, and I knew he was no living thing.

"One day I was following the goat, to get a sup of milk from her, and she turned into the field and up into the castle of Lydican, and went up from step to step up the stairs to the top, and I followed, and on the stairs a woman passed me, and I knew her to be Ryan's wife that died. And when I got to the top I looked up, and there standing on the wall was a woman looking down at me, long-faced and tall, and with bracket clothes, and on her head something yellow and slippery, not hair, but like marble. And I called out to ask her wasn't she afraid to be up there, and she said she was not, And a herd that used to live below in the castle saw the same woman one night he went up to the top, and a room and a fire, and she sitting at it, but when he went there again there was no sign of her or of the room.

"I know that I used to be away with them myself, but how they brought me I don't know; but when I'd come back, I'd be cross with my husband and with all; and I believe that I was cross with *them* when they wouldn't let me go. I met a man on the road one time, he had striped clothes like the others, and he told me why they didn't keep me altogether was because they didn't like cross people to be with them. The husband would ask me where I was, and why I stopped so long away; but I think he knew I was taken, and it fretted him; but he never spoke much about it. But my mother knew it well, but she'd try to hide it. The neighbours would come in and ask where was I, and she'd say I was sick in the bed, for whatever was put there in place of me would have the head in under the clothes. And when a neighbour would bring me in a drink of milk, my mother would put it by, and say, "Leave her now, maybe she'll drink it tomorrow.' And, maybe, in a day or two I'd meet a friend, and she'd say, 'Why wouldn't you speak to me when I went into the house to see you?' And I was a young, fresh woman at that time. Where they brought me to I don't know; nor how I got there; but I'd be in a very big house, and it round, the walls far away that you'd hardly see them, and a great many people all round about. I would see there neighbours and friends that I knew, and they in their own clothing, and with their own appearance, but they wouldn't speak to me, nor I to them, and when I'd meet them again, I'd never say to them that I saw them there. But the others had all long faces, and striped (bracket) clothes of blue and all colours, and they'd be laughing and talking and moving about. What language did they speak? Irish, of course; what else would they speak? And there was one woman of them, very tall, and with a long face, standing in the middle, taller than anyone you ever saw in this world, and a tall stick in her hand: she was the Mistress. She had a high yellow thing on her head—not hair—her hair was turned back under it, like the woman I saw at the window of the castle, and she had a long yellow cloak hanging down behind, and down to her feet."

I showed her a picture of a spirit, by the seer I have already spoken of, and made her look at the halo, which is made up of rods of light, with balls of gold light upon their ends, and asked if she had anything like that on her head. She answered, "It was not on her head, it was lower down here about the body," and by body she seemed to mean the waist. The old epic tales talk constantly of golden apples being used as ornaments. She looked at the brooch in the picture, a great wheel brooch, and said, "She had a brooch like that in the picture, but hanging low down like the other." I took up a different picture, a picture of a gigantic spirit, with the same rod-like head-dress, leaning over a sleeping man. It was painted in dull blue and grey, and very queer. She did not wait for me to question her, but said, "And that picture you have there in your hand, I saw one like it on the wall. It was a very big place and very grand, and a long, long table set out, and grand food offered me, and wine, but I never would touch it. And sometimes I had to give the breast to a child; and there were cradles in the room. I didn't want to stop there, and I began crying to get home, and the tall woman touched me here on the breast with the stick in her hand; she was vexed to see me wanting to go away.

"They have never brought me away since the husband died, but it was they took him from me." She has much fear of "the Others," and tells of many mischiefs they have done her. She went on to tell of her husband's death. "It was in the night, and he lying beside me, and I woke and heard him move, and I thought I heard someone with him. And I put out my hand, and what I touched was an iron hand, like knitting needles it felt. And I heard the bones of his neck crack, and he gave a sort of a choked laugh; and I got out of the bed and struck a light, and saw nothing, but I thought I heard someone go through the door. And I called to Honor, and she didn't come, and I called again, and she came; and she said she struck a light when she heard me calling, and was coming, and someone came and struck the light from her hand. And when we looked in the bed he was dead, and not a mark on him."

They have taken also two of her children. "There was a child of my own, and he but a year and a-half old, and he got a quinsy and a choking in the throat, and I was holding him in my arms beside the fire, and all in a minute he died. And the men were working down by the river washing sheep, and they heard the crying of a child pass over them in the air, and they said, 'That's Sheridan's child that's brought away.' So I know, sure enough, that he was taken."

Another fell under their power through being brought to Biddy Early by a neighbour. "There was a woman, Mrs. Merrick, had something wrong with her, and she went to Biddy Early, and nothing would do her but to bring my son along with her. And I was vexed—what call had she to bring him there? And when Biddy Early saw him she said, 'You'll travel far, but wherever you go, you'll not escape.' The woman he went up with died about six months after; but he went to

America, and he wasn't long there, when what was said came true and he died. They followed him sure enough as far as he went. And one day since then I was on the road to Gort, and Macan said to me, 'Your son is on the road before you.' And I said, 'How can that be and he dead?' But for all that, I hurried on. And on the road I met a little boy and I asked did he see anyone, and he said, 'You know well who I saw.' But I got no sight of him at all myself."

They have injured her and annoyed her in all kinds of ways. "Even when I was a child I could see them, and once they took my walk from me and gave me a bad foot. And my father cured me, and if he did, in five days after he died. But there's not much harm at all in them, not much harm." She said there was not much harm in them for fear they might be listening. "Three times when I went for water to the well the water was spilled over me, and I told Honor after that, they must bring the water themselves, I'd go for it no more. And the third time it was done there was a boy—one of the Healys—was near, and when he heard what happened me, he said, 'It must have been the woman that was at the well along with you that did that.' And I said, 'There was no woman at the well along with me.' 'There was,' he said: 'I saw her there beside you, and she with two tin cans in her hand.' One time after I came to live here, a strange woman came into the house, and I asked what was her name; and she said, 'I was in it before you were in it;' and she went into the room inside, and I saw her no more. But Honor and Martin saw her coming in the door, and they asked me who she was, for they never saw her before. And in the night, where I was sleeping at the foot of the bed, she came and threw me out on the floor, that the joint of my arm has a mark on it yet. And every night she'd come, and she'd spite and annoy me in some way. And at last we got Father Boyle to come and to drive her out. And as soon as he began to read, there went out of the house a great blast, and there was a sound as loud as thunder. And Father Boyle said, 'It's well for you she didn't have you killed before she went.'"

And another time a man said to her in a forth, "'Here's gold for you, but don't look at it till you go home.' And I looked and saw horse-dung, and I said, 'Keep it yourself, much good may it do you.' They never gave me anything did me good, but a good deal of torment I had from them." She is afraid that the cat by her hearth may be one of *them* in disguise, come to work her some evil. "There's something that's not right about an old cat, and it's well not to annoy them. I was in the house one night, and one came in, and he tried to bring away the candle that was lighting in the candlestick, and it standing on the table. And I had a little rod beside me, and I made a hit at him with it, and with that he dropped the candle, and made at me, as if to kill me. And I went on

my two knees, and I asked his pardon three times, and when I asked it the
third time he got quiet all of a minute, and went out the door. But when
you speak of them, you should always say the day of the week. Maybe
you didn't notice that I said, 'This is Friday,' just as we passed the gate."

I did not see her again, but last winter my friend heard she was ill,
and went to see her. She said: "It's very weak I am, and took to my
bed since yesterday. *They* have changed now out of where they were,
near the castle, and it's inside the demesne they are. It was an old man
told me that; I met him on the road there below. First I thought he was
a young man, and then I saw he was old, and he grew very nice-looking
after, and he had plaid clothes. 'We've moved out of that now,' he
said, 'and it's strangers will be coming in it. And you ought to know
me,' he said.

"It's about a week ago, one night someone came in the room, in the
dark, and I knew it was my son that I lost, he that went to America—
Mike. He didn't die; he was whipped away. I knew he wasn't dead, for
I saw him one day on the road to Gort on a coach, and he looked down
and he said, 'That's my poor mother.' And when he came in here I
couldn't see him, but I knew him by his talk. And he said, 'It's asleep
she is,' and he put his two hands on my face, and I never stirred. And he
said, 'I'm not far from you now.' For he is with the Others, inside Coole,
near where the river goes down. To see me he came, and I think he'll
be apt to come again before long. And last night there was a light about
my head all the night, and no candle in the room at all."

W. B. Yeats

# Irish Language and Irish Literature

Although he contributed an amiable letter on "Irish Language and Irish
Literature" to the first issue of *The Leader*, on September 1, 1900, Yeats soon
found himself squabbling with the nationalist paper's flinty editor, D. P.
Moran. In his second issue, Moran agreed to disagree with Yeats, insisting
"that nothing can be Irish literature that is not written in the Irish language"
and anticipating that "we still have sufficient difference . . . to lend zest,
perhaps, to many a future exchange". Moran proved ever ready to correct lapsed nationalists as in the matter of Yeats's attendance at the "Corinthian Club Dinner" in 1907 (p. 355 below).

Moran often helped with the work of the Gaelic League but he criticized
its preoccupation with the language for its own sake. He came to view much
of the work of the Irish literary revival as shallow commercialism and Yeats's

emergence as a representative of the national renaissance seemed, to Moran,
"one of the most glaring frauds that the credulous Irish people have ever
swallowed" (quoted in O'Brien, ed., *The Shaping of Modern Ireland*, London,
1960, p. 111).

Galway, August 26th

DEAR SIR,
    I look upon the appearance of THE LEADER as of importance,
for it will express, I understand, and for the first time, the loves and
hates, the hopes and fears, the thoughts and ideals of the men who have
made the Irish language a political power. *Claideamh Soluis* and *Fainne an
Lae*,[1] because of their preoccupation with the language itself, have been
unable to make that free comment on the life about them, which the
times require, if illusions that were, perhaps, truths in their day are not
to cling about us and drown us. Ireland is at the close of a long period
of hesitation, and must set out before long under a new policy, and it is
right that any man who has anything to say should speak clearly and
candidly while she is still hesitating. I myself believe that unless a great
foreign war comes to re-make everything, we must be prepared to turn
from a purely political nationalism with the land question as its lever, to
a partly intellectual and historical nationalism like that of Norway, with
the language question as its lever. The partial settlement of the land
question has so limited the number of men on whom misrule presses
with an immediate pressure, and ten years of recrimination have so
tarnished the glory that once surrounded politics as a mere game, that
the people of Ireland will not in our time give a full trust to any man
who has not made some great spectacular sacrifice for his convictions,
or that small continual sacrifice which enables a man to become himself
Irish, to become himself an embodiment of some little of the national
hope. We will always have politics of some kind, and we may have
to send members of Parliament to England for a long time to come,
but our politics and our members of Parliament will be moved, as I
think, by a power beyond themselves, though by one which they will
gladly obey, as they were moved by a power beyond themselves, which
they gladly obeyed, in the recent debate on the report of the Commissioners of Education.[2] We need not feel anxious because the new move-

[1] *An Claideamh Soluis* (*The Sword of Light*), edited by Eoin MacNeill (1867–1945) and
Padraig Pearse (1879–1916), was the official organ of the Gaelic League, the declared objects
of which were: the preservation of Irish as the national language of Ireland, the extension of
its use as a spoken tongue, the study and publication of Gaelic literature, and the cultivation
of a modern literature in Irish. *An Claideamh Soluis* absorbed the earlier publication *Fainne an
Lae* (*Dawn*), which name was adopted again briefly in 1908 and again in 1922–30.
[2] The Viceregal Commission on Intermediate Education, whose hearings Yeats had
drawn attention to in his letter on "The Academic Class and the Agrarian Revolution" on
March 11, 1899, above, reported on August 14 of that year. In subsequent debate in the

ment has taken a firmer hold in the towns than in the country places, for very many of the priesthood are coming to understand that the Irish language is the only barrier against the growing atheism of England, just as we men of letters have come to understand that it is the only barrier against the growing vulgarity of England; and the priesthood can do what they like with the country places. In ten years or in fifteen years or in twenty years the new movement will be strong enough to shake governments, and, unlike previous movements that have shaken governments, it will give continuity to public life in Ireland, and make all other righteous movements the more easy.

I do not think that I am likely to differ very seriously from you and from your readers about this movement, and for the very reason that it is a national movement, a movement that can include the most different minds. I must now, however, discuss another matter, about which I have differed and may still differ from you and from many of your readers. Side by side with the spread of the Irish language, and with much writing in the Irish language, must go on much expression of Irish emotion and Irish thought, much writing about Irish things and people, in the English language, for no man can write well except in the language he has been born and bred to, and no man, as I think, becomes perfectly cultivated except through the influence of that language; and this writing must for a long time to come be the chief influence in shaping the opinions and the emotions of the leisured classes in Ireland in so far as they are concerned with Irish things, and the more sincere it is, the more lofty it is, the more beautiful it is, the more will the general life of Ireland be sweetened by its influence, through its influence over a few governing minds. It will always be too separate from the general life of Ireland to influence it directly, and it was chiefly because I believed this that I differed so strongly in 1892 and 1893 from Sir Charles Gavan Duffy and his supporters, who wished to give such writing an accidental and fleeting popularity by uniting it with politics and economics.[3] I believe that Ireland cannot have a Burns

---

House of Commons on July 19, 1900, John Redmond (1856–1917), John Dillon (1851–1927) and T. M. Healy (1855–1931) raised the long-simmering question of the teaching of the Irish language, along with complaints that, under the proposed system, Irish funds would be diverted to teachers' pensions and that money would be denied certain parochial schools. Their attempts to amend the bill on July 19 and again on July 26 resulted only in the expansion of the membership of the controlling board.

[3] Sir Charles Gavin Duffy (1816–1903), journalist and statesman, had been a leader of the Young Ireland movement in the 1840s. He emigrated to Australia in 1855 and did not return to Ireland until 1880. Yeats had opposed his titular leadership of the publishing scheme undertaken by the Irish Literary Society and the National Literary Society in 1892, fearing Duffy "wanted 'to complete the Young Ireland movement'—to do all that had been left undone because of the Famine, or the death of Davis, or his own emigration" (*Autobiography*, p. 152), rather than encourage imaginative works by younger writers.

or a Dickens, because the mass of the people cease to understand any
poetry when they cease to understand the Irish language, which is the
language of their imagination, and because the middle class is the great
supporter and originator of the more popular kind of novels, and we
have no middle class to speak of; but I believe that we may have a
poetry like that of Wordsworth and Shelley and Keats, and a prose like
that of Meredith and Pater and Ruskin. There will be a few of all classes
who will read this kind of literature, but the rest will read and listen to
the songs of some wandering Raftery,[4] or of some poet like Dr. Hyde,[5]
who has himself high culture, but makes his songs out of the thoughts
and emotions he finds everywhere about him, and out of the circumstances of a life that is kept poetical by a still useful language, or they
will go to perdition with their minds stuffed full of English vulgarity;
till perhaps a time has come when no Irishman need write in any but
his own language.

We can bring that day the nearer by not quarrelling about names, and
by not bringing to literary discussion, which needs a delicate and careful temper, the exasperated and violent temper we have learned from a
century of political discussion. You have decided, and rightly, consider-
ing your purpose, to call all "literature concerning Ireland written in
English," "Anglo-Irish literature," and I shall certainly do the same
when I would persuade a man that nothing written in English can unite
him perfectly to the past and future of his country, but I will certainly
call it Irish literature, for short, when I would persuade him that "Farewell to Ballyshannon and the Winding Banks of Erne" should be more
to him than "The Absent-Minded Beggar,"[6] or when I am out of

---

[4] The blind Gaelic poet, Anthony Raftery (*c.* 1784–1835) was Yeats's lifelong exemplar of
the popular poet. In 1899, he had heard Raftery's verses on Mary Hynes and had begun, in
"'Dust Hath Closed Helen's Eye'" both the identification of Raftery and Mary with Homer
and Helen and the creation of the tower at Ballylee, near which she had lived and died, as his
personal symbol. Yeats expands this conception of popular poetry's importance to Ireland
in his essay on "Literature and the Living Voice", where he describes a pilgrimage, probably
in 1903, to Raftery's grave in Killeenan, Co. Mayo (see *Explorations*, New York, 1962, pp.
202–21).

[5] See p. 217 above.

[6] When it first appeared in 1865, "The Winding Banks of Erne; or, The Emigrant's
Adieu to Ballyshanny", by William Allingham, bore the notation, "A Local Ballad".
Although he omitted the notation when it was included in *A Book of Irish Verse* (1895),
Yeats obviously cites it here to draw attention to the authenticity of such ballads. The
contrast could hardly be greater between this gentle catalogue of relinquished pleasures and
Kipling's "ballad", "The Absent-Minded Beggar", which exhorts the hearer to pay up for
the girls and families that "Tommy's left behind him":

> *When you've shouted "Rule Britannia", when you've sung "God save the Queen,"*
> *When you've finished killing Kruger with your mouth,*
> *Will you kindly drop a shilling in my little tambourine*
> *For a gentleman in khaki ordered South?*

temper with all hyphenated words, or with all names that are a mixture of Latin and English. Such things are governed by usage and convenience, and I do not foresee a day when there will not be Englishmen who will call Walt Whitman English literature, and merely because they like him, and Englishmen who will call him American literature, and merely because they dislike him. And I would be sorry to see a day when I should not find a certain beautiful sermon of St. Columbanus, which compares life to a roadway on which we journey for a little while, and to the rising and falling of smoke,[7] in accounts of Irish literature, as well as in accounts of the Latin literature of the Early Church.

Whether we dispute about names or not, the temper of our dispute is perhaps of more importance than the subject, and it is certainly of especial importance when we discuss those among our writers who have any rank, however small, in that great household I have spoken of. Ruskin, Meredith, Pater, Shelley, Keats, Wordsworth, had all to face misunderstanding and misrepresentation, and sometimes contumely, for they spoke to an evil time out of the depths of the heart, and if England had been accustomed to use in literary discussion the coarse methods of political discussion, instead of descending to them in rare moments of excitement, she would not now have that remnant which alone unites her to the England of Shakespeare and Milton. In Ireland, too, it may be those very men, who have made a subtle personal way of expressing themselves, instead of being content with English as it is understood in the newspapers, or who see all things reflected in their own souls, which are from the parent fountain of their race, instead of filling their work with the circumstance of a life which is dominated by England, who may be recognised in the future as most Irish, though their own time entangled in the surfaces of things may often think them lacking in everything that is Irish. The delicate, obscure, mysterious song of my friend, "A.E.," which has, as I know, comforted the wise and beautiful when dying, but has hardly come into the hands of the middle

---

*He's an absent-minded beggar, and his weaknesses are great—*
*But we and Paul must take him as we find him!*
*He is out on active service, wiping something off a slate—*
*And he's left a lot of little things behind him!*

(*Rudyard Kipling's Verse*, New York, 1944, p. 457.)

[7] Saint Columban (543?-615)—also known as Colum, Columbanus, Columba and Colman—was born in Leinster and wrote in Latin on various subjects. Yeats refers here to his Sermon V which begins: "Oh human life, feeble and mortal, how many have you deceived, beguiled, and blinded! While you fly, you are nothing, while you are seen, you are a shadow, while you arise, you are but smoke. . . . You are the roadway of mortals, not their life, beginning from sin, enduring up till death . . . you have allotted all your travellers to death." (G. S. M. Walker, *Sancti Columbani Opera*, Dublin, 1957, p. 85.)

class—I use the word to describe an attitude of mind more than an accident of birth—and has no obviously Irish characteristics, may be, or rather must be, more Irish than any of those books of stories or of verses which reflect so many obviously Irish characteristics that every newspaper calls them, in the trying phrase of 1845, "racy of the soil!"

Now, sir, you and I have paid each other a very pretty compliment, for when you wrote to me for a letter, you must have thought that I would not be influenced by the many attacks you have made upon me and upon the movement I represent,[8] while I, on my side, have written this letter because I am convinced from what I have read of your writings, that you are one of the few in Ireland who try to go down to the root of public events and who seek the truth with earnestness and sincerity. For you and me, as for all others, it may be wholesome to dispute about a real issue, but if we dispute about misunderstandings or about names we can only destroy that clear ardour of life which is as necessary to your cause as to mine, and never long exists without precision and lucidity. I have, therefore, dealt at length with the public issues which lie between us, and must say some few words on a purely personal issue. You have been misled, doubtless, by reading what some indiscreet friend or careless opponent has written, into supposing that I have ever used the phrases "Celtic note" and "Celtic Renaissance" except as a quotation from others, if even then, or that I have quoted Matthew Arnold's essay on Celtic literature "on a hundred platforms" or elsewhere in support of the ideas behind these phrases, or that I have changed my opinions about the revival of the Irish language since a certain speech in Galway. I have avoided "Celtic note" and "Celtic renaissance" partly because both are vague and one is grandiloquent, and partly because the journalist has laid his ugly hands upon them, and all I have said or written about Matthew Arnold since I was a boy is an essay in "Cosmopolis,"[9] in which I have argued that the characteristics he has called Celtic, mark all races just in so far as they preserve the qualities of the early races of the world. And I think I need not say, after the first part of this letter, that I still believe what I believed when I made that speech in Galway; but none of these matters are likely to interest your readers. I will, therefore, close this long letter with a hope that *The Leader* may enable you to complete the power-

8 In her diary for December 29, 1900 (NYPL Berg Ms. 65B1810), Lady Gregory speculated about Moran's attacks on Yeats and others, noting that Douglas Hyde had told him he shouldn't attack friends "whereat M said: 'Your enemies don't mind what you say, but if you attack your friend, he is the boy that will feel it.'"

9 This essay, "The Celtic Element in Literature", appeared in *Cosmopolis* for June, 1898. It is the first section of the essay of the same name which Yeats included in *Ideas of Good and Evil* (1903). (See *Essays and Introductions*, New York, 1961, pp. 173–88.)

ful analysis of Irish life which you have begun in the *New Ireland
Review*.[10]

Yours truly,

W. B. Yeats

# The Great Enchantment

Standish O'Grady launched his nationalist paper, the *All Ireland Review*, in
January, 1900, and throughout the early months he conducted a serial editorial on "The Great Enchantment" that had seemingly come over Irish
political feeling since the failure of Wolfe Tone's insurrection of 1798. From
time to time, he urged Yeats, Lady Gregory, George Russell and Douglas
Hyde, among others, to contribute to the paper; and from time to time he
threatened to discontinue the series on the "Enchantment". By Spring, Russell and T. W. Rolleston had engaged in controversy in his columns but
O'Grady was obliged, in the issue for May 19, to ask ". . . why does not
Fiona M'Leod or W. B. Yeates [*sic*] send me a poem or two? They send plenty
to the Philistines."

Yeats's first contribution was a letter signed "Y" in the issue for September
22, to which O'Grady attached a lengthy comment which broadly hints at
Yeats's authorship. The letter continues an attack on Trinity College and the
Anglo-Irish class which Yeats had begun in 1886 in his essay on "The Poetry
of Sir Samuel Ferguson" (see *Uncollected Prose*, vol. I, pp. 88 ff.) and which he
had intensified in the nineties. No doubt, such outbursts as this were in Yeats's
mind when he regretted, more than thirty years later, having at this time
"seen nothing in Protestant Ireland as a whole but its faults" (p. 489 below).
The sentiments are Yeats's and, while it is difficult to sense the "personal
savour and flavour", it was often O'Grady's practice to append tantalizing
and transparent signatures; his allusion to Edward Martyn, with whom
Yeats was collaborating in the Literary Theatre, further encourages attribution of the letter to Yeats.

I HOPE you will give us more and more of your opinions. What we
want from you is a kind of Irish 'Fors Clavigera.'[1] You are about the

---

[10] Beginning in 1898, two years before his founding of *The Leader*, Moran's articles
appeared in the Dublin monthly, *The New Ireland Review*.

[1] Between 1871 and 1884, John Ruskin published his views on many topics in a sporadic
periodical he called *Fors Clavigera*, the private title Yeats used when, at the end of his life, he
undertook in *On the Boiler* a project similar to that he urges here on O'Grady (see *Letters*
pp. 900 and 901).

best fighter we have against that Death whose most manifest expression in this country is Trinity College (should we not add Alexandra College?)[2] and which has already turned our once intelligent gentry into readers of the Irish Times!

I fear that you cannot awake the dying mind of a dying class; but people can keep it from dying right out till another class is ready to take its place.

Y.

Dear Y., The initial will not hide you; the distinctive personal savour and flavour are so strong.

Thanks for desiring to get more of my opinions. I know you do, for you had always the courage to be sincere; but I am by nature properly more a storyteller than a propounder of views and opinions.

What I work against, for my 'fighting' days, if I ever had any, are, I think, over, is 'The Great Enchantment' whose modes of operation are past counting and whose subtlety transcends the human faculties to discern.

I have watched its presence and power in our politics and public life generally! You are more aware of it as it manifests itself in education and things literary.

. . . I would ask you to use your influence with Mr. Edward Martyn to write some such satire upon Ireland as he wrote upon England in that excellent book, Morgante the Lesser.[3] . . . The Enchantment must be assailed from many points, and writing is only food as a preparation for action, for it is only by action that the power of the spell can be effectually broken. The true deliverers will be the doers not the sayers . . . .

# Mr. Yeats's Jug

In *The Leader* for November 3, 1900, an article signed "Seang Siúir" and entitled "Mr. Yeats's Jug" commented caustically on an interview with Yeats in a society paper called *M.A.P.* (Mainly About People), which was edited by T. P. O'Connor (1848–1929), the Irish-born journalist and Nationalist M.P. for Liverpool. While asserting that Yeats's "Anglo-Irish" poetry was beneath troubling to understand, the author expressed ironic gratitude that, unlike those of the great Irish writers of the dim past, Yeats's "looks,

---

[2] Probably O'Grady's insertion.
[3] Edward Martyn published *Morgante the Lesser, His Notorious Life and Deeds* in 1890, under the pseudonym "Sirius".

longings and guise" would be lovingly preserved, so that "from his 'butterfly tie' to his boots, the race of Rhodes and Harmsworth may know the 'elusive' singer who retold the Wanderings of Oisin". The title of the piece refers to the author's mocking suspense as to just how Yeats, leaving his interviewer for a moment, brought back the milk for their tea. "So to us the supreme appeal of this wonderful Society idyll is the mystery of the milk-jug. In our reverie on lonely moors, or under the moon o'nights in the cities of the stranger, we shall try, ever try, to visualise it. Was it of earth, or after earth, or of Orchill's under-earth, manufacture, that Jug which, 'with reverent hands,' the poet bore out into the spellful night what time the blithe nymph was tea-thirsty?"

Despite Yeats's chilly comment on the "interview" in his letter to *The Leader*, November 10, 1900, a nearly identical version appeared in *The Gael* (New York) for January, 1901 (p. 27).

SIR,

A sentence in your article, "Mr. Yeats's Jug." may have led your readers to suppose that I welcomed knowingly, and possibly invited, an interviewer from Mr. O'Connor's paper, *M. A. P.*[1] I did neither, nor do I know who wrote the paragraphs you have quoted.

Yours sincerely,

W. B. Yeats

# A Postscript to a Forthcoming Book of Essays by Various Writers

Yeats's first acknowledged contribution to Standish O'Grady's *All Ireland Review* was "A Postscript to a Forthcoming Book of Essays by Various Irish Writers", in the issue for December 1, 1900. Despite the accommodating attitude in Yeats's last paragraph, O'Grady's editorial note, thanking Yeats for "the beautiful and eloquent little discourse which you were good enough to send me", tartly observed that it "was not written for me or written for Ireland; it was written for London, for all your clever friends over there, and all your clever enemies, for I know that you are carrying on a sort of war there . . .". O'Grady resented Yeats's exportation and explanation of the "Irish move-

---

[1] The "sentence" to which Yeats refers is presumably that in which the interviewer seems to "shake his long bony hand—it might break, it feels so brittle—and follow his long, thin figure, dressed in black, up the narrow wooden staircase . . .".

ment", and was particularly disturbed that "among the other interesting barbarians whom you are exhibiting to the Philistines I, too, am being trotted out and made to show my paces". Nonetheless, excerpts from O'Grady's editorials appeared along with pieces by D. P. Moran, George Moore, Douglas Hyde and Yeats in Lady Gregory's *Ideals in Ireland* (1901), to which this essay, with minor modifications, is the "Postscript".

WHEN I have stood before some Irish crowd, speaking of something, that seemed to me an immediate duty, if the popular hope, the life of all our hopes, as I think, was not to be weakened, I have said to myself "how bewildered, how angry, perhaps, everybody would be if any thoughtful person on any platform spoke out all his mind." Though it may well be that no man can ever speak out all his mind, for the mind is half silence and even the subtless [*sic*] words lay their bonds on truth, a work like this helps men, who spend much of their lives in the midst of a movement of enthusiasm, where one can but speak as if one wrote upon the dark with a burning stick, to tell what permanent quarrel, as of good and evil angels, has thrown upward what may seem to be[1] the indifferent and the weary but a passing clamour. Though I doubt not that all but all one's convictions go deeper than reason, I think that our Irish movements have always interested me in part, because I see in them the quarrel of two traditions of life, one old and noble, one new and ignoble. One undying because it satisfies our conscience though it seemed dying and one about to die because it is hateful to our conscience, though it seems triumphant throughout the world. In Ireland wherever the Gaelic tongue is still spoken, and to some little extent where it is not, the people live according to a tradition of life that existed before the world surrendered to the competition of merchants and to the vulgarity that has been founded upon it; and we who would keep the Gaelic tongue and Gaelic memories and Gaelic habits of our mind would keep them, as I think, that we may some day spread a tradition of life that would build up neither great wealth nor great poverty, that makes the arts a natural expression of life that permits even common men to understand good art and high thinking and to have the fine manners these things can give. Almost every one in Ireland on the other hand, who comes from what are called the educated and wealthy classes, that is to say, every man who has read a little Homer for the grammar, and many vulgar books for his pleasure, or who thinks his stable of more importance than all libraries, seeks, and often with fervour, to establish a tradition of life perfected and in part discovered by

[1] This sentence is more intelligible if "be" is omitted. The version in *Ideals in Ireland* reads: "thrown upward what may seem a passing clamour, to the indifferent and the weary" (p. 105).

the English speaking peoples, which has made great wealth and poverty and which would make the arts impossible were it not for the self-sacrifice of a few who spend their lives in the bitterness of protest, and has already made the understanding of the arts and of high thinking impossible outside of a small cultivated class. They do this because they are entangled in the subtle net of bribery, which England has spread among us by courts, and colleges and Government offices, and by a social routine, and they fould [*sic*] and unfold their net before us that they make us like themselves, and we have answered by discovering an idea, by creating a movement of intellect, whose ever growing abundance, whose ever deepening energy, would show their education its sterility, their wealth, its raggedness. There has been no notorious self-seeker these twenty years, no seller of causes for money down, but he has arisen amongst them; and there has been no man that has lived poorly that he might think well, no master of lofty speech, no seeker of subtle truth, but he has arisen among us; and abundance in these things comes now as always from the hand of the Future already half lifted in blessing.

Part of the power of this movement is that unlike the purely political movement, it can use every talent and leave every talent in freedom. It has need of the violence of the mob that it may sometimes tear that subtle net, and it has need of every delicate talent for it would discover, as would all such movements, the form of the nation made perfect, the fiery seed as upon the divine hand, in the ideas and passions of the nation, and as all religions have built upon hope and desire and terror of death, changing them to sacraments that are like flames rustling up into one white point; it would build upon their ideas and passions an idea, a passion, as little to be reasoned over, as little to be doubted or analysed as any simple love or hate though it is that form of perfection, that fiery seed, as in a mirror.

# On a Letter to the *Daily Mail*

As Yeats's personality became more interesting to the general public, he found himself "correcting" views of it in more varied contexts. In addition to mediating between the nationalist biases of the *Leader* and the affectations of such society papers as *M.A.P.*, above, and the *Free Lance*, below, he had also to clarify his notion of poetry spoken to music as reported by the *Saturday Review* (see Wade, *Letters*, p. 348). In this letter to the *Daily Mail*, Yeats is "correcting" the notorious halfpenny paper, the success of which, since its founding in 1896 by Alfred Harmsworth—later Lord Northcliffe—(1865–1922), had astounded and disturbed established literary and journalistic circles. Perhaps this is the reason Yeats chose also to send his note to the *Academy*—certainly a journal of "men of breeding"—where it appeared on May 4, 1901.

MR. W. B. YEATS writes: "I have just sent the following letter to the Editor of the *Daily Mail*:[1] 'Sir, I have been sent a cutting from the *Daily Mail* of April 26, beginning: "A representative of the *Daily Mail* had a short conversation yesterday with Mr. W. B. Yeats the poet, who, with Mr. George Moore and Mr. Robert Martin, is practically responsible for the Irish Literary Movement." It is no part of my purpose to correct the inaccuracies in this sentence or in the report of my opinions which follows it, but I think it my duty to state that your representative did not ask permission to publish my opinions. It is obvious that the practice of quoting in the Press private conversations, however unimportant in themselves, if generally adopted, would make it impossible to receive a representative of the Press as the equal of men of good breeding.' "

[1] The editor of the *Daily Mail* was Thomas Marlowe (1868–1935).

# At Stratford-on-Avon

Of the two essays on the 1901 productions at Stratford-on-Avon written for *The Speaker*, Yeats reprinted the first two parts of the first and all of the second in *Ideas of Good and Evil* (1903). (See *Essays and Introductions*, pp. 96–110.) The original version of the first essay, which appeared in the issue for May 11, is presented here.

## I

I HAVE been hearing Shakespeare, as the traveller in "News from Nowhere"[1] might have heard him, had he not been hurried back into our noisy time. One passes through quiet streets, where gabled and red-tiled houses remember the Middle Age, to a theatre that has been made

[1] In William Morris's "utopian romance", *News from Nowhere* (1890), the narrator visits, in a dream vision, a twenty-first century England reformed by Socialist "fellowship" into a version of Morris's ideal medieval society.

not to make money, but for the pleasure of making it, like the market houses that set the traveller chuckling; nor does one find it among hurrying cabs and ringing pavements, but in a green garden by a river side. Inside I have to be content for a while with a chair, for I am unexpected, and there is not an empty seat but this; and yet there is no one who has come merely because one must go somewhere after dinner. All day, too, one does not hear or see an incongruous or noisy thing, but spends the hours reading the plays, and the wise and foolish things men have said of them, in the library of the theatre, with its oak-panelled walls and leaded windows of tinted-glass; or one rows by reedy banks and by old farm-houses, and by old churches among great trees. It is certainly one's fault if one opens a newspaper, for Mr. Benson[2] gives one a new play every night, and one need talk of nothing but the play in the inn-parlour, under the oak beams blackened by time and showing the mark of the adze that shaped them. I have seen this week *King John*, *Richard II*, the second part of *Henry IV*, *Henry V*, the second part of *Henry VI*, and *Richard III* played in their right order, with all the links that bind play to play unbroken; and partly because of a spirit in the place, and partly because of the way play supports play, the theatre has moved me as it has never done before. That strange procession of kings and queens, of warring nobles, of insurgent crowds, of courtiers, and of people of the gutter has been to me almost too visible, too audible, too full of an unearthly energy. I have felt as I have sometimes felt on grey days on the Galway shore, when a faint mist has hung over the grey sea and the grey stones, as if the world might suddenly vanish and leave nothing behind, not even a little dust under one's feet. The people my mind's eye has seen have too much of the extravagance of dreams, like all the inventions of art, before our crowded life had brought moderation and compromise, to seem more than a dream, and yet all else has grown dim before them.

In London the first man one meets puts any high dream out of one's head, for he will talk to one of something at once vapid and exciting, some one of those many subjects of thought that build up our social unity. But here he gives back one's dream like a mirror. If we do not talk of the plays, we talk of the theatre, and how more people may be got to come, and our isolation from common things makes the future become grandiose and important. One man tells how the theatre and the library were at their foundation but part of a scheme the future is to fulfil. To them will be added a school where speech, and gesture, and

<hr>

[2] F. R. Benson (1858–1939), the English actor and director, staged productions at Stratford-on-Avon from 1886 until 1919. "The Benson company," Yeats wrote to Lady Gregory at this time, "are playing wonderfully and really speaking their verse finely" (*Letters*, p. 349).

fencing, and all else that an actor needs will be taught, and the council which will have enlarged its Festivals to some six weeks, will engage all the chief players of Shakespeare, and perhaps of other great dramatists in this and other countries. These chief players will need to bring but few of their supporters, for the school will be able to fill all the lesser parts with players who are slowly recovering the lost tradition by musical speech. Another man is certain that the Festival, even without the school, which would require a new endowment, will grow in importance year by year, and that it may become with favouring chance the supreme dramatic event of the world; and when I suggest that it may help to break the evil prestige of London he becomes enthusiastic.

Surely a bitter hatred of London is becoming a mark of those that love the arts, and all that have this hatred should help anything that looks like a beginning of a centre of art elsewhere. The easiness of travel, which is always growing, began by emptying the country, but it may end by filling it; for adventures like this of Stratford-on-Avon show that people are ready to journey from all parts of England and Scotland and Ireland, and even from America, to live with their favourite art, as shut away from the world as though they were "in retreat," as Catholics say. Nobody but an impressionist painter, who hides it in light and mist, even pretends to love a street for its own sake; and could we meet our friends and hear music and poetry in the country, none of us that are not captive would ever leave the thrushes. In London, we hear something that we like some twice or thrice in a winter, and among people who are thinking the while of a music-hall singer or of a member of parliament, but there we would hear it and see it among people who liked it well enough to have travelled some few hours to find it; and because those who care for the arts have few near friendships among those that do not, we would hear and see it among near friends. We would escape, too, from those artificial tastes and interests we cultivate, that we may have something to talk about among people we meet for a few minutes and not again, and the arts would grow serious as the Ten Commandments.

## II

I do not think there is anything I disliked in Stratford, beside certain new houses, but the shape of the theatre; and as a larger theatre must be built sooner or later, that would be no great matter if one could put a wiser shape into somebody's head. I cannot think there is any excuse for a half-round theatre, where land is not expensive, or no very great audience to be seated within earshot of the stage; or that it was adopted for a better reason than because it has come down to us, though from a

time when the art of the stage was a different art. The Elizabethan
theatre was a half-round, because the players were content to speak
their lines on a platform, as if they were speakers at a public meeting,
and we go on building in the same shape, although our art of the
stage is the art of making a succession of pictures. Were our theatres
of the shape of a half-closed fan, like Wagner's theatre, where the
audience sit on seats that rise towards the broad end, while the play is
played at the narrow end, their pictures could be composed for eyes at a
small number of points of view, instead of for eyes at many points of
view, above and below and at the sides, and what is no better than a
trade might become an art.[3] With the eyes watching from the sides of
a half-round, on the floor and in the boxes and galleries, would go the
solid built houses and the flat trees that shake with every breath of air;
and we could make our pictures with robes that contrasted with great
masses of colour in the back cloth and such severe or decorative forms
of hills and trees and houses as would not overwhelm, as our naturalistic scenery does, the idealistic art of the poet, and all at a little price.
Naturalistic scene-painting is not an art, but a trade, because it is, at
best, an attempt to copy the more obvious effects of nature by the
methods of the ordinary landscape painter, and by his methods made
coarse and summary. It is but flashy landscape painting and lowers the
taste it appeals to, for the taste it appeals to has been formed by a more
delicate art. Decorative scene-painting would be, on the other hand, as
inseparable from the movements as from the robes of the players and
from the falling of the light; and being in itself a grave and quiet thing
it would mingle with the tones of the voices, and with the sentiment of
the play, without overwhelming them under an alien interest. It would
be a new and legitimate art appealing to a taste formed by itself and
copying nothing but itself. Mr. Gordon Craig[4] used scenery of this
kind at the Purcell Society performance the other day, and despite
some marring of his effects by the half-round shape of the theatre, it
was the first beautiful scenery our stage has seen. He created an ideal

---

[3] The theatre in which Yeats saw the 1901 productions was that in the semi-Gothic
Shakespeare Memorial, built in 1877. Wagner's innovative theatre at Bayreuth was opened
in 1876.

[4] The influence on Yeats of Gordon Craig (1872–1957), the English actor, producer and
theatrical designer, begins with Craig's production, on March 26, 1901, of *Dido and Aeneas*
and *The Masque of Love* for the Purcell Society in London. "You have created a new art," he
wrote Craig on April 2, "I would like to talk the thing over with you" (Craig, *Index to the
Story of My Days*, New York, 1957, p. 239). And the following year Yeats publicly ranked
the Purcell productions "among the important events of our time" (*Letters*, p. 366). He
cooperated with Craig and his sister Edith—the children of Ellen Terry and E. W. Godwin
—on several productions of his plays and many of his notions of the impersonal presentation of themes and of a theatre without characters were influenced by this collaboration.
(See pp. 384–94 and 397–401 below.)

country where everything was possible, even speaking in verse, or
speaking in music, or the expression of the whole of life in a dance, and
I would like to see Stratford-on-Avon decorate its Shakespeare with like
scenery. As we cannot, it seems, go back to the platform and the curtain,
and the argument for doing so is not without weight, we can only get
rid of the sense of unreality, which most of us feel when we listen to the
conventional speech of Shakespeare by making scenery as conventional.
Time after time his people use at some moment of deep emotion an
elaborate or deliberate metaphor, or do some improbable thing which
breaks an emotion of reality we have imposed upon him by an art that
is not his, nor in the spirit of his. It also is an essential part of his method
to give slight or obscure motives of many actions that our attention
may dwell on what is of chief importance, and we set these cloudy
actions among solid looking houses, and what we hope are solid looking
trees, and illusion comes to an end, slain by our desire to increase it. In
his art, as in all the older art of the world, there was much make believe,
and our scenery, too, should remember the time when, as my nurse used
to tell me, herons built their nests in old men's beards! Mr. Benson did
not venture to play the scene in *Richard III* where the ghosts walk,[5] as
Shakespeare wrote it, but had his scenery been as simple as Mr. Gordon
Craig's purple back cloth that made Dido and Æneas seem wandering
on the edge of eternity, he would have found nothing absurd in pitch-
ing the tents of Richard and Richmond side by side. Goethe has said,
"Art is art, because it is not nature!" It brings us near to the archetypal
ideas themselves, and away from nature, which is but their looking-
glass.

## III

Of Mr. Benson and his players one need say little, for they have been in
London till a few weeks ago, but one or two things one must say. They
speak their verse not indeed, perfectly, but less imperfectly than any
other players upon our stage, and the stage management is more imaginative than that of other companies. Richard II beating time to the
music at the end of the abdication scene and his leaning on Bolinbroke
[*sic*] for his protection at the end of the scene before Flint Castle are
dramatic in the highest sense. Of Mr. Benson's playing as Richard II one
need not speak, for most people who are likely to read this have seen it,
but only those who have been to Stratford have seen Mr. Weir's admirable, though too benevolent and cleanly, Falstaff, or Mr. Ash's Jack
Cade, and Mrs. Benson's Doll Tearsheet, which had the extravagance
and energy one desires and seldom finds in the representations of the

[5] *Richard III*, Act V, scene iii.

most extravagant of poets. Mr. Rodney and Mr. Sweet[6] played Falcon-
bridge and King John with a barbaric simplicity that was entirely admirable, and helped with a certain bareness and simplicity in the costumes
to contrast meaningly with the playing and costuming in *Richard II*,
which describes a time when, as Shakespeare knew from Hollingshead,
life became more splendid and luxurious than it had been before in
England. I thought Mr. Benson's Henry V nearly as good as his Richard
II, and admired how he kept that somewhat crude king, as Mr. Waller[7]
did not, from becoming vulgar in the love scene at the end, when the
language of passion has to become the instrument of policy; but I will
speak of Henry V, when I speak of the cycle as a whole, as I believe his
character, when contrasted with that of Richard II, lets out a little of
Shakespeare's secret, and all but all the secret of his critics.'[8]

W. B. Yeats

# A Correction

In two letters to the press in August and September, 1901, Yeats sought to
untangle yet another representation of his views. The issue of the *Free Lance*
for the week ending July 20 had printed an account of a conversation between
"a correspondent" and "Mr. W. B. Yeats, the young Irish poet in whose
brain the [Irish literary movement] first suggested itself". This "Popular
Society and Critical Journal", a penny weekly founded in 1901 by the influential dramatic critic of the eighties and nineties, Clement Scott (1841–
1904), quoted Yeats in regard to his learning Irish: ". . . I am acquiring my
native tongue by degrees . . . and I hope I may live to see Irish becoming the
language of the artistic and intellectual world of Anglo-Saxondom. Of course,
it will take centuries, but I have no doubt as to the ultimate result. . . . The
few intelligent people will always rule the many unintelligent." Quotation
from the "interview" in the *Daily Express* prompted Yeats's "correction",
which appeared in the *Daily Express* for August 5.

[6] George R. Weir (1854–1909). Oscar Asche (1872–1936). F. R. Benson married Gertrude
Constance Samwell in 1886. Mrs. Benson frequently appeared in her husband's productions
under the stage name of Constance Featherstonhaugh. Frank Rodney (1859–1902). E. Lyall
Swete (1865–1930).
[7] Lewis Waller (1860–1915).
[8] Yeats attacks the "schoolboy" view of Shakespeare as exemplified by his father's friend,
Edward Dowden, by which "Shakespearian criticism became a vulgar worshipper of
success", in the second of these essays (*Essays and Introductions*, pp. 102–5). In a letter to Lady
Gregory at the time of the composition of this essay he formulated this important distinction: "The more I read the worse does the Shakespeare criticism become and Dowden's
about the climax of it. I[t] came out [of] the middle class movement and I feel it my legitimate
enemy." (Wade, *Letters*, p. 349.)

TO THE EDITOR OF THE *DAILY EXPRESS*

SIR,

I find in your issue of July 19, which I have but just seen, a paragraph copied from an English paper. The paragraph makes me say, on the evidence of a supposed interview in a paper called the "Free Lance," that "I hope to see Irish becoming the language of the artistic and intellectual world of Anglo-Saxondom," and that, "of course, it will take centuries."

It then comments—"Mr. Yeats is anxious to beat Methusaleh's record." As the Irish opposition to movements of enthusiasm and of intellect has always found anonymous anecdotes among the chief of its weapons, I will take the trouble to contradict this one. The interview in the "Free Lance" never took place. It is not the first time this year I have had to complain of a spurious interview in an English paper.[1]

Yours truly,

W. B. Yeats

August 2

---

[1] In addition to the "correction" of the *Daily Mail* in May of 1901, above, Yeats had complained in the *Saturday Review* for March 16 of the attribution to him by J. F. Runciman (1866–1916), the music critic, of the term "Cantilation". ". . . you will permit me to say", he wrote, "that Mr. Runciman invented the word. I never used it, and I don't mean to, and I don't like it, and I don't think it means anything" (*Letters*, p. 348).

# About an "Interview"

THE *FREE LANCE*, SEPTEMBER 21, 1901

MR. W. B. YEATS in Answer:

Mr. W. B. Yeats, the well-known Irish poet and organiser of the Pan-Celtic movement, if I mistake not (writes a correspondent), sends me the following letter, dated September 6, from Coole Park, Gort, Co. Galway. I hope you, Mr. Editor, will give it due space verbatim et literatim:—

"Dear Sir, Your letter of August 15[1] has only just reached me, as I

---

[1] In some details, this exchange is confusing. Apparently, someone wrote to Yeats on August 15, complaining that the "interview" had indeed been an interview and that Yeats's etter seemed to attribute to it the comparison with Methuselah which had been an addition by the *Daily Express*.

While Scott maintains here the distinction between himself, as editor, and his "correspondent", it is likely that he wrote the original article himself. Otherwise, Yeats's commiseration with "an editor" who, facing the "state of degradation" of London journalism,

have been moving about. My letter to 'Express' (sic) did not attribute to your paper (sic), but to the comment in 'Express' paragraph the remark about Methuselah. This matter is unimportant, as my objection was to an interview, which never took place. I have no doubt that some person sent you a careless report of some private conversation of mine, but a private conversation is not an 'interview,' even when accurately quoted. You are probably as much a victim as I am in these matters. London journalism has sunk into such a state of degradation that I can well understand that an editor must find it almost impossible to keep his pages clean of offence. Even had I wished to ignore the matter I could not, as the silly extravagance your correspondent attributed to me was certain to be used, as it has been (the last time in last week's 'Spectator'),[2] against the cause I represent.

Yours, etc.,

W. B. Yeats

An Answer to Mr. Yeats:

May I be allowed to say a few words in reply (continues my correspondent)? I don't know why Mr. Yeats beats about the bush: I have no need to, nor should I have thought that a person of Mr. W. B. Yeats' reputation would have needed to. His letter is very ingenious, though, unfortunately, not ingenuous. It is a poor soul that cannot admit the truth. Contrary to Mr. Yeats' expectation, I know the difference between a private conversation and an interview. I saw him manifestly, and, as I told him, for the purpose of interview. To assert the opposite is to say the thing which is not. As for "the pages clean of offence" of London journalism and the "silly extravagance," I imagine there will be more pages clean of offence and less silly extravagance when Mr. Yeats stops writing for the ill-used Press.

---

must accept "a careless report of some private conversation" from "some person" makes no sense in a letter supposedly, in the present context, sent on by the "correspondent".

[2] The concluding paragraph of a letter on "the Pan-Celtic Congress" in the issue of *The Spectator* for August 31, 1901, had contained an allusion to Yeats's "interview", "*A propos* of this extreme Celtomania among us, there is a story to the effect that one of the leaders of the Celtic movement recently declared that since the language of the cleverer race tended to oust that of the less gifted (*sic?*), he confidently expected that Irish would be the language of culture in the erstwhile English-speaking world. But perhaps the great man had his tongue in his cheek."

# John Eglinton

Yeats used the provocative writings of "John Eglinton" (W. K. Magee, 1868–1961), whom he had known first as a classmate at Erasmus Smith High School in Dublin and later as a fellow Theosophist, to clarify his own ideas of literary nationalism. In 1898, Magee's essay in the *Daily Express* initiated the controversy which resulted in *Literary Ideals in Ireland* (1899) (see p. 128 above). There, as in "John Eglinton", a review of *Pebbles from a Brook* (1901) in *The United Irishman* for November 9, 1901, Yeats pays Magee the tribute of sharp, critical appreciation. In 1905 Yeats edited, not entirely to Magee's liking, a selection of his friend's writings for the Dun Emer Press.

WHEN I got "Two Essays on the Remnant" some years ago, I am ashamed to say that I read but a few pages and threw it aside, irritated by superficial characteristics, and that although I afterwards tried to make people read it, I did not do so until somebody else had written in its praise.[1]

And now, again, I have been irritated by superficial characteristics and have let months go by before I discovered that "Pebbles from a Brook" was all but as beautiful and as weighty. I do not, indeed, agree with John Eglinton about, perhaps, the most important matters, but to differ from a writer of so much precision is to discover a truth for oneself, to enrich one's conscience. A single argument is to be found in all these essays, and in spite of their curious, furtive style, this argument is so formidable that if a few thousand people believed in it and tried to arrange their lives as it would have them, they would become like the foxes that dragged the torches into the Philistines' corn. He thinks that States and every other institution of man begin by fostering men's lives, and then gradually perfect themselves at the expense of men's lives, becoming more and more separated from life, until at last they become fixed as by a kind of frost, so that men, if they would keep alive and not be frozen, must fly from them as the Children of Israel fled from Egypt. He imagines that the children of Israel, the idealists, are now wavering between Egypt, comfort, civilisation, as they call it, and the wilderness, the unworldly life; and he would persuade them to hesitate no longer.

[1] Yeats's reference is probably to his review entitled "Dublin Mystics" in *The Bookman* in 1895 (*Uncollected Prose*, vol. I, pp. 356–8), which listed *Two Essays on the Remnant* (1894), along with two editions of a book by "A.E.", as its subjects. Noting that Magee's book was already in a second edition, Yeats briefly characterized it as "a passionate and lofty appeal to the 'idealists' to come out of the modern world, as the children of Israel came out of Egypt".

He looks at this thought from many sides, and he looks at books and men under its light. He is now eloquent and now ironical about it. He often seems to have forgotten it, and then in a moment he is in the midst of it again. He describes in beautiful words the youth of States when "the young men exercise in the fields, the old men sit in council, and at sunset the daughters leap down the street to the dance,"[2] and how the faculties and works of men perfect themselves until, "as the rosebud becomes a rose," "its expanded petals fall away in a shower of dramas and epics,"[3] and how at last the flower withers and the State dies. He writes—"The test of the state of civilisation is therefore quite simple, whether in assisting it the individual is astride of his proper instincts. If in gratifying his deepest and truest inclinations he is subserving the general end, then of that civilisation it may be said it is growing and prospering, and that nature is in it. When, on the other hand, a man does some violence to his nature in adhering to the parent bulk, when its character and aspirations are not repeated in him, when his duty to himself runs counter to his outward obligations; when the component parts of the State, its institutions, must have mainstays passed round them to hold them together; when the family is no longer the State in miniature, and woman demurs to what is expected of her; when the populace breaks over its natural barriers; when the faculty of building ceases; when the ideal and the practical seem mutually antagonistic, and the youth must crush his genius into his cleverness if he will catch on as a citizen—then of that State it may be said that its day as a State is over; that nature is no longer in it, and that endless disintegration is its portion."[4]

When this day has come, patriotism changes its nature, for the State has accomplished its purpose, which is "to enrich the life of each with the life of all; to form, fashion, educate and finally to liberate an individual," and henceforth the patriot must be a giver instead of a receiver, and ever readier to drink the hemlock than to carry a sword. He must honour his nation, "parent and nurse of men," but he must live his own life, for she is about "to die, being full of wisdom as of days."[5]

He often speaks of Wordsworth and of devout readers of Wordsworth who live a tranquil country life, unmindful of most things that men care for, when he would tell us how these "liberated individuals" should live their own lives.

[2] *Two Essays on the Remnant* (1894), p. 17.
[3] *Two Essays*, p. 14, for "petals fall away" has "petals were falling".
[4] *Two Essays*, p. 16, has "violence to his own nature" for "violence to his nature".
[5] The essay on "Regenerate Patriotism" in *Pebbles from a Brook* (1901) has on p. 27 "educate, and finally"; p. 81, "as of days!".

## II

Nobody can write well, as I think, unless his thought, or some like thought, is moving in other minds than his, for nobody can do more than speak messages from the spirit of his time. Thoughts, not all unlike these of John Eglinton, passed through my mind when I was growing up; some of them I wrote out a few years later in a lecture for the National Literary Society, though not with the beauty and precision of these essays;[6] but that which has made John Eglinton turn from all National ideas and see the hope of the world in individual freedom, in "the individual grown wiser than his institutions," has made me a Nationalist and has made me see the hope of the world in re-arrangements of life and thought which make men feel that they are part of a social order, of a tradition, of a movement wiser than themselves. Perhaps I might think as he does had I not lived more than he has among those "liberated individuals" and come to understand that their life never seems natural and seldom seems happy to them. He would not deny the name of "the Remnant" to the men and women I have in mind. They certainly refused to crush their genius into their cleverness, and they have almost all been outcasts of some kind. One, whom I know very well, lived for a long while on bread and shell conch to escape from hack work, and another, a very fine scholar whom I know slightly, spent some ten years selling matches in the Strand; while another, worn out by the bitterness of a struggle not to live, but to live and work finely, and by some of the bad habits of the miserable, died of starvation because he had ceased to care enough for life to be at the trouble to buy sufficient food. Then, too, I have known two or three men of philosophic intellect like Wilde or Beardsley[7] who spent their lives in a fantastic protest against a society they could not remake. Huysmans has once and for all summed up the life of such men in a famous novel.[8] He tells of a ma

---

[6] In a disclaiming note to Yeats's 1905 edition of passages from his essays, Magee regrets his use of a "metaphor" which compares the plight of the creative remnant of the declining Egyptian and Greco-Roman societies with that of Irish artists at the turn of the century ("The Chosen People at Work", *Two Essays*, pp. 29–49). The problem and the approach, though not the conclusion, are similar to Yeats's in his lecture before the National Literary Society on May 19, 1893 (see *Uncollected Prose*, vol. I, pp. 266–75).

[7] Yeats's attempts to identify his feelings about Wilde (1854–1900) and Beardsley (1872–98) culminate in *The Trembling of the Veil*. He sympathetically associates the former with Cellini, "who, coming after Michael Angelo, found nothing so satisfactory as to turn bravo and quarrel with the man who broke Michael Angelo's nose" (*Autobiography*, p. 93.) Wilde is "an audacious Italian fifteenth-century figure" (*Autobiography*, p. 87; cf. *A Vision*, New York, 1956, pp. 148–51), and Beardsley is the tragic saint and victim of the thirteenth phase whose nature is "on the edge of Unity of Being, the understanding of that Unity by the intellect his one overmastering purpose" (*Autobiography*, p. 221; cf. *A. Vision*, pp. 129–31).

[8] Duc Jean des Esseintes, the hero of *A Rebours* (1884) by J. K. Huysmans (1848–1907), was the model for many disillusioned escapists in late nineteenth century French and

whose "individual freedom" has been increased by great wealth, and who is more miserable than a squirrel in a cage, because the society he lives in is too far towards its death to send a living stream into his intellect and his heart: "None of us liveth to himself and no man dieth to himself." [9] I have known but two that were certainly happy men and yet were men of the Remnant—William Morris, [10] who believed that society was about to be remade according to his heart's desire, and that his own hands were helping to remake it; and a rather vulgar lad, who found in the East what he calls wisdom, but might call with perhaps greater accuracy a society that is still simple and joyous. He was in bad health and very poor, and his friends sent him to Ceylon for his health, and in a little while he wrote home a beautiful letter, of which I have made a copy, to tell them that he was dressed in white clothes and sitting at a little table two feet high in a Buddhist monastery, saying his prayers before an offering of white flowers. He described in words of simple piety the beautiful life, full of pity and reverence, he was now a part of, and seemed in everything a new man, except that he still spelled "veranda" with an "r" at the end. When I knew him he was full of the restlessness of poverty, and I have no doubt a good deal despised by neighbours and relations, but now that he had found a welcome amongst the heathen, his letters were full of merry and beautiful conversations with children and old men and with the wise men of the villages.

## III

If John Eglinton had found any one of these people of the Remnant I can imagine what they would have said to one another. He would have begun perhaps with: "You and I should be singularly happy, for the State has been put to a lot of trouble making us. We are perfected individualities, and ever since Hengist and Horsa [11] it has been making

---

English writing. Among them are the George Moore of *Confessions of a Young Man* (1888) and Dorian Gray, whose creator identified "Huysmans's over-realistic study of the artistic temperament" (Hart-Davis, ed., *Letters of Oscar Wilde*, New York, 1962, p. 313) as the book Dorian had read in which the "things he had dimly dreamed of were suddenly made real to him" (Wilde, *Picture of Dorian Gray*, London, 1949, p. 139).

[9] Romans, 14:7.

[10] The influence of William Morris (1834–1896) on Yeats and Yeats's admiration for the man he epitomized as "The Happiest of the Poets" (*Essays and Introductions*, pp. 53–64) began in childhood and intensified when the young poet frequented lectures and suppers at Kelmscott House in the late 1880s. Morris's accommodation of magic and fantasy, which qualifies him here as one of "the Remnant", explains Yeats's observation that Morris's late prose romances "were the only books I was ever to read slowly that I might not come too quickly to the end" (*Autobiography*, p. 94).

[11] The legendary first Anglo-Saxon settlers of Britain, Hengist and Horsa, were two brothers who, according to Geoffrey of Monmouth, landed in 499 to aid the British King Vortigen in his war with the Picts.

imperfect ones. Indeed, it has been put to so much trouble that it is all but dead." The other, fresh from a walk down Tottenham Court-road, would answer: "How can I be happy when I see nothing that is pleasant or comely all day long. If one lived in the age of Chaucer, when people were handsomely dressed and had handsome houses, and sang charming songs and had not to work very hard, that might be different." John Eglinton would answer: "But Chaucer's individuality must have been very imperfect. I know what is wrong with you. You should go into the wilderness. You will be happy when you are in the wilderness."

"But what is the wilderness?"

"The wilderness is a country life."

"And when I get into the country what am I to do?"

"Why! read Wordsworth."

"But I can read all the Wordsworth I think good poetry in a couple of days, and besides I am of an active disposition, I haven't a country clergyman among my ancestors for ten generations, nothing but soldiers. There was one of them that—"

"You can fish?"

"But I don't want to fish. I want to pull down Totenham Court-road, and to build it nearer to the heart's desire."[12]

Then as likely as not he would go on, for the Remnant is not prejudiced: "If I belonged to your country I could do something. There one has a chance. Your national life is not old and decadent as it is with us. One might help to build a better civilisation over there. But you must get rid of the English first. We are the makers of all vulgarity."

"The sword is really quite obsolete, but one should always be ready to drink the hemlock. I have always admitted that."

"Oh, the hemlock is a sedentary drink. I have just been hearing Prince Kropotkin[13] lecture; he, too, is for the Remnant, and I am for the sword."

The truth is that John Eglinton is too preoccupied with English literature and civilisation to remember that the decadence he has described is merely the modern way, because it is the English way, because it is the commercial way. Other countries only share it in so far as they are commercial. Here and there over Europe there are countries that preserve a more picturesque and elastic life. He forgets, too, that in the East, where civilisation is older than recorded history, and where there

[12] Yeats echoes, perhaps unintentionally, the yearning of Omar Khayyám "To grasp this sorry Scheme of Things entire . . . and . . . Re-mould it nearer to the Heart's desire" (Fitzgerald ♯XCIX), which was a motto of Fabian Socialism.

[13] Yeats had met the exiled Russian geographer and anarchist, Prince Peter Kropotkin (1842–1921), "perhaps but once or twice" at supper at Kelmscott House in the 1880s (*Autobiography*, p. 94).

have always been "liberated individuals," there have been, perhaps, other kinds of decadence, but not his kind.

I believe him right in thinking that the great movement of our time is a movement to destroy modern civilisation, but I cannot but believe him wrong in thinking that it will be ended by "liberated individuals" who separate themselves from the great passions, from the great popular interests, from religion, from patriotism, from humanitarianism. The movement against it takes the form now of collectivist, now of anarchist, now of mystical propagandas, now of groups of artists who labour to make the things of daily life, plates and candlesticks and the like, beautiful again; now of the awakening of the smaller nations who preserve more of the picturesque life of the ancient world than do the big nations. "The Remnant," the men and women who have learned whatever modern life has to teach and grown weary of it, should be the leaders of these movements. They are a small body, not more than one in five thousand anywhere, but they are many enough to be a priesthood, and in the long run to guide the great instinctive movements that come out of the multitude. They should be, as Walter Pater said of Leonardo de Vinci, like men "upon some secret errand,"[14] and in sharing in a great passion, should look beyond the passion to some remote end; and they must be as ready to sacrifice themselves as those are who have never seen beyond the passion. Their labour must be to live as the blind do for the most part, to live as if they had but one idea, who have so many; but there will be times when they may have to bear witness for the end for some far-off thing, and seemingly against the passion itself, the idea itself, and John Eglinton may call this being ready to drink the hemlock. I think that if they have not this simplicity, this singleness of mind, they may do many beautiful things, write madrigals and the like, and be good critics, but they will not, while the world remains what it is to-day, make the most weighty kind of literature, or give the world the impulse it is waiting for.

John Eglinton tells how, when Rome was decadent, when there was no longer an elastic and vigorous "civic life," the new impulse came from the early Christians. That impulse is coming to-day from the seemingly contradictory propagandas and persons I have described, and though the external forms of their activities are doubtless as mortal as the social and religious experiments of the early Christians, I cannot doubt that they are about to make the world change its image like a cloud.

[14] In the first paragraph of his essay on Leonardo da Vinci in *The Renaissance*, Pater says of Leonardo that "he is so possessed by his genius that he passes unmoved through the most tragic events, overwhelming his country and friends, like one who comes across them by chance on some secret errand" (Pater, *The Renaissance*, London, 1910. p. 99).

# IV

I was kept from reading Eglinton's essays for many months by certain petulances which are strange in so scrupulous a writer. In Ireland, where we have no mature intellectual tradition, and are in imperfect sympathy with the mature tradition of England, the only one we know anything of, we sometimes carry with us through our lives a defiant dogmatism like that of a clever schoolboy. I remember sitting all day in a Dublin garden trying to persuade myself that Walter Pater was a bad writer, and for no better reason than that he perplexed me and made me doubtful of myself. Keats, who was a sensitive, brooding man, says in one of his letters: "When I am among women I have evil thoughts, malice and spleen. I am full of suspicion, and, therefore, listen to nothing; I am in a hurry to be gone."[15] We approach the great masters and the great things of the world when they are a little difficult to us in just this spirit: we listen to nothing, we are in a hurry to be gone. Exaggerate this spirit a little and you have Shakespeare's Jack Cade, who wanted to hang everybody who could read and write because he had once put his name to a bond and was never his own man after. We learn more slowly than other people to understand that everything that has ever interested large numbers of men is very worthy of study and reverence. A journalist must be content often with opinions that have no importance beyond some controversy of the hour, but a writer like John Eglinton, who must know that his words will outlive him and us, has no business writing such a phrase as "vulgarity ritual," "and all that riff-raff," or writing a too notorious sentence about the crucifix, or declaring that philosophy takes only a "pathological and perfunctory" interest in a certain kind of poetry, which he defines as Belles Lettres, and which was certainly the kind that was written by Keats, or in writing that Wagner and Shelley "saw in art a refuge from the squalid reality," an inaccuracy which implies in his system of thought an equally careless condemnation, or in describing a certain book, which decides by perfectly logical deductions from a too narrow premises that Shakespeare and the Greek tragedians are bad art and Mrs. Beecher Stowe is good art, as "a formidable book, the doom of the cliques."[16] He does

[15] Keats makes this observation in a letter of July 18, 1818, to Benjamin Bailey in which he discusses his fears of not having "a right feeling towards Women" (Forman and Forman, eds., *Poetical Works and Other Writings of John Keats*, New York, 1939, vol. VII, p. 80).

[16] Yeats's concluding volley at *Pebbles from a Brook* is aimed first at Magee's calling the consideration of beauty, truth, art and God "as facts outside experience" the "beginning of formalism, incredulity, vulgarity, ritual and of all that riff-raff which incumbers the paradise of a true life" (p. 37). His next targets are Magee's portrayal of the true patriot as one who will turn against his motherland, saying, "I will persist in seeing thee a virgin mother . . . will still behold thee beautiful and unprofaned, no palsied beldam with whiskey on thy breath

not believe these things. He does not even want us to believe that he believes them. He is merely irritated. He sees a great complicated tradition which weighs upon his spirits, and is full of that kind of defiant timidity which some of us never get over when we are among strange people whose life we do not understand.

W. B. Yeats

# Literature and the Conscience

In October of 1901, the Irish Literary Theatre produced *Diarmuid and Grania*, the result of an erratic collaboration between Yeats and George Moore which had stretched over nearly three years. As presented by F. R. Benson's company, who had trouble with the Irish names, and augmented by Edward Elgar's music, the play drew sharp criticism from Irish nationalists, who denounced it as yet another English imposition and, worse, a ransacking of an Irish theme. In an interview with the *Freeman's Journal* at this time, Moore suggested that censorship, perhaps by the Church, would be appropriate to a national theatre, to which suggestion Yeats responded in a letter to the *Journal* of November 14. Pointing out that he would refuse to join Moore in any project established with ecclesiastic censorship, Yeats added that he would "watch the adventure with the most friendly eyes" and that he had "no doubt that a wise ecclesiastic, if his courage equalled his wisdom, would be a better censor than the mob . . ." (*Letters*, p. 356). The statements by Moore and Yeats prompted the shrewd and pseudonymous commentator of *The United Irishman*, "Irial", to chide both men in an article which appeared on November 23. Moore's attitude was cowardly and Yeats had not only failed to "take the highest ground" in not denouncing the despotism of censorship but had also impoliticly betrayed a certain amorality in his elevation of literature as "the principal voice of the conscience" over "the special moral-

---

and a crucifix in thy hand—two things I never loved" (p. 80) and his assertion that philosophy rarely recognizes the heights of "eternal wisdom" in poetry, having an interest in art which is "otherwise mainly pathological and perfunctory" (p. 93). Yeats then attacks Magee's declaration that "The criticism of such ardent but harassed idealists as Shelley and Wagner, who saw in art the refuge from a squalid reality, can hardly satisfy those who have learned from Wordsworth . . . to regard poetry simply as a fact of life" (p. 89). His final allusion is to Magee's praise of Tolstoy's *What is Art?* (1898), which lists *Uncle Tom's Cabin* among its "examples of the highest art flowing from love of God and man" (Tolstoy, *What is Art?*, trans. A. Maude, London, 1959, p. 242).

Yeats's final paragraph was probably the major provocation for Eglinton's retort in *The United Irishman* for November 16 that it was "strange that one who makes so little of modern civilization as Mr. Yeats could think of nothing but fishing and reading Wordsworth as possible occupations for idealists of the school of Rousseau and Tolstoy. . .".

ities" of churches, governments, and "peoples". Yeats responded, in a letter on "Literature and the Conscience" in *The United Irishman* for December 7, 1901, to "Irial's" assertion that "fine writing is not by any means always on the side of the true and the just" and his charge that Yeats's statement allows any "smart young man in the *Telegraph* . . . to turn it to the use of the reactionaries".

A PHRASE in my letter to the *Freeman's Journal* about the proposed clerical censorship of the National Theatre has caused a good deal of misunderstanding. "Irial," for instance, objects to my description of literature as "the principal voice of the conscience," and himself defines literature as "any piece of writing which in point of form is likely to secure permanence." If "Irial" will recall the names of a few masterpieces he is much too intelligent not to see that his description is inadequate. Let him recall to mind "Don Quixote," or "Hamlet," or "Faust," or Tolstoi's "War and Peace" and "Anna Karenina," or almost any novel by Balzac or Flaubert, or any play by Ibsen, his "Enemy of the People" let us say. If he will do so, he will understand why literature seems to me, as indeed it seems to most critics of literature, to be the principal voice of the conscience. A great writer will devote perhaps years, perhaps the greater part of a lifetime, to the study of the moral issues raised by a single event, by a single group of characters. He will not bemoralise his characters, but he will show, as no other can show, how they act and think and endure under the weight of that destiny which is divine justice. No lawgiver, however prudent, no preacher, however lofty, can devote to life so ample and so patient a treatment. It is for this reason that men of genius frequently have to combat against the moral codes of their time, and are yet pronounced right by history. "Irial" will recall many examples, of which the most recent is Ibsen. A play or a novel necessarily describes people in their relation to one another, and is, therefore, frequently concerned with the conscience in the ordinary sense of that word, but even lyric poetry is the voice of what metaphysicians call innate knowledge, that is to say, of conscience, for it expresses the relation of the soul to eternal beauty and truth as no other writing can express it. That apparently misleading sentence of mine was, indeed, but an echo of a sentence of Verhaeren's,[1] the famous Belgian poet. He says that a masterpiece is a portion of the conscience of the world. An essay on poetry by Shelley and certain essays by Schopenhauer are probably the best things that have been written on the subject by modern writers, but Mr. George Santayana has written a book called

[1] Arthur Symons introduced Yeats to the work of the Belgian poet, Emile Verhaeren. See p. 131, above.

"The Sense of Beauty,"[2] which deals profoundly with the whole philosophy of aesthetics. "Irial" should read it. He can buy it for half-a-crown if he is lucky.

Now, another matter. I am doing an historical note on the various versions of the Diarmuid and Grainne legend, of which there are many. The critics who have objected to Mr. Moore's treatment and mine only seem to know one version and that a late literary form of the story, and this version they misunderstand. They have not even consulted so obvious a source as J. G. Campbell's book, "The Fians," which gives several Highland folk-lore versions of the legend which are also current in Ireland. I may send my note to you when I have time to finish it, but, in any case, if Mr. Moore consents, as I have no doubt he will, it shall go with the printed text of the play.[3]

W. B. Yeats

P.S. I must add a sentence or two to what I have said about the conscience. It is made sensitive and powerful by religion, but its dealings with the complexity of life are regulated by literature. "Irial" spoke of a book which discusses problems of the hour and yet seems to him at once literature and iniquitous. He is certainly mistaken. Literature, when it is really literature, does not deal with problems of the hour, but with problems of the soul and character.

# Favourite Books of 1901

Yeats responded in the issue of *Academy* for December 7, 1901—along with Edmund Gosse, Theodore Watts-Dunton, Katharine Tynan, Richard Garnett, Arthur Symons and others—to the review's annual request for their choices among the year's books. His selections, in the year of such works as Hardy's *Poems of the Past and Present*, Meredith's *A Reading of Life* and Santayana's *Poetry and Religion*—as well as H. G. Wells's sociological essays,

[2] *The Sense of Beauty* by George Santayana (1863–1952) was published in New York and London in 1896.

[3] Just before "Irial's" note appeared, Yeats wrote to Lady Gregory about the several versions of the story of Diarmuid and Grania, including that in *The Fions* (1891), by John Gregorson Campbell (1836–91), whose work Yeats had admired since the eighties. Noting that Campbell's Grania is "not very particular in the choice of her lovers" and that "Finn in one version has her buried alive", Yeats said he was "half inclined to write for the printed text of the play a preface describing the various versions of the tale—and so dispose of Irish criticism once for all . . ." (*Letters*, p. 359). However, the play was not printed until 1951, when it appeared with a note by William Becker in *The Dublin Magazine*.

*Anticipations*, and Kipling's *Kim*—suggest his loyalty to his friends as well as the specialization of his reading.

Both Robert Laurence Binyon (1869–1943), whose *Odes* had appeared in December of 1900, and Thomas Sturge Moore (1870–1944), a poet and designer, were Yeats's friends of long standing. Binyon, whose work as an art historian and critic Yeats had praised and whom Yeats unsuccessfully urged to succeed Hugh Lane in 1916 as Director of the Irish National Gallery, had introduced Yeats to Moore in 1898. Moore's designs embellished many of Yeats's books and their friendship endured until Yeats's death.

## MR. W. B. YEATS

BINYON'S ODES, because of the poem in it about Tristram and Iseult, which seems to me perhaps the most noble and pathetic love poem on an old theme written in my time; and Sturge Moore's *Aphrodite Against Artemis*, which is powerful, with a beautiful constrained passion. I have read only one other book[1] published during the year, but cannot think, from what I hear, that had I read many I would have thought otherwise.

# Egyptian Plays

In his only contribution to the independent London paper, the *Star*, founded in 1888 by T. P. O'Connor, Yeats undertook to praise faintly the collaboration of Florence Farr and Olivia Shakespear, his close friends and for a time his lovers. An actress, Miss Farr (d. 1917), was the wife of Edward Emery. She was Yeats's fellow student in the Order of the Golden Dawn and together they worked on dramatic productions and readings of his poetry to music. Yeats had met Mrs. Shakespear, a novelist and the niece of Lionel Johnson, in 1894. He wrote of his liaison with her in the unpublished "Memoirs", calling her "Diana Vernon", and in 1934, when composing the section of his autobiography which was to become *Dramatis Personae*, he lamented to her that her image, "the most significant . . . of those years", had to be left out (*Letters*, p. 820). He learned of her death on October 7, 1938, and wrote to Dorothy Wellesley on the following day that Olivia Shakespear had been "for more than forty years" the center of his life in London "and during all that time we have never had a quarrel, sadness sometimes but never a difference" (*Letters*, p. 916).

[1] The only other work mentioned in his correspondence or his writings during 1901 is "John Eglinton's" *Pebbles from a Brook* (see pp. 255 above).

The plays Yeats saw, "The Beloved of Hathor" and "The Shrine of the Golden Hawk", were produced January 20 and 21, 1902, and his review appeared on January 23. Wade (*Letters*, p. 372) says that the texts were on sale at the theatre but that they were never published.

THE EGYPTIAN SOCIETY, whose object is to illustrate the life and thought of Ancient Egypt by plays and lectures, gave two plays at the Victoria Hall on Monday night and on Tuesday afternoon. The plays, which are the work of Miss Florence Farr and of Mrs. Shakespear, interested me by being an attempt to do a new thing. They are not only new in their subject, but in the rigorously decorative arrangements of the stage, which imitated the severe forms of Egyptian mural painting. The plays themselves are less plays than fragments of a ritual—the ritual of a beautiful forgotten worship. The characters are priests and priestesses of Ancient Egypt, and the names and mysteries of a religion that was one with magic are perpetually in their mouths. Their tribulations are the unearthly tribulations of the weavers of enchantments and of the moulders of talismans, and when the Ka, or double, of a priestess stands beside her in the sanctuary we do not find its manifest flesh and blood too earthly for a spirit, as we so often do upon the stage, for flesh and blood itself have begun to seem unearthly. This effect was, indeed, to me the chief merit of the plays, and it came, I think, more from the scenic arrangements, which did not grossen the imagination with realism, and from the symbolic costumes and from the half-chanting recitation of phrases of ritual, than from anything especially dramatic. If I except one final dramatic moment when a priestess, who has just been shrinking, in terror before her God, the Golden Hawk, dances in ecstasy before his image, neither play stirred in me a strictly dramatic interest. The too realistic acting was to blame for this in the second play, but "The Beloved of Hathor" was not ill-acted, and yet it irritated me from time to time by its chaos of motives and of motiveless incidents. When the irritation was over one listened contentedly enough. One understood that something interesting was being done—not very well done, indeed—but something one had never seen before, and might never see again.

Miss Farr and Miss Paget[1] played often picturesquely, and sometimes with sweetness and gravity, and always with that beauty of voice, which

---

[1] Dorothy Paget (*c.* 1886–?) was the niece of Florence Farr. Yeats had written *The Land of Heart's Desire* for her debut which took place, under the management of her aunt, in 1894. She had read the prologue which Lionel Johnson wrote for the first production of *The Countess Cathleen* by the Irish National Theatre in 1899.

becomes perhaps the essential thing in a player when lyrical significance
has become the essential thing in a play. They spoke their sentences in
adoration of Heru, or Hathor, copied or imitated from old Egyptian
poems, as one thinks the Egyptian priestesses must have spoken them.
They spoke with so much religious fervour, with so high an ecstasy, that
one could not but doubt at times their Christian orthodoxy. Miss Paget
has, in addition to a beautiful voice, still a little lacking in the richness of maturity, the beauty of extreme youth, and a fluent charm as of
one who had put on womanhood and not yet put off childhood. If
they had had "The Shrine of the Golden Hawk" to themselves, with a
couple of priests who would have been content to speak and not to act,
I might feel that an interesting thing had not only been done, but done
well, or well enough. Some imperfections one must always expect in
work out of the ordinary track, for there the worker finds nothing ready
to his hand. He has to make everything afresh.

W. B. Yeats

# Away

This article is the last of the group of six which Yeats organized from the
folk material gathered by himself and Lady Gregory. It appeared in *Fortnightly Review* in April, 1902.

## I

THERE is, I think, no country side in Ireland where they will not tell
you, if you can conquer their mistrust, of some man or woman or child
who was lately or still is in the power of the gentry, or "the others," or
"the fairies," or "the sidhe," or the "forgetful people," as they call the
dead and the lesser gods of ancient times. These men and women and
children are said to be "away," and for the most part go about their
work in a dream, or lie all day in bed, awakening after the fall of night
to a strange and hurried life.

A woman at Gort, in County Galway, says: "There was an old
woman I remember was living at Martin Ruanes, and she had to go with
them two or three hours every night for a while, and she'd make great
complaints of the hardships she'd meet with, and how she'd have to
spend the night going through little boreens, or in the churchyard at
Kinvara, or they'd bring her down to the sea shore. They often meet

with hardships like that, those they bring with them, so it's no wonder they're glad to get back; this world's the best." And an old pensioner from Kiltartan, a village some three miles from Gort, says: "There is a man I knew that was my comrade after, used to be taken away at nights, and he'd speak of the journeys he had with them. And he got severe treatment and didn't want to go, but they'd bring him by force. He recovered after, and joined the army, and I was never so astonished as I was the day he walked in, when I was in Delhi." There are a boy near Gort and a woman at Ardrahan close at hand, who are "away," and this same man says of them: "Mary Flaherty has been taken, and whenever she meets old Whelan the first thing she asks is for his son. She doesn't go to see him in the house, but travelling of nights they meet each other. Surely she's gone. You have but to look in her face to see that. And whatever hour of the night she wants to go out, they must have the horse harnessed to bring her wherever she likes to go."

The commonest beginning of the enchantment is to meet some one not of this earth, or in league with people not of this earth, and to talk too freely to them about yourself and about your life. If they understand you and your life too perfectly, or sometimes even if they know your name, they can throw their enchantment about you. A man living at Coole near Gort says: "But those that are brought away would be glad to be back. It's a poor thing to go there after this life. Heaven is the best place, Heaven and this world we're in now. My own mother was away for twenty-one years, and at the end of every seven years she thought it would be off her, but she never could leave the bed. She could but sit up, and make a little shirt or the like for us. It was of the fever she died at last. The way she got the touch was one day after we left the place we used to be in, and we got our choice place on the estate, and my father chose Kilchreest. But a great many of the neighbours went to Moneen. And one day a woman that had been our neighbour came over from Moneen, and my mother showed her everything and told her of her way of living. And she walked a bit of the road with her, and when they were parting the woman said: "You'll soon be the same as such a one." And as she turned she felt a pain in the head. And from that day she lost her health. My father went to Biddy Early, but she said it was too late, she could do nothing, and she would take nothing from him." Biddy Early was a famous witch.

If you are taken you have always, it is said, a chance of return every seven years. Almost all that go "away" among them are taken to help in their work, or in their play, or to nurse their children, or to bear them children, or to be their lovers, and all fairy children are born of such marriages. A man near Gort says: "They are shadows, and how could a shadow have power to move that chair or that table? But they have

power over mankind, and they can bring them away to do their work."
I have told elsewhere[1] of a man who was "away" with Maibh Queen of
the western Sidhe as her lover, and made a mournful song in the Gaelic
when she left him, and was mournful till he died.

But sometimes one hears of people taken for no reason, as it seems,
but that they may be a thing to laugh at. Indeed, one is often told that
unlike "the simple" who would do us an evil, "the gentle" among "the
others" wish us no harm but "to make a sport of us."

And a man at Gort says: "There was one Mahony had the land taken
that is near Newtown racecourse. And he was out there one day building
a wall and it came to the dinner hour, but he had none brought with
him. And a man came by and said, 'Is it home you'll be going for your
dinner?' And he said, 'It's not worth my while to go back to Gort, I'd
have the day lost . . .' And the man said, 'Well, come in and eat a bit with
me.' And he brought him into a forth and there was everything that was
grand, and the dinner they gave him of the best, so that he eat near two
plates of it. And then he went out again to build the wall. And whether
it was with lifting the heavy stones I don't know, but with respects to
you, when he was walking the road home he began to vomit, and what
he vomited up was all green grass."

You may eat their food, if they put it out to you, and indeed it is
discourteous to refuse and will make them angry, but you must not
go among them and eat their food, for this will give them power over
you.

## II

Sometimes one hears of people "away" doing the work of the others
and getting harm of it, or no good of it, but more often one hears of
good crops or of physical strength or of cleverness or of supernatural
knowledge being given and of no evil being given with it except the
evil of being in a dream, or being laid up in bed or the like, which
happens more or less to all who are "away." A woman near Craugh-
well says: "There's a boy now of the Lydons, but I wouldn't for all the
world let them think I spoke of him. But it's two years since he came
from America and since that time he never went to Mass, or to Church,
or to market, or to fair, or to stand at the cross roads, or to the hurling.
And if anyone comes into the house, it's into the room he'll slip not to
see them. And as to work, he has the garden dug to bits and the whole
place smeared with cowdung, and such a crop as was never seen, and
the alders all plaited that they looked grand. One day he went as far as
Peterswell Chapel, but as soon as he got to the door he turned straight

[1] Yeats tells this story in " 'Maive', and certain Irish beliefs" (see p. 205 above). The
story of the "woman from the North", one of the "Ingentry", which follows here is, with
minor alteration, taken from the same place.

round again as if he hadn't power to pass it. I wonder he wouldn't get
the priest to read a mass for him or some such thing. But the crop he
has is grand, and you may know well he has some that help him."

Indeed, almost any exceptional cleverness, even the clever training of
a dog may be thought a gift from "the others." I have been told of a
boy in Gort "who was lying in the bed a long time, and one day, the
day of the races, he asked his father and mother were they going to the
course, and they said they were not. Well, says he, 'I'll show you as
good sport as if you went.' And he had a dog and he called to it and
said something to it, and it began to take a run and to gallop and to
jump backwards over the half door, for there was a very high half door
to the house. 'So now,' says he, 'didn't you see as good sport as if you
were on Newtown racecourse?' And he didn't live long, but died soon
after that." And the same man whose mother had been away for twenty-
one years says: "There was one of the Burkes, John, was away for
seven years, lying in his bed but brought away at nights. And he knew
everything. And one Kearney up in the mountain, a cousin of his own,
lost two hoggets and came and told him. And he knew the very spot
where they were and told him, and he got them back again. But *they*
were vexed at that, and took away the power, so that he never knew
anything again, no more than another. There was another man up near
Ballylee could tell these things too. When John Callan lost his wool he
went to him, and next morning there were the fleeces at his door. Those
that are away know these things. There was a brother of my own took
to it for seven years, and he at school. And no one could beat him at the
hurling and the games. But I wouldn't like to be mixed with that
myself." The wool and perhaps the hoggets had been taken by "the
others" who were forced to return them.

When you get a "touch" you feel a sudden pain, and a swelling comes
where you have felt the pain. I have been told that there is a fool and a
queen "in every household of them," and that nobody can cure the touch
of the fool or the queen, but that the touch of anyone else among them can
be cured. A woman at Kiltartan says: "One time a woman from the
North came to our house, and she said a great deal of people is kept
below there in the lisses. She had been there herself, and in the night
time in one moment they'd be all away at Cruachmaa, wherever that
may be, down in the north I believe. And she knew everything that
was in the house, and told us about my sister being sick, and that there
was a hurling match going on that day, as there was, at the Isabella
Wood in Coole. And all about Coole house she knew, as well as if she
spent her life in it. I'd have picked a lot of stories out of her, but my
mother got nervous when she heard the truth coming out and bid me
be quiet. She had a red petticoat on her, the same as any country woman,

and she offered to cure me, for it was that time I was delicate and her ladyship sent me to the salt water. But she asked a shilling, and my mother said she hadn't got it. 'You have,' says she, 'and heavier metal than that you have in the house.' So then my mother gave her the shilling and she put it in the fire and melted it, and says she, 'After two days you'll see your shilling again,' but we never did. And the cure she left I never took it—it's not safe, and the priests forbid us to take their cures, for it must surely be from the devil their knowledge comes. No doubt at all she was one of the Ingentry, that can take the form of a woman by day and another form by night. After that she went to Mrs. Finnegan's house and asked her for a bit of tobacco. 'You'll get it again,' she said, 'and more with it.' And sure enough that very day a bit of meat came into Mrs. Finnegan's house."

The people of the North are thought to know more about the supernatural than anybody else, and one remembers that the good gods of the Celts, the children of Danu, and the evil gods of the Celts, the Fomor, came from the North in certain legends. The North does not mean Ulster, but any place to the north, for the people talk of the people of Cruachmaa, which is but a little north of Galway, as knowing much because they are from the North—one cannot tell whether the woman from the North in this tale was a mortal or an immortal. People "away," like people taken by "the others" from their death-beds, are confounded with the immortals, the true children of Danu, or the Dundonians, as I have heard them called in Clare. I have never heard the word "Ingentry" for "the others" at any other time.

Sometimes people who are "away" are thought to have, like the dead who have been "taken," that power of changing one thing into another, which is so constantly attributed to the Children of Danu in the Gaelic poems. The Children of Danu were the powers of life, the powers worshipped in the ecstatic dances among the woods and upon the mountains, and they had the flamelike changeability of life, and were the makers of all changes. "The others," their descendants, change the colours of their clothes ever moment, and build up a house "in the corner of a field" and "in ten minutes," "finer than any gentleman's house." An Irishwoman from Kildare that I met in London told me: "There was a woman used to go away at night, and she said to her sister, 'I'll be out on a white horse, and I'll stop and knock at your door as I pass,' and so she used to do sometimes. And one day there was a man asked her for a debt he owed, and she said, 'I have no money now.' But then she put her hand behind her, and brought it back filled with gold, and then she rubbed it in her hand, and when she opened her hand again, there was nothing in it but dry cow-dung, and she said, 'I could give you that, but it would be of no use to you.' "

Those who are "away" have sometimes, too, it seems, the power of changing their size and of going through walls as "the others" themselves do. A man on Inisheer says: "There was a first cousin of mine used sometimes to go out of the house through the wall, but none could see him going. And one night his brother followed him, and he went down a path to the sea, and then he went into a hole in the rocks that the smallest dog wouldn't go into. And the brother took hold of his feet and drew him out again. He went to America after that, and is living there now, and sometimes in his room they'll see him beckoning and laughing and laughing, as if some were with him. One night there, when some of the neighbours from these islands were with him, he told them he'd been back to Inishmaan, and told all that was going on, and some would not believe him. And he said, 'You'll believe me next time.' So the next night he told them again he had been there, and he brought out of his pocket a couple of boiled potatoes and a bit of fish, and showed them; so then they all believed it." And an old man on Inisheer, who has come back from the State of Maine, says of this man: "I knew him in America, and he used often to visit this island, and would know what all of them were doing, and would bring us word of them all, and all he'd tell us would turn out right. He's living yet in America."

It often seems as if these enchanted people had some great secret. They may have taken an oath to be silent, but I have not heard of any oath, I am only certain that they are afraid or unable to speak. I have already told of Whelan[2] and his nightly rides. I got a friend, with whom I was staying, to ask Whelan's father, who is a carpenter, to make a box and send it by his son. He promised to "try and infatuate him to come," but did not think it would be of any use. It was no use, for the boy said, "No, I won't go, I know why I am wanted." His father says that he did not tell him, but that "the others" told him, when he was out with them.

A man said to a friend of mine in the Abbey of Corcomroe among the Burren hills in County Clare: "There was one O'Loughlin that lies under that slab there, and for seven years he was brought away every night, and into this Abbey. And he was beat and pinched, and when he came home he'd faint. He told his brother-in-law, that told me, that in that hill beyond, behind this Abbey, there is the most splendid town that ever was seen, and grander than any city. Often he was in it and ought not to have been talking about it, but he said he wouldn't give them the satisfaction of it, he didn't care what they'd do to him. One night he was with a lot of others at a wake, and when he heard them coming for him he fainted on the floor. But after he got up he heard

---

[2] *i.e.* earlier in this essay.

# AWAY

them come again and he rose to go, and the boys all took hold of him, Peter Fahey was one of them, and you know what a strong man he was, and *he* couldn't hold him. Drawn out of the door he was, and the arms of those that were holding him were near pulled out of their sockets."

And a woman near Loughrea says: "My mother often told me about her sister's child, my cousin, that used to spend the nights in the big forth at Moneen. Every night she went there, and she got thin and tired like. She used to say she saw grand things there, and the horses galloping and the riding. But then she'd say, 'I must tell no more than that or I'll get a great beating.' She wasted away, and one night they were so sure she was dead they had the pot full of water boiling on the fire to wash her. But she recovered again and lived five years after that."

And an old man on the north isle of Arran says: "I know a good many on the island have seen *those*, but they wouldn't say what they're like to look at, for when they speak of them their tongue gets like a stone."

The most of what the country people have to tell of those who have been "taken" altogether, and about the ways and looks of the "others," has come from the frightened and rare confidences of people upon whom "the others" cast this sleepy enchantment.

A man in the Burren hills says: "That girl of the Connors that was away for seven years, she was bid tell nothing of what she saw, but she told her mother some things, and told of some she met there. There was a woman, a cousin of my own, asked was her son ever there, and she had to press her a long time, but at last she said he was. And he was taken too, with little privication [*sic*], fifty years ago."

And a woman near Ardrahan says: "There was a girl near Westport was away, and the way it came on her was she was on the road one day, and two men passed her, and one of them said, 'That's a fine girl,' and the other said, 'She belongs to my town.' And there and then she got a pain in her knee, and she couldn't walk home but had to be brought home in a cart, and she used to be away at night, and thorns in her feet in the morning, but she never said where she went. But one time the sister brought her to Kilfenora, and when they were crossing a a bog near to there she pointed to a house in the bog and she said, 'It's there I was last night.' And the sister asked did she know anyone she met there, and she said, 'There was one I knew that is my mother's cousin,' and told her name. And she said, 'But for her they'd have me ill-treated, but she fought for me and saved me!' She was thought to be dying one time, and my mother sent me to see her, and how she was. And she was lying on the bed, and her eyes turned back, and she was speechless, and I told my mother when I came home she hadn't an hour to live. And the next day she was up and about and not a thing on her. It might be the mother's cousin that fought for her again then. She went to America after."

This girl fell under the power of "the others" because the two men looked at her with admiration, "overlooked her," as it is called, and did not say "God bless her." "The others" can draw anything they admire to themselves by using our admiration as a bond between them and it.

## III

In some barbarous countries no one is permitted to look at the king while he is eating, for one is thought to be less able to drive away malicious influence when one is eating, and most mortal influence must be malignant when one is the representative and instrument of the gods. I have sometimes been told that nobody is ever allowed to see those who are "away" eating. A woman near Gort says of Whelan the carpenter's son, "He's lying in bed these four years, and food is brought into the room but he never touches it, but when it's left there it's taken away." And a man at Coole says: "I remember a boy was about my own age over at Cranagh on the other side of the water, and they said he was away for two years. Anyhow, for all that time he was sick in bed, and no one ever saw bit or sup pass his lips in all that time, though the food that was left in the room would disappear, whatever happened it. He recovered after and went to America."

They are sometimes believed to hardly eat our food at all, but to live upon supernatural food. An old man from near Loughrea says: "There was Kitty Flannery at Kilchreest, you might remember her. For seven years she had everything she could want, and music and dancing could be heard round her house every night, and all she did prospered. But she ate no food all that time, only she'd take a drink of the milk after the butter being churned. But at the end of the seven years all left her, and she was glad at the last to get Indian meal."

But often one hears of their fearing to eat the food of "the others" for fear they might never escape out of their hands. An old man on the Gortaveha mountain says: "I knew one was away for seven years, and it was in the next townland to this she lived. Bridget Kinealy her name was. There was a large family of them, and she was the youngest, a very nice-looking fair-haired girl she was. I knew her well, she was the one age with myself. It was in the night she used to go to them, and if the door was shut she'd come in by the keyhole. The first time they came for her she was in bed between her two sisters, and she didn't want to go, but they beat her and pinched her till her brother called out to know what was the matter. She often spoke about them, and how she was badly treated because she wouldn't eat their food, and how there was a red-haired girl among them that would throw her into the river she'd get so mad with her. But if she had their food ate, she'd never have got away from them at all. She got no more than about three cold potatoes she could eat the whole time she was with them. All the old people about her put out food every night, the first of the food before they have any of it tasted themselves. She married a serving man after, and they went to Sydney, and if nothing happened in the last two years they're doing well there now."

# IV

The ancient peoples from whom the country people inherit their belief had to explain how, when you were "away," as it seemed to you, you seemed, it might be, to your neighbours or your family, to be lying in a faint upon the ground, or in your bed, or even going about your daily work. It was probably one who was himself "away" who explained, that somebody or something was put in your place, and this explanation was the only possible one to ancient peoples, who did not make our distinction between body and soul. The Irish country people always insist that something, a heap of shavings or a broomstick or a wooden image, or some dead person, "maybe some old warrior," or some dead relative or neighbour of your own, is put in your place, though sometimes they will forget their belief until you remind them, and talk of "the others" having put such and such a person "into a faint," or of such and such a person being "away" and being ill in bed. This substitution of the dead for the living is indeed a pagan mystery, and not more hard to understand than the substitution of the body and blood of Christ for the wafer and the wine in the mass; and I have not yet lost the belief that some day, in some village lost among the hills or in some island among the western seas, in some place that remembers old ways and has not learned new ways, I will come to understand how this pagan mystery hides and reveals some half-forgotten memory of an ancient knowledge or of an ancient wisdom. Time that has but left the lesser gods to haunt the hills and raths, has doubtless taken much that might have made us understand.

A man at Kiltartan, who thinks evil of "the others," says: "They have the hope of heaven or they wouldn't leave one on the face of the earth, and they are afraid of God. They'll not do you much harm if you leave them alone, it's best not to speak to them at all if you should meet them. If they bring anyone away they'll leave some good-for-nothing thing in its place, and the same way with a cow or a calf or such things. But a sheep or a lamb it's beyond their power to touch, because of our

Lord." And a woman near Ardrahan says: "There was a cousin of my own was said to be 'away,' and when she died I was but a child, and my mother brought me with her to the house where she was laid out. And when I saw her I began to scream and to say, 'That's not Mary that's in it, that's some old hag.' And so it was, I know well it was not Mary that was lying there in the bed." And a woman from near Loughrea says: "Sure there was a fairy in a house at Eserkelly fourteen years. Bridget Collins she was called, you might remember Miss Fanny used to be bringing her gooseberries. She never kept the bed, but she'd sit in the corner of the kitchen on a mat, and from a good stout lump of a girl that she was, she wasted to nothing, and her teeth grew as long as your finger, and then they dropped out. And she'd eat nothing at all, only crabs and sour things. And she'd never leave the house in the daytime, but in the night she'd go out and pick things out of the fields she could eat. And the hurt she got, or whatever it was touched her, it was one day she was swinging on the Moneen gate, just there by the forth. She died as quiet as another, but you wouldn't like to be looking at her after the teeth fell out."

And a man from Cahirglissane says: "There was one Tierney on the road to Kinvara, I knew him well, was away with them seven years. It was at night he used to be brought away, and when they called him he should go. They'd leave some sort of a likeness of him in his place. He had a wart on his back, and his wife would rub her hand down to feel was the wart there before she'd know was it himself was in it or not. Himself and his pony used to be brought up into the sky, and he told many how he used to go riding about with them, and that often and often he was in that castle you see below. And Mrs. Hevenor asked him did he ever see her son Jimmy that died, among them, and he told her he did, and that mostly all the people that he knew that had died out of the village were amongst them now. And if his wife had a clutch of geese they'd be ten times better than any other one's, and the wheat and the stock and all they had was better and more plentiful than what anyone else had. Help he got from them of course. But at last the wife got in the priest to read a mass and to take it off him. And after that all that they had went to flitters."

And a girl at Coole says of a place called "The Three Lisses," where there are three of those old clay remnants of ancient houses or encampments so much haunted by "the others": "There must in old times have been a great a great deal of fighting there. There are some bushes growing on them, and no one, man or woman, will ever put a hand to cut them, no more than they would touch the little bush by the well beyond, that used to have lights shining out of it. And if anyone was to fall asleep within in the Liss, himself would be taken away, and the spirit of some old warrior would be put in his place, and it's he would know everything in the whole world. There's no doubt at all but that there's the same sort of things in other countries, sure *these* can go through and appear in Australia in one minute, but you hear more about them in these parts because the Irish do be more familiar in talking of them."

The chief way of bringing a person out of this state of dream is to threaten the dead person believed to have been put in his place. A man from county Clare says: "I heard of a woman brought back again. It was told me by a boy going to school there at the time it happened, so I know there's no lie in it. It was one of the Lydons, a rich family in Scariff, whose wife was sick and pining away for seven years. And at the end of that time one day he came in, he had a drop of drink taken, and he began to be a bit rough with her. And she said, 'Don't be rough with me now, after bearing so well with me all these seven years. But because you were so good and so kind to me all the time,' says she, 'I'll go away from you now, and I'll let your own wife come back to you.' And so she did, for it was an old hag she was. And the wife came back again and reared a family. And before she went away she had a son that was reared a priest, and after she came back she had another that was reared a priest, so that shows a blessing came on them."

The country people seldom do more than threaten the dead person put in the living person's place, and it is, I am convinced, a sin against the traditional widsom to really ill-treat the dead person. A woman from Mayo who has told me a good many tales and has herself both seen and heard "the royal gentry," as she calls them, was very angry with the Tipperary countryman who burned his wife, some time ago, her father and neighbours standing by. She had no doubt that they only burned some dead person, but she was quite certain that you should not burn even a dead person. She said: "In my place we say you should only threaten. They are so superstitious in Tipperary. I have stood in the door and I have heard lovely music, and seen the fort all lighted up, but I never gave in to them." "Superstitious" means to her "giving in" to "the others," and "giving in" means, I think, letting them get power over you, or being afraid of them, and getting excited about them, and doing foolish things. One does hear now and then of "the dead person" being really ill-treated, but rarely. When I was last in Western Galway a man had just been arrested for trying to kill his sister-in-law, because he thought she was one of "the others," and was tempting him to murder his cousin. He had sent his cousin away that she might be out of his reach in case he could not resist the temptation. This man was merely out of his mind, and had more than common reasons for his anger besides. A woman from Burren tells a tale more like the Tipperary tale. "There was a girl near Ballyvaughan was away, and the mother used to hear horses coming about the door every night. And one day the mother was picking flax in the house and of a sudden there came in her hand an herb with the best smell and the sweetest that ever anyone smelled. And she closed it into her hand and called to the son that was making up a stack of hay outside, 'Come in Denis, for I have the best smelling herb that ever you saw.' And when he came in she opened her hand and the herb was gone, clear and clean. She got annoyed at last with the horses coming about the door, and some one told her to gather all the fire into the middle of the floor and to lay the little girl upon it, and to see would she come back again. So she did as she was told, and brought the little girl out of the bed and laid her on the coals, and she began to scream and to call out, and the neighbours came running in, and the police heard of it, and they came and arrested the mother and brought her to Ballyvaughan, before the magistrate, Mr. Macnamara, and my own husband was one of the police that arrested her. And when the magistrate heard all, he said she was an ignorant woman, and that she did what she thought right, and he would give her no punishment. And the girl got well and was married, and it was after she married I knew her."

I was always convinced that tradition, which avoids needless in-humanity, had some stronger way of protecting the bodies of those, to whom the other world was perhaps unveiling its mysteries, than any mere command not to ill-treat some old dead person, who had maybe been put in the room of one's living wife or daughter or son. I heard of this stronger way last winter from an old Kildare woman, that I met in London. She said that in her own village, "there was a girl used to be away with them, you'd never know when it was she herself that was in it or not till she'd come back, and then she'd tell she had been away. She didn't like to go, but she had to go when they called to her. And she told her mother always to treat kindly whoever was put in her place, sometimes one would be put and sometimes another, for, she'd say 'If you are unkind to whoever is there, they'll be unkind to me.'"

Sometimes the person is thought to be brought back by some one who meets him on his wanderings and leads him home. A woman near Kinvara says: "There was a child was dying in some house in Burren by the sea, and the mother and all around it, thinking to see it die. And a boy came in, and he said when he was coming through a field beyond the house he heard a great crying, and he saw a troop of *them* and the child ran out from among them, and ran up to him and he took hold of its hand, and led it back, and then he brought it safe and well into the house. And the thing that was in the bed he took up and threw it out, and it vanished away into the air."

An army pensioner says: "My family were of the Finns of Athenry. I had an aunt that married a man of the name of Kane, and they had a child was taken. So they brought it to the Lady Well near Athenry, where there's patterns every 15th of August, to duck it. And such a ducking they gave it, that it walked away on crutches, and it swearing. And their own child they got back again, but he didn't live long after." I have one tale in which a visit to Knock, the Irish Lourdes, worked the cure. "There was a girl was overlooked got cured at Knock, and when she was cured she let three screams out of her, it was a neighbour of mine saw her and told me. And there are a great many cures done at Knock, and the walls thick with crutches and sticks and crooked shoes. And there was a gentleman from America was cured there, and his crutch was a very grand one, with silver on it, and he came back to bring it away, and when he did, he got as bad as ever he was before." It was no doubt the old person who gave the three screams.

And sometimes a priest works the cure. A piper who wanders about county Galway says:—"There was a girl at Kilkerran of the same name as my own, was lying on a mat for eight years. When she first got the touch the mother was sick, and there was no room in the bed; so they laid a mat on the floor for her, and she never left it for the eight years, but the mother died soon after. She never got off the mat for anyone to see, but one night there was a working man came to the house and they gave him lodging for the night. And he watched her from the other room, and in the night he saw the outer door open, and three or four boys and girls come in, and with them a piper or a fiddler, I'm not sure which, and he played to them, and they danced, and the girl got up off the mat and joined them. And in the morning, when he was sitting at breakfast, he looked over to her where she was lying, and said, 'You were the best dancer among them last night.' "

Many stories of the old Gaelic poems and romances become more fully intelligible when we read them by the light of these stories. There is a story about Cuchullain in *The Book of the Dun Cow*, interpreted too exclusively as a solar myth by Professor Rhys,[3] which certainly is a story of Cuchullain "away." The people of Uladh, or Ulster, were celebrating the festival of the beginning of winter that was held the first day of November, on the days before and after. A flock of wild birds lighted upon a lake near where Cuchullain and the heroes and fair women of Uladh were holding festival, and because of the bidding of the women Cuchullain caught the birds and divided them among them. When he

---

[3] The Celtic scholar, John Rhys, retells this story in "The Sun Hero", the fifth of his *Lectures on the Origin and Growth of Religion as Illustrated by Celtic Heathendom*, which Yeats had read at the time of its publication in 1888. He used much of the story of Cuchullain "away", as he recounts it here, in *The Only Jealousy of Emer* (1919).

*Leabhar na h-Uidhre* (The Book of the Dun Cow), the oldest of the Irish miscellaneous manuscripts, was composed around 1100.

came to his own wife Emer, he had no birds left, and promised her the finest two out of any new flock. Presently he saw two birds, bound one to the other with a chain of gold, and they were singing so sweetly that the host of Uladh fell in a little while into a magic sleep. Cuchullain cast a stone out of a sling, but missed them, and then another stone, but missed them, and wondered greatly, because he had not missed a cast from the day when he took arms. He threw his spear, and it passed through the wing of one of the birds, and the birds dived out of his sight. He lay down in great sorrow, because of his bad casting, and fell asleep and dreamed that two women, one dressed in green and one dressed in red, came to him and first one and then the other smiled and struck him with a whip, and that they went on beating him until he was nearly dead. His friends came while he was still dreaming, but only saw that he slept and must not be awakened, and when at last he awoke, he was so weak that he made them carry him to his bed. He lay in his bed all through the winter, the time of the power of the gods of death and cold, and until the next November Eve, when those who watched beside him suddenly saw a stranger sitting upon the side of his bed. This stranger was Ængus, perhaps that Ængus, the master of love, who had made four birds out of his kisses, and he sang that Fand, the wife of Mannannan, the master of the sea, and of the island of the dead, loved Cuchullain, and that, if he would come into the country of the gods, where there was wine and gold and silver, she would send Leban, her sister, to heal him. Having ended his song, the stranger vanished as suddenly as he had come. Cuchullain having consulted with his friends, went to the place where he had seen the swans and dreamed his dream, and there the woman dressed in green came and spoke with him. He reproached her, and she answered that she wished him no harm, but only to bring him to her sister Fand, who had been deserted by Mannannan, and who loved him passionately, and to bring him to help her own husband Labraid of the Swift Hand on the Sword in a one-day's battle against his enemies. After hearing what another mortal who had been to the country of Labraid had to tell, Cuchullain mounted into his chariot, and went to the country of Labraid, and fought a one-day's battle, and had Fand to wife for a month. At the month's end he made a promise to meet her at a place called "The Yew at the Strand's End," and came back to the earth. When Emer, his mortal wife, heard of the tryst, she went with other women to the Yew at the Strand's End, and there she won again the love of Cuchullain. When Fand saw that she had lost his love she lamented her happy days with Mannannan when their love was new. Mannannan heard and came swiftly and carried her away to his own country. When Cuchullain saw her leaving him his love for her returned, and he became mad and went into the mountains,

and wandered there a long time without food or drink. At last the King
of Uladh sent his poets and his druids to cure him, and though he tried
to kill them in his madness, they chanted druid spells, so that he became
weak. He cried out for a drink in his weakness, and they gave him a
drink of forgetfulness; and they gave Emer a drink of forgetfulness,
so that she forgot the divine woman.

Mr. Frazer discusses in, I think, the second volume of *The Golden
Bough*—I am writing in Ireland and have not the book at hand and
cannot give the exact reference—the beating of the divine man in ancient
religious ceremonies, and decides that it was never for a punishment but
always for a purification, for the driving out of something.[4] I am inclined, therefore, to consider the beating of Cuchullain by the smiling
women, as a driving out or deadening, for a time, of his merely human
faculties and instincts; and I am certain it should be compared with the
stories told by the country people, of people over whom "the others"
get power by striking them (see my article in the *Nineteenth Century* for
January, 1898, p. 69, for one such story);[5] and with countless stories of
their getting power over people by giving them what is called "the
touch"—I shall tell and weigh a number of these stories some day—and
perhaps with the common habit of calling a paralytic attack a "stroke."
Cuchullain wins the love of Fand just as young, handsome countrymen are believed to win the love of fair women of "the others," and
he goes to help Labraid as young, strong countrymen are believed to
help "the others" who can do little, being but "shadows" without a
mortal among them, at the hurling and in the battle; and November
Eve is still a season of great power among the spirits. Emer goes to the
Yew at the Strand End just as the wife goes to meet her husband who
is "away" or has been "taken," or the husband to meet his wife, at midnight, at "the custom gap" in the field where the fair is held, or at some
other well known place; while the after madness of Cuchullain reminds
me of the mystery the country people, like all premature people, see in
madness, and of the way they sometimes associate it with "the others,"
and of the saying of a woman in the Burren hills, "Those that are away
among them never come back, or if they do they are not the same as
they were before." His great sorrow for the love of Fand reminds me
of the woman told of in Arran, who was often heard weeping on the
hill-side for the children she had left among "the others." One finds
nothing in this tale about any person or thing being put in Cuchullain's
place; but Professor Rhys has shown that in the original form of the
story of Cuchullain and the Beetle of Forgetfulness, Cuchullain made the

---

[4] It is the ninth volume of *The Golden Bough* (1890) by J. G. Frazer (1854–1941), "The
Scapegoat", which contains several instances of beating as a purifying process (pp. 259 ff.).
[5] "The Prisoners of the Gods", p. 80 above.

prince who had come to summon him to the other world, take his place at the court of Uladh. There are many stories everywhere of people who have their places taken by Angels, or spirits, or gods, that they may live another life in some other place, and I believe all such stories were once stories of people "away."

Pwyll and Arawn in the Mabinogian change places for a year, Pwyll going to the court of the dead in the shape of Arawn to overcome his enemies, and Arawn going to the court of Dyved. Arawn said, "I will put my form and semblance upon thee, so that not a page of the chamber, not an officer nor any other man that has always followed me, shall know that it is not I . . . And I will cause that no one in all thy dominions, neither man nor woman, shall know that I am not you, and I will go there in thy stead." Pwyll overcomes Arawn's enemy with one blow, and Arawn's rule in Dyved was a marvel because of his wisdom, for in all these stories strength comes from among men, and wisdom from among gods who are but "shadows."

Professor Rhys has interpreted both the stories of Cuchullain and the story of Pwyll and Arawn as solar myths, and one doubts not that the old priests and poets saw analogies in day and night, in summer and winter; or perhaps held that the passing away for a time of the brightness of day or of the abundance of summer, was one story with the passing of a man out of our world for a time. There have been mythmakers who put the mountain of the gods at the North Pole, and there are still visionaries who think that cold and barrenness with us are warmth and abundance in some inner world; while what the Arran people call "the battle of the friends" believed to be fought between the friends and enemies of the living among the "others," to decide whether a sick person is to live or die, and the battle believed to be fought by "others" at harvest time, to decide, as I think, whether the harvest is to stay among men, or wither from among men and belong to "the others" and the dead, show, I think, that the gain of the one country is the other country's loss. The Norse legend of the false Odin that took the true Odin's place, when the summer sun became the winter sun, brings the story of a man who is "away" and the story of the year perfectly together. It may be that the druids and poets meant more at the beginning than a love story, by such stories as that of Cuchullain and Fand, for in many ancient countries, as even among some African tribes today, a simulated and ceremonious death was the symbol, or the condition, of the soul's coming to the place of wisdom and of the spirits of wisdom; and, if this is true, it is right for such stories to remind us of day and night, winter and summer, that men may find in all nature the return and history of the soul's deliverance.

W. B. Yeats

# Mr. Yeats' New Play

The first productions of *Deirdre* by A.E. and Yeats's *Cathleen ni Houlihan*, with Maud Gonne as the "Poor Old Woman", in Saint Teresa's Hall, Dublin, on April 2, 3 and 4, 1902, were great popular successes. This resulted in a brief truce between the National Theatre and Arthur Griffith's *United Irishman*, where angry speculation on the "failure" or "betrayal" of national drama had become a regular feature. The note on "Mr. Yeats' New Play", in the issue for April 5, reflects this mood, as Yeats speaks of his play as "the call of country" and as he anticipates the "play about the call of religion" which was to become *The Hour-Glass* and which, he told Lady Gregory, would not "offend anybody" but might "propitiate Holy Church" (*Letters*, p. 370).

MR. YEATS, who returned to Dublin a few days ago to attend the final rehearsals of his new play, in answer to some questions we submitted to him has kindly sent us the following reply:

My subject is Ireland and its struggle for independence. The scene is laid in the West of Ireland at the time of the French landing. I have described a household preparing for the wedding of the son of the house. Everyone expects some good thing from the wedding. The bridegroom is thinking of his bride, the father of the fortune which will make them all more prosperous, and the mother of a plan of turning this prosperity to account by making her youngest son a priest, and the youngest son of a greyhound pup the bride promised to give him when she marries. Into this household comes Kathleen Ni Houlihan herself, and the bridegroom leaves his bride, and all the hopes come to nothing. It is the perpetual struggle of the cause of Ireland and every other ideal cause against private hopes and dreams, against all that we mean when we say the world. I have put into the mouth of Kathleen Ni Houlihan verses about those who have died or are about to die for her, and these verses are the key of the rest. She sings of one yellow-haired Donough in stanzas that were suggested to me by some old Gaelic folk-song:

> *I will go cry with the woman,*
> *For yellow-haired Donough is dead,*
> *With a hempen-rope for a neck-cloth,*
> *And a white cloth on his head.*

> *I am come to cry with you woman,*
> *My hair is unbound and unwound;*
> *I remember him ploughing his field,*
> *Turning up the red side of the ground.*

> *And building his barn on the hill,*
> *With the good-mortared stone;*
> *Oh, we'd have pulled down the gallows,*
> *Had it happened at Enniscrone.*

And just before she goes out she sings:

> *Do not make a great keening*
> *When the graves have been dug to-morrow;*
> *Do not call the white-scarfed riders*
> *To the buryings that shall be to-morrow;*
> *Do not spread food to call strangers,*
> *To the wakes that shall be to-morrow,*

And after a few words of dialogue she goes out crying:

> *They shall be remembered for ever;*
> *They shall be alive for ever;*
> *They shall be speaking for ever,*
> *The people shall hear them for ever.*

I have written the whole play in the English of the West of Ireland, the English of people who think in Irish. My play, "The Land of Heart's Desire," was, in a sense, the call of the heart, the heart seeking its own dream; this play is the call of country, and I have a plan of following it up with a little play about the call of religion, and printing the three plays together some day.[1]

# The Acting at St. Teresa's Hall

Yeats followed his explanatory note on *Cathleen ni Houlihan* with a note on "The Acting at St. Teresa's Hall" in *The United Irishman* for April 12, 1902, in which he praised the acting of A.E.'s *Deirdre* by an all-Irish cast. For the 1901 season of the Irish Literary Theatre, Yeats's and Moore's *Diarmuid and Grania* had been produced by F. R. Benson's English company and Douglas Hyde's *Casadh an tSugain* (The Twisting of the Rope) had been done in Gaelic by members of the Gaelic League. Partly because of nationalist objections to the English production of a play by Irish writers on an Irish theme, and also because the ability of the League members seemed limited, the 1902 productions were given by the Irish National Dramatic Company of W. G. Fay (1872–1947). According to Gerard Fay (*The Abbey Theatre*, London, 1958,

---

[1] This edition never appeared. The text of *Cathleen ni Houlihan* appeared in *Samhain* and in book form in October of 1902 and was printed, along with *The Hour-Glass* and *The Pot of Broth* as "Volume Two of Plays for an Irish Theatre" in 1904.

p. 34), Yeats had praised the company's "grave acting" in some nationalist tableaux at the Antient Concert Rooms in August of 1901, and he had been corresponding with Fay's brother and collaborator, Frank (1870–1931), since the latter's series of essays on an Irish Theatre had begun appearing in *The United Irishman* in May of 1901. The Fays continued their collaboration with Yeats and Lady Gregory through the Irish National Dramatic Company and the Irish National Theatre Society until January 1908.

THE acting of "Deirdre" delighted me by its simplicity. It was often a little crude, it showed many signs of inexperience, but it was grave and simple. I heard somebody say "they have got rid of all the nonsense," the accumulated follies of the modern stage. An amateur actor, as a rule, delights even more than a professional actor, in what is called "business," in gesture and action of all kinds that are not set down in the text. He moves restlessly about, he talks in dumb show with his neighbours, and so on. He wishes to copy at every moment the surface of life, to copy life as he thinks the eye sees it, instead of being content with the simple and noble forms the heart sees. The result is that he, like the professional actor, can act modern comedy, but he cannot act any kind of drama that would waken beautiful emotions. Beautiful art is always simpler and graver and quieter than daily life, and, despite many defects, the acting of "Deirdre" has left to me a memory of simplicity and gravity and quietness. The actors moved about very little, they often did no more than pose in some statuesque way and speak; and there were moments when it seemed as if some painting upon a wall, some rhythmic procession along the walls of a temple had begun to move before me with a dim, magical life. Perhaps I was stirred so deeply because my imagination ignored, half-unconsciously, errors of execution, and saw this art of decorative acting as it will be when long experience may have changed a method into a tradition, and made Mr. Fay's company, in very truth, a National company, a chief expression of Irish imagination. The Norwegian drama, the most important in modern Europe, began at a semi-amateur theatre in Bergen, and I cannot see any reason in the nature of things why Mr. Fay's company should not do for Ireland what the little theatre at Bergen did for Europe. His actors, now that he has set them in the right way, need nothing but continuous experience, and it should be the business of our patriotic societies to give them this experience. The audience is there, for an audience that could be moved by the subtleties of thought and sentiment of a play like "A.E.'s" "Deirdre," that could take pleasure in a beauty that was often as imponderable as the odour of violets, cannot be less imaginative than the men of the Rennaissance. Victor Hugo said somewhere: "It is in the Theatre that the mob becomes a people,"[1] and it is certain that nothing but a victory on the battlefield could so uplift and enlarge the imagination of Ireland, could so strengthen the National spirit, or make Ireland so famous throughout the world, as the creation of a Theatre where beautiful emotion and profound thought, now fading from the Theatres of the world, might have their three hours' traffic once again.

W. B. Yeats

P.S. I have said nothing of the acting of "Kathleen Ni Houlihan," for though altogether excellent of its kind, it was not of a new kind. The play tried to give the illusion of daily life, and the actors therefore acted it in the usual way, and quite rightly. That they did so well in two so different plays is a good promise for the future.

# The Gaelic Movement and the Parliamentary Party

*Cathleen ni Houlihan*, with its overt nationalism, was a great success in Dublin during its opening run in April, 1902. "There is continual applause", Yeats wrote to Lady Gregory (*Letters*, p. 368) and, despite his recent trouble with English interviewers (see pp. 243, 253 above), he spoke with unusual directness about the state of Irish politics in an interview which appeared on April 25 in *The Echo*, a London paper. While Yeats's description of the period following Parnell's fall resembles those in his address at the Robert Emmet celebration in New York in 1904 (see pp. 320-1 below) and in "The Trembling of the Veil", he is much more explicit here in his evaluation of such political figures as T. W. Russell and John Redmond, Parnell's heir.

## MR. WM. BUTLER YEATS TALKS ABOUT THE GAELIC MOVEMENT AND THE PARLIAMENTARY PARTY

ONE of the most interesting Movements of the last few years is the Gaelic Movement, a kind of Irish Renaissance; a stirring among the dry

[1] Yeats's reference is probably to Hugo's observation, in the section called "Tas de Pierres, iii" of the posthumous *Post-Scriptum de Ma Vie*, that in "the theatre the poet and the multitude gaze into each other's eyes; sometimes they touch each other, sometimes they insult each other, sometimes they mix with one another: fecund mingling. On one side a crowd, on the other a soul. That something of a crowd which enters into a soul, that something of the soul which enters into the crowd is dramatic art in its completeness." (Lorenzo O'Rourke, ed. and trans., *Victor Hugo's Intellectual Autobiography*, London, 1907, pp. 369-70.)

bones of the Irish people, whose past is full of painful memories of oppression and tyranny. On the intellectual side, no one better represents this movement than William Butler Yeats, who was born in Dublin thirty-six years ago. His father was an artist, and so he rather naturally followed in his footsteps, but when only 21 he left art for literature, and since then has deserved and won that most honourable of titles, "a man of letters." It was he who suggested and helped to found the Irish Literary Society and the National Literary Society of Dublin, while he has, with a genius for the literature of his people, awakened an enthusiasm for the Irish language which grows from day to day. As a poet and an essayist he is among the choicest spirits young Ireland has produced. We see signs on every hand—in music, literature, and art—of this intellectual awakening. Lough Rea Cathedral at the present moment is being decorated by Irish artists. The interest aroused by the new Movement, especially on the intellectual side, led me to call upon Mr. Yeats and ask him for some information on a subject with which Englishmen are, for the most part, totally unacquainted.

### THE SITUATION IN IRELAND

"May I preface anything I have to say," Mr. Yeats began, "with the remark that I make no pretence to criticise the politician, not because I am destitute of opinions, but because it is beyond the limits of literature, and so whatever remarks I may make will be with this qualification?"

"I quite understand your position, Mr. Yeats, but still, I should like to ask, plunging *in medias res* with a big question, what the situation is in Ireland at the present moment?"

"Very much like it was in the time of the 'Young Ireland' Movement: Redmond takes the place of O'Connor.[1] The Gaelic and its allied Movements in many ways ressemble 'Young Ireland.' There are two sides, one the intellectual, and the other the political, although they overlap to some extent, as I will explain later. Redmond and the Nationalists hold the agrarian districts, together with the older men in the towns. The younger men are not so much hostile as aloof. They are not thinking of the politics of the hour."

"I suppose this is due to the dissensions in the Irish Party for so many years?"

---

[1] Probably through reportorial or typographical error, "O'Connor" is substituted for the name of Daniel O'Connell, "The Liberator" (1775–1847), who in 1844 found himself—many years after his winning of Catholic emancipation—an established and conservative resister to the views on educational reform and revolutionary repeal of the Articles of Union advanced by the young intellectuals known as the Young Ireland movement.

## THE FADING OF ROMANCE

"Yes, that is so. Ten years of discord accomplished a good deal. It took away the air of romance that had gathered round Parliamentary politics. The fading of romance from Parliamentary life has had this good effect; it has liberated all the other pent-up forces of the nation—all the forces, in fact, which were absorbed by revolutionary politics of past time. The Member of Parliament in olden days was idealised and counted an authority upon almost every subject. It is better, perhaps, that our politics should be done in a more humdrum spirit, and so the Gaelic Movement sprang out of the orgie of criticism into which our Members plunged."

"Put it briefly to me: What is the Gaelic Movement, or what are its essential features? I presume language is the most important element?"

"Let me begin with that. A language procession took place about a month ago in our chief towns, to collect money for the teaching of the Irish language. In Dublin it was three miles long, and £1,500 was collected. There are about 25,000 people learning the language in various classes, quite exclusive of the schools, and the census shows a considerable increase on all sides. In addition to this the Gaelic League has become a large publishing concern, and books from 1d. to 1s. now have an enormous sale."

## PRACTICAL ISSUES

"Please excuse the practical turn of my mind. What does the Irish Movement aim at? What do you expect to get or do? Our readers would like to know the practical issues."

"If you don't object, I should like to begin with something that seems the reverse of practical—the sentimental reasons. The Gaelic Movement is helping to preserve the national character of the people, and to prevent the country from becoming an imitation England. When an Irishman begins to resemble an Englishman, it is the very worst type that he resembles. It is not Shakespeare and Milton that have been superseding the Gaelic poets in Ireland, but the half-penny comics; in fact, Anglicisation has meant vulgarisation."

## THE LANGUAGE QUESTION

"And now, how about the more practical side; the side which appeals to the politician? In what direction do you think the Gaelic Movement has had most effect?"

"The leaders of the Movement in Ireland claim that the language question has, in several European countries, preceded a general revival of national life, and particularly the revival of manufacturing industries.

A powerful Irish weekly, the 'Leader,' urges constantly that as soon as a country forgets its past language and literature it becomes unproductive.[2] Manufacturers have been ruined, not merely by unjust laws, but by the lack of self-reliance caused by perpetual imitation and by the feeling among the people that English wares and English fashions are a sign of good form. The Gaelic Movement synchronises with the increase of manufactures in Ireland."

"But you would hardly say that the 'Leader' represents the whole of the Movement?"

## UNITED IRISHMAN

"Certainly not. There is another important section of the Gaelic revival which finds expression in the 'United Irishman.' It is more avowedly political, and on the whole more influential in the large towns. The difference between the two chiefly consists in the definition of 'nationality.' Both sections are for language and industries, but the 'United Irishman' locates the driving energy of national life, largely in political memories and political hopes. The 'Leader' thinks that Davis and Emmet, Wolfe Tone and Parnell, were but anglicised Irishmen at the best, while the 'United Irishman' sees in them the patron saints of nationality. The latter paper has more ideas, and is more literary in tone, and yet this paper, which represents the national aspirations of a large section, was three times suppressed by the Government the year before last."[3]

"How about the present Parliamentary Party, and how far have they the backing of the Nationalists?"

## THE PARLIAMENTARY PARTY

"I think I may say, without straining the point, that the general *vis inertia* [sic] of the Nationalists supports the Parliamentary Party. It is supported by the middle-aged Nationalists, and by men both young and old in the agricultural districts."

"May I ask why the young men in the towns do not support it so heartily?"

"They were discouraged by the failure of the Parnellite Movement and disillusioned by the many dissensions of the party in the House of Commons. Accordingly they turned their eyes elsewhere."

"Will they return to their allegiance?"

"I cannot prophesy. It depends on things more or less outside the control of any man. I can, however, conceive of events that would make

[2] See pp. 236–7 above for Yeats's differences with *The Leader* and its editor, D. P. Moran.
[3] Yeats's contribution to the controversy surrounding the seizure of several issues of Arthur Griffith's *United Irishman* in 1900 is reprinted on pp. 213–16 above.

the larger part of Ireland avowedly Fenian, and nobody can say what would happen if Redmond were to make some great spectacular Parliamentary 'coup,' or if the agrarian agitation in the West were to increase."

"How about the revival of the Coercion Act?[4] What effect will it have?"

### EFFECT OF THE COERCION ACT

"In the opinion of most young men I have spoken to, it will greatly strengthen Redmond's hand, increase the power of the League, and bring him money from America. Yet those who believe this are his opponents, and want to have the field clear for the intellectual movement, so you may be sure there is a good deal in it."

"What is your opinion of Redmond—if you feel at liberty to state it?"

"When I heard him first, some years ago at Dublin, he seemed to lack that note of personal conviction which we are accustomed to in our leaders. Harrington,[5] who spoke immediately after, impressed me more favourably. Redmond struck me as an advocate doing his best for his client, according to the traditions of his profession. I think the young men in Dublin felt this too, and that is why he has not touched their imagination. Now I am beginning to think that the seeming defect is perhaps the secret of his power. He is able to take a larger view, a wider outlook, to see further ahead than most of our Parliamentary leaders, because he is less interested in the argument of the moment."

"One more question, Mr. Yeats, before I cease to heckle, and leave you in peace. Is Mr. T. W. Russell[6] going to play a large part in the future national life?"

"I heard him state his policy at Dublin at a private gathering a few days ago. I had not heard him for many years, when oddly enough, I met him at the same house. At that time he was the most bitter, most anti-Irish, the most fanatical of our opponents. Now I find him, at any rate, just, sympathetic, and friendly. On the land question he is practically at one with those against whom he used to speak."

---

[4] In an attempt to check crimes arising from land agitation, the "Coercion Bill" of March, 1881, had authorized the arrest and detention without trial of persons suspected of fomenting violence. Both Parnell and John Dillon were imprisoned under this Act before enforcement of it was relaxed in May, 1882.

Certain counties were "proclaimed" under it again in April of 1902 because of agitation in Sligo, Tipperary, Clare, and particularly that at the De Freyne property in Roscommon in which Maud Gonne took part.

[5] Stanley Harrington (1856–1949) had been a Member of Parliament since 1885 and was later Privy Councillor for Ireland.

[6] T. W. Russell (1841–1920), a Liberal Member of Parliament since 1886, opposed Home Rule in the eighties, but was primarily responsible for the Land Acts Commission of 1894 which created the Land Act of 1896. In 1907 he became Vice-President of the Department of Agriculture and Technical Instruction for Ireland.

# The Acting at St. Teresa's Hall

"Martyn has rather irritated me", Yeats wrote to Lady Gregory after reading Edward Martyn's article in *The United Irishman* of April 19, 1902 on the Irish National Theatre productions. "I got him to write to *U I* about the plays and he has written rather abusing the actors, whom one wants to encourage" (*Letters*, p. 370). Martyn had praised both *Deirdre* and *Cathleen ni Houlihan*, noting that Maud Gonne outshone the other players in the title-role of Yeats's play. He thought *Deirdre* was "in the right key" but wanting in intensity and, seeking to explain the inopportune laughter from the audience during *Cathleen ni Houlihan*, he blamed W. G. Fay for playing Peter Gillane as a low-comedy character. An editorial note which followed defended Fay and, noting that the audience the following evening did not laugh, asserted that the relaxation during Yeats's play of the tensions wrought in the opening night audience by AE's solemn drama had been responsible. Yeats's defense of his players appeared in *The United Irishman* for April 26. "I want," he wrote Frank Fay on April 21, "to make people understand the importance of the St. Teresa's Hall experiment, and to prepare them for future work" (*Letters*, p. 371).

## I

I PARTLY agree with you that the "laughter" that Mr. Martin [*sic*][1] says "greeted every word however serious that fell from Peter Gillane's lips" was due on the night of the first production to the relaxation of tension to which the audience had been brought by "Deirdre," but there were other causes. Many phrases that have a tragic meaning in Connacht have no meaning or even a comic meaning in Dublin. "He looks like somebody that has got the touch" is, for instance, tragic in Connacht. In Dublin it means somebody that is not right in his head. The stroke of the fairy wand and the touch of a fairy hand are only remembered where folk tradition lingers, though we still talk everywhere of "a stroke of paralysis" and of being "touched." Another reason for the laughter was that Mr. Fay has so long delighted Dublin audiences with excellent humorous acting that they are ready to laugh even before he speaks, as they did on the first night. I do not write to you, however, to argue with Mr. Martyn, but to say that if he had been in the theatre on Friday he would have seen Mr. Fay again and again rob himself of the laughter and applause that is the legitimate reward of the actor lest the play as a whole might suffer. Instead of trying to make points, he tried with admirable self-sacrifice to make his effect as subdued as possible.

[1] The spelling of Edward Martyn's name varies throughout this article.

I need hardly say that I do not agree with Mr. Martin as to the acting of "Deirdre." I think the difference between us comes from the difference of our arts. Mr. Martyn likes a form of drama that is essentially modern, that needs for its production actors of what is called the "natural school," the dominant school of the modern stage. The more experience an actor has had of that stage the better he is for Mr. Martyn's purpose, and almost of a certainty the worse for mine. English actors or Irish actors trained in England, for years to come, must serve his turn far better than Irish-trained Irish actors who are likely to be extravagant, romantic, oratorical, and traditional, like Irish poetry and legend themselves. I can only repeat that I was delighted with the acting of Mr. Fay's company, that I cannot see any reason in the nature of things why it should not be the foundation for a National Drama. I have plans for a somewhat elaborate essay on the Theatre, and am also lecturing on the subject at Oxford next month, and I shall probably speak of that acting in both lecture and essay as the first example of right method that I have come upon.[2] Its defects were the defects of inexperience and of all new things. A poet, or painter, or actor who is trying to make his art afresh in always more imperfect than one whose art is founded upon the current art of his time. One sees it in the imperfect drawing of the imaginative painters of a time when painting, like acting, has come to be founded upon observation rather than upon imagination. Until the stream of the world has begun to flow in a different direction, a Rossetti will always draw worse than a Millais.

## II

When Mr. Fay's company have the time and money, and it will need little of either, I hope that they will apply the same principles that they have applied to acting to the scenery and the stage itself. The scenery of a play as remote from real life as "Deirdre" should, I think, be decorative rather than naturalistic. A wood, for instance, should be little more than a pattern made with painted boughs. It should not try to make one believe that the actors are in a real wood, for the imagination will do that far better, but it should decorate the stage. It should be a mass of deep colour, in harmony with the colours in the costumes of the players. I was, I think, the first to commend this kind of scenery, and now Mr. Gordon Craig has used it to make certain old English operas the most

---

[2] Yeats lectured at Oxford, with demonstrations by Florence Farr, on his notions of dramatic speech set to music on June 10, 1902. His text no doubt resembled his essay on "Speaking to the Psaltery", which appeared in May and which is reprinted in *Essays and Introductions*.

beautiful sight that has been seen upon the modern stage.[3] I do not think that he was influenced by me; but the reaction against the scientific age is setting decorative art in the stead of naturalistic art everywhere, and it was bound to come upon the stage.

I would try and make a theatre where realism would be impossible. I am not at all certain, but I think I would bring the floor out in front of the proscenium, as it was in the old theatres before the "natural school" drove out poetry. All the great poetical dramatists of the world wrote for a theatre that was half platform, half stage, and for actors that were, at least, as much orators as actors. William Morris once said to me of an eminent dramatist of our time, "He will never understand any art because he does not understand that all art is founded upon convention." It has been our pride, hitherto, to destroy the conventions of the Stage, and until we have restored them we will never have a dramatic art which the Englishman of the time of Shakespeare and the Greek of the time of Sophocles and the Spaniard of the time of Calderon and the Indian of the time of Kaladasa[4] would have recognised as akin to their own great art.

W. B. Yeats

# Mr. Churton Collins on Blake

A letter in *The Times Literary Supplement* for May 30, 1902, is Yeats's only sortie in a battle which had begun with a letter from the writer and lecturer, J. Churton Collins (1848–1908) in the *Literary Supplement* for May 9. Defending his praise of the work of Stephen Phillips in reply to an article in the *Quarterly Review*, Collins had disparaged the reviewer's quotation from Blake as an example of great poetry. On May 16, "The Writer in the Quarterly Review," replied that, by rejecting his touchstone, Collins was "confessing to the world, proudly, his lack of that sense by which poetry is apprehended". Yeats's letter is in reply to Collins's response in the issue for May 23 in which he attacked the "dithyrambic or hysterical school of criticism of which Mr. Swinburne was unhappily the founder" and in which he spoke of the "falsetto" in the reviewer's tone and of the "fanfarade—nonsense pure and absolute" of Blake's lines taken out of the context of the piece in which they

---

[3] In the year which had elapsed since he saw them, Yeats had frequently referred to the Purcell Society productions of *Dido and Aeneas* and *The Masque of Love* which Craig staged in 1901. See, for examples, his essay "At Stratford-on-Avon" (p. 250 above) and the letter, written a few weeks before this article, in which he spoke of the productions as being "among the important events of our time" (*Letters*, p. 366).

[4] Of the three plays of Kālidāsa, the great Hindu dramatist and poet (*fl.* fifth century A.D.), the most famous is *Sakuntalā*.

might be "intelligible and excusable as the extravagant and hysterical expression of rapt enthusiasm".

TO THE EDITOR OF THE TIMES

SIR,

Mr. Churton Collins has for many years commended accurate learning and the University teaching of literature as the only certain guides to good taste. It is, therefore, interesting to know that he himself, the accuracy of whose learning is notorious, thinks Blake's lines ending "Did He who made the lamb make thee?" not only "falsetto" but, when taken from their context, "nonsense pure and absolute." When I was a boy my father was accustomed to read to me passages of verse that seemed to him and to his friends great poetry, and this very stanza was among them; and now that I have edited Blake, and thought much over every line that he wrote, I cannot think that cry "Did He who made the lamb make thee?" less than a cry out of the heart of all wisdom. A recent article of Mr. Churton Collins about the importance of learning as a guide to taste almost converted me to his opinion, but now I return to my own opinion that many a cultivated woman without learning is more right about these matters than all the professors.

I am, Sir, your obedient servant,<br>W. B. Yeats

# The Hill of Tara

In the summer of 1900 the annual meeting of the Royal Archeological Institute had been held in Ireland and an expedition from Dublin had discovered the unauthorized excavations of the Hill of Tara, the seat in County Meath of the ancient Irish kings, by a group of English enthusiasts who were looking for the Ark of the Covenant. The Institute was told that the earthwork known as the King's Chair had been almost completely destroyed and, shortly after its president, Sir Henry Howorth (1842–1923), denounced the digging as "a perfectly monstrous thing", the work was stopped.

When Yeats learned that the excavation had begun again, in June of 1902, he, Douglas Hyde and George Moore wrote a letter on "The Hill of Tara", which appeared in *The Times* of London on June 27. While Yeats's part in the composition of the note cannot be determined, his concern here, as does his antipathy for Edward VII (p. 212 above), gives specific meaning to the lines from the title poem of *In the Seven Woods* (1904): ". . . I have forgot awhile / Tara uprooted, and new commonness / Upon the throne . . ." (*Variorum Poems*, p. 198). The poem is dated "August 1902" in almost all editions.

SIR,

We have just returned from a visit to the Hill of Tara, where we found that the work of destruction, abandoned a year or two ago, has begun again. Labourers are employed to dig through the mounds and ditches that mark the site of the ancient Royal duns and houses. We saw them digging and shovelling without any supervision, hopelessly mixing the different layers of earth and altering the contour of the hill.

This is not being done through any antiquarian zeal, but, apparently, that the sect which believes the English to be descended from the Ten Tribes may find the Ark of the Covenant.

We are assured that the Commissioners of Public Works in Ireland can do nothing in this case, for by the Ancient Monuments Protection Act of 1882 they can only interfere when the "owner" has himself "constituted" them "the guardians of such monument."[1]

All we can do under the circumstances is to draw the attention of the public to this desecration. Tara is, because of its associations, probably the most consecrated spot in Ireland, and its destruction will leave many bitter memories behind it.

We are, Sir, yours truly,

Douglas Hyde, LL.D.

George Moore

W. B. Yeats

Dublin, June 24

# The Freedom of the Theatre

In the fall of 1902, the collapse of a joint project of Yeats's and George Moore's resulted in a permanent alteration of their friendship. "We were never cordial again," Yeats wrote many years later; "on my side distrust remained, on his disgust" (*Autobiography*, p. 305). They had talked about a play, whose hero was to be modeled on a mystical friend of A.E. in which an idealistic atheist carries his convictions into action. In *Dramatis Personae*,

---

[1] These excavations seem to have been halted by the intervention of Yeats's old friend, T. W. Rolleston (1857–1920), who reported in a letter to *The Times* on July 1, 1902, that he had spoken to the owner of the land on which Tara stood, "my friend Mr. Briscoe", and to a Mr. Boylan, "the present lessee". According to Rolleston, all work was to be stopped at Tara until arrangements could be completed with the Royal Society of Antiquaries (Ireland) to "undertake the further exploration of the site under proper scientific direction and control".

Yeats claims that the idea was his and that Moore's suggestions were limited to such details as the main character's having a brother who seduces the housemaid. Yeats let the project lapse and sometime later, Moore wired him: "I have written a novel on that scenario we composed together. Will get an injunction if you use it" (*Autobiography*, p. 304).

Yeats retired to Coole where, with the help of Lady Gregory and Douglas Hyde, he composed the five acts of *Where There is Nothing* in a fortnight. Meanwhile, having discovered through the neutral A.E. that Moore had written no novel on the theme but that some dramatic work was getting under way, Yeats arranged for immediate publication of his play in Griffith's *United Irishman*. He wrote to Lady Gregory around September 26 that the play was completed, and on October 4 he wrote: "All is arranged with the *United Irishman* and Moore had no suspicions. I have not told Russell my plans but have told him about things generally" (*Letters*, p. 380). Two weeks later, Yeats wrote to Russell: "Many thanks for note about Moore. Of course I will publish play. Tell Moore to write his story and be hanged. Yours sincerely, W. B. Yeats" (*Letters*, p. 381).

*Where There is Nothing*, which Yeats later recognized as "a bad play" (*Autobiography*, p. 305), was never produced in Dublin. Paul Ruttledge, the hero, would most probably have provoked a riot with his "plucking off the rags and tatters of the world" (*Variorum Plays*, p. 1143), his testing and destroying of conventional beliefs, and his dying pronouncement that "where there is nothing there is God" (*Variorum Plays*, p. 1164). The text appeared as a supplement to *The United Irishman* for November 1, 1902, in which Yeats published his article on "The Freedom of the Theatre". While the essay anticipated precisely most of the criticisms his play was to provoke, the thin cordiality of Yeats's postscript betrays the strategic purpose it played in his squabble with Moore. Even the choice of *The United Irishman* was calculated to increase Moore's discomfort, Allan Wade (*Bibliography*, p. 58) recalled Yeats's telling him, because Yeats "knew Moore would not dare to issue an injunction against a Nationalist newspaper for fear of getting his windows broke". Despite Moore's retort when he learned that Yeats's hero had a brother—"Then Yeats has stolen the spoons" (*Autobiography*, p. 305)—there was no legal action and the two writers were partially reconciled by John Quinn, then on his first visit to Ireland. The tenacity of Yeats's distrust, however, is reflected in his note to *The Unicorn from the Stars*, in 1908, in which he explained that in writing *Where There is Nothing*, "I wrote at such speed that I might save from a plagiarist a subject that seemed worth the keeping . . ." (*Variorum Plays*, p. 712). Modifying this note in 1922, Yeats said only that he "had to write at great speed to meet a sudden emergency" (*Variorum Plays*, p. 713). His postscript to the incident came in 1935, two years after Moore's death; in *Dramatis Personae* he admitted to looking back with some remorse. "Had I abandoned my plot and made him write the novel, he might have put beside *Muslin* and *The Lake* a third masterpiece, but I was young, vain, self-righteous, and bent on proving myself a man of action" (*Autobiography*, p. 305).

IN my play, "Where There is Nothing," I have put my stick into so many beehives that I feel a little anxious. Someone is sure to say I have written a mischievous attack upon the Law, upon Church and State, upon Sobriety, upon Custom and even upon the Sun in his strength. I have some reason to expect this, for ingenious theatre-goers both in London and America have found my poor little "Land of Heart's Desire" to be both clerical and anticlerical; and when "The Countess Cathleen" was acted, the opinions of my demons were said to be my own opinions, and there was thought to be something dangerous and demoralising in the spectacle of a woman so intoxicated with compassion that she sold her own soul that she might give the money to the poor. It was thought that she was setting a dangerous example. I was described as unpatriotic, too, because I pictured Irish men and women selling their souls to keep death from their houses. It was well-known, I was told, that they had never done such a thing, and yet I think that I have known some few Irish men and women who sell their souls daily for a much smaller price.[1]

Then, too, I cannot keep from thinking of the experience of other dramatists, for the drama has always been a disturber. The plays of Shakespeare and his contemporaries had to be acted on the Surrey side of Thames to keep the Corporation of London from putting them down by law. The Corporation of London represented in those days that zealous class who write and read the *Freeman's Journal*, and the *Independent* and the *Irish Times* in our day. I myself, can remember when Wagner was the worst of those that had fallen from heaven, when people used to ask one another how could an audience who had witnessed "Tristan and Isolda" resist temptation. And even the youngest of my readers will remember the indignant noise when Ibsen's "Ghosts" was played in London.

I hope nobody will think that I am comparing my powers with those of these great men. I am trying to show that it is impossible to write plays in a spirit of sincerity without sometimes putting one's stick into the beehives. The reason is that drama is a picture of the soul of man, and not of his exterior life. We watch Coriolanus with delight, because he had a noble and beautiful pride, and it seems to us for the moment of little importance that he sets all Rome by the ears and even joins himself to her enemies. Shakespeare makes a wise hearer forget everything except what he wants him to remember. But those citizens of the Corporation, hungry to have the law of him, saw nothing it may be but a bad example. They saw the exterior life plainly enough, for their little petty businesses taught them that, but they could not see clearly any

[1] Yeats summarizes here the attack on *The Countess Cathleen* by Frank Hugh O'Donnell. See p. 337 below.

picture of the soul. It is the same with all tragedies, we watch the spectacle of some passion living out its life with little regard for the trouble it is giving.

Drama describes the adventures of men's souls among the thoughts that are most interesting to the dramatist, and, therefore, probably most interesting to his time. Shakespeare's age was interested in questions of policy and kingcraft, and so he and his contemporaries played shuttle-cock with policy and kingcraft. We are interested in religion and in private morals and personal emotion, and so it is precisely out of the rushing journey of the soul through these things that Ibsen and Wagner get the tumult that is drama. Doubtless, the character must always have something of the dramatist when it is a character that is pictured from within. It has been said that Shakespeare could not have written the part of Iago unless he had something even of Iago in him. If he had given himself up to his amorous emotions he would have been Romeo, if to his hatred of the world he would have been Timon, if to his Philis-tinism he would have been Henry the Fifth, and if to the near ally of his wit he would have been King Lear.

Some of our idealists have thought to help their cause by crying out lately that certain English plays are immoral. If they had only cried out that they were vulgar and stupid we would have all joined in the cry. But immoral? That is a dangerous cry.

If one wants to know what is vulgar and stupid one can turn to certain admirable writers. There is a recognised criticism. But every newspaper man, every crossing-sweeper, thinks himself a moralist. The reign of the moralist is the reign of the mob, or of some Jack-in-office. It is always either one or the other, or both of them. I have just read in the morning paper that the Turkish Censor has altered "Othello" beyond recognition, because among other reasons, the play speaks of Cyprus "as if it was not an integral part of the Turkish Empire." There you have them both. Jack-in-office appeals to the patriotism of the mob.

Ireland is, I suppose, more religious than any other European coun-try, and perhaps that is the reason why I, who have been bred and born here, can hardly write at all unless I write about religious ideas. In "The Land of Heart's Desire," a dreamy girl prefers her own dreams and a wandering voice of the night to the priest and his crucifix. In "The Hour Glass," which is soon to be acted, it is the proud spirit that is defeated by the belief that has seemed folly to the wise. And in "The Countess Cathleen" the commandment of mercy is followed to the forgetting of all else. In "The Shadowy Waters" human love, and in "Cathleen ni Houlihan" love of country, become through their mere intensity a cry that calls beyond the limits of the world. In "Where There is Nothing," Paul, because he is a seeker after God, desires the destruction of all things. So far as I am a dramatist, so far as I have made these people alive, I watch them with wonder and pity, and I do not even ask myself were they right to go upon that journey.

W. B. Yeats

P.S. "Where There is Nothing" is founded upon a subject which I suggested to George Moore when there seemed to be a sudden need of a play for the Irish Literary Theatre; we talked of collaboration, but this did not go beyond some rambling talks. Then the need went past, and I gradually put so much of myself into the fable that I felt I must write on it alone, and took it back into my own hands with his consent. Should he publish a story upon it some day, I shall rejoice that the excellent old custom of two writers taking the one fable has been revived in a new form. If he does I cannot think that my play and his story will resemble each other. I have used nothing of his, and if he uses anything of mine he will have so changed it, doubtless, as to have made it his own.

# A Canonical Book

In a note of 1922 to *A Pot of Broth* (1904), Yeats recalled, as he often did when looking back to his work around the turn of the century, the thoroughness of his collaboration at that time with Lady Gregory. "I hardly know how much of the play is my work, for Lady Gregory helped me as she has helped in every play of mine where there is dialect, and sometimes where there is not (*Variorum Plays*, p. 254). For his part, Yeats missed no opportunity in those years to prepare an audience for his friend's books. He contributed prefaces to both *Cuchulain of Muirthemne* (1902) and *Gods and Fighting Men* (1904) and in a note to his "Baile and Aillinn" in *The Monthly Review* for July, 1902, he called *Cuchulain* "the most important book that has come out of Ireland in my time" (*Variorum Poems*, p. 188), an estimation questioned by his friend Clement Shorter (see p. 327 below) and commended for Stephen Dedalus's imitation, in the "Library" episode of *Ulysses*, by Buck Mulligan:

"Couldn't you do the Yeats touch?
He went on and down, mopping, chanting with waving graceful arms:
—The most beautiful book that has come out of our country in my time. One thinks of Homer."

Yeats reviewed Lady Gregory's *Poets and Dreamers: Studies and Translations from the Irish* (1903) first in an article in the *New Liberal Review* for March, 1903, which was reprinted as "The Galway Plains" in *Ideas of Good and Evil*, and then, breaking four years' silence in *The Bookman*, he praised her "canonical book" in the issue of May, 1903.

SOMETIMES I have made a list of books for some friend who wanted to understand our new Irish movement, but the list has seldom been much to my mind. One book would show the old poetry through the dark glass of a pompous translator, and another's virtue was in a few pages or even in a few lines. There was, however, one book that was altogether to my mind, "The Love Songs of Connacht,"[1] for it was all about beautiful things, and it was simply written; and now I know of two other books, which will be always a part of our canon, Lady Gregory's "Cuchulain of Muirthemne," which it is no longer necessary to praise, and this new book of hers, "Poets and Dreamers" (Dublin: Hodges and Figgis; London: John Murray). It is not as important as "Cuchulain of Muirthemne," but it should be read with it, for it shows the same spirit coming down to our own time in the verses of Gaelic poets and in the stories of the country people. Her chapters on Raftery, the wandering poet of some ninety years ago, on Irish Jacobite ballads, and old country love songs, and on the spells that are in herbs and the like, are necessary to anybody who would understand Ireland. She translates the ballads and love songs into prose, but it is that musical prose full of country phrases, which is her discovery and Dr. Hyde's; and her own comments, for all their simplicity and charm, cannot hide from discerning eyes an erudition in simple things and a fineness of taste in great things, that are only possible to those who have known how to labour.

The towns, for our civilisation has been perfected in towns, have for a long time now called the tune for the poets, even as, I think, for the Lake poets. And because one is not always a citizen there are moods in which one cannot read modern poetry at all; it is so full of eccentric and temporal things, so gnarled and twisted by the presence of a complicated life, so burdened by that painful riddle of the world, which never seems inexplicable till men gather in crowds to talk it out. I could not imagine myself, though I know there are some who feel differently, reading modern poetry when in love or angry or stirred by any deep passion.[2] It is full of thoughts, and when one is stirred by any deep passion one does not want to know what anybody has thought of that passion, but to hear it beautifully spoken, and that is all. Some seventeenth century lyric, where the subtleties are of speech alone, or some old folk tale that had maybe no conscious maker, but grew by the almost

---

[1] Yeats had begun by 1903 the deprecation of his Irish propaganda of the mid-nineties. Two of his lists survive (*Letters*, pp. 246–7, and *Uncollected Prose*, I, pp. 383–7), and both include Douglas Hyde's *The Love Songs of Connacht* (1893), which Yeats had reviewed enthusiastically in *The Bookman* in 1893. (See *Uncollected Prose*, I, pp. 292–5.)

[2] Yeats echoes here his earliest published critical opinion. In his 1886 essays on Sir Samuel Ferguson he lamented that the nature description of poets of the previous age merely half-concealed ". . . the sad soliloquies of a nineteenth century egoism" (*Uncollected Prose*, I, p. 103).

accidental stringing together of verses out of other songs, commingle one's being with another age, or with the moods of fishers and turf-cutters. Sometimes, indeed, being full of the scorn that is in passion, one is convinced that all good poems are fruit of the Tree of Life, and all bad ones apples of the Tree of Knowledge. I find in this book many fruits of the Tree of Life, and am content that they offer me no consolation but their beauty.

A friend of mine once asked some Irish-speaking countrymen, who were learning to write and read in Irish, what poem they liked the best out of a bundle that had been given them. They said, "The Grief of a Girl's Heart," an Aran poem, which is among those Lady Gregory has translated, and they added that the last verse of it was the best. This is the last verse: "You have taken the east from me; you have taken the west from me; you have taken what is before me and what is behind me; you have taken the moon, you have taken the sun from me; and my fear is great that you have taken God from me." A few years ago, before the modern feeling for folk-thought on the one hand, and for certain schools of esoteric poetry on the other hand, had brought a greater trust in imagination, a verse like that would have seemed nonsense to even good critics, and even now a critic of the school represented by most of the writing in, let us say, the *Spectator*,[3] would probably call it vague and absurd. The poet who made it lived when poetry, not yet entangled in our modern logic, a child of parliaments and law courts, was contented with itself, and happy in speaking of passions almost too great to be spoken in words at all. The poet had bitten deeply into that sweet, intoxicating fruit of the tree that was in the midst of the garden, and he saw the world about him with dim, unsteady eyes. Another verse of the Aran song, and all the song is lovely, would seem, I think, more wicked than foolish. The girl would give everything to her lover, and at last cries out: "O, aya! my mother[4] give myself to him; and give him all that you have in the world; get out yourself to ask for alms, and do not come back and forward looking for me." A critic to whom the hidden life of the soul is of less importance than those relations of one person to another that grow in importance as life becomes crowded would find it hard to sympathise with so undutiful a daughter. He might, indeed, if he had learnt his trade in that singular

[3] While the *Spectator* for April 18, 1903, had given *Poets and Dreamers* a favourable review, in which the only objection was to the inclusion of such politically controversial material as Boer poems, the magazine's reviewers had often troubled over these qualities in Yeats's poetry of the nineties. Thus, the *Poems* of 1895 were weakened because Yeats was "tempted to rely on the sound and rush of his words" and the reviewer of *The Wind Among the Reeds* (1899) had warned that "a poet, if he is to be a poet of any consequence, has thoughts that he wants to convey; the most that Mr. Yeats does is to give us his dreams."

[4] Lady Gregory reads: "my mother, give . . .".

criticism of Shakespeare, which has decided that "Hamlet" was written for a warning to the irresolute, and "Coriolanus" as a lesson to the proud, persuade himself that the poem was written to show how great passion leads to undutifulness and selfishness. He could hardly come to understand that the poet was too full of life to concern himself with that wisdom, which Nietzsche has called an infirmary for bad poets,[5] that if he had known of it he would have scorned it as deeply as any true lover, no matter how unhappy his love, would scorn the wizard drug, that promised him easy days and nights untroubled by his sweetheart's eyes. I would send any man who wants to be cured of wisdom to this book, and to 'Cuchulain of Muirthemne," and to books like them. The end of wisdom is sometimes the beginning of heroism, and Lady Gregory's country poets have kept alive the way of thinking of the old heroic poets that did not constrain nature into any plan of civic virtue, but saw man as he is in himself, as an amorous woman has seen her lover from the beginning of the world. Raftery, the peasant poet, praises one man, "because he had pleasantness on the tops of his fingers,"[6] "because in every quarter that he ever knew he would scatter his fill and not gather. . . . He would spend the estate of the Dalys, their beer and their wine";[7] and he praises another because "He did not lower himself or humble himself to the Gall, but he died a good Irishman, and he never bowed the head to any man."[8] In the presence of thoughts like these two aristocracies have passed away. The one, hearing them sung in its castles, perished fighting vainly against the stranger, and the other, hearing them in the praise and dispraise of the Celtic poor, felt without understanding what it felt, the presence of a tribunal more ancient and august than itself, and became spendthrift, and fought duels across handkerchiefs, and at last, after a brief time of such eloquence that the world had hardly seen its like, passed away ignobly.

Lady Gregory finishes her book with translations of Dr. Hyde's little plays. These plays, which are being constantly acted throughout Ireland, are typical of the new movement, so far as it is a movement in Irish. Acted for peasants, and sometimes by them, and full of the peasant

[5] In section 30 of *Thus Spake Zarathustra*, "The Famous Wise Ones", Zarathustra charges the hearer with having "out of wisdom . . . made an alms-house and a hospital for bad poets" (. . . *und aus der Weisheit machet ihr oft ein Armen—und Krankenhaus für schlechte Dichter*) (*Werke in Drei Bänden*, Munich, 1965, vol. ii, p. 362).

[6] Gregory: "The swans on the water are nine times blacker than a strawberry since the man died from us that had pleasantness on the tops of his fingers."

[7] Gregory: "In every quarter that he ever knew he would scatter his fill and not gather. He would spend the estate of the Dalys, their beer and their wine."

[8] Gregory: "And that is the true man, that didn't humble himself or lower himself to the Gall; Anthony O'Daly, O Son of God! He was that with us always, without a lie. But he died a good Irishman; and he never bowed the head to any man. . . ." This and the above two quotations are from poems by Raftery.

mind, they show how it keeps to-day the thoughts of Raftery and his predecessors back to the beginning of history. One play is about Raftery himself, one is about an imaginary poet, Hanrahan,[9] one is about an old saint, one is a very beautiful Nativity. They have an impartial delight in the sinless wandering saint, and in the drunken wandering poet with his mouth full of curses. Are not both of them fine creatures, and what does it matter if one has hard claws and the other carries no burdens? Is it not an illusion that man exists for man? Was he not made for some unknown purpose, as the stones and the stars and the clouds, or made, it may be, for his Maker's pleasure? I think the old poets thought that way, and the Irish countryman, who is prosaic enough in himself, is the clay where one finds their footsteps even yet.

W. B. Yeats

# Irish Plays and Players

On May 2, 1903, the Irish National Theatre Society gave two very successful performances of plays by Yeats, Lady Gregory and Fred Ryan before London audiences, its first appearances outside Dublin. "Lady Aberdeen, Henry James, Michael Field . . . and I don't know how many other notables were there," Yeats wrote to Lady Gregory, "and all I think were moved" (*Letters*, p. 400). Among the notables was E. K. Chambers (1866–1954), who wrote a warm and appreciative review in the *Academy* for May 9 of the plays and of one of the series of lecture-performances which Yeats and Florence Farr were giving of Yeats's "new art", the reading of poems to the accompaniment of the psaltery. Although he was pleased by Chambers's apprehension of the dramatic movement, "under the direction of Mr. Yeats", as "only one expression of the growing and widening national consciousness', Yeats corrected his reviewer in a letter on "Irish Plays and Players" which appeared in the issue for May 16.

SIR,

Your sympathetic notice of our Irish plays and players has it that they were produced under my direction. They were produced under the direction of Mr. W. Fay our stage manager, and Mr. F. Fay our teacher of speech, and by the committee of our dramatic society. Mr. W. Fay is the founder of the society, and from the outset he and I were so agreed

[9] Translations of Hyde's *The Marriage*, *The Lost Saint* and *The Twisting of the Rope*, a play based on the same folktale as Yeats's story of the same name in *The National Observer* for December 24, 1892, were included in the last section of *Poets and Dreamers*.

about first principles that no written or spoken word of mine is likely to have influenced him much.[1] I, on the other hand, have learned much from him and from his brother, who knows more than any man I have ever known about the history of speech upon the stage. Yours, &c.,

W. B. Yeats

[1] The actual staging of the productions remained in the hands of the Fay brothers, although since the founding of The Irish National Theatre Society in February, 1903, with Yeats as its president, the acting company had appeared under that name rather than as "W. G. Fay's Irish National Dramatic Company".

# The King's Visit

As it coincided with the effective settlement of the long and bitter land agitation by the Land Bill of 1903, the visit of Edward VII to Ireland in July brought forth calls in the press both for a cordial reception and for demonstrations pressing the next goal—for some writers Home Rule and for others complete independence. Edward Martyn urged that "to show disrespect for the King would prove that we are in earnest" and in a letter on "The King's Visit" in the *Freeman's Journal* for July 13, Yeats joined the debate, noting that the settlement was of Irish origin.

## TO THE EDITOR OF THE *FREEMAN'S JOURNAL*

DEAR SIR,

I have noticed that somebody has said, in most of the discussion about the King's visit, that the King has given us the Land Bill. I have even read that he is going to give us Home Rule. When George the IV came to Ireland he got a great reception, because it was believed that he was about to give Catholic emancipation. A friend of mine has lately been through all the private correspondence of George the IV about his visit to Ireland and found there much about the dinners he was to eat and the cooks that were to cook them, but nothing about Catholic emancipation.[1] Whenever Royalty has come to Ireland rumours of this kind have been spread and spread with an object. The Land Bill has not been given to us by English Royalty but won by the long labours of our own people.[2]

Yours, etc.,

W. B. Yeats

[1] George IV visited Ireland in August, 1821. The relief bill of April, 1829, which accomplished Catholic emancipation, was largely a result of English recognition of the growing political strength of the Catholics, led by Daniel O'Connell, "the Liberator".

[2] The Land Bill, called "Wyndham's Act", after Prime Minister Balfour's chief secretary, George Wyndham, came about through the efforts of John Shawe-Taylor (1866–1911), a

# Flaubert and the National Library
## *THE IRISH TIMES*, OCTOBER 8, 1903

### TO THE EDITOR OF *THE IRISH TIMES*

SIR,

A writer in to-day's *Irish Times* quotes from my magazine "Samhain" as follows: "I have found some time ago that though it (the National Library) had two books on the genius of Flaubert it had refused on moral grounds to have any books written by him."[1] Your reviewer then comments as follows: "One does not know exactly what date 'some time ago' can mean, but as a matter of fact during the past four years five of Flaubert's masterpieces have been added to the catalogue." Your reviewer, who is in all else so sympathetic, then complains that I have "lightly aspersed" "The National Library." Now some of those four or five masterpieces of Flaubert were added because of my protest, and the others, and one of these the most famous of all Flaubert's books, were only added some four months ago. Someone wrote in the suggestion book that every other national library in Europe had them, and at that the trustees surrendered. At this moment "the National Library" refuses to have any book written by Nietzsche, although it has a book upon his genius. Of course I agree with all that anyone has said about the serviceable work of this library. Its librarian[2] is the most zealous man I know, and even its Committee of Selection is doing as well as the admirable moral characters of its members will permit.

Yours, etc.,

W. B. Yeats

---

Galway landlord and Lady Gregory's nephew, whom Yeats memorialized in "The Cutting of an Agate" (see *Essays and Introductions*, pp. 343–5). His call on September 2, 1902, for a conference to discuss the acquisition by tenants of land at fair prices, resulted in a meeting in December, presided over by Lord Dunraven, a landlord from Limerick. The conference's recommendation was accepted by Wyndham because it satisfied both the English concern for the interests of the landlords and the Balfour government's aim of weakening pressure for Home Rule by such conciliatory gestures.

[1] The essay from which this quotation is taken, "Moral and Immoral Plays", appeared in *Samhain* for September, 1903, and is reprinted in *Explorations*, pp. 111–13.

[2] Thomas William Lyster (1855–1922), the urbane, purring "Quaker librarian" of Joyce's *Ulysses*, was the director of the National Library of Ireland from 1895 to 1920. He encouraged both Joyce and Yeats in their early efforts and Yeats acknowledged his aid and advice in an address delivered at the unveiling of the memorial to him at the Library on March 27, 1926. (See below, pp. 470–72.)

# The Irish National Theatre and Three Sorts of Ignorance

In October, 1903, Yeats wrote three articles for *The United Irishman* in answer to the attack upon the Irish National Theatre by *The Irish Independent*, a Nationalist paper founded in 1891 in support of Parnell. By 1903, however, the paper was under the control of the Roman Catholic businessman William Martin Murphy (1844–1919), the denouncer of Parnell whom Yeats was to immortalize in "To a Shade" as "old foul mouth". On October 8, a few hours before the opening of *In the Shadow of the Glen*, the *Independent* had impugned Synge's honesty and the motives and judgment of the Theatre's directors: "Mr. Synge did not derive his inspiration from the Western Isles. We do not for a moment think that all the members of the Irish National Theatre Society can be held accountable for the eccentricities of Mr. Yeats and his friends. But . . . we hold that those who ambition the uprise of a dramatic art that shall be true, pure and National, should make their voices heard against the perversion of the Society's avowed aims. . . ."

Although Yeats took the high road in his first reply, "An Irish National Theatre" (*Explorations*, pp. 114–18) on October 10, his curtain speech on opening night was in another key, "his usual thumpty-thigh, monotonous, affected, preachy style", as Joseph Holloway (1861–1944), the tireless Dublin playgoer, grumbled to his journal. Yeats made "a fool of himself in 'going' for an article that appeared in this morning's *Independent*. He generally makes a mess of it when he orates" (Hogan and O'Neill, eds., *Joseph Holloway's Abbey Theatre*, Carbondale, 1967, p. 27).

In his second essay, "The Theatre, The Pulpit, and the Newspapers" (*Explorations*, pp. 119–23) on October 17, Yeats warmed to the growing discussions in the press, calling the *Independent* the new "leader and voice" of "those enemies of life, the chimeras of the Pulpit and the Press". In his final article, "The Irish National Theatre and Three Sorts of Ignorance" in *The United Irishman* for October 24, he categorized the "obscurantism" against which he struggled.

MUCH that has happened lately in Ireland has alarmed Irishmen of letters for the immediate future of the intellectual movement. They would sooner do their work in peace, writing out their speculations or telling the stories that come into their heads without being dragged into a battle, where the worst passions must of necessity be the most conspicuous for perhaps a long time. I have listened of late to a kind of thought, to which it is customary to give the name "obscurantism," among some who fought hard enough for intellectual freedom when we were all a few years younger. Extreme politics in Ireland were once the politics of intellectual freedom also, but now, under the influence of a violent contemporary paper, and under other influences more difficult to follow, even extreme politics seem about to unite themselves to hatred of ideas. The hatred of ideas has come whenever we are not ready to give almost every freedom to the imagination of highly-cultivated men, who have begun that experimental digging in the deep pit of themselves, which can alone produce great literature, and it has already brought the bad passions, when we accuse old friends and allies of changing their policy for the sake "of the servants of the English men who are among us," or when we pervert their work out of all recognition or split hairs to find a quarrel. It will save some misunderstandings in the future if I analyse this obscurantism.

1st. There is the hatred of ideas of the more ignorant sort of Gaelic propagandist, who would have nothing said or thought that is not in country Gaelic. One knows him without trouble. He writes the worst English, and would have us give up Plato and all the sages for a grammar. 2nd. There is the obscurantism of the more ignorant sort of priest, who, forgetful of the great traditions of his Church, would deny all ideas that might perplex a parish of farmers or artisans or half-educated shopkeepers. 3rd. There is the obscurantism of the politician and not always of the more ignorant sort, who would reject every idea which is not of immediate service to his cause. He lives constantly in that dim idol-house I described last week.[1] He is more concerned with the honour and discipline of his squad than with the most beautiful or the most profound thought, and one has only right to complain when he troubles himself about art and poetry, or about the soul of man. One is under the shadow of his darkness when one refuses to use, even in the service of one's own cause, knowledge acquired by years of labour, when that knowledge is an Englishman's and is published in a London paper. Nor is one out of that shadow when one complains that someone has found a Cleopatra in the villages. Everyone knows who knows the country-places intimately, that Irish countrywoman [*sic*] do sometimes grow weary of their husbands and take a lover. I heard one very touching tale only this summer. Everyone who knows Irish music knows that "The Red-haired Man's Wife"[2] is sung of an Irish woman, and I do not

---

[1] In the essay of October 17, Yeats gave a vivid description of the habitat of ideological conformity, a "great dim temple where the wooden images sit all round upon thrones, and where the worshippers kneel. . . . In the idol-house every god, every demon, every virtue, every vice, has been given its permanent form, its hundred hands, its elephant trunk, its monkey head. The man of letters . . . swings his silver hammer and the keepers of the temple cry out, prophesying evil, but he must not mind their cries and their prophesies, but break the wooden necks in two and throw down the wooden bodies" (*Explorations*, p. 120).

[2] Two versions of "The Red Man's Wife" had been included in *Love Songs of Connacht* by Douglas Hyde, who noted the ballad was "to be found every place throughout the country". The texts catalogue the joys to be expected and deeds to be done in order "to be stretched / For the while of a night by the wife of the Red-haired man" (5th edn., London, 1909, p. 95).

think anybody could gather folk-tales along the Galway coast without coming on the ancient folk-tale (certainly in no way resembling the Widow of Ephesus as it is told by Pogius of Florence) which Mr. Synge has softened in his play.[3] These things are inconvenient one thinks when one is under that heavy shadow, for it is easier to go on believing that not only with us is virtue and [*sic*] Erin, but that the virtue has no bounds, for in that way our hands may not grow slack in the fight. It will be safer to go on, one says, thinking about the Irish country people, as if they were "picturesque objects," "typical peasants," as the phrase is, in the foreground of a young lady's water-colour.

Now, I would suggest that we can live our national life without any of these kinds of ignorance. Men have served causes in other lands and gone to death and imprisonment for their cause without giving up the search for truth, the respect for every kind of beauty, for every kind of knowledge, which are a chief part of all lives that are lived, thoughtfully, highly, and finely. To me it seems that ideas, and beauty and knowledge are precisely those sacred things, an Ark of the Covenant as it were, that a nation must value even more than victory.

W. B. Yeats

# We are Unlike the English in All Except Language

Yeats's first speaking tour in America, from November, 1903, until March, 1904, had been arranged for the most part by his friend, the Irish-American attorney, John Quinn (1870–1924). After appearances in New York, New Haven and surrounding cities, he travelled to Philadelphia, Chicago, Saint Paul, Saint Louis, San Francisco, and into Canada. Shortly before his departure for Dublin he contributed a farewell note, "We Are Unlike the English in All Except Language", to *The New York Daily News* for March 4, 1904. The tone of this piece is peculiarly un-Yeatsian, and rather American. One suspects that it is "based" on an interview with Yeats.

---

[3] While the outline of Synge's story does resemble the tale of the Widow of Ephesus as it occurs in Petronius Arbiter and the Florentine, Gian Francesco Poggio Bracciolini (1380–1459), Synge's direct source is the Aran story-teller, Pat Dirane, whose version appears in "The Aran Islands" (*Collected Works*, vol. II, pp. 70–2). Synge's use of the story was the subject of the controversy in *The United Irishman* in January and February of 1905. (See pp. 331–38 below.)

I MUST say that I shall leave this great country and its hospitable people with sincere regret. The warmth of the welcome given me wherever I went—and I have covered a good deal of ground during the three months I have been here, going as far West as the Pacific coast—has far outstripped anything I could have hoped for or had a right to hope for. I landed a total stranger I may say, and I go back to my beloved Dublin feeling as though I had known America and Americans all my life.

The only similarity between Americans and Englishmen that I have been enabled to discover is that they speak the same language. For the rest, they are as unlike as any two peoples you can think of. Their habits of thought, their forms of expression, their shops, their methods of travel, their hotels, their homes, the clothes they wear, the food they eat, the current of daily talk, the newspapers they print by the million, and scan with such devouring assiduity—all, all remind one of America and of no other country under the sun. Solid, massive and splendid surely is this republic. And it is unique at the same time.

While standing alone as a whole, certain phases of life in America bear a marvelous resemblance to those of her great sister republic of France. The enthusiasm of the two peoples is very much alike. The American has an imagination not alone lively but palpable as well— exactly as has the Frenchman, and he has unrestrained enthusiasm at the proper moment. This I feel impelled at times to describe as a God-given inheritance.

An American not alone sees the point, but also seizes the point of an argument with lightning speed; or, to use one of your own clever phrases, "quick as a wink." You don't need to draw a diagram to furnish him with a key to a joke, which, I am afraid, is more or less the case in the land where the Saxon dwells. The American may jump to conclusions now and again, it is true, but his conclusions are in the main correct, being based, for the most part, like those of the French and Irish, on natural impulse rather than the crabbed waywardness of conventional laws. And so, as I've heard New Yorkers often declare, he "gets there every time."

Well, good luck to him, I say! The great interest in education has surprised me more than all else. In England, the cultivated class is, in the main, confined to London, and those who compose it are by no means numerous. I found it different in America, where you have, not one, but many centers of thought diffused throughout the land—New York, Philadelphia, Boston, Chicago, Baltimore, Washington, Indianapolis, St. Paul, St. Louis and San Francisco.

And how wonderful are your seats of learning—and as numerous as they are wonderful. Indeed, it was inspiring to witness all this. How generous, too, appear the rich among you in supporting these institutions, vying with each other in their lavish distribution of money both in cash and endowments.

And what a democratic spirit is over all! The President of the republic I found less pretentious than many a little village Dogberry of an English official in Ireland, who sits on a tuppenny throne. Mr. Roosevelt has a fine memory and a fine mind, and is I should judge, an omnivorous reader.

Much of the poetry written by women here I would describe as organized sentiment. The women themselves—and I have met many types in many places—are adorable and inspiring. It is a delight to talk to them and a happiness little less than enduring to hear them talk. I hope to renew my recollections of all this by making a return visit to the United States at no distant day.

# Emmet the Apostle of Irish Liberty

Although it was not his final appearance, certainly the highlight of Yeats's American tour was his address in the Academy of Music in New York on Sunday, February 28, 1904, at the celebration of the 126th anniversary of the birth of the Irish patriot, Robert Emmet (1778–1803). An estimated 4,000 people attended the meeting, which was sponsored by the *Clan-na-Gael* (Family of the Gaels), an Irish-American organization founded in New York in the 1870s. The *Clan* had supported the Irish Republican Brotherhood with both men and funds and, in the eighties, had split into factions favouring either the terrorist tactics of Alexander Sullivan or the programme of political and economic pressures advocated by John Devoy (1842–1928). Devoy's main concern at the Emmet celebration was a set of resolutions denouncing the alliance by Secretary of State John Hay (1838–1905), of the United States with England in opposition to Russian claims in Manchuria. The resolutions, under the title "Stand by America's Friend Russia", shared the front page of the March 5 issue of Devoy's newspaper, *The Gaelic American*, with this account of Yeats's speech.

Yeats had agreed to this speech under the urging of John Quinn but, as the day approached, he doubted that he could speak his mind before an audience which included Devoy, the exiled Fenian Jeremiah O'Donovan Rossa (1831–1915), Quinn and Yeats's old friend and fellow student, Charles Johnston (1867–1931), the president of the Irish Literary Society of New York. "It is indeed, as you say, a sword dance," he wrote Lady Gregory on February 26, "and I must give to it every moment. I had no idea until I started on it how completely I have thought myself out of the whole stream of traditional Irish feeling on such subjects. I am just as strenuous a Nationalist as ever, but I have got to express these things all differently" (*Letters*, p. 432). The address is thus a mixing of the most comprehensive account he had given to date of the state of Irish affairs with a rare example of Yeats's platform rhetoric.

# W. B. YEATS DELIVERS A GREAT SPEECH ON THE PATRIOT AND HIS LEGACY
## *Memorable and Significant Meeting*

### IRISHMEN SOUND THE TOCSIN AGAINST ENGLISH ALLIANCE AND PROCLAIM FRIENDSHIP FOR RUSSIA

THE Emmet celebration at the Academy of Music last Sunday evening was a magnificent and most significant demonstration. Fully 4,000 people, the cream of the Irish race in New York and vicinity, were packed into the great hall, in spite of the fact that it had rained all day and that the weather was still threatening up to the time the doors were opened. The address delivered by William Butler Yeats was a great intellectual treat that was fully appreciated by the audience and will long be remembered.

But it was from another point of view that the meeting was most significant. Believers in the principles and policy for which Robert Emmet gave his life, the Irish people in the United States have realized that one of the chief aims of the movement to bring about an alliance between this country and England is to strangle with the aid of America the movement for Irish independence. They realize that the concerted assault on Russia by the State Department and in the press is intended to destroy, if possible, the only great power whose policy has been steadily anti-English and pro-American, and that the time has come for strong speech and vigorous action to defeat the "Anglo-Saxon" plotters. Hence the resolutions dealing with the situation and the scene of enthusiasm when they were read to the meeting. Notice was served on the "Anglo-Saxons" that their challenge has been taken up and that the fight will be fought to the bitter end until the army of British agents in America is crushed.

For the first time in the history of these celebrations this significance of the attitude of the Irish people was recognized by the New York press. For the first time also the Russian flag was displayed, side by side with the Stars and Stripes and the flag of Ireland.

### A MOST REPRESENTATIVE GATHERING

No speaker ever had a finer audience. There was not a discordant note and the vote on the resolutions was a scene never to be forgotten. There were more prominent citizens present than at any Irish meeting held in New York for twenty-five years and their demeanor showed that they were in complete accord with the sentiments expressed in the speeches and resolutions. Among them were Dr. Thomas Addis Emmet, William Temple Emmet, Grenville T. Emmet, Judge Martin J. Keogh, of the Appellate Division of the Supreme Court; Judges James Fitzgerald and James A. Blanchard, of the Supreme Court; Hon. Leonard A. Giegerich, Justice of the Supreme Court and President of the Catholic Club; Recorder John W. Goff, Captain James Mitchel, son of John Mitchel; ex-Mayor Hugh J. Grant, ex-District Attorney Philbin, Judge George M. Van Hoesen, ex-Senator Charles A. Towne, Judge Edward M. McCall, William Astor Chanler, Louis Stuyvesant Chanler, Colonel C. F. Murphy, veteran of the Mexican and of the Civil War and recently Commissioner to Russia for the State of Iowa; Daniel Buckley, Dr. J. P. Henry, Daniel F. Cohalan, Joseph I. C. Clarke, James Clancy, Daniel V. Clancy, John Devoy, Thomas H. Kelly, treasurer Irish Industrial League of America; Police Commissioner McAdoo, J. M. Wall, John Quinn, Charles Johnston, president Irish Literary Society; James Byrne, Senator Victor J. Dowling, Michael J. Jennings, Timothy Cohalan, Sr., O'Donovan Rossa, John P. Cohalan, Park Commissioner Pallas, Corporation Counsel Minturn, Hoboken; the Rev. Fathers M. G. O'Farrell, Thomas McMillen, John W. Powers, the Rev. Dr. Henry A. Brann, the Rev. Dr. Charles McCready, P. J. Hannon, of Dublin, representing the Irish Industrial League; M. Clune, Judge Daniel J. Kenefick, Senator James J. Frawley, Thomas J. O'Sullivan, P. J. McNulty, County Prest. Ancient Order of Hibernians; Patrick J. Conway, Commissioner Dalton, Senator Thomas C. O'Sullivan, Brother Leontine, of the Catholic Protectory; Thomas M. Mulry, Major Charles J. Crowley, of the Irish Volunteers; Commissioner Edward C. Sheehy, Peter McGinn, John B. Manning, Commissioner James S. Coleman, Hon. Farrell O'Dowd, Thomas F. Churchill, Alfred M. Downes, Peter Doelger, J. K. Caddigan, Judge Edward Browne, William J. Fanning, Hon. John P. O'Connell, Van Cortlandt House; Dr. John T. Nagle, Judge Amend, William O'Connor, Edward Hassett, Thomas Hassett, Michael Cohalan, Brother Potamia, Manhattan College; Police Captain John F. Flood, Captain W. H. Hodgins, Captain Stephen McDermott, Captain O'Connor, Captain Robert A. Tighe, William N. Penney, Senator Daniel J. Riordan, Thomas F. Foley, Frank Goodwin, Tenement House Commissioner T. C. T. Grain and Commissioners Haffen, Oakley, Ahearn, Darlington, Hayes Featherson and Brady, Dr. J. J. Walsh, Colonel Henry L. Swords, Colonel Abraham Gruber.

A delegation of noted Russian ecclesiastics—something before unheard of at an Irish meeting—occupied conspicuous places on the platform. The delegates were the Right Rev. Bishop Tickhon, head of the Orthodox Greek Church in America; the Rev. A. A. Hotovitzky, archpriest, and the Rev. Elias T. Zotikoff.

Comptroller Edward M. Grout[1] presided and in a short speech introducing Mr. Yeats said that Emmet's career, short as it was—apparently a useless sacrifice of a young life—had done more to strengthen the feeling of patriotism and love of liberty, not only among his own people, but among other peoples, than many efforts to secure freedom which have been successful in other lands.

Comptroller Grout received a great ovation from the meeting. An American without any Irish affiliations, he did not hesitate to put himself on record as being not alone in sympathy with the Irish national cause, as represented by the Clan-na-Gael, but also resolutely opposed to the pro-British propaganda that would have the United States depart from the time-honored traditional policy and make an alliance with England. His courageous and timely action will not be forgotten by Irish citizens of New York, nor by the ever increasing number who have grown sick of the "hands across the sea" rubbish.

After some of the musical numbers, Mr. Daniel F. Cohalan read the resolutions, every one of which was greeted with a storm of applause, and at the conclusion of the reading passed unanimously.

### ADDRESS OF MR. YEATS

Comptroller Grout then introduced William Butler Yeats, who received a welcome that will tingle pleasantly in his ears as long as he lives. He spoke as follows:

One nation is bound to another by all kinds of subtle threads and no two nations are bound more closely together than Ireland and America. In this present century every Irish movement has had to look to America for a principal means of its support and every Irishman looks to Irish-Americans for a principal encouragement. And even before emigration had made a second Ireland the example of America was of great importance to Ireland. When the Irish Parliament won its freedom in 1782 it was encouraged and strengthened by the example of America. Indeed it is doubtful if Grattan could have accomplished that great task if he had not had the example of America before him—so powerful is any great achievement for liberty, even far off. And when we think of the whole history of Ireland for the last seven hundred years, there is perhaps only one epoch that we look upon with entire joy and pride—the ten or fifteen years after the declaration of the independence of the Irish Parliament.[2]

During that brief period the manufactures of Ireland awoke; pros-

---

[1] Edward M. Grout (1861–1928) was elected Comptroller of New York City in 1901 and served until 1904.

[2] The Irish Parliament, established under the leadership of Henry Grattan in 1782, was disbanded in 1800.

perity began to come upon the land. Lord Clare,[3] no friendly witness, said that no country in Europe became so prosperous during so short a period. The Irish gentry suddenly cast off their irresponsibility and became a great class, creating an eloquence whose like has not been in any modern nation. There arose in Dublin a brilliant social life. Many books were published. Many beautiful houses were built—public buildings and great country houses. The nation was growing to greatness and it was precisely because it was so growing that England became afraid and decided to overthrow it. She fomented a rebellion by quartering the soldiers upon the people, and then when the land was struck with terror by that rebellion and by the means that had been used to crush it, she bribed with tithes and with money till she was able to extinguish our Parliament and to cut off all that splendid, growing life. So desolate was the land made, so many atrocities were committed, so many thousands were killed and left unburied by the roadside, that I have read that in that day people feared to eat bacon for fear the hogs might have fed on human flesh.

But more criminal than the crimes that were committed to bring about the extinction of our nationality, was that extinction itself The day will some day come when the world will recognize that to destroy a nation, a fountain of life and civilization, is the greatest crime that can be committed against the welfare of mankind An old Dutch traveler has said of the Elizabethan Englishmen that they were witty, boastful and corrupt [4] Alas! how they have changed They are no longer witty. They still, however, understand how to use the most corrupt means in their public life, and how to boast. I have seen in the parlors of an English inn a cartoon of the year 1800 representing Ireland and England as clasping hands in an eternal friendship and prosperity descending upon Ireland pouring her gifts out of a cornucopia. And in the English Parliament of that time a common theme was the prosperity which England in her wisdom and her greatness had conferred upon Ireland.

### EMMET'S TIMELY SACRIFICE

Out of that self-complacency the rebellion of Robert Emmet awoke the English people. Just when it seemed that they had bribed all that

[3] John Fitzgibbon, 1st Earl of Clare (1749–1802), was Lord Chancellor of Ireland from 1789 until his death. He was a stern anti-Catholic and resisted attempts to weaken Irish ties to England. In 1780, he had denounced Grattan's efforts to gain independence for the Irish Parliament.

[4] Yeats's reference is probably to the description of the Elizabethan English by the Antwerp merchant, historian and statesman, Emanuel Van Meteren (1535–1612), who traveled in England in 1575 and who was Dutch consul for England from 1583 until his death. In his "History of the Netherlands" (1599), he noted that the English of his day were "not vindictive, but very inconstant, rash, vain-glorious, light, and deceiving, and very suspicious, especially of foreigners whom they despise" (in W. B. Rye, *England as Seen by Foreigners*, London, 1865, p. 70).

mattered in Ireland, this young man came and he laid down his life. He showed that there was something in Ireland which not all the wealth of the world could purchase. He seemed to say to England: How can you permanently triumph? What can you offer to us if we do not fear to leave even life itself?

But England had always another weapon against Irish nationality besides bribery. She knows how to slander. As the greatest preacher of Emmet's ideals, John Mitchel, says, England has the ear of the world. She says, as it were, to our young men: If you only will serve me, this will be done for you. You will find preferment, you go to the bar; maybe you will rise to be a judge. If you serve me well against the interests of your country, wealth will come to you in some shape or other. But if that young man go against her and unite himself to the Irish people, then England will follow him with every kind of slander. Her representatives in Ireland, the class who depend upon her, will whisper against him all kinds of subtle accusations; or it may be he may have to meet some charge such as that Parnell had to meet when the *Times* newspaper accused him of recommending assassination.[5] Like all tyranny, she knows how to make what she admires seem great and what she fears seem despicable. She has tried to persuade us that Robert Emmet was but a wild, hair-brained, vain young man, and some of our own people out of weakness have repeated the slander.

It is well, therefore, that we should examine and find out why Ireland has placed him foremost among her saints of nationality; why she honors him most of all those who have laid down their lives to serve her. The Catholic Church has a curious ceremony which precedes the canonization of a saint. One states all that can be said against him and then another refutes these accusations. The saint's life is carefully examined, and so I would have you examine with me the life of Emmet.

### TESTIMONY OF HIS CONTEMPORARIES

When the rebellion of 1798 was stirring Ireland he was a youth of nineteen, an undergraduate of Trinity College, and we have still the opinions of his contemporaries about him. They tell us that when he stood up to debate in the College Debating Society all thronged in to

[5] Yeats refers to the infamous "Pigott letter" which *The Times* had printed on April 18, 1887, concluding a series of articles on "Parnellism and Crime". The letter, allegedly by Parnell, implicated him and his party in the murders, on May 6, 1882, of the incoming Chief Secretary for Ireland, Lord Frederick Cavendish, and the Under-Secretary T. H. Burke, as they were walking through the Phoenix Park. A Parliamentary Commission in 1889 cleared Parnell and revealed the forger, Richard Pigott, a newspaper man, who fled to Spain and committed suicide. Yeats's feelings on the matter were characteristically complicated. "Poor Pigott!" he had written to Katharine Tynan, "One really got to like him, there was something so frank about his lies. They were so completely matters of business, not of malice. . . . The poor domestic-minded swindler!" (*Letters*, pp. 112–13).

hear him; and one, the most famous of his admirers, the poet Thomas Moore, has spoken of the greatness of his eloquence, saying that he had heard no eloquence since then that seemed to him loftier or purer than the eloquence of that boy of nineteen, and he adds: "He was altogether a noble fellow and as full of imagination and tenderness of heart as of manly bearing." [6]

And another famous contemporary has said of him: "He was gifted with abilities and virtues that rendered him an object of universal esteem and admiration. His mind was fed from the pure fountain of classic literature, and he lived not so much in the scenes around him as in the society of the illustrious and sainted dead. The poets of antiquity were his companions, its patriotism his methods, and its republics his admiration." [7]

And another who knew him well has written: "So gifted a creature does not appear in a thousand years." [8] Indeed, all that knew him speak of him in what would seem an extravagant eulogy.

"Were I to remember," Moore has said, "the men among all I have ever known who appear to me to contain in the greatest degree pure moral worth and intellectual power, I should among the highest of the few place Robert Emmet." [9] And many of those who speak of him praise his great modesty and speak of a diffidence that was curiously mingled with self-reliance. In any other land he would have risen to the highest position and have lived honored by all men. But in Ireland he was expelled from his college without a degree because of his treasonable opinions.

He went to France and was almost immediately in communication with Napoleon and Talleyrand. He was then but twenty-four, and yet these men, the mightiest in Europe, listened to his plans and discussed with him the liberation of Ireland. Napoleon was then the most victorious conqueror the world had ever seen. No check had come to his power. He had conquered many European nations and had their power mingled with his own and he was turning all this great power against England. He had just collected an enormous fleet for the invasion of England; 360,000 men were to be flung on the English coast.

[6] This observation by Moore appears in his "Memoirs of Myself" in the Russell edition (London, 1853) of *Memoirs, Journal, and Correspondence,* vol. I, p. 58.

[7] Yeats's source for this appreciation and those which follow is, ultimately, the portrait of Emmet in the second edition of *The United Irishmen* (1858–60) by Richard R. Madden (1798–1886). He may, however, have used the condensation of Madden's material by his friend D. J. O'Donoghue (1866–1917) whose *Life of Robert Emmet* had appeared in 1902. This remark is, with some minor changes, that which Madden (2nd edn., p. 287) quotes from the *Recollections of Curran* (1818), by Charles Phillips (1787?–1859).

[8] Madden (p. 269) quotes this passage from a letter by Rev. Archibald Douglas.

[9] This quotation, from Moore's *Life and Death of Lord Edward Fitzgerald* (1831), is also in Madden (p. 266).

Emmet returned to Ireland to raise there a rebellion which was to strike at Dublin Castle when Napoleon struck at England. He acted in consultation with others, with the survivors of the rebellion of 1798, and it is manifest that his plan was their plan. The organization of the United Irishmen had been immense, but its very size had been a difficulty in its way, for it had been full of spies. The hardest and strongest fight had been made in Wexford, where the United Irishmen organization was very weak, and Emmet and his friends decided to do without any such organization, to substitute surprise for great numbers. They believed that all Ireland was so disaffected to English rule that if they could suddenly seize the centre of government in Dublin all Ireland would rise to help them.

## PLANNED TO TAKE THE CASTLE

Emmet established in Dublin two depots for the manufacture of pikes and for the storing of ammunition almost under the walls of the Castle. He set to work in March, 1803, and was to strike in the autumn, when he expected Napoleon's fleet to disembark its troops upon the English coast. All, however, went wrong almost from the beginning. An explosion in one of the depots forced him to make his attempt before all his plans were ready, and then by what was either an extraordinary succession of accidents or treachery, nothing happened as it was expected to happen. Large bodies of men were to have been assembled on Saturday night, July 23d, in Thomas Street, Dublin—so many hundred from Wexford, so many hundred from Kildare, so many hundred from Wicklow. The Wicklow men under Michael Dwyer did not come because a messenger had turned treacherous or cowardly. The Kildare men came but were met with a rumor that all was postponed and went home again. Some eighty men alone answered the call. The officers who should have led them—young men of fashion whose names have not come down to us—failed him at the last moment. The crowd became a disorderly mob and was dispersed by the soldiers. Emmet took refuge in the mountains with Michael Dwyer.

And yet he might have easily escaped to France had he not waited for a last interview with his sweetheart, Sarah Curran. That was a weakness more touching than any strength. He was taken and put upon his trial and at his trial spoke those words that are a part of Irish imagination for ever. He had the eloquence of the great generation he belonged to.

On the day of his execution a coach was seen waiting near the prison. In it was a lady with her face buried in her handkerchief; it was Sarah Curran. When he ascended the scaffold he had a braid of her hair pleated over his heart. But others who were bound to him by no such passionate ties were almost as deeply moved by his fate. It has been recorded that as he went to execution he passed the turnkey in whose care he had been, a man accustomed to the tragedies of a prison. The tears were streaming down the man's cheeks. Robert Emmet's hands were pinioned, but he leaned forward and touched him on the cheek with his lips. The turnkey fell fainting to the ground. When he awoke from his faint Robert Emmet's life had been snatched away.

I need not remind you of how Ann Devlin was tortured by the soldiers who sought to make her reveal his hiding place, and how she kept silent through it all.[10]

## A MAN OF GREAT ABILITY

This young lad of twenty-five had certainly won the confidence of all, the love of all. Old men and men of middle life obeyed him and served him unquestioningly. In one thing only was he foolish. He was a very young man. He had not that distrust of human nature which is the bitterest part of wisdom and only comes to men by long experience. He trusted too easily. Men failed him through weakness, through idleness, through all kinds of little petty weaknesses. Some, too, perhaps, were treacherous. His mind was in a flame with his own thoughts, with his own purposes. But such men, though they see often less into human nature than others until the world has schooled them, have often been the very masters of the world.

Nor did his scheme lack historical precedents. He took few men into his counsel. He had no great army. But Portugal won her freedom from Spain in 1640 by the help of only two-score men. Two score of conspirators spent the night praying in the cathedral, and then seized the Vice-Queen of Portugal, the representative of Spain, and the whole country rose about them and became free. It may well have seemed to Robert Emmet that Ireland could do as much. He showed, too, by the details of his plan that he had studied military science very deeply. He had indeed mastered everything but human nature.

And when he failed he did not repine. Our age has seen no loftier courage. In letters that he wrote, in the speech that he made, there is no regret for his own death, no sorrow for the loss of the beautiful world and the loss of love. He goes to his death full of a kind of ecstacy of self-sacrifice and all the time his mind is as athletic, is as clear, as if he were sitting quietly in his study. The man who reported his death scene for an English paper—a hostile witness—said that he had not thought

---

[10] Anne Devlin (*c.* 1780–1851), Emmet's housekeeper and a niece of the Wicklow "mountaineer", Michael Dwyer, was arrested at Emmet's house after his escape and steadfastly refused, although tortured by bayonets and subjected to a mock hanging in the courtyard, to reveal his hiding place. She was imprisoned, along with her father, a partisan of Emmet's, from 1803 until 1806. Richard Madden discovered her, living in poverty, in 1842, and questioned her, the last living member of Emmet's company.

any man could die so.[11] Emmet had hoped to give Ireland the gift of a victorious life, an accomplished purpose. He failed in that, but he gave her what was almost as good—his heroic death. The fear and malice of his enemies followed him even after death. The English authorities denied him a last known resting place. His burial place, like the burial place of the great French orator, Miribeau [*sic*], remains unknown. His enemies seemed to have wished that his dust might mingle with the earth obscurely; that no pilgrimages might come to his tomb and keep living the cause he served. And by so doing they have unwillingly made all Ireland his tomb.

## LEFT IRELAND AN IDEAL

And out of his grave his ideal has arisen incorruptible. His martyrdom has changed the whole temper of the Irish nation. England celebrates her successes. She celebrates her victorious generals. Her music halls have sung the praises of the victors of Omdurman and South Africa. They have not sung of the noble sacrifice of Gordon.[12] In Ireland we sing the men who fell nobly and thereby made an idea mighty. When Ireland is triumphant and free, there will yet be something in the character of her people, something lofty and strange, which shall have been put there by her years of suffering and by the memory of her many martyrs. Her martyrs have married her forever to the ideal. When the poetry of Young Ireland came some forty years after Emmet's death, his memory was one of its principal inspirations. And in a little while it came about that his picture hung in thousands of Irish cottages beside the picture of St. Patrick and the picture of the Mother of God.

There is a street ballad that always sounds very touching to my ears. It was made by no professing poet, but by some obscure rhymer of the streets, written immediately after the exile of John Mitchel, the greatest disciple of Emmet in the last century. His name comes in at the end of nearly every stanza, but it seems to one as if that latest tragedy moved the writer of the poem too deeply for him to give it many words.

(Then Mr. Yeats read the old song with the refrain: "Here's the memory of the friends that are gone.")[13]

[11] Madden (p. 466) quotes the account, in *The London Chronicle* for September 24–7, 1803, of Emmet's execution. "He seemed to scoff at the dreadful circumstances attendant on him; at the same time, with all the coolness and complacency that can be possibly imagined— though utterly unlike the calmness of Christian fortitude. Even as it was, I never saw a man die like him; and God forbid I should see many with his principles."

[12] Charles George Gordon (1833–85), known as "Chinese" Gordon, was the heroic but futile defender of Kartoum during the siege of April, 1884–January, 1885.

[13] This anonymous poem, "By Memory Inspired", had been included by Yeats in *A Book of Irish Verse* (1895). Described as a "Street Ballad", it toasts the memories of Irish patriots, among them O'Connell, Emmet and John Mitchel.

## THE LESSON OF OUR RECENT HISTORY

Sometimes in our Irish politics we have forgotten for a brief period the example of our martyrs, and in the end we have always suffered for that forgetfulness. Sometimes we have become so absorbed in the politics of the hour, in the pursuit of some great political measure, that we have forgotten the more eternal and ideal elements of nationality.

When I was a young lad all Ireland was organized under Parnell. Ireland then had great political power; she seemed on the verge of attaining great amelioration, and yet when we regret the breaking up of that power—and we may well regret it—we must remember that we paid for that power a very great price. The intellect of Ireland died under its shadow. Every other interest had to be put aside to attain it. I remember the *Freeman's Journal* publishing an article which contrasted the Parnell movement with the movement that had gone before it by saying: "The last movement was poetry plus cabbage garden" (meaning poetry and the failure of Smith O'Brien)[14] "but this movement is going to be prose plus success." When that was written Ireland was ceasing to read her own poetry. Ireland was putting aside everything to attain her one political end.

I sometimes think that O'Connell was the contrary principle to Emmet. He taught the people to lay aside the pike and the musket, the song and the story, and to do their work now by wheedling and now by bullying. He won certain necessary laws for Ireland. He gave her a few laws, but he did not give her patriots. He was the successful politician, but it was the unsuccessful Emmet who has given her patriots. O'Connell was a great man, but there is too much of his spirit in the practical politics of Ireland. That great Parnellite movement tried now to bully England by loud words and now to wheedle England by soft words, and Ireland herself, her civilization and her ideals, were forgotten in the midst of it all. She was ceasing to have her own thoughts, to speak her own language, to live her own life. Idealists and poets had once been of importance to her, but I can remember some verses in a daily paper which gave the prevailing feeling of that time. They were addressed to the poet and they wound up by saying: "Take a business tour through Munster; Shoot a landlord; be of use." We poets were expected to be of use. The day had come when Ireland was to be content with prose plus success; but then it turned out to be not prose plus success but prose plus Committee Room Number 15.

[14] William Smith O'Brien (1803–64) was a political leader of the "Young Irelanders", the party of the early 1840s which was associated with such "poets of the *Nation*" as Mangan and Davis.

## THE NEW INTELLECTUAL LIFE

Then suddenly Parnell fell. The new school of practical and ecclesiastical politicians sold him to the enemy for nothing. Let us mourn his tragic fall, but let us remember that it brought, besides much evil, also a new life into Ireland. To you Irishmen in America what followed must have seemed a time of sheer desolation, of mere ignorable quarrelling. To us it was the transformation of the whole country. We saw that the imaginations of our young men would be directed away from the politics of the hour; that a time had come when we could talk to them of Davis, and of Emmet, when we could talk to them of Irish history and Irish culture, when we could make them think of Ireland herself. We would take up the work of young Ireland; and direct the imaginations of our young men towards Irish nationality, as Thomas Davis and the young Irelanders understood Irish nationality. Then we founded the Irish Literary Society of London and the National Literary Society of Dublin.

In a few years great numbers of books were published about Ireland —more books, it has been said, with but little exaggeration than during the whole hundred years that went before. We appealed to the people as Davis had appealed to the people. But it was not that movement which was destined to rouse the people. They were not to be roused by any words spoken in English.

One day the man whose name will mark this epoch, Dr. Douglas Hyde, went to a little country town bringing with him certain friends and he urged that all who had the Irish language should keep it living and all that had lost it should learn it. He told them that while Ireland had been agitating for a single necessary political measure, she had been giving up the battle in all else. The little country town had sent its member of Parliament to Westminster, but it had sent also a man or woman to London to bring back to the little local shop the latest London fashions. We were even giving up our own cloth; we were dressing like Englishmen in all things; and what was true of our clothes was true of all our thoughts. We were reading little English papers—the *Police News*, vulgar English story papers and comic papers. We were no longer reading Irish history; no longer reading the *Young Irelander*. We had become too practical for all that. We did, indeed, read the debates at Westminster to know what our vigorous members of Parliament were doing there and that only absorbed us the more in what was taking place beyond the channel.

## GREAT WORK OF DOUGLAS HYDE

Some of the politicians who had been most active in that struggle had even Anglicized their names; had given up their old Gaelic names that had a place in the history of Ireland. Dr. Hyde gave long lists of such names. He told the people that the native culture of Ireland was in the Irish language; that the history of Ireland could only be understood through that native language; that the Irish nation would die if it lost its language. His appeal had an immediate and wonderful success. What could have seemed more impracticable than that the people should begin to learn a language in which no business of the modern world is transacted, in which no thought peculiar to the modern world is expressed? And yet his movement succeeded with the most amazing rapidity. And after all, is not that always so? Is it not the impracticable dreamer that conquers the world? Is it not the impracticable dreamers who take the world up out of its course and turn it from one way to another? Who else are the founders of schools of philosophy? The founders of religions?

Ireland is being transformed from end to end by that impracticable dream. In every country [*sic*] now there are held what are called Feises— assemblies little and big for the singing of Irish poems, for the telling of Irish stories, for the playing of Irish plays, and these Feises are centres for the re-awakening of the national life. There comes very vividly before my mind the picture of the Galway Feis of last year and of an old man 104 years of age, repeating there his own poems in the high shrill voice of age. He had been found in the workhouse and had been brought out of it to be honored and cherished by his countrymen in his old age.

But I need not waste many words to prove to you that this language movement has become a great power in Ireland, a great moral power. Last spring the Gaelic League decided to hold its procession to collect money for the language cause on St. Patrick's Day. They decided that the public houses must close. They invited them to do so. At first they were scornful. Then girls waited outside the different houses, each distributing leaflets telling the people to pass by. On the morning of St. Patrick's Day there were streams of publicans outside the doors of the Gaelic League, come there to make their submission and to receive the little cards announcing that they had closed by order of the Gaelic League. As the result of this there were not six public houses open in all Dublin.

A movement that stirs the people deeply when those people have ancient culture like the Irish, can hardly fail to produce memorable poetry. Ireland in the old time was celebrated among the nations for her poets and the revival of the Gaelic language has brought with it a new living poetry. If I were asked to choose a poem in which Ireland's hate of English tyranny had found its most memorable expression, I would not choose a poem that came out of any of our professedly political movements but a certain poem written in Irish the other day by an anonymous writer. I know no expression of political hatred quite so splendid and passionate. I am a man of letters. It is difficult for me to hate anything very deeply. My life is too quiet for that. But I know that a nation cannot be powerful, cannot be ready for necessary battle, unless it has hatred as well as love in its heart. A nation is like a great tree and it must lift up its boughs towards the cold moon of noble hate no less than to the sun of love, if its leaves are to be thick enough to shelter the birds of heaven. Nor can its fruit be worthy to be eaten by men unless it have a harsh as well as a sweet savour.

(Mr. Yeats here read a translation from the Irish of the poem referred to.)

### RISE OF THE NATIONAL THEATRE

When this great movement appeared in Ireland, it looked for a time as if there was nothing for men like myself to do. We had learned English in the nursery. We thought in English. A man can only write well in the language he thinks in. We might learn Irish, but we would never learn it well enough to write good poetry or good prose in it. It seemed at first as if there was nothing for us to do except tell everyone to learn Irish. And then it became clear to us that when we experienced any beautiful emotion or saw any truth, it was right for us to tell others about it in whatever language we could use the best. And then we discovered the theatre. We found that we could reach our people, through the theatre. One of the most powerful instruments for the Anglicizing of Ireland was the English theatre in Ireland. It was no use merely denouncing it. It was necessary to put something in its place. A young artisan, Mr. William Fay, whose name will some day be known in the history of Irish drama, got together a company of young men and women and he has taught them to act very beautifully and very simply, so beautifully and so simply that one of the most celebrated dramatic critics in England has said of them that they have given him more pleasure than anything he has seen in the regular theatre for a long time.[15] They perform every month now in Dublin and are drawing appreciative audiences and all their plays are taken from the history of Ireland or from the heroic age of Ireland or are satires or comedies on contemporary Irish life. This little theatre fears nothing and the doctrines of Emmet have found upon its stage a vivid expression. We are producing in Ireland a school of dramatists writing both in Irish and in English. Three years ago we produced a play in Irish by Dr. Douglas Hyde. It was called "The Twisting of the Rope." It was immediately taken up

[15] Yeats's reference is to the appreciation of the Literary Theatre by Arthur Bingham Walkley. See pp. 46–7 above.

through the country in many places and from that has risen a whole vigorous dramatic literature in Irish.

One day I was going through a street in London when two tall lads and a big tall country girl came up to me. They began speaking all at once. I could not make out anything of their story, except that they were manifestly from County Cork. I brought them into a little restaurant and got them to speak one at a time, and then they told me that they had recognized me; that they had seen me once at a meeting, and that they had stopped me to tell me the latest theatrical news from Ireland. Father Peter O'Leary, their parish priest, had turned playwright at the age of seventy. The whole countryside was excited about his play. It was about a rogue who had lived in that parish forty years before and one reason why the people were so excited was that the descendants of the rogue were there and the descendants of the man he cheated were there, and the descendants of the rogue had taken it so badly that poor Father Peter O'Leary had been compelled to change his name in the play.

There are now many Gaelic playwrights and many little companies performing their plays. A year ago a little company came up from Ballinadereen with a play of Dr. Hyde's and another little company came up from County Cork with a play of Father Peter O'Leary's and they performed in the round room of the Rotunda for a week, filling that great hall which holds some three thousand people, night after night. Instead of the metropolis sending travelling companies to the country to Anglicize the country, we have now little companies coming up from the villages to the town to make the town Irish. It is as though the very sods had begun to sing to us.

None of these actors or these dramatists are paid anything for their work. They give to their art a disinterested service which they would hardly be ready to give if Ireland had not been trained in self-sacrifice by her political martyrs. Some of them have their sufficient reward, for it is no light thing to become a part of the proudest aristocracy upon earth, the aristocracy of the artists, the only aristocracy which has never oppressed the people and against which the people have never arisen.

### FOSTERING IRISH INDUSTRIES

But it is not only intellectual movements that have been created by this new moral fervor that has come into the country with the revival of the Irish language. When a man believes in his own nation, in the culture of his own nation, in the products of his own nation, his belief very soon has a practical outlet in many directions. Wherever the Gaelic League goes you will find in the shop windows, in out of the way country towns even, printed notices saying that goods of Irish manufacture can be got there. These printed notices are all the work of the Gaelic League. A somewhat celebrated sentence puts the doctrine of the Gaelic League upon this subject very briefly: "'Ireland can never be conquered,' said a certain orator. Ten thousand hats made in England were lifted to applaud that sentiment."

Side by side with the work of the League, created out of the enthusiasm which has been mainly inspired by the League, has grown a most vigorous industrial movement. The cloth mills of Cork, for instance, have doubled their product in the last five or six years. The paper mills of Sagart have increased their business six-fold. They are employing, I believe, six times as many hands as they did before the rise of this movement. The movement for the organization of agriculture upon scientific principles, goes forward side by side with the League, helped by its organizers and helping its organizers. Ten years ago Irish butter was being beaten from the market. To-day the societies organized by this movement are alone exporting $10,000,000 worth of butter every year, which means a profit of $3,000,000 to Irish farmers. Two hundred and fifty co-operative banks have been established in the country places to rescue the farmer from the money lender, and it is certainly a tribute to the moral worth of the people of Ireland that not one of these banks has ever lost a shilling. There have been no bad debts.

But I need not speak further upon this side of the movement, for my friend Father O'Donovan has already spoken to many of you upon it, and my friend Mr. Patrick Hannon is here in America now and will also, I have no doubt, speak to you most eloquently and convincingly upon it.

## REVIVED ECCLESIASTICAL ART

But most interesting of all to me, an artist, has been the rise of a school of ecclesiastical art in Ireland. One of the papers of the movement discovered that the Irish priests and parsons sent $150,000 every year to Munich to buy the worst possible stained glass. We have no good maker of stained glass in Ireland, but a certain very well known Irish artist opened there a workshop, and got the most famous maker of stained glass of the time to come and to superintend the work and to send there his best pupil, and now, really beautiful stained glass is being made in Dublin for the new Cathedral of Loughrea and for many other churches throughout Ireland.[16]

And this is only a part of the work. Beautiful windows are being made; young Irish sculptors are at work; and surely the people of

[16] The "Tower of Glass' stained glass cooperative was established in 1903 by Edward Martyn and Sarah Purser (1848–1943), the Irish portrait painter. For their first commission, the windows at Loughrea Cathedral, they were aided by A. E. Child, the English master.

Ireland will not be the less devout because the windows of their cathedrals celebrate in beautiful colors saints who lived their lives in Ireland and for the people of Ireland and because the artists of Ireland sculptured from them St. Patrick or St. Brendan with Irish hands. Nor will the church be less powerful if it became again, as it was everywhere in the middle ages, a patron of the arts.

This new movement has touched the moral life, the intellectual life, the material life of the country. If I were asked to put into a single sentence what it has done, I would say that it has made Irish intellect occupy itself with Ireland. I began by telling you how England bribed the Irish Parliament, but that bribery did not cease with the Irish Parliament. It has gone on all the while. England by an elaborate system of preferment, of offices drew away the intellect of Ireland, hypnotized it as it were, and turned it to her own purposes. She keeps up a vast legal establishment, to take but one instance, far greater than the nation needs, and that is but a bribe to Irish intellect to occupy itself with anything rather than with Ireland. This new movement that I speak of, has brought back Irish intellect to Ireland.

## INTENSE INTELLECTUAL ACTIVITY

An intense intellectual activity has arisen throughout the whole country. The old books of Ireland have been translated into beautiful and simple English. Surely it is no exaggeration to say that the last ten or twelve years—years which to the merely political observer have been years of defeat and desolation—have produced in Ireland an intellectual and moral activity the like of which has not been seen there for a century. Ireland is thinking about herself, is living her life within her own borders. A political movement can only give occupation to some two or three thousand of the people of a nation. The others can only join some organization and subscribe a little money. But a movement like that of Irish Ireland and the intellectual awakening of the people gives occupation to every man and woman and child in the country. The activity of such a movement is continuous. It has been one of the curses of Irish public life that we have had but an intermittent activity. We have had a period of intense life—Fenianism, Parnellism, whatever it may be—and then it dies down again. But once you have an organization of the whole people, you give to every man some occupation that suits him, to one man the awakening of an industry, to another man the learning of a language, you prepare for a political activity so powerful, you create leaders so full of resource, that one may say without fear that such a nation will be master of its own destiny; that no power outside itself will ever be able to check its development; that if it desires complete nationality it will attain it at the last, for it will be full of an inflexible power, full of an unconquerable energy, and for the future of my nation now that its new life has come, I feel entirely confident. Man's life is short, but the life of the nation is long. Even a century of failure need not discourage it; this is but a moment in the life of a nation.

The nations of the world are like a great organ. A little while ago, the organ pipe that we call the Empire of Spain was sounding and it had filled the world with its music; and then that life fell silent and the divine hand moved to another stop of the organ and the pipe that we call the Empire of England began to sound. And we need not doubt that the divine hand will move again and that the pipe that is called Ireland will once more begin to sound and that its music will fill the world.

# The Best Book from Ireland

Yeats's praise of Lady Gregory's *Cuchulain of Muirthemne* as "the most important book that has come out of Ireland in my time" (see p. 299 above) returned to haunt him in a three-way exchange in *The Daily News*. In the issue for April 29, 1904, the *News* had chided Yeats's friend of many years, the English journalist and editor Clement Shorter (1857–1926), for his reference to Yeats's and Lady Gregory's "inclination to mutual admiration and log-rolling" in an article in *The Sphere*. As the husband of the Irish poet Dora Sigerson and son-in-law of Dr. George Sigerson, one of the earlier generation of collectors of Irish literature (see p. 359 below), Shorter seems to have intended only to point out that the Irish literary movement was not entirely Yeats's and Lady Gregory's doing. However, in his reply to the *News*, in the issue for May 4, he provoked Yeats to enter in, not only by inserting "best" for "most important" in Yeats's remark about *Cuchulain* and expanding its praise to include all Irish books, but also by forcing him to discriminate between his work and that of the great eighteenth-century Anglo-Irish writers with whom Yeats was in later years to feel close kinship. "That Mr. Yeats," he wrote, "has written delightful poetry and excellent plays I take for granted; that he is more distinguished than some other literary Irishmen of this age must, I assume, be a matter of opinion. It is not, however, a matter of opinion to define Sir Charles Gavan Duffy's position in the Irish literary movement. To speak of him, as Lady Gregory does, as having 'helped' Mr. Yeats to found the Irish library, is absurd; equally absurd is it when Mr. Yeats defines Lady Gregory's 'Cuchulain of Muirthemne' as 'the best book that has come out of Ireland in my time—perhaps I should say the best book that has ever come out of Ireland.' Apart from the many great writers, Burke, Goldsmith, Sheridan, and Sterne, and a hundred others of whom England and Ireland may be equally proud . . . several of those very stories from the Irish language have been translated many times before they were given to us by Lady Gregory." Yeats's reply appeared in *The Daily News* for May 11.

TO THE EDITOR OF THE DAILY NEWS

SIR,

I have just seen in your issue of May 4 a letter from my friend, Mr. Clement Shorter, objecting to my description of Lady Gregory's "Cuchulain of Muirthemne" as "the best book that has come out of Ireland in my time."

I have come to agree with him: I withdraw that description; it is no longer true. Her "Gods and Fighting Men" is a better book, containing, as it does, an even greater amount of the heroic foundations of the race.

All is personal preference in the end, and Mr. Shorter, who is very modern in his interests, naturally prefers Swift, Burke, and Goldsmith, who hardly seem to me to have come out of Ireland at all. I, on the other hand, having found but one thing in Ireland that has stirred me to the roots—a conception of the heroic life come down from the dawn of the world and not even yet utterly extinguished—would give all those great geniuses for the first book that has retold the old epic fragments in a style so full at once of dignity and simplicity and lyric ecstasy, that I can read them with entire delight. And what is it to the point that others have translated these stories into less admirable language? I read them, and they were the chief influence of my youth; but I had to put them into better English as I read. How could one be interested in a hero who "ascended to the apex of an eminence" unless one had reminded oneself that he had but climbed a hill?

Yours, etc.,<br>W. B. Yeats

# The Irish National Theatre

After its success in London in 1903, the Irish National Theatre Society had been invited by the organizers to the Louisiana Purchase Exposition which was to be held in Saint Louis in 1904. Under pressure from influential members of the *Clan-na-Gael* to approve the venture, Yeats had visited Saint Louis in January. When the Society declined the offer, productions were proposed by a few of the players, including the leading male actor, Dudley Digges, who had left the company during the controversy over Synge's *In the Shadow of the Glen* in the fall of 1903 (see p. 306, above). An announcement of this project in *The Gael* (*An Gaodhal*), an Irish-American New York monthly, provoked Yeats's letter on "The Irish National Theatre" in the issue for June, 1904.

London, May 7, 1904

EDITOR *THE GAEL*

DEAR SIR,

I see in an article in THE GAEL that the holders of the Irish Concession at St. Louis have named their theatre "The Irish National Theatre."

This choice of name is unfortunate, as a certain number of people will confuse it with the original Irish National Theatre, on which I spoke a good deal in my lectures in America. It has no connection with it.

The article states that certain of my plays are to be acted at St. Louis. This is not the case. In accordance with the wish of the Irish National Theatre Society, of which I am president, I, together with others of our playwriters, refused permission.

The society does not wish to be identified with any other body of players. I hope America may have an opportunity of seeing their own fine and characteristic work within the next two or three years.

Yours faithfully,

W. B. Yeats

# Note on the Performing Rights of his Plays

*THE UNITED IRISHMAN*, JUNE 4, 1904

MR. YEATS sends us the following:

Some confusion has arisen about the right to perform my plays. Some societies wishing to act them have written to the Secretary of the Irish National Theatre Society, one has written to the Editor of a newspaper, one or two have performed them without writing to anybody. It will spare me and others some correspondence if you will allow me to say that all my plays are copyright, but that the National Theatre Society can give leave for their performance when it seems advisable, and on payment of a small fee towards the work of the society.

# Mr. George Moore and the Royal Hibernian Academy

Yeats briefly renewed his alliance with George Moore in 1904 in his efforts to extend the exhibition at the Royal Hibernian Academy of a group of modern French paintings gathered together by the successful young art dealer, Hugh Lane (1875–1915), who was Lady Gregory's nephew. In *Hail and Farewell* Moore depicts his Irish friends' suspicions of Lane's "collecting": "He is a collector who weeds out his collection. Let us call him a weeder; and let us never speak of the lavatory but of the cloak-room . . ." (*Vale*, p. 95). None the less, Moore and Yeats—along with J. B. Yeats and others—wrote appreciations and organized meetings, hoping both to keep the exhibition open and to begin raising the £30,000 needed to buy the paintings for Dublin. The high point of their efforts was Moore's talk on December 8, 1904, "Reminiscences of the Impressionist Painters", which he printed as a pamphlet in 1906 and in *Vale* (pp. 99–113), where he includes a sketch of Yeats, "lately returned to us from the States with a paunch, a huge stride, and an immense fur overcoat". In his impressions of the evening, of which Yeats's letter to the Dublin *Daily Express* on December 7 was one preliminary, Joseph Holloway remarked that Yeats proposed the vote of thanks to Moore "in his earnest, excitable way. . . . Mr. Yeats . . . said that, 'Mr. Moore and I are sometimes great friends and sometimes great enemies,' and I may say myself I was astonished to see them on the same platform, because I thought they were at daggers drawn" (*Joseph Holloway's Abbey Theatre*, p. 48). This letter marks Yeats's entry into the prolonged controversy over the Lane collection (see pp. 414–15 below).

### TO THE EDITOR OF THE *DAILY EXPRESS*

SIR,

I see by Mr. Catterson Smith's letter in to-day's "Express" that he did not know of Mr. Hugh Lane's Exhibition project until the Academy received Mr. Lane's formal application on September the 7th. His letter implies that had he been aware of the project he would have done his best to keep the Academy at Mr. Lane's disposal for the winter. One is glad to know this, but Mr. Smith will find it easier to understand Mr. George Moore's point of view if I run over certain facts and dates. It was at an informal meeting at the end of June, or in early July—it was the week before the death of Watts—and at this meeting it was decided that Mr. Lane should issue a circular and ask Sir Thomas Drew to sign it, as representing the Hibernian Academy.[1] This circular, of which I

---

[1] S. Catterson Smith (1849–1912), a portrait painter, served as Secretary to the Royal Hibernian Academy from 1890 until 1910, and Sir Thomas Drew (1838–1910), the Irish architect, was President of the Academy from 1900 until his death.

George Frederick Watts, the English painter and sculptor, died on July 1, 1904. See Yeats's appreciation of him, p. 342, below.

have a copy, was signed and issued a few days later, and in the week that followed a great part of Mr. Lane's work was done. Had Mr. Lane known that he could only have the Academy for a little more than a month, instead of the whole winter, I doubt if he would have undertaken the great expense and labour of gathering together the finest collection of modern French painting which has been seen out of Paris. He certainly believed that he had the whole winter before him. He sent in his formal application at the request of Sir Thomas Drew, merely to regularise, as he believed, an understanding arrived at with Sir Thomas Drew and other Academicians when the circular was issued. I believe that even after September the 7th, however, possibly even as late as last week, the paper-hangers could have been persuaded to forego their contract if the Academy had approached them. The attempt should, at any rate, have been made. It is certain, if Mr. Catterson Smith's letter represents the general feeling of the Academicians, that they would have supported him had Sir Thomas Drew acted on his own responsibility. Perhaps it is not still too late. The Lord Mayor would probably be willing to give the paper-hangers the use of the Round Room at the Mansion House.

I myself am for the first time beginning to feel that I understand French Art a little. I go almost every day to the Exhibition, and I know of others who will think the closing of this great Exhibition a personal misfortune.

Yours truly,<br>W. B. Yeats

December 6th, 1904

# J. M. Synge's "The Shadow of the Glen"

For its first performances at the Abbey Theatre, on December 27, 1904, the Irish National Theatre Society introduced Lady Gregory's *Spreading the News* and Yeats's *On Baile's Strand*, along with revivals of *Cathleen ni Houlihan* and Synge's *In the Shadow of the Glen*. On January 7, 1905, Griffith's *United Irishman* renewed the controversy begun with the original performances of Synge's play (p. 306 above) charging that "Mr. Synge's adaptation of the old Greek libel on womankind—'The Widow of Ephesus'—has no more title to be called Irish than a Chinaman would have if he printed 'Patrick O'Brien' on his visiting card . . .". Yeats's letter to *The United Irishman* for January 28, 1905, is the first of his three contributions to the renewed dispute.

MR. YEATS writes to us—we owe him an apology for the delay in the insertion of the letter—a delay occasioned through the borough elections:

Dear Sir,

You say of Mr. Synge's "Shadow of the Glen" in one of your paragraphs on the performances at the Abbey Theatre, "The story is two thousand years old—it was invented by the decadent Greeks—the reputation of womankind has suffered in every century from it. Mr. Synge heard the story, he called the Greek dame Nora Burke; her husband, Dan Burke; and the robber with whom in the original, she goes away, while the Greek husband and the Greek lover remain, 'a Tramp.' He calls Ephesus, a Wicklow Glen, and lo! the thing is staged and dubbed an Irish play." If the names have been changed from Greek to Irish, they have not been changed by him, but by the unknown Irish peasant who first told the story in Ireland. You will find the Irish form of the story in Mr. Synge's forthcoming book on the Aran Islands.[1] You, yourself, once suggested that it was imported by the hedge schoolmasters. I do not, myself, see any evidence to prove what country it first arose in, or whether it may not have had an independent origin in half-a-dozen countries. The version of the Widow of Ephesus that I know differs from Mr. Synge's plot, and also from the Irish folk-story on which he has founded his play. I would be very much obliged if you would give me the reference to the story referred to by you in the paragraph I have quoted. I do not remember it in the "Decameron," which I have lately read. This story may, however, be exactly the same as some Greek or Italian story, and we be no nearer its origin.

Among the audience at the last performance of "On Baile's Strand" there was a famous German scholar who had just edited the old German version of the world-wide story of the king who fights with his own son. Yet, no man can say whether that story came from Ireland to Germany or from Germany to Ireland, or whether to both countries from some common source.

There is certainly nothing in the accounts that travellers give of mediaeval Ireland or in Old Irish or Middle Irish literature to show that Ireland had a different sexual morality from the rest of Europe. And I can remember several Irish poems and stories in which the husband feigns death for precisely the reason that the husband does in Mr.

[1] The manuscript of Synge's *The Aran Islands* had circulated for some time but, despite the efforts of Yeats and Lady Gregory, it was not published until 1907. It contains the story Synge was told by the Aranman Pat Dirane, in the first person, of his being welcomed into the cottage of a young widow and having been drawn into a conspiracy with her husband, who is feigning death to catch her in adultery. (See *J. M. Synge: Collected Works*, vol. II, ed. Alan Price, London, 1966, pp. 70–2.)

Synge's play; one of them a very beautiful ballad found in the Aran Islands by Mr. Fournier.[2]

But after all, if Mr. Synge had found the story in some Greek writer and had changed the names into Irish names, or even if he had found it in the "Decameron" itself, as you suggest, he would have precedents to encourage him. Shakespeare laid the scene of Cymbeline in his own country, but he found the story in the "Decameron."

I do not reply to the matters of opinion in dispute between us, for to do so would be to repeat what I have already written in my introduction to "A Book of Irish Verse," in the Irish part of "Ideas of Good and Evil," and in the last number of "Samhain."[3] It is no bad thing that our two so different points of view should find full and logical expression, for as William Blake says: "All progress is by contraries"[4]; but differences that arise out of mistakes of fact are useless.

---

[2] Edmund Edward Fournier d'Albe (1868–1933), an English physicist and lexicographer, published works on both physical and psychical research and, in 1903, an Irish dictionary and phrase book. It is not clear if the version of this story which he heard on Tory Island was published. It was, however, known at this time, as were versions collected by Jeremiah Curtin in Munster and Alice Milligan in Ulster.

[3] Yeats's list is a bibliography of his developing view of "national" literature. He had distinguished, in *A Book of Irish Verse* (1895), between the "practical and political . . . poets who gathered about Thomas Davis" and such ones as Samuel Ferguson and William Allingham who had, partly by studying other literatures, advanced Irish literature. He redefined the relation of nationality to art when, in "Ireland and the Arts", an essay of 1901 which was reprinted in *Ideas of Good and Evil* (1903), he addressed himself "especially to those who are convinced, as I was convinced [sixteen years ago], that art is tribeless, nationless, a blossom gathered in No Man's Land. . . . I would have our writers and craftsmen of many kinds master [Irish] history and . . . legends, and fix upon their memory the appearance of mountains and rivers and make it all visible again in their arts, so that Irishmen, even though . . . thousands of miles away, would still be in their own country . . ." (*Essays and Introductions*, pp. 205–6). The universality of such seemingly localized art was Yeats's subject in "First Principles", the essay in the 1904 issue of *Samhain*, the periodical publication of the Irish National Theatre Society. There, he described the function of Irish national literature, as it exemplifies the national temperament. "It will influence the life of the country immeasurably more, though seemingly less, than have our propagandist poems and stories. It will leave to others the defence of all that can be codified for ready understanding . . . but it will bring all the ways of men before that ancient tribunal of our sympathies" (*Explorations*, p. 161).

[4] Blake, "The Marriage of Heaven and Hell," pl. 3: "Without Contraries is no progression." (Keynes, ed., p. 182).

# J. M. Synge's "The Shadow of the Glen"

*THE UNITED IRISHMAN,* FEBRUARY 4, 1905

MR. YEATS writes:

Two or three weeks ago you wrote of Mr. Synge's "Shadow of the Glen:" "The story is two thousand years old—it was invented by the decadent Greeks—the reputation of womankind has suffered in every century from it. Mr. Synge heard the story, he called the Greek dame Nora Burke; her husband, Dan Burke, and the robber with whom in the original she goes away, while the Greek husband and the Greek lover remain, 'a tramp.' He calls Ephesus a Wicklow Glen, and lo! the thing is staged and dubbed an Irish play." I wrote to you that I would be very much obliged if you would give me the reference to the story referred to by you in the paragraph I have quoted. You replied, "Mr. Yeats is mistaken in supposing the story of the Ephesian widow a folk-story. It is a story invented by the wits of decadent Greece, and introduced, with amendments, into Latin literature by the most infamous of Roman writers, Petronius Arbiter, the pander of Nero. But Mr. Synge could not have ventured to produce Petronius's version on the stage of any civilised country."

You have wasted some of my time. There is no such story in Petronius, and I must again ask you for your reference. He does, indeed, tell the well-known story of the Ephesian widow. You will find a rather full paraphrase of his version in chapter 5 of Jeremy Taylor's "Holy Living."[1] It is an admirable fable. It has been described by a good scholar and masterly writer as "the very model of its kind, and withal the perfection of ironic humour," but it is not Mr. Synge's story nor the story of your paragraph.

Here it is: "A widow mourning on the tomb of her husband surrenders to the love of a soldier who has been sent to watch over the hanged body of a robber. In the night the robber's friends steal his body away, and the widow hangs her husband's body in its place to save the life of the soldier who had otherwise been executed for neglect of duty." This is a bare summary, and does no justice to a fable that has gone through the whole world. It was not invented by the decadent Greeks, for you will find, if you look in Dunlop's "History of Fiction,"[2] that it

---

[1] Yeats's reference should have been to *The Rule and Exercise of Holy Dying* (sect. 8 ch. 5) by Jeremy Taylor (1613–67), where the story of the Ephesian woman is told, with the admonition that the soldier afterward possessed "a love which might change as violently as her grief had done" (Taylor, *Works,* London, 1867, vol. i, p. 606).

[2] *The History of Fiction,* by John Dunlop (1785–1842) was first published in London in 1814 and was, at this time, in its fifth edition.

is one of the oldest of Eastern tales. It is in that most ancient book of fables, "The Seven Wise Masters," and is extant in a very vivid form in old Chinese writings. Ireland may, I think, claim all the glory of Mr. Synge's not less admirable tale. The only parallels I can remember at this moment to the husband who pretends to be dead that he may catch his wife and his wife's lover, are Irish parallels. One is in a ballad at the end of "The Love Songs of Connacht,"[3] and the other in a ballad taken down in Tory Island by Mr. Fournier.[4]

In everything but the end of the play Mr. Synge has followed very closely the Aran story, which he has, I believe, sent to you; but it is precisely the end of the play that puts him at once among men of genius For this there is no parallel in any story that I know of. The sitting down together of the husband and the lover is certainly "the perfection of ironic humour."

It is not my business to dispute with you about the character of Petronius. I know little about him, but I do know that his identification with Arbiter Elegantarium is considered very uncertain by good scholars, and that little that is certain is known of either Petronius or Arbiter. Mr. Charles Whibley,[5] a sound critic and, as I have always understood, a sound scholar, has said of Petronius, "One thing only is certain, he was a gentleman, and incomparably aristocratic."

The Aran story and the Ephesian story are alike stories of wrong-doing; but so, too, is Bluebeard, and we are none of us a penny the worse.

\* \* \* \* \* \* \*

Mr. Yeats is wasting his time, but he is doing so voluntarily. It is not at our request he indulges in logrolling. If Mr. Yeats refers again to our reply to his question, Where he may procure the prurient Greek story Mr. Synge has dubbed "In a Wicklow Glen," [sic] he will find the answer, In the Palais Royale. Mr. Yeats, who informs us there is no such story in Petronius, has never read Petronius. He has learned, however, from one Whibley, that it is doubtful whether Petronius was Petronius, but that it is certain he was a gentleman and an aristocrat. We advise Mr. Yeats not to trust too implicitly in Mr. Whibley's scholarship and his definitions. If Mr. Yeats had read Petronius and his editors he would not have been put to the necessity of referring to Dunlop's

---

[3] "The Roman Earl", the last poem in Douglas Hyde's collection of *Love Songs of Connacht* (1894), tells of a wealthy Roman who feigns death to test his wife, whose greatest subsequent lapse is that she has his "corpse" dressed in a shroud "of canvas coarse; / (To his hips it did not come)" (9th edn., London, 1909, p. 147).

[4] See note 2, p. 333 above.

[5] This assessment of Petronius appears in the essay on him in *Studies in Frankness* (1910), by Charles Whibley (1859–1930), the English scholar and litterateur, who also cites Jeremy Taylor's use of the story of the widow of Ephesus.

History of Fiction, which takes equal rank for accuracy and learning with Chamber's Book of Days. He would have found that Petronius brought the story out of Greece, where it had been invented by the decadents, and altered it. Mr. Yeats fails to tell us who the 'mediaeval travellers' were he spoke of in his last letter, who led him to believe that Irishwomen were of the same class with the Ephesian dame, and where in Old or in Middle Irish literature he found confirmation for the impression these "mediaeval travellers" made upon him. In future we advise him to catch his traveller before quoting him for we fear his imagination has carried him away in this matter as it did in America when he told his audiences the Castle lived in fear of his theatre and sent forty baton-bearing myrmidons down to its each performance. Mr. Synge forwards us a tale he states he took down in Aran, which is essentially different to the play he insolently calls "In a Wicklow Glen." In the Aran story the wife appears as a callous woman—in Mr. Synge's play the wife is a strumpet. In the interests of the National Theatre Society, we advise its writers to leave that kind of "drama" to the "Theatre of Commerce," where Mr. Synge's "genius" may entitle him to a seat beside the author of "Zaza." [6]

# J. M. Synge's "The Shadow of the Glen"

*THE UNITED IRISHMAN*, FEBRUARY 11, 1905

MR. YEATS writes to us:

I don't see how we can go on with the controversy about the origin of the "Shadow of the Glen" until you have printed Mr. Synge's letter to you, with its enclosure giving the Irish original, and given me a more definite reference than "The Palais Royal." [1] I must, however, contradict a statement you have made about myself. You say, "In America he told his audiences the Castle lived in fear of his Theatre, and sent forty baton-bearing myrmidons down to its each performance." This is as true as the statement made to me by an American journalist that you were paid by the British Government to abuse the Irish Party. I des-

---

[6] *Zaza*, the popular opera by Ruggiero Leoncavallo (1858–1919), was first produced in 1900. It was based on the play by Pierre Berton and Charles Simon.

[1] Griffith's reference is in his exchange with Yeats on January 28 (p. 335 above), which is also the source of the allusion to the "mediaeval travellers". References to Synge's sojourn in Paris were touchstones of Griffith's Nationalist rhetoric.

cribed in many of my American lectures the attack made upon the "Countess Cathleen" by Mr. F. H. O'Donnell and the *Nation* newspaper.[2] I have my exact words among my papers in London. This seems to be the origin of your extravagant charge, doubtless sent to you by some imaginative correspondent, or copied from some inaccurate newspaper. I mentioned neither Dublin Castle nor politics of any kind.

In deciding not to continue the controversy he began, we think Mr. Yeats is acting wisely. To remove the misapprehension Mr. Yeats' letter is calculated to create, we may say that this is the first intimation we had that Mr. Synge intended his letter for publication, and not for our personal enlightenment. Since we find we have erred, we subjoin it:

Sir,

I beg to enclose the story of an unfaithful wife which was told to me by an old man on the Middle Island of Aran in 1898, and which I have since used in a modified form in "The Shadow of the Glen." It differs essentially from any version of the story of the "Widow Ephesus" with which I am acquainted. As you will see, it was told to me in the first person, as not infrequently happens in folktales of this class.

Yours,

J. M. Synge

Mr. Synge's story, which, as we said last week, depicts the wife as a callous woman, whilst his Ephesian play depicts her as a strumpet, is, we regret to say, of insufficient merit to entitle it to a place in our columns. We presume Mr. Yeats' "American journalist" is a blood relation of

---

[2] In 1899, prior to the presentation of Yeats's *The Countess Cathleen* as the first program of the Irish Literary Theatre, a controversy had arisen over its orthodoxy. Leading the attack was Frank Hugh O'Donnell, a sometime member of Parliament and political opportunist. Hoping both to gain in the esteem of conservative Nationalists and to avenge his expulsion from John O'Leary's circle (at the suggestion of Yeats and Maud Gonne), O'Donnell published a pamphlet, *Souls for Gold*, on the cover of which were the words of one of the demons in Yeats's play: "There soon will be no man or woman's soul unbargained for in five score baronies". Below this was the attribution: "Mr. W. B. Yeats on Celtic Ireland". O'Donnell's attack was aided by the *Daily Nation*, controlled then by William Murphy, whose *Irish Independent* launched the attack in 1903 on Synge (see p. 306 above). The *Nation* solicited and printed this opinion from Michael Cardinal Logue (1840–1924): "All I know of this play is what I could gather from the extracts given in Mr. O'Donnell's pamphlet and your paper. . . . I have no hesitation in saying that an Irish Catholic audience which could patiently sit out such a play must have sadly degenerated, both in religion and patriotism" (quoted in Lennox Robinson, *Ireland's Abbey Theatre*, London, 1951, p. 6).

Despite these attacks, Yeats managed to calm his pious collaborator, Edward Martyn, who had sought theological counsel at the height of the controversy and had nearly withdrawn his play, *The Heather Field*, and curtailed his support. Yeats's citation of the earlier controversy in the present note has an ironic edge, because one of his worries at that time was the offer by Arthur Griffith of the presence and support of "a lot of men from the Quays" who would "applaud anything the church did not like" (*Autobiography*, p. 279).

those "mediaeval travellers" from whom he learned that the mediaeval Irishwomen were akin to the Ephesian dame, and that we shall request his name from Mr. Yeats with the same ill-success we have requested the names of the mediaeval slanderers. The statement which Mr. Yeats contradicts is taken from one of those English papers which latterly Mr. Yeats delights to quote—the *Daily News*. Mr. Yeats will notice that it purports to give his exact words, and that, therefore, if untrue, it is a deliberate forgery. This is the paragraph:

Mr. W. B. Yeats has been lecturing in America upon the intellectual revival in Ireland under the auspices of the Irish Literary League of America. In the course of his remarks he said about the Irish National Theatre: "There is a deeper and bitterer tone in the new Irish literature than there ever was in the old Irish ballads. The Gaelic League has developed passion where there was once apathy. Our dramatists now study what the people want, and then we give it to them in such form that thirty or forty police must often be stationed inside the theatre to prevent riots. You can do something with people like that."

That Mr. Yeats never mentioned Dublin Castle nor politics of any kind in America is all the more wonderful in view of the fact that he delivered a public address to a Nationalist audience on Robert Emmet there.[3] An address on Robert Emmet with all reference to the Castle and politics left out eclipses the record of the stage-manager who successfully produced "Hamlet" with the part of the Prince of Denmark omitted.

# America and the Arts

An article in *The Metropolitan Magazine* for April, 1905, reflecting Yeats's interest in what he had seen of American education during his 1903–4 tour, is his only contribution to this popular New York monthly.

THE other day I was dining with some friends in a little restaurant in Soho and somebody asked me what I thought of America, where I had been lecturing for some four months. I spoke of America as the best educated country I had met with, of its clean, well-dressed people, so

---

[3] See pp. 310–327 above for the text of Yeats's speech at the Emmet celebration and a note on his wishes to avoid politics in it.

unlike the people of London or Dublin; of charming houses where one saw the tradition of William Morris commingled with a native tradition, come down from Colonial days; of Western college buildings where one saw the architecture of the old Spanish Mission House adapted to new purposes; of colleges that led their districts in all intellectual things; of women who were not argumentative, although they had been to college; of all that vivid life where everything is more intense than elsewhere—a thirst for money, for ideas, for power, beyond our understanding. I had come back, I said, believing as never before in the future of the world, not merely the remote future when beauty and leisure shall have returned to men, but the immediate future of labor and disorder.

Everything, I said, had been a delight to me except American poetry, which had followed the modern way of Lowell, who mistook the imaginative reason for poetry, not that ancient way Whitman, Thoreau and Poe had lit upon.

Presently, an Englishman who was there said: "You and I would soon quarrel, for I am a good Englishman." And he got up and went away. I had forgotten I was speaking of a civilization that has influenced my country so constantly, that it is as natural for an Irishman to like it as it seems natural for an Englishman to dislike it, or to like it with something of condescension. Friends had said to me that in America I should of a certainty find nothing likable, and I had set out thinking that for me at any rate—an artist—there would be nothing. And yet I found there what is surely the root of all pleasure to an artist, many cultivated people in every town, with whom one could discuss the most interesting things. In England one finds hardly such people anywhere but in London. One sometimes comes upon some charming town with an old cathedral in the midst of it and some fragment of the old wall that once kept it in safety, and for a moment one thinks that it had been a better place to winter in than in London. Then one remembers that one could not live there where the only intellectual preoccupation would be, whether it was the church-goer or the chapel-goer that is lost. But everywhere in America—Indianapolis, Minneapolis, Chicago, St. Louis, New York and far western San Francisco—one finds people who are of one's own tribe, liberated souls, partakers of the mysteries as it were. The words of Morris and of Ruskin have found hearers who have listened better because of Thoreau and Emerson; and everywhere one finds one's own table of values. A man could set up house without fear wherever the skies are bluest and the shadows deepest. I had got to think it a necessary part of modern life that my tribe should be very small and that I should look at most men with a little hostility because of their hatred for what I love and their love for all that I hate. Half of the beauty of old romance is that it made men to be of one kind and so could find a worthy adventure behind every wall. I once indeed knew a romantic looking Hindu poet who lived in London as it were Bagdad or Samerkand or ancient Delhi, and he would speak of his life there, and very eventful it was, with the same emotion I have heard him put into the words: "There was a princess of Delhi, and she had a purple parrot"; but he had not our thoughts and one thing was like to another where all were strange.

Perhaps the absence of an hereditary aristocracy has something to do with this intellectual curiosity. An American will boast to you of the seven generations of his fathers that have been to college, as an Englishman of relations in the peerage. He has even invented the words "college-bred" and one can see that education opens to man or woman doors that only birth or wealth would open here. Education is a national passion, and everywhere one finds some college having its own distinct life, differing from that of other colleges and getting its endowments out of its own countryside. And everywhere quite poor people pare and save to send their children to college, understanding that their country offers all forms of wealth and power to the disciplined mind. I was in many colleges, and I went to them expecting to find vigorous teaching of whatever leads to professional success, but not expecting to find imaginative teaching. And yet here also the lack of an hereditary order had brought fire and vigor. A teacher must interest his pupils, for if he bore them no unassailable tradition will keep them to listen. In many places I found students who are set to analyze the modern novel for the whole of their first year in literature, and in one great school the pupils read nothing but the Norse Sagas for a long time, for the Sagas, the headmaster told me, stirred their blood the most. The principal of a college said to me, "The English have sent out a Commission to find out how we teach Science, thinking that our commercial success depends upon that, but I told them it came from all our life and that the Imagination was more than Science." The men are for the most part too busy to show their imaginative side outside their business, but one finds the women, just in so far as they have been well educated, according to the accepted meaning of the word, imaginative, impulsive, and curious about ideas. I spoke at many Women's Colleges and I met few women who had not been to some college or other, and yet I never met that typical argumentative woman of the English college, who was meant, it may be, to have a happy natural charm but has learned an unhappy pose. Ever censorious, ever doing battle for the commonplace, her mind fashioned for joy and triumph, is full of virulent peevish negation; one would as soon sit down to supper with a host who dropped tin tacks into the soup tureen as converse with her; but these American women are as charming, as well-educated in all necessary things, as if they had spent their youth in the impulsive laborious ignorance of the studio. By what secret have these teachers learned so to enlarge the imagination and the sympathies of those who have been born to no creative art, and to make them as human as if they had held the paint brush and the chisel. The principal of a great college for women said to me, "I have noticed the difference between the English educated women and ours, and it is because they teach them to teach in England and we prepare them for life."[1] Certainly it was a great joy to speak before so many fair heads that are learning and yet not unlearning life, about the queens of old Irish romance who were fitted to be the perfect mistress and the perfect wife, and yet when the need called for it to carry a bow through the wilderness.

One wonders why America has not created more beautiful art. It is not, as I think, that she lacks the emotion of antiquity. Is not England for all practical purposes but of yesterday? If one leave out a few buildings here and there, is not London as new as Baltimore or even as New York? Indeed, one finds throughout America a sense of an immediate stirring past that should arouse the imagination as much as an age of romance, from which an early Victorian deluge divides us. In the Capitol at Washington there is a dome painted for four-fifths of its circle with historical frescoes, while one-fifth is but bare wall. It was felt that but one event, the Civil War, was important enough to fill that space, but that it was not right to commemorate civil war. A country that did not feel imaginatively about its past would have filled it with some state ceremony, some trivial noisy event.

America has made many charming houses and some good novels, and there is Poe and Thoreau and Whitman, and there is Emerson, who seems to me of a lesser order because he loved the formless infinite too well to delight in form, and there is Whistler. But New England has passed away, and Whistler was shaped far from America. One cannot think that this new America which has robbed culture of its languor and yet kept its fineness has found an adequate expression. Is it because it is an America of women, and women have not yet been abundant creators of the arts? Is it because, as several university teachers said to me, America has to assimilate with herself millions of immigrants who not only come with alien traditions but speak English coldly and unimaginatively because it is still a foreign tongue? Or is it that America has flung herself into the private wars of commerce and must be silent

[1] This passage echoes Yeats's letter of December, 1903, to Lady Gregory. Writing from Bryn Mawr, "the chief women's college of America", he marvelled at the attendance at his talk and added, "Do you know I have not met a single woman here who puts 'tin tacks in the soup'? and I found that the woman who does is recognized as an English type. One teacher explained to me the difference in this way, 'We prepare the girls to live their lives but in England they are making them all teachers'" (*Letters*, p. 414).

till they are over, as England was during the Wars of the Roses? I was in some beautiful and quiet towns, but I stayed in one town where a railway train went up and down the main street ringing a bell once every hour or so through the day and night. Perhaps the arts await until some Apollo slay that python. Yet here and there one could almost hear the footsteps of the Muses: in that beautiful San Francisco, for instance, under a sky of untroubled blue, by the edge of that marble Greek theater at Berkeley College, or in those ornamental gardens a little southward where the policemen ride among the pepper trees and the palm trees with lassoes before them on the saddle. Perhaps it was only the enchantment of a still sea, of a winter that endured the violets, and of a lovely book of verses from Petrarch, sent me by a young writer, that made me fancy that I found there a little of that pleasure in the Arts, which brings creative art and not scholarship, because it is delight in life itself.

When life grows beautiful and joyful, when men are ready with a blow and women dream extravagantly, the Muses come in secret under the shadows that they may hurriedly consume upon their treacherous altar what many generations have gathered. The scholar and the connoisseur are friends of the artist indeed, but he is of a different race, for are not we artists but soldiers, merchants, malcontents and lovers who have turned from life because she has nourished us in desires that she cannot satisfy. Nobody can tell where life is going to catch fire and become art, and all our prophecies are but as a child's make-believe; but certainly should it come into those half Latin places that will be well, for the Northern voices of the world seem to be getting a little fainter and they do not, it may be, delight us as they did.

# The Watts Pictures

On January 25, 1906, Yeats gave the second of a series of lectures on an exhibition at the Royal Hibernian Academy which Hugh Lane had organized in memory of George Frederic Watts (1817–1904), the English artist. In his definition of "The Ideal in Art", as it was reported the following day in the Dublin *Daily Express*, Yeats obviously used the example of Watts to discuss the complicated relation between the artist, a man "of finer sensations", and his necessarily popular and national materials and aims. The treatment of this idea in *Ideas of Good and Evil* (1903) is echoed throughout this appreciation, as when, for example, Yeats attributes to Watts a recognition of the viability of Irish myths as materials for expression at once both personal and possessed of the "emotion of multitude".

## LECTURE     MR. W. B. YEATS

LAST night the second of a series of lectures arranged in connection with the Watts Exhibition was delivered by Mr. W. B. Yeats in the Royal Hibernian Academy, his subject being "The Ideal in Art." There was again a very large attendance.

The chair was occupied by Mr. R. C. Orpen,[1] who briefly introduced the lecturer. They knew the high position he occupied in the world of poetry, and he felt quite sure that anything he had to say on the subject before them would be worth saying, and, furthermore, that it would be well said.

Mr. Yeats, who was cordially received, said it was so many years since he was an art student that he approached his present subject with a good deal of diffidence. He was supposed to talk of the ideal in art, but when he came to consider it he found that the artist was, above all others, concerned with the realities of experience. Art was simply the pursuit of the one central reality of them all—the discovery of themselves and the representation in poetry, in poem, and music of themselves. He was going to try and apply to painting certain fundamental principles of art which he had found true of poetry. He was convinced that all the arts were fundamentally one art, and that what was true of one art was, if properly understood, true of them all. As he took it, poets were men who were content to express the sensations and experiences which they themselves received, being face to face with the world. They were men of finer sensations, and more settled experiences than others, and they gave us simply those sensations and experiences. The popular poet was the man who mixed with what were his finer experiences maxims,[2] thought, story, anecdote, enthusiasm, and so forth, which the ordinary man has already accepted and made a part of himself. There were two kinds of artists; the one like some mysterious priesthood, living, as it were, in the obscure depths of the temple, carrying on the offices of their religion for themselves and their brother priests; and there was another order that spoke to the people, taking up the images that already lay in their minds, giving them additional beauty and additional power. Aesthetic poetry had its equivalent in emotional painting, and popular poetry in subject painting. Watts lived in moral—over-moral and over-zealous England. He had for his contemporaries Ruskin, George Elliot [sic], and not only Morris, the poet, but Morris, the Socialist agitator. He was troubled with the idea that he would fail in his duty if he did not succeed in being one of that outer priesthood to appeal

---

[1] R. Caulfield Orpen (1862–1938), the Dublin architect, was the brother of Yeats's friend, William Orpen (1878–1931), the painter.

[2] The *Daily Express* prints "maximums" for "maxims" throughout this report.

to the people. Full of a moral restlessness and dissatisfaction, he saw that the great painters and sculptors and poets who had conquered the mass of men had done so by admitting some other element than themselves into their aesthetic nature, and he looked also for some element that he could make part of his own. There were no longer any myths amongst the people, or any religious symbols common to his mind and common to theirs. Only one thing remained, namely, moral zeal, which all men had in some degree, even the worst. So Watts took moral legends and maxims for his pictures—things that could be explained to a child or an imbecile. It seemed to him (Mr. Yeats) that Watts was seeking restlessly, and, as he thought, vainly, for some element that he, the great artist, would share with the mass of the people. He was as conscious and as deliberate in his pursuit of the multitude for noble ends as Tolstoi. The greatest joy that ever came to the artist—the highest element in his creative joy was to contemplate his own personality, enlarging itself, completing itself with the mirror of his writings and of his paintings, and he could imagine Watts looking back upon his life, and thinking to himself that he was very like those old artists of ancient times or the Middle Ages; and as he did so it could be easily imagined that it was not, perhaps, his pictures that were the most beautiful that came to his mind, but those moral allegories that were done consciously that he might become the master of the people. Yet these were very different from the old myths and the old legends and symbols in this, that they were consciously made. The old people believed in their old symbols and their old legends, and accepted them as to a certain extent realities. When Watts was not thinking that he was a preacher or a prophet, but painted from the image that he was moved by simply because he was a man of culture and because he belonged to a certain imaginative and poetic tradition which overshadowed the minds of all cultured people—when he was not painting out of a conscious moral effort, then they seemed to have the mark of his best genius and his best art upon them. In his (Mr. Yeats') opinion, one could not in art do anything deliberately, consciously. Nature was the mother of the artist, and nature was very zealous. She demanded that the artist should permit her to do all. She gave nothing to self-control; everything to self-surrender. She murmured to her children, "Leave all to me." It was because of that that the lives of artists had suffered so many shipwrecks. She was the great temptress, and out of her temptations had been created poetry, painting, sculpture—the glory of the world. But although, so far as cultivated Europe was concerned, the days of symbols and myths had gone, something had been gained as well as lost. Individuality stood out in stronger relief, and painters as well as poets had all learned to sing the song of themselves—the song of their own souls, more gladly, more confidently than ever before. Here in Ireland they had still myths and beliefs among the people. They had still left some of the element of the middle ages, and he thought if Watts had been an Irishman he would not have painted these allegories but would have devoted himself to the celebration of the national legends and heroes. He did happen to know that in the last year of his life, he got some of the old Irish legends done in translation in Lady Gregory's books, and he knew also that Watts had declared them to be the books of the year—the great literary sensation of the last year of his life. In that enthusiasm he (Mr. Yeats) believed he was expressing his desire for a means of communication with the multitude. Let some of those who might be reached by his words, and who were artists, take up this great tradition that they called a nation—that great mass of thoughts, of hereditary feelings, of hereditary hopes, of hereditary legends, beliefs, and so on, and give them pictorial expression. In doing so they need not be afraid of raising old controversies. A work of art silences discussion; it does not awaken it (applause).

# A Note on "The Mineral Workers", and Other Notes

Between October, 1906, and August, 1909, Yeats edited five issues of *The Arrow*, a pamphlet which was distributed with the programs at the Abbey Theatre. In the first issue, on October 20, 1906, he introduced *The Mineral Workers* by William Boyle (1853–1922), a civil servant whose *The Building Fund* had been part of the 1905 season of the Irish National Theatre Society. Earlier in 1906, Boyle's comedy, *The Eloquent Dempsey*, a political satire which Yeats had privately called "impossibly vulgar", had pleased the Abbey's audience, as did *The Mineral Workers*, according to Joseph Holloway. Boyle withdrew his plays from the Abbey repertory during the controversy over Synge's *Playboy of the Western World* in January, 1907, and no plays by him were produced there until 1912.

AS we wish our work to be full of the life of this country our stage manager has almost always to train our actors from the beginning, always so in the case of peasant plays, and this makes the building up of a theatre like ours the work of years. We are now fairly satisfied with the representation of peasant life, and we can afford to give the greater part of our attention to other expressions of our art and of our life. Our romantic work and poetical work once reasonably good, we can, if but the dramatist arrive, take up the life of our drawingrooms, and see if there is something characteristic there, something which our nationality may enable us to express better than others, and so create plays of that life and means to play them as truthful as a play of Hauptmann's or of Ibsen's upon the German or Scandinavian stage. I am not myself interested in this kind of work, and do not believe it to be as important as contemporary critics think it is, but a theatre, such as we project, should give a reasonably complete expression to the imaginative interests of its country. In any case, it was easier, and therefore wiser, to begin where our art is most unlike that of others, with the representation of country life.

It is possible to speak the universal truths of human nature whether the speakers be peasants or wealthier men, for

> *Love doth sing*
> *As sweetly in a beggar as a king.*[1]

So far as we have any model before us it is the national and municipal theatres in various Continental towns, and, like the best of these, we must have in our repertory masterpieces from every great school of dramatic literature, and play them confidently, even though the public be slow to like that old stern art, and perhaps a little proudly, remembering that no other English-speaking theatre can be so catholic. Certainly our weather-cocks will not turn those painted eyes of theirs too long to the quarter of the Scandinavian winds. If the wind blow long from the Mediterranean, the paint may peel before we pray for a change in the weather.

W. B. Y.

### A NOTE ON *THE MINERAL WORKERS*

Mr. Boyle has used the struggles of an Irish-American engineer who is trying to smelt ore in Ireland, as a symbol to represent the difficulties of any enthusiast who attempts, in a country demoralized by failure, to change anything or establish anything that would mean a break with settled habits and interests. He knows the country well—or rather the

---

[1] These lines are a variation of a stanza by Robert Greene (*c.* 1560–92) in "The Shepheards Wives Song" (1590):

> *Ah what is loue? It is a pretty thing,*
> *As sweet vnto a shepheard as a king,*
> *And sweeter too:*
> *For kings haue cares that waite vpon a Crowne,*
> *And cares can make the sweetest loue to frowne:*

(J. Churton Collins, ed., *The Plays and Poems of Robert Greene*, Oxford, 1905, vol. ii, p. 273.)

countryside where he was born and bred, and no man knows more of
the world than that, if the knowledge one means, is that instinctive kind
that goes to making plays of character. His people are individuals, but
they are also types, and there is something of the national tragedy in the
play. Every man is ready, in Mr. O'Grady's phrase, to break ranks and
go hunting hares, because no man believes that the marching is going
to bring him to anything better than a night's sleep. But if you have no
mind for meanings, you can take the play, and I hope any play we
produce, as a story, and be content.

W. B. Y.

# Notes

Most of Yeats's editorials in *Samhain*, the occasional publication of the Irish
National Theatre Society which he edited between October, 1901 and
November, 1908, were revised into the collection entitled "The Irish Dramatic Movement", which was published in volume four of *The Collected Works*
(1908) and reprinted in *Explorations* (1962). An exception is "Notes", which
appeared in the issue for December, 1906.

I HAVE re-printed from the *Contemporary Review* with the kind permission of the Editor, an essay of mine on the art of the Player, the
Singer, and the Reciter, in relation to literature and to the art of the
Abbey Theatre.[1] It was written shortly after the opening of the Theatre,
though through an accident it was not published until October of this
year, and it gives a better account than anything I have written of
certain dreams I hope the Theatre may in some measure fulfil. Our
work has developed more quickly upon one side, and more slowly upon
another, than I had foreseen. We have done little, though we have done

---

[1] For the *Samhain* of 1906, Yeats reprinted his essay, "Literature and the Living Voice",
which had appeared in the October issue of the *Contemporary Review*. In that essay, which is
reprinted in *Explorations* (pp. 202–21), Yeats develops the distinction between spoken and
written literature and, recalling the blind poet, Anthony Raftery, asserts that Irish literature
is more deeply based than English literature on oral tradition. "Irish poetry and Irish
stories were made to be spoken or sung, while English literature, alone of great literatures,
because the newest of them all, has all but completely shaped itself in the printing-press"
(*Explorations*, p. 206). When the essay was included in "The Irish Dramatic Movement",
Yeats noted that it was written at the outset of the Abbey Theatre but was not printed "until
the art of the Abbey had become an art of peasant comedy. It tells of things we have never
had time to begin. We still dream of them" (*ibid.*, p. 202).

something, to find music that would not obscure the meaning and the rhythm of words, and we have done nothing for the story-tellers, but now that our country comedies, with their abundant and vivid speech, are well played and well spoken, we may try out the whole adventure. We cannot of a certainty try it all at one time, and it will be easier for our audience to follow fragmentary experiments, now that the dream is there upon the paper.

Our main business is to create an Irish dramatic literature, and a list of plays from the outset of our movement, printed at the end of *Samhain* will show that we have done something towards it. The movement was begun by the Irish Literary Theatre, which produced or promoted the performance of Irish Plays and English Players, there being no others to be had at the time, for one week a year, for three years, Mr. Benson's Company playing for it in its last year. After that, a company of Irish players, with Mr. William Fay to stage-manage them, and Mr. Frank Fay to teach them elocution, took up the work, and Lady Gregory and Mr. Synge and myself have been responsible or mainly responsible for the choice of plays and the general policy of the National Theatre Society, as this Company is now called, from the opening of the Abbey Theatre, the Company's first permanent home, in 1904. We have a small subsidy from Miss Horniman,[2] the generous friend who has given us the free use of the Theatre, and are the only directors of an English-speaking Theatre who can say, as the artist can in every other art, "we will give you nothing that does not please ourselves, and if you do not like it, and we are still confident that it is good, we will set it before you again, and trust to changing taste." All true arts, as distinguished from their commercial and mechanical imitation, are a festival where it is the fiddler who calls the tune.

# The Controversy over the Playboy

In *The Arrow* for February 23, 1907, Yeats reprinted some of the documents which concern themselves with the week of riots and performances under police protection of Synge's *The Playboy of the Western World* after its premiere on Saturday, January 26. His major public statement was the speech which he delivered at a public debate on the *Playboy* at the Abbey on February 4. The concluding section of this speech is included in "The Irish Dramatic Movement", as is a part of the introductory matter of this essay (*Explorations*, pp. 225–8).

[2] See pp. 357, 379 and 486, below.

I HAVE reprinted in the present *Arrow* my speech at the Debate in the Abbey Theatre on the 4th February upon the Playboy, and the measures taken to preserve order, and certain extracts from the "Samhain" of 1905, and from patriotic papers of various dates. These quotations show how old is the attack and how old the defence, and that no satirical writer of the Theatre—certainly not Mr. Boyle, who has left us because we fought Mr. Synge's battle[1]—has escaped a misunderstanding unavoidable where certain crude general ideas and propagandist emotions have taken the place of every other kind of thought. If we had withdrawn the play those that hissed or cried "stage Irishman" at the performance of "The Mineral Workers" would have tried to drown the next play of Mr. Boyle's, that they objected to, by the stamping of their feet and the blowing of tin trumpets. We have claimed for our writers the freedom to find in their own land every expression of good and evil necessary to their art, for Irish life contains, like all vigorous life, the seeds of all good and evil, and a writer must be free here as elsewhere to ripen weed or flower, as the fancy takes him. No one who knows the work of our Theatre as a whole can say we have neglected the flower;[2] but the moment a writer is forbidden to show the weed without the flower, his art loses energy and abundance. In the great days of English dramatic art the greatest English writer of comedy was free to create "The Alchemist" and "Volpone," but a demand born of Puritan conviction and of bourgeois timidity and insincerity, for what many second-rate intellects thought to be noble and elevating events and characters had already at the outset of the eighteenth century ended the English drama as a complete and serious art. Sheridan and Goldsmith, when they restored comedy after an epoch of sentimentalities, had to apologise for their satiric genius by scenes of conventional lovemaking and sentimental domesticity that have set them outside the company of all, whether their genius be great or small, whose work is pure and whole. The quarrel of our Theatre today is the quarrel of the Theatre in many lands; for the old Puritanism, the old bourgeois dislike of power and reality have not changed, even when they are called by some Gaelic name.

[Yeats reprinted paragraphs attacking Synge, William Boyle, and Padraic Colum from *The Leader* and *The United Irishman* in 1905 and 1906. Also, under the title "Answers to Some of these Criticisms from the 'Samhain' of 1905", he reprinted an excerpt from his defense of these writers. With the exception of one passage which he deleted, this

---

[1] See p. 345 above.
[2] A section of this essay reprinted by Yeats in "The Irish Dramatic Movement" (*Explorations*, p. 225) begins with this sentence and continues to the end of this paragraph.

excerpt is the text in *Explorations* (pp. 187–93, "The sentimental mind
. . . against the walls of the world").]

## MR. YEATS' OPENING SPEECH AT THE DEBATE OF FEBRUARY 4TH, AT THE ABBEY THEATRE

"During the performances every now and then some one got up in his
place and tried to make a speech. On Saturday night an old gentleman
stood up in the front row of the pit after the opening of the third act,
and is probably very indignant that the police did not allow him to
speak. I hope he is here to-night, and all those other speakers. We have
never desired anything but the most free discussion that we may get at
last some kind of sound criticism in this country. But before the discussion commences I will do my best to answer a few of the more
obvious arguments, for there is no use wasting our time on stupidities
or on misunderstandings of each other's point of view. I see it said
again and again that we have tried to prevent the audience from the
reasonable expression of dislike. I certainly would never like to set
plays before a theatrical audience that was not free to approve or
disapprove, even very loudly, for there is no dramatist that does not
desire a live audience. We have to face something quite different from
reasonable expression of dislike. On Tuesday and on Monday night it
was not possible to hear six consecutive lines of the play, and this
deafening outcry was not raised by the whole theatre, but almost
entirely by a section of the pit, who acted together and even sat
together. It was an attempt to prevent the play from being heard and
judged. We are under contract with our audiences, we receive money
on the understanding that the play shall be heard and seen; we consider
it is our duty to carry out our contract.

"It has been said in to-day's 'Freeman' that the forty dissentients in
the pit were doing their duty because there is no government censor in
Ireland. The public, it is said, is the censor where there is no other
appointed to the task. But were these forty—we had them counted upon
Monday night and they were not more—alone the public and the
censor? What right had they to prevent the far greater number who
wished to hear from hearing and judging? They themselves were
keeping the plays from the eyes and ears of its natural censor. We called
to our aid the means which every community possesses to limit the
activities of small minorities who set their interests against those of the
community—we called in the police. There is no stalwart member of the
Sinn Fein party who would not do the same if he were to find a representative of that active minority—the burglars—fumbling with the lid
of his strong box. We think it folly to say that we cannot use the laws

common to all civilised communities to protect ourselves and our audience against the tyranny of cliques. At no time would we have ever hesitated to do what we have done. When 'The Countess Cathleen' was denounced with an equal violence we called in the police. That was in '99, when I was still President of the '98 Association of Great Britain.[3]

"I would indeed despise myself if for the sake of popularity or of a vague sentiment I were to mar the task I have set my hands to, and to cast the precious things of the soul into the trodden mire. A deputation of young Catholic students came to see me the other day, and the one who spoke their thoughts the most thanked us especially for this, for he said that the little domineering cliques presume upon the fear of lost popularity that keeps a Nationalist from calling to his aid those powers which hold together every community of the world, and silence the rattling bells on the cap of the fool. The struggle of the last week has been long a necessity; various paragraphs in newspapers describing Irish attacks on Theatres had made many worthy young men come to think that the silencing of a stage at their own pleasure, even if hundreds desired that it should not be silenced, might win them a little fame, and, perhaps, serve their country.[4] Some of these attacks have been on plays which are themselves indefensible, vulgar and old-fashioned farces, or demoded comedies. But the attack being an annihilation of civil rights was never anything but an increase of Irish disorder. The last I heard of was in Liverpool, and there a stage was rushed, and a priest, who had set a play upon it, withdrew his play and apologised to the audience. We have not such pliant bones, and did not learn in the houses that bred us a so suppliant knee. But behind the excitement of example there is a more fundamental movement of opinion. Some seven or eight years ago the National movement was democratised and passed from the hands of a few leaders into those of large numbers of young men organized in clubs and societies. These young men made the mistake of the newly enfranchised everywhere; they fought for causes worthy in themselves with the unworthy instruments of tyranny and violence. Comic songs of a certain kind were to be driven from the stage, everyone was to wear Irish cloth, everyone was to learn Irish, everyone was to hold certain opinions of political policy, and these ends were sought by personal attack, by virulent caricature and violent derision. It needs eloquence to persuade and knowledge to expound; but the coarser

[3] In regard to the controversy surrounding *The Countess Cathleen* see p. 337 above.

The year-long series of events which were planned to commemorate Wolf Tone's insurrection of 1798 had begun on April 13, 1898, with Yeats's address on "The Union of the Gael".

[4] This sentence begins the account of Yeats's speech which was reprinted in "*The Irish Dramatic Movement*" (*Explorations*, pp. 226–8).

means come ready to every man's hand, as ready as a stone or a stick, and where these coarse means are all, there is nothing but mob, and the commonest idea most prospers and is most sought for.

"Gentlemen of the little clubs and societies, do not mistake the meaning of our victory; it means something for us, but more for you. When the curtain of "The Playboy" fell on Saturday night in the midst of what the "Sunday Independent"—no friendly witness—described as 'thunders of applause,' I am confident that I saw the rise in this country of a new thought, a new opinion, that we had long needed. It was not all approval of Mr. Synge's play that sent the receipts of the Abbey Theatre this last week to twice the height they had ever touched before. The generation of young men and girls who are now leaving schools or colleges are weary of the tyranny of clubs and leagues. They wish again for individual sincerity, the eternal quest of truth, all that has been given up for so long that all might crouch upon the one roost and quack or cry in the one flock. We are beginning once again to ask what a man is, and to be content to wait a little before we go on to that further question: What is a good Irishman? There are some who have not yet their degrees that will say to friend or neighbour, 'You have voted with the English, and that is bad;' or 'you have sent away your Irish servants, or thrown away your Irish clothes, or blacked your face and sung a coon song. I despise what you have done, I keep you still my friend; but if you are terrorized out of doing any of these things, evil things though I know them to be, I will not have you for my friend any more.' Manhood is all, and the root of manhood is courage and courtesy."

The only practical suggestion made in the long disorderly debate that followed was that the management of the Theatre might have tired out the opposition, and so get a hearing for the play without calling in the police. Mr. Yeats replied to this as follows:—"Have you any idea as to the effect of all that noise and insult upon the nerves of the players? Do you think we would submit them to all that wear and tear of nerve night after night when we had the means of ending it? Our business was to secure quiet and silence, and we secured it as soon as possible."

# Notes

Given the uproar over Synge's *Playboy of the Western World* in Dublin, the play was a calculated risk among the National Theatre Society's offerings on their tour of Scotland and England in May and June of 1907. Anticipating demonstrations by Irish emigrants in the audiences, Yeats at first planned to omit the play from the program in Glasgow and Birmingham and present it only in Cambridge, Oxford and London. The Lord Chamberlain's reader's hesitation in granting an English license for the *Playboy* added to the company's nervousness and finally it was scheduled for Oxford and Cambridge only. Yeats's precautions, which included the reprinting of his speech at the Playboy debate and the publication of a new essay on the play as "Notes" in *The Arrow* on June 1, proved unnecessary. The Oxford performance on June 5 and the subsequent appearance in London were unqualified successes.

I NEED add but little to the argument raised by the production of "The Playboy" in Dublin, for my own statement, made in "The Arrow" at that time, is on sale in the theatre. The failure of the audience to understand this powerful and strange work has been the one serious failure of our movement, and it could not have happened but that the greater number of those who came to shout down the play were no regular part of our audience at all, but members of parties and societies whose main interests are political. We have been denounced with even greater violence than on the first production of the play for announcing that we should carry it to London. We cannot see that an attack, which we believe to have been founded on a misunderstanding of the nature of literature, should prevent us from selecting, as our custom is, whatever of our best comes within the compass of our players at the time, to show in some English theatres. Nearly all strong and strange writing is attacked on its appearance, and those who press it upon the world may not cease from pressing it, for their justification is its ultimate acceptance. Ireland is passing through a crisis in the life of the mind greater than any she has known since the rise of the Young Ireland party, and based upon a principle which sets many in opposition to the habits of thought and feeling come down from that party, for the seasons change, and need and occupation with them. Many are beginning to recognise the right of the individual mind to see the world in its own way, to cherish the thoughts which separate men from one another, and that are the creators of distinguished life, instead of those thoughts that had made one man like another if they could, and have but succeeded in setting hysteria and insincerity in place of confidence and self-possession.

To the Young Ireland writers, who have the ear of Ireland, though not its distracted mind, truth was historical and external and not a self-consistent personal vision,[1] and it is but according to ancient customs that the new truth should force its way amid riot and great anger.

The plays we bring to London are a selection from a considerable number which have been produced at the Abbey Theatre, and sometimes we have have to choose some particular one, not because it is the best, but because it suits our players or as many as can travel. I would myself sooner have been represented by "Deirdre" or "The King's Threshold," than by "The Shadowy Waters," which may not seem a play to any but the lovers of lyric poetry, or "On Baile's Strand," which is part of a cycle of plays on the life of the ancient hero Cuchulain. The training of verse speakers has become the most laborious part of our work, for a player may be excellent in all else and yet have all to learn in verse or be altogether unfitted for it. In the first state of our theatre it proved to be impossible, no matter how great the enthusiasm of individuals, to keep to work so arduous and prolonged players who had to earn their living in some workshop or office. Even yet we have only made a beginning, and with the exception of one or two speakers, cannot claim more than the rightness of our methods. Good speech of some kind has always, whatever the play, been our principal preoccupation—for only when there is musical, finely articulated, delicate, varied, deliberate speech, can style, whether the play be in verse, or, as are the greater number of ours, in dialect have any effect upon the fortunes of a play, and as St. Beuve has said, style is the only thing that is immortal in literature.[2] It is to set arbitrary limits to the office of the player, to grant it gesture and facial expression, but to deny it, as some do, a fine speaking of fine things, or to think that the stage has become

---

[1] In the introductory essay to *A Book of Irish Verse* (1895), entitled "Modern Irish Poetry", Yeats had invoked poetic "sincerity" in order to distinguish between the young men who were associated with Thomas Davis and *The Nation* in the 1840s—the Young Irelanders—and less well-known poets—principally Samuel Ferguson and William Allingham—whose example he valued more. The poets of "Young Ireland", he wrote, "were full of earnestness, but never understood that though a poet may govern his life by his enthusiasms, he must, when he sits down at his desk, but use them as the potter the clay. Their thoughts were a little insincere, because they lived in the half illusions of their admirable ideals; and their rhythms not seldom mechanical because their purpose was served when they had satisfied the dull ears of the common man. . . . No man was more sincere, no man had a less mechanical mind than Thomas Davis, and yet he is often a little insincere and mechanical in his verse." (pp. xiv–xv)

[2] While this statement has not been found in Saint-Beuve, Alexander Smith (1830–1867) makes the following observation in the second chapter, "On the Writing of Essays", of his *Dreamthorp*: "And style, after all, rather than thought, is the immortal thing in literature" (London, 1866, p. 43).

more really the stage, more consistent with itself, in forgetting the feeling for fine oratory that made possible the rogues and clowns of Ben Jonson and the Princes of Corneille and of Shakespeare.

W. B. Yeats

# A Corinthian Club Dinner

Towards the end of 1907, Yeats found himself again at odds with D. P. Moran, the Nationalist editor of *The Leader*. The Corinthian Club gave a dinner at the Gresham Hotel on September 14 in honor of Lady Aberdeen (1857–1939), the wife of the Lord Lieutenant of Ireland and Yeats's participation, along with Aberdeen and the Provost of Trinity College, in the evening's toasts was the instigation for Moran's heavily ironic editorial note in *The Leader* for November 23. "'Cathleen,' we suppose, is all right in theory; but then a dinner is a dinner even to a poet. . . . The toast of 'the King,' which in this country means for the most part 'to hell with the Irish nation,' was drunk [and] Mr. Yeats was amongst the speakers at this feed. . . ." While Yeats's toast, as reported in the Dublin *Daily Express* the following day, was a mild plea for the help of "cultured and educated people in Ireland" in his attempt to renew in the nation's mind "the noble images of its past and the noble images of its present", Moran's real target was the Abbey Theatre, "the theatre that was once a morgue" and the scene of "the 'Playboy' atrocity". The Theatre's practice of offering "Professional" Friday matinees where visiting English companies were invited to perform was to Moran a betrayal of Yeats's "hoity-toity talk about the mere 'Commercial Theatre'" and thus of national dramatic art.

Moran was mollified by a letter from Yeats which appeared in *The Leader* for November 30, along with an editorial in which Moran discussed the whole question of "the attitude Ireland ought to adopt before the institution, the figment of the imagination, or whatever one like to call it, known by the phrase 'The King'". Although he chided Yeats for his innocence in expecting a "Bohemian gathering", Moran did not renew his attack on the Abbey and, in the issue for December 7, he concluded this skirmish by printing a letter signed "Idolator" which suggested that during Yeats's enumeration of Irish causes—among them a Catholic University which the *Express* report did not mention—the dinner's chairman, Sir Charles Cameron (1841–1924), an Irish newspaper owner, "spent the most agonizing eight minutes of his life . . . though many of the guests were annoyed and a few delighted."

Abbey Theatre,
Nov. 21[1]

DEAR SIR,

I see in your issue of to-day a series of paragraphs beginning "The author of Cathleen Ni Houlihan, we see, was at a God save the King dinner one night last week". The dinner you refer to was given in honour of Lady Aberdeen by the Corinthian Club, and my presence there was accident.

I met Sir Charles Cameron for the first time at a theatrical supper party; he asked me to dine with him at the Corinthian Club a few days later, and to reply to the toast of the guests, but did not mention who they were. I knew nothing of the Corinthian Club, except from a report in the papers of a luncheon party which it had given for Mr. Tree.[2] I expected to find a Bohemian gathering of perhaps twenty or thirty people. I found two or three hundred, and was already sitting in my place when I heard that Lord and Lady Aberdeen were expected. That I have met Viceroyalty at a public dinner is the fault, doubtless unintentional, of Sir Charles Cameron. If it should happen again it will be my fault.

I have long ceased to be an active politician, but that makes me the more anxious to follow with all loyalty the general principles defined by Mr. Parnell and never renounced by any Nationalist party. He directed Ireland on the occasion of a Royal visit in 1885 or 1886 to pay no official honour to any representative of English rule until a sufficient National independence had made possible a new treaty. I could have slipped away and so avoided attack, or won a little vain glory by making some protest, but I chose rather to follow those old rules of courtesy in which, as Balzac has said, we are all Conservatives.

Yours sincerely,
W. B. Yeats

---

[1] Yeats evidently dated his letter incorrectly, since the notice to which he responds did not appear until November 23.

[2] Herbert Beerbohm Tree (1853–1917), the famous actor-manager, had recently appeared in Dublin and was among several "stars" of the "Commercial Theatre" Moran listed in his original editorial note as Yeats's imported patronizers of Irish drama.

# W. Fay's Resignation

On January 10, 1908, W.G. and Frank Fay resigned from the Abbey Theatre after nearly six years of collaboration with Yeats and Lady Gregory. The causes of their departure were the results of differences within the company of years' duration and were not being understood, evidently, by any of the principals at the time. Since 1905, Yeats had been moderating between the demands of Miss Annie E. F. Horniman (1860–1937), the Abbey's bene-factress, that the Fays be replaced and the commitment, still strong with Lady Gregory and to a lesser degree with Synge, that had been made to W. G. Fay in 1902. Yeats admired Fay both as a producer of some kinds of Irish drama and as a comic actor. But, while he resisted Miss Horniman's demands, he seems to have favored some reduction of Fay's responsibilities, as he noted in a letter to Synge in August, 1907. "You know of old that I don't believe that Fay is a very competent man to run a theatre, that in fact I think him particularly unfitted for it . . ." (Greene and Stephens, *J. M. Synge*, New York, 1961, p. 274).

A new manager of Miss Horniman's choosing, Ben Iden Payne (b. 1881), was installed in May, 1907, by dint of elaborate diplomacy involving Fay's being paid more while his responsibility was limited to the production of Gaelic or "peasant" plays. When Payne resigned, after five inconclusive months, Fay drafted a five-point proposal under which he would resume full management. The Abbey directors, Yeats, Synge and Lady Gregory, met on December 4 and agreed to reject the proposal, the chief provision of which was the termination of the players' contracts with the Theatre and their reengagement under contract to Fay. The directors' decision was not imme-diately announced and plans were made to hear the players' views on the matter. Apparently Yeats did not suspect that Fay would resign, since a long memorandum he wrote at this time, while it restated Miss Horniman's hopes for the evolution of a more varied and international range of drama, insisted that "William Fay must be freed from all work except his artistic work so that the comedies may be as fine as possible" (quoted in Gerard Fay, *The Abbey Theatre*, pp. 130–1).

News of the resignation spread quickly and speculations were soon every-where as to the reasons. The recent public controversy over *The Playboy of the Western World*, in regard to which the directors, the management and the players had been in almost total agreement, was often cited, but another charge, that the directors were suppressing good plays, was also current. Yeats responded to this charge in his letter to *The Dublin Evening Mail* for January 14. A letter, signed "W.", had appeared in the issue for January 13 and Yeats undertook to answer it both by publication of a paragraph in praise of Fay which he had written for *Samhain* and by challenging the dissidents to name a worthy play the Abbey had turned down. While nothing seems to have come of his challenge, Yeats did not allay the charge. In his diary entry for January 17, Joseph Holloway thought it "of interest to jot down the . . . list of authors amongst others whose plays have been rejected . . ." (*Joseph Holloway's Abbey Theatre*, p. 99) and Frank Fay, although he and his brother had no comment for the *Mail*'s interviewer at this time, repeated the charge in interviews in England and America (see p. 363 below).

## TO THE EDITOR OF THE *EVENING MAIL*

SIR,

I enclose a paragraph written for a forthcoming number of "Samhain."[1] It was written before I saw your article of last night, in which you describe the "internal dissensions," "serious rupture," etc., in the Abbey Theatre. I send it to you with the consent of Mr. William Fay, and it is sufficient to show the spirit in which we part. I see no necessity to discuss in public details of organisation and re-organisation, for our plays concern the public, the rest ourselves. You make one statement, however, which challenges the justice of our administration in the selection of plays, and that needs an answer. You state that we have not given "a fair field and no favour," and imply that we have suppressed excellent plays in favour of our own work or of our friends' work. I challenge you to appoint three persons chosen from the literary men of the city, who shall invite rejected dramatists to send them their plays. If they find amongst the plays rejected by the Abbey Theatre during the last twelve months any play which they consider worthy of production we will produce it for three nights at the Abbey Theatre and allow the public to judge.

Yours sincerely,

W. B. Yeats

Abbey Theatre, Dublin
January 14, 1908

# The Abbey Theatre

Yeats's response to the criticisms of "W" provoked several new critics, most of them using only their initials, to join in the discussion of the Fays' departure. Yeats pressed his "challenge" in a letter to *The Dublin Evening Mail* for January 16, 1908, and "W" kept the quarrel alive by responding, in the same

[1] Although Yeats sent his note to several papers, there were no issues of *Samhain* until November, 1908, when he reprinted it, with amplification. (See p. 374 below.)

issue, to two other correspondents. In this letter, he renewed his charge that the Abbey's directors, "not content with endeavouring to force an objectionable play down the throats of an indignant public by means of the baton . . . persisted in performing what even the most cultured section of playgoers had no desire for, and went to excessive pains to shelve what it approved". This "challenge", which is initiated on page 358, seems to have come to nothing.

### TO THE EDITOR OF THE *EVENING MAIL*

SIR,

I have asked Dr. Sigerson,[1] President of the National Literary Society, if he will ask his Society to make the necessary arrangements for the judgment of plays, and to bring the matter to the knowledge of the authors concerned. It is essential from the point of view of the Abbey Theatre that some responsible newspaper association should appoint the judges or give them authority. The production of a play means several weeks of rehearsal, and costs a good deal of money, and the contest would be useless from our point of view if the public did not believe in its reality. They will only do that if the details are arranged by some body like the National Literary Society. My challenge was given to the "Mail," but as it will not take the matter up, I am glad to find that Dr. Sigerson is ready to do so, and I know that if your correspondent would go to see him, Dr. Sigerson will consider his suggestions. I am satisfied with the judges your correspondent has suggested, but one or more of them may refuse to act, and another judge or judges have to be chosen. The terms of the challenge as given by me and accepted by your correspondent are: That we will produce for three nights in the Abbey Theatre any play rejected by us during the last twelve months, and considered worthy of production by any three Dublin men of letters who, however, must be properly appointed for the purpose.

Yours truly,

W. B. Yeats

P. S. I have just seen Maunsell and Co., and they undertake to publish the play selected by the judges, at the time of its performance. This will secure an appeal to an even larger public than could performance.

W. B. Y.

---

[1] Dr. George Sigerson (1838–1925) was Professor of Botany and Zoology at University College, Dublin. He also made translations and collections of Irish poetry, beginning with *The Poets and Poetry of Munster* in 1860. He had been the first president of the National Literary Society, in 1892, and his daughter, the poet Dora Sigerson, was married to Yeats's friend Clement Shorter. In *The Trembling of the Veil*, Yeats remembered Dr. Sigerson as "learned, artificial, unscholarly, a typical provincial celebrity, but a friendly man" (*Autobiography*, p. 135).

# A Correction

The contributions by Yeats and his antagonist, "W", to the January 17, 1908, issue of *The Dublin Evening Mail* were a perfect rhetorical contrast. Yeats busied himself with correcting the text of his proposal of Sigerson or some "responsible" newspaper or association as judge in his "contest", apparently to avoid seeming to specify the Irish Newspaper Society, a group of publishers which had been formed in 1907. "W" denounced Yeats's fickleness, asserting that the whole question of rejected plays had been brought up by Yeats "in his shuffling way" to avoid discussion of the gradual weakening of the Abbey through the defection of such important members as the Fays. Declaring his "ruggedly independent spirit" irked by Yeats's "insatiable desire for domination", "W" withdrew from the fray, pointing out that "no self-respecting dramatist would re-submit his play on the off chance of having its value completely destroyed by the inefficiencies of a number of raw amateurs", and leaving "the Mutual admiration (alas the National Literary Theatre) Society to run headlong on that rapid dissolution which will now righteously be its due".

### TO THE EDITOR OF THE *EVENING MAIL*

SIR,

There is a misprint in my letter of to-day. I wrote: "It is essential from the point of view of the Abbey Theatre that some responsible newspaper or association should appoint the judges," etc. The "or" has fallen out, and I have been made to write "Newspaper Association," which seriously alters the meaning of my letter.

Yours truly,<br>W. B. Yeats

United Arts Club,
Lincoln Place, Dublin

# The Abbey Theatre

*THE DUBLIN EVENING MAIL*, JANUARY 18, 1908

### TO THE EDITOR OF THE *EVENING MAIL*

SIR,

I have no desire to slake my "insatiable thirst for domination" upon your correspondent's "ruggedly independent spirit," and should he change his mind again, and carry his suggestions to Dr. Sigerson, he will find that so far from appointing my own judges, I will object to no one and suggest no one. Should he, upon the other hand, prefer, to the National Literary Society, some other association of like authority, it is all one to me, so long as I hear from him, or it, in the next few days. In any case I hope he will bring his "ruggedly independent spirit" to the Abbey Theatre, when it re-opens some three weeks hence with new plays by new writers. We have confidence in our company, and know that whatever has been lost they have still humour, charm, and sincerity.

Yours truly,

W. B. Yeats

Abbey Theatre, Dublin
18th January, 1908

# Mr. W. B. Yeats and "The Piper"

On February 13, 1908, the Abbey Theatre presented *The Piper*, a fantasy sub-titled "An Unended Argument in One Act", by Norreys Connell (Conal O'Riordan) (1874–1948) who was one of the "new writers" Yeats had promised for the 1908 season and who later became the Abbey's stage manager. Partly because of its strangeness and partly because of frequent mild blasphemies in the dialogue, the play, a tale in which three Irishmen squabble over an English prisoner during the 1798 insurrection until they are shot, was hissed and booed. After the second performance, on February 14, Joseph Holloway noted that "*The Piper* has proved another *Playboy of the Western World*", and added that "Yeats told me the author meant *The Piper* for a satire on Parnell. How or why I could not tell" (*Joseph Holloway's Abbey Theatre*, pp. 103–4). Yeats explained the play to the audiences at both per-formances the next day and on February 17 the Dublin *Daily Express*, among other papers, carried an account of his talk.

BOTH at the matinee and the evening performances at the Abbey Theatre on Saturday Mr. W. B. Yeats came before the curtain and made a speech to the audience, in which he explained the point of view which, he suggested, should be adopted in regard to Mr. Norreys Connell's play, "The Piper," the production of which on Friday night had given rise to noisy expressions of disapproval from some parts of the house. "Some years ago," said Mr. Yeats, "when I was in Paris I went to a little intellectual theatre where a play was being performed which aroused some heated feelings, and I remember someone came in front of the curtain before the play and told the audience what it meant to him, and what the meaning of the play was for the management of the theatre. So, therefore, you will not think that I am insulting your intelligence by appearing to talk to you about Mr. O'Connell's play. [sic] I have no right to tell you what it is Mr. Connell had in his mind when he wrote the play—his explanation, his attitude of mind—it is for you to judge"—(A Voice—"It is judged already," and interruption). "I have every right to tell you what the play meant to me when I read it. It seemed to me a fine play to set before the people of this country"—(A Voice—"Fudge," and hear, hear). "I think when you have heard me and you have heard the play you will be in a better position to judge" (loud applause). "The play meant to me a satire on those dreadful years of the Parnellite split—those years of endless talk, of endless rhetoric, and drivelling folly—years which were taken out of the history of this nation and made nothing of, because of the folly of this nation. It meant to me something else. My imagination went back to the rebellion of Robert Emmett—to that heroic figure, the folly that surrounded him, the slackness that was as bad as treachery. I suppose that is also satirised in this play. We are all agreed the thing I speak of is worthy of satire— is worthy of the most bitter satire. There is not a man in this audience who does not think that a National Theatre is right in satirising such endless, useless talk through which the life-blood of the nation is wasting away. There is only one possible difference between us— whether that has been done in this play or not. That is for you to judge. But I say more than that. In Mr. Connell's play I see the generous impulses, the underlying heroism, which is in the midst of all that folly. I see the ceaseless heroic aspirations of the Irish people imaged in the character of the Piper. I see a figure which had deeply impressed my boyhood in the character of Black Mike. I see in that character Charles Stewart Parnell. I see that angry, heroic man once again as I saw him in my boyhood face to face with Irish futility. I see in the whole play simply a satire on all that dreadful epoch. The day has not come when the men of Dublin do not desire to see that satirised on the stage; nor do I think the play less worthy of their attention because the Englishman is acting nobly, unaware of the heroism which, through good or evil fortune, he has overcome" (applause).

The play then proceeded, and was given a respectful hearing, although there were some occasional expressions of disapproval. At its conclusion there was a great outburst of applause, and loud cries of "Author." Mr. Connell came before the curtain and bowed his acknowledgements.[1]

# Mr. W. Fay and the Abbey Theatre

Shortly after leaving the Abbey Theatre, W. G. Fay, along with his brother and wife, the actress Brigit O'Dempsey, were contracted by Charles Frohman (1840–1915), the American impresario, to appear in London. Almost immediately, they were sent instead to New York, where they made their American debut in Yeats's *The Pot of Broth* on February 18, 1908. The American tour was only marginally successful but, as W. G. Fay recalled, "it was some consolation that we got great space in the Chicago newspapers . . ." (W. G. Fay and Catherine Carswell, *The Fays of the Abbey Theatre*, London, 1935, p. 246). An interview with Fay by Burns Mantle (1873–1948) in the *Chicago Sunday Tribune* for May 10 renewed the charges against the directors of the Abbey, and quotation of this interview in *The Dublin Evening Mail* for May 20, 1908, provoked Yeats's letter to the paper on May 21. In the *Tribune* interview, Fay was described as "the inspiration, and, until recently, the life of the Irish National Theatre movement in Dublin" and he was quoted repeating the familiar charge that Yeats, Synge, and Lady Gregory had been "so near sighted as to be almost blind" in recognizing promising work by younger playwrights. After quoting his discussion with Fay of the controversy over "the piece by Boyle called 'The Playboy of the Western World [*sic*]'", Mantle offered a summation of Fay's break with the Abbey: "When Mr. Fay reached the conclusion that he could no longer work to advantage with the National Theatre organization in Dublin—with poets to the right of him choosing the plays, literati to the left of him running the stage, geniuses before him, behind him, and all about him with daily hints on the saving of Ireland's drama—he folded his traps, took his wife and his brother with him, and traveled away to London."

[1] In his speech Connell took the blame on himself as "the author who has so offended you tonight" (*Joseph Holloway's Abbey Theatre*, p. 104), thanking the audience for its treatment of the players. While Yeats, too, expressed private misgivings about the play, he characteristically arranged for three more performances the following week.

TO THE EDITOR OF THE *EVENING MAIL*

SIR—I see a quotation in to-night's "Mail" from the "Chicago Sunday Tribune," which attributes to Mr. William Fay the statement that he left the Abbey Theatre because the directors had discouraged the work of young writers. I hope Mr. William Fay said nothing of the kind, for it is entirely untrue. We have only twice, as far as we can remember, refused plays recommended by Mr. Fay—one some years ago, because it had no dramatic merit whatever, and another about a year ago, because its promise, though considerable, did not justify its subject, which would have offended many, a discussion between a priest with an immoral past and a country girl who had left her home for an immoral life in the Dublin streets. Mr. Fay's reason for leaving us was precise and entirely different. Having quarrelled with the company on tour, he wrote to us that he would resign if we did not dismiss the company, and tell its members to re-engage personally with him. Our refusal was the reason of his resignation.[1]—

Yours sincerely,

W. B. Yeats

Abbey Theatre, May 21st, 1908.

# British Association Visit to the Abbey Theatre

On September 4, 1908, the Abbey presented a matinee program for the British Association for the Advancement of Science, which met that year in Dublin. Yeats, whose play *The Hour-Glass* was part of the program, addressed the delegates both in a program note, "The Abbey Theatre", and in a speech on "The Abbey Theatre—Its Aims and Works". The note is largely retrospective, but the text of the address, issued as a special program four days later, gives an early identification of his dramatic theory with the art of Japan. And the declaration that "All the highest business of man is to do valiantly in some fight or other" shows his continuing awe of the poet speaking "with such airs / That one believed he had a sword upstairs" (*Variorum*

---

[1] Yeats gives the essentials of Fay's proposal here. But Fay clearly intended for the players to be contracted to him as stage manager, rather than to him personally, in order to restore his control of the company. A letter, signed by Sara Allgood, Arthur Sinclair, J. M. Kerrigan and Maire O'Neill, accompanied Yeats's letter to the *Mail*. The players declared their agreement that "acceptance of the proposals of Mr. W. G. Fay by the directors would have led to the dissolution of the company" and that they "certainly would not have rejoined under Mr. Fay's proposed conditions".

*Poems*, p. 267), despite the poem rejecting the image, written a few weeks earlier.

## THE ABBEY THEATRE

THE movement out of which the Abbey Theatre and the Abbey Theatre Company were born began in 1898. A few Irish writers, among whom were Lady Gregory and myself, wrote or collected a certain number of Irish plays, and brought over English actors to play them. There was not at that time any Irish Company, but in 1901 performances were given by a little company of Irish amateurs, who did what amateurs seldom do—worked desperately. They had only their evenings for rehearsals; and at first playwrights and players formed a single body, deciding on everything together, and paying the expenses amongst them. Meanwhile new playwrights had joined us, one of these, J. M. Synge, has since become a very well-known dramatist. We gave our plays in various Dublin lecture halls, where the level floor of the auditorium made it difficult to see the stage, and as neither player nor playwright received any money, considered ourselves very wealthy. In 1904 Miss Horniman, who had seen us playing in London, where critics told us that we had found out a new, simple and sincere art of the stage, rebuilt for us the Abbey Theatre, and gave us the free use of it; and a little later, finding that the double work was becoming too hard for our principal players, gave us a small annual subsidy.[1]

We are the first subsidized theatre in any English-speaking country, the only theatre that is free for a certain number of years to play what it thinks worth playing, and to whistle at the timid. We make a concession now and then, but grant to ourselves for a compensation joyous defiance a little later on; and if we are not popular we can at any rate say that what support we have is from the shilling and sixpenny seats, and not from a coterie in the stalls. The stalls are generally empty, but again and again we have not sixpenny seats for all that come and I think that in spite of some complaints, which are not lacking in energy, our following likes us the better because we know our own mind. When we are anxious for a change, and would see the dearer seats as full as the cheap ones we go to the most intellectual places, where dramatic literature is a serious study, and fill a house in London, Oxford and Cambridge.[2] Our Patent, for as the laws in Ireland are frequently old-fashioned, we come

---

[1] Miss Horniman's subsidy for players' salaries was established at £600, but she usually paid out more than this annually between 1905 and 1910, when it was withdrawn.

[2] The Abbey company performed in London, Oxford and Cambridge in November, 1905, and again in June, 1907.

under the patent system, confines us to plays by Irishmen or upon Irish subjects, or to foreign masterpieces (and among these we may not include anything English). This limitation was put in at the request of the other theatres that we might not be their rival, the counsel for one of them being particularly anxious to keep us from playing Goldsmith and Sheridan, who were, he believed, Englishmen. It does not inconvenience us, however, for we believe that good art, whether in acting, play-writing, or anything else, arises from the shock of new subject-matter. We are trying to put upon the stage in playing as in playwriting the life of this country, not a slavish copy of it as in a photograph, but a joyous, extravagant, imaginative image as in an impressionist painting.

In Japan there are some who believe very erroneously that we are a great success, and even making money, and one of their distinguished critics uses our example to urge upon his countrymen the support of their native drama; and the Transvaal has begun to pirate us.[3]

## W. B. YEATS' SPEECH AT THE MATINEE OF THE BRITISH ASSOCIATION FRIDAY, SEPTEMBER 4TH, 1908

To some of you, who may perhaps have heard of the Abbey Theatre for the first time, it is necessary that I should tell a little how it all came about.

Some years ago a group of Irish writers, among whom were Lady Gregory and myself, noticing that the Irish people cared more for oratory than for reading (for a nation only comes slowly to the reading habit) resolved to express ourselves through a Theatre. At first we brought over English Actors, because there was no Irish Company in existence; but there was always something incongruous between Irish words and an English voice and accent. Presently with the help of a very able actor, who has lately left us, an electric light fitter by occupation, we got together a group of young men and young women here in Dublin, who were prepared to give their entire leisure to the creation of an Irish Theatre.[4] They worked for their living during the day, and

---

[3] The editors have been unable to discover the Transvaal pirates. The Japanese critic is probably Hōgetsu Shimamura (1871–1918), who had written an evaluation of Yeats's influence on the Irish revival in *The Tokyo Daily News* in March, 1906.

[4] Either rhetorical purposes or their recent differences (see p. 357 above) cause Yeats to portray W. G. Fay somewhat unfairly. The theatre had been the first interest of Fay and his brother since childhood, according to his autobiography, *The Fays of the Abbey Theatre* (London, 1935). He became an electrician, after stints as a scene builder and a theatrical advance man because his brother "urged electricity was a new motive power that was sure to be used more and more. . . . I was not making my fortune as an actor and I wanted to have some means of living that would leave me free to devote more time to the theatre" (p. 99).

for their art during the evening. At first we played in little inconvenient halls, but after a few years a generous friend gave us the use of this Theatre, and, finding that our people were becoming overworked, gave us enough money to free them from their shops and offices. In this way, quite apart from the traditions of the ordinary Theatre, we had built up an art of acting which is perhaps peculiar to ourselves; our players, instead of specialising, as most other actors do to represent the life of the drawingroom, which is the same all over the world, have concentrated themselves upon the representation of what is most characteristic in one nation. I think I can say with perfect sincerity that, until our people learnt their business, what is most characteristic in Irish life had never been set upon the stage at all. I doubt if the Irish accent had ever been accurately spoken there. It does not seem to us any drawback that we have limited ourselves, with the exception of a few foreign masterpieces, to the expression of the life of our own country. Art has, I believe, always gained in intensity by limitation, and there are plenty of other Theatres for the other things. In rehearsing our Plays we have tried to give the words great importance; to make speech, whether it be the beautiful and rhythmical delivery of verse, or the accurate speaking of a rhythmical dialect, our supreme end, and almost all our play-wrights in the same way give to the vividness and pictur-esqueness of their style a principal consideration. We believe words more important than gesture, that voice is the principal power an actor possesses; and that nothing may distract from the actor, and what he says, we have greatly simplified scenery. When we wish to give a remote poetical effect we throw away realism altogether, and are con-tent with suggestion; this is the idea of the Japanese in their dramatic art; they believe that artificial objects, the interior let us say of some modern house, should be perfectly copied, because a perfect copy is possible; but that when you get to sea and sky you should only suggest, and when they wish to suggest a sea they are content to put before you merely a pattern of waves. Good realistic scenery is merely bad land-scape painting, an attempt to do something which can only be done properly in an easel painting; but if you are content to decorate the stage, to suggest, you create something which is peculiar to the stage, for you put before your audience a scene that only wakes into life when the actors move in front of it. The "Hourglass" was our first experi-ment of this kind and our simplest; but I think the effect of the purple dresses against the green may have interested you. This play, by the by, is one of our very earliest, and I notice, somewhat to my alarm, that it means one thing to myself, and often quite a different thing to my audience. To me it is a parable of the conscious and the sub-conscious life, an exposition of ideas similar to those in Ernest Myers [*sic*] great book; but the other day it converted a music hall singer, and kept him going to Mass for six weeks, after which he relapsed, and was much worse than before.[5]

But we are not always so orthodox. We have been denounced at one time or another by every party in Ireland. One of the plays which we give to-night, "The Rising of the Moon," has roused the enmity of two parties.[6] A daily paper described it as a slander upon the police, for it represented a policeman letting off a Fenian prisoner, whereas some nationalist friends of mine were equally indignant because they said it was an unpatriotic act to represent a policeman as capable of any virtue at all. How could the Dublin mob fight the police, I was asked, if it looked upon them as capable of any patriotic act, and, Are not morals more than literature? At another time we were offered support from what are called "the classes," and at a time we greatly needed it, if we would withdraw my own play, "Kathleen ni Houlihan." We have always refused to listen to any of these demands, for we claim always the entire independence of the artist from everything except the high traditions of his craft. And our trouble has not always come from Ireland.

Any of you who have heard of us at all will have heard how a year and a half ago some hundreds of police were called out to quell a riot over one of our plays. We brought that play to London, and a little while before we produced it there we received a letter from your Censor —(we have no official censor in Ireland)—saying that as the play, though harmless in itself, was likely to raise a riot, he was consulting the Home Office as to whether it should be forbidden. Now your English Censor is a very much worse person than our Irish censors are, for your man has got the police on his side. However, actors and authors consulted together, and after calculating ways and means and raising sufficient capital, we decided, if necessary, to give an illegal performance in London, and all go to prison. However, the Home Office had more sanity than your Censor, and we were allowed to give our play, which was taken very peaceably.[7]

---

[5] Yeats's reference should probably be to the pioneer in psychical research, F. W. H. Myers (1843–1901), and his famous *Human Personality and Its Survival of Bodily Death* (2 vols., 1903). This study of subliminal consciousness bears more closely on the subject of Yeats's *Hour-Glass*, the prose version of which was first produced in March, 1903, than anything by Myers's brother Ernest (1844–1921), a poet, translator and editor of Milton. In a "Preface" to the revised version of the play, in 1913, Yeats claimed he "began a revision of the words from the moment when the play converted a music hall singer and sent him to mass and confession" (*Variorum Plays*, p. 577).

[6] By most accounts, Lady Gregory's *The Rising of the Moon* was respectfully received when it was first produced on March 9, 1907.

[7] At the outset of the Abbey's tour in June, 1907, Yeats tried to avert a repetition of the Dublin disturbances over the *Playboy* by such means as his publication of "Notes" on the whole affair in *The Arrow* (see p. 353, above). None the less, George Redford, the Lord

That play has been our "Belfast Address";[8] for just as history has shown that you are not the peaceable people you look, we are not either. No matter what great question you take up, if you are in earnest about it, you come to the great issues that divide man from man. Everything is battle. All the highest business of man is to do valiantly in some fight or other, and often when one looks into it, battles that seem fought about the most different things change their appearance and become but one battle.

When I was coming up in the train the other day from Galway, I began thinking how unlike your work was to my work, and then suddenly it struck me that it was all the same.[9] A picture arose before my mind's eye: I saw Adam numbering the creatures of Eden; soft and terrible, foul and fair, they all went before him. That, I thought, is the man of science, naming and numbering, for our understanding, everything in the world. But then I thought, we writers, do we not also number and describe, though with a difference? You are chiefly busy with the exterior world, and we with the interior. Science understands that everything must be known in the world our eyes look at; there is nothing too obscure, too common, too vile, to be the subject of knowledge. When a man of science discovers a new species, or a new law, you do not ask the value of the law, or the value of the species before you do him honour; you leave all that to the judgment of the generations. It is your pride that in you the human race contemplates all things with so pure, so disinterested an eyesight that it forgets its own necessities and infirmities, all its hopes and fears, in the contemplation of truth for the sake of truth, reality for the sake of reality.

We, on the other hand, are Adams of a different Eden, a more terrible Eden perhaps, for we must name and number the passions and motives

---

Chamberlain's Examiner of Plays, licensed the production only after Pegeen Mike's allusion in Act I to the "looséd kharki cut-throats" was struck out. Yeats omits mention here of his removal of the play from the program in Glasgow and Birmingham, at the Lord Chamberlain's urging, because, as Yeats explained to Synge, there were "enough slum Irish in Birmingham to stir up a row" (quoted in Greene and Stephens, *J. M. Synge*, p. 269).

[8] Yeats refers to the speech given in Belfast on February 22, 1886, by Lord Randolph Churchill (1849–1895) immediately following his famous declaration at Larne that "Ulster will fight, and Ulster will be right". While his analogy between the performance of the *Playboy* in London and Churchill's dramatic playing of "the Orange card" in Belfast is somewhat askew, Yeats's speech and Churchill's conclude in a similar mood, Yeats praising the sweet music of "the stroke of the sword" and Churchill paraphrasing Thomas Campbell:

> *The combat deepens; on, ye brave,*
> *Who rush to glory or the grave.*
> *Wave, Ulster—all thy banners wave,*
> *And charge with all thy chivalry.*

(Quoted in Winston S. Churchill, *Lord Randolph Churchill*, New York, 1906, vol. ii, p. 63.)

[9] The last part of this essay, beginning with this sentence, is reprinted in *Samhain* for 1908 (see *Explorations*, pp. 241–3).

of men. There, too, everything must be known, everything understood, everything expressed; there, also, there is nothing common, nothing unclean; every motive must be followed through all the obscure mystery of its logic. Mankind must be seen and understood in every possible circumstance, in every conceivable situation. There is no laughter too bitter, no irony too harsh for utterance, no passion too terrible to be set before the minds of men. The Greeks knew that. Only in this way can mankind be understood, only when we have put ourselves in all the possible positions of life, from the most miserable to those that are so lofty that we can only speak of them in symbols and in mysteries, will entire wisdom be possible. All wise government, depends upon this knowledge not less than upon that other knowledge which is your business rather than ours; and we and you alike rejoice in battle, finding the sweetest of all music to be the stroke of the sword.

# Events

Despite the uncertainty and confusion at the end of 1907, of which the departure of the Fays was but one indication, 1908 was a year with which Yeats could be pleased as he reviewed its "Events" in the November issue of *Samhain.* The eight volumes of his *Collected Works in Verse and Prose* appeared between September and December and his career as a dramatist had been advanced by the appearance of Mrs. Patrick Campbell (1865–1940) in the title role of his *Deirdre,* on November 9. On November 15 he wrote excitedly to John Quinn that Mrs. Campbell had acquired the English and American rights to the play for the next five years and that he felt a turning point had been reached. "There has not been one hostile voice here and I am now accepted as a dramatist in Dublin. Mrs. Campbell was magnificent" (*Letters,* p. 512). The Abbey had done well, drawing an audience that almost made its subsidy from Miss Horniman unnecessary, and even Joseph Holloway, who had worried on January 13 that the theater might "come smash over the present crisis", ended the year in rapt admiration of *Deirdre.* On November 10, he attended the supper for Mrs. Campbell at the Gresham Hotel, noting that Yeats began his remarks "by saying that for once in his life he had nothing to say, and then went on to say it at some length" (*Joseph Holloway's Abbey Theatre,* pp. 99, 122).

THERE has been no *Samhain* for a couple of years, principally because an occasional publication, called *The Arrow,* took its place for a time.

Some twelve months ago Mrs. Patrick Campbell was so well pleased by some performances of our Company that she offered to come and play with it in my *Deirdre*; coming, I need hardly say, for the love of our people's art, and bringing her service as a gift. She let me announce this from the stage, and afterwards announced it herself from the stage of the Gaiety in kind and gracious words. We all feel that this great actress who has played in the one play with Bernhardt, will confer upon us in November a supreme honour. When we and all our players are with the dead players of Henley's rhyme,[1] some historian of the Theatre, remembering her coming and giving more weight to the appreciation of a fellow artist than even to the words of fine critics, will understand that if our people were not good artists one of the three or four great actresses of Europe would never have come to where the oldest player is but twenty-six. To the sincere artist the applause of those who have won greatness in his own craft is often his first appreciation, and always the last that he forgets. When I had just published my first book, I met William Morris in Holborn Viaduct, and he began to praise it with the words, "That is my kind of poetry," and promised to write about it, and would have said I do not know how much more if he had not suddenly caught sight of one of those decorated lamp posts, and waving his umbrella at the post, raged at the Corporation. As the years pass I value those words of his not less but more, understanding, as I could not at that time, how much I learned from the daily spectacle of that great, laborious, joyous man.[2]

The *Freeman* of September 18th contained a leading article on the passing of the Gaiety Theatre and the Theatre Royal into the hands of a trust. After pointing out the way in which all such trusts lead in the long run to musical comedy, and this alone, and regretting what it thinks to be the errors of "the only independent theatre left to us," the article wound up with:—"The Abbey patent expires in 1910, so there is no time to lose, . . . would it one day be possible for the Corporation to take it over as a municipal theatre? Municipalisation is the method by which the Germans have successfully fought monopoly and saved their stage from decadence. But is dangerous even to mention such a thing in these days of punctilious auditors."

At the expiration of our patent our present arrangement with Miss Horniman will also have come to an end. We hope, however, before that day comes, to have made the theatre either self-supporting or nearly so, and to be able to hand it over to some management that will

---

[1] William Ernest Henley's (1849–1903) "Ballade of Dead Actors" was published in *A Book of Verse* (1888).

[2] On Yeats's friendship with William Morris, see p. 258 above. He recalls Morris's praise of *The Wanderings of Oisin* (1889) in "The Trembling of the Veil" (*Autobiography*, p. 98).

work it as a business, while keeping its artistic aim. We shall be able to hand over to that management a great mass of plays, and we shall have accustomed audiences and dramatists alike to the freedom necessary for vigorous literature. Whatever form of organization takes the place of the present, it is not likely to be subsidized, or at any rate subsidized to any large extent, and will, therefore, be much more in the hands of the public than we are. Before that time, however, all the plays which have caused disturbance with us will have been accepted as matters of course; the *Playboy* and the *Piper* will trouble their audiences no more than the *Well of the Saints*, at one time so much disliked, or the *Shadow of the Glen*, against which a newspaper once used all its resources.[3] We know that we have already created a taste for sincere and original drama and for sincere, quiet [*sic*] simple acting. Ireland possesses something which has come out of its own life, and the many failures of dramatic societies which have imitated our work without our discipline and our independence, show that it could not have been made in any other way. But when the new management comes we hope that we, the present Directors, may be able to return to our proper work without the ceaseless distraction of theatrical details.

Before the present Patent of our Theatre comes to an end we hope to visit America. We believe that the success of our players here and in England would repeat itself in America, and upon a larger scale. In fact it was a part of our original calculation when we set out to form an Irish stock company, that it would spend a certain portion of every year among the Irish in America. It has been lack of money that has prevented us going there, and kept us playing a greater number of months in Dublin than we had thought possible. A good deal of touring is desirable, for it is difficult with a company so small as ours to put on new plays at short enough intervals to hold a Dublin audience for nine or ten months in the year. If we were to do no worse than we already do during the most fortunate part of each Dublin season, for, say ten months in the year, we should be more than independent of subsidy. Some three months touring every year with the same amount of success we have had in London, and Oxford, Glasgow and Manchester, and somewhat better stalls in Dublin than we get at present, would pay expenses and allow for all necessary widening of activity.

Last spring the hoardings of New York showed placards announcing that The Irish National Theatre Company of Dublin was performing

---

[3] The controversies over Synge's *Playboy of the Western World* and *The Piper* are discussed on pp. 348, 361 above. See p. 306 for the attack by Arthur Griffiths's *United Irishman* on Synge's *In the Shadow of the Glen*.

there. A great many who had seen or had heard of our work in Ireland crowded to the theatre, and some of them have written to us of their disappointment, for the *Pot of Broth* and *The Rising of the Moon* were given, not by our whole company, but by three of our players who had left us, and by other players who, though they had played in a few of our performances, had been in America for many years. We allowed Mr. William Fay to take these plays to America, as his engagement with Mr. Frohman was conditional on his getting them, but it was on the understanding that Mr. Frohman was not to use the name of our Society. Not only was it used (at first with the alteration of a word) but a programme headed with the words "Mr. Frohman presents the Irish National Theatre Company of Dublin," was otherwise copied so accurately from our Dublin programme that the names of actors who never left the Abbey Theatre were set down as playing in New York. Everything was done by Mr. Frohman's agent through advertisements, interviews and portraits to identify the New York experiment with us, and after the programmes had been stopped in New York under threat of legal proceedings, and the plays had been withdrawn, "Mr. Frohman presented the Irish National Theatre Society" (not Company this time) in a play by Mr. William Boyle to the people of Chicago.[4] The speculation was a failure. The plays were produced on large stages and in large theatres, instead of the little theatres they are written for, and as curtain-raisers to some French farce that drew its own audience; and the section of the literary and the Irish public who had heard something about us expected our whole company and a selection of plays as representative as we send to London and Oxford and Cambridge. We had hoped to have gone to America this autumn, but this failure has delayed us.

Last January Mr. William Fay, his wife and brother, left us, but, great as their loss has been, their places have been taken by other players, and the general efficiency of the Company has not suffered. We have never produced so many plays in so short a time as we did last spring, nor had such good audiences as in August, September and October this year.

When Mr. Fay was leaving us I wrote this paragraph for a *Samhain*

---

[4] Shortly after their debut in America, the Fays were joined on tour by Dudley Digges, the former Abbey actor. On February 19, 1908, Frank Fay wrote to his friend W. J. Lawrence from New York, "We are described on the advertising bills as 'The Irish National Theatre Co. from Dublin' . . . and they have used Yeats's name to boom the thing, all I needn't say against my wishes, but one can't interfere" (quoted in Gerard Fay, *The Abbey Theatre*, p. 135). Charles Frohman, Fay's manager, altered the company's advertisements only after legal action on Yeats's behalf was threatened by John Quinn.

we had thought to bring out immediately, read it to him, and, with his approval, published it in certain papers at the time:[5]

"We are about to lose our principal actor. William Fay has had enough of it, and we don't wonder, and is going to some other country where his exquisite gift of comedy and his brain teeming with fancy will bring him an audience, fame, and a little money. He has worked with us now since 1902, when he formed his company 'to carry on the work of the Irish Literary Theatre,' and feels that he must leave to younger men the long laborious battle. We have his good wishes, and he will return to us if at all possible to play his old parts for some brief season, or seasons, and may possibly rejoin us for a London or an American tour. We believe that William Fay is right to go, and he will have our good will and good wishes with him, though we have lost in losing him the finest comedian of his kind upon the English-speaking stage."

*—Irish Times*, Jan. 5, 1908.

Last May a performance of *Measure for Measure* was given by the Elizabethan Stage Society at Stratford. Mr. Poël asked us to lend him Miss Sara Allgood to play the part of Isabella. I confess that she surprised me very much. I had not thought her capable of tragedy unless where, as in *Dervorgilla* and *Cathleen ni Houlihan*, she has a character element to help her, and was altogether astonished at a performance full of simplicity and power, where the elements were purely passionate.[6]

[5] Yeats's reprinting of this tribute (see p. 357 above) is probably a sincere attempt to pay respect to the Fays. It comes, however, after the threatened injunction against their calling their company the Irish National Theatre Company and after other unpleasantness. In March of 1908, Frank Fay had written from New York to W. A. Henderson, the Abbey's business manager, complaining about the fees being charged his company for plays by Yeats and Lady Gregory, "two snippets that have not been and never will be successes here. The magnanimous Yeats, who shed crocodile tears over our leaving, has evidently his eyes to business" (*Joseph Holloway's Abbey Theatre*, p. 108). And in a letter to W. J. Lawrence on April 10, Fay had copied the letter from Synge, acting as Secretary of the Irish National Theatre Society, which informed them that, at a meeting attended by him, Yeats and U. Wright, they had been suspended from membership. Moreover, Frank Fay's son, Gerard Fay, suggests in *The Abbey Theatre* that Yeats is insincere in the causes he attributes to W. G. Fay's resignation. "There had never been a question of Willie Fay's wanting to leave to earn more money. He had only a few days before the Directors' meeting pointed out that for his latest contract he accepted less salary than before. As he was well under 40 and a demon for work the suggestion that he wanted to leave the battle to younger men was meaningless . . . the 'Samhain' paragraph contained such inaccuracies that it is hard to see why Willie Fay agreed to its publication" (p. 133).

[6] Sara Allgood (1883–1950) had joined the Irish National Theatre Society in 1903 and was becoming recognized as the Abbey's leading actress. On April 11, 1908, she appeared in a production of *Measure for Measure*, under the direction of the innovative founder of the Elizabethan Stage Society, William Poel (1852–1934). This production, at the Gaiety Theatre, Manchester, was sponsored by Miss Horniman.

On October 21, 1907, Sara Allgood had appeared in the title role of Lady Gregory's *Dervorgilla* and when she appeared again in this play, in May, 1908, Joseph Holloway re-

One of our hopes for the Abbey Theatre was that it would encourage dramatic enterprise apart from our own company. Rivalry should be a help in matters of art, for every good work increases the public interest in all similar work. This hope has only been fulfilled by the two visits of the Ulster Literary Theatre, which have given us a very great pleasure. I was away at the time of their last visit, but I remember vividly in the performance of a year ago the absence of the ordinary conventions, the novelty of movement and intonation.[7] I saw a play of Cockney life the other day. The actors were incomparably more experienced, the playwright was one of the new school who go directly to life, and one felt that the players were conscientious enough to do their best to go to life also. But I felt that though there was observation in detail, there was in every case a traditional representation in the player's mind. He hung his observation about some old type as a dressmaker hangs a new dress upon the *Mannequin d'Osier* that is in every dressmaker's room. I believe, furthermore, that these Ulster players, like ourselves, are doing something to bring to an end the charlatanism of International acting. I saw a while ago a performance of *The Corsican Brothers*, which, but for its Corsican peasantry, had been excellent.[8] The Brothers themselves, essentially traditional types of romance, were played with sincerity, but when the other Corsicans began to quarrel, I went straight back to the days when my uncles and aunts helped me to dress up in old tablecloths. When we have a sincere dramatic art there will be in every country actors who have made a study of the characteristics of its different classes. This will make "adaptions from the French," let us say, more difficult, but not more than the translation of a fine poem, which somebody says is impossible. You can re-create it, making an English poem of a French or a German, and in the same way it will be necessary to re-create drama as we do when we play *Le Medecin Malgre Lui* in "Kiltartanese."[9] The inaccuracy of detail, the persistence of conventional types, has arisen from the same causes, which have destroyed in modern drama eloquence, poetry, beauty, and all the reveries of widsom, and given us in their place a more or less logical mechanism.

---

corded that "The reception accorded Sara Allgood after the fall of the curtains . . . was quite embarrassing to the young artist. . . . Her acting was always impressive and on occasion extremely beautiful" (*Joseph Holloway's Abbey Theatre*, p. 112). Miss Allgood left the Abbey in 1913 for a long and distinguished career in England and America.

[7] Yeats attended a performance of the Ulster Literary Theatre on March 30, 1907, at which the major production was *The Turn of the Road* by Rutherford Mayne [Samuel Waddell] (b. 1878), who played the lead and who was later to write for the Abbey Theatre.

[8] Dion Boucicault (Dionysius Bourcicault) (1820?–1890), the Irish actor and author, adapted *The Corsican Brothers* from the French in 1848.

[9] The Abbey Theatre first produced Lady Gregory's translation of Molière's *Le Médecin malgré lui* on April 16, 1906.

When I saw the Ulster players, upon the other hand, it was in their mechanism that their playwrights failed. It was in their delight in the details of life that they interested one. I hear, however, that their plays upon their last visit showed much more unity. In any case it is only a matter of time, where one finds so much sincere observation, for the rest to follow.

The Ulster players are the only dramatic society, apart from our own, which is doing serious artistic work. Two other performances were lamentable; that of the Independent Theatre Society showed little sign of work or purpose. One or two of the players had a gift for acting, and working upon new material among hard workers might have struck out something new and forcible. But the performance as a whole made me wonder why so much trouble was taken to put on something not finer at its finest moments and much worse at every other moment than a third-rate touring company. The Theatre of Ireland made me indignant, because although the playwrights had found more of themselves than Count Markiewicz struggling with the difficulties of a strange language and strange circumstance, there was even less evidence of work and purpose.¹⁰ Such adventures can do nothing but injury to the drama in Ireland. They all show talent here and there, for Ireland has talent in plenty, but it is brought to nothing by lack of work and lack of subordination to a single aim. Though I used to speak with the greatest freedom of the performances given by the Gaelic League, I have not hitherto touched upon the work of these societies, and would not now, but for my real pleasure in the Ulster Theatre. One feels that in a country like this, where there is so little criticism with any special knowledge behind it, it is a wrong to the few fine workers to omit anything that may help to separate them from the triflers. I have a right to speak, for I

¹⁰ While Yeats's criticisms of these productions are supported by contemporary records, considerable personal differences also lie beneath them. The Theatre of Ireland had been founded in 1908. Its president was Yeats's one-time collaborator Edward Martyn and its players and writers were also, largely, defectors from the Abbey. Among its directors was Padraic Colum (1881–1972), who had sided with Maire Nic Shiubhlaigh [Maire Walker], the leader of the group who had left in 1905, charging that the aesthetics of Yeats and Lady Gregory—with Miss Horniman's support—were taking the Theatre away from its Nationalist beginnings. The Theatre of Ireland, which lasted six years, also had the support of A.E., who had withdrawn from the Theatre Society in 1904.

There is little record of Yeats's feelings about Casimir Joseph Dunin-Markievicz (1874–1932), the flamboyant Polish painter, who in 1900 had married Constance Gore-Booth (1868–1927), the young noblewoman from County Sligo, whom Yeats had first met in 1894. This note marks the beginning of Markievicz's flirtation with the Irish theater. He and his wife staged several plays, including his own *The Dilettante*, in the fall in Dublin and later —as a Christmas carnival—in Sligo. In 1910, he founded the Dublin Repertory, a company which sometimes included his wife in productions ranging from plays of his own to those of Shaw and Maeterlinck. Markievicz's productions were marked by fanatical attention to realistic detail and, apparently, by lack of discipline.

asked our own company to give up two of our Saturday performances that we might give the Independent Theatre and the Theatre of Ireland the most popular days. I see some talk in the papers of those two societies uniting. If they do so, there is only one means of success, the appointment of some competent man who will be able to cast parts with no thought but efficiency, and to insist upon regular attendance at rehearsals. The Gaelic League companies must do the same if they would raise the Gaelic drama out of its present decline, for theatres cannot be democracies. The Gaelic League has difficulties one must respect, for the Gaelic League can hardly spare many of its thoughts for any art till its battle is more nearly won, and this single purpose gives to even their most clumsy performance a little simplicity and entire lack of pretense. The same excuse applies to the National Players, whose representation of *Robert Emmet* in St. Cecilia's Hall some years ago, interested me and touched me. It was frankly propagandist, had the dignity of a long national tradition, and carried my imagination to Davis and to Mitchel. All work which is done without selfishness for something beyond one's self has moral beauty.

# The Shewing-Up of Blanco Posnet
## Statement by the Directors

When the Lord Chamberlain had refused to allow Bernard Shaw's *The Shewing-Up of Blanco Posnet* to be performed in England, Yeats and Lady Gregory had eagerly agreed to produce it at the Abbey. Rehearsals, supervised by Lady Gregory herself, were well under way when the Lord Lieutenant moved to establish himself as a censor, threatening to withdraw the theater's patent. After several conferences, including one with Lord Aberdeen himself, Yeats and Lady Gregory had decided that the production must be halted. But during the course of what was to have been the final rehearsal, on Saturday, August 21, 1909, each came privately to the decision that the play had to be given. As Lady Gregory recalls, "We found that during those two or three hours our minds had come to the same decision, that we had given our word, that at all risks we must keep it or it would never be trusted again; that we must in no case go back, but must go on at any cost" (Lady Gregory, *Our Irish Theatre*, New York, 1913, p. 163). On August 25, the play was performed without hindrance and an issue of *The Arrow* was published containing a "Statement by the Directors", which was composed on August 22 and released to several papers, a long editorial on the play from *The Nation*, and a concluding note by Yeats.

ON Sunday night the following explanation was issued on behalf of the Abbey Theatre Company:

The statement communicated to certain of Saturday's papers makes the following explanation necessary: During the last week we have been vehemently urged to withdraw Mr. Shaw's play, which had already been advertised and rehearsed, and have refused to do so. We would have listened with attention to any substantial argument; but we found, as we were referred from one well-meaning personage to another, that no one would say the play was hurtful to man, woman or child. Each said that someone else had thought so, or might think so. We were told that Mr. Redford[1] had objected, that the Lord Chamberlain had objected, and that, if produced, it would certainly offend excited officials in London, and might offend officials in Dublin, or the law officers of the Crown, or the Lord Lieutenant, or Dublin society, or Archbishop Walsh,[2] or the Church of Ireland, or "rowdies up for the Horse Show", or newspaper editors, or the King.

In these bewilderments and shadowy opinions there was nothing to change our conviction (which is also that of the leading weekly paper of the Lord Lieutenant's own party),[3] that so far from containing offence for any sincere and honest mind, Mr. Shaw's play is a high and weighty argument upon the working of the Spirit of God in man's heart, or to show that it is not a befitting thing for us to set upon our stage the work of an Irishman, who is also the most famous of living dramatists, after that work had been silenced in London by what we believe an unjust decision.

One thing, however, is plain enough, an issue that swallows up all else, and makes the merit of Mr. Shaw's play a secondary thing. If our patent is in danger, it is because the decisions of the English Censor are being brought into Ireland, and because the Lord Lieutenant is about to revive on what we consider a frivolous pretext, a right not exercised for 150 years, to forbid, at the Lord Chamberlain's pleasure, any play produced in any Dublin theatre, all these theatres holding their patents from him.

We are not concerned with the question of the English censorship, now being fought out in London, but we are very certain that the conditions of the two countries are different, and that we must not, by accepting the English Censor's ruling, give away anything of the liberty of the Irish theatre of the future. Neither can we accept, without protest, the revival of the Lord Lieutenant's claim at the bidding of the Censor or otherwise. The Lord

---

[1] George Alexander Redford (d. 1916), the Examiner of Plays from 1895 until 1911, is the "Censor" of whom Yeats spoke in his speech to the British Association for the Advancement of Science in 1908 (p. 368 above).

[2] William J. Walsh (1841–1921) had been Archbishop of Dublin and Primate of Ireland since 1885.

[3] Shaw noted in a telegram to Lady Gregory on August 12 that the play "had been declared entirely guiltless and admirable by the leading high class journal of [the Lord Lieutenant's] own party", in reference to the editorial in *The Nation (Our Irish Theatre,* p. 152).

Lieutenant is definitely a political personage holding office from the party in power, and what would sooner or later grow into a political censorship cannot be lightly accepted.

W. B. Yeats, *Managing Director*.
A. Gregory, *Director and Patentee*.
ABBEY THEATRE, *August 22nd, 1909*

The Managing Director of the Abbey Theatre has received a letter from Mr. Bernard Shaw, dated August 22nd, which contains the following passage:

"To-day the papers have arrived . . . You can make a further statement to the Press, that since the last statement Lady Gregory has written to me, pointing out that a certain speech was open to misconstruction, and that I immediately re-wrote it much more strongly and clearly; consequently the play will now be given exactly as by the author, without concessions of any kind to the attacks that have been made upon it, except that to oblige the Lord Leiutenant, I have consented to withdraw the word 'immoral' as applied to the relations between a woman of bad character and her accomplices. In doing so I wish it to be stated that I still regard these relations as not only immoral but vicious; nevertheless, as the English Censorship apparently regards them as delightful and exemplary, and the Lord Lieutenant does not wish it to be understood as contradicting the English Censorship, I am quite content to leave the relations to the unprompted judgment of the Irish people. Also, I have consented to withdraw the words, 'Dearly beloved brethren,' as the Castle fears that they may shock the nation. For the rest, I can assure the Lord Lieutenant that there is nothing in the other passages objected to by the English Censorship that might not have been written by the Catholic Archbishop of Dublin, and that in point of consideration for the religious beliefs of the Irish people, the play compares very favourably indeed with the Coronation Oath."

[Here, Yeats inserted under the title *"The Nation* on Blanco Posnet" the editorial from *The Nation* of May 29, 1909, which attacked the censorship because it encouraged bad drama and suppressed good drama. According to the editorial writer, whom Shaw had let see the manuscript of the play and the Censor's letter of suppression, Shaw had given in on one passage but refused to alter another very important one. The writer identified the mood of the play with that of Bret Hart's "The Luck of Roaring Camp" and then summarized the play, defending its basic morality. He quoted and commented at length on the controversial dialogue on Divine Providence between Blanco and Elder Daniels, comparing the rantings of Blanco to the Book of Job in that both deal with the implacable love of God. The editorial writer defended the right of the playwright to treat of serious religious questions on the stage, asserting in conclusion that the Censor's "theory of British drama . . . is to warn off the artist and the preacher, and to clear the path for the scoffer and the clown."]

## THE RELIGION OF BLANCO POSNET

The meaning of Mr. Shaw's play, as I understand it, is that natural man, driven on by passion and vain glory, attempts to live as his fancy bids him but is awakened to the knowledge of God by finding himself stopped, perhaps suddenly, by something within himself. This something which is God's care for man, does not temper the wind to the shorn lamb, as a false and sentimental piety would have it, but is a terrible love that awakens the soul amidst catastrophes and trains it by conquest and labour.

The essential incidents of the play are Blanco's giving up the horse, the harlot's refusal to name the thief, and the child's death of the croup. Without the last of these Mr. Shaw's special meaning would be lost, for he wants us to understand that God's love will not do the work of the Doctor, or any work that man can do, for it acts by awakening the intellect and the soul whether in some man of science or philosopher or in violent Posnet.

W. B. Y.

# The Irish National Theatre

The Abbey's failure, due to a series of mistakes, to close in tribute when Edward VII died on May 7, 1910, was the crowning exasperation for its English benefactress, Miss Horniman. Thus, as the renewal of the Theatre's patent came due in November, Yeats and Lady Gregory found themselves sharing control of the new National Theatre Society Limited, along with full responsibility for raising an endowment to secure its future. In a letter to *The Times* on June 16, they sought publicly to add to the some £2,000 they had already raised. Despite this appeal and the good offices of such friends as Shaw and Edmund Gosse, their fund amounted to £2,169 when the new patent was granted on November 26, 1910.

## TO THE EDITOR OF *THE TIMES*

SIR.—In some of the many discussions of late upon the possibility and uses of repertory theatres, kind words have been spoken about our Irish one. Mr. Walkley,[1] in his speech at the dinner of the Royal Theatrical Fund last Sunday, said that the promoters of the Shakespeare National Theatre and all who might think of starting a repertory theatre "could not have a better example of the real value of a modest enterprise than that afforded by the Irish National Theatre, which they owed to Mr. Yeats and his comrades". For eleven years past we have worked very hard in the attempt to found and to put on a permanent footing this enterprise. Six years ago we were enabled by a generous subsidiary [*sic*] to play on a regular stage.[2] We have had to fight against apathy and prejudice, and at one time or another against patriotic cliques and against Government officials. But our Dublin audience is steadily increasing, and we find support and a welcome not only in the chief towns of Ireland, but in the English intellectual centres, London (our company is now playing at the Court Theatre), Manchester, Oxford, and Cambridge.

A school of Irish writers and actors has been founded, which has given a distinguished and powerful representation of Irish country life. The works of our fellow director, the late Mr. Synge, are recognized everywhere now by students of dramatic literature as among the most important that have been given to the theatre in our time. We play also and find an audience for translations of foreign masterpieces, especially those of Molière, akin to the folk drama, and of Goldoni.[3] All the laborious building up, the slow amassing of a large repertory of Irish plays, the training of actors, the making of a reputation with the general public, has been accomplished or all but accomplished. Our takings in our last financial year are almost three times what they have been in any previous year, and we believe that within a few years we shall be independent of outside aid. We need not be ashamed of having to wait these few years, for after ten years the celebrated Moscow Art Theatre is still carried on at a loss.

Our subsidy, including the free use of the Abbey Theatre, comes to an end, as well as our patent, in this year. We have saved enough money

[1] For Yeats's appreciation of the change in A. B. Walkley's criticisms of the Abbey Theatre, see pp. 46–7 above.

[2] Yeats's reference is to the acquisition of the hall of the Mechanics' Institute, Abbey Street, in 1904 and the creation of the Abbey Theatre through the endowment of Miss Horniman.

[3] Productions of Lady Gregory's translations of Molière; which had begun in 1906, had continued with *The Rogueries of Scapin* in 1908 and *The Miser* in 1909. Her translation of *Mirandolina* by the Italian playwright, Carlo Goldini (1707–1793), was produced in February, 1910.

(about £1,900) to take over the Abbey Theatre and to pay for a new patent, a somewhat heavy expense. Our business advisers tell us that the sum of £5,000, which would hardly support a London theatre for a season, would enable us to keep our theatre vigorous, intellectual, and courageous for another half dozen years. Towards this endowment we have already been given £2,000, among the donors being Mr. J. M. Barrie, Mr. A. Birrell, Colonel Hutcheson Poe, Lord Pirrie, Lord Iveagh, Mr. Wilfrid Blunt, Lady Bell, Lord Dunsany, Mr. F. Huth Jackson, the Duke of Leinster, and the Duchess of Sutherland. Lady Tennant, 34, Queen Anne's Gate, herself a large subscriber, is kind enough to act as our treasurer. Should we receive no more than this £2,000 we shall still go on for as long as we can, but we shall be crippled, and not able to carry out plans for the strengthening and widening of our work, and we shall have, as in the years past, to give up to the actual business of the theatre so great a part of our own time as to interfere with our personal and creative work. We feel we have almost pushed the ball up the hill. We shall be grateful to any friends of our enterprise who will help us to keep it from rolling down again.

Yours faithfully,
W. B. Yeats
A. Gregory

Court Theatre, June 14.

# The Art of the Theatre

Along with Bernard Shaw, Cecil French, Gordon Craig and others, Yeats took part in a symposium on "The Art of the Theatre" which appeared in A. R. Orage's weekly review, *The New Age*, in 1910. His brief comments, which appeared in the issue for June 16, suggest the growing distinction he made between realistic and suggestive stage decoration.

THE following questions are being put by THE NEW AGE to many persons connected with the theatre, both in this country and abroad:—

1. Have recent developments, in your opinion, shown any advance in the direction of increasing the beauty of the stage picture?
2. Do you think that managers and producers are yet using to the full all the advantages offered by the modern studio?
3. Would you say that artists are availing themselves as fully as they might of the opportunities open to them in the modern theatre?

In the last two issues we printed some of the replies received from prominent producers and painters. Next week we shall print those received from prominent authors and critics, among them Messrs. Bernard Shaw, E. A. Buaghan, J. T. Grein, and further series will be published as they arrive.

### MR. W. B. YEATS (ABBEY THEATRE, DUBLIN)

I would answer your second question first, and say that managers and producers in this country are certainly not using to the full "the advantages offered by the modern studio," nor is it desirable that they should do so. We should use in every art but that which is peculiar to it, till we have turned into beauty all things that it has, and cease to regret the things that it has not. That which the stage has, as distinguished from easel painting, is real light and the moving figures of the players. We should begin our reform by banishing all painted light and shadow, and by clearing from round the stage and above the stage everything that prevents the free playing of light. Once we have done this, and it may mean a re-shaping of the theatre, we shall discover a something very startling and strange—the beauty of the moving figure. We shall no longer dwarf them as Mr. Tree does and Mr. Trench[1] does, and every other popular producer, with a vast meretricious landscape, which has everything the easel painting has except its subtlety and distinction. We shall have abolished realism except in interiors, which can be exactly reproduced, and created a new art—the art of stage decoration.

I will answer your first and third questions together. Only two artists have done good work upon the English stage during my time, Mr. Craig[2] and Mr. Ricketts,[3] and the first of these is the originator throughout Europe of almost every attempt to reform the decoration and mechanism of the stage, and all that these artists have done has had beauty, some of it magnificent beauty. I cannot judge of the work done in France by Fortuni and Apia,[4] but what work I have seen in England

[1] Herbert Trench (1865–1923), the poet and playwright, was director of the Haymarket Theatre, a position held earlier by Sir Herbert Beerbohm Tree, the actor-manager, who was at this time the owner and manager of His Majesty's Theatre, London. Yeats had frequently mentioned Tree's elaborate stagings as examples of the sort of futile ingenuity which his theatre avoided. While his public citations were, as in this instance, courteous, his private antipathy to Tree's method was strong as, for example, in his footnote to a letter written to Lady Gregory in November of the preceding year: "I have just written to Mrs. Pat Campbell refusing to consider Tree in writing my play [*The Player Queen*]. I have described his ideal of beauty as thrice vomited flesh" (*Letters*, p. 539).

[2] For Yeats's collaboration with Gordon Craig see pp. 384–94 below.

[3] Yeats's friend of long-standing, Charles Ricketts (1866–1931), the artist, writer, book and stage designer, had designed the sets for the Abbey's revival of Synge's *The Well of the Saints*, which had opened on May 14, 1908.

[4] Mariano Fortuni (1871–1949), the Italian theatrical designer, had been experimenting since 1902 with a revolutionary lighting system featuring a movable dome over the stage

by artists, other than those I have named, has but increased the confusion between the stage and easel painting, for we gain nothing by substituting modern touch and handling for the touch and handling of the landscape painters of fifty years ago still in use among commercial scene-painters, and we lose by seeming to gain.

# The Tragic Theatre

Throughout 1910, Yeats was elaborating his theory of an embodiment of dramatic speech which drew as little as possible on any concept of "character". His experiments were intensified by the "'place' or whatever one should call his invention", (*Letters*, p. 546) which Gordon Craig unveiled for him on January 7. Apparently agreeing to Craig's insistence that all his poetic plays in future be produced on his system of enclosed monochromatic screens and lights, Yeats had a model built. By July, he was consulting with a dubious Joseph Holloway for alterations in the Abbey to accommodate what Holloway called "the Gordon Craig scheme for reducing the size of stage pictures by an arrangement that expands or contracts from sides and top automatically" (*Joseph Holloway's Abbey Theatre*, p. 140).

Yeats's most thorough explanation of his hopes for this method of presentation appear in the essay on "The Tragic Theatre", which was written at Coole in July and August of 1910. The essay was first published in the October issue of *The Mask*, the periodical which Craig edited in Florence, under the pseudonym, "John Semar". In revised forms the essay constitutes the "Preface" to *Plays for an Irish Theatre* (1911) and is included in *The Cutting of an Agate* (1912).

I NOTICED in all but all the printed criticisms of Synge's "Deirdre of the Sorrows" that none of the things that made certain moments seem to me the noblest tragedy were written of, but that the play was judged by things that seemed to me but wheels and pulleys necessary to the effect, but in themselves nothing.

---

which allowed for greater illusions of depth and ranges of effect. Fortuni's system was perfected in 1910, coincident with the development of a similar system by Max Reinhardt in Berlin.

Yeats had expressed interest in the experiments of Adolphe Appia (1862–1928), the Swiss set designer, in the essay "The Play, the Player and the Scene" which had appeared in the *Samhain* for December, 1904. In that essay, Yeats had admitted that he understood little of Appia's concept of lighting as a unifying force. It is likely that Yeats learned more about Appia from Sturge Moore, whose wife was Appia's cousin.

Upon the other hand, those who spoke to me of the play never spoke of these wheels and pulleys, but if they cared at all for the play, cared for the things I cared for. One's own world of painters, of poets, of good talkers, of ladies who delight in Ricard's[1] portraits or Debussey's [sic] music, all those whose senses feel instantly every change in imagination, in our mother the moon, saw the stage in one way; and those others who look at plays every night, who tell the general playgoer whether this play or that play is to his taste, saw it in a way so different that there is certainly some body of dogma whether in the instincts or in the memory, pushing the ways apart. A printed criticism for instance found but one dramatic moment, that when Deirdre in the second act overhears her lover say that he may grow weary of her; and not one, if I remember rightly, chose for praise or explanation the third act which alone had satisfied the author, or contained in any abundance those sentences that were quoted at the fall of the curtain and for days after.

Deirdre and her lover, as Synge tells the tale, returned to Ireland though it was nearly certain they would die there, because death was better than broken love, and at the side of the open grave that had been dug for one and would serve for both, quarreled, losing all they had given their life to keep. "Is it not a hard thing that we should miss the safety of the grave and we trampling its edge?"[2] That is Deirdre's cry at the outset of a reverie of passion that mounts and mounts till grief itself has carried her beyond grief into pure contemplation. Up to this the play had been a Master's unfinished work, monotonous and melancholy, ill arranged, little more than a sketch of what it would have grown to, but now I listened breathless to sentences that may never pass away, and as they filled or dwindled in their civility of sorrow, the player, whose art had seemed clumsy and incomplete, like the writing itself, ascended into that tragic ecstasy which is the best that art . . . perhaps that life . . . can give. At last when Deirdre, in the paroxysm before she took her life, touched with compassionate fingers him that had killed her lover, we knew that the player had become, if but for a moment, the creature of that noble mind which had gathered its art in waste islands, and we too were carried beyond time and persons to where passion living through its thousand purgatorial years, as in the wink of an eye, becomes wisdom; and it was as though we too had touched and felt and seen a disembodied thing.

One dogma of the printed criticism is that if a play does not contain

[1] At the time of this essay the work of Louis Gustave Ricard (1823–73), the French portrait painter, was receiving new attention as a contribution to the development of modern painting in France.

[2] In the printed text of *Deirdre of the Sorrows*, Deirdre says, in Act III: "In a little while we've lived too long, Naisi, and isn't it a poor thing we should win the safety of the grave, and me trampling its edge?" (*The Complete Plays of John M. Synge*, New York, 1960, p. 259).

definite character, its constitution is not strong enough for the stage, and that the dramatic moment is always the contest of character with character. In poetical drama there is, it is held, an antithesis between character and lyric poetry, for lyric poetry however beautiful when read out of a book can but, as these critics think, encumber the action.[3] Yet when we go back a few centuries and enter the great periods of drama, character grows less and sometimes disappears, and there is much lyric feeling, and at times a lyric measure will be wrought into the dialogue, a flowing measure that had well befitted music, or that laboured one of the sonnet. Suddenly it strikes us that character is continuously present in comedy alone, and that there is much tragedy, that of Corneille, that of Racine, that of Greece and Rome, where its place is taken by passions and motives, one person being jealous, another full of love or remorse or pride or anger. In writers of tragi-comedy (and Shakespeare is always a writer of tragi-comedy) there is indeed character, but one notices that it is in the moments of comedy that character is defined, in Hamlet's gaiety let us say; but that in the great moments, when Timon orders his tomb, when Hamlet cries to Horatio "absent thee from felicity awhile", when Cleopatra names "Of many thousand kisses the poor last" all is lyricism, unmixed passion, 'the integrity of fire'. Nor does character ever attain to complete definition in these lamps ready for the taper, no matter how circumstantial and gradual the opening of events, as it does in Falstaff who has no passionate purpose to fulfill, or as it does in Henry the Fifth whose poetry, never touched by lyric heat, is oratorical like a speech at a general election, like an article in some daily paper; nor when the tragic reverie is at its height do we say "How well that man is realised, I should know him were I to meet him in the street", for it is always ourselves that we see upon the stage, and should it be a tragedy of love we renew, it may be, some loyalty of our youth, and go from the theatre with our eyes dim for an old love's sake.

I think it was while rehearsing a translation of "Les Fourberies de Scapin"[4] in Dublin, and noticing how passionless it all was, that I saw what should have been plain from the first line I had written, that tragedy must always be a drowning and breaking of the dykes that separate man from man, and that it is upon these dykes comedy keeps house. But I was not certain of the site; (one always doubts when one knows no testimony but one's own); till somebody told me of a certain letter of Congreve's. He describes the external and superficial expres-

---

[3] This sentence begins the version of this essay which is the "Preface" to *Plays for an Irish Theatre* and which, with three paragraphs omitted, is substantially the present text.

[4] Lady Gregory's adaptation of Molière's *Les Fourberies de Scapin*, entitled *The Rogueries of Scapin*, was produced at the Abbey in April, 1908.

sions of "humour" on which farce is founded and then defines "humour" itself, the foundation of comedy, as "a singular and unavoidable way of doing anything peculiar to one man only, by which his speech and actions are distinguished from all other men" and adds to it that "passions are too powerful in the sex to let humour have its course",[5] or as I would rather put it, that you can find but little of what we call character in unspoiled youth, whatever be the sex, for as he indeed shows in another sentence, it grows with time like the ash of a burning stick, and strengthens towards middle life till there is little else at seventy years.

Since then I have discovered an antagonism between all the old art and our new art of comedy and understand why I hated at nineteen years Thackery's [sic] novels and the new French painting. A big picture of cocottes sitting at little tables outside a Cafe, by some follower of Manet's, was exhibited at The Royal Hibernian Academy while I was a student at a life class there, and I was miserable for days. I found no desirable place, no man I could have wished to be, no woman I could have loved, no Golden Age, no lure for secret hope, no adventure with myself for theme out of that endless tale I told myself all day long. Years after I saw the Olympia of Manet at the Luxembourg and watched it without hostility indeed, but as one might some incomparable talker whose precision of gesture gave one pleasure, though one did not understand his language. I returned to it again and again at intervals of years, saying to myself "some day I will understand" and yet it was not until Sir Hugh Lane brought the Eva Gonzales to Dublin, and I had said to myself "How perfectly that woman is realized as distinct from all other women that have lived or shall live" that I understood I was carrying on in my own mind that quarrel between a tragedian and a comedian which the Devil on Two Sticks showed to the young man who was climbing through the window.[6]

There is an art of the flood, the art of Titian when his Ariosto and

[5] Yeats quotes from the essay "*Concerning Humour in Comedy*", which William Congreve (1670–1729) wrote in the form of a letter to John Dennis dated July 10, 1695: "I take [humor] to be, *A singular and unavoidable manner of doing, or saying any thing, Peculiar and Natural to one Man only; by which his Speech and Actions are distinguish'd from those of other Men*" (John C. Hodges, ed., *William Congreve: Letters and Documents*, New York, 1964, p. 182). Yeats's rather confusing further quotation is an excerpt of Congreve's subsequent discussion of the relative powers of passions and humors in men and women: ". . . I have never made an observation of what I Apprehend to be true Humours in Women. Perhaps Passions are too powerful in that Sex, to let Humour have its Course . . ." (*ibid.*, p. 183).

[6] Manet's portrait of his student Eva Gonzalès, painted in 1869–70, was owned by Hugh Lane, who is shown sitting beneath it, along with George Moore and others, in William Orpen's famous *Homage to Manet* (1909).

In the fourteenth chapter of *Le Diable Boiteux* (1707) by Alain René Le Sage (1668–1747), the "devil upon two sticks" explains a quarrel between a tragic poet and a comic author to the rogue-hero, Don Cleophas.

his Bacchus and Ariadne gave new images to the dreams of youth, and
of Shakespeare when he shows us Hamlet broken away from life by
the passionate hesitations of his reverie. And we call this art poetical,
because we must bring more to it than our daily mood if we would take
our pleasure; and because it delights in picturing the moment of exaltation, of excitement, of dreaming (or in the capacity for it, as in that still
face of Ariosto's that is like some vessel soon to be full of wine). And
there is an art that we call real, because character can only express itself
perfectly in a real world, being that world's creature, and because we
understand it best through a delicate discrimination of the senses,
which is but entire wakefulness, the daily mood grown cold and crystal-
line.

We may not find either mood in its purity, but in mainly tragic art
one distinguishes devices to exclude or lessen character, to diminish the
power of that daily mood, to cheat or blind its too clear perception. If
the real world is not altogether rejected it is but touched here and there,
and into the places we have left empty we summon rhythm, balance, pattern, images that remind us of vast passions, the vagueness of past
times, all the chimeras that haunt the edge of trance; and if we are
painters, we shall express personal emotion through ideal form, a
symbolism handled by the generations, a mask from whose eyes the
disembodied looks, a style that remembers many masters, that it may
escape contemporary suggestion; or we shall leave out some element
of reality as in Byzantine painting, where there is no mass, nothing in
relief, and so it is that in the supreme moment of tragic art there comes
upon one that strange sensation as though the hair of one's head stood
up. And when we love, if it be in the excitement of youth, do we not
also, that the flood may find no wall to narrow, no stone to convulse it,
exclude character or the signs of it by choosing that beauty which seems
unearthly because the individual woman is lost amid the labyrinth of its
lines as though life were trembling into stillness and silence, or at
last folding itself away? Some little irrelevance of line, some promise
of character to come, may indeed put us at our ease, 'give more interest'
as the humour of the old man with the basket does to Cleopatra's dying.
But should it come as we had dreamed in love's frenzy to our dying for
that woman's sake, we would find that the discord had its value from
the tune.

Nor have we chosen illusion in choosing the outward sign of that
moral genius that lives among the subtlety of the passions, and can for
her moment make her of the one mind with great artists and poets. In
the studio we may indeed say to one another "character is the only
beauty" but when we go to the gymnasium to be shaped for woman's
eyes, as when we choose a wife, we remember academic form, even

though we enlarge a little the point of interest and choose "a painter's beauty", finding it the more easy to believe in the fire because it has made ashes.

When we look at the faces of the old tragic paintings, whether it is in Titian or in some painter of medieval China, we find there sadness and gravity, a certain emptiness even as of a mind that waited the supreme crisis (and indeed it seems at times as if the graphic art, unlike poetry which sings the crisis itself, were the celebration of waiting). Whereas in modern art, whether in Japan or in Europe, 'vitality' (is not that the great word of the studios?) the energy that is to say that is under the command of our common moments, sings, laughs, chatters or looks its busy thoughts.

Have we not here then the Tree of Life and that of the knowledge of Good and Evil which is rooted in our interests, and if we have forgotten the differing forms of leaf and fruit, it is surely because we have taken delight in a confusion of crossing branches. Tragic art, passionate art, the drowner of dykes, the compounder of understanding, moves us by setting us to reverie, by alluring us almost to the intensity of trance. The persons upon the stage, let us say, greaten till they are humanity itself. We feel our minds expand convulsively or spread out slowly like some moon-brightened image crowded sea. That which is before our eyes perpetually vanishes and returns again in the midst of the excitement it creates, and the more enthralling it is the more do we forget it.[7] When I am watching my own Deirdre I am content with the players and myself, when I am moved for a while not by the contrasted sorrows of Deirdre and Naoise, but because the words have called up before me the image of the sea-born woman so distinctly, that her unshaken eyelids that had not the sea's cold blood seem by contrast what I had wished her to seem, a wild bird in a cage.

It was only by watching my own plays upon the stage that I came to understand that this reverie, this twilight between sleep and waking, this bout of fencing, alike on the stage and in the mind, between man and phantoms, this perilous path as on the edge of a sword, is the condition of tragic pleasure, and to understand why it is so rare and so brief. If an actor becomes over emphatic, picking out what he believes to be the important words with violence, and running up and down the scale, or if he stresses his lines in wrong places, or even if an electric lamp that should have cast but a reflected light from sky or sea, shows from behind the post of a door, I discover at once the proud fragility of dreams.

At first I was driven into teaching too statuesque a pose, too monotonous a delivery, that I might not put "vitality" in the place of the

[7] This sentence concludes the version of this essay in *The Cutting of an Agate*.

sleep walking of passion in these things, and for the rest became a little deaf and blind.

But alas! it is often my own words that break the dream. Then I take the play from the stage and write it over again, perhaps many times. At first I always believed it must be something in the management of events, in all that is the same in prose or verse, that was wrong, but after I had reconstructed a sene with the messenger in Deirdre in many ways, I discovered that our language must keep at all times a certain even richness. I had used "traitor", "sword", "suborned" words in a too traditional usage, without plunging them into personal thought and metaphor, and I had forgotten in a moment of melodrama that tragic drama must be carved out of speech as a statue is out of stone.

It is certain therefore that should suggestion run thin, should some one move violently, should there be a sudden noise, any one out of a thousand accidents that would hardly trouble the robust pleasure of comedy, the climbing shoulders will come from under the stone. Perhaps there is in tragic art something womanish come from the continual presence of the Muses who have given Comedy a later and a slighter love, and we know that men can have their day's work amid the abrupt, the common, the foolish even without utter loss, but that women cannot keep their fineness lacking a fine company.

But train our players and our mechanists as we will and if we have not thought out the art of stage decoration afresh every brush stroke of our scene painters will mix into the reverie the monotonous or the irrelevant. We will hire some journeyman to accompany the poet's description with a painted landscape which, because it must give all to the first glance and yet copy nature, will alone copy what is obvious, and which even if it could keep the attention and give it pleasure could but keep it to the poet's loss:—

> *A vapour, sometime, like a bear, or lion,*
> *A tower'd citadel, a pendant rock,*
> *A forked mountain, or blue promontory*
> *With trees upon't that nod unto the world.*
> *And mock our eyes with air.*[8]

I have heard Antony speak those lines before a painted cloth that, though it could not make them nothing, left in the memory the sensation of something childish, theatrical as we say. Words as solemn, and having more for the mind's eye than those of the Book of Common Prayer must be spoken where no reformer has cast out the idolatrous mummery and no tradition sanctified.

[8] *Antony and Cleopatra*, Act IV, scene xiv, ll. 3-7.

In no art can we do well unless we keep to those effects that are peculiar to it or that it can show better than the other arts. We no longer paint wood with a grain that is not its own, but are content that it should display itself or be covered with paint that pretends to be but paint, and if we paint a design upon a vase or a plate, we are careful not to attempt something that can be better done in easel painting. But in the art of the theatre we imitate easel painting, even though we ignore or mar for its sake the elements we should have worked in, the characteristics of the stage, light and shadow, speech, the movement of the players. Our tree-wings . . . let us say . . . can only be given mass and detail by painted light and shadow and these will contradict, or be in no relation to the real light, and this real light will be so cut up and cut off by wings and borders arranged for effects of painting that we shall be content to use it in but a few obvious ways. Then too our background will be full of forms and colours, instead of showing an even or almost even surface whereon the players are outlined clearly that we may see their movements and feel their importance; and all the while the background, even if it were fine painting and had no false light and shadow and did not reduce the players to a picturesque group in the foreground of a water colour painting by my grandmother,[9] could but insist on the unreality we are anxious to forget, for every time a player stood close to that garden scene we would but feel over again on how flat a surface they had painted that long garden walk dwindling away into the distance.

If we would give our theatre the dignity of a church, of a Greek open air theatre, of an Elizabethan platform stage, and cannot be content with any of these we must have a scene where there is no painted light and shade, and that is but another way of saying, no realism, no objects represented in mass unless they can be copied exactly as we can copy an interior, and the mechanism of this scene must as little as possible prevent the free and delicate use of light and shadow.

When we have made this change in obedience to a logic which has been displayed in the historical development of all the other arts, we shall have created a theatre that will please the poet and the player and the painter. An old quarrel will be ended, the stage will be beautifully decorated, every change will be full of meaning and yet it will never create a competing interest, or set bounds to the suggestions of speech and motion, and liberated from the necessity of an always complete realization, the producer, recovering caprice, will be as free as a modern

---

[9] In "Reveries Over Childhood and Youth", Yeats recalls that his grandmother, Elizabeth Pollexfen (1819–92) would, in his childhood, "choose some favourite among her flowers and copy it upon rice-paper. I saw some of her handiwork the other day and I wondered at the delicacy of form and colour . . ." (*Autobiography*, p. 4).

painter, as Signor Mancini[10] let us say, to give himself up to an eliptical imagination. Gloster [*sic*] will be able to fall but from his own height and think that he has fallen from Dover cliff, and Richard's and Richmond's tents can face one another again. We shall have made possible once more a noble, capricious, extravagant, resonant, fantastic art.

All summer I have been playing with a little model, where there is a scene capable of endless transformation, of the expression of every mood that does not require a photographic reality. Mr. Craig . . . who has invented all this, . . . has permitted me to set up upon the stage of the Abbey another scene that corresponds to this, in the scale of a foot for an inch and henceforth I shall be able, by means so simple that one laughs, to lay the events of my plays amid a grandeur like that of Babylon, and where there is neither complexity nor compromise nothing need go wrong, no lamps become suddenly unmasked, no ill-painted corner come suddenly into sight.[11] Henceforth I can all but produce my play as I write it, moving hither and thither little figures of cardboard through gay or solemn light and shade, allowing the scene to give the words and the words the scene. I am very grateful for he has banished a whole world that wearied me and was undignified and given me forms and lights upon which I can play as upon some stringed instrument.

This essay is an introduction to a volume of Mr. Yeats' plays which is in preparation and which will contain stage designs by Mr. Gordon Craig. [This note in *The Mask* refers to *Plays for an Irish Theatre*, which appeared in December, 1911, with four drawings by Gordon Craig.]

[10] In January of 1908 Yeats wrote enthusiastically to John Quinn about the portrait by Antonio Mancini (1852–1930) which was ultimately to appear in the fifth volume of *The Collected Works* (1908). "Mancini, who filled me with joy, has turned me into a sort of Italian bandit, or half bandit half café king, certainly a joyous Latin, impudent, immoral, and reckless" (*Letters*, p. 502). Later, in a letter to A. H. Bullen, urging their original plan of presenting several portraits at the beginning of the first volume, Yeats praised the Italian extravagantly. "The Mancini, if you had enough knowledge of painting to see it, is a great chance. It costs nothing and it is a master work of one of the greatest living painters" (*Letters*, p. 504).

[11] His experiments with Craig's model convinced Yeats of the system's potential. In November, he wrote to his father that "the Craig scenery will give us a very strange and beautiful stage. . . . I shall get all my plays into the Craig scene" (*Letters*, p. 555). When Joseph Holloway visited the Abbey late in the month, Craig's scene seemed to him "as like as peas, only on a big scale, of the blocks I as a child built houses of. As Yeats never played with blocks in his youth, Gordon Craig's childish ideas give him keen delight now . . ." (*Joseph Holloway's Abbey Theatre*, p. 146). On January 12, 1911, the Craig scenes were introduced in productions of Lady Gregory's *The Deliverer* and Yeats's *The Hour Glass*.

# Abbey Theatre
# New System of Scenery

Yeats's enthusiasm, as he anticipated the inauguration of Gordon Craig's system of scenery in an interview in the *Evening Telegraph* on January 9, 1911, is tempered by Joseph Holloway's description of the performances, three nights later. "With a great flourish of egotistical trumpets on the part of the management and Yeats in dress clothes with crush opera hat in hand, the Gordon Craig freak scenery and lighting were tried at the Abbey. . . . And while most voted the innovation an affected failure with possibilities for effective stage pictures, none considered it in any way an improvement on the old methods . . ." (*Joseph Holloway's Abbey Theatre*, p. 148).

## ABBEY THEATRE
## NEW SYSTEM OF SCENERY
### INVENTED BY FAMOUS THEATRICAL MANAGER
### TO BE TRIED ON THURSDAY
### INTERESTING INTERVIEW WITH MR. YEATS

THURSDAY night promises to be a memorable occasion in the history of the Abbey Theatre, for then, for the first time on the stage, a new experiment will be tried in regard to scenic effect. The plays [*sic*] produced will be "The Deliverer," by Lady Gregory, an Egyptian drama, the scene of which takes place outside a vast pillared Egyptian palace. The depicting of this scene will be carried out on the new system, and should prove extremely effective, judging by what a representative of the Evening Telegraph saw at the theatre this afternoon. The other play to be produced on Thursday night will be Mr. Yeats's well-known "Hour-Glass," with a new staging on the new principle, and with costumes all designed, and the scenery arranged by Mr. Gordon Craig, the originator of this remarkable theatrical innovation, who has given permission to the Abbey to make use of it.

Mr. Yeats informed our representative that Mr. Craig is a son of Ellen Terry, the famous actress, and stated that he is the greatest stage inventor in Europe. The scenery, he said, differs entirely from the old style of scenery, and consists chiefly of portable screens, by means of which beautiful decorative effects can be obtained, the working of the screens being based on certain mathematical proportions by which the stage manager can make walls, pillars, etc.—a palace almost in a moment, a palace of great cyclopean proportions, and which can be changed again almost in a moment into a room with long corridors, and be changed again into a third and very different scene just as quickly.

But the old kind of scenery, said our representative, can nowadays be changed very quickly?

Mr. Yeats paused for a moment and thought, and walking up and down in front of the proscenium, stated the advantages of Craig's conception as follows:—

"The primary value of Mr. Craig's invention is that it enables one to use light in a more natural and more beautiful way than ever before. We get rid of all the top hamper of the stage—all the hanging ropes and scenes with prevent the free play of light. It is now possible to substitute in the shading of one scene real light and shadow for painted light and shadow. Continually, in the contemporary theatre, the painted shadow is out of relation to the direction of the light, and what is more to the point, one loses the extra-ordinary beauty of delicate light and shade. This means, however, an abolition of realism, for it makes scene-painting, which is, of course, a matter of painted light and shade, impossible. One enters into a world of decorative effects which give the actor a renewed importance. There is less to compete against him, for there is less detail, though there is more beauty."

Mr. Yeats expressed himself as sanguine in regard to the future of the Abbey Theatre, and seemed to look forward to a long run of artistic, dramatic, and literary prosperity, and to the house being able to do good work in the future for dramatic literature in this country.

# The Folly of Argument

"The Folly of Argument", Yeats's first public use of the diary he kept in late 1908 and 1909, appeared in the June, 1911, issue of *The Manchester Playgoer*, a journal published by the Manchester Playgoer's Club between 1910 and 1914. These paragraphs, as well as his views on this form of prose, underwent subtle modification as they passed from the diary and through this publication to emerge fifteen years later in the Cuala Press volume entitled *Estrangement*, which constitutes one section of the *Autobiography*. The first three of these extracts appear as sections 2, 1 and 5, respectively, in *Estrangement*.

ONCE some years ago at some crisis in our Theatre's affairs, because I found that I could do no premeditated writing, I began a diary of casual meditations. Having no set form I could begin and end them when I liked, and as they were but for my own reading, it was not necessary to write them over again. The Diary is now a considerable book and I find that I turn to it continually to find out my own settled opinions. I send you some passages about argument, for the argumentative drama presses upon you in England.

## I

December 13, 1908. Last night there was a debate on a political question at the club. I was for a moment inclined to use arguments merely to answer something said by one speaker or another. I resisted the temptation however and said but personal and fanciful things that I might escape from combat. I noticed that all the arguments which had occurred to me were said by somebody or other. Logic is a machine. One can leave it to itself, and unhelped it will force those present to exhaust the subject. The fool is as likely as his betters to speak the appropriate answer to any assertion. If an argument is forgotten, somebody will go home miserable. You throw your money on the table and you take up so much change. Style, personality, deliberately adopted and therefor a mask, is the only escape from the heat of the bargaining, from all but the sight of the money changers.

## II

To keep these notes natural and useful to me in my life, I must keep one note from leading to another, for that is to surrender oneself to literature. Every note must first have come as a casual thought. Then it will be my life. If Christ or Buddha or Socrates had written, they would have surrendered life for a logical process.

## III

January 22. To oppose the new ill breeding of Ireland, which may in a few years destroy all that has given Ireland a distinguished name in the world ("O Ireland, Mother of the bravest soldiers and of the most beautiful women," cried Borrow[1] when he thought of the hospitality he had had, distributor of Bibles that he was, from the Irish monks in Spain), the artist can only set up a secondary or interior personality

[1] George Henry Borrow (1803–81), the English traveller and writer, was an early cultural philologist, one of the first foreign correspondents and a student of gypsies. During much of his travel through England, France, Germany, Russia, and the Far East, he was an agent for the British and Foreign Bible Society.

created out of the tradition of himself, and this personality (alas if it be only in his writings) must be always gracious and simple. It must have that slight separation from immediate interests which makes charm possible, while remaining near enough for fire. Is not charm what it is perhaps because it is an escape from mechanism? So much of the world as is dominated by the contest of interests is a mechanism. The newspaper is the roar of the machine. Argument the moment acknowledged victory is sought becomes a clash of interests. One should not, above all not in those books that sigh for immortality, argue at all if one is not ready to leave to another apparent victory. In daily life one becomes rude the moment one grudges to the clown his perpetual triumph.

## IV

February 12. The modern audience dislikes the free mind, the mind that plays with life, expressing great things lightly. It dislikes all that is not plainly organised and determined, all that is not plainly logical. A play with a purpose or a moral is as much a part of social organization as a newspaper or a speech. It likes to see the railway tracks of thought. It is afraid of the wilderness. It would go down a steep place into the sea if it accepted the devilish doctrine from which arises the seeming frivolity of noble minds, that truth is a state of mind and not a thought nor a remembered syllogism nor an opinion. It dreads all liberated things and is half fascinated by what it dreads. It loves rhetoric because rhetoric is impersonal and predetermined, and it hates poetry whose suggestions cannot be foreseen. It does not hate the freedom of the rich and the highbred more bitterly than the phantasy of the poor. It holds to all rules because it cannot live without them and it would turn all art and literature into a blackboard for its own instruction. Fortunately noble thought when it has been a long time in the world is so written about and so obscured by common minds that it seems at last safe reading for slaves and even worthy to instruct them.

W. B. Yeats

# The Theatre of Beauty

Although he had been reluctant at first, Yeats was convinced by the prospect of trouble in presenting *The Playboy of the Western World* to Irish-American audiences and by casting problems to join the Abbey company when they embarked on an American tour on September 13, 1911. Lady Gregory, who followed in a few days and who remained with the players until the tour ended in March, 1912, recorded their troubles and successes in Chapter VII of *Our Irish Theatre*. Although Yeats was unsuccessful in his attempt to collect the essays which were to constitute *The Cutting of An Agate* (1912) in time for their publication while he was in America, both he and Lady Gregory were much sought after for interviews and personal appearances, particularly at colleges where the Irish plays, especially those of Synge, were already class-room texts. Lady Gregory spoke at Smith and Vassar, and Yeats spoke, on October 5, at Harvard. The text of his address on "The Theatre of Beauty" was published in *Harper's Weekly* on November 11, 1911.

The opening section is a variation on the discussion of "character" as a distinguishing factor between comic and tragic writing with which he began "The Tragic Theatre" (see pp. 384–92 above) No doubt the greater concentration here on the mechanics of stage arrangement reflect Yeats's extensive experimentation with Gordon Craig's system in the intervening year.

### AN ADDRESS DELIVERED BEFORE THE DRAMATIC CLUB OF HARVARD UNIVERSITY

ONE day when I was watching a player, a leading character in Lady Gregory's "C[a]navans,"[1] I made a discovery. I said to myself, "That is beautiful comedy. He is displaying the fear of death, that is the subject of the play in all its forms, and yet it is all comedy, a game, all like a child's game."

Then I said to myself, that because he was really never in fear of death—he was passionless. The discovery filled me with excitement; I had discovered a new thing about comedy. Presently I was producing Molière's "Miser,"[2] and there also I saw it was all a child's game. Those persons did not really love and hate. I began puzzling myself to find out what comedy had if it left the passion to tragedy, and I saw it was

---

[1] *The Canavans*, by Lady Gregory, was produced by The Abbey Theatre in December, 1906. Yeats's reference is probably to W. G. Fay's portrayal of Peter Canavan, an Elizabethan miller who is mistakenly imprisoned as a deserter and who, at the opening of Act II, is seen awaiting his execution.

[2] *The Miser*, a translation by Lady Gregory of Molière's *L'Avare*, was produced by the Abbey Theatre in January, 1909.

character. Then I found in a letter of Congreve's[3] the statement that
humor was that which one man had as distinguished from all other men.
Humor was with him clearly the same thing as character. He said, too,
that you could not give character to the young women in a play, because they had too much passion. It was clear that he saw the antithesis.
I realized that when I watched Falstaff on the stage; I said to myself,
"How unlike all other men he is! I would know him if I met him in the
street." But when I saw one of Shakespeare's tragic characters in a supreme moment—Hamlet, let us say, when he says to his friend: "absent
thee from felicity awhile"; or Antony when he names "of many million
kisses the poor last"; or Timon when he orders his tomb—at such times
I do not say: "How like that man is to himself," but rather: "That man
is myself." All humanity is there in one man. Shakespeare expresses
something that is common to all, something that is like a liquid that can
be poured into vessels of every shape; whereas writers of comedy (and
in all but his supreme moments Shakespeare is a writer of comedy)
were occupied with the shape of the vessel. Corneille and Racine, who,
like Shakespeare, were tragedians alone, substitute for character different motives—one man is jealous, another man hates, another loves.
The persons of their plays are but contrasted or opposing passions,
and with a right instinct they generalize the surroundings of these passions. To express character, which has a great deal of circumstance, of
habit, you require a real environment; some one place, some one moment of time: but in tragedy, which comes from that within us which
dissolves away limits, there is a need for surroundings where beauty,
decoration, pattern—that is to say, the universal in form—takes the
place of accidental circumstance.

The practical workers of the European theatres are at this moment
seeking to create a method of representation that will make the theatre
more beautiful, and some are striving to make possible there a stately
unreal scenery; because they would find adequate staging for musical
drama, which, like tragedy, is all passion, or because they desire to
bring poetry on the stage again. If one would work honestly in any art,
it is necessary to ask oneself what that art possesses as distinguished from
all other arts. If you are going to decorate a plate you do not put upon
it something which would look better in an easel painting. You think
of the color, surface, shape, and use of the plate, and set something upon
it which will look well there and nowhere else. It is the same if you were
asked to put a great painting in a public building. You remember that
this is to be seen from far away by people in many different moods, and
that it is a part of the architecture. You avoid detail and a painted per-

[3] Yeats's reference to Congreve's letter as well as his touchstones from Shakespeare are
repeated from his essay on "The Tragic Theatre", pp. 386-7 above.

spective that would make a hole in your wall—at least you do if you are Puvis de Chavannes. Now the art of the stage has three things which the easel painting has not. It has real light and shade, it has real perspective, and it has the action of the player. It is absurd when you have these things to use a painting of light and shade with painted perspective, and a landscape so elaborate that your players are reduced to a picturesque group in the foreground of an old-fashioned picture. It is absurd to paint and set before an audience a meretricious easel painting, a bad academy picture which is so full of fussy detail that the players do not stand out in a clear outline against it, and that takes to itself also some of the attention which should be given to their actions and to their words. I have seen painted shadows again and again in the theatre contradict the real light; but even when they did not contradict it— when by some surprising conjuring trick the real light comes from the same point as the painted light does, or, as is more general, from all points—you have lost one of the most beautiful dramatic effects: change of light. We should banish all those painted shadows, and light the stage, as far as possible, as Nature does: from a single point. Very often a reflecting surface will give one, as it does in Nature, all the effusion of light one needs.

Nothing alarms the ordinary producer so much as a real shadow, yet it may be an infinitely expressive thing. In a play I am writing at this moment I shall represent the passing crowd by a row of huddled shadows on the wall.[4] Professor Reinhardt, one of the men of the New Movement, in a production that he brought to London the other day, brought certain of his players down a raised platform through the auditorium, and before they reached the stage one saw there their shadows of an immense size.[5] It was the finest thing in a production that a little disappointed me. In the same way you can use light and compose with it. You have a great, bare wall that seems to you monotonous. Instead of painting a commonplace window upon it, you can cast a shaft of light across it and so have something living and changing, which is all delightful to watch.

[4] Yeats's reference is probably to the penultimate scene of *The Green Helmet*, produced in February of the preceding year, in which he had treated the "Horse Boys and Scullions" as scuffling shadows before a wall. While a printed version of the play had been included in *The Green Helmet and Other Poems* in December, 1910, the separate edition of the play was in preparation when this address was being written.

[5] Just after the turn of the century, Max Reinhardt (1873–1943), the Austrian actor, had become an experimental producer. Working with technicians, architects, choreographers, musicians, and young actors trained in his methods, he created a stylized theatre with the avowed intention both of freeing the stage from the requirements of realistic literature and of greatly intensifying the contact between actors and audience. In December, 1911, Reinhardt and his company had produced Vollmöller's *The Miracle* at the Olympic Theatre, London.

Easel painting is no natural part of the theatre. It was imposed upon it at the end of the Renaissance by the graphic genius of Italy. Up to that moment the theatre had used its real perspective and its real light almost wholly. For a time all art dwindled before painting, but now that the proportions have returned, we have restored the theatre to its normal state. This in the end will bring about a change in the shape of the building, for our theatrical architecture is at present arranged for effects of painting and does not admit of free play of light. If we are to get either ideal beauty or reality in our stage landscapes, we should change its shape. At present, narrow strips of painted canvas arranged in lines parallel to the footlights hang from the gridiron of the theatre to prevent the audience observing that gridiron, and on this the sky is painted, or the branches of trees. These borders are the ugly, obvious convention. They have no beauty and they create no illusion, and, what is worse, they make natural lighting—light from one point, as in Nature —impossible. The lights must be hung in rows between them; so, too, we have to fill up the sides of the stage that the audience may not see the walls of the building, and so we use there what are called "wings": three or four frames of canvas on each side, one behind the other, from the proscenium to the back drop. They can hardly represent anything but trees—and what trees! Is there a picture gallery in the world that would accept such a painting? Every open place must be a bare place in a forest and lit by streaks of light from every direction.

Synge gave up his intention of showing upon the stage a fight in a plowed field between "The Playboy" and his father, because he would not have six large trees, three on each side, growing in the middle of a plowed field. The stage directors of Europe have tried various experiments to amend this. One method would be to extend the platform behind the proscenium to a great distance on each side, until the shape of the building would be that of an immense T. I heard this discussed by a great stage director. It would have the advantage that any spectators sitting toward one side in the first rows would be prevented from seeing the side walls of the stage. No wings would be necessary, nothing but the back drop would be visible. We could get rid not only of our side wings, but of all those built-up scenes which make the stage so expensive. I am told that Herr Kemendy,[6] of Budapest, has carried out something like this scheme. He has bent the back wall of the top of his stage, a T, into an arc that brings it almost around the ends of the pro-

---

[6] The continuous wall which Yeats describes here was only one of the innovations introduced by the Hungarian stage designer, Jeno Kemendy, at the National Theatre in Budapest. In addition to piercing the wall to allow for various back-lighting effects, he divided the front half of the stage into three sections and provided for either of the side sections to be rolled off and on stage to allow for changes of setting.

scenium opening and gives it a curve. There are two opinions as to whether such a curve (which a friend of mine says makes him feel as if he were sitting in the middle of a balloon) better represents Nature than the flat surface or straight line which we are ready to accept as a simple convention. Herr Reinhardt and Mariano Fortuny[7] have adopted another scheme that has much the same effect, and at the same time gives the arc of the sky instead of the canvas borders. They use a great hood of canvas, a half-dome, that curves from one side of the proscenium to the other, and from the back of the stage to the top of the proscenium arch. Nothing is visible but a great curved surface, much like the dome of the sky, upon which lights in color may be thrown. Monsieur Fortuny's lighting arrangements are very curious. He does not use painting at all, I understand, when he has everything in his own hands, and is applying his methods in his own way. He creates color by the throwing of colored light upon the object, and he shows his audience a clear or cloudy day by throwing into the hood, through a curved slot in the floor that goes around the base of the hood, lights reflected from rolls of colored silks. Monsieur Fortuny is very ingenious. His dome folds up like the hood of a perambulator, but in the opposite direction, from the bottom. The chief difficulty about this method is that, owing to the rolling of the canvas, creases soon appear across the sky.

All of these methods based upon the curved-back scene aim, I think, to give one a beautiful, realistic effect, reproducing as exactly as possible the sense of the open air—they aim to do what the Japanese theatre has always considered an impossibility. In Japan an interior will be exactly represented, because it can be reproduced on the stage so as to be indistinguishable from what it is in a house; but an exterior is only suggested. For instance, the Japanese will represent the sea by surrounding not only the stage but the auditorium with the well-known Japanese wave pattern. Being a writer of poetic drama, and of tragic drama, desiring always pattern and convention, I would like to keep to suggestion, to symbolism, to pattern like the Japanese. Yet realism, too, is a legitimate thing, and a necessary thing for all plays that seek to represent the actual environment of a man, and to reflect the surface of life in words and actions. We should not stage Galsworthy and Shakespeare in the same way. Realism also may be beautiful, but it is well that its mechanism be made perfect.

[7] See note 4, pp. 383-4 above.

# The Story of the Irish Players

Yeats departed for Ireland on October 17, 1911, after the largely uneventful opening of *The Playboy of the Western World* in Boston on the 16th. Under the direction of Lady Gregory, the Abbey company concluded their tour in Chicago in February, 1912, after triumphs and troubles which included their arrest in Philadelphia. Yeats's name continued to be associated with the touring players by means of such devices as his contribution to a series on "The Story of the Irish Players", which occupied the front page of the Drama section of Chicago's *Sunday Record–Herald* on February 4, 1912. Both in tone and content, Yeats's paragraphs, entitled "What We Try to Do", are rather thin glosses of many of his previous writings. This piece was accompanied by "Not for Money" by Sara Allgood, "Thanking God for Synge" by T. W. Rolleston, "Our Trials and Triumphs" by Lady Gregory and "From the Beginning" in which George Moore praises "the indefatigable Yeats" who had asked him to help with the Irish theater. ". . . but I was haughty, whereas Yeats knew how to stoop and conquer, and he conquered because he was possessed of an idea, and an idea is always sufficient to secure success".

## THE STORY OF THE IRISH PLAYERS
## WHAT WE TRY TO DO

WHEN the idea of giving expression on the stage to the dramatic literature of Ireland was about to be carried out in 1899 it was found that no Irish actors were to be had. So we brought an English company to Dublin and Irish plays were presented by them for a short period.[1] This method, however, did not produce the results we had hoped for; the English actors lacked the proper feeling for the Irish spirit. In 1902 there was a nearer approach to a realization of a truly national Irish theatre, for a company of amateurs produced Irish plays in small halls in Dublin.[2] The players received nothing, nor did they ask remuneration. Since they had to gain a living by another work to carry on the work they were interested in the double burden told heavily on them.

When it looked as if all might have to be given up my friend Miss

---

[1] All the major parts in the Literary Theatre's production of *The Countess Cathleen* were played by Englishmen and this was true also of the three plays produced in 1900. The next year, F. R. Benson's company, which was imported to play in *Diarmuid and Grania*, was disappointing and the Theatre's critics were quick to draw attention to the comparative success of the members of the Keating branch of the Gaelic League, who played in Douglas Hyde's Gaelic play, *Cásadh an tSugáin*.

[2] The members of W. G. Fay's Irish National Dramatic Company acted in the 1902 season and became the Irish National Theatre Society later that year.

Horniman[3] arranged for a little theatre in connection with the Mecha-anics' Institute and after a struggle the idea of a national Irish theatre became an assured fact. The National Theatre Society now has the Abbey Theater in Dublin and it is entirely independent and paying its way. But this does not mean that we did not have a hard fight. Our great difficulty was that in our first years our income was mostly from six-penny and one shilling seats in the gallery and pit. Clerks, shop boys, shop girls and workmen—audiences of much enthusiasm but little money—came to see our plays, which appealed to them. Our theater had its beginnings not among the rich, as did the New Theater in New York,[4] but right in the masses of the people. The working people showed the way and now that all classes come to us we constantly fill the Abbey Theater.

## THE PREDOMINANT PEASANT

With us the Irish peasant is predominant for the moment, as was the peasant in the Norwegian movement. During the youth of Ibsen and Bjornson their phrase was "To understand the peasant by the saga and the saga by the peasant." Our whole movement could apply to itself the same phrase. Lady Gregory, the author of our most amusing come-dies, is also the author of the standard translation of the Irish epic stories, which she has translated into the speech of the Irish peasant.[5] Synge, too, when he put an old heroic tale into dramatic play made use of dialect.

Speaking of Synge, we have two opposite types of characters in Ireland that both seem peculiarly national. One is the gentle, harmless —you might call it saintly—type, that knows no wrong, and goes through life happy and untroubled, without any evil or sadness. Gold-smith was an Irishman of that type, a man without any real knowledge apparently of sadness or evil. And that kind of Irishman is common in Ireland, chiefly among the better-off people, but among the country people you find it too. There are a surprising number of constitutionally happy people in Ireland.

The other type that is also so characteristically Irish is represented by

---

[3] The good works of Annie Horniman, the English tea heiress and the difficult but generous benefactress of the Irish National Theatre Society, culminated in her purchase and refurbishing, in 1904, of the building which became the Abbey Theatre. For a note on Yeats's later differences with Miss Horniman, see p. 485 below.

[4] In 1909 the New Theater, a richly endowed experiment in national theater, had been founded in New York by Winthrop Ames (1871–1937). It was imitative of the European art-theaters and although it listed many of the country's richest men as its patrons, the project collapsed in 1911, with a deficit of $400,000.

[5] Lady Gregory had rendered the Cuchulain legends into the Kiltartan dialect in *Cuchulain of Muirthemne* (1902). For Yeats's earlier commentary on the work, see p. 299 above.

Swift. It is true he had little or no Irish blood, but in bringing up he was an Irish product. And that type is terribly bitter, hostile, sarcastic.

Now Synge belonged to this bitter, sarcastic type in so far as he was a satirist. He was no incarnation of Goldsmith, but rather the opposite. Yet his personality, his emotions were remarkably sane and healthy, even though they were not placid. Only the other day I heard a paper read in which he was described as the embodiment of a healthy mentality.

That was the truth, and I agreed with it. But the strange part was that Synge gained his healthiness from living for years facing death. He faced death in his own body, for he was constitutionally weak. And in going to the Aran Islands he found a people that faced death, and he lived with them. The islanders are all the time being picked off by the sea, from which they make their livelihood, yet they are a strong, healthy people. And so, in his life facing death, Synge in the end gained a wonderful mental healthiness, though only after a struggle.

### FIRST MEETING WITH SYNGE

When I first met Synge in 1897 I found that he wanted to write about French literature. He had been studying Molière, Corneille, and Racine. I told him that if he was to write for the English papers he would find that they demanded something about modern French literature. Of the latter he knew nothing. If he was influenced by French writers they were of the pre-Molière period, and about them there was certainly nothing decadent.

He was a nationalist, but he never spoke of politics. Nothing interested him but the individual man. It was no malice, no love of mischief, that made him imagine, instead of colleens of the old sort and the good young men of Boucicault, blind Martin and his wife, in "The Well of the Saints," the erring wife in "The Shadow of the Glen," the fantastic mistaken hero-worship of the people in his "Playboy of the Western World." Dublin for a time saw but one-half his meaning and rejected him, rioting for a week after the first performance of his greatest play,[6] rejecting him as most countries have rejected their greatest poets. But Dublin has repented sooner than most countries have repented, and today "The Playboy" is played constantly in Dublin to good houses, drawn from all political and social sections.

[6] The *"Playboy* riots" are discussed on p. 347 above.

# Stage Scenery

An appreciation of an exhibition of Gordon Craig's designs for several productions in *The Times* for September 10, 1912, prompted Yeats's letter in the issue for September 13. Apparently, the reviewer's regretful note that Craig's ideas must generally be understood from drawings, rather than in production, seemed to Yeats to slight the Abbey's use of them.

## TO THE EDITOR OF *THE TIMES*

SIR,—You say in your issue of September 10 of Mr. Gordon Craig's substitution of screens for painted scenery:—"Except *The Hour Glass* at the Abbey Theatre, Dublin, the Moscow *Hamlet*[1] is the only play, we believe, in which they have been chiefly or exclusively used." We have used them in *The Canavans*, a comedy in three acts; in *The Deliverer*, a tragedy in one act, as well as in *The Hour Glass*;[2] and only the long American tour of our company has prevented us using them in other plays. They gave out beautiful effects, light, and impressive form.

Yours truly,

W. B. Yeats

Abbey Theatre, Dublin, Sept. 11

# Dublin Fanaticism

A strike by Irish transportation workers in late August, 1913, initiated the famous struggle between the Irish Transport and General Workers' Union led by James Larkin (1876–1947) and the Dublin employers whose spokesman was William Martin Murphy, Yeats's old antagonist (see p. 306 above). The employers' devastating lock-out increased the desperation of the workers and their families, and there was frequent violence at depots and loading docks. Further tensions arose in October, when a plan was announced, and immediately opposed by both the Catholic Church and the Nationalists, for the wives and children of workers to go to England to live. Consequently, in addition to the random violence there were demonstrations by the Nationalists, with the unusual condonation of the Unionist officials, aimed at turning the emigrants back physically. On October 27 Larkin was sent to prison.

Yeats's letter on "Dublin Fanaticism", which appeared in *The Irish Worker*,

---

[1] The revolutionary production of *Hamlet* at the Moscow Art Theatre on January 8, 1912, concluded a collaboration of more than three years' duration between Gordon Craig and Konstantin Stanislavsky (1863–1938).

[2] See pp. 384, 392 above, for the Abbey's use of Craig's scenes in *The Deliverer* and *The Hour-Glass*. Yeats's mention of Lady Gregory's *The Canavans* is probably a mistake, as neither the authoritative *Edward Gordon Craig* by Denis Bablet (Paris, 1962; New York, 1966) nor any records of the Abbey's activities mention designs by Craig for this play.

Larkin's paper, on November 1, was his only interruption of the disillusioned detachment from public events reflected by such poems of this period as "September, 1913". The even-handed condemnation of all parties seems eccentric in the company of contributions like Constance Markievicz's "In Jail", Maud Gonne's "The Real Criminals", and a brief note signed "Eileen", which refers to the Lord Mayor of Dublin as "the 'Mountjoy Midget'". For "A.E.", however, who had spoken on November 1 along with Larkin's sister, James Connolly, and Bernard Shaw at a rally at the Albert Hall, Yeats's letter was welcome support. "I have differed from you in many things", he wrote a few days later, "but I felt all my old friendship and affection surging up as I read what you said" (*Letters from AE*, p. 91).

I DO not complain of Dublin's capacity for fanaticism whether in priest or layman, for you cannot have strong feeling without that capacity, but neither those who directed the police nor the editors of our newspapers can plead fanaticism. They are supposed to watch over our civil liberties, and I charge the Dublin Nationalist newspapers with deliberately arousing religious passion to break up the organisation of the workingman, with appealing to mob law day after day, with publishing the names of workingmen and their wives for purposes of intimidation. And I charge the Unionist Press of Dublin and those who directed the police with conniving at this conspiracy. I want to know why the "Daily Express," which is directly and indirectly inciting Ulster to rebellion in defence of what it calls "The liberty of the subject"[1] is so indifferent to that liberty here in Dublin that it has not made one editorial comment, and I ask the "Irish Times" why a few sentences at the end of an article, too late in the week to be of any service, has been the measure of its love for civil liberty? I want to know why there are only (according to the Press reports) two policemen at Kingsbridge on Saturday when Mr. Sheehy Skeffington[2] was assaulted and a man prevented from buying a ticket for his own child? There had been tumults every night at every Dublin railway station, and I can only assume that the police authorities wished those tumults to continue. I want to know why the mob at North Wall and elsewhere were permitted to drag children from their parents' arms, and by what right one woman was compelled to open her box and show a marriage certificate; I want

[1] The great debate over the Home Rule Act and whether it could include Unionist Ulster was raging at this time, amid threats of armed resistance from the Ulster Volunteers.

[2] Francis Sheehy-Skeffington (1878–1916), the political journalist, was a socialist, a pacifist and—along with his wife, Hannah Sheehy—a leading feminist. In the face of the violence which developed during the Transport Workers' strike, Sheehy-Skeffington urged conciliation between the strikers and management. He was an inveterate lamp-post orator, which perhaps bears on the attack to which Yeats refers here.

to know by what right the police have refused to accept charges against rioters; I want to know who has ordered the abrogation of the most elementary rights of the citizens, and why authorities who are bound to protect every man in doing that which he has a legal right to do—even though they have to call upon all the forces of the Crown—have permitted the Ancient Order of Hibernians[3] to besiege Dublin, taking possession of the railway stations like a foreign army. Prime Ministers have fallen, and ministers of State have been impeached for less than this. I demand that the coming Police Inquiry shall be so widened that we may get to the bottom of a conspiracy, whose like has not been seen in any English-speaking town during living memory. Intriguers have met together somewhere behind the scenes that they might turn the religion of Him who thought it hard for a rich man to enter into the Kingdom of Heaven into an oppression of the poor.

# Mr. W. B. Yeats and Ghosts

On All-Hallows' Eve, 1913, Yeats lectured on "Ghosts and Dreams" before the Dublin Branch of the Psychical Research Society. His involvement with psychical research, as distinct from his interest in philosophical and esoteric mysticism, had begun around 1911. In 1912 he began to record the results of his experiments with a young medium, Elizabeth Radcliffe, whose automatic writing often contained languages entirely unknown to her, among them Hebrew, Greek, Welsh, Provençal, Chinese and Coptic. At about the same time he became acquainted with the work of the Society for Psychical Research and with its president, Dr. Everard Fielding. It is likely that Yeats's lecture to the Society was a report on his experiments with Bessie Radcliffe.

A wry report of his lecture in *The Irish Times* the following day concluded with the advice that Yeats should not so easily disclose that his poems were "inspired" by "some kind of super-dream . . .". In his letter to the editor in the issue for November 3, Yeats ignores this taunt, contenting himself with correcting the report of his experiments with languages.

---

[3] The Ancient Order of Hibernians, an Irish-American Roman Catholic organization, was founded in 1836 and claimed to be derived from a fourteenth-century religious group. Although it was often involved in social and political matters, its greatest influence seems to have been exerted through secret and often terrorist support of Irish Catholic policies.

SIR,—In a well-meaning article on my lecture at the Psychical Research Society yesterday, you say: "He stated that he had communicated with ghosts in no less than five different languages—Greek, Hebrew, Latin, Irish, and Welsh. We feel that we must congratulate both him and his friends, the spirits, upon their linguistic accomplishments." I have claimed no such accomplishment. I am very ignorant of languages. I hope you will not take it as a discourtesy that I do not explain what I did say. Life is short.—Yours, etc.,

W. B. Yeats

Abbey Theatre, Dublin,
1st November, 1913.

Our reporter's exact note of Mr. Yeats's statement is as follows:—"I myself have read writings written in a medium's hand. I have had writings in Greek, in Hebrew, in Latin, in German, some in Welsh, some in Irish, a great mass of tongues—certainly unknown to the medium, who is a personal friend of mine, a young girl."

We agree with Mr. Yeats that life is too short for explanations of his psychical adventures.—ED. I.T.

# The Playboy

*The Playboy of the Western World* continued to arouse controversy and to draw Yeats to its public defense. Disruption of the Abbey's performances at the Liverpool Repertory Theatre on November 24 and 27, 1913, caused the Theatre's management, under pressure from the authorities, to withdraw the play from the matinee program on Saturday, November 29. This action provoked a letter from Yeats in *The Times* of London on December 1, which was answered by the manager of the Repertory Theatre, Godfrey Edwards, in a letter which appeared in *The Times* for December 3. Edwards' reply, that "Having succeeded in giving the play a fair hearing, the management decided entirely upon their own responsibility to alter the programme", was the subject of Yeats's second letter, in *The Times* on December 4.

## ACTION OF THE LIVERPOOL POLICE

MR. W. B. YEATS writes from Stone Cottage, Coleman's Hatch, Sussex, under Saturday's date:—

"The Irish Players have been giving a number of plays during the last week at the Repertory Theatre, Liverpool. The *Playboy* was performed on Monday and on Thursday evenings. The audience, on the whole, were exceedingly enthusiastic, but from time to time fervoured Irish patriots, who are a little old-fashioned in their opinions, interrupted and were thrown out. Yesterday our manager received a message from the police asking that the play should not be produced at the Saturday *matinée*. If the police are to be allowed to suppress plays at their will, a very serious issue has been raised affecting the reputations and financial interests of managers and dramatic authors. That for the first time a performance of the *Playboy* should have been prevented by the mob, reinforced by the police, matters little to the Irish players. They have a large repertory and can substitute almost always for any play another not less popular and nothing to-day can injure the fame of a work of art already a classic. But like action by the police might well ruin a company touring but one play and looking to Saturday, the most profitable day of the week, to pay its weekly salaries. If a play is immoral, it is subject to prosecution, but it is to no man's interest that it should be subject to the irresponsible will of the police. The Liverpool police were alarmed because a crowd gathered in the street, a crowd of men and women, not one of 50 of whom had read or seen the play . . .

"It cannot be in the interest of the public or the police that the police should be left under the temptation to suppress the victim to avoid the trouble of suppressing the more formidable malefactor. They might as well forbid a man whose watch had been stolen to leave his house because of the indignation his complaint had caused among the thieves, as forbid without process of law or public inquiry the production of a famous play which lies under no charge of immorality and is held by most educated Irishmen to be the master-work of the dramatic literature of Ireland."

# "The Playboy" at Liverpool

THE TIMES, DECEMBER 4, 1913

SIR,—Mr. Godfrey Edwards says in *The Times* of to-day that the police of Liverpool did not "request," but "simply suggested" the withdrawal of *The Playboy of the Western World*, and the "management" of the Repertory Theatre accepted the police suggestion "entirely upon their own responsibility."

*The Playboy* has been played in many towns in America, in England,

and in Ireland, and besides those, always increasing in number, who consider the play a classic, others resenting the sarcastic genius of its creator have organized demonstrations. But nowhere outside Liverpool have the police made "suggestions" which are a precedent for mob law and a menace to all playwrights who would serve their art and not their purse and have enough imagination and power to be loved and hated.

I am yours sincerely,

W. B. Yeats

Stone Cottage, Coleman's Hatch, Sussex, Dec. 3.

# Mr. W. S. Blunt

On January 18, 1914, at the instigation of Ezra Pound, Yeats, Pound, F. S. Flint (b. 1885), Richard Aldington (1892–1962), Sturge Moore and Victor Plarr (1863–1929) dined with Wilfrid Scawen Blunt (1840–1922) in honor of his seventy-fourth birthday. Yeats had known Blunt much earlier, when Blunt had joined in Irish agitation against absentee-landlordism, and in 1907 the Abbey Theatre had produced Blunt's *Fand*, a verse play on "the only jealousy of Emer" (*Letters*, p. 376). The two men had met from time to time, although Blunt's outspoken anti-Imperialism had forced his retirement from public life. Yeats's contributions to the birthday celebration consisted of the inspiration for the main course—a peacock served in full plumage—and an unsigned notice, attributed to him by Hone (*W. B. Yeats*, p. 291), which appeared in *The Times* for January 20.

AT Newbuildings Place, Sussex, on Sunday, a committee of poets consisting of W. B. Yeats, Sturge Moore, John Masefield, Victor Plarr, Frederic Manning, Ezra Pound, F. S. Flint, and Richard Aldington, presented to Mr. Wilfred Scawen Blunt, in token of homage for his poetry, a carved reliquary of Pentelican marble, the work of the sculptor Gaudier Brzeska.[1] It bears a recumbent female figure and an inscrip-

---

[1] Hilaire Belloc joined the company after dinner. In his excellent account of this gathering ("A Peacock Dinner: The Homage of Pound and Yeats to Wilfrid Scawen Blunt", *Journal of Modern Literature*, March, 1971, pp. 303–10) William T. Going notes that Masefield and Manning did not finally attend the dinner, although Masefield sent a poem. Apparently Robert Bridges, then Poet Laureate, declined to attend because of Blunt's politics and Going states that Blunt thought the reliquary by Henri Gaudier-Brezeska (1891–1915), with its recumbent female figure figure, was "in bad taste, and he was obliged later to turn it with its face to the wall" (p. 305).

tion. The committee had intended to give a dinner in Mr. Blunt's honour, but he preferred to receive them at Newbuildings.

The following verses of address were read:

*To Wilfred Blunt.*
*Because you have gone your individual gait,*
*Written fine verses, made mock of the world,*
*Swung the grand style, not made a trade of art,*
*Upheld Mazzini and detested institutions:*
*We, who are little given to respect,*
*Respect you, and having no better way to show it,*
*Bring you this stone to be some record of it.*[2]

Mr. Blunt said in his reply that he was to some extent an impostor. He had been all sorts of other things, but never a poet. He was not brought up that way at all. He was never at a public school, nor at a college. He had written a certain amount of verse, but only when he was rather down on his luck and had made mistakes either in love or politics or some branch of his active life. He found that it relieved his feelings. He never thought in the least of getting it published: he did not even show it to his friends. His first little anonymous work was published when he was 35 or 36—and it was not much of a thing even then. He did not publish a single verse over his own name till he was about 43. His life had been an active one in various connexions, and people wrote to him sometimes, "We have great admiration for you". But it was never about his poetry. It had been either because he had taken up the cause of the Indian or the Egyptian, or more generally because he bred horses, that he was generally known. In one of the very first things he wrote he was ill-advised enough to say that he would not be called a poet, and that had stuck to him ever since. However, he had come round rather from that now. Within the last year or two he had washed his hands of politics and all forms of public life, and had withdrawn to a great extent from horse-breeding, and, having nothing to do, he had taken up with verse-writing to console him for a new disappointment. He had been writing a certain amount in the last year, and was very pleased now to be considered a poet.

There was then some general discussion of rhyme, blank verse, and assonance as Mr. Blunt's speech became less formal and was mingled with replies from individual members of the committee.

[2] In this poem, Pound confuses Giuseppe Mazzini (1805–72), the Italian revolutionary with Ahmed Arabi (1841?–1911), the Egyptian rebel with whom Blunt had been associated. Going (*ibid.*) cites Blunt's comment on this confusion as it is quoted in Edith Finch's *Wilfrid Scawen Blunt: 1840–1922* (London, 1938, p. 337): "But I really did not understand the address they read me or perceive till afterwards that they had confused Arabi with Mazzini in it, and I was afraid of committing myself in reply to anything serious."

# Poetry's Banquet

*Poetry*, the magazine of verse, had been founded in Chicago in 1912 by Harriet Monroe (1860–1936). At the end of its first season, the journal had awarded a prize of £50 for the best poem to Yeats for "The Grey Rock". Wade (p. 584) prints a letter in which Yeats returned £40, hoping that it might be used to help a younger poet, and another (p. 585) in which he suggests Ezra Pound as the recipient. When he visited America in 1914, Yeats was honored at a banquet given on March 1 by the Poetry Society of Chicago at the "Cliff Dwellers". An account of his speech appeared in the April issue of *Poetry*.

AT the dinner given in honor of Mr. William Butler Yeats by the guarantors, contributors and editors of *Poetry*, in the rooms of the Cliff-Dwellers, Chicago, on the evening of March first, the Irish poet took occasion to warn his confreres in America against a number of besetting sins. He said, in part:

"Twenty-five years ago a celebrated writer from South Africa said she lived in the East End of London because only there could she see the faces of people without a mask. To this Oscar Wilde replied that he lived in the West End because nothing interested him but the mask.[1] After a week of lecturing I am too tired to assume a mask, so I will address my remarks especially to a fellow craftsman. For since coming to Chicago I have read several times a poem by Mr. Lindsay,[2] one which will be in the anthologies, "General Booth Enters Into Heaven." This poem is stripped bare of ornament; it has an earnest simplicity, a strange beauty, and you know Bacon said, "There is no excellent beauty without strangeness.'[3] . . .

"I have lived a good many years and have read many writers. When I was younger than Mr. Lindsay, and was beginning to write in Ireland, there was all around me the rhetorical poetry of the Irish politicians. We young writers rebelled against that rhetoric; there was too much of it

---

[1] In "The Trembling of the Veil" (*Autobiography*, p. 111) Yeats recalls Wilde's having told of this encounter with Olive Schreiner (1855–1920).

[2] The American poet, Vachel Lindsay (1879–1931), had published "General William Booth Enters into Heaven" in 1913. Joseph Hone notes that Lindsay cited this remark nearly twenty-five years later, in a letter to Yeats, as "the literary transformation scene of my life". ". . . you did me the honour to speak well of one piece of my work in public, and by the magic of your name, everything that I have written since has been too much praised, whether you saw it or not, or whether it was worthy of your eyes" (*W. B. Yeats*, p. 298).

[3] In his essay, "Of Beauty" (1625), Bacon observes that "There is no excellent beauty that hath not some strangeness in the proportion".

and to a great extent it was meaningless. When I went to London I found a group of young lyric writers who were also against rhetoric. We formed the Rhymers' Club; we used to meet and read our poems to one another, and we tried to rid them of rhetoric.

"But now, when I open the ordinary American magazine, I find that all we rebelled against in those early days—the sentimentality, the rhetoric, the "moral uplift"—still exist here. Not because you are too far from England, but because you are too far from Paris.

"It is from Paris that nearly all the great influences in art and literature have come, from the time of Chaucer until now. Today the metrical experiments of French poets are overwhelming in their variety and delicacy. The best English writing is dominated by French criticism; in France is the great critical mind.

"The Victorians forgot this; also, they forgot the austerity of art and began to preach. When I saw Paul Verlaine in Paris, he told me that he could not translate Tennyson because he was 'too *Anglais*, too noble' —'when he should be broken-hearted he has too many reminiscences.'[4]

"We in England, our little group of rhymers, were weary of all this. We wanted to get rid not only of rhetoric but of poetic diction. We tried to strip away everything that was artificial, to get a style like speech, as simple as the simplest prose, like a cry of the heart. . . .

"Real enjoyment of a beautiful thing is not achieved when a poet tries to teach. It is not the business of a poet to instruct his age. He should be too humble to instruct his age. His business is merely to express himself, whatever that self may be. I would have all American poets keep in mind the example of François Villon.

"So you who are readers should encourage American poets to strive to become very simple, very humble. Your poet must put the fervor of his life into his work, giving you his emotions before the world, the evil with the good, not thinking whether he is a good man or a bad man, or whether he is teaching you. A poet does not know whether he is a good man. If he is a good man, he probably thinks he is a bad man.

"Poetry that is naturally simple, that might exist as the simplest prose, should have instantaneousness of effect, provided it finds the right audience. You may have to wait years for that audience, but when it is found that instantaneousness of effect is produced."

To illustrate his points, Mr. Yeats read a few poems. Of "An Epitaph," by Mr. Walter De La Mare, he said, "There is not an original sentence in this short poem, yet it will live for centuries." He spoke of Mr. T. Sturge Moore as "one of the most exquisite poets writing in England; his poetry is a glorification of instinct." "Our Lady," by

4 Yeats recalls this remark in the fourth section of "The Trembling of the Veil" (*Autobiography*, p. 229).

Miss Mary E. Coleridge, he read as an example of "poetry as simple as daily speech." [5] Continuing, he said:

"We rebelled against rhetoric, and now there is a group of younger poets who dare to call us rhetorical. When I returned to London from Ireland, I had a young man go over all my work with me to eliminate the abstract. This was an American poet, Ezra Pound. [6] Much of his work is experimental; his work will come slowly, he will make many an experiment before he comes into his own. I should like to read to you two poems of permanent value, "The Ballad of the Goodly Fere" and "The Return." This last is, I think, the most beautiful poem that has been written in the free form, one of the few in which I find real organic rhythm. A great many poets use *vers libre* because they think it is easier to write than rhymed verse, but it is much more difficult.

"The whole movement of poetry is toward pictures, sensuous images, away from rhetoric, from the abstract, toward humility. But I fear I am now becoming rhetorical. I have been driven into Irish public life—how can I avoid rhetoric?"

Mr. Yeats then read a few poems from a group which will be printed next month in *Poetry*. Mr Nicholas Vachel Lindsay followed with his powerful poem, "The Congo," an interpretation of the African race, which will soon appear in the *Metropolitan Magazine*; also, by request, "General Booth Enters into Heaven."

# A Chance for the National Gallery

The campaign for the return to Dublin of French paintings gathered together by Hugh Lane began on November 14, 1916, when Lady Gregory gave testimony in London at a meeting of the Trustees of the National Gallery. Lane had suggested that the collection belonged in Dublin as early as 1904 (see p. 330 above) but had been frustrated by the municipal mistrust, spite and ignorance which Yeats bitterly personifies as "Paudeen" in two poems on this controversy. Lane died in the sinking of the Lusitania on May 7, 1915, leaving

---

[5] This poem by Mary Elizabeth Coleridge (1861–1907), whose grandfather was S. T. Coleridge's nephew, is included in Yeats's edition of *The Oxford Book of Modern Verse* (1936) (p. 62).

[6] Yeats had first become acquainted with "this queer creature" (*Letters*, p. 543) Ezra Pound (1885–1972) in 1909, when Pound was on his first visit to Europe. His brash inventiveness and the wide range of his enthusiasms appealed to Yeats and the two men lived together at Stone Cottage, Coleman's Hatch Sussex, during the fall and winter of 1913–14, Pound serving as Yeats's secretary.

behind an unwitnessed codicil to his will revoking an earlier decision and bequeathing his paintings, after all, to Dublin.

Lane's vexation with the Dublin officials was well known and he had been, moreover, solicited for some time by many prominent figures in English art circles. Thus, when the decision to honor the admittedly invalid codicil fell to the National Gallery Trustees, Yeats and Lady Gregory brought Dublin's case to public attention in a series of letters and articles. Lady Gregory summarized her case in a letter to *The Times* (London) on December 6 and Yeats, whose major contribution was a letter-essay in *The Observer* on January 21, 1917 (see *Letters*, pp. 616 ff.), entered the fray on December 10 with a letter to *The Observer* headed "A Chance for the National Gallery" and signed "Y", which is attributed to him by Allan Wade (*Bibliography*, p. 377).

A temporary settlement of the dispute was effected in 1959 in an agreement whereby London and Dublin share the pictures under a continuing loan. Lady Gregory's recollections of Lane and of this controversy are in her *Hugh Lane's Life and Achievement* (1921) and Lane's friend, Thomas Bodkin (1887–1961), contributed a very valuable study in *Hugh Lane and His Pictures* (1932; 2nd ed., 1934).

## IRELAND AND SIR HUGH LANE

THE TRUSTEES of the National Gallery have at this moment a great opportunity. Sir Hugh Lane, at a moment of irritation with the Dublin Corporation, made a will bequeathing his Modern French pictures, which he had intended for Dublin, to the English National Gallery. He made his will in 1913, and a little later became Director of the National Gallery of Ireland. His resentment died away and a more vivid feeling against the London National Gallery took its place. He seemed to think that if Dublin had slapped him on the one cheek the London trustees had slapped him on the other. Before starting for the visit to America from which he never returned, he wrote—coming back to his original purpose—a codicil, leaving his pictures once more to Dublin. It is not legal, for it had no witness, but the handwriting and signature are not disputed, and it leaves no doubt as to his intention. His friends testify to conversations which leave this beyond doubt, and had he not been drowned in the Lusitania he would doubtless have given it legal form. We are confident that the National Gallery Trustees will not claim a strict legal right and that Parliament will give them the necessary freedom for a gracious action.

The creation of a great gallery of modern painting in Dublin was the preoccupation of Sir Hugh Lane's life. He was a passionately patriotic man, whose patriotism never took a political form. He was typical of many men and women to-day who are giving to an educational movement the passion which previous generations gave to some sterile form of politics. The future of Ireland to a very great extent depends on the growing influence of these men and women. We cannot help or mar that influence, but we may be quite certain that any lack of generosity towards the life-work of one of them would be remembered for generations. It would be recorded in all those little popular books of history and patriotic feeling which have always had a chief part in the shaping of young Irish minds. The young men were Hugh Lane's supporters from the beginning; his quarrel was with the older men. The Dublin Corporation treated him badly. It is for our National Gallery to do honour to the memory of one of whom it has been said, "he brought into the profession of a picture dealer the magnanimity of the Medici."

Y.

# Sir Hugh Lane's Pictures

A.E. and Hugh Lane's sister, Mrs. Ruth Shine, who had been his confidential secretary, published letters in *The Times* (London) on December 12, 1916, apparently in response to a *Times* article on December 11, "Sir Hugh Lane's Pictures", which argued that the National Gallery's Trustees had no legal choice but to accept the paintings for London while urging support for a bill which would allow the Gallery to "share" them with Dublin. A.E.'s attempt to distinguish between the claims of "Law" and those of "Justice" were dismissed on December 11 as a "deplorable specimen of Irish political controversy", in a letter to *The Times* from Robert Clermont Witt (1872–1952), a lawyer and a Trustee of the National Gallery.

Witt had been a friend of Lane's and was apparently responsible for introducing him to two other figures involved in the present dispute, Charles Aitken (1869–1936), Keeper of the Tate Gallery, and Dougald Sutherland MacColl (1859–1948), Aitken's predecessor and a Tate Trustee. Thomas Bodkin quotes Lane's letter, written on January 14, 1913, less than a week after he and Yeats had agreed that they "hated" Dublin for its treatment of Lane: "I am to dine with the Robert Witts on Thursday to meet MacColl and Aitken. They are making love to me—to try and get the Dublin pictures to found a *new* Gallery in London" (*Hugh Lane and His Pictures*, 2nd ed., p. 38). Yeats replied to Witt in an interview, "Sir Hugh Lane's Pictures", which appeared in *The Observer* on December 17, 1916. For his response to the suggestion of the *Times* article, see p. 426 below.

## MR. W. B. YEATS'S REPLY

FROM a letter and an inspired paragraph in "The Times," it appears that the Trustees of the National Gallery are still obdurate over Sir Hugh Lane's group of French pictures. They are standing by the letter of the law that the codicil to the will which left them to Dublin was unwitnessed and therefore invalid. The moral claim of Dublin to the pictures, founded on the often expressed wishes of Sir Hugh, which must be known to them, they ignore.

"One of the arguments in 'The Times,'" Mr. W. B. Yeats said yesterday in a fireside interview with a representative of THE OBSERVER, "was that if Sir Hugh Lane had lived it is understood that he would have been invited to become director of the English National Gallery, which was shortly to become vacant. In the past one has often seen some poet or artist derided or neglected during his own life and honoured immediately upon his death and it is curious to discover that a man who simply collected beautiful things may sometimes meet with a similar fate. Everyone now is anxious to do honour to Sir Hugh Lane and to recognise the great unselfish nobility of his life.

"The only thing, however, which is germane to the matter in the paragraph in 'The Times'—and it has since been repeated by Mr. Witt—is that if Sir Hugh Lane 'had wished to complete the codicil he could have done so at once and that, not having done so, he evidently intended to leave the matter open.'

"I can only repeat that Sir Hugh Lane wrote the codicil very carefully in his own handwriting, fastened it up in an envelope, and left it in his desk in Dublin addressed to his sister. He was going on a dangerous journey. He had already spoken to her of making a new will. For what conceivable purpose could he have put that envelope in his desk if it was not to be used in case of his death?

"They say he was a businesslike man, and would have known that it was necessary in law to have the codicil witnessed. He certainly was not a businesslike man in any sense in which they use the word. Even the very will on which they rely was not drawn up by a lawyer, but was dictated to his sister, and she tells me that but for her persistence neither that will, nor a will made a few years before, would have been witnessed.

"Mr. Witt in his letter says we make a moral claim, and that even on a moral claim the British public has some right to be considered. He also goes on to explain how very much the French pictures are needed in London.

"In the claim we make the British public will not expect to be considered. We simply claim that, whether people like it or not, the clearly expressed wish of a donor, written in his own handwriting, must be accepted by a great British institution, and that it is against the traditions of such an institution to plead legality against justice. If anyone found a man in what he believed to be the wrongful possession of his property, I doubt if he would permit that man to argue that being needy he also had a moral right to the goods.

"We are offered a compromise: they will lend us some of the pictures. We cannot accept this compromise. Sir Hugh Lane described these pictures as complementary to the collection in Dublin, and he refused in the past to allow the National Gallery to make a selection.

"I have great sympathy with Mr. Witt. He was constantly urging Sir Hugh Lane to leave his pictures to the National Gallery of London, and he naturally feels that they should be where there is the larger public. I feel, however, that, on the contrary, Ireland, which has few pictures, and not London, which has many, has the greater need. Besides, I have based my whole life on the conviction that it is more important to give fine examples of high art to a country that is still plastic, still growing, than to an old country where national character has been formed for centuries.

"The possession by Dublin of the great collection which Sir Hugh Lane planned for Ireland has a chance of far more profoundly influencing the national mind than it could ever do in England. It will be a great matter of national pride and a great nursing place for students.

"I think Mr. Witt, on further consideration, will see that the National Gallery Trustees cannot in justice refuse to Sir Hugh Lane, who was drowned by a German act of war, the privilege that is granted to every soldier who is killed in the trenches. Directions that are written in their own handwriting, even though they are not witnessed, are regarded as legal. Furthermore, Sir Hugh's sister is prepared to testify that on a certain date, which she can verify from her diary and about the time that he wrote the codicil, he refused to consider a request to bequeath his collection to London, using the words, 'London is rich enough to buy its own pictures.' After all he was of Irish birth, his father's family connected with Cork and his mother's with Galway County for generations, and he wished to benefit his own country."

# Sir Hugh Lane's Pictures

As the question of Hugh Lane's real intentions about his collection assumed central importance, testimony emerged from many sources. A letter to *The Morning Post* from Charles Aitken on December 14, 1916, claiming that Lane had indicated he "was prepared to give at any rate his French pictures to whichever city seemed first ready to show some appreciation", provoked a response from Yeats in the *Post* for December 19.

TO THE EDITOR OF *THE MORNING POST*

SIR,—I have just seen Mr. Aitken's letter in the *Morning Post* of Thursday. It argues that had Sir Hugh Lane lived to know of certain plans and the probability of carrying them out to create a Gallery of Modern Continental Art in London he would have given to that gallery the French pictures he had collected for Dublin. If he had lived he would certainly have given some generous gift to such a scheme, though not, I think, to the impoverishment of Dublin. But all that is irrelevant, for we are only concerned with what he planned before his death in the *Lusitania* on the 7th of May. Mrs. Duncan, Curator of the Gallery of Modern Art in Dublin,[1] writes:

He spoke to me at length upon the subject just before he sailed for America. He said he was anxious to remove the pictures from the National Gallery in London, where they were not even seen by the public, and that he wished to bring them back to Dublin. He spoke of the need of a new building, but said that he would be content if the Corporation made good their promise to build a gallery within a reasonable time, leaving the choice of a site to them. Meanwhile he intented to rehang the pictures in the Dublin Municipal Gallery on his return from America. My recollection of this conversation is particularly clear, as it made a deep impression upon me.

Mr. John Quin [*sic*], the well-known lawyer and connoisseur of New York, and one of the members of the governing bodies there, offers to make statutory declaration of a similar conversation. Sir Hugh Lane told him on the very eve of his leaving New York on the *Lusitania* that if the Dublin Corporation would make a building, "not necessarily the

---

[1] The sworn declarations of Ellen Duncan, the Curator of the Dublin Municipal Gallery, and of Ruth Shine, Lane's sister, made in February, 1917, are reprinted by Lady Gregory in "Appendix IV" of her book on Hugh Lane. Lane had succeeded in establishing a temporary home for his "modern classics" in the Municipal Gallery which opened on January 18, 1908, at 17 Harcourt Street, Dublin. In 1927, the Gallery moved to its present site, Charlemont House, Parnell Square.

Bridge site," he would give Dublin the pictures, "as he had always wanted them to be there." His sister, Mrs. Shine, and I myself can quote similar conversations, but I claim that no such quotations are necessary. We have the codicil written very carefully, his sister believes after several preliminary drafts, sealed in an envelope, addressed to the sister to whom he had dictated his previous wills, and left in his desk in Dublin on the eve of a dangerous voyage. He felt so much the danger of that voyage that at first he had refused to go upon it, unless those that invited him agreed to insure his life for £50,000 to clear his estate of certain liabilities in case of death. He had already spoken of making a new will, and his family do not doubt that he considered his codicil legal. For what other purpose could he have written it than that it should be found and given effect to in case of his death? It was not witnessed, but neither would the will that the National Gallery relies upon, nor a will made some years before, have been, but for Mrs. Shine's persistency. When he made his second will he had forgotten all she had told him about the necessity. I cannot imagine a document with a stronger moral claim, and we invite the Parliamentary action that will make that claim legal.

Perhaps Sir Hugh Lane meant, had he lived, to keep "an open mind" —though I doubt it. Perhaps Mr. Witt or Mr. Aitken might have persuaded him that their project was better than his. I do not doubt that he listened to them sympathetically, but they did not persuade him to destroy the codicil, and it remains to show what he desired us to do with his estate if he did not live.—Yours, &c.,

W. B. Yeats

Dec. 18

# Sir Hugh Lane's Pictures

An editorial note in *The Spectator* for December 16, 1916, expressing "the very strongest sympathy with those who say that the National Gallery ought to give over to the National Gallery in Dublin Sir Hugh Lane's Collection of Continental pictures", urged that the Trustees, should there be legal problems involved, seek the passage of legislation which would allow the transfer. Yeats's letter in the issue for December 23 was in response to this suggestion, as well as the note's further conclusion that the Government, "if for any reason the trustees are unable to do this", should "pass a short act carrying out the transfer".

TO THE EDITOR OF *THE SPECTATOR*

SIR,—I am not the only friend and fellow-worker of the late Sir Hugh Lane who will be grateful for your note in last week's issue. May I give you a somewhat more detailed account of the circumstances than has yet been published? Some influential reader of yours may help to accomplish an act of generosity and of justice. Sir Hugh Lane had for many years as his chief preoccupation the formation of a great collection of modern art in Dublin. He was of Irish birth, and his father's family had been connected with Cork and his mother's with Galway County for generations. In Dublin he was the victim of an ill-mannered Press campaign, and more, as Dr. Hayden Brown,[1] with whom he discussed the matter, has testified, as "a retaliation and inducement for the future" than as a final decision, he made a will leaving his famous collection of French pictures to the London National Gallery. These pictures had been collected for Dublin, and were, in his own words, "comple-mentary to the collection already there." I saw him at the time, and he made to me a promise, which his aunt and close friend, Lady Gregory, to whom I wrote, must have somewhere among her papers. After a lapse of time he would once more offer to Dublin the same or better pictures, but he wished his decision for the present, for diplomatic reasons, to seem final. I remember one sentence with, I believe, verbal accuracy: "You may be quite certain I will not leave the present Dublin Municipal Gallery to represent me; it is not good enough."[2] He was a man of the most vehement feelings, irascible and generous beyond any man I have ever known. And presently there came a new quarrel to occupy his thoughts. It was with the Trustees of the London National Gallery about a proposed loan exhibition of his pictures there, and I am convinced, having lately gone through his papers, that he was entirely

---

[1] Lane's physician was Haydn Brown (1864–1936), the neurologist and author of books on psychology, spiritualism and medical advice. His testimony in regard to Lane's last wishes is cited in all arguments for the return of the pictures to Dublin.

[2] This passage was one of Yeats's most serious strategic errors in the Lane controversy. His version of this exchange was taken up in the "Postscript" to the essay in *Nineteenth Century* for February, 1917, entitled "The National Gallery Bill and Sir Hugh Lane's Bequest" by D. S. MacColl, who compared Yeats's "highly coloured recollection" with the quotation from his report to Lady Gregory which he had subsequently published in the letter-essay in the *Observer*.

"'All should be allowed to rest for the present'," Yeats had written, "he wanted 'time to recover his enthusiasms . . . but you may be very sure,' he said, 'I have no desire to leave the present Dublin collection to represent me'" (*Letters*, p. 618). MacColl offered a passage from a letter to Lady Gregory from Lane which does, in several respects, seem to explain Lane's intention at that time more clearly than Yeats's version in this letter. "You give me much too much credit for my intentions toward Dublin:" Lane had written. "I hate the place, the people and the 'gallery' . . . and would like to make it really good of a kind. I don't think that I will ever bring back these same pictures, as I could best work up a fresh interest (to myself and Dublin) by making a fresh collection." (Vol. LXXI, p. 397.)

in the right. From that time on, he spoke of the London Trustees with
a bitterness I have never heard in any speech about his Dublin enemies.
A little later he was appointed Director of the Dublin National Gallery,
and his thoughts and his affections returned to Dublin. In February,
1915, he wrote a codicil leaving his French pictures to Dublin. He signed
it, but it was not witnessed. He was a man of no business habits in the
ordinary sense of the word, and his sister (to whom he had dictated his
previous wills, the earliest leaving everything to Dublin and the later
leaving the French pictures to London) has no doubt that he considered
it in the light of a postscript to an already witnessed will and therefore
in itself legal. She has testified that neither of his wills would have been
witnessed but for her persistency, and that at the making of the second
he had forgotten all that she had told him at the making of the first. He
never forgot the least detail about any picture that had once interested
him, but nothing else seemed to stay in his mind. He sealed this codicil
in an envelope addressed to his sister and left it in his desk in Dublin on
the eve of a dangerous voyage. He realized the danger of that voyage
so clearly that at first he had refused to go unless those who invited him
to America insured his life for £50,000 to free his estate of certain
liabilities in the case of death. He wrote this codicil with great care
and, his sister believes, after several rough drafts, for it was well written
and he composed even a letter with difficulty.

Nor did he change his purpose during the few weeks that passed
between the writing of it and his sailing from New York in the 'Lusitania.' Mrs. Duncan, Curator of the Dublin Municipal Gallery of
Modern Art, writes:—

"He spoke to me at length on the subject just before he sailed for
America. He said he was anxious to remove his pictures from the
National Gallery (they had been stored there since the public loan
exhibition fell through), where they were not even seen by the public,
and that he wished to bring them back to Dublin. He spoke of the need
of a new building, but said that he would be content if the Corporation
made good their promise to build a gallery in a reasonable time, leaving the choice of a site to them. Meanwhile he intended to rehang the
pictures in the Dublin Municipal Gallery on his return from America.
My recollection of this conversation is particularly clear as it made a
deep impression upon me at the time."

His friend Mr. Martin,[3] who travelled to Liverpool with him when
he was leaving England, is about to publish his recollection of a similar

---

[3] Alec Martin (1884–1971) was, along with Lady Gregory, among Lane's closest confidants.
Having joined Christie's, the art dealers, at the age of twelve, he became the Managing
Director in 1940, a position he held until 1958. In 1959, he was knighted. Lady Gregory's
book on Lane, which reprints Martin's deposition in "Appendix IV", is dedicated to "Alec
Martin, Hugh's Friend and Mine".

conversation which took place, I believe, in the train. Mr. John Quinn, the well-known New York lawyer and art collector and one of the governing body of the Metropolitan Museum, writes that Sir Hugh Lane told him just before the 'Lusitania' sailed that "if they would make some provision for a gallery, and I remember his saying 'not necessarily the bridge site,' he would give them the pictures as he always meant them to go there." Mr. Quinn is prepared to make a statutory declaration before the British Consul. Sir Hugh Lane's proposal to set the gallery upon a bridge over the Liffey was the only question at issue between him and the Dublin Corporation, and the moment he abandoned it all difficulty was at an end. I gave evidence some twelve months ago before, I think, the Finance Committee of the Dublin Corporation, and at my request the Lord Mayor renewed the promise already upon the books of the Corporation of a suitable building. The Lord Mayor and the Corporation of Dublin and representatives of all the principal educational and learned Societies in that city, and such distinguished men as Mr. William Orpen,[4] Sir Horace Plunkett, Mr. George Russell ("AE"), and Mr. George Bernard Shaw, have sent memorials to the Trustees of the London Gallery, and we shall invite Parliament to give to those Trustees the necessary power to treat the codicil as legal, so that, in the words of the Lord Mayor of Dublin, "the last wishes of Sir Hugh Lane may be carried out."

There are no politics in the matter. Both the Irish parties are at one upon it, and the only danger is that in the press of war Parliament may not find the time or the thought for a concession in accordance with its own great traditions.—I am, Sir, &c.

W. B. Yeats

# The Hugh Lane Pictures

D. S. MacColl was at work on an authorized biography of Hugh Lane and, thus, his views on the probable destination of Lane's French collection assumed considerable importance. In letters to *The Observer* for December 24, 1916, Lady Gregory and Yeats attempted to counter the assertions of MacColl, who, ultimately, abandoned the project during the controversy over the codicil.

---

[4] At this time William Orpen was an Associate of the Royal Academy and a member of the Royal Hibernian Academy.

## LETTER FROM LADY GREGORY
### TO THE EDITOR OF *THE OBSERVER*

SIR,—My nephew Hugh Lane, having named me in the codicil leaving his French pictures to Dublin as "sole trustee in this matter," I have but to endeavour to carry out what I know to have been his intention when that was written in February, 1915, and later, in Easter week, 1915, and yet three weeks later, before he left America in the Lusitania. This was his last charge to me; I cannot, as others do, speak confidently of a possible change of mind had he lived to know an addition was to be built to the Tate Gallery. The codicil arranged what was to be done did he not live.

When I was asked to choose his biographer I passed over nearer friends and persuaded Mr. McColl[1] to undertake the task. I was, perhaps foolishly, preoccupied with Dublin opinion; I wanted ignorant dispraise of the offered group of French pictures put an end to by the impartial judgment of so brilliant a critic. And such is the irony of Fate, this has been done apart from the writing of the book, for the biographer, joining with those who would keep the pictures in London for the yet unbuilt Tate extension, gives his opinion that, "without Lane's pictures this most important national project would be crippled at its start;" and I am well content with this appreciation.

A paragraph sent to the Press states as a reason why Hugh Lane would have inclined towards London projects had he lived that he would probably have been offered the Directorship of the London National Gallery. I may say that one evening, somewhere about Christmas, 1913, he told me that this offer had already been made to him, though unofficially. He said: "I went there to-day and spent a long time going round it with this in mind; but it is so rich, so well cared for, so well arranged, that I did not see there was much I could do in it; it would not interest me." And he begged me to write to Dr. Mahaffy,[2] then Chairman of the Dublin Trustees, urging his appointment there. He said, "Tell him that if I get the Dublin Gallery I will make it my adopted child." We know now how whole-heartedly this promise was carried out.

I know the high traditions of the London Trustees. My husband was one of their number; and so I appeal to them, now at Christmas time, to stop an argument that is on the way to turn to wrangling, by themselves offering to bring into Parliament the Bill that will set them free

[1] MacColl's name is misspelled throughout.

[2] Sir John Pentland Mahaffy was a powerful figure in Irish intellectual affairs for forty years. The Provost of Trinity College, Dublin, he was also, at this time, president of the Royal Irish Academy.

to carry out what all of them must feel would be an act of grace, even if all are not convinced it is an act of justice.

Yours, etc.,

Augusta Gregory

Galway, December 21, 1916.

Dear Sir,—It was I who suggested to Lady Gregory that Mr. McColl be asked to write the life of Sir Hugh Lane. I thought that his style fitted him to deal firmly with Sir Hugh Lane's Dublin enemies; and I still think so. He was never, however, among Sir Hugh Lane's more intimate friends and has had to go to others for all his material. Why does he claim a special knowledge and why, above all, does he suggest that he is more impartial than other men? Mr. Witt, Mr. Aitken, and and Mr. McColl, by constantly seeing one another and acting together, have been able greatly to benefit the London picture galleries. Very rightly, from their point of view, and again acting together, they tried for years to persuade Sir Hugh Lane to leave his pictures to London and not to Dublin; and now once more acting together they write to "The Times," the "Morning Post," and *The Observer* respectively to say that they did get a conditional promise or half promise of the pictures. If the codicil is declared law, a dear and legitimate hope of theirs will be defeated. No, Mr. McColl is no more impartial than I am. I think they deceive themselves, for I do not think Sir Hugh Lane would have even half promised to make a compact behind the back of friends and fellow-workers and nearest kin and behind the back of the Dublin Corporation, which was to lose the pictures if it did not observe a condition it did not know; and to make this compact with three critics who were so little in his confidence that he told them neither of the will he had made in favour of the National Gallery nor of the codicil revoking it.

All three letters are vague and they can weigh them in their own minds against Sir Hugh Lane's later statements, which are not vague, and against the codicil itself. He told Mrs. Duncan, the Curator of the Dublin Municipal Gallery, two days before he left for America that he had abandoned all claim for any special site (the only question at issue between him and the Dublin Corporation) and that "he intended to re-hang the pictures in Dublin on his return from America." He told his friend, Mr. Martin, who travelled to Liverpool with him and who was certainly the last man to see him before he left England, that he was giving the pictures to Dublin, and he told Mr. John Quinn, the well-known New York lawyer, and one of the governing body of the New York Metropolitan Museum, just before the Lusitania sailed, that "if they would make some provision for a gallery—and I remember his saying 'not necessarily the bridge site'—he would give them the pictures, as he always meant them to go there." If Sir Hugh Lane ever contemplated leaving the pictures to London (for even the will in favour of the National Gallery was, according to one friend, Dr. Hayden Brown, but "a retaliation and inducement for the future," made to impress Dublin) he did it in momentary irritation. The Dublin Gallery had been the main work of his life and the creation of his own fancy.

Since your interviewer came to see me last week I have discovered two new facts which make the moral claim of the codicil even stronger. When he wrote it he did not expect to leave London after seven or eight weeks as he did, but at the utmost in three or four, and he felt so acutely the danger of the voyage that he had at first refused to go unless those who had invited him would insure his life for £50,000 to clear his estate of certain liabilities in the event of death. He wrote the codicil with the thought of death in mind. Mr. Hind[3] suggests that we share the pictures with Mr. Aitken's, Mr. Witt's, and Mr. McColl's new London Gallery, and Mr. McColl suggests that we borrow some of them. No: but we are about to ask Parliament to declare that the codicil is legal, believing that it contains Sir Hugh Lane's last wishes.

Yours truly,<br>W. B. Yeats

Dec. 20, 1916

# Sir Hugh Lane's Pictures

The decision of the Trustees of the National Gallery about the Lane collection resembled the plan suggested by *The Times* to which Yeats had responded on December 17, 1916 (see p. 416 above). In the interim, he had amassed further evidence, which he included in a letter to *The Times* on December 28, that Hugh Lane had never intended the collection to be divided.

## TO THE EDITOR OF *THE TIMES*

SIR,—If the arrangement hinted at in *The Times* of December 11 as "a substantial concession to Sir Hugh Lane's friends" is the same proposed in the formal answer of the National Gallery Trustees to Lady Gregory's plea for the acceptance of Sir Hugh Lane's codicil, I may say

---

[3] Yeats's reference is probably to Charles Lewis Hind (1862–1927), the art critic and journalist. None of the commentators on the Lane controversy identifies this suggestion and it evidently was not reprinted in Hind's works.

that it certainly would not "open the way to a friendly solution of the the Irish claim." This proposal was:—"Should the enhanced powers of loan for which the Trustees are now asking Parliamentary sanction be granted to them, they will be in a position and will certainly desire to respond favourably to any requests for the loan of some of these pictures which might reach them from the authorities in Dublin." Any such breaking up of the collection would have been contrary to Sir Hugh Lane's wishes. There is no guesswork here. I take this extract from a letter written by him to Sir C. Holroyd,[1] July 27, 1913:— "These pictures are complementary to the collection I have already given them (the Dublin Corporation) and the other pictures given and subscribed for by others . . . I think that if they were hung at the National Gallery or the Tate Gallery it might encourage the Corporation to fulfil my conditions." In 1913, in reply to a proposal to exhibit in the National Gallery upon loan a portion of this collection he writes: "I should never have dreamed of submitting my pictures for selection to members of the Board." He wanted all his pictures for Dublin. After he had taken them away from there one of the London Trustees writes to ask him if there is any prospect that the National Gallery may profit at a later date by his generosity "or would the loan if accepted be a loan in reality for the aid of Dublin?" He answers to this, "The situation in regard to my pictures has not changed very much . . . As I still hope that my work in Dublin will not prove a failure I cannot think of giving them to any other gallery at present. But the gallery that not having such, refused the loan of them for one or two years would appear to be quite unworthy of them as a gift. I confess to being quite out of sympathy with the English National Gallery." Two months after writing this letter in a fit of anger against the Dublin Corporation he made the will upon which the London National Gallery bases its claim; but four months later, or, to be exact, in January, 1914, he once more refused to allow the National Gallery to make selection of the pictures for a loan exhibition, and refused to promise to give or leave them to the Gallery. His feeling for Dublin had returned, and he thought, as he expressed himself to some who urged him, that "London was quite rich enough to buy its own pictures."

Yours,<br>W. B. Yeats

Royal Societies Club, St. James's street, S. W.

[1] Sir Charles Holroyd (1861–1917), the painter and etcher, was the first Keeper of the Tate Gallery. He served from 1897 until 1906.

# Dublin and the Hugh Lane Pictures

As parliamentary action on the bill to return Hugh Lane's pictures to Dublin became imminent, Yeats wrote to *The Observer* on February 3, 1918, to review the main points in the dispute.

TO THE EDITOR OF *THE OBSERVER*

SIR,—An influential meeting was held in Dublin on January 29 to invite the Government to make it legal for the trustees of the National Gallery to return to Dublin the pictures collected by Sir Hugh Lane for the Dublin Municipal Gallery.

You permitted me some twelve months ago to state the case to your readers,[1] but by this time it may be getting somewhat dim in their memories. Sir Hugh Lane left certain French pictures, at a moment of irritation with Ireland, to the English National Gallery, and then at a moment when he was setting out on a voyage which filled him with anxiety he wrote a codicil once more leaving the pictures to Dublin. That codicil was signed but unwitnessed, but immediately before leaving Ireland for America, in conversation with the curator of his Dublin gallery, Mrs. Duncan, he was perfectly clear as to his intention that Dublin should have the pictures; and while travelling from London to take ship at Liverpool made the same statement to his friend, Mr. Martin.

On leaving New York for the voyage on which he was lost he made the same statement to Mr. John Quinn, one of the governors of the Municipal Art Gallery of New York.[2]

Since the controversy in your paper last winter I received from the Right Hon. W. F. Bailey[3] the record of a precisely similar conversation with him just before Sir Hugh Lane left Ireland. Against this, the head of the Tate Gallery remembers certain words, leaving him under the impression that Sir Hugh Lane was undecided whether London or Dublin was to have the pictures, and he suggests that he may possibly, while signing the codicil, have left it unwitnessed on purpose.

No one, however, I think, believes that Sir Hugh Lane would have

---

[1] Yeats refers to the letter-essay in the *Observer* of January 21, 1917 (Wade, *Letters*, pp. 616 ff.).

[2] *i.e.*, The Metropolitan Museum of Art.

[3] William Frederick Bailey (1857–1917), the Irish jurist and man of letters, was Governor of the National Gallery at this time. He was a shareholder in the Abbey Theatre, having been appointed to its Financial Committee in 1911, at the time of Miss Horniman's withdrawal.

given these pictures to England if circumstances made it impossible for him to gather another collection for Dublin.

Dublin Gallery would always bear his name and be the chief testimony of his taste. We are convinced that he considered the codicil legal, as it would be in France, and that it directs what he would have wished done in case of his death, and we appeal to the Government to take the necessary steps to make it legal.—Yours, etc.,

W. B. Yeats

45 Broad-street, Oxford
January 30, 1918

# Major Robert Gregory

Lady Gregory's son, William Robert (1881–1918), was killed in action on January 23, 1918. In the months immediately following, Yeats wrote three poems on the subject of his death: "In Memory of Major Robert Gregory", "An Irish Airman Foresees his Death", and "Shepherd and Goatherd". A few years later he wrote a fourth poem, the bitter "Reprisals". Yeats's earliest tribute, however, was a prose appreciation in *The Observer* for February 17, 1918. In this essay, Yeats studies, as he does in the elegies, the blending of accomplishment and active achievement which he first remarked in a letter to John Quinn written a few days after Gregory's death: "His paintings had majesty and austerity, and at the same time sweetness. He was the most accomplished man I have ever known; I mean that he could do more things well than any other" (*Letters*, p. 646).

## A NOTE OF APPRECIATION

I HAVE known no man accomplished in so many ways as Major Robert Gregory, who was killed in action a couple of weeks ago and buried by his fellow-airmen in the beautiful cemetery at Padua. His very accomplishment hid from many his genius. He had so many sides: painter, classical scholar, scholar in painting and in modern literature, boxer, horseman, airman—he had the Military Cross and the Légion d'Honneur—that some among his friends were not sure what his work would be. To me he will always remain a great painter in the immaturity of his youth, he himself the personification of handsome youth. I first came to understand his genius when, still almost a boy, he

designed costumes and scenery for the Abbey Theatre.[1] Working for a
theatre that could only afford a few pounds for the staging of a play, he
designed for Lady Gregory's "Kinkora" [sic] and her "Image" and for
my "Shadowy Waters" and for Synge's "Deirdre of the Sorrows"
decorations which, obtaining their effect from the fewest possible lines
and colours, had always the grave distinction of his own imagination.
When he began to paint, accustomed to an older school of painting, I
was long perplexed by what seemed to me neglect of detail. But in a few
years I came to care for his paintings of the Clare coast, with its cloud
shadows upon blue-grey stony hills, and for one painting of a not very
different scenery by his friend, Innes,[2] more than for any contemporary
landscape painting. A man of letters may perhaps find in work such as
this, or in old Chinese painting, in the woodcuts and etchings of Calvert
and Palmer,[3] in Blake's woodcuts to Thornton's Virgil,[4] in the landscape
background of Mr. Ricketts'[5] "Wise and Foolish Virgins," something
that he does not find in the great modern masters, and that he cares for
deeply. Is it merely that these men share certain moods with great
lyric poetry, with, let us say, the "Leach Gatherer" of Wordsworth;[6]
or that their moods, unlike those of men with more objective curiosity,
are a part of the traditional expression of the the soul? One always
understood by something in his selection of line and of colour that he
had read his Homer and his Virgil and his Dante; that they, while
giving something of themselves, had freed him from easy tragedy and
trivial comedy.

Though he often seemed led away from his work by some other
gift, his attitude to life and art never lost intensity—he was never the
amateur. I have noticed that men whose lives are to be an ever-growing
absorption in subjective beauty—and I am not mainly remembering

[1] Robert Gregory's first designs for the Abbey, the stylized settings and costumes for his
mother's play about Brian Boru, Kincora, were warmly received when the play opened on
March 25, 1905.

[2] In his letter to John Quinn, Yeats had referred to Robert Gregory's friend, James
Dickson Innes (1887–1914). "Certainly", he wrote of Gregory, "no contemporary landscape moved me as much as two or three of his, except perhaps a certain landscape by Innes,
from whom he had learnt a great deal" (Letters, p. 646).

[3] Yeats notes in a letter, written shortly after this essay, to Lady Gregory that he has been
studying the woodcuts of Edward Calvert and Samuel Palmer in the Bodleian Library
(Letters, p. 646).

[4] Blake rendered seventeen woodcuts—his only work in that medium—for the edition of
Virgil's Bucolica (1821) by the English physician, botanist and classicist, John Robert
Thornton (c. 1758–1837).

[5] Yeats had been a friend of the English artist and designer, Charles Ricketts, since the
late eighties. For his praise of Ricketts's stage designs, see p. 383 above.

[6] Wordsworth's "Resolution and Independence" (1802) was called by the Wordsworth
family "The Leech-Gatherer", after the central figure, an aged peasant. It bears this title in
Matthew Arnold's immensely popular edition of Wordsworth which first appeared in 1879.

Calvert's philosophy of myth and his musical theory, or Verlaine's sensuality, or Shelley's politics—seek through some lesser gift, or through mere exceitement, to strengthen that self which unites them to ordinary men. It is as though they hesitated before they plunged into the abyss. Major Gregory told Mr. Bernard Shaw, who visited him in France, that the months since he joined the Army had been the happiest of his life. I think they brought him peace of mind, an escape from that shrinking, which I sometimes saw upon his face, before the growing absorption of his dream, the loneliness of his dream, as from his constant struggle to resist those other gifts that brought him ease and friendship. Leading his squadron in France or in Italy, mind and hand were at one, will and desire.

# Sir Hugh Lane and the National Gallery

A review in *The Times Literary Supplement* of Lady Gregory's *Hugh Lane's Life and Achievement* provoked a letter, which Lady Gregory labeled the "audacious untruth signed 'X'" (Lennox Robinson, ed., *Lady Gregory's Journals*, N.Y., 1947, p. 299), in the issue for March 17, 1921. This letter, which she suspected to have come from Robert Witt, asserted that Lane was, "at the time of his departure for America . . . bound by promises to Mr. D. S. MacColl, Mr. Charles Aitken, and other friends in England to give the pictures to London if a Modern Foreign Gallery could be founded there". Further, "X" claimed that the facts in the case had been reviewed impartially and that it had "been decided on the highest authority that to upset the will would be contrary to the principles of justice". Lady Gregory and her friends were pressing their case at this time for just such a review. Thus, she sent notes on March 22 requesting two letters, "one from the old letters of Aitken and MacColl from Yeats, and a fiery one of moral indignation from 'A.E.'" (*Journals*, p. 300). The letters appeared, under the heading "Sir Hugh Lane and the National Gallery", in *The Times Literary Supplement* on March 31, 1921.

SIR,—Your correspondent "X." is mistaken, or has but a dim memory of the controversy over the Lane pictures in 1916–17. I wrote at that time a summary of it in the *Observer* of January 21, 1917,[1] a part of which is quoted in Lady Gregory's "Life of Hugh Lane." I said in it: " 'He was prepared,' says Mr. Aitken in the *Morning Post*, 'to give, at any

[1] This is the letter-essay reprinted by Wade (*Letters*, pp. 616 ff.).

rate, his French pictures to whichever city seemed first ready to show some appreciation.' And Mr. MacColl says that on March 5, 1914, he promised to wait and see what appreciation of them was shown, the test being the foundation of a gallery.' These sentences are vague. There was clearly nothing in the nature of a compact. It was plain that he reserved for his own judgment what constituted 'some appreciation.' "

There was no assertion made at the time that Lane was "bound by promises to Mr. MacColl, Mr. Charles Aitken, and other friends in England to give the pictures to London if a modern foreign gallery could be founded there." This amazing claim goes far beyond that made by those named. Their assertion was that he was prepared to give certain pictures "to whichever city seemed first ready to show some appreciation." Lady Gregory refers to this in her book as "an idea that had for a short time tempted him." But we know by the sworn statement of the curator of the Harcourt-street Gallery that on his last day in Ireland he said that he wished to bring these pictures to Dublin; that "he would be content if the Corporation reaffirmed their already expressed intention of building a gallery." (And this they have since done.) He said also, "I wish to bring the pictures back to Dublin as soon as possible, and they might be rehung here pending the building of any gallery the Corporation may decide on." It is absolutely impossible that Sir Hugh Lane, when he said this and spoke to others in England and America of a like intention, was bound by a promise to anyone.

Your correspondent "X." says the facts in their legal aspect have been impartially reviewed more than once. We are aware that an un-witnessed codicil is not legal in England as it would be in Scotland. The facts, as they appeared to us, and as printed in a pamphlet issued by "The Lane Picture Committee," were put before the then Chief Secretary for Ireland, the Right Honourable Ian Macpherson,[2] the representatives of the London National Gallery at the same time laying before him their fully considered statement or defence. Mr. Macpherson, himself a lawyer, having considered and weighed the evidence on both sides, expressed, as Lady Gregory tells us in her book, his conviction that Hugh Lane had "intended that codicil to be carried out at the time he wrote it, and at the time of his death," and prepared the Bill to legalize that codicil which we are confident will eventually become law.

Yours sincerely,
W. B. Yeats

[2] Lennox Robinson has reprinted the passages from *Lady Gregory's Journals* (pp. 298–9) in which she recounts the details of her interview with Macpherson (1880–1937).

# From Democracy to Authority

On February 17, 1924, *L'Otage* by the French poet and playwright Paul Claudel (1868–1955) was produced in Dublin. Yeats and Iseult Gonne had read Claudel, Charles Péguy, and other members of the French Catholic literary revival in Normandy in the winter of 1916–17, and for Yeats, disillusioned by the chaos which followed the establishment of the Free State in 1922, these writers' mystical reevaluation of the individual seemed prophetic. As a Free State Senator, Yeats was committed to the policies of the so-called "Irish Mussolini", Kevin O'Higgins (1892–1927), who, as vice-president and minister for Home Affairs under W. T. Cosgrave (1880–1965), was repressing Republican activity with great severity. Moreover, Yeats had begun the speculation which was to result in *A Vision* and was thus inclined to combine political and aesthetic observations, as he did in an interview in *The Irish Times* for February 16, 1924, entitled "From Democracy to Authority: Paul Claudel and Mussolini—A New School of Thought".

## PAUL CLAUDEL AND MUSSOLINI—A NEW SCHOOL OF THOUGHT

"Authoritative government is certainly coming, if for no other reason than that the modern State is so complex that it must find some kind of expert government, a government firm enough, tyrannical enough, if you will, to spend years in carrying out is plans."

Such is the belief of Dr. W. B. Yeats as expressed in the course of an interview which he gave to an *Irish Times* representative yesterday.

He began with a reference to to-morrow's production by the Dublin Drama League of Paul Claudel's *L'Otage*, a play which, he declared, was not only of great literary importance, but of great importance to anybody studying modern European thought. "It expresses," he said, "something which is apparent all over the world to-day. What Péguy put into speeches and essays is now being expressed in political and democratic[1] forms by other writers. They are giving expression in literature to the same movement that has brought Mussolini into power in Italy, and that threatens France.

"Ibsen's 'Enemy of the People' opposed individualism against autocracy of public opinion. *L'Otage*, like everything else typical of European thought, reverses the process; that which in the mass is an inherited nation[2]—something that is not ours. The characters are those

---

[1] This sentence is more intelligible if "poetic and dramatic" is substituted for *The Times*'s "political and democratic".

[2] "Notion" ought perhaps to be substituted for "nation" here.

that sacrifice themselves for those terms. One finds the same thoughts expressed with more complexity by Péguy in that wonderful trilogy, 'Joan of Arc'. We find in these plays the same emotions which give Mussolini his great audiences in Italy. When I was under thirty it would seem an incredible dream that 20,000 Italians, drawn from the mass of the people, would applaud a politician for talking of the 'decomposing body of liberty,' and for declaring that his policy was the antithesis of democracy.[3]

"Everything seems to show that the centrifugal movement which began with the Encyclopædists and produced the French Revolution, and the democratic views of men like Mill, has worked itself out to the end. Now we are at the beginning of a new centripetal movement.[4] It has appeared more clearly because of the war, but it was not made by the war. L'Otage and Péguy's great work were published before [it] even began, and Charles Maurras, the political philosopher of the movement in France, had already written his principal works.[5]

"Such surprising things such as the amazing popularity of Roosevelt, simply because of his authoritative manner, show that the movement had its beginning earlier. Individualism had produced vulgarity— commonness.

"The astonishing thing about Mussolini's utterances is not that he should think or say those things—other men have thought them before —but that he should be applauded for saying them. We may see the importance of that without admiring Mussolini or condemning him. Socialists in modern Europe have as little respect as he for the decomposing body of liberty. One observes the change in European thought as one observes the day changing into night or the night changing into day.

"Movements that had for their aim the setting free of the individual were found to produce anarchy in the end. Now they say that a Royalist coup d'etat may come in France any day. And in Russia the very contrary opinions have gone even further from democracy—there are

[3] Yeats repeated, with somewhat more admiration, his respect for this declaration by Mussolini (1883–1945) in a public address which is quoted by Richard Ellmann in Yeats— the Man and the Masks (New York, 1958, pp. 244–5): ". . . a great popular leader has said to an applauding multitude 'We will trample upon the discomposing body of the Goddess of Liberty.'"

[4] This sentence is apparently the model of one in the note which, later in 1924, accompanied "Leda and the Swan", and which explained that the poem was written "because the editor [A.E.] of a political review asked me for a poem. I thought, 'After the individualist, demagogic movement, founded by Hobbes and popularized by the Encyclopaedists and the French Revolution, we have a soil so exhausted that it cannot grow that crop again for centuries'" (Variorum Poems, p. 828).

[5] Charles Maurras (1868–1952), co-founder of L'Action française, published L'Enquête sur la monarchie in 1900 and L'Avenir de l'intelligence in 1905.

100,000 Communists controlling one hundred million who are indifferent or hostile.

"When the democratic movement was in its beginning Burke opposed it in speeches and in essays, and what he did vainly when the movement was in its sunrise, Péguy and Claudel have done in poems and plays in its sunset.

"Authoritative government is certainly coming, if for no other reason than that the modern State is so complex that it must find some kind of expert government—a government firm enough, tyrannical enough, if you will, to spend years in carrying out its plans. The Marxian Socialist wants to re-create the world according to a scientific theory, while men like Péguy, Claudel, and Maurras—whom one can admire as a thinker without admiring his practical politics—see the nation as something like a growing child or an old man, as the case may be, and not an automaton, as Socialists would make it.

"I see the same tendency here in Ireland towards authoritative government. What else can chaos produce even though our chaos has been a very small thing compared with the chaos in Central Europe? The question in Ireland, as elsewhere in Europe, is whether the authoritative government which we see emerging is the short reaction that comes at the end of every disturbance, lasting ten or fifteen years, or whether it is, as I think, a part of a reaction that will last one hundred or one hundred and fifty years. Not always of the same intensity, it is, still, a steady movement towards the creation of a nation controlled by highly trained intellects."

Asked what effect the new movement would have on the social fabric generally, and what weapons it would use to enthrone authority, Dr. Yeats shook his head. "I'm afraid," he said, "it will be busy with very crude things during my lifetime. I shall be a very old man if I live to see it capable of taking up the tasks for which I care and of which I dream. My son may live to see it ready to take up those tasks. One of them certainly is to make a Dublin as worthy of our new Parliament as the great buildings, like the Bank of Ireland, were worthy of the old one.[6] I am only afraid that they will start this task before they are capable of carrying it out.

"I should like to see the best teaching in architecture, in metal work, in mosaic work, and in everything else necessary for the establishment of a fine school of building here in Dublin. I should like to see the most competent teachers brought in from abroad, where necessary, so that in

[6] In 1802, following the dissolution of the Irish Parliament by the Act of Union, Parliament House—the great achievement of Sir Edward Lovett Pearce (d. 1733) and, later, of James Gandon (1743–1823)—on College Green, Dublin, was sold to the Bank of Ireland, with the secret provision that the interior and exterior be altered so that both the facility for and the public's memory of a local Parliament would be effaced.

ten or fifteen years' time we might train a generation of students to
become capable of designing and decorating great public buildings.

"One thing we might do at once is to get proper teaching in the
designing of lace. We had a fine lace industry once, but it perished
through poor modern designing or through hurried execution of good
old designs."

Discussing the trend of modern Irish literature in relation to the
Claudel–Péguy school, Dr. Yeats remarked that the Irish mind did not
go into any political question at present without treating it in satirical
vein. "We were bitter," he commented, "before our late experiences,
and we are not likely to grow any less bitter because of them." All
James Joyce's work, except "that first exquisite little book of lyrics" was
a satire on Irish life in its different phases.[7] The satiric element was
present in the works of most of the other Irish writers, but it only
reached philosophic consciousness in James Joyce.

# A Memory of Synge

In 1923 Horace Plunkett revived *The Irish Statesman* largely with Irish-
American contributions. A.E. was the editor and Yeats contributed, on
July 5, 1924, "A Memory of Synge", which introduced "John Synge as I
Knew Him", a short reminiscence by Cherry Matheson Horton, Synge's first
love.

A CORRESPONDENT has sent me the following little essay with
the comment "A short time ago I read Synge's life, and it seemed to me
rather lacking in the personal touch, so I wrote down these few memories." Where we have so little with that "touch," I am grateful as an
old friend of Synge's, and I have asked the IRISH STATESMAN
to put the essay into print that it may remain for some future biographer.
John Synge was a very great man, and in time to come every passing
allusion that recalls him, whether in old newspaper articles or in old
letters, will be sought out that historians of literature may mould, or
try to mould, some simple image of the man. Even before the war,
invention had begun, for a tolerably well-known American journalist,[1]

---

[7] Yeats had made this distinction in Joyce's work when, in 1915, he had corresponded
with Edmund Gosse about Joyce's being aided by the Royal Literary Fund. "He has
written *Dubliners* a book of satiric stories of great subtlety . . . and *Chamber Music* a book of
verse, a little of it very beautiful and all of it very perfect technically" (*Letters*, p. 597).

[1] James Huneker (1860–1921), the American journalist and critic, had written warmly of
Synge just after his death. His essay was reprinted in 1913 as part of "The Celtic Awakening"
in *The Pathos of Distance*.

who had never been under the same roof with Synge, or even set eyes
upon him, published scenes and conversations, that were all, from no
malicious intention but because of his gross imagination, slander and
travesty. He based all upon what he supposed the inventor of so many
violent and vehement peasants must be like, knowing so little of human
character that he described, without knowing it, Synge's antithesis. I
have left my correspondent's notes as they came from her unpractised
hand, trivial and important alike. That praise of Wordsworth, for
instance, is nothing in itself. To say that "Wordsworth is more at one
with Nature" than some other, is too vague to increase our knowledge,
but it recalls some early work of Synge's, certain boyish reveries, that I
excluded from his collected edition but not from material that his
biographers might use, in which he described minutely brook or coppice—I have forgotten which—a shadowed, limited place, such as
children love.[2] I had not known of his passion for Wordsworth, and to
know it completes the image. Then again, his liking for Patrick Street
has reminded me that a little before his death he planned to make it the
scene of a play. I remember that "little house" in Paris; it was one room
which cost him two or three francs a week, yet was not in a slum, but
had its own front door and even, I think, some kind of little hall between the front door and room door, and was at the top of a decent
house full of flats near the Luxembourg. Paris, as an old astrologer
said to me once, is a good town for a poor man, or so it was twenty
years ago. I do not know why I have not crossed out that allusion to
*Dana*, a very short-lived but delightful paper . . . "too remote from the
world of thought," except that it might give pleasure to *Dana's* em-
bittered editor.[3] C. H. H. has lent me the photograph she speaks of, but
the IRISH STATESMAN has no means of publishing such things.
It shows a face less formed and decisive than the face of later years.

W. B. Yeats

---

[2] Yeats's reference is probably to the "boyish verses" written in 1894 which Synge noted
were "not to be printed under any circumstances" (Greene and Stephens, *J. M. Synge*, p. 50).

[3] John Eglinton had founded *Dana* in 1904 with Fred Ryan. Ryan, who had been associated with W. G. Fay's company and with the Irish National Theatre Society, died shortly
afterwards. The periodical ceased publication in 1905. Of Eglinton's temperament at this
time, AE noted, in a letter to Ernest Boyd, that he was "still sulking in Wales hiding away
from the world. I think he is cursed by the 'Dusk of the Perverse' which Poe imagined sheer
opposition to everybody and everything ordinary" (*Letters from AE*, p. 168).

# To All Artists and Writers

In August, 1924, Yeats contributed a leading article to the first issue of *To-Morrow*, a review edited by the artist Cecil Salkeld (b. 1910), the novelist Francis Stuart (b. 1902), and F. R. Higgins (1896–1941), the poet who was to become Yeats's collaborator and "favourite crony" (*Letters*, p. 867) in his last years. Stuart had succeeded where Yeats had failed by marrying Maud Gonne's daughter Iseult, the "girl that knew all Dante once / [who] live[d] to bear children to a dunce" (*Variorum Poems*, p. 626).

The group had sought Yeats's encouragement and, on June 20, he had toasted their success. "I got a bottle of Sparkling Moselle, which I hope youthful ignorance mistook for champagne, and we swore alliance. . . . My dream is a wild paper of the young which will make enemies everywhere and suffer supression, I hope a number of times, with the logical assertion, with all fitting deductions, of the immortality of the soul" (*Letters*, p. 706). The paper was suppressed, after two issues, because of the controversy over Lennox Robinson's story which Yeats discusses on pp. 463–5 below.

Although this note was signed by Stuart and Salkeld, Mrs. Yeats confirmed the attribution of it to Yeats by Richard Ellmann, who discusses it in *Yeats— the Man and the Masks* (pp. 245–7).

WE are Catholics, but of the school of Pope Julius the Second and of the Medician Popes, who ordered Michaelangelo and Raphael to paint upon the walls of the Vatican, and upon the ceiling of the Sistine Chapel, the doctrine of the Platonic Academy of Florence, the reconciliation of Galilee and Parnassus. We proclaim Michaelangelo the most orthodox of men, because he set upon the tomb of the Medici "Dawn" and "Night," vast forms shadowing the strength of antideluvian Patriarchs and the lust of the goat, the whole handiwork of God, even the abounding horn.

We proclaim that we can forgive the sinner, but abhor the atheist, and that we count among atheists bad writers and Bishops of all denominations. "The Holy Spirit is an intellectual fountain," and did the Bishops believe that Holy Spirit would show itself in decoration and architecture, in daily manners and written style.[1] What devout man can read the Pastorals of our Hierarchy without horror at a style rancid, course and vague, like that of the daily papers? We condemn the art and literature of modern Europe. No man can create, as did Shakespeare,

---

[1] Yeats converted Blake's rhetorical question, from the introduction to the fourth book of *Jerusalem*, into this assertion in 1896, in his review of Richard Garnett's *William Blake* (see *Uncollected Prose*, I, p. 401). This sentence is more intelligible if read as a rhetorical question.

Homer, Sophocles, who does not believe, with all his blood and nerve, that man's soul is immortal, for the evidence lies plain to all men that where that belief has declined, men have turned from creation to photography. We condemn, though not without sympathy, those who would escape from banal mechanism through technical investigation and experiment. We proclaim that these bring no escape, for new form comes from new subject matter, and new subject matter must flow from the human soul restored to all its courage, to all its audacity. We dismiss all demagogues and call back the soul to its ancient sovereignty, and declare that it can do whatever it please, being made, as antiquity affirmed, from the imperishable substance of the stars.

H. Stuart<br>Cecil Salkeld

# Compulsory Gaelic

In a wry dialogue entitled "Compulsory Gaelic", which appeared in A.E.'s *The Irish Statesman* on August 2, 1924, Yeats drew upon his long experience with the problems of casting popular or "national" imagination into the official language of the Free State. Since the early days of the Gaelic League and his forays among Lady Gregory's Galway story-tellers, the dilemma had fascinated and aggravated him and, in his role as a Senator, he had lately taken the positions of both "Paul", the proponent of increased Governmental encouragement of Gaelic, and "Peter", who resists it. Compulsory instruction in the language was already established by law and Yeats had been chairman of a Senate Committee which had returned its report on June 4, urging that some £5,000 be vested in the Royal Irish Academy, for increased activity in seven separate fields of research and recovery of the language. On July 2, however, he had denounced a proposal that railway tickets, signs and notices be printed bilingually as "a form of insincerity that is injurious to the general intellect and thought of this country and . . . an irritation against the Gaelic language" (Donald R. Pearce, ed., *The Senate Speeches of W. B. Yeats*, Bloomington, Indiana, 1960, p. 79). "Timothy", the "elderly student" who concludes the dialogue with a characteristic appeal to "courtesy" and whose politics are "in reality . . . more anarchic than a sparrow" (*Letters*, p. 896), represents that side of Yeats which might have prophesied, as it happened, that the Committee's proposal would be passed and never acted upon while the provisions of the amendment on bilingual signs and notices—although the amendment was on this occasion withdrawn—would become permanent features of Irish life.

*Persons*: *Peter, a Senator*
*Paul, a Deputy*
*Timothy, an elderly student*

PETER

WE will catch nothing, so I may as well listen to you. They have dynamited the fish, and several seasons will pass before there are enough trout to make a day's fishing. Let us put our rods against a tree and eat our lunch. I see Timothy coming along the river path, and I do not suppose he has had any better luck. While I am making the fire, you can explain that incredible doctrine of yours.

PAUL

Which doctrine, for I have a number which you consider incredible.

PETER

I mean what you said in the train, when you told me that you were about to vote scholarships or something of that kind for Gaelic speakers.

PAUL

Our general culture cannot be better than that of the English-speaking world as a whole, and is more likely to be worse. We are on the banks of a river that flows through an industrial town and bathe in its waters. But visit certain small nations—one of the Scandinavian nations, let us say—and you will notice at once that not only education, but general well-being are better distributed there, and when you ask how they manage it, somebody says "our people are so few that we can reach everybody." Everybody you meet speaks several languages well enough for commercial purposes and travel, but only one well enough for intimacy. Kings, nobles, farmers, professional men, socialists and reactionaries, novelists and poets grow up with a common life, from which nothing can separate them. Their rich or able men seldom drift away permanently, for if they find themselves in London or New York or Paris, they feel but strangers there. They may perhaps be less rich than men of equal ability, who belong to some English-speaking nation, and so manipulate greater resources, material or living, but their ability or their riches create in their own country a habit of energy and a tradition of well-being. No bond constrains, because no man compels; they but accept a limitation like that imposed upon a sculptor by the stone in which he works. Would not Ireland have gained if Mr. Bernard Shaw and Oscar Wilde, let us say, and the various Ryans and O'Briens who have enriched America, had grown up with such a limitation, and thought they were strangers everywhere but in Ireland. Then, too, I could discover with a little research the names of actors and singers who might at this moment be performing in some Dublin State Theatre or State Opera House, but for the damnable convenience of the English tongue.

PETER

If we have no State Theatre or State Opera House, we have the Abbey Theatre, and have all commended *Juno and the Paycock*.

PAUL

We may keep the author of the play, but how long shall we keep the players that give it so great a part of its life? A great Empire buys every talent that it can use and for the most part spoils what it buys. If we keep a good comedian, it is generally because his art, being an art of dialect, interests few but ourselves. A play called *Peg o' my Heart*—a stage mechanism without literary value—because it contained one dialect part, robbed the Abbey Theatre of four actresses, and almost brought it to an end.[1] If they had been bound to Ireland by a separate language, they would not have gone, they would not have desired to go.

PETER

You mean that if enforced bonds make hatred those that are obeyed though not enforced, make love.

PAUL

Norway could never have created the greatest dramatic school of modern times if it had spoken a world-wide language.

PETER

But surely a nation like Ireland or Norway should be able to pay an actress enough to keep her at home in comfort.

PAUL

World-wide commercial interests exploit whatever form of expression appeals to the largest possible audience; that is to say, some inferior form; and will always purchase executive talent. The chief actress of Norway, some few years ago, had to threaten to stop acting altogether

---

[1] The fabulously successful light comedy, *Peg o' My Heart*, by the American dramatist, J. Hartley Manners (1870–1928), opened in 1912. By 1922 it had been played over 8,000 times in North America and Great Britain and had been translated into three languages. In addition, over 245,000 copies of the novel based on the play had been sold.

Among the Irish actresses who played the role of Peg, the Irish girl who inherits a fortune and goes to live in London, was Sarah Allgood, who left the Abbey at the end of 1913 and toured in the play throughout 1915 and 1916.

to get her salary raised from £200 a year. If she had spoken English she could have earned more than that in a week, at some English or American music-hall.

PETER

Your point seems to be that no nation can prosper unless it uses for itself the greater portion of its talent.

PAUL

I am not thinking only of talent. The greater part of its creative life—that of the woman of fashion, not less than that of the founder of a business or of a school of thought, should be the jet of a fountain that falls into the basin where it rose.

PETER

That may or may not be true, but what has it to do with practical affairs? I have heard a man discuss for an hour what would have happened if the library of Alexandria had never been burnt, and another bored me through a windy day on an outside car by describing what Europe might have been if Constantinople had never fallen. The Irish language can never again be the language of the whole people.

PAUL

Why not?

PETER

Because the Irish people will not consent that it should, having set their hearts on Glasgow and New York.

PAUL

We shall have to go slowly, making our converts man by man, and yet Ireland should become bilingual in three generations.

PETER

Those three generations may be the most important since the foundation of Christianity. Architecture, and all the arts associated with architecture are being re-born as though to express a new perception of the inter-dependence of man. Drama and poetry are once more casting out photography, becoming psychological and creative. The experimental verification of a mathematical research—research made possible by the Irishman Rowan Hamilton[2]— has

---

[2] William Rowan Hamilton (1805–65), the Irish mathematician and man of letters, was a professor at Trinity College, Dublin. His studies dealt with higher mathematics, optics and astronomy.

changed the universe into a mathematical formula, and a formula so astounding that it can but alter every thought in our heads. Psychical research interpreted by that formula in thirty years will once more set man's soul above time and change, and make it necessary to reconsider every secular activity. Nations are made neither by language nor by frontier, but by a decision taken in some crisis of intellectual excitement like that which Italy took at the Renaissance, Germany at the Reformation, moments of fusion followed by centuries of cooling and hardening. The whole world draws to such a crisis, and you would cut Ireland off from Europe and plunge it into a controversy that will be incredibly bitter, because it can be fought without ideas and without education.

PAUL

I see no reason why the Gaelic movement should cut Ireland off from Europe, and I have never spoken a bitter word about an opponent.

PETER

I know a man who, after certain years of dependence in a great house, has set up as a picture-framer in a country town. He employs a young man, poverty-stricken like himself at the same age, and though this young man is as well educated as himself, compels him to take his meals in the kitchen with the servants. The great house had not driven him to the kitchen, but his offended dignity has demanded an offering. Spinoza thought that nations were like individuals, and that it was no use pulling down a tyrant, for a tyrant is what he is, because of something in the nation. "Look at the people of England," he said, or some such words. "They have pulled down Charles, but have had to push up Cromwell in his place." [3] Can you read an Irish propagandist newspaper, all those threatenings and compellings, and not see that a servitude, far longer than any England has known, has bred into Irish bones a stronger sub-conscious desire than England ever knew to enslave and to be enslaved? There is no public emotion in the country but resentment, and no man thinks that he serves his cause who does not employ that emotion. If we praise, the praise is unreal, and but given to some reflection of ourselves, but our vituperation is animated and even joyous. We think it effeminate to trust in eloquence and patience, and prefer to make

---

[3] In Part IV of Chapter XVIII of the *Tractatus Theologico-Politicus*, Spinoza observes the "melancholy instance" of the English in support of his notion that ". . . peoples, though often able to change their tyrants, have never been able to abolish them and replace monarchy by a different form of constitution. . . . They tried to find plausible legal grounds for removing their king; but having removed him, they still found it quite impossible to change the form of the state. Indeed, after much bloodshed they got the length of calling their new king by a different name (as though the name alone had been the whole question at issue!)" (*The Political Works*, A. G. Wernham, ed., Oxford, 1958, p. 201.)

men servile, rather than permit their opinions to differ from our own, and if there is a man notable for intellect and sincerity, we fit some base motive to his every act that he may not prevail against us. We had eloquence some hundred years ago, and had, it seems, when we spoke in Gaelic, popular poetry, but now we have neither—possessing indeed every quality of the negro but his music. We were a proud people once, but have grown so humble, that we have no method of speech or propaganda that the knave cannot use and the dunce understand.

PAUL

There are a great many people in this country who neither threaten nor impute base motives, and besides what you say, in so far as it is true, describes half the democracy of Europe.

PETER

Yes, all those who have pulled down a tyrant and would put another in his place.

PAUL

All this passion means, I suppose, that you object to our teaching Gaelic to those who do not want it.

PETER

I object to every action which reminds me of a mediaeval humorist compelling a Jew to eat bacon. Especially as in this case Jew compels Jew.

PAUL

Yet, if a Government can enforce Latin it has a right to enforce Gaelic.

PETER

I do not deny the right, but I deny that it should be employed in this country except within the narrowest limits.

PAUL

Ruskin once contended that reading and writing should be optional because what a fool reads does himself harm, and what a fool writes does others harm. That may be a convincing argument, but as our Government accepts the modern theory, I do not see why Gaelic should not be compulsory also. I have had nothing to do with that, however. My work, if I have a work, is to keep it from stupefying. I want the

Government to accept the recommendation of the Senate and spend
£5,000 a year on Gaelic scholarship; to train a small number of highly-
efficient teachers of the living tongue, who should have general European culture; to found scholarships for the best pupils of those teachers;
to endow a theatre with a Gaelic and English company, and to make
Gaelic an instrument of European culture. There is already a Gaelic
company performing *Tchekov*,[4] and there is much European literature,
especially that of countries like Spain and Italy which have a long-
settled peasantry that would go better into Gaelic than into English.
After all, Sancho Panza is very nearly a Munster farmer. I want the
Government to find money for translation by ceasing to print Acts in
Gaelic that everybody reads in English.

### PETER

As soon as a play or book is translated, which goes deep into human
life, it will be denounced for immorality or irreligion. Certain of our
powerful men advocate Gaelic that they may keep out the European
mind. They know that if they do not build a wall, this country will
plunge, as Europe is plunging, into philosophic speculation. They
hope to put into every place of authority a Gaelic speaker, and if
possible, a native speaker, who has learned all he knows at his mother's
knee.

### PAUL

I have always opposed the making of Irish obligatory for any post not
connected with the language. I want everywhere the best man with the
knowledge appropriate to his post.

### PETER

Once you make Gaelic a political question you are helpless. They have
made it obligatory, and will continue to do so.

### PAUL

That will last a few years. We are all new to public life, but the choice
between wisdom and fanaticism will be good for our intelligence.

### PETER

We are agreed that the future of Ireland depends upon the choice.

4 Yeats's reference is probably to the productions of *An Comhar Drámníochta* (The
Dramatic Union), which had been successful in its presentation of both original works and
translations in Gaelic since 1922. See also n. 5, p. 469, below.

PAUL

If Gaelic cannot become as I would make it, a disturbing intellectual force, it means . . .

PETER

A little potato-digging Republic.

PAUL

No, but Ireland a dull school-book, consequent apathy and final absorption in the British Empire.

PETER

You are ready to chance all that?

PAUL

I believe in the intellectual force created by years of conflict as by a flint and steel.

[*They are joined by Timothy*]

TIMOTHY

I see that you have the kettle boiling.

PAUL

Had you any luck?

TIMOTHY

Not a rise, but I saw some good fish floating with their bellies up. I am glad to sit down, for I am old enough to grow tired standing with a useless rod in my hand. What were you disputing about? Peter, you looked a moment ago as if you would fling the kettle into Paul's face, and Paul's face is red.

PETER

At present we speak English and Gaelic is compulsory in the schools, but Paul wants us to speak Gaelic and make English compulsory in the schools, and I am not sufficiently attracted by the change to plunge the country into a permanent condition of bad manners.

TIMOTHY

Whatever imagination we have in Ireland to-day, we owe to Gaelic literature or to the effect of Gaelic speech upon the English language. Think of the dialect plays of Synge and of Lady Gregory—of Lady

Gregory's translations of the stories of Fionn and of Cuchulain, which have given new classics to the English tongue. I can read a little Gaelic, but I often think I would give some years of life if I could read in the original one of those old poems translated by Kuno Meyer,[5] and the lamentations of *Deirdre*, and read well enough to feel the quality of their style. We can only feel the full beauty of a poem in another language when we can understand without translating as we read, when we can become for the time being a Frenchman, a German, or a Gael, and I sometimes wonder if that is really possible. Those lamentations of *Deirdre* have a poignancy unlike anything in any other European tongue. Surely, there must be something in the vocabulary, in the cadence, corresponding to it, and when I think that these poems were written in this country and by and about its people, it seems to me unbearable that I should be shut out, or partly shut out, from it all.

PAUL

Then you want to make Gaelic the language of the country?

TIMOTHY

But, Paul, I am so uncertain about everything, and there is so much to be said upon every side. English literature is, perhaps, the greatest in the world, and I am not in politics. If I were in politics, I would have to be certain, whereas I am an elderly student. I cannot even call myself a scholar, for I know nothing properly. Politics are a roulette wheel with various colours, and if a man is to take a part in the game, he must choose. If he prefers some colour that is not there, or if he be quite undecided, he must put that away and bang down his money firmly. So Peter must oppose the Gaelic movement and you must defend it.

PAUL

If Ireland gives up Gaelic, it will soon be a suburb of New York.

PETER

Like somebody in Shakespeare, I think nobly of the soul and refuse to admit that the soul of man or nation is as dependent upon circumstance as all that.

[5] In the report of the Senate Committee on Irish Manuscripts, which he wrote with the Irish historian Mrs. Alice Stopford Green (1848–1929), Yeats pays tribute to Kuno Meyer (1858–1919), the German philologist and Celtic scholar. Yeats had reviewed Meyer's translation of *The Vision of MacConglinne* in 1893 for *The Bookman* (see *Uncollected Prose*, vol. I, pp. 261–3) and, while he seems not to have met Meyer for some years, the scholar was acquainted with many of his friends, including Lady Gregory. In *Salve*, George Moore recalled Meyer's visits from Liverpool, where he taught, to Dublin "to shepherd the little flock that browses about the Celtic erudition" (p. 165). In 1903 Meyer had founded the School of Irish Learning, which was later absorbed into the Royal Irish Academy.

### TIMOTHY

I have held both opinions in the same hour, perhaps in the same minute. It sometimes seems to me, too, that there must be a kind of politics where one need not be certain. After all, imitation is automatic, but creation moves in a continual uncertainty. If we were certain of the future, who would trouble to create it?

### PAUL

I cannot see any means whereby a Parliament can pass uncertainty into law.

### TIMOTHY

I have no practical experience, but perhaps it might be possible to choose a schoolmaster as we choose a painter or a sculptor. "There is so-and-so," we would say, "who thinks that Ireland should be Gaelic-speaking, and because he is a very able, cultivated and learned man we will give him a school and let him teach. We ourselves think that he may be wrong, but after all, what does anybody know about it?" I think the knowledge of the Greek language must have come to Renaissance Italy in much that way. No two men, perhaps, would have agreed about its future. To some it meant a better knowledge of the New Testament, and to others—some at the Platonic Academy of Florence, for instance—a re-established worship of the Homeric gods. I am not sure that I like the idea of a State with a definite purpose, and there are moments, unpractical moments, perhaps, when I think that the State should leave the mind free to create. I think Aristotle defined the soul as that which moves itself, and how can it move itself if everything is arranged beforehand?

### PETER

Do you mean to say that you would appoint a schoolmaster, not only to teach Irish, but that it must be the living language of Ireland, although you thought what he attempted neither desirable nor possible?

### TIMOTHY

Perhaps neither desirable nor possible, but remember I would not appoint him if I did not like him, and because I have always liked Peter, if he wanted to teach that English was the only proper language for the Irish people, I would appoint him also. I generally dislike the people of Ulster, and want to keep them out—when I was in Belfast a few years ago they had only one bookshop—but I am told the Government wants to bring them in, so it might be well to give a school to some likeable Orangeman and let him teach Orangeism there. In fact, I am almost certain that the Education Office that would please me best, would choose schoolmasters much as a good hostess chooses her guests. It should never invite anybody to teach who is a bore or in any way disagreeable.

PETER

Timothy, you have not shed any light upon the subject.

PAUL

None whatever.

# An Undelivered Speech

As civil pressures on the Cosgrave government eased, the many issues which separated the supporters of the Free State began to surface. Thus, in the Senate debate on divorce on June 11, 1925, Yeats spoke passionately against legislation which would in effect make laws about divorce impossible to pass, seeing this as the Catholic majority's subtle imposition of its morality on the whole nation (see *Senate Speeches*, pp. 89–102). Yeats had been prepared to speak on this question earlier, in February, when a resolution came to the Senate from the Dáil which requested a rule proscribing even the introduction of any bills dealing with divorce *a vinculo matrimonii*. When the chairman of the Senate ruled this resolution out of order, Yeats published "An Undelivered Speech" in *The Irish Statesman* for March 14, 1925.

(Expecting a debate upon the problem of Divorce in the Senate on March 4, I had made notes for a speech. As the Message from the Dáil was ruled out of order, debate was impossible. As I think that whoever can should help to inform public opinion before the matter comes round again, I sent you my notes.—W. B. Yeats)

I SHALL vote against the resolution sent up to us by the Dáil, not because I am interested in the subject of divorce, but because I consider the resolution an act of aggression. We have the right to assume—it was indeed declared in so many words at a meeting of the Catholic Truth Society—that no Catholic would avail himself of opportunities for divorce; and President Cosgrave had before him the example of

Quebec, where, though the proportion of Catholics is greater than in Ireland, facilities of divorce are permitted to the minority, but he had preferred to impose his Catholic convictions upon members of the Church of Ireland and upon men of no church. I know that at the present stage of the discussion a large part of the Irish public, perhaps a majority, supports him, and I do not doubt the sincerity of that support —the sincerity that has heard only one side is invariably without flaw— and I have no doubt even that if he and they possessed the power they would legislate with the same confidence for Turks, Buddhists, and followers of Confucius. It is an impressive spectacle, so quixotically impressive, indeed, that one has to seek its like in mediaeval Spain. I wonder, however, if President Cosgrave and his supporters have calculated the cost—but no, I am wrong to wonder that, for such enthusiasm does not calculate the cost. This country has declared through every vehicle of expression known to it that it desires union with the North of Ireland, even that it will never be properly a nation till that union has been achieved, and it knows that it cannot bring that union about by force. It must convince the Ulster Protestants that if they join themselves to us they will not suffer injustice. They can be won, not now, but in a generation, but they cannot be won if you insist that the Catholic conscience alone must dominate the public life of Ireland. The Catholic Church fought for years against the Unity of Italy, and even invited recruits from this country to help it in that fight, and though it had the highest motives, history has condemned it, and now it is about to fight against the Unity of Ireland. But there is another cost which I will remind you of, though I am sure the Irish Bishops and President Cosgrave, whether they have calculated it or not, are prepared to pay it, and I shall speak of it, not to influence them, but because various journalists have charged those who favour divorce with advocating sexual immorality. The price that you pay for indissoluble marriage is a public opinion that will tolerate illegal relations between the sexes. Some time ago I was talking to an Italian of an illustrious Catholic house, from which have come Cardinals and, I believe, one Pope, and he spoke of what he considered the extreme harshness of American public opinion to illicit relations between the sexes, and explained it by the ease of divorce in America, which made such relations seem inexcusable. He thought that Italy was wiser, and said that the indissoluble marriage of Italy, of which he approved, caused great tolerance towards such relations. In describing Italy, he described, I think, every country where marriage has been indissoluble, Spain, France of the eighteenth century, and all mediaeval Europe. I will call Balzac as evidence, and not merely because he was the greatest of French novelists, but because he prided himself in recording the France of his own day. He was writing about aristocratic France which, though divorce was permitted since the French Revolution, was ardently Catholic, and did not recognise the laws of the Revolution. One of the most charming of his heroines is about to be married, and her mother takes her aside that she may speak these words: "Remember, my child, that if you love your husband that is the most fortunate of things, but if you do not, you will no doubt take a lover. All I say to you is, do nothing against the family." Then Balzac uses these remarkable words: "She went to the altar with the words of that noble woman ringing in her ears." I have just read the book in which my friend Mr. Chesterton puts the Catholic case with so much ability,[1] and I find nothing incompatible with the advice of that French mother; he is too wise an advocate of indissoluble marriage not to base it upon the family and the family only. It is a protection to the family, a protection to the children, or it is believed to be so, and its advocates think that the price is worth paying. I am certainly not going to reason against that conviction, I certainly do not think that I have anything to say that can affect an issue that has been debated by men of the greatest sincerity and intellect for generations. I shall merely put another point of view, that we may understand each other the better, a point of view which is held with passion by men who follow the teachings of some Church that is not under Rome, or like myself, believe as little in an infallible book as an infallible Church. For a long time there has been a religious truce in Ireland, men like myself have kept silent about all those matters that divide one religion from another, but President Cosgrave has broken that truce, and I will avail myself of the freedom he has given me. Marriage is not to us a Sacrament, but, upon the other hand, the love of man and woman, and the inseparable physical desire, are sacred. This conviction has come to us through ancient philosophy and modern literature, and it seems to us a most sacrilegious thing to persuade two people who hate one another because of some unforgettable wrong, to live together, and it is to us no remedy to permit them to part if neither can re-marry. We know that means the formation of ties which are commonly unhappy because transitory, and immoral because separated from the rest of life, and which, if there are children, may send the wrong into the future. We believe, too, that where such ties are not formed the emotions and therefore the spiritual life may be perverted and starved. The Church of Ireland permits the remarriage of such persons, and the Head of the Church of England has accepted the present Divorce Law of England. Neither would, perhaps, extend that law, but it will be extended in the future, for no nation which dates its public life

---

[1] Chesterton's essay "Questions of Divorce", a review of Florence Farr's *Modern Woman: Her Intentions* (1910), had appeared in *Uses of Diversity* (1921).

from the Reformation will permanently compel a man or woman to remain solitary if husband or wife has been condemned to life-long imprisonment or has been certified as an incurable lunatic. We do not think that children brought up in a house of hatred, where the parents quarrel perpetually, are the better for it, and we are certain that a step-mother is better than no mother, even if the real mother is but in gaol or mad or bad beyond reformation, or estranged beyond recall, and we put our faith in human nature, and think that if you give men good education you can trust their intellects and their consciences without making rules that seem to us arbitrary. Some rules there have to be, for we live together in corporate society, but they are matters of practical convenience, and we think that they should be made by statesmen and not by a celibate clergy, however patriotic or public-spirited.

I do not think that my words will influence a single vote here, nor am I thinking of this House, I am thinking only of a quarrel which I perceive is about to commence. Fanaticism having won this victory, and I see nothing that can prevent it unless it be proved to have overstepped the law, will make other attempts upon the liberty of minorities. I want those minorities to resist, and their resistance may do an overwhelming service to this country, they may become the centre of its creative intellect and the pivot of its unity. For the last hundred years Irish nationalism has had to fight against England, and that fight has helped fanaticism, for we had to welcome everything that gave Ireland emotional energy, and had little use for intelligence so far as the mass of the people were concerned, for we had to hurl them against an alien power. The basis of Irish nationalism has now shifted, and much that once helped us is now injurious, for we can no longer do anything by fighting, we must persuade, and to persuade we must become a modern, tolerant, liberal nation. I want everything discussed, I want to get rid of the old exaggerated tact and caution. As a people we are superficial, our Press provincial and trivial, because as yet we have not considered any of those great political and religious questions which raise some fundamental issue and have disturbed Europe for generations. It must depend upon a small minority which is content to remain a minority for a generation, to insist on those questions being discussed. Let us use the weapons that have been put into our hands.

# The Bounty of Sweden

"The Bounty of Sweden", Yeats's account of his receiving the Nobel Prize in 1923, first appeared in *The London Mercury* and *The Dial* in September, 1924. However, the distribution of the Cuala Press edition in the summer of 1925 provoked a chiding review of it in *The Sunday Times* by Yeats's friend of thirty years' standing, Edmund Gosse, who had been anxious that the prize go to Thomas Hardy. Yeats replied in a letter headed "The Bounty of Sweden" in *The Sunday Times* on August 9, 1925.

Gosse's review was an exercise in mocking condescension. Aside from the fact that Yeats was chosen over Gosse's candidate, an additional irritant was the inference which Gosse drew that the pro-German Swedes had chosen Irish Yeats to spite the British. The following passages from Gosse's review will give some sampling of his spite:

> His lecture, apart from these touches of political ornament, contained nothing with which we are not perfectly familiar. Mr. Yeats revolves, like a squirrel in a cage, inside his globular recollections of the Gallic [*sic*] League and the late Mr. Synge, the Abbey Theatre, and the White-Headed Boy. He has told us all this, over and over and over again. He has now told it to the Swedes, in exactly the same terms.

After recounting the beginnings of Yeats's career, stressing his place in English literary traditions, Gosse concluded the review as follows:

> The successive lyrics and lyrical dramas of the new poet displayed a genius which rapidly rose to its height, and achieved permanent recognition. But if there ever lived a dreamer who ought not to meddle in public affairs, who ought never to have left "the hills above Glen-Car," never to have stooped to the monotonous wranglings of faction, it is William Butler Yeats. Will he never learn that he knows all there is to know about fairies and mahatmas, and nothing whatever about international polemics?

Yeats's poem "Politics", written in 1938, seems to take Gosse's side in this argument.

SIR,—I am astounded at the article my friend Sir Edmund Gosse has written upon my little book "The Bounty of Sweden." I can only conclude that he read no page through, but picked sentences and half-sentences here and there without troubling himself with their context. It is not true that I described Strindberg as still living; it is not true that I described the Nobel prize-winner as "received with salvos of artillery";

it is not true that the "interesting memorials of Swedish culture" which I saw "left no impression," seeing that I have written many pages upon them.

I would not, however, write merely to correct inaccuracies which Sir Edmund Gosse perhaps considers journalistic vivacity. I write because I received, when in Stockholm, much courtesy from the English Minister,[1] and Sir Edmund Gosse accuses me of making statements which must have made the minister reflect "as he listened to the burning orator that good taste and historical accuracy were in equal danger of being neglected." The "burning words" were, he says, "amazing things about the Anglo-Irish War." My only words upon that subject were as follows:—

A trumpery dispute about an acre of land can rouse our people to monstrous savagery, and if in their war with the English Auxiliary Police they were shown no mercy, they showed none; murder answered murder.[2]

Sir Edmund Gosse declares this statement was made "because Mr. Yeats had to consider his own return to Dublin." Does he mean that a citizen of a British Dominion must be always more careful of the sensitiveness of England than that of his own country, or does he mean that no man belonging to a British Dominion may speak impartial truth without discourtesy? I think I can assure Sir Edmund Gosse that the English Minister to Stockholm took no such view.

W. B. Yeats

# The Child and the State

Yeats's visits to primary schools, late in 1925 and in the early months of 1926, as a representative of the Irish Senate, precipitated several remarkable expressions on themes that had occupied him for some time. At least as early as 1922, he had written of his interest in the "efficient" government emerging in Italy, and his dialogue on "Compulsory Gaelic" (see pp. 439–49 above) had approached the questions of freedom, discipline, national identity and national purpose in education. Early in 1925, he had discovered the theories of education of Giovanni Gentile (1875–1944), the Italian metaphysician and Minister of Education. Characteristically, Yeats found in Gentile's *La Riforma*

---

[1] The English Minister to Sweden in 1923 was Sir Colville A. d. R. Barclay (1869–1929).
[2] This passage is included in "The Irish Dramatic Movement", Yeats's text of his lecture in Stockholm, in *The Autobiography* (p. 379).

*dell' Educazione*, which he came to know first through summaries made by his wife, the perfect method for the introduction into Irish education of the "two great classics of the eighteenth century", Bishop Berkeley, who "proved that the world was a vision, and Burke that the State was a tree . . .".

The culmination of Yeats's readings, his visit—in February, 1926—to a Montessori school, St. Otteran's in Waterford, and his Senate speeches (see *Senate Speeches*, pp. 106–16) in "Among School Children" is traced by D. T. Torchiana in his excellent "'Among School Children' and the Education of the Irish Spirit" (Jeffares and Cross, eds., *In Excited Reverie*, New York), 1965, pp. 123–50). Yeats's first public formulation of this subject, however, was his lecture on November 30, 1925, to the Irish Literary Society on "The Child and the State", which was published in *The Irish Statesman* in two parts, on December 5 and 12, 1925.

PERHAPS there are some here, one or two, who were present some thirty-six years ago at a meeting in my house, at which this society was first proposed. I think that meeting was the beginning of what is called the Irish Literary Movement. We and Dr. Hyde and his movement, which began three or four years later with the foundation of the Gaelic League, tried to be unpolitical, and yet all that we did was dominated by the political situation. Whether we wrote speeches, or wrote poems, or wrote romances or wrote books of history, we could not get out of our heads that we were somehow pleading for our country before a packed jury. And that meant a great deal of strain, a great deal of un-reality, and even a little hysteria. Now there is no one to win over, Ireland has been put into our hands that we may shape it, and I find all about me in Ireland to-day a new overflowing life. To this overflowing life I attribute that our audiences at the Abbey Theatre have doubled, that the interest in music is so great that the Royal Dublin Society, which a few years ago was content with a hall that held seven hundred people, finds its new hall that holds some fifteen hundred so much too small, that every afternoon concert has to be repeated in the evening. Nor is it only appreciation that has grown, for where there is the right guidance and the right discipline, young men are ready for the hardest work. Colonel Brasé[1] does not find it hard to get his young men to practise many hours a day, his difficulty is sometimes to get them to cease work.

I know no case where the best teaching has been brought to Ireland in vain, and to-day there is a greater desire than ever before for ex-pression, I think I may also say for discipline. The whole nation is

[1] Colonel Fritz Brasé was a German officer employed by the Irish Government as head of the Army School of Music.

plastic and receptive, but it is held back, and will be held back for some time to come by its lack of education, education in the most common and necessary subjects.

For that reason I put so much reliance in your patriotism and your patience that I am going to talk to you about education in the Primary Schools. Perhaps, indeed, I but speak of it because it is so running in my head that I would speak badly of anything else. I have been going round schools listening at a school attendance committee, talking to schoolmasters and inspectors. Many of you have influence in Ireland, influence through the Press, or through your friends, and I want to impress upon you that the schools in Ireland are not fit places for children. They are insanitary, they are out of repair, they are badly heated, and in Dublin and Cork they are far too small. The Government inherited this state of things, this old scandal; they want to put it right, but they will not be able to do so unless public opinion is with them, above all perhaps, unless just the kind of people who are here to-night are prepared to defend them and support them. The Government is introducing a Compulsory Education Bill, but we have all our individual responsibility, and we must see to it that compulsory education does not come into force—I do not say does not pass—until those schools are fitted for their work. And if the children are going to be forced to school you must not only see that those schools are warm and clean and sanitary, but you must do as other countries are doing more and more, and see that children during school hours are neither half-naked nor starved.

You cannot do this by money alone, you must create some body of men with knowledge, that can give enough attention to see that all does not go to ruin again. Many of us think that you can only accomplish this by having a county rate struck, and by having county committees to supervise the spending of the money. No one proposes to interfere with the present manager's right to appoint and dismiss teachers. That right is cherished by the clergy of all denominations, but the ablest managers would, I believe, welcome popular control if confined to heating, housing, clothing, cleaning, etc. The old system has broken down, and all know that it has.

Only when the schools have been made habitable will the question arise that most interests us—what are you going to teach there? Whether Gaelic be compulsory or voluntary, a great deal of it will be taught. At present Gaelic scholars assure me that there is nothing to read in modern Irish except for very young children who love fairy-tales. You must translate, you must modernise. A committee of the Senate, of which I was chairman, has made a recommendation to the Government asking it to endow research into old, middle and modern Irish.[2] Nothing is decided, but I think the Government will make this grant. Probably most of the books so produced will be in middle or ancient Irish, and in any case unsuitable for young children. They will, however, supply the material from which in some degree a vivid modern literature may be created. I think the Government should appoint some committee of publication and so make possible a modern Gaelic literature. Let us say, Dr. Douglas Hyde, Mr. James Stephens, who is always working at his Irish, and Mr. Robin Flower,[3] who is a great scholar and a fine critic. They would not have to do much of the great work themselves, but they could put others to it. Up to, say, ten years old, a child is content with a wild old tale, but from ten years on you must give it something with more of the problems of life in it. I would like to see the great classics, especially of the Catholic Latin nations, translated into Gaelic.

The tendency of the most modern education, that in Italy, let us say, is to begin geography with your native fields, arithmetic by counting the school chairs and measuring the walls, history with local monuments, religion with the local saints, and then to pass on from that to the nation itself. That is but carrying into education principles a group of artists, my father among them, advocated in art teaching. These artists have said: "Do not put scholars to draw from Greek or Roman casts until they have first drawn from life; only when they have drawn from life can they understand the cast." That which the child sees—the school—the district—and to a lesser degree the nation—is like the living body: distant countries and everything the child can only read of is like the cold Roman or Greek cast. If your education therefore is efficient in the modern sense, it will be more national than the dreams of politicians. If your education is to be effective you must see to it that your English teaching also begins with what is near and familiar. I suggest therefore another commission or committee to find writers who can create English reading books and history books, which speak of Ireland in simple vivid language. Very few such books exist, indeed I can only think of Mr. Standish O'Grady's *Bog of Stars*, published at the suggestion of this Society many years ago.[4] That book is a fine piece of writing, and the books I think of should be fine pieces of

[2] This is the recommendation described on p. 439 above.

[3] James Stephens (1882–1950) had been, with Joyce, one of the two "most promising people . . . in Ireland", whom Yeats had commended to Edmund Gosse in a letter of August 21, 1915 (*Letters*, p. 600).

Robin E. W. Flower (1881–1946), the poet, scholar and Celticist, was at this time Assistant in the Department of Manuscripts of the British Museum.

[4] For a note on the Literary Society's publication scheme, see p. 238 above. *The Bog of Stars*, which Yeats recalled in "The Trembling of the Veil" as one of the "two or three good books" (*Autobiography*, p. 153) published in the series, had appeared in 1893.

writing, written by men of letters, chosen by men of letters; yet I do not think that I would exclude from the children's books any simple masterpiece of English literature. Let them begin with their own, and then pass to the world and the classics of the world.

There are two great classics of the eighteenth century which have deeply influenced modern thought, great Irish classics too difficult to be taught to children of any age, but some day those among us who think that all things should begin with the nation and with the genius of the nation, may press them upon the attention of the State. It is impossible to consider any modern philosophical or political question without being influenced knowingly or unknowingly by movements of thought that originated with Berkeley, who founded the Trinity College Philosophical Society, or with Burke, who founded the Historical.[5] It would be but natural if they and those movements were studied in Irish colleges, perhaps especially in those colleges where our teachers themselves are trained. The Italian Minister of Education has advised his teachers continually to study the great classics, and he adds that those great classics will be as difficult to them as is the lesson to the child, and will therefore help them to understand the mind of a child.

In Gaelic literature we have something that the English-speaking countries have never possessed—a great folk literature. We have in Berkeley and in Burke a philosophy on which it is possible to base the whole life of a nation. That, too, is something which England, great as she is in modern scientific thought and every kind of literature, has not, I think. The modern Irish intellect was born more than two hundred years ago when Berkeley defined in three or four sentences the mechanical philosophy of Newton, Locke and Hobbes, the philosophy of England in his day, and I think of England up to our day, and wrote after each, "We Irish do not hold with this," or some like sentence.[6]

[5] Yeats combines two of his most important Anglo-Irish models in noting the founding, in 1705, of the Philosophical Society by Berkeley (1685-1753) and that of the Historical Society by Burke (1729-97) in 1761.

[6] In a note, Yeats explicated a favorite passage of his which occurs toward the end of the penultimate section of the *Commonplace Book* kept by Berkeley when he was a student at Trinity College:

Note—The passage in the *Commonplace Book* is as follows:—"There are men who say there are invisible extensions. There are others who say that the wall is not white, the fire is not hot." (Meaning that there is a substratum differing from the appearance and outside mind.) "We Irishmen cannot attain to these truths. The mathematicians think there are insensible lines. About these they harangue: these cut at a point in all angles: these are divisible *ad infinitum*. We Irish can conceive no such lines. The mathematicians talk of what they call a point. This they say is not altogether nothing, nor is it downright something. Now we Irishmen are apt to think something" (meaning the mathematicians' "something" which is an abstraction) "and nothing are near neighbours. . . . I publish this . . . to know whether other men have the same ideas as Irishmen."

Feed the immature imagination upon that old folk life, and the mature intellect upon Berkeley and the great modern idealist philosophy created by his influence upon Burke who restored to political thought its sense of history, and Ireland is reborn, potent, armed and wise. Berkeley proved that the world was a vision, and Burke that the State was a tree, no mechanism to be pulled in pieces and put up again, but an oak tree that had grown through centuries.[7]

Teacher after teacher in Ireland has said to me that the young people are anarchic and violent, and that we have to show them what the State is and what they owe to it. All over the world during the Great War the young people became anarchic and violent, but in Ireland it is worse than elsewhere, for we have in a sense been at war for generations, and of late that war has taken the form of burning and destruction under the eyes of the children. They respect nothing, one teacher said to me, "I cannot take them through Stephen's Green because they would pull up the plants." Go anywhere in Ireland and you will hear the same complaint. The children, everybody will tell you, are individually intelligent and friendly, yet have so little sense of their duty to community and neighbour that if they meet an empty house in a lonely place they will smash all the windows. Some of the teachers want lessons on "Civic Duty," but there is much experience to show that such lessons, being of necessity dry and abstract, are turned to mockery. The proper remedy is to teach religion, civic duty and history as all but inseparable. Indeed, the whole curriculum of a school should be as it were one lesson and not a mass of unrelated topics. I recommend Irish teachers to study the attempt now being made in Italy, under the influence of their Minister of Education, the philosopher Gentile, the most profound disciple of our own Berkeley,[8] to so correlate all subjects of study. I would have each religion, Catholic or Protestant, so taught that it permeate the whole school life, and that it may do so, that it may be good education as well as good religion, I would have it taught upon a plan signed, as it is in Italy, by the representative of the Government as well as by the religious authority. For instance, the Italian teachers are directed by the Minister to teach "no servile fear." Up to three years ago in Ireland religion could not be taught in school hours, and even now, though that regulation is no longer binding, it is often nothing but a daily lesson in the Catechism. In Italy it takes four forms, that it may not be abstract, and that it may be a part of history and of life itself, a part, as it were, of the foliage of Burke's tree. First, praying, the learn-

---

[7] This sentence concludes the part of this essay in *The Irish Statesman* for December 5.

[8] Several years after this essay, in a letter to Olivia Shakespear, Yeats recommends Gentile's "dry difficult beautiful book", *Teoria Generale dello Spirito come Atto puro*, "for that founds itself on Berkeley" (*Letters*, p. 782).

ing and saying of simple prayers; second, singing, the learning and singing of famous religious songs; third, narration, the reading, or perhaps among the younger children the hearing, and writing out in the child's own words of stories out of the Bible, and stories of the great religious personages of their own country; fourth, contemplation, by which I mean that dogmatic teaching which stirs the mind to religious thought. The prayers and songs for an Irish school exist in abundance. There are, for instance, many religious songs in Gaelic with their traditional music, and they are already published in little books.

Every child in growing from infancy to maturity should pass in imagination through the history of its own race and through something of the history of the world, and the most powerful part in that history is played by religion. Let the child go its own way when maturity comes, but it is our business that it has something of that whole inheritance, and not as a mere thought, an abstract thing like those Graeco-Roman casts upon the shelves in the art-schools, but as a part of its emotional life.

One never knows where one's words carry, and I, in speaking, though I speak to you all, am thinking perhaps of some one young man or some one young girl who may hear my words and bear them in mind years hence. Even he and she may do nothing with my thought, but they may carry it, or some other amongst you may carry it, as a bird will carry a seed clinging to its claws. I am thinking of an Egyptian poem, where there are birds flying from Arabia with spice in their claws.[9] I do not think any of you are millionaires, and yet permit me to dream that my words may reach one that is. If the Government were to do all that I suggest, if after the schools are put in good repair it were to get together the right editors and they find the right authors, if all the textbooks necessary to create a religious and secular culture in Irish and English were published, there would still be much that no Government, certainly no Government of a poor country, can accomplish. England has had great educational endowments for centuries, everyone

[9] Yeats's reference is probably to the Egyptian love songs in Harris Papyrus 500 of the British Museum. The writer and theatrical producer Terence Gray (b. 1895) had published translations in *And in the Tomb were Found* in 1923:

> *I am come to prepare my snare with my hands,*
> *My cage, and my hiding place for all the birds of Puanit,*
> *They swoop upon the Black Land laden with incense.*
> *The first which cometh, he shall seize my worm-bait,*
> *Bearing from Puanit the fragrance which he exhales,*
> *His claws full of sweet-smelling resins.*
> *My heart desires that we take them together,*
> *I with thee alone.*

knows with what lavish generosity the rich men of America have endowed education. Large sums of money have been sent to Ireland for political ends, and rich Irish-Americans have largely contributed, and we all hope, I think, that there is no further need for that money. If societies like this interest themselves in Irish education and spread that interest among the Irish educated classes everywhere, money may be sent to us to cheapen the price of school-books for the poor, or to clothe the poorer children, or to make the school buildings pleasanter to a child's eyes, or in some other way to prepare for an Ireland that will be healthy, vigorous, orderly, and above all, happy.

W. B. Yeats

# The Need for Audacity of Thought

Yeats's thoughts on education, his historical speculations and his exasperation with the pompous ignorance he encountered in the Senate and elsewhere in public life came together in a critique he composed for A.E.'s *Irish Statesman*, ostensibly provoked by the recent suppression in Ireland of a paper containing a version of "The Cherry-Tree Carol". When A.E. declined the essay because it might "endanger" the *Statesman*, Yeats published his declaration of "The Need for Audacity of Thought" in *The Dial* for February, 1926.

SOME weeks ago, a Dublin friend of mine got through the post a circular from the Christian Brothers, headed A Blasphemous Publication and describing how they found "the Christian number[1] of a London publication in the hands of a boy"—in the hands of innocence. It contained "a horrible insult to God . . . a Christian Carol set to music and ridiculing in blasphemous language the Holy Family." But the Editor of a Catholic Boys' Paper rose to the situation; he collected petrol, roused the neighbourhood, called the schoolboys about him, probably their parents, wired for a film photographer that all might be displayed in Dublin, and having "bought up all unsold copies . . . burned them in the public thoroughfare." However, he first extracted the insult—the burning was to be as it were in effigy—that he might send it here and there with the appeal: "How long are the parents of Irish children to tolerate such devilish literature coming into the country?"

"The devilish literature" is an old Carol of which Dr. Hyde has given

[1] Doubtless, a "Christmas" number is meant.

us an Irish version in his Religious Songs of Connacht.[2] The version
enclosed with the circular was taken down by Mr. Cecil Sharpe,[3] and
differs in a few unessential phrases from that in The Oxford Book of
English Ballads

> *Then up spake Mary,*
> *So meek and so mild;*
> *Oh, gather me cherries Joseph*
> *For I am with child.*
>
> *Then up spake Joseph,*
> *With his words so unkind*
> *Let them gather cherries*
> *That brought thee with child.*
>
> *Then up spake the little child,*
> *In his Mother's womb;*
> *Bow down you sweet cherry tree,*
> *And give my Mother some.*
>
> *Then the top spray of the cherry tree,*
> *Bowed down to her knee;*
> *And now you see Joseph*
> *There are cherries for me.*

The poem is a masterpiece, because something of great moment is
there completely stated; and the poet who wrote the English words—
it may exist in every European tongue for all I know—certainly wrote
before the Reformation. It has been sung to our own day by English
and Irish countrymen, but it shocks the Christian Brothers. Why?

The actual miracle is not in the Bible, but all follows as a matter of
course the moment you admit the Incarnation. When Joseph has uttered
the doubt which the Bible also has put into his mouth, the Creator of
the world, having become flesh, commands from the Virgin's womb,
and his creation obeys. There is the whole mystery—God, in the indignity of human birth, all that seemed impossible, blasphemous even, to
many early heretical sects, and all set forth in an old "sing-song" that
has yet a mathematical logic. I have thought it out again and again and I
can see no reason for the anger of the Christian Brothers, except that

[2] Hyde's version is in volume 1 of *The Religious Songs of Connacht* (London and Dublin,
1906, pp. 279–85).

[3] Yeats misspells the name of Cecil Sharp (1859–1924), the collector of folk songs and
dances, who published several series of collected songs beginning with *A Book of British
Songs* (1902). With slight difference, the text Yeats gives is that in Sharp's *English Folk-Carols*,
London, 1911, pp. 7–8).

they do not believe in the Incarnation. They think they believe in it, but they do not, and its sudden presentation fills them with horror, and to hide that horror they turn upon the poem.

The only thoughts that our age carries to their logical conclusion are deductions from the materialism of the seventeenth century; they fill the newspapers, books, speeches; they are implicit in all that we do and think. The English and Irish countrymen are devout because ignorant of these thoughts, but we, till we have passed our grain through the sieve, are atheists. I do not believe in the Incarnation in the Church's sense of that word, and I know that I do not, and yet seeing that, like most men of my kind these fifty years, I desire belief, the old Carol and all similar Art delight me. But the Christian Brothers think that they believe and, suddenly confronted with the reality of their own thought, cover up their eyes.

Some months ago Mr. Lennox Robinson gave to a paper edited by young poets a story written in his youth. [4] A religious young girl in the west of Ireland, her meditations stirred perhaps by her own name of Mary, begins to wonder what would happen if Christ's second coming were in her own village. She thinks first that the people are so wicked they would reject him, and then that they might accept him and grow good. She is pursued by a tramp, becomes unconscious, is ravished, and returns to consciousness in ignorance of what has happened. Presently she finds herself with child and believes, and persuades her parents, that a miracle has taken place, and gradually the neighbours believe also and turn good. At last she dies bringing forth a girl-child; and the tramp arrives in the village knowing nothing of what has happened, gets drunk, and boasts of his crime.

This story roused as much horror as the Cherry Tree Carol. Yet countless obscure Mothers have so dreamed, have been so deceived; some of them born in Protestant communities have become Johanna Southcotts[5] and lost our sympathy, but if we imagine such a mother as a simple country girl living amongst settled opinions, the theme grows emotional and philosophical. I have myself a *scenario* upon that theme which

---

[4] In 1924, Lennox Robinson (1886–1958), playwright, editor, manager (1910–14, 1919–23) and director (1923–56) of the Abbey Theatre, had published "The Madonna of Slieve Dun", in the first issue of *To-Morrow* (see p. 438 above). Robinson's story—along with Yeats's "Leda and the Swan" and a story by the wife of a Trinity professor which concerned miscegenation—caused an uproar in which both Father Thomas Finlay (1848–1940) and John Henry Bernard (1860–1927), the Provost of Trinity, resigned from a Carnegie Library Advisory Committee, of which Robinson was secretary and treasurer. Lady Gregory, who was also on the committee, tells of "The Carnegie Row" in her *Journals* (pp. 272–82).

[5] As early as 1802 Johanna Southcott (1750–1814), the English prophetess and fanatic, had proclaimed herself "the Lamb's wife" and announced that she was to give birth to the second Christ. This prophecy, magnified by her followers, aroused great indignation. While she displayed signs of pregnancy in her last illness, an autopsy revealed nothing.

I shall never turn into a play because I cannot write dialect well enough, and if I were to set it where my kind of speech is possible, it would become unreal or a mere conflict of opinion. Mr. Lennox Robinson and I want to understand the Incarnation, and we think that we cannot understand any historical event till we have set it amidst new circumstance. We grew up with the story of the Bible; the Mother of God is no Catholic possession; she is a part of our imagination.

The Irish Religious Press attacked Mr. Lennox Robinson, and a Catholic Ecclesiastic and an Ecclesiastic of the Church of Ireland resigned from the Committee of the Carnegie Library, because it would not censure him. I think that neither the Irish Religious Press nor those Ecclesiastics believe in the Second Coming. I do not believe in it—at least not in its Christian form—and I know that I do not believe, but they think that they do. No minds have belief who, confronted with its consequence—Johanna Southcotts, deluded peasant girls, and all the rest—find those consequences unendurable. The minds that have it grow always more abundant, more imaginative, more full of fantasy even, as its object approaches; and to deny that play of mind is to make belief itself impossible.

I have worked with Mr. Lennox Robinson for years and there are times when I see him daily, and I know that his mind plays constantly about the most profound problems, and that especially of late his Art, under the mask of our brisk Dublin comedy, has shown itself akin to that of writers who have created a vision of life Tertullian would have accepted. I think of Strindberg in his Spook Sonata, in his Father, in his books of autobiography, as mad and as profound as King Lear; of James Joyce in his Ulysses lying "upon his right and left side" like Ezekiel and eating "dung" that he might raise "other men to a perception of the infinite"; of John Synge, lost to the "dazzling dark" of his Well of the Saints and of the last act of his Deirdre. I cannot deny my sympathy to these austere minds though I am of that school of lyric poets that has raised the cry of Ruysbroeck[6] though in vain: "I must rejoice, I must rejoice without ceasing, even if the world shudder at my joy."

The intellect of Ireland is irreligious. I doubt if one could select from any Irish writer of the last two hundred years until the present generation a solitary sentence that might be included in a reputable anthology of religious thought. Ireland has produced but two men of religious genius: Johannes Scotus Erigena[7] who lived a long time ago, and Bishop Berkeley who kept his Plato by his Bible; and Ireland has for-

---

[6] Jan van Ruysbroeck (1293–1381), the Flemish mystic.

[7] Yeats was rereading the Celtic theologian Johannes Scotus Erigena (815?–77?) at this time.

gotten both; and its moral system, being founded upon habit, not intellectual conviction, has shown of late that it cannot resist the onset of modern life. We are quick to hate and slow to love; and we have never lacked a Press to excite the most evil passions. To some extent Ireland but shows in an acute form the European problem, and must seek a remedy where the best minds of Europe seek it—in audacity of speculation and creation. We must consider anew the foundations of existence, bring to the discussion—diplomacies and prudences put away—all relevant thought. Christianity must meet to-day the criticism, not, as its ecclesiastics seem to imagine, of the School of Voltaire, but of that out of which Christianity itself in part arose, the School of Plato: and there is less occasion for passion.

I do not condemn those who were shocked by the näive faith of the old Carol or by Mr. Lennox Robinson's naturalism, but I have a right to condemn those who encourage a Religious Press so discourteous as to accuse a man of Mr. Lennox Robinson's eminence of a deliberate insult to the Christian religion, and so reckless as to make that charge without examination of his previous work; and a system which has left the education of Irish children in the hands of men so ignorant that they do not recognise the most famous Carol in the English language.

Note: The Irish periodical which has hitherto published my occasional comments on Irish events explained that this essay would endanger its existence. I have therefore sought publication elsewhere.

# A Defence of the Abbey Theatre

Yeats's last Abbey Theatre controversy was marked by almost every feature of all those that had gone before. Even before the opening of O'Casey's *The Plough and the Stars* on February 8, 1926, a director of the Theatre and one of the actresses had threatened to desert the production, much as Edward Martyn had in the case of Yeats's *Countess Cathleen* in 1899. And Joseph Holloway was on hand on February 11 to record Yeats's vain efforts to lecture the crowd amid a tumult during which "Some of the players behaved with uncommon roughness to some ladies who got on the stage, and threw two of them into the stalls" and "One young man thrown from the stage got his side hurt by the piano" (*Joseph Holloway's Abbey Theatre*, p. 254). As had happened with the first production of the *Playboy*, performances continued under police surveillance and were accompanied by a raging battle in the press. O'Casey, however, was more than able to conduct his own defence and he did so in an exchange of public letters with Hannah Sheehy-Skeffington which are reprinted in *Holloway's Abbey Theatre* (pp. 255–65).

Yeats delivered his major commentary on the disturbances in "A Defence of the Abbey Theatre" on February 23 at a meeting of the Dublin Literary Society. Little is known of Norman Reddin, with whom he evidently shared the platform, and all that survives of Reddin's remarks is Joseph Holloway's note, in his diary, that they consisted of "a short paper on the need of a national theatre in which he said a lot of controversial things . . ." (Holloway, Ms., 1900, p. 358, National Library). Although he rises to Reddin's taunt at his ancestry, Yeats's speech, as published in *The Dublin Magazine* for April–June, 1926, is remarkably pointed and tempered; he speaks as if to a younger self when he observes that "Mr. Reddin is too abstract; he has a theatre in his head, a kind of spiritual substance out of time and space."

* A SPEECH DELIVERED AT A MEETING OF THE DUBLIN
LITERARY SOCIETY, ON FEBRUARY 23RD

MR. REDDIN complains that the Abbey Theatre has produced many bad plays; that its Directors and play-writers are a "cult"; that it cannot be national, not being "the expression of the entire people"; that it uses the English language; that we Directors, being not only "Cromwellians," but "stout Cromwellians," have invented a form of dialect that he who has "lived with the people of the western south has never heard"; and, on top of all our other offences, that we have neither produced foreign masterpieces nor predominantly religious and political plays.

Now the last matter first. I do most anxiously assure Mr. Reddin that the Cromwellian mind has always loved religion and politics. We Cromwellian Directors laid down this principle twenty-five years ago, and have not departed from it: never to accept or reject a play because of its opinions. When we began our work, it was the accepted principle that an artistic or a literary society should have nothing to do with religion or politics. We could have had far greater support—greater financial support—had we made the usual declaration, but we refused to do so, because we considered all thought legitimate dramatic material. A good many years had to pass before people understood that we were sincere, that we were not trying to undermine anybody's political or religious opinions. Indeed that was only understood when many plays of different tendencies had been shown. Our first trouble was with the Unionists, but we have had to fight all parties, and are prepared to go on doing so. "Kathleen ni Houlihan," "The Piper," "The Rising of the

* One cannot recall an impromptu speech with verbal accuracy, nor is it necessary that one should. This is, however, the substance of what I said.—W. B. Y.

Moon," "The Lost Leader," "The Plough and the Stars," Miss Mc-
Ardle's revolutionary plays,[1] and many others are political, but political
in different ways. We have no object but good plays, made out of whatever thought is most exciting to the minds of those who make them.

At first, especially, many of our plays were in dialect, for what first
attracted our dramatists was that life of "folk," which in every country
is most obviously national, most obviously historical and ancient. The
Norwegian dramatists did precisely the same. "Understand the saga by
the peasant, and the peasant by the saga," that was their phrase. But we
are, he says, Cromwellians, and can, therefore, know nothing of the
matter. All, at this late day, have mixed strains of blood—even Mr.
Reddin, I imagine—but I think we Abbey Directors can find strains of
our blood that came into this country before Cromwell. I think the
first Synges came in the time of Elizabeth; but whatever the date, and
whatever their strains of blood, Lady Gregory and John Synge were
the first educated man and woman who spoke their whole souls in the
dialect of the people; the first to see in that dialect not a vehicle of
farce, but of intellect. That dialect—the dialect spoken in the west and
south of Ireland—is an ancient form of the English language. It has a
history of some hundreds of years, and is derived from two main sources.
Its syntax is partly that of Irish, and its vocabulary is partly that of
Tudor English. Synge and Lady Gregory had enough Irish to understand the syntax. Synge studied ancient Gaelic under H. d'Arbois de
Jubainville and, though always half an invalid, modern Irish in the
hardship of an Arran cottage. Lady Gregory had, in her "Cuchulain
of Muirthemne" and her "Gods and Fighting Men," made the most
famous translations ever made from the Irish language,[2] and she had,
before writing a word of her plays, filled notebook after notebook with
the English of her neighbourhood. Furthermore Synge and Lady Gregory knew Tudor English—Lady Gregory especially, for when I knew
her first, the *Morte d'Arthur* was her book of books. I do not believe
that Mr. Reddin's knowledge equals that of either; but if it does, that is
not sufficient for me—the farmer and the sailor have knowledge, but we
do not accept their opinion as to the merits of a landscape or a sea-scape.
I should want to be certain that he had an equal understanding before I
weighed his opinion against that of Lady Gregory and John Synge. Of

[1] Yeats's list of "political plays" alludes to both triumphs and controversies. While his
*Cathleen ni Houlihan* (1902), Lady Gregory's *The Rising of the Moon* (1907), and *The Lost
Leader* (1918) by Lennox Robinson were all popular and artistic successes, *The Piper* by
Norreys Connell had embroiled Yeats in public dispute (see p. 361 above). *The Old Man*
(1925), one of three plays by Dorothy Macardle (1899-1958) produced at the Abbey, had
been cited as one of its inoffensive political plays in Sean O'Casey's letter to *The Irish Times*
on February 19, 1926, at the time of the controversy over *The Plough and the Stars*.

[2] For a note on Yeats's praise of these books, see p. 299 above.

course, Synge and Lady Gregory no more reproduce dialect like a phonograph than a great painter copies land and sea like a photograph— "art is art because it is not Nature." [3] They have selected, but selected from a knowledge few dialect writers of any country have equalled. Sir Walter Scott made a single lowland Scottish dialect serve for all Scotland; and the Irish novelists, or the greater number of them, made Munster, Leinster and Connaught talk like a Dublin jarvey. Scott and the Irish novelists did their work according to their knowledge and their purpose, and were justified.

It is a recognised rule of criticism that you should never criticise at all till you have seen or tried to see what your author has done or tried to do. Let Mr. Reddin take down some anthology of prose—English, French or German—I care not what the language, and ask himself if he cannot find passages equal to any there of a like species—I do not mean by this in dialect—in Synge's "Playboy," in the last Act of his "Deirdre," in Lady Gregory's "Jail Gate," or here and there among her comedies, or among the slight dialect of her translations from the Gaelic. He will find that these passages are not only expressed in a way peculiar to this country, but that they are the classic prose of modern Ireland.

But he has more than our dialect against us—there are all those bad plays. Of course we have produced bad plays, some to give their authors experience, and some—and in these there is always good—because they are popular. Until a year ago the Abbey was practically bankrupt. It had survived war and civil war, and I assure you an audience gets very thin when there is firing in the streets. Time and again we Cromwellians had to go to our friends, some of these Cromwellians too, and raise money; but a time came when we could do this no longer. When we were an independent nation, it did not become the dignity of that nation that we should go to London, where we got £2,000 the last time, to save the dramatic movement of Ireland. Then the Government gave us our subsidy, and peace restored our audience. From that moment we began weeding out poor plays, improving our scenery, and bringing into our repertory plays from other countries. We have always played a certain number of foreign masterpieces, and for a long time we guided ourselves in this by the principle that, as our object was to create an Irish theatre, we would translate such foreign masterpieces as threw light upon our Irish plays. Because of their likeness in a part of their method to the work of Synge and Lady Gregory, we have long had plays by Molière in our repertory; and while we still hoped for an Irish religious drama, we produced a number of medieval "mysteries" and "moralities." Lately we have chosen foreign masterpieces without first think-

[3] This aphorism, a favourite of Yeats's, appears on p. 251 above as well as in "Notes" in *Samhain* for October, 1902 (*Explorations*, p. 88).

ing of our Irish plays, because an Irish school of drama has been created and does not need the same anxious fostering. We have always wished to do more foreign masterpieces than we have been able to, but they seldom succeed with the audience—I think I see signs of a change in that matter, but it will come slowly. It takes even longer to train an audience than a company of actors. You cannot have a national theatre without creating a national audience, and that cannot be done by the theatre alone, for it needs the help of schools and newspapers, and of all teachers of the people. The theatre can go only a little ahead of the people, and it can only continue to do that if Directors and shareholders agree not to take a penny in profits.

But I had forgotten. We play and act in English because we are Cromwellians, and that is the worst charge of all. Mr. Reddin is mistaken—we play and act in English because that is the language in which our audience thinks. Years ago Lady Gregory and I persuaded that other Cromwellian, Dr. Hyde, to write—I know he will not mind my saying this—those admirable little plays of his, those plays where there is often a humour so beautiful and an eloquence so touching.[4] We thought that we were helping to create a Gaelic theatre in country villages where Gaelic is the language of thought. That theatre almost came into existence, but it was destroyed because subordinated* to propaganda, for the natural man is bored by propaganda. But now a new Gaelic theatre has arisen which will not commit that error. We are glad it uses the same stage that we do, and we wish it success.[5] If the mass of the people come to think in Gaelic, it will become the national theatre of Ireland, but not till then. People can only act and sing and write well or enjoy these things well in the language of their thought.

Mr. Reddin is too abstract; he has a theatre in his head, a kind of spiritual substance out of time and space. An intellectual movement of any kind moves in narrow limits—a few people, a spot of the earth—and it grows out of the knowledge that it finds and does, not what it should according to any man's theory, but what it can or must. If those few

* Subordinated also, as I pointed out in *Samhain* at the time, to bad stage management and worse rehearsal. (See my *Plays and Controversies*, pages 35 and 36, and elsewhere). The first Gaelic play ever performed in a theatre, "The Twisting of the Rope," was performed under our management. It had no successor, because it is impossible to specialise in two languages.—W. B. Y.

[4] The Gaelic plays by Douglas Hyde which had been produced in their original form in the Abbey were *Casadh an t-Sugain* (The Twisting of the Rope) in October of 1901 and *An Tinnceur agus an tSidheóg* (The Tinker and the Fairy) in January, 1912. A third play by Hyde, *An Pósadh* (The Marriage) had been produced in November, 1911, in a translation by Lady Gregory.

[5] *An Comhar Drámuíochta* (The Dramatic Union) had been formed shortly after the establishment of the Free State in 1922. In 1925, it was granted a government subsidy to produce plays in Irish and it was using the Abbey stage at this time.

people are interested in the villages, it goes to villages for its vehicle of experssion; and if they are interested in slums, it must go there for a vehicle, and when that interest is exhausted it turns to something else, and always the greater the success, the more marked are the limits. A master is known, somebody has said, by the fact that he works within limits. Of one thing we may be quite certain: at no time, neither in the beginning nor in its final maturity, does an intellectual movement express a whole people, or anybody but those who are built into it, as a victim long ago was built into the foundation of a bridge. Sometimes if those few people are great enough, if there is amongst them a Sophocles or a Shakespeare, or even some lesser genius who has the sincerity of the Great Masters, they give their character to the people.

# Memorial to the Late T. W. Lyster

On March 27, 1926, Yeats spoke at the unveiling, in the National Library, of the memorial to T. W. Lyster, the late Librarian (see p. 305 above). Yeats had collaborated with Louis Claude Purser (1854–1932), on the simple inscription and the memorial was designed by George Atkinson (?–1941), the Director of the National College of Art. Yeats's remarks were published in June, 1926, in a pamphlet for the subscribers and this text was reprinted in *The Irish Book* in Autumn, 1960.

WHEN, after the late Mr. Lyster's death in 1922, some friends of his decided to put up a memorial to commemorate his long service in the National Library, it was quite clearly in their minds that the memorial must be in the Library, or, at any rate, just outside its door. For forty-two years Mr. Lyster was in the service of the Library, and for thirty-two of those forty-two years in this building. When, as quite a young man, he became a librarian, the reading room was the large room in Leinster House where the Senate now meets. When he was ten years there, the Library was moved into the present building. He became full Librarian in 1895; up to that he had been Assistant Librarian to Mr. W. Archer, F.R.S.,[1] who was Head Librarian before him. When Mr. Lyster became Head Librarian, he put aside all other work, and made this Library the business of his life—this Library and the municipal

[1] William Archer (1830–97).

libraries of Dublin, to which he was of great service, conducting examinations, for instance.

He also served in connection with the Royal Dublin Society Library. Libraries became his passion—he knew all about them, and how to make them efficient; he read notable papers upon that subject at library congresses. At the same time he was what a librarian was not always—he was a great scholar in books. He read perpetually, and had a vast memory. He read in English literature and in German literature. If he had not entered into the service of this Library, he would have done works of scholarship of very great value.

As it is, we owe to him that very fine translation of Düntzer's 'Life of Goethe,' much more readable than the original.[2] I remember that he gave me a copy of it when I was a very young man. I still read it for its exhaustive and vivid account of one of the greatest men who ever lived. He was, I think, something which we have not now in Dublin—a great scholar in literature. We have great scholars in various subjects; but he was our last great scholar in literature for itself. He inherited that passion from a great friend of his youth, Edward Dowden, and from him also his interest in German and in German literature. I myself would like to say that I am deeply indebted to Mr. Lyster. When I was a very young man, I read literature in the National Library—at that time it was in Leinster House—and it was Mr. Lyster who guided me. He had a great knowledge of Elizabethan literature, and I read that constantly under his guidance in that magnificent eighteenth-century room.

I am indebted to him also for something else. My first published work owed much to his correction. I wrote a long pastoral play, which was accepted by the short-lived 'Dublin University Review.'[3] When a young man writes his first poems, there will often be a good line followed by a bad line, and he should always go to a scholar to be advised; and Mr. Lyster did that for me. I used to go to his house, and he would go over the manuscript of my play with me, and help me to correct the bad lines.

I have said that we were quite clear in our minds that the memorial must be in this building. He had, I think, strong affection for it, not only because it was the place where he spent his life, but because it was

[2] Lyster published his translation of *Goethes Leben* (1880) by Heinrich Düntzer (1813–1901) in 1883.

[3] Yeats's *The Island of Statues*, an "Arcadian Faery Tale—in Two Acts", appeared in April–June, 1885, in *The Dublin University Review*, the journal founded in February, 1885, by Charles Hubert Oldham (?–1926), a Professor of Commerce and nationalist leader at Trinity College. Later in 1885, Oldham also founded the Contemporary Club, a discussion group before which Yeats often spoke. Many of Yeats's early poetic fragments and his second published essay (see *Uncollected Prose*, I, pp. 87–104) appeared in the *Review*, which ceased publication in June, 1887.

the place where he was surrounded by the young men whom he loved. Many young men owed a great deal to his guidance here. The Library was full of young students. On one occasion some person wished to prevent the students from sitting on the steps outside, and he said: 'No; they must be allowed to sit there, because this is their building.' And that was always his attitude towards the young men who surrounded him.

When we came to think of what kind of memorial we would erect, we sadly gave up some charming schemes because of the difficulty of light. Some of us, for instance, were anxious to have a little mosaic with Mr. Lyster in the Library, surrounded by those young men; but the light was too dim for that. Then we thought of some sculptured memorial, and that, too, seemed impossible. We played with the idea of a stained-glass window, because that is one of the things which Dublin artists can produce so beautifully; but it would have been out of keeping with the other windows: so the Committee decided on the simple lettered memorial to Mr. Lyster's achievements and his scholarship, and they asked Mr. George Atkinson, R.H.A., to carry out that decision; and I will now hand over Mr. Atkinson's dignified, simple design to Sir Philip Hanson,[4] who represents the Board of Works.

# The Hugh Lane Pictures

Concurrent with their literary and dramatic careers and throughout the civil tumult in Ireland between 1916 and 1925, Yeats and Lady Gregory doggedly pressed on in the matter of Hugh Lane's French pictures (see pp. 414-28 above). At one time or another, they drew on the likes of Bernard Shaw, Eamon DeValera and W. T. Cosgrave, who included the issue in several negotiations at the time of the establishment of the Free State. A persistent ally was the Ulster Unionist leader, Edward Carson (1854-1935), who promised to introduce a Bill legalizing Lane's codicil and whose speech in Parliament in July, 1924, prompted the formation of a Committee of Inquiry to decide the matter. The Committee's report in June of 1925 found, paradoxically, that while Lane had indeed thought he was making a legal disposition, no legalizing action should be taken because of the grave precedent that would be established. The Committee's further observation, that in the intervening years Dublin had built no suitable building for the paintings, as Lane had required in the codicil, whereas the Tate addition to the National Gallery had

---

4 At the time of this address, Sir Philip Hanson (1871-1955) was Acting Chairman of the Board of Public Works.

been built in London, seemed to Yeats "exactly as if the Forty Thieves were to say they had a right to their treasure because they had been to the trouble of digging a cavern to contain it" (quoted in *Lady Gregory's Journals*, p. 306.).

Lady Gregory's objection, that the Committee had exceeded its mandate by finding on other matters than Lane's legal intention, was confirmed by Carson, who added that he had himself "had a hand" in the alteration of Queen Victoria's will, so that the Committee's concern for precedent was groundless. Thus, she determined "to frame an answer at once, for Cosgrave to write, indignant at their straying outside the questions asked them. . . . And we must make a strong national as well as ethical claim" (*ibid.*). Part of this claim was the resolution passed by the Irish Senate on July 14, 1926, seeking return of the Lane pictures. Yeats was of course among the speakers (see *Senate Speeches*, pp. 118–24), as was another long-time ally, S. L. Brown (?–1939), whose speech drew forth a friendly letter to *The Times* of London on July 21 from Lord Aberdeen, the ex-Lord Lieutenant.

The response by Yeats's old antagonist, D. S. MacColl, in *The Times* for July 23, denouncing "The very small body of Irish opinion which still maintains this ten years' agitation", provoked the letter signed by Yeats and Lady Gregory on "The Hugh Lane Pictures, Dublin's Chance" in *The Times* for July 29. This letter, largely a quotation of sworn evidence, is Yeats's only contribution to the controversy which raged in the "Correspondence" column of the *Times* until August 3, when "G.A.F." concluded it, praising the results of the Committee's findings: "England has the pictures, which she values highly; Ireland has the grievance, which she values still more highly."

## THE HUGH LANE PICTURES
## DUBLIN'S CHANCE

### TO THE EDITOR OF *THE TIMES*

SIR,—Mr. MacColl writes in *The Times* of July 23 of Sir Hugh Lane's last interview with Mr. Aitken, which took place some time in March, 1915. Mr. Aitken had himself written of that interview in a letter to the *Morning Post*, December 14, 1916:—

Lady Gregory and others have spoken with assurance as to what were Sir Hugh's latest intentions. As a matter of fact, I feel sure that he was himself undecided. I had several conversations with Sir Hugh Lane about the final destination of the group of French pictures, and I can testify that his intentions were not settled then. [The date of this conversation had been erroneously given by Mr. Aitken as "a few days before he sailed for America," but, this being pointed out as erroneous, was later stated to have been about March 25.]

But neither Mr. MacColl nor any other opponent of our claim nor the committee in their report have mentioned the later, more definite, and conclusive testimony as to Hugh Lane's final decision in favour of Dublin sworn to in the affidavits made by some of his friends to whom he had spoken on the matter in the last week (April 3 to April 10) before he sailed for New York on Sunday, April 11, 1915. I give some extracts from these in order of date of the conversations.

Mr. A. W. West, of Leixlip House, Co. Kildare, a Land Commissioner and a cousin of Hugh Lane says:—

On Saturday, April 3, 1915, he took me to see some pictures he had newly hung in the National Gallery, Dublin. I have a vivid recollection of our conversation—my last with Hugh Lane. He told me definitely and unequivocally that he had decided after all to let Dublin have the pictures that he had sent to London. On my interrogating him as to the much-vexed question of the site and architect of the proposed gallery, he stated that he was willing to waive his requirements in regard to those matters, but added:—"I do not wish that to be known at present." I turned to him and said:—"You are the most forgiving man I ever met." He then informed me that he felt he had not long to live, and gave certain grounds for his belief. He also mentioned that he was leaving for New York on the following Friday, and referred to the risk of being torpedoed. Personally, I do not consider that Dublin deserves the pictures, and I have no interest in making this declaration beyond a strong desire that what I look upon as the dying wish of a great friend and relative whose memory I revere should be respected, and, having regard to the circumstances of his death, treated with the sanctity of that of a soldier on the battlefield.—July 21, 1924.

Mrs. Duncan, the Curator of the Dublin Municipal Gallery, says in her affidavit:—

I last saw Sir Hugh Lane on the last day of his stay in Dublin before he sailed for America. He came to the Gallery that day and had a conversation with me about his collection of Continental pictures which were then stored in the London National Gallery. He said that he wished to bring these pictures to Dublin. That with regard to the building of a new Gallery he did not wish now to insist on any special plan, but would be content if the Corporation reaffirmed their already expressed intention of building *a* gallery. He asked me whether I thought I could get the Corporation to give some assurance to this effect. The words he used were, "I do not wish to appear to have climbed down about a new gallery building, but I do not wish to revive any of the old controversies. I wish to bring the pictures back to Dublin as soon as possible, and they might be hung here pending the building of any gallery the Corporation might decide upon."—Feb. 12, 1917.

Mr. G. W. Russell (AE), now editor of the *Irish Statesman*, declared:—
I met Sir Hugh Lane on the day previous to his departure from

Dublin for the last journey to the United States. I asked Lane at once:—
"Are we to lose the pictures?" He replied, "Oh, Dublin will get the
pictures all right. I made threats to frighten people here and to get them
to move." I believe those to be actually the words he used. I remembered them precisely because I was most anxious that those pictures
should be in some Dublin gallery. I was despondent because of the
rumours and was greatly cheered by Lane's confident reply. The words
I have quoted certainly represent the full sense of his words. . . . I had
not the slightest doubt after my conversation that it was Sir Hugh
Lane's will to give the pictures now in the National Gallery, London,
either to the Municipal Gallery or to the Gallery in Merrion-square, and
all he said to me was in harmony with the codicil to his will.—July 24,
1924.

Although those three witnesses are Irish, it is not likely their word
will be questioned or that they will be accused of having exaggerated
the statements made to them. The next affidavit is that of Mr. Ralph
Freeman Smith, of 31, Old Burlington-street, who cannot be suspected,
being English, of any prejudice in our favour. The last is also by an
English witness, and he also is not likely to be suspected of having tilted
the balance against London.

Mr. Freeman Smith says:—

I was an intimate friend of the late Sir Hugh Lane for some years
before his death, and on the day before sailing for America he called at
my office on a matter of business. In the course of general conversation
he spoke of the journey to New York and of the dangers of travelling at
that time, and, referring to the pictures now in dispute, he said: "I have
altered my will, so that the pictures at the National Gallery shall after all
go to Dublin." I have no personal feeling as to the ultimate destination
of the pictures, but I make this declaration to support those who are
interested in giving effect to his last wishes.—July 28, 1924.

Mr. Alexander Martin makes oath:—

I have been asked to state in a word my impression of Sir Hugh
Lane's wishes regarding these pictures in so far as I gathered it in
conversation with him when I accompanied him to Liverpool. I am
pleased to accede to this request, and I should like to preface it with the
remark that it was the more strongly fixed in my mind because his
wishes as he expressed them were not those with which I had most
sympathy. Personally I should have preferred to have seen the pictures
placed in London rather than in Dublin. From earlier conversations I
was aware, of course, of Sir Hugh Lane's deep interest in Ireland, and
was not therefore at all surprised when on this occasion he spoke of it,
and of his recent visit to Dublin, with the greatest affection. He spoke
to me also of the Modern Gallery, referring again to the ambition he had

entertained when collecting the pictures of seeing them housed in Dublin, and he gave me to understand that his mind was made up that it should, after all, be the destination of his pictures, and I make this declaration conscientiously believing the same to be true and by virtue of the Statutory Declaration Act, 1835.—Feb. 27, 1917.

These affidavits have not been published. Copies were sent to the committee, and some copies have been kept in our High Commissioner's office in London.

Yours faithfully,
W. B. Yeats
A. Gregory
Coole Park, Gort, Co. Galway, July 26

# Sympathy with Mrs. O'Higgins

The shooting by Republican gunmen of Kevin O'Higgins (see p. 433 above) on July 10, 1927, was a great blow to Yeats, who wrote later to Olivia Shakespear (*Letters*, pp. 726-7) of the premonitory vision of the murder which he and Mrs. Yeats had had the night before. His first public response, in a letter of "Sympathy with Mrs. O'Higgins", which was published in *The Irish Times* on July 14, betrays some of the stunned bitterness which emerged later, when Yeats was "roused to write *Death* and *Blood and the Moon* by the assassination of . . . O'Higgins, the finest intellect in Irish public life" (*Variorum Poems*, p. 831).

### MESSAGES FROM W. B. YEATS AND "AE"

MR. W. B. YEATS, writing to Mrs. O'Higgins said:—

"What can one say? I think of these words in an old Irish poem: 'The sorrowful are dumb for her'. What one can say is that the country has lost the man it needed, its great builder of a nation. When obscure men die in battle we say 'Their country will never forget them,' and it forgets them before daybreak; but a martyred intellect is the most powerful of all things. One remembers that when men write the history of this generation they will tell his life and know that all is told; one tries to find consolation in that thought, and then one remembers all that he had still to do.

"I have during these last four and twenty hours tried again and again to find something less inadequate to say, but before certain events one feels most of all the helplessness of human life."

"AE" (G. W. Russell) wrote:— "My dear Mrs. O'Higgins. May I add my sympathy and profound regret at the loss of the great statesman to the multitude you have received? I had but slight personal knowledge of your husband, but I had watched with increasing admiration his career as a public man, knowing that he was the moral architect of the new state; and I had the belief that if he lived, he would have moulded the Free State into the image of his imagination, but a state we would all have been proud of."

# The Censorship and St. Thomas Aquinas

Yeats's health declined towards the end of his term as Senator. His final speech, on July 18, 1928, was a short, characteristic plea for the priority of personal ability to abstract representativeness in the selection of Senators, about which he wrote to Lady Gregory: "Probably I have made my last Senate appearance. A little speech, three sentences, was followed by a minute of great pain . . ." (*Letters*, p. 744). Thus, in September, as the Senate prepared to take up a subject of great importance to him in the "Censorship of Publications Bill", Yeats presented his views in two essays, "The Censorship and St. Thomas Aquinas" in *The Irish Statesman* on September 22, 1928 and "The Irish Censorship" in *The Spectator* on September 29. In these essays, Yeats continued the synthetic method of several of his later prose pieces, combining his reading of the new French critics (see pp. 433–6 above), and the recent controversy over the "Cherry Tree Carol" (see p. 461 above) with the current political debate and "the Platonizing theology of Byzantium" which motivates several poems of this period.

## I

"THE Censorship of Publications Bill" declares in its preliminary section that "the word 'indecent' shall be construed as including 'calculated to excite sexual passion.'" I know something of the philosophy of St. Thomas, the official philosophy of the Catholic Church. Indeed, the new Thomist movement in literary criticism has made such knowledge almost essential to a man of letters,[1] and I am convinced that this defini-

---

[1] Yeats's reference is probably to the work of such neo-Thomists as Jacques Maritain (1882–1973) and Charles Maurras, which had been appearing in *The Criterion*, and to that of

tion, ridiculous to a man of letters, must be sacrilegious to a Thomist. I cannot understand how Catholic lawyers, trained in precision of statement and ecclesiastics, who are supposed to be trained in philosophy, could have committed such a blunder. Had Professor Trench[2] made it I would understand, for his sort of evangelical belief, whatever it owes to the ascetic Platonism of the seventeenth century, owes nothing to Aquinas.

## II

Cardinal Mercier[3] writes in his *Manual of Modern Scholastic Philosophy*, Vol. 1, p. 314, English Edition: "Plato and Descartes, who both considered the soul as a substance completely distinct from the body, make it reside in some central part whence, like a pilot at the helm, it can control the movements of the whole organism. By Plato the rational soul is placed in the brain, whilst Descartes relegates it to the minute portion of it called the pineal gland. St. Thomas's opinion, to which we adhere, is entirely different; he lays down that the soul is wholly present in the whole body and in all its parts—'anima rationalis est tota in toto corpore et tota in qualibet parte corporis.'"

For centuries the Platonizing theology of Byzantium had dominated the thought of Europe. Amidst the abstract splendour of its basilicas stood saints with thought-tortured faces and bodies that were but a framework to sustain the patterns and colours of their clothes. The mosaics of the Apse displayed a Christ with face of pitiless intellect, or a pinched, flat-breasted virgin holding a child like a wooden doll. Nobody can stray into that little Byzantium chapel at Palermo, which suggested the chapel of the Grail to Wagner,[4] without for an instant renouncing the body and all its works and sending all thought up into that heaven

---

Wyndham Lewis (1884–1957) whose *Time and Western Man* Yeats had been reading, at the time of this essay, with great enthusiasm. In November, 1927, he wrote to Olivia Shakespear that he wanted to meet Lewis: "we are in *fundamental* agreement" (*Letters*, p. 733). And in January of the next year he wrote, "You will see from this that *Time and Western Man* still fills my imagination. . . . I read the last chapter again and again. He reminds me of a Father of the Church . . ." (*Letters*, p. 734).

[2] Dr. Wilbraham Trench (1873–1939) had been appointed, at the death of Edward Dowden in 1913, to the chair of English Literature at Trinity College Dublin for which Yeats had also been considered. In his "Introduction" to P. A. Ussher's translation of *The Midnight Court* (1926), Yeats had alluded to Trench's solemnity in wishing "that a Gaelic scholar had been found or, failing that, a man of known sobriety of manner and of mind—Professor Trench of Trinity College, let us say—to introduce to the Irish reading public this vital, extravagant, immoral, preposterous poem" (*Explorations*, p. 281).

[3] D. F. F. J. Cardinal Mercier (1851–1926), the Archbishop of Malines, Belgium, and founder of the Institute of Philosophy, had published his *Manual of Modern Scholastic Philosophy* in 1917.

[4] For Miss Horniman's comment on this attribution, see p. 485 below.

the pseudo Dionysius, the Areopagite, fashioned out of the Platonic ideas.

## III

Within fifty years of the death of St. Thomas the art of a vision had faded, and an art of the body, an especial glory of the Catholic Church, had inspired Giotto. The next three centuries changed the likeness of the Virgin from that of a sour ascetic to that of a woman so natural nobody complained when Andrea del Sarto chose for his model his wife, or Raphael his mistress, and represented her with all the patience of his "sexual passion." A corresponding change in technique enabled him to imagine her, not as if drawn upon a flat surface, but as though moulded under the hand in bas-relief. Painters liberated from a conviction that only ideas were real, painted, from the time of Orcagna, bodies that seemed more and more tangible till at last Titian saw grow upon his canvas an entirely voluptuous body.[5] "Anima est in *toto corpore*" (the italics are Cardinal Mercier's). "The breast's superb abundance where a man might base his head." [6] The lawyers who drew up the Bill, and any member of the Dáil or Senate who thinks of voting for it, should study in some illustrated history of Art Titian's *Sacred and Profane Love*, and ask themselves if there is no one it could not incite to "sexual passion," and if they answer, as they are bound to, that there are many ask this further question of themselves. Are we prepared to exclude such art from Ireland and to sail in a ship of fools, fools that dressed bodies Michael Angelo left naked, Town Councillors of Montreal who hid the Discobulus in the cellar?[7]

## IV

There is such a thing as immoral painting and immoral literature, and a criticism growing always more profound establishes that they are bad

---

[5] The mosaics at Palermo date from around 1180. St. Thomas died in 1274 and the decoration of the chapel of the Virgin of the Annunciation in Padua by Giotto (c. 1267–1337) was begun around 1306. Andrea del Sarto lived from 1486 until 1531 and Raphael from 1483 until 1520. Orcagna lived from c. 1308 until 1368 and Titian (1477–1576) painted his "Sacred and Profane Love" around 1503.

[6] This line is from the fifth section of Browning's "A Toccata of Galuppi's":

> *Was a lady such a lady, cheeks so round and lips so red,—*
> *On her neck the small face buoyant, like a bell-flower on its bed,*
> *O'er the breast's superb abundance where a man might base his head?*

(H. E. Scudder, ed., *The Complete Poetical Works of Robert Browning*, Boston, 1895, p. 175.)

[7] The neglect of a plaster cast of the Discobolus of Myron of Eleutherae (c. 450 B.C.) in the Montreal Museum of Natural History is the inspiration for "A Psalm of Montreal" (1884) by Samuel Butler (1835–1902).

paintings and bad literature,[8] but though it may be said of them that they sin always in some way against "in *toto* corpore," they cannot be defined in a sentence. If you think it necessary to exclude certain books and pictures, leave it to men learned in art and letters, if they will serve you, and, if they will not, to average educated men. Choose what men you may, they will make blunders, but you need not compel them to with a definition.

W. B. Yeats

# The Irish Censorship

*THE SPECTATOR*, SEPTEMBER 29, 1928

THE other night I awoke with a sense of well-being, of recovered health and strength. It took me a moment to understand that it had come to me because our men and women of intellect, long separated by politics, have in the last month found a common enemy and drawn together. Two days before I had gone to see an old friend, from whom I had been separated for years, and was met with the words, "We are of the same mind at last."[1] The Free State Government has in a month accomplished what would, I had thought, take years, and this it has done by drafting a Bill which it hates, which must be expounded and defended by Ministers full of contempt for their own words.

Ecclesiastics, who shy at the modern world as horses in my youth shied at motor-cars, have founded a "Society of Angelic Welfare." Young men stop trains, armed with automatics and take from the guard's van bundles of English newspapers. Some of these ecclesiastics

---

[8] Yeats echoes Wilde's famous pronouncement, in the "Preface" to *The Picture of Dorian Gray*, that "There is no such thing as a moral or an immoral book. Books are well written, or badly written."

[1] The "old friend" is probably George Russell. The estrangement which had become public in Russell's withdrawal from the Abbey in 1904 and which both writers felt came from irreconcilable differences in their natures had been suspended on several occasions. The Censorship Bill temporarily eased their separation, as had William Martin Murphy's lock-out in 1913 (see p. 405 above) and the Conscription Act of 1918. Yeats's first public statement on the Censorship Bill had appeared in Russell's paper (see p. 477 above). Debate of the bill continued in the columns of *The Irish Statesman* and, on November 9, 1928, Russell wrote to Yeats, who was then at Rapallo, sending him the four issues from October 20 through November 10 and adding that Bernard Shaw had sent "a devastating article on the censorship" which would appear on November 17 (*Letters from AE*, p. 180).

are of an incredible ignorance. A Christian Brother publicly burnt an English magazine because it contained the Cherry Tree Carol, the lovely celebration of Mary's sanctity and her Child's divinity, a glory of the mediaeval church as popular in Gaelic as in English, because, scandalized by its *näiveté*, he believed it the work of some irreligious modern poet; and this man is so confident in the support of an ignorance even greater than his own, that a year after his exposure in the Press, he permitted, or directed his society to base an appeal for public support, which filled the front page of a principal Dublin newspaper, upon the destruction of this "infamous" poem.

> *Then out and spoke that little Babe*
> *Which was within Her womb:*
> *"Bow down, bow down thou cherry tree*
> *And give my Mother some."* [2]

The Bill is called "Censorship of Publications Bill, 1928," and empowers the Minister of Justice to appoint five persons, removable at his pleasure, who may, if that be his pleasure, remain for three years apiece, and to these persons he may on the complaint of certain "recognized associations" (The Catholic Truth Society and its like) submit for judgment book or periodical. These five persons must then say whether the book or periodical is "indecent," which word "shall be construed as including calculated to excite sexual passions or to suggest or incite to sexual immorality or in any other way to corrupt or deprave," or whether, if it be not "indecent" it inculcates "principles contrary to public morality," or "tends to be injurious or detrimental to or subversive of public morality." If they decide it is any of these things the Minister may forbid the post to carry it, individual or shop or library to sell or lend it. The police are empowered by another section to go before a magistrate who will be bound by the Bill's definition of the word "indecent" and obtain, without any reference to the committee or the Minister, a right to seize in a picture-dealer's shop, or at a public exhibition where the pictures are for sale, an Etty, or a Leighton[3]—the police have already objected to "The Bath of Psyche"—and fine or imprison the exhibitor. Another section forbids the sale or distribution of any "appliance to be used for," or any book or periodical which advocates or contains an advertisement of any book or periodical

---

[2] See p. 461 above.
[3] William Etty (1787-1849), the English colorist and history painter, often painted the female nude. "The Bath of Psyche", by the English portraitist and history painter, Sir Frederick Leighton (1830-1896), is a quite representative and sensuously coloured female nude.

which advocates "birth control." The *Spectator*, the *Nation*, the *New Statesman*, and *Nature*, are, I understand, liable to seizure.[4]

This Bill, if it becomes law, will give one man, the Minister of Justice, control over the substance of our thought, for its definition of "indecency" and such vague phrases as "subversive of public morality," permit him to exclude *The Origin of Species*, Karl Marx's *Capital*, the novels of Flaubert, Balzac, Proust, all of which have been objected to somewhere on moral grounds, half the Greek and Roman Classics, Anatole France and everybody else on the Roman index, and all great love poetry. The Government does not intend these things to happen, the Commission on whose report the Bill was founded did not intend these things to happen, the holy gunmen and "The Society of Angelic Welfare" do not intend all these things to happen; but in legislation intention is nothing, and the letter of the law everything, and no Government has the right, whether to flatter fanatics or in mere vagueness of mind to forge an instrument of tyranny and say that it will never be used. Above all, they have no right to say it here in Ireland, where until the other day the majority of children left school at twelve years old, and where even now, according to its own inspectors, no primary schoolmaster opens a book after school hours.

It will, of course, appoint a "reasonable committee," and, unless the Minister of Justice decides to remove one or more of its members, four out of five must agree before anything happens. I know those reasonable committee-men who have never served any cause but always make common cause against the solitary man of imagination or intellect. Had such a committee, with even those two Protestant clergymen upon it somebody suggests, censored the stage a while back, my theatre, now the State Theatre, would never have survived its first years. It now performs amid popular applause four plays, of which two, when first performed, caused riots, three had to be protected by the police, while all four had to face the denunciation of Press and pulpit. Speaking from the stage, I told the last rioters—to-day's newspaper burners—that they were not the first to rock the cradle of a man of genius.[5] By such conflict

---

[4] Despite the efforts of Yeats, A.E., Shaw, and many others, the Censorship of Publications Bill which became law in 1929 was, in most particulars, that which Yeats describes here.

[5] Rioting less severe than that over *The Playboy of the Western World* in 1907 had broken out during the second performance of O'Casey's *The Plough and the Stars* in 1926. On both occasions—as he had done at the time of the controversy over his *Countess Cathleen* in 1899—Yeats had called for police protection. The fourth disputed play referred to here is probably Synge's *In the Shadow of the Glen* (see pp. 306, 331–8 above).

In his speech to the audience of *The Plough and the Stars*, Yeats had chided his countrymen with characteristic sharpness: "You have disgraced yourselves again. Is this to be an ever-recurring celebration of the arrival of Irish genius? Once more you have rocked the cradle of genius. The news of what is happening here will go from country to country. You

truth, whether in science or in letters, disengages itself from the past. The present Bill does not affect us, but if it passes into law the next will bring the stage under a mob censorship acting through "recognized associations."

The well-to-do classes practise "birth control" in Ireland as elsewhere, and the knowledge is spreading downwards, but the Catholic Church forbids it. If those men of science are right, who say that in a hundred years the population will overtake the food supply, it will doubtless direct the married to live side by side and yet refrain from one another, a test it has not imposed upon monk or nun, and if they do not obey—well, Swift's "Modest Proposal" remains, and that, at any rate, would make love self-supporting.

Although it was almost certain that Catholic Ireland, thinking "birth control" wrong in principle, would follow the lead of countries that, being in sore need of soldiers and cheap labour, think it undesirable and legislate against it, those who belong to the Church of Ireland or to neither Church should compel the fullest discussion. The Government is forbidden under the Treaty to favour one religion at the expense of another, which does not mean that they may not propose legislation asked for by one Church alone, but that they must show that the welfare of the State demands it. "You Mahommedans must not quote your Koran because the Christians do not believe in it, you Christians must not quote your Bible," said the chairman at the religious meeting in ancient Damascus—or was it Bagdad?—which scandalized the Spanish Traveller. Those who think it wrong to bring into the world children they cannot clothe and educate, and yet refuse to renounce that "on which the soul expands her wing," can say "no man knows whether the child is for love's sake, the fruit for the flower, or love for the child's sake, the flower for the fruit"; or quote the words of St. Thomas: "*Anima est in toto corpore.*" [6]

The enthusiasts who hold up trains are all the better pleased because the newspapers they burn are English, and their best public support has come from a newspaper that wants to exclude its rivals; but their motives may be, in the main, what they say they are, and great numbers of small shopkeepers and station-masters who vaguely disapprove of their methods approve those motives. A Government official said of these station-masters and shopkeepers the other day: "They are defending their sons and daughters and cannot understand why the good of the nine-tenths, that never open a book, should not prevail over the

---

have once more rocked the cradle of reputation. The fame of O'Casey is born tonight" (quoted in Saddlemyer and Skelton, eds., *The World of W. B. Yeats*, rev. ed., Seattle, 1967, p. 107).

[6] See Yeats's citation of this passage, p. 478 above.

good of the tenth that does." Twenty years ago illegitimacy was almost unknown, infanticide unknown, and now both are common and increasing, and they think that if they could exclude English newspapers, with their police-court cases which excite the imagination, their occasional allusions to H. G. Wells which excite the intellect, their advertisements of books upon birth control which imply safety for illicit love, innocence would return. They do not understand that you cannot unscramble eggs, that every country passing out of automatism passes through demoralization, and that it has no choice but to go on into intelligence. I know from plays rejected by the Abbey Theatre that the idealist political movement has, after achieving its purpose, collapsed and left the popular mind to its own lawless vulgarity. Fortunately, the old movement created four or five permanent talents.

There are irresponsible moments when I hope that the Bill will pass in its present form, or be amended by the Republicans, as some foretell, into a still more drastic form, and force all men of intellect, who mean to spend their lives here, into a common understanding. One modern-minded Catholic writer has been hawking a letter round the Press threatening anti-clericalism; but if that come, and I do not expect it in my time, it will not come in the old form. No Irishman wants the fourteenth century, even though most damnably compromised and complicated by modern Rathmines, driven from his back door so long as the front door opens on the twentieth. Our imaginative movement has its energy from just that combination of new and old, of old stories, old poetry, old belief in God and the soul, and a modern technique. A certain implacable and able Irish revolutionary soldier[7] put me to read Berkeley with the phrase: "There is all the philosophy a man needs"; and I have long held that intellectual Ireland was born when Berkeley wrote in that famous note-book of his after an analysis of contemporary mechanistic thought: "We Irish do not think so," or some such words.[8] The power to create great character or possess it cannot long survive the certainty that the world is less solid than it looks and the soul much solider—"a spiritual substance" in some sense or other—and our dramatists, when they leave Ireland, or get away from the back door in some other fashion, prefer cause or general idea to characters that are an end to themselves and to each other.[9] Synge's "Playboy" and O'Casey's

[7] D. T. Torchiana (*W. B. Yeats and Georgian Ireland*, p. 222) has identified the "implacable and able Irish revolutionary soldier" as the Reverend Jephson Byrne O'Connell, a Catholic priest. Yeats refers to O'Connell's recommendation of Berkeley on p. 489 below.

[8] See p. 458 above.

[9] Yeats's reference is probably to O'Casey, who had published earlier in 1928 Yeats's letter explaining the Abbey's rejection of *The Silver Tassie*. "The mere greatness of the world war has thwarted you," Yeats wrote. "Dramatic action is a fire that must burn up everything but itself. . . . The whole history of the world must be reduced to wallpaper in front of which the characters must pose and speak" (*Letters*, p. 741).

"Plough and the Stars" were attacked because, like "The Cherry Tree Carol," they contain what a belief, tamed down into a formula, shudders at, something wild and ancient.

W. B. Yeats

# Wagner and the Chapel of the Grail

"The strange thing", Yeats wrote to Florence Farr in 1907 in reference to Annie Horniman, "is that any old hatred years after you think it dead will suddenly awaken" (*Letters*, p. 490). Just such hatred had formed when Yeats refused in 1908 to leave the Abbey and write poetical dramas for Miss Horniman's Manchester Repertory Theatre. Disillusioned with Yeats and the Abbey and jealous of Lady Gregory, Miss Horniman had withdrawn from the Theatre in 1910. Nearly twenty years later, an article by Yeats in *The Irish Statesman* (p. 478 above) provoked a letter from her which appeared in the *Statesman* for October 6, 1928, chiding his learning: "It would be unreasonable to expect you to correct the mistakes of your contributors, but you may like to know that the Byzantium Chapel at Palermo, spoken of in the article on The Censorship and St. Aquinas, has nothing whatever to do with the Grail Temple scene in 'Parsifal' at Bayreuth." In conclusion she noted that her copy of the paper went "to a learned gentleman in Munich, and perhaps he will be amused to read that anyone who has heard of Wagner and the Grail should mix up Pavia and Palermo."

Yeats's response, a letter on "Wagner and the Chapel of the Grail" in the issue of October 13, limits itself to Miss Horniman's confusion of Wagner's inspiration for the Grail Temple scene in *Parsifal* with his staging of it.

### TO THE EDITOR OF THE *IRISH STATESMAN*

DEAR SIR,—Miss Horniman is in the right when she says that Wagner got part of the painted scene, that represents the Chapel of the Grail, from the Certosa of Pavia, part from the Alhambra, and she might have added part from that fine Cathedral in Siena which is striped like a zebra. But she is wrong in supposing that I spoke of his deplorable stage scenery. Wagner paid a visit to Palermo towards the end of his life, and, though Ellis' translation of Glasenapp's biography[1] makes no

---

[1] W. Ashton Ellis (d. 1919), whom Yeats had known in the late eighties, was the translator of Wagner's prose works, his letters and the biography by C. F. Glasenapp (1847–1915). He was a close friend of Miss Horniman who, Yeats had written to Arthur Symons in 1905, spoke "as his voice" (*Letters*, p. 460).

mention of the journey, it is recorded on the wall of the Hotel des Palmes, and should Miss Horniman visit there the manager will show her Wagner's room and I think the pen he wrote with, and some guide will bring her to the Capella Palatina where Wagner went day after day seeking—unless local patriotism deceive itself—an idea powerful enough to call into his hearer's mind the Chapel of the Grail.—Yours, faithfully,

W. B. Yeats

42 Fitzwilliam Square, Dublin

# Ireland, 1921–1931

Despite the assassination in 1927 of Kevin O'Higgins, "the one strong intellect in Irish public life" (*Letters*, p. 727), Yeats continued to develop his concept of "a nation controlled by highly trained intellects". His identification of these minds with the great Anglo-Irishmen of the eighteenth century had begun as early as his attribution in 1925 of the ideas of Giovanni Gentile to Berkeley (see p. 459 above) and is traced in detail in D. T. Torchiana's *W. B. Yeats and Georgian Ireland*. As the general elections of February, 1932, approached, Yeats was named by Aodh De Blacam (1890–1932) in the *Irish Press* as part of "the attempt now being made by certain 'Anglo-Irish Leaders' to bring back the Irish Eighteenth Century" (*Letters*, p. 790). A few days earlier, Yeats had compared the "hold on Irish imagination" of Berkeley and Swift to that of O'Connell in "Ireland, 1921–1931", which appeared in *The Spectator* for January 30. "De Blacam's passing mention is valuable", he wrote to Joseph Hone, for whose book on Berkeley (1931) he had supplied an "Introduction", "as it conveys an idea that something is happening, and that may get it [into] some undergraduate's head" (*ibid.*).

## I

I WALKED along the south side of the Dublin quays a couple of years ago; looked at the funnels of certain Dublin steamers and found that something incredible had happened; I had not shuddered with disgust though they were painted green on patriotic grounds; that deep olive green seemed beautiful. I hurried to the Parnell Monument and looked at the harp. Yes, that too was transfigured; it was a most beautiful symbol; it had ascended out of sentimentality, out of insincere rhetoric, out of mob emotion. When I reached home I took from the mantelpiece a bronze medal of myself and studied the little shamrock the American medallist had put after the date. But there there had been no transformation; the disgust that will always keep me from printing that portrait in any book of mine, or forgiving its creator, had increased, as though the ascent of the other symbols had left the shamrock the more alone with its associations of drink and jocularity.

## II

What had happened to those other symbols? What had gone down into my subconsciousness? What had changed the foundations of my mind? Five or six years ago an old Galway farmer told me that he supported the Government because it had given us the only peace Ireland had known in his lifetime. A month ago a Thomist philosopher who is an experienced politician said to me: "Nothing can bring Europe to its senses but an epoch of Bolshevism; the people ask the impossible and the governments are afraid to govern." Our Government has not been afraid to govern, and that has changed the symbols, and not for my eyes only. We are on the edge of a general election and nobody in either party is confident, for it is hard to foretell anything about an election held under a scheme of proportional representation except that neither side will have more than a bare majority.[1] If the Republicans come into power we shall have a few anxious months while they discover where they have asked the impossible, and then they in their turn will govern. An Irishman is wild in speech, the result of centuries of irresponsible opposition, but he casts it off in the grip of fact with a contempt beyond the reach of sober-speaking men.

The Government of the Free State has been proved legitimate by the only effective test; it has been permitted to take life. The British Government, after the Rebellion of 1916, executed some sixteen or seventeen men and it was out of the country in five years. In the middle of our Civil War a Republican prisoner said to his fellow-prisoners: "We have won. I have news: they have executed their first man." They executed more than seventy and not a vote changed.[2] These dead cannot share the glory of those earlier dead; their names are not spoken aloud to-day except at those dwindling meetings assembled in O'Connell Street or at some prison gate by almost the sole surviving friend of my

---

[1] In the election on February 16, 1932, the Republican *Fianna Fáil* party of Eamon De Valera defeated the incumbent *Cumann na nGaedhal* party of W. T. Cosgrave. Yeats's vote was, of course, for the incumbents.

[2] Kevin O'Higgins's enforcement of the Army Emergency Powers Resolution of September 28, 1922, resulted in the execution of seventy-seven Republican "Irregulars", including the author and statesman, Erskine Childers (1870-1922).

early manhood, protesting in sybilline old age, as once in youth and beauty, against what seems to her a tyranny.[3]

## III

When I think of the legislation of those ten years I think first of the roads which have brought lorry and bus, the newspaper, and here and there books, to remote villages; then of the electrical works at Ardna-crusha. These works are successful; the demand has exceeded the prophecy of the Minister.[4] The Minister and his Board have quarrelled as to whether they should pay their way from the start or sell cheap until the whole power of the Shannon is employed; but of the works themselves there has been no criticism. They were the Government's first great practical success, a first object-lesson in politics. Planned by German engineers, they were attacked in the English Press, and still more vigorously by men and newspapers in Ireland, which the Irish public associated, often mistakenly, with English interests. When the Government seized the Republican headquarters they found letters from men all over Ireland resigning from Republican posts because such a project, carried against such opposition, proved our economic independence.

Nothing remains the same and there have been few mistakes. My six years in the Irish Senate taught me that no London Parliament could have found the time or the knowledge for that transformation. But I am less grateful to the Government for what it has done than because its mere existence delivered us from obsession. No sooner was it established, the civil war behind it, than the musician, the artist, the dramatist, the poet, the student, found—perhaps for the first time—that he could give his whole heart to his work. Theatre and concert audiences increased, the Royal Dublin Society built a new hall double the size of the old and doubled the number of performances; and this vigorous life stayed unimpaired until the European economic crisis.

## IV

Freedom from obsession brought me a transformation akin to religious conversion. I had thought much of my fellow-workers—Synge, Lady

---

[3] Yeats refers, of course, to Maud Gonne. "When Lady Gregory goes," he had written to Olivia Shakespear in September of 1929, "and she is now very frail, I too shall have but one old friend left. (M.G. has been estranged by politics this long while.)" (*Letters*, p. 769).

[4] Yeats's description is of the "Shannon Scheme", a massive and spectacularly successful hydroelectric project championed by Patrick McGilligan (1889–1961) Minister for Industry and Commerce from 1924 to 1932.

Gregory, Lane—but had seen nothing in Protestant Ireland as a whole but its faults,[5] had carried through my projects in face of its opposition or its indifference, had fed my imagination upon the legends of the Catholic villages or upon Irish mediaeval poetry; but now my affection turned to my own people, to my own ancestors, to the books they had read. It seemed we had a part to play at last that might find us allies everywhere, for we alone had not to assume in public discussion of all great issues that we could find in St. Mark or St. Matthew a shorthand report of the words of Christ attested before a magistrate. We sought religious conviction by a more difficult research:

> *How charming is divine philosophy!*
> *Not harsh and crabbed, as dull fools suppose,*
> *But musical as is Apollo's lute.*[6]

Now that Ireland is substituting traditions of government for the rhetoric of agitation our eighteenth century had regained its importance. An Irish Free State soldier, engaged in dangerous service for his Government, said to me that all the philosophy a man needed was in Berkeley. Stirred by those words I began to read *The Dialogues of Hylas and Philonus*.[7] From Berkeley I went to Swift, whose hold on Irish imagination is comparable to that of O'Connell. The Protestant representatives in Dáil and Senate were worthy of this past; two or three went in danger of their lives; some had their houses burnt; country gentlemen came from the blackened ruins of their houses to continue without melodrama or complaint some perhaps highly technical debate in the Senate. Month by month their prestige rose. When the censorship of books was proposed certain Protestant Bishops disassociated themselves from it, and had the Government persisted with the Bill in its first form and penalized opinion we might have had a declaration, perhaps from the Episcopacy as a whole, that private judgement implied access to the materials of judgement. Then, just when we seemed a public necessity, our Episcopacy lost its head. Without consulting its representatives in Dáil or Senate, without a mandate from anybody, in the teeth of a refusal of support from Trinity College, terrified where none threatened, it appealed, not to the Irish people, but to the Colonial Conference, to keep the Irish Courts in subordination to the Privy Council, thereby seeming to declare that our ancestors made the independence of the legislature and the Courts the foundation of their politics, and of Ireland's from that day, because those Courts and that

---

[5] See p. 484 above.
[6] Milton, *Comus*, ll. 472–4.
[7] The Free State soldier is J. B. O'Connell (see p. 484 above). Berkeley's *Dialogues Between Hylas and Philonous* appeared in 1713.

legislature protected not a nation but a class.[8] When these blind old men turned their backs upon Swift and Grattan, at a moment too when the past actions of the Colonial Conference itself had already decided the issue, they had forgotten, one hopes, or had never learnt, that their predecessors sat in the Irish House of Lords of 1719, when it sent the Irish Court of Exchequer to prison for accepting a decision of that Privy Council.

## V

If I were a young man I would start an agitation to show them their task in life. As a beginning I might gather together the descendants of those who had voted with Grattan against the Union that we might ask the British Government to return his body; it lies in Westminster Abbey under a flat plain stone since it was laid there, despite the protests of his followers, less to commemorate his fame than to prevent a shrine and a pilgrimage. Then I would ask the Irish Government to line the streets with soldiers that we might with all befitting pomp open the pavement of St. Patrick's for one last burial.

# Gypsy Prize Winners, 1932

During tours of America, Yeats—in addition to A.E., Padraic Colum, Lennox Robinson and others—had stayed at "Freelands", the Kentucky estate of W. T. H. Howe (*c.* 1873–1939), the president of the American Book Company and the bibliophile whose library became, after his death, the basis of the Berg Collection in the New York Public Library. Among Howe's interests was a poetry prize in *The Gypsy*, an "all poetry magazine" published between 1925 and 1937 by a Cincinnati newspaperwoman, Miss George Elliston (d. 1946). In "Gypsy Prize Winners, 1932" in the issue for March, 1933, Yeats, who judged the contest, noted the reason for his choice of "Moon", by Dorothy Marie Davis:

---

[8] In order to regularize what had become a common practice, a Bill amending the Free State Constitution by abolishing the right of appeal from Free State Courts to the Judicial Committee of the Privy Council had been introduced towards the end of the Cosgrave administration. Despite the strong opposition of the Protestant Episcopacy which Yeats cites here, the Bill was enacted shortly after the election of De Valera.

MOON

*Oh, is there no one who will set the moon free?*
*She is caught in the lobster-pot of the tree.*
*Oh, is there no one to save the moon's daughter?*
*She is being dragged down in the arms of the water!*

A FOUR line poem, arresting for its fresh and spontaneous treatment of a topic so long sung, that it is extremely difficult to arrive at any originality regarding it, has been awarded the $100 offered by W. T. H. Howe for the best lyric in the 1932 series of The Gypsy.

The poem is entitled "Moon," and is the work of Dorothy Marie Davis, Pomona, Cal.

W. B. Yeats, who judged The Gypsy verses gave the $50 for the best sonnet to Carmelite Janvier of New Orleans, La., "Aunt Cissy Sits Down" and the $50 for the best free verse piece to Nolanne O'Hair, Greencastle, Indiana, for "Birch Woods."

Yeats gives his decisions in the following letter to Mr. Howe, who offers the three prizes annually:

Dear Mr. Howe:

I have read the poems with surprise; they are so spontaneous, natural and simple. Even when they are not good poems they are interestering [*sic*] as the record of some moment of life.

I decide that "Moon," by Dorothy Marie Davis, is the best of the lyrics. Because it is such a little thing, I have told myself that it must be my love for folk rhyme and nursery rhyme that makes me pitch upon it.

In doubt of myself I have gone over the poems again and hesitated between it and "Mystery," by Laurie Bruenn, which attempts so much more. But no: a small thing is done so perfectly in "Moon" that I must give it the prize.

The best sonnet is undoubtedly "Aunt Cissy Sits Down," by Carmelite Janvier, and I decide with less confidence that the best free verse is "Birch Woods," by Nolanne O'Hair, although "Silence" by Gee Kaye, runs it close. "Silence," however, has a rhythm which is rather that of prose than of verse.

Yours,
(Signed) W. B. Yeats

# The Great Blasket

Yeats recognized "The Great Blasket", an appreciation in *The Spectator* for June 2, 1933, of the English translation of *Twenty Years A-Growing* by Maurice O'Sullivan, as "the last [review] I shall ever write. I haven't the gift," he wrote on May 21, "my writings have to germinate out of each other. I spent about ten days on the thing and it's not worth the trouble. It is something else altogether, dressed out to look like a review" (*Letters*, p. 809). Nevertheless, the autobiographical narrative of O'Sullivan (1904–50), a Civic Guard in Connemara who had been raised in the Blasket Islands, a remote chain off the Dingle Peninsula, renewed in Yeats some enthusiasms of the nineties. "Read *Twenty Years a-Growing* [*sic*] or some of it," he wrote in a postscript to Olivia Shakespear a few days later. "I once told you that you would be happy if you had twelve children and lived on limpets. There are limpets on the Great Blasket" (*Letters*, p. 811).

ARAN was John Synge's first choice. There he thought himself happy for the first time, "having escaped the squalor of the poor and the nullity of the rich".[1] There he and Lady Gregory saw one another for the first time, looked at one another with unfriendly eyes without speaking, not knowing that they were in search of the same thing.[2] Then others came and he fled to the Great Blasket. He told me upon his return that he found an old crippled pensioner visiting there, that they had come away together, stayed in the same little hotel in Ventry or Dingle. One morning the pensioner was not to be found. Synge searched for him everywhere, trying to find out if he had gone back to the Island, jealous as if the Island had been a woman. A few years ago the Irish Government, lacking texts for students of modern Irish, asked

---

[1] Near the end of Part I of *The Aran Islands*, Synge describes his feelings when returning from the Arans. "I have come out of an hotel full of tourists and commercial travellers, to stroll along the edge of Galway Bay, and look out in the direction of the islands. The sort of yearning I feel toward those lonely rocks is indescribably acute. This town, that is usually so full of wild human interest, seems in my present mood a tawdry medley of all that is crudest in modern life. The nullity of the rich and the squalor of the poor give me the same pang of wondering disgust; yet the islands are fading already and I can hardly realise that the smell of the seaweed and the drone of the Atlantic are still moving round them" (*Collected Works*, vol. II, pp. 102–3).

[2] In her essay on "Synge", in *The English Review* for March, 1913, Lady Gregory recalls first seeing Synge "in the North Island of Aran. I . . . felt quite angry when I passed another outsider walking here and there, talking also to the people. I was jealous of not being alone on the island among the fishers and seaweed gatherers. I did not speak to the stranger, nor was he inclined to speak to me; he also looked on me as an intruder, I only heard his name" (p. 556).

Mr. Robin Flower to persuade one of its oldest inhabitants to write his life.[3] After much toil he got the main facts on to a sheet of notepaper and thought his task at an end. Then Mr. Flower read him some chapters of Gorki's Reminiscences. Now all was well, for to write like that was to write as he talked, and he was one of the best talkers upon the Island where there is no written literature. Then came a long delay; scholars had to pronounce upon the language, moralists upon the events; but when the book was published the few Gaelic speakers of my acquaintance passionately denied or affirmed that it was a masterpiece. Then a Blasket Islander settled in Dublin began to read out and circulate in manuscript poems that pleased a Gaelic scholar whose judgement I value, but were too Rabelaisian to please the eye of Government. Then Mr. Maurice O'Sullivan, a young Civic Guard, who had lived upon the Island until he reached manhood, wrote his life, called it *Twenty Years A-Growing*, and Chatto and Windus have published a translation.

All this writing comes from the sheep runs and diminishing fisheries of an Island seven or eight miles long and a mile broad, from its hundred and fifty inhabitants who preserve in their little white cottages, roofed with tarred felt, an ancient culture of the song and the spoken word, who consult neither newspaper nor book, but carry all their knowledge in their minds. A few more years and a tradition where Seventeenth Century poets, Mediaeval storytellers, Fathers of the Church, even Neoplatonic philosophers have left their traces in whole poems of fragmentary thoughts and isolated images will have vanished. "The young people are no use," said an old man to Synge. "I am not as good a man as my father was and my son is growing up worse than I am."

Mr. Maurice O'Sullivan, by a series of episodes, his first days at school, his first day puffin hunting, a regatta at Ventry, a wake, a shipwreck, a night upon a deserted neighbouring Island, calls up a vision of the sea, dark or bright, creates by the simplest means a sense of mystery, makes us for the moment part of a life that has not changed for thousands of years. And he himself seems unchanging like the life, the same when a little boy playing truant as when a grown man travelling by rail for the first time. It is not a defect that there is no subjectivity, no development; that like Helen during the ten years' siege he is untouched by time. Upon this limitation depend the clarity and the gaiety of his work. Fate has separated his people from all that could not sustain their happiness and their energy, from all that might confuse the

---

[3] Robin Flower had translated the reminiscences of a Blasket Islander, Tomás Ó Crohan, as *The Islandman* in 1929.

soul, given them the protection that monks and nuns find in their traditional rule, aristocrats in their disdain.[4]

Much modern Irish literature is violent, harsh, almost brutal, in its insistence upon the bare facts of life. Again and again I have defended plays or novels unlike anything I have myself attempted, or anything in the work of others that has given me great pleasure, because I have known that they were medicinal to a people struggling against second-hand thought and insincere emotion. Mr. O'Sullivan's book is not a great book, the events are too unrelated, but it is perfect of its kind, it has elegance; Mr. E. M. Forster compares it with a sea-bird's egg; and I am grateful.[5] He has found admirable translators—Mrs. Llewellyn Davies and Professor George Thompson, who teaches Greek through the vehicle of Gaelic in Galway University. They have translated his Gaelic into a dialect that has taken much of its syntax from Gaelic. Dr. Douglas Hyde used it in the prose of his *Love Songs of Connaught*; he was the first. Then Lady Gregory, in her translation of old Irish epics; then Synge and she in their plays. In late years it has superseded in the works of our dramatists and novelists the conventional speech nineteenth-century writers put into the mouth of Irish peasants. To Lady Gregory and to Synge it was more than speech, for it implied an attitude towards letters, sometimes even towards life, an attitude Lady Gregory was accustomed to define by a quotation from Aristotle: "To think like a wise man but to express oneself like the common people."

[4] Yeats echoes here the distinction he made in the essay, "What is 'Popular Poetry'?" dated 1901 in *Ideas of Good and Evil*. "Indeed, it is certain that before the counting-house had created a new class and a new art without breeding and without ancestry, and set this art and this class between the hut and the castle, and between the hut and the cloister, the art of the people was as closely mingled with the art of the coteries as was the speech of the people ... with the unchanging speech of the poets" (*Essays and Introductions*, pp. 10-11).

[5] In his "Introductory Note" to O'Sullivan's book, E. M. Forster notes the author's pleasure that the book will appear in the original Irish, "because it will be read on the Blasket. They will appreciate it more there than we can, for whom the wit and poetry must be veiled. On the other hand, we are their superiors in astonishment. They cannot possibly be as much surprised as we are, for here is the egg of a sea-bird—lovely, perfect, and laid this very morning" (p. v).

# The Growth of a Poet

Yeats's radio broadcasts began in September 1931 and continued through 1937, ranging in form from reminiscences and readings to the elaborate stagings, with musical interludes, of "In the Poet's Pub" on April 12, 1937, and "In the Poet's Parlour" on April 22. His description of "The Growth of a Poet" was broadcast from the Belfast studios of the British Broadcasting Company on March 17, 1934, and was published in *The Listener* on April 4.

WHEN I was a young man poetry had become eloquent and elaborate. Swinburne was the reigning influence and he was very eloquent. A generation came that wanted to be simple, I think I wanted that more than anybody else. I went from cottage to cottage listening to stories, to old songs; sometimes the songs were in English, sometimes they were in Gaelic—then I would get somebody to translate. Some of my best known poems were made in that way. "Down by the Salley Gardens," for instance, is an elaboration of two lines in English somebody sang to me at Ballysadare, County Sligo.[1] In my poetry I tried to keep to very simple emotions, to write the natural words, to put them in the natural order. Here is a little poem in which an old peasant woman complains of the young. There is music for it written to what is called the Irish gapped scale. The poem is called "The Song of the Old Mother:"

> *I rise in the dawn, and I kneel and blow*
> *Till the seed of the fire flicker and glow;*
> *And then I must scrub and bake and sweep*
> *Till stars are beginning to blink and peep;*
> *And the young lie long and dream in their bed*
> *Of the matching of ribbons for bosom and head,*

[1] In a note to "Down by the Salley Gardens" in *The Wanderings of Oisin and Other Poems* (1889) Yeats mentioned "an old peasant woman" as the source for this poem and in *Words for Music* (Cambridge, 1941, p. 65) V. C. Clinton-Baddeley, who collaborated with Yeats on his radio broadcasts, identified the song as "The Rambling Boys of Pleasure", an Anglo-Irish ballad. Yeats delights in this revivification of an example of "popular poetry" in a letter to Dorothy Wellesley (1889–1956) of September 25, 1935, which anticipates the broadsides, ballads and broadcasts of his last years: "The work of Irish poets, quite deliberately put into circulation with its music thirty and more years ago, is now all over the country. The Free State Army march to a tune called 'Down by the Salley Garden' without knowing that the march was first published with words of mine, words that are now folklore. Now my plan is to start a new set of 12 next Spring with poems by English as well as Irish poets. . . . I want to make another attempt to unite literature and music." (Dorothy Wellesley, ed., *Letters on Poetry from W. B. Yeats to Dorothy Wellesley*, London, 1940, p. 32.)

> *And their day goes over in idleness,*
> *And they sigh if the wind but lift a tress:*
> *While I must work because I am old,*
> *And the seed of the fire gets feeble and cold.*

A poem called "A Faery Song" was typical of that period. Diarmuid and Grania are the Irish Paris and Helen. Some countryman told me that they slept under the cromlechs. For that reason I called my poem "A song sung by the people of Faery over Diarmuid and Grania in their bridal sleep under a Cromlech." I call the people of faery "old and gay," not "old and grey" as it is sometimes misprinted. Time cannot touch them:

> *We who are old, old and gay,*
> *O so old!*
> *Thousands of years, thousands of years,*
> *If all were told:*
>
> *Give to these children, new from the world,*
> *Silence and love;*
> *And the long dew-dropping hours of the night,*
> *And the stars above:*
>
> *Give to these children, new from the world,*
> *Rest far from men.*
> *Is anything better, anything better?*
> *Tell us it then:*
>
> *Us who are old, old and gay,*
> *O so old!*
> *Thousands of years, thousands of years,*
> *If all were told.*

But the best known of these very simple early poems of mine is "The Fiddler of Dooney." The places mentioned in the poem are all in County Sligo. Dooney Rock is a great rock on the edge of Lough Gill. I had been to many picnics there and in gratitude called my fiddler by its name:

> *When I play on my fiddle in Dooney,*
> *Folk dance like a wave of the sea;*
> *My cousin is priest in Kilvarnet,*
> *My brother in Mocharabuiee.*
>
> *I passed my brother and cousin:*
> *They read in their books of prayer;*
> *I read in my book of songs*
> *I bought at the Sligo fair.*

*When we come at the end of time*
*To Peter sitting in state,*
*He will smile on the three old spirits,*
*But call me first through the gate;*

*For the good are always the merry,*
*Save by an evil chance,*
*And the merry love the fiddle,*
*And the merry love to dance:*

*And when the folk there spy me,*
*They will all come up to me,*
*With 'Here is the fiddler of Dooney!'*
*And dance like a wave of the sea.*

Years later I tried to return to this early style in "Running to Paradise." Some Gaelic book tells of a man running at full speed, who, when asked where he is running, answers "to Paradise." I think you will notice the difference in style. The poem is more thoughtful, more packed with little pictures:

*As I came over Windy Gap*
*They threw a halfpenny into my cap,*
*For I am running to Paradise;*
*And all that I need do is to wish*
*And somebody puts his hand in the dish*
*To throw me a bit of salted fish:*
And there the king is but as the beggar.

*My brother Mourteen is worn out*
*With skelping his big brawling lout,*
*And I am running to Paradise;*
*A poor life, do what he can,*
*And though he keep a dog and a gun,*
*A serving-maid and a serving-man:*
And there the king is but as the beggar.

*Poor men have grown to be rich men,*
*And rich men grown to be poor again,*
*And I am running to Paradise;*
*And many a darling wit's grown dull*
*That tossed a bare heel when at school,*
*Now it has filled an old sock full:*
And there the king is but as the beggar.

*The wind is old and still at play*
*While I must hurry upon my way,*

*For I am running to Paradise;*
*Yet never have I lit on a friend*
*To take my fancy like the wind*
*That nobody can buy or bind:*
And there the king is but as the beggar.

In later life I was not satisfied with these simple emotions—though I tried, and still try, to put the natural words in the natural order. I had founded Irish literary societies, an Irish Theatre, I had become associated with the projects of others, I had met much unreasonable opposition. To overcome it I had to make my thoughts modern. Modern thought is not simple; I became argumentative, passionate, bitter; when I was very bitter I used to say to myself, "I do not write for these people who attack everything that I value, not for those others who are lukewarm friends, I am writing for a man I have never seen." I built up in my mind the picture of a man who lived in the country where I had lived, who fished in mountain streams where I had fished; I said to myself, "I do not know whether he is born yet, but born or unborn it is for him I write." I made this poem about him; it is called "The Fisherman:"

*Although I can see him still,*
*The freckled man who goes*
*To a grey place on a hill*
*In grey Connemara clothes*
*At dawn to cast his flies,*
*It's long since I began*
*To call up to the eyes*
*This wise and simple man.*
*All day I'd looked in the face*
*What I had hoped 'twould be*
*To write for my own race*
*And the reality;*
*The living men that I hate,*
*The dead man that I loved,*
*The craven man in his seat,*
*The insolent unreproved,*
*And no knave brought to book*
*Who has won a drunken cheer,*
*The witty man and his joke*
*Aimed at the commonest ear,*
*The clever man who cries*
*The catch-cries of the clown,*
*The beating down of the wise*
*And great Art beaten down.*

*Maybe a twelvemonth since*
*Suddenly I began,*
*In scorn of this audience,*
*Imagining a man,*
*And his sun-freckled face,*
*And grey Connemara cloth,*
*Climbing up to a place*
*Where stone is dark under froth,*
*And the down-turn of his wrist*
*When the flies drop in the stream;*
*A man who does not exist,*
*A man who is but a dream;*
*And cried, 'Before I am old*
*I shall have written him one*
*Poem maybe as cold*
*And passionate as the dawn.'²*

² The script of this broadcast, among Yeats's papers, concludes: "Now you will hear my poem 'Down by the Salley Gardens' sung to an old Irish air".

# Abbey Theatre and the Free State

While the government subsidy granted in 1923 eased its financial problems, public apathy forced the Abbey Theatre to undertake longer and more frequent American tours. When such venerable standards of its repertory as *The Playboy of the Western World, Juno and the Paycock* and *In the Shadow of the Glen* were still able to arouse the anger of Irish-American groups, Yeats found himself defending the Theatre's integrity before a government at once more responsive to pressure from America and more directly in a position of power within the Abbey. In April of 1933, the De Valera government reduced the subsidy by one-fourth and a year later, as the company prepared for a tour which was to extend from October until June of the following year, De Valera announced in the Dáil that he had told the Theatre's Directors "if they produce certain plays that are on the list for production in America . . . they will damage the good name of Ireland and they will cause shame and resentment to the Irish exiles" (quoted in Peter Kavanagh, *The Story of The Abbey Theatre*, New York, 1950, p. 161). Just prior to the players' departure, Yeats announced a mutually agreeable solution, whereby the Abbey undertook to make clear that its subsidy did not imply either selection or approval of its plays by the Government. A report of his announcement in *The Sunday Times* for September 30, 1934, cast him somewhat into his old role as the fighter against entrenched ignorance and intolerance and prompted his letter, entitled "Abbey Theatre and the Free State—A Misunderstanding Corrected", in the issue for October 7.


# A MISUNDERSTANDING CORRECTED

### TO THE EDITOR OF *THE SUNDAY TIMES*

SIR,—The SUNDAY TIMES, September 30, in a friendly comment on the departure of the Irish Players for America, and on the enthusiasm of the Abbey audience on their farewell night, makes a statement which I must correct. Mr. de Valera has not "demanded" the withdrawal of any play by Synge or by O'Casey from our American repertory, nor have I "insisted" on their presence there.

We are on friendly terms with the Irish Government. The agents who were responsible for the last tour inserted in the programmes a statement which, though true to fact as far as words went, led many people to think that the Irish Government had something to do with the selection of the plays, which was anything but true to fact. The Irish Government drew our attention to this misunderstanding, and suggested that our future programmes should explain that though we had a Government subsidy the plays were our selection. We accepted that suggestion, and the matter ended.

Your paragraph contains these words: "Mr. Yeats is reported to have retorted that rather than submit to the dictation of politicians or to the idea that the Abbey Theatre is a minor branch of the Civil Service, he would reject the State subsidy." No such statement was necessary; no such statement was made.

(Signed) W. B. Yeats

Dublin

[We accept, of course, Mr. Yeats' statement of the position, and regret that the facts were not accurately stated by our correspondent.— Ed. S. T.]

# Poems: by Margot Ruddock
# with Prefatory Notes on the Author

Although he had determined in 1933 to write no more reviews (see p. 492 above), Yeats was obliged to undertake one most delicate appreciation in "Poems: by Margot Ruddock with Prefatory Notes on the Author" in the July, 1936, issue of *The London Mercury*. Almost immediately after their first meeting in October, 1934, Yeats and the troubled young English actress and writer, Margot Ruddock Collis Lovell (1907–1951) had become involved in the complex relationship which is set forth in Roger McHugh's edition of their correspondence, *Ah, Sweet Dancer* (New York, 1971). In May, 1936 Margot Ruddock suffered a nervous collapse during which she came to Casa Pastor in Majorca, where Yeats was recuperating from an illness. The events of the next two days which Yeats recounts in his letter of May 22 to Olivia Shakespear and which are recreated by Margot Ruddock in "Almost I Tasted Ecstasy" (McHugh, *op. cit.*, pp. 91–8) led to excited reports in the press, where scrutiny of the "failing" poet had already been considerable. "She walked in at 6.30," Yeats wrote, "her luggage in her hand and, when she had been given breakfast, said she had come to find out if her verse was any good. I had known her for some years and had told her to stop writing as her technique was getting worse. I was amazed by the tragic magnificence of some fragments and said so. She went out in pouring rain, thought, as she said afterwards, that if she killed herself her verse would live instead of her. Went to the shore to jump in, then thought that she loved life and began to dance. . . . Next day she went to Barcelona and there went mad, climbing out of a window, falling through a baker's roof, breaking a kneecap, hiding in a ship's hold, singing her own poems most of the time. The British consul in Barcelona appealed to me, so George and I went there, found her with recovered sanity sitting up in bed at a clinic writing an account of her madness. . . . Will she stay sane? it is impossible to know" (*Letters*, p. 856).

Yeats accepted financial responsibility for the young woman, grumbling that he thus wouldn't "be able to afford new clothes for a year" (*ibid.*), but was anxious to avoid publicity in the matter. "When I am in London," he wrote in the same letter to Mrs. Shakespear, "I shall probably hide because the husband may send me journalists and because I want to keep at a distance from a tragedy where I can be no further help." Yeats's situation was complicated by his having promised an introduction and a selection of Margot Ruddock's poems for the July issue of the *Mercury*. At the end of May, he received her "account of her madness" which he at first thought to include in this selection but which both he and the magazine's editor, R. A. Scott-Jones (1878–1959), finally thought it best to leave out. "Let me," Yeats wrote to her on June 10, "conduct your 'publicity' for a little" (McHugh, ed., *op. cit.*, p. 105). The "account" was included in Margot Ruddock's *The Lemon*

*Tree* (1937) along with this appreciation, to which Yeats added another section, dated December, 1936.

Despite a period of stability during which she took part in three of Yeats's radio broadcasts in 1937, the "girl who is quite a beautiful person" (*Letters*, p. 856) collapsed again towards the end of the year and was committed to an asylum, where she spent the rest of her life. Yeats idealized her in "Sweet Dancer" and "A Crazed Girl"—originally called "At Barcelona" and first published in *The Lemon Tree*—in which she becomes

> *That crazed girl improvising her music,*
> *The poetry dancing upon the shore*
> *. . .*
>
> *Climbing, falling she knew not where,*
> *Hiding amid the cargo of a steamship,*
> *Her knee-cap broken, that girl I declare*
> *A beautifully lofty thing, or a thing*
> *Heroically lost, heroically found.*
>
> (*Variorum Poems*, p. 578)

But his association of Margot Ruddock with his father, Standish O'Grady, Lady Gregory and Maud Gonne—the "Beautiful Lofty Things" remembered elsewhere—is countered by his association of her with his guilt, in "The Man and the Echo", at having invoked the violence of Easter Week and failed to prevent the destruction of Coole:

> *Did that play of mine send out*
> *Certain men the English shot?*
> *Did words of mine put too great strain*
> *On that woman's reeling brain?*
> *Could my spoken words have checked*
> *That whereby a house lay wrecked?*
> *And all seems evil until I*
> *Sleepless would lie down and die.*
>
> (*Variorum Poems*, p. 632)

I WAS breakfasting in bed at 7.30 when my wife announced that Margot Ruddock had arrived. A woman in whom I had some two years ago divined a frustrated tragic genius. Some two years ago she had asked my help to found a poets' theatre. Of distinguished beauty of face and limb she had been a successful provincial actress, managing her own company, but had come to London because her husband, Raymond Lovell, hoped for a career on the London stage.[1] Her father's name was

---

[1] Before her marriage to the actor, Raymond Lovell (1900–1953), in 1932, Margot Ruddock had been married to Jack Collis, whose name she kept as her stage name.

Ruddock, and she wishes, when we speak of her as a poet, to be called Margot Ruddock. I brought her to Dulac the painter, and Ashton the creator and producer of ballets, subtle technical minds with an instinctive knowledge of the next step in whatever art they discussed.[2] I asked her to recite some poems. She had all the professional elocutionist's bag of tricks, but rehearsed by Ashton and Dulac substituted a musical clarity pleasant to a poet's ear. In a few days she had lost it and returned unconsciously to the bag, but what can be done once can be done again. I had never seen her act, but after thirty years' experience I know from the mind of man and woman what they can do upon the stage when they have found their legs, judging that mind perhaps from the way they sink into a chair or lift a cup. There was something hard, tight, screwed-up, in her, but were that dissolved by success she might be a great actress, for she possessed a quality rare upon the stage or, if found there, left unemployed—intellectual passion. She had set her heart upon my *Player Queen* where the principal character might give the opportunity she had lacked, seemed indeed in some sense of the word herself.

I gave Margot Ruddock permission to arrange for a performance of the *Player Queen* wherever she could, said all I cared about was that she should play the principal part, and returned to Ireland. Such a performance was arranged for, but owing to some error or misunderstanding, Margot Ruddock, or, to use her stage name, Margot Collis, had but a minor part which she played with precision and distinction.[3]

Meanwhile I had discovered her poetry. She sent me passionate, incoherent improvisations, power struggling with that ignorance of books and of arts which has made the modern theatre what it is. I criticized her with some vehemence and the improvisations became coherent poems. I selected "The Child Compassion," "Autumn," which have something of Emily Brontë's intensity, and some others for an anthology

---

[2] In 1933, Yeats dedicated *The Winding Stair and Other Poems* to Edmund Dulac (1882–1953), whom he had admired since 1916, when the English artist and musician had designed the masks and costumes for the first performance of Yeats's first play in the "Noh" manner, *At the Hawk's Well*. In a friendship and collaboration which lasted until the poet's death, Dulac provided illustrations for several of Yeats's books and made musical settings for several of his poems, including "He and She", which was performed in the BBC broadcast of Yeats's works on July 3, 1937, in which Margot Ruddock took part.

Roger McHugh (*op. cit.*, p. 10) has noted the recollection of Sir Frederick Ashton (b. 1906), the English choreographer, that, "being asked by Yeats to rehearse Margot Ruddock in speaking verse", he felt "she had 'definite potential as an actress but had obviously never fallen into the right hands', though he found her very intense and she seemed 'a lost soul'".

[3] According to McHugh (pp. 52–6), after protracted arrangements *The Player Queen* was produced for three matinees at the Little Theatre, London, on October 28, 29 and 31, 1935. Although Margot Ruddock seems to have had the title role at the last performance, Yeats praised the "precision and passion" (McHugh, *op. cit.*, p. 57) of her portrayal of the real Queen which he saw on the first day.

I have compiled for the Oxford University Press.[4] She wrote from time to time, most letters contained a poem or poems, but these poems seemed to have lost form; had she fallen back as after the Ashton and Dulac rehearsal? It was not now a falling back into convention but an obsession by her own essential quality; passion followed passion with such rapidity that she had no time for deliberate choice; she seemed indifferent to scansion, even to syntax. I got angry and told her to stop writing. After that almost every day brought some big packet of verse; I was busy with Shree Purohit Swami, we were translating *The Upanishads*;[5] I left the packets unopened, or thrust the contents into some drawer unread. And now she had come to defy me and to cover my table with her thoughts. I sat down with boredom but was soon amazed at my own blindness and laziness. Here in broken sentences, in ejaculations, in fragments of all kinds was a power in the expression of spiritual suffering unique in her generation. "O Song, song harshened, I have leashed you to harshness." . . . "I will shut out all but myself and grind, grind myself down to the bone." . . . "Follow, follow lest that which you love vanishes. Let it go, let it go." . . . "Shape me to Eternal Damnation to rid me of the phlegm that spits itself from unbearable cold." . . . "Bleed on, bleed on, soul, because I shall not cease to knife you until you are white and dry." . . . "Almost I tasted ecstasy and then came the Blare, and drowned perfection in perfection." . . . "I cannot endure it when I see you asleep, having carefully tucked your teddy bear beside you. I cannot endure it. Even if you would have been born anyhow. Even if you did choose me. Even if it was because I cannot endure it you chose me!" . . . "Good nature, sweet nature and you'll have to be crushed. You shall not be; by God you shall not be. Whatever you do I will see that you are not crushed. I will not stand that you be crushed." "It is because I love you that I will not let my life into yours." "Feed the cat! feed the cat, you can't starve people though they can starve you. Might as well eat as I feed the cat, now the cat wants my food." "Consider and consider and always come back to what

---

[4] Yeats included seven of Margot Ruddock's poems in *The Oxford Book of Modern Verse*, which was published in November, 1936.

[5] Yeats had met his "religious man", Shree Purohit Swami (b. 1882), in the winter of 1931–2. His introduction to the Swami's *An Indian Monk* (1932) was the first of several joint projects, the most important of which was *The Ten Principal Upanishads, Put into English by Shree Purohit and W. B. Yeats*, which appeared in April, 1937. In her account of the episode in Majorca, Margot Ruddock recalled visiting the Swami, whom she had met through Yeats in 1934, just after leaving Casa Pastor: "I got a room where Shree Purohit Swami was staying. He lent me clothes for I was wet through, I had come away without money; I thought 'if I stay here people will think I came to see him before he left for India and not knowing that he is beyond all human interests blame him. I will go and see my friends in Barcelona where my baby was born two years ago'" (McHugh, *op. cit.*, p. 93).

Shortly after these events, the Swami returned to India.

you said in a flash and to what you knew when you saw it." "Give me
power to choose to keep wisdom." "I will scald myself to cool."[6]

> *O sky harshen, O wind blow cold,*
> *O crags of stony thought be steep*
> *That mind may ache and bleed,*
> *That mind be scattered to the wind.*

> *All is true of all*
> *For all that is is true;*
> *But Truth is not;*
> *To become Truth*
> *Is not to be.*

> *Grief is not in Truth*
> *But Truth in grief must live grief*
> *Yet know no grief;*
> *For Truth is proof against all but itself.*

> *When all thought is gathered into the heart*
> *And set out to ripen like good fruit;*
> *And that which might have been eaten withered,*
> *And that which were better withered eaten;*
> *I sit and sit*
> *And marvel at the itch of it.*

> *I have counted all that may happen*
> *And it will not happen,*
> *I have said all that shall be*
> *And it will not be.*

> *O song, no tears but thine*
> *Be sung, no thought*
> *That is not secret,*
> *Shut out all others*
> *For all earth must lie*
> *But thou, and I.*

[6] The fragments which Yeats quotes here, part of what Margot Ruddock called "Moments. Snatchings—Probings", are discussed in McHugh's "Appendix A" (pp. 127–30).

# 'I Became an Author'

Yeats's last radio broadcast, with Margot Ruddock, was "My Own Poetry Again" on October 29, 1937. While none of the three programs proposed for 1938 were broadcast, Yeats had written the text for one of them, a reminiscence called "I Became an Author", part of a BBC series in which contemporary writers, including Hilaire Belloc (1870–1953), J. B. Priestley (b. 1894) and Agatha Christie (b. 1891), told "how they began to write and what obstacles they had to overcome to achieve publication". "I Became an Author" appeared in *The Listener* on August 4, 1938, and was Yeats's last publication, with the exception of *The Autobiography*, which appeared on August 30. Yeats died on January 28, 1939.

HOW did I begin to write? I have nothing to say that may help young writers, except that I hope they will not begin as I did. I spent longer than most schoolboys preparing the next day's work, and yet learnt nothing, and would always have been at the bottom of my class but for one or two subjects that I hardly had to learn at all. My father would say: 'You cannot fix your mind on anything that does not interest you, and it is to study what does not that you are sent to school.' I did not suffer from the 'poetic temperament,' but from some psychological weakness. Greater poets than I have been great scholars. Even today I struggle against a lack of confidence, when among average men, come from that daily humiliation, and because I do not know what they know. I can toil through a little French poetry, but nothing remains of the Greek, Latin and German I tried to learn. I have only one memory of my schooldays that gives me pleasure; though in both my English and Irish schools I was near the bottom of the class, my friends were at the top, for then, as now, I hated fools. When I would find out if some man can be trusted, I ask if he associates with his betters. In the Irish school my chief friend was Charles Johnston, son of the Orange leader.[1] He beat all Ireland in the Intermediate examinations, and when I met him in America years afterwards he said: 'There is nothing I cannot learn and nothing that I want to learn.' Some instinct drew us together, it was to

---

[1] Charles Johnston, a schoolmate and later a fellow theosophist with Yeats, was the founder of the Hermetic Society in Dublin. Johnston was responsible for Yeats's introduction to Madame Blavatsky, whose niece he had married in 1888. He entered the Indian Civil Service in the same year and eventually settled in America. While he and Yeats seem not to have sustained the friendship which had flourished in the eighties, when Yeats had been a visitor at the home in County Down of Johnston's father, William (1829–1902), a Member of Parliament from Belfast, Johnston was on the platform for Yeats's address on Robert Emmet in New York in 1904 (see p. 310 above).

him I used to read my poems. They were all plays—except one long poem in Spenserian stanzas, which some woman of whom I remember nothing, not even if she was pretty, borrowed and lost out of her carriage when shopping. I recall three plays, not of any merit, one vaguely Elizabethan, its scene a German forest, one an imitation of Shelley, its scene a crater in the moon, one of somebody's translations from the Sanscrit, its scene an Indian temple. Charles Johnston admired parts of these poems so much that I doubt if he ever thought I had fulfilled their promise. A fragment, or perhaps all that was written, of the Indian play, I put near the opening of my *Collected Poems* because when I put it there he was still living, and it is still there because I have forgotten to take it out.[2] I have sometimes wondered if I did not write poetry to find a cure for my own ailment, as constipated cats do when they eat valerian.[3] But that will not do, because my interest in proud, confident people began before I had been much humiliated. Some people say I have an affected manner, and if that is true, as it may well be, it is because my father took me when I was ten or eleven to Irving's famous 'Hamlet.' Years afterwards I walked the Dublin streets when nobody was looking, or nobody that I knew, with that strut Gordon Craig has compared to a movement in a dance, and made the characters I created speak with his brooding, broken wildness.[4] Two months ago, describing the Second Coming, I wrote this couplet:

> *What brushes fly and gnat aside?*
> *Irving and his plume of pride.*[5]

Nobody should think a young poet pathetic and weak, or that he has a lonely struggle. I think some old and famous men may think that they had in their schooldays their most satisfying fame; certainly I had about

[2] None of the available descriptions of the plays Yeats wrote in the early 1880s helps to identify the "vaguely Elizabethan play". The "imitation of Shelley", however, was a play written in 1886 which, according to Richard Ellmann (*Yeats—the Man and the Masks*, pp. 46–7), was "entitled variously *The Blindness*, *The Epic of the Forest* and *The Equator of Wild Olives*". The "fragment . . . of the Indian play" is "Anashuya and Vijaya". Yeats had alluded, in his "Notes" to *Early Poems and Stories* (1925), to Charles Johnston's fondness for these lines. "Every time I have reprinted them I have considered the leaving out of most, and then remembered an old school friend who has some of them by heart, for no better reason, as I think, than that they remind him of his own youth" (*Variorum Poems*, p. 841).

[3] Yeats expresses a similar idea in "The Circus Animals' Desertion" (*Variorum Poems*, p. 629), written about the same time as this essay.

[4] In his biography of Sir Henry Irving (1838–1905), *Henry Irving* (New York, 1930), Gordon Craig notes that "In dancing a role, Irving went to the extreme limits possible to an actor of the nineteenth century, of preserving the last tingle of a mighty Greek tradition" (p. 71).

[5] "A Nativity" (*Variorum Poems*, p. 625, ll. 7–8).
Yeats's "Two months ago" is questionable. Jeffares (*Commentary*, p. 502) suggests this poem may have been written in August, 1936.

me a little group whose admiration for work that had no merit justified my immense self-confidence.

When eighteen or nineteen I wrote a pastoral play under the influence of Keats and Shelley, modified by that of Jonson's 'Sad Shepherd,' and one of my friends showed it to some Trinity undergraduates who were publishing the *Dublin University Review*, an ambitious political and literary periodical that lasted for a few months—I cannot remember who, except that it was not Charles Johnston, who had passed for the Indian Civil Service, gone to India, and would stay there until he tired of it.[6] I was at the Art Schools because painting was the family trade, and because I did not think I could pass the matriculation examination for Trinity. The undergraduates liked the poem and invited me to read it to a man four or five years older than the rest of us, Bury, in later years a classical historian and editor of Gibbon.[7] I was excited, not merely because he would decide the acceptance or rejection of my play, but because he was a schoolmaster and I had never met a schoolmaster in private life. Once when I was at Edward Dowden's the head of my old school was announced, but I turned so pale or so red that Dowden brought me into another room. Perhaps I could get Bury to explain why I had been told to learn so many things that I had not been able to fix my attention upon anything.

I thought a man brought his convictions into everything he did; I had said to the photographer when he was arranging his piece of iron shaped like a horseshoe to keep my head in position: 'Because you have only white and black paper instead of light and shadow you cannot represent Nature. An artist can, because he employs a kind of symbolism.' To my surprise, instead of showing indignation at my attack upon his trade, he replied: 'A photograph is mechanical.' Even today I have the same habit of thought, but only when thinking of pre-eminent men. A few days ago I read of some University meeting where, when somebody said: 'Nobody today believes in a personal devil,' Lord Acton said: 'I do'; and I knew that because the *Cambridge Universal History*, which he had planned, contains nothing about a personal devil's influence upon events Lord Acton was a picturesque liar.[8] For some

---

[6] See p. 471 above for the publication of *The Island of Statues* and for *The Dublin University Review*.

Ben Jonson's unfinished last play, *The Sad Shepherd, or, A Tale of Robin Hood* was published in 1641.

[7] John Bagnell Bury (1861–1927), the classical scholar and historian, taught at Trinity College Dublin and, later, at Cambridge. His edition of Gibbon's *Decline and Fall* appeared between 1896 and 1900.

[8] Describing his plans for *On the Boiler* (1939) in a letter to Dorothy Wellesley on June 22, 1938, Yeats used this same example—there as here using the popular rather than the actual title of *The Cambridge Modern History* (1902–12), which was conceived by the Cambridge Professor of Modern History, John E. E. D. Acton (1834–1902). "This is the proposition on

reason which I cannot recollect I was left alone with Bury and said, after a great effort to overcome my shyness: 'I know you will defend the ordinary system of education by saying that it strengthens the will, but I am convinced that it only seems to do so because it weakens the impulses.' He smiled and looked embarrassed but said nothing.

My pastoral play 'The Island of Statues' appeared in the review. I have not looked at it for many years, but nothing I did at that time had merit. Two lyrics from it are at the beginning of my *Collected Poems*,[9] not because I liked them but because when I put them there friends that had were still living. Immediately after its publication, or just before, I fell under the influence of two men who were to influence deeply the Irish intellectual movement—old John O'Leary the Fenian leader, in whose library I found the poets of Young Ireland and Standish O'Grady, who had re-written in vigorous romantic English certain ancient Irish heroic legends. Because of the talk of these men, and the books the one lent and the other wrote, I turned my back on foreign themes, decided that the race was more important than the individual, and began my 'Wanderings of Oisin'; it was published with many shorter poems by subscription, John O'Leary finding almost all the subscribers. Henceforth I was one of the rising poets. I lived in London and had many friends, and when I could not earn the twenty shillings a week which in those days bought bed and board for man or boy, I could stay with my family or a Sligo relative. In this I was more fortunate than Isadora Duncan who was to write of her first London years: 'I had renown and the favour of princes and not enough to eat.'[10] As a professional writer I was clumsy, stiff and sluggish; when I reviewed a book I had to write my own heated thoughts because I did not know how to get thoughts out of my subject; when I wrote a poem half-a-dozen lines sometimes took as many days because I was determined to put the natural words in the natural order, my imagination still full of poetic diction. It was that old difficulty of my school work over again, except that I had now plenty of time.

---

which I write: 'There is now overwhelming evidence that man stands between two eternities, that of his family and that of his soul.' I apply those beliefs to literature and politics, and show the change they must make. Lord Acton said once that he believed in a personal devil, but as there is nothing about it in the Cambridge Universal History which he planned, he was a liar" (*Letters*, p. 911).

[9] In *Collected Poems* (1933), "The Song of the Happy Shepherd" and "The Cloak, the Boat, and the Shoes" survive, with some changes, from "The Island of Statues".

[10] Remembering her days in Paris in Chapter Nine of *My Life* (1927), the dancer Isadora Duncan (1878–1927) notes that "Neither the appreciation of princes, nor my growing fame, brought us enough to eat" (p. 86).

# Appendix to Volume One

# Poems by Miss Tynan

This review of Katharine Tynan's *Ballads and Lyrics* appeared in the *Evening Herald* for Saturday, January 2, 1892. A shortened version of the review was reprinted in Roger McHugh's edition, *W. B. Yeats, Letters to Katharine Tynan*, New York, 1953. For information on Yeats's literary relationship with Katharine Tynan, see pp. 119–20 of Volume I of this edition.

A GREAT change has come over our Irish writers in recent years. In '48 they made songs and ballads from some passionate impulse of the moment. Often the same song would contain poetry of the most moving power, side by side with flaccid and commonplace lines. Men like Doheny,[1] under the stress of strong excitement, would strike off a ringing ballad and then sink into tuneless silence. We can reproduce now neither the merits nor defects of that poetry, in which all was done from sudden emotion, nothing from deliberate art. It was like the days of the Arabs before Mahometanism, when the same man led the tribe to war and wrote its songs of love and battle. Such periods cannot last. If literatures are to go on they must add art to impulse and temper their fire with knowledge. Literary Ireland is going through such a training. The days of Davis were followed by those of Allingham's Ballyshannon songs and De Vere's "Innisfail" and his "Legends of St. Patrick," and Ferguson's[2] later and greater work, his "Deirdre"[3] and "Conary." These men were all experimenters, trying to find out a literary style that would be polished and yet Irish of the Irish. Those who follow them have their work made more easy through their experiments.

In reading this new book of Miss Tynan's, "Legends and Lyrics"[4] (Kegan Paul, Trench, Trubner and Co), I feel constantly how greatly she has benefited by study both of the old Irish ballads and of the modern writers I have named. Her first book, "Louise de La Valliere," was too full of English influences to be quite Irish, and too laden with

---

[1] Michael Doheny (1805–63), who was chiefly famous for his song, "Bright Vein of My Heart".

[2] *Evening Herald* printed "Fergusson".

[3] *Evening Herald* printed "Deordre".

[4] The title of the book was *Ballads and Lyrics*, by which name Yeats refers to it below.

garish colour to be quite true to the austere Celtic spirit. "Shamrocks"[5]
was better, and now "Ballads and Lyrics" is well nigh in all things a
thoroughly Irish book, springing straight from the Celtic mind, and
pouring itself out in soft Celtic music. Though perfectly original, I can
yet feel in it the influence of more than one master of Celtic speech, and
in thus gaining nationality of style Miss Tynan has found herself and
found the world about her. The landscapes are no more taken from the
tapestry-like[6] scenery of Rossetti and his imitators, but from her own
Clondalkin[7] fields, and from the grey Dublin hills. She apologises for
this charming provincialism in an "Apologia" as exquisite as Allingham
at his best, but with an added richness—

> *Here in my book there will be found*
> *No gleanings from a foreign ground:*
> *The quiet thoughts of one whose feet*
> *Have scarcely left her green retreat;*
> *A little dew, a little scent,*
> *A little measure of content,*
> *A robin's song, perchance to stir*
> *Some heart-untravelled traveller.*
>
> *A low horizon hems me in,*
> *Low hills, with fields of gold between,*
> *Woods that are waving, veiled with grey,*
> *A little river far away,*
> *Birds on the boughs and on the sward,*
> *Daisies that dancing praise the Lord.*[8]
>
> \*     \*     \*     \*     \*
>
> *And in my garden, all in white*
> *The Mary-lilies take the light,*
> *And southern wood and lavender*
> *Welcome the bee in golden fur,*
> *A splendid lover, and on high*
> *Hovers the spangled butterfly,*
> *Where roses*[9] *old and sweet, dream on,*
> *Fading to rich oblivion.*[10]
>
> \*     \*     \*     \*     \*
>
> *So in my book there will be found*
> *No gleanings from a foreign ground,*

---

[5] See Vol. I, pp. 119–22 of this edition for Yeats's review of *Shamrocks*.
[6] *Evening Herald* printed "tapestery".
[7] *Evening Herald* printed "Cloudalkin".
[8] Yeats omitted two stanzas at this point.
[9] *Ballads and Lyrics* reads "roses, old and sweet".
[10] Yeats omitted one stanza here.

*If such you seek, go buy, go buy*
*Of some more travelled folk than I.*
*Kind Master Critic, say not, please,*
*How that her world so narrow is,*
*Since here she warns expectant eyes*
*That homely is her merchandise!*[11]

In Miss Tynan's earlier books colour was too often sought for its own sake, as if an artist were to rest satisfied with the strange and striking combinations of the colours spread upon his palettes, instead of using them to make manifest the beautiful things about him. In this book, however, is many a fine landscape[12] and much fine portraiture of noble woods. How well suggested is the gloomy landscape in "The Children of Lir,"[13] and how subtly[14] expressed are their wistful human souls wrapped round with the birds' bodies.

How rare a thing is good religious poetry is known to all reviewers, and yet some of the most successful poems in this book are on the most hackneyed symbols of Christianity. Miss Tynan draws from them even some new and quaint beauty. Some of[15] her religious poems have the *näiveté*[16] of mediæval song; nor is their simplicity any the less genuine for being conscious—for being a product quite as much of art as of impulse. Some fourteenth [century] monk[17] might have murmured, as he bent over an illuminated missal, lines like these:—[18]

*The sheep with their little lambs*
*Passed by me*[19] *on the road;*
*All in the April evening*
*I thought on the Lamb of God.*

*The lambs were weary, and crying*
*With a weak, human cry,*
*I thought on the Lamb of God*
*Going meekly to die.*

*Up in the blue, blue mountains*
*Dewy pastures are sweet;*
*Rest for the little bodies,*
*Rest for the little feet.*[20]

[11] *Evening Herald* printed "morchandise".
[12] *Evening Herald* printed "landscapes".
[13] *Evening Herald* printed "Lis".
[14] *Evening Herald* printed "subtely".
[15] *Evening Herald* printed "of of".
[16] *Evening Herald* printed *naivette.*
[17] In the *Evening Herald* this phrase read "Fourteenth monk".
[18] Yeats omitted the first stanza of this poem.
[19] Tynan's poem reads "me by".
[20] Tynan's stanza does not end with a period.

> *But for the Lamb of God,*
> *Up on the hill-top green,*
> *Only a cross[21] of shame*
> *Two stark crosses between.*
>
> *All in the April evening,*
> *April airs were abroad;*
> *I saw the sheep with their lambs,*
> *And thought on the Lamb of God."[22]*

Good, too, is "Rose in Heaven,"[23] a memorial song for the late Miss Rose Kavanagh; but best of all is, perhaps, "In a Cathedral," the story of a wood-carver who lived all his life unknown and solitary amid the cathedral shadows, content to serve God by the beauty of art, by the grace of the carven roof where "he fashioned many a singing bird, whose lovely silence praised the Lord."

> *The patient carver toiled apart;*
> *The world roared on—a world away.*
> *No earthly ties were round his heart,*
> *No passion stirred his quiet day;*
> *His carvings in the cloisters[24] dim*
> *Made home, and wife, and child for him.[25]*
>
> *He was so young when he began—*
> *A fair-haired boy, whose wistful eyes*
> *Saw earth and heaven, and scarcely man,*
> *But weighed large issues and was[26] wise:*
> *The years that all unheeded[27] sped*
> *Shook their grey dust upon his head.*

Here and there is a poem that leaves me cold, a song, that does not seem to me to sing, a ballad where art has become artificial and stifled impulse instead of guiding it; but what need is there to single them out, when there is so much beauty, so many verses that may well be dear to the hearts of our people, when I[28] who write and you who read are under the green grass or "where[29] the thistles grow."

W. B. Yeats

[21] Tynan's poem reads "Cross".
[22] *Evening Herald* printed closing quotation marks only.
[23] Tynan's title is "To Rose in Heaven".
[24] Tynan's poem reads "cloister".
[25] Tynan's poem reads "to him".
[26] Tynan's poem reads "were".
[27] *Evening Herald* printed "unheed".
[28] *Evening Herald* printed "I when".
[29] *Evening Herald* printed "when".

# The Chain of Gold.

# By Standish O'Grady (T. Fisher Unwin.)

This unsigned review of *The Chain of Gold* by Standish O'Grady appeared in *The Bookman* of November, 1895. Allan Wade listed it in his first bibliography of Yeats's writings, that which appeared in the eighth volume of the 1908 collected edition of Yeats's work, so we may presume that Yeats acknowledged authorship.

MR. STANDISH O'GRADY has a habit of returning on his ideas and incidents, and manifestly out of sheer love for them, and not from any poverty of imagination, for the second telling is for the most part the better. He has, for instance, told the story of Cuchullin twice over, and the second version is the more minute in finish, the more rich in beautiful detail; and now he returns upon the central accident of "Lost on Du Corrig," and builds out of it the far more potent "Chain of Gold." "Lost on Du Corrig" was a boy's story of a boy who fell through a crevice in a cliff and found an immense cavern, and being there entrapped, supported himself by many fascinating shifts, and encountered the ghost of an ancient Irish hero; while "The Chain of Gold" is a history of two boys who go out fishing, and are hurled, boat and all, into the mouth of a cave far above the sea level, by one of the best storms raised in modern fiction, and there keep body and soul together by contrivances as excellent as any of Crusoe's, and encounter the phantom of an ancient Irish hermit, or else endure a strange delirium from hardship and thirst—for we are left in doubt—and return at last to common things and safety. Parts of the earlier book were curiously careless and ill-built, despite its general vigour and freshness, but Mr. O'Grady has now learnt to admiration the difficult art of writing for boys, and of doing so not by warping or imprisoning his own mature imagination, but simply by delighting in such things as were a delight to men and women at the dawn of the world. If Finn and Cuchullin lived in our day they would be much like these masterful, resourceful cave-dwellers, and if Usheen came alive to write of them he would write in no very different spirit from Mr. O'Grady.

# Errata to Volume I

p. 11, l. 32 should read "Columbia University Press".

p. 39, l. 26 and p. 40, l. 2: "Irish Literary Society" should read "National Literary Society".

p. 40, l. 8: "Richard Garnett" should read "Edward Garnett".

p. 44, note 27: reference should be to Edmund Spenser. The source of the phrase is *Faerie Queene*, Book I, Canto VI, stanza 2.

p. 61, l. 14: "angles" should read "angels".

p. 87, l. 17: "Spencer" should be followed by [*sic*].

p. 87, note 21: The reference should be to the poet Spenser, not the philosopher Spencer. See correction to p. 44, note 27 above, for source of the quotation.

p. 104, l. 34: "Ancient" should read "Old".

p. 105, l. 5: this statement is inaccurate. Joyce is mentioned in "Popular Ballad Poetry of Ireland", p. 161 of Volume I, this edition.

p. 118, note 8, l. 2: "continues" should read "continue".

p. 142, l. 28: "pp. 116" should read "pp. 166".

p. 227, note 5: "Callirrhoi" should read "Callirrhoë".

p. 259, l. 32: "Frazer" should be followed by [*sic*]. Yeats refers to *Fraser's Magazine*.

p. 285, l. 17: omit [*sic*] after Thistelton Dyer.

p. 288, l. 4: "spirits" should read "spirit".

p. 288, l. 9: "instructive" should read "instinctive".

p. 289, l. 26: quotation is from Emerson's "Saadi".

p. 327, l. 11: "tale" should be followed by [*sic*]. Yeats apparently meant "tail".

# Index to Volumes One and Two

Page numbers in italics refer to mention in the text of Yeats's prose. Otherwise, page numbers refer to the introduction, to the headnotes or footnotes, or to quotations from other Yeats works. Entries from Volume One follow roman numeral I; entries from Volume Two follow roman numeral II.

INDEX 539

Lectures:
"British Association Visit to the Abbey
Theatre", Abbey Theatre program,
Sept. 4, 1908, II, *364–70*, 378
"The Child and the State", *The Irish
Statesman* (in two parts), Dec. 5 and
12, 1925, II, *455–61*
"A Defence of the Abbey Theatre",
delivered to a meeting of Dublin
Literary Society, *The Dublin Maga-
zine*, April–June, 1926, II, *466–70*
"Emmet the Apostle of Irish Liberty",
*The Gaelic American*, March 5, 1904,
II, 286, *310–27*, 338, 506
"Irish Literary Theatre, Lecture by Mr.
W. B. Yeats", *The Irish Literary
Society Gazette*, June, 1899, II, *153–8*,
162, 163
"Memorial to the Late T. W. Lyster", re-
printed in *The Irish Book*, autumn,
1960, II, 305, *470–2*
"Nationality and Literature", *United
Ireland*, May 27, 1893, I, 52, 53, 250,
251, *266–75*, 302, 306; II, 119, 257
"Poetry's Banquet", for the Poetry
Society of Chicago on March 1, in
*Poetry*, April, 1914, II, *412–14*
"An Undelivered Speech", *The Irish
Statesman*, March 14, 1925, II, *449–52*
"The Watts Pictures", Dublin *Daily
Express*, Jan. 25, 1906, II, 194, *342–5*
"Mr. W. B. Yeats and 'The Piper'",
Dublin *Daily Express*, Feb. 17, 1908,
II, *361–3*

Letters:
"The Abbey Theatre", *The Dublin Evening
Mail*, Jan. 16, 1908, II, *358–9*
"The Abbey Theatre", *The Dublin Evening
Mail*, Jan. 18, 1908, II, *361*
"Abbey Theatre and the Free State", *The
Sunday Times*, Oct. 7, 1934, II, *500*
"About an 'Interview'", *The Free Lance*,
Sept. 21, 1901, II, *253–4*
"Academic Class and the Agrarian Revo-
lution, The", *Daily Express*, March
11, 1899, II, *148–52*
"Best Book from Ireland, The", *The
Daily News*, May 11, 1904, II, 157,
299, *327–8*
"Bounty of Sweden, The", *The Sunday
Times*, Aug. 9, 1925, II, *453–4*
"Carleton as an Irish Historian", *Nation*
(Dublin), Jan. 11, 1890, I, *166–9*
"'98 Centenary, The", *United Ireland*,
March 20, 1897, II, *37–8*
"Chance for the National Gallery, A",
*The Observer*, Jan. 21, 1917, II, *415–
16*
"Mr. Churton Collins on Blake", *The
Times Literary Supplement*, May 30,
1902, II, *293–4*
"Corinthian Club Dinner, A", *The
Leader*, Nov. 30, 1907, II, 236, *355–6*

"Correction, A", Dublin *Daily Express*,
March 21, 1900, II, *207–8*
"Correction, A", Dublin *Daily Express*,
Aug. 5, 1901, II, *252–3*
"Correction, A", *The Dublin Evening
Mail*, Jan. 17, 1908, II, *360*
"De-Anglicising of Ireland, The", *United
Ireland*, Dec. 17, 1892, I, *254–6*
"Dublin and the Hugh Lane Pictures",
*The Observer*, Feb. 3, 1918, II, *428–9*
"Dublin Fanaticism", *The Irish Worker*,
Nov. 1, 1913, II, *406–7*
"Favourite Books of 1901", *Academy*,
Dec. 7, 1901, II, *264–5*
"Mr. W. Fay and the Abbey Theatre",
*The Dublin Evening Mail*, May 21,
1908, II, *363–4*
"W. Fay's Resignation", *The Dublin
Evening Mail*, Jan. 14, 1908, II,
*357–8*
"Flaubert and the National Library", *The
Irish Times*, Oct. 8, 1903, II, *305*
"Freedom of the Press in Ireland, The",
*The Speaker*, July 7, 1900, II, *213–16*,
289
"Mr. George Moore and the Royal
Hibernian Academy", Dublin *Daily
Express*, Dec. 7, 1904, II, *330–1*
"Great Enchantment, The", *All Ireland
Review*, Sept. 22, 1900, II, *242–3*
"Hill of Tara, The", *The Times*, June 27,
1902, II, *294–5*
"Hugh Lane Pictures, The", from Lady
Gregory and W.B.Y., *The Observer*,
Dec. 24, 1916, II, *424–6*
"Hugh Lane Pictures, Dublin's Chance,
The", from W. B. Yeats and Lady
Gregory, *The Times*, July 29, 1926,
II, *473–6*
"Important Announcement—Irish Liter-
ary Theatre", Dublin *Daily Express*,
Jan. 12, 1899, II, 128, *137–9*
"Irish Language and Irish Literature",
*The Leader*, Sept. 1, 1900, I, 58; II,
*236–42*
"Irish Literary Society, London, The",
*United Ireland*, July 30, 1892, I, *230–
1*
"Irish Literary Theatre, The", *Irish
Literary Society Gazette*, Jan., 1900,
II, *196–7*
"Irish National Theatre, The", *The Gael*
(New York), June, 1904, II, *328–9*
"Irish National Theatre, The", *The Times*,
June 16, 1910, II, 47, *381–2*
"Irish Plays and Players", *Academy*, May
16, 1903, II, *303–4*
"King's Visit, The", *Freeman's Journal*,
July 13, 1903, II, *304*
Letter, to Dublin *Daily Express*, March 8,
1895, I, 56
Letter, to *Leader*, Sept. 1, 1900, I, 58
Letter, to *United Ireland*, Dec. 17, 1892,
I, 57